"There's certainly no shortage of entertainingly thorough books documenting the early '90s alt-rock boom and What Kurt Hath Wrought. But for exhaustive detail about Seattle's unlikely, meteoric stint as the center of the universe—from Cat Butt to Candlebox and all points in between—this is hard to beat."

—*Spin*

"For hardcore fans or people just curious about what the fuss was all about, Mark Yarm's excellent new book *Everybody Loves Our Town: An Oral History of Grunge* is well worth the read. Yarm has done an admirable job of assembling an engaging, funny and ultimately sad narrative by letting the people who helped create the Jet City sound talk about what happened in their own words."

—*Seattle Post-Intelligencer*

"A deeply funny story, as well as a deeply sad story—the glorious '90s moment when a bunch of punk rock bands from Seattle accidentally blew up into the world's biggest noise. Mark Yarm gives the definitive chronicle of how it all happened, and how it ended too soon."

—Rob Sheffield, author of *Love Is a Mix Tape* and *Talking to Girls About Duran Duran*

"I came away from this book with a big smile on my face. Lots of it is like a gray day in western Washington; you've been kicked out of yet another band, and your girlfriend is spending far too much time with the drummer from the Melvins or the Screaming Trees. In the end, though, *Everybody Loves Our Town* made me want to be young, stupid and lucky again. Mainly, it made me want to be young."

—*The Washington Post*

"Mark Yarm has assembled the gospels of grunge music. Here is a warts-and-elbows refresher course for those of us who still find our memories of the era a little hazy."

—Chuck Palahniuk, author of *Fight Club*

"There's a wealth of insider gossip to savor. . . . [Filled] with quotes that burst with passion and candor."

—*New York Daily News*

"Details the dramatic rise of the grunge movement and all of its players, including Cobain, Love and Vedder, told through the voices of the people that lived through it."

—*The Hollywood Reporter*

"Yarm's account captures the essential tension that made the era so compelling."

—Greg Kot, *Chicago Tribune*

"A comprehensive, entertaining and exceptionally readable account of the musicians and supporting cast who permanently altered the course of rock."

—*The Times-Picayune*

"Exhilarating . . . Mark Yarm's brilliant and exhaustive oral history of grunge is full of . . . vivid observations. Some 250 interviews with those intimately associated with the most unlikely musical sensation of all time piece together a story that is hilarious and tragic and utterly gripping."

—*Sunday Times* of London

"A Herculean work of interviewing and editing which gives everyone a voice, from the biggest stars to the lowliest foot soldiers. . . . Though the Seattle scene's stew of folly, feuding, rampant drug addiction and a startling number of fatalities might have made for a voyeuristic tale, Yarm leaves the reader full of empathy for young men and women swept up in a cultural moment they couldn't control."

—*The Guardian* (U.K.)

"[A] lively, funny, melancholy and exhaustive oral history . . . For all its eventual compromise and dissolution, Seattle was briefly an exhilarating pop cultural moment to rank with the greats. Yarm's labour of love has well and truly done it justice."

—*Time Out London*

"A rip-roaring melodrama fuelled by musical passions, youthful insolence, oscillating fraternal and romantic allegiances, alcohol, tall stories and, increasingly towards its demise, drugs."

—*The Telegraph* (U.K.)

"From basement shenanigans to grunge's MTV peak and its subsequent descent into drug-fuelled darkness, Yarm's book is at once hilarious, enlightening and heartbreaking—a masterful, comprehensive reminder of how an entire musical community became the victim of its own unexpected success. An absolute must-read for music fans."

—*The Vancouver Sun*

"A very noble record of the grunge scene—and an excellent addition to the growing library of oral history music books."

—Legs McNeil, coauthor of *Please Kill Me: The Uncensored Oral History of Punk*

The New *Mksh*

Quality Rock 'n' Roll

1025 FM

RTHWEST AU
STEREO SUI

AN ORAL
HISTORY OF
GRUNGE

THREE RIVERS PRESS
NEW YORK

EVERY BODY LOVES OUR TOWN

MARK YARM

Library of Congress Cataloging-in-Publication Data
Yarm, Mark.
Everybody loves our town : an oral history of Grunge / Mark Yarm.
p.   cm.
1. Grunge music—United States—History and criticism.   2. Grunge
groups—Interviews.   I. Title.
ML3534.3.Y37 2011
781.66—dc22   2011009192

ISBN 978-0-307-46444-6
eISBN 978-0-307-46445-3

Printed in the United States of America

Photo research by Christine Reilly
Text design by Maria Elias
Cover design by Gregg Kulick
Cover photograph © JJ Gonson/Contributor

10 9 8 7 6 5 4 3 2 1

First Paperback Edition

To Bonnie and Dad

In loving memory of Clair Yarm

Everybody loves us
Everybody loves our town
That's why I'm thinking lately
The time for leaving is now

—Mudhoney, "Overblown" (1992)

CONTENTS

INTRODUCTION

First, let's get that word out of the way. *Grunge.* Yes, this is a book about grunge. The term that bedeviled and, let's face it, benefited (at least temporarily) many a Seattle rock musician in the early to mid-1990s. I cannot count how many times, when I described to an interviewee what exactly it was I was working on, I'd get back, "I hate that word . . ." And here they would go one of two ways: spit out "that word" *grunge* or insist, "I don't even like to say it," as if uttering that one syllable would somehow validate a now decades-old coinage. (For a thorough, yet inconclusive, probe into how grunge got its name, see chapter 17.) Others reacted to the term thusly: "rubs me raw," "a marketing tool," "it's all just music," "fuckin' concocted bullshit." And this: "When I see the word *grunge*, especially on books, I kind of go"—and at this point, the guy I was interviewing made a rather convincing vomiting sound.

Of course, most people don't like to be reduced to a label (retch-inducing or otherwise), particularly when it's applied seemingly indiscriminately by the media, as *grunge* often was after Nirvana broke into the mainstream with *Nevermind*'s lead single, the loud-quiet-loud anthem "Smells Like Teen Spirit," in fall 1991. As more than one person asked me over the course of my putting this book together, how is it that a band like Pearl Jam—a well-polished musical outfit whose sound owes more to classic rock than punk rock—was labeled grunge, a word that evokes scuzzy guitar tones and all-around rawness? The answer, it would seem, comes down to genealogy (two of Pearl Jam's members come from what many cite as the first grunge band, Green River) and, more simply, geography (they are, after all, from Seattle). "If you lived in Seattle and were under 30 at that point, you were grunge," is how Ben London, who fronted the not particularly grungy Seattle band Alcohol Funnycar, described the early '90s to me. Though in short order, the term would transcend geography, being applied to the Stone Temple Pilots (from San Diego), Bush (the U.K.), and Silverchair (Australia), all multiplatinum, "corporate rock" bands accused of jumping on the grunge bandwagon.

We could argue forever—and people on Internet message boards do—about what bands are grunge, because the label is entirely subjective. Are Alice in Chains grunge or heavy metal or both? Were 7 Year Bitch punk or grunge or Riot Grrrl? How about contemporary Canadian arena rockers Nickelback: Post-grunge? Neo-grunge? But with the passage of time, some in the Seattle music community have come to grudgingly accept the g-word. "We never considered anybody to be grunge," guitarist Steve Turner of Mudhoney—the band whose raw, scabrously funny single "Touch Me I'm Sick" epitomizes the so-called Seattle sound—told author Clinton Heylin a number of years back. "In 1995, we came out of the closet and said, 'Fine, we're grunge. If anybody fuckin' is, we are.'"

Nirvana frontman Kurt Cobain once posed for a famous photo clutching his infant daughter, Frances Bean, and wearing a T-shirt bearing the words GRUNGE IS DEAD. This sentiment—then merely a joke/wishful thinking on the wearer's part—also has become a point of vibrant debate, particularly since Cobain's April 1994 suicide, which provided a convenient end to an era for some. But in the current decade, grunge seems to be quite animated: The Melvins, Mudhoney, and Candlebox are still kicking, and three of the big four grunge bands are also active concerns: Pearl Jam are celebrating their 20th anniversary this year; as of this writing, Alice in Chains are planning another studio album with their second singer; and Soundgarden are back together after a 13-year break. Meanwhile, surviving Nirvana members Dave Grohl and Krist

Novoselic reunited with *Nevermind* producer Butch Vig to record a song for the latest album by Grohl's Foo Fighters.

While Turner's bandmate Mark Arm (no relation to this author, by the way) professes not to know what grunge is, he says, "I hate it when people say a particular type of music is dead. That's a retarded notion. That's viewing music as fashion"—and anyone who remembers the heyday of flannel and Doc Martens knows that grunge *was* viewed as fashion. "It doesn't make any sense. It's not dead as long as somebody's playing it or writing songs in that style."

So grunge, whatever it may be, is not dead. But enough from me—after all, I'm just a music writer from Brooklyn. This is a book made up almost entirely of the words of more than 250 musicians, producers, managers, record executives, video directors, photographers, journalists, publicists, club owners, roadies, scenesters, and hangers-on—people with firsthand knowledge of a truly remarkable era in rock-and-roll history. I hope their stories and commentary—at turns silly and insightful, hilarious and harrowing—affect you as profoundly as they affected me.

—Mark Yarm, May 2011

CHAPTER 1
SOMETHING CRAZY'S GONNA HAPPEN

LARRY REID (U-Men manager; co-owner of Roscoe Louie/Graven Image galleries; Tracey Rowland's husband) This was Labor Day weekend of 1985. Here's how I remember it. The U-Men's roadie, Mike Tucker, thinks it was my idea; I think it was Charlie Ryan's idea. And it's not that I don't want to take credit for it, because it was brilliant. But I'm sure it was Charlie's idea because Charlie had a fetish for Zippo lighters.

MIKE TUCKER (U-Men roadie) The idea, I do believe, was born out of a conversation between Larry and me. I remember going with Larry and getting the lighter fluid, which someone poured into Mickey's brand malt-liquor bottles.

JIM TILLMAN (U-Men/Love Battery bassist) I'm fairly positive it was John's idea. Suffice it to say that we all thought it was brilliant.

CHARLIE RYAN (U-Men/Cat Butt/the Crows drummer) It was *my* idea. I collected lighters. I was the firebug. I was the pyro. *My idea!*

LARRY REID The U-Men were the first real punk band ever booked at the Bumbershoot Festival. I managed to sell them as a performance-art combo. God bless 'em, the producers trusted me, and they shouldn't have—and never did after this!

CHARLIE RYAN Larry says, "We're on Bumbershoot." And we're like, "Oh, my God. Okay. This is going to be the ultimate showcase for us." I start thinking about the fact that there's the moat, this body of water in front of the stage. I wondered, Could we light it on fire?

LARRY REID Nobody was quite sure it would work, so we filled up my bathtub, poured some lighter fluid on it, and . . .

CHARLIE RYAN We took a match and threw it in, and it went *boom!* Flames.

LARRY REID There was a curtain on the window above the bathtub and it fucking went up, man. If we would've thought about it, we probably would've tried it outside using a bucket of water. The alarm went off, all hell broke loose—they had to empty the building, but it didn't catch the apartment on fire. We were all high-fiving each other, and like, "Yes, this was a good thing. This is gonna work!"

So skip to the gig, a couple weeks later. Bumbershoot was held at an outdoor venue called the Mural Amphitheatre, which is on the grounds of this large city-owned property called the Seattle Center. There were hundreds of people in the audience because it was free.

KURT BLOCH (Fastbacks/Young Fresh Fellows guitarist) I was right there in the front. They're setting up and everybody's like, "Something crazy's gonna happen, something crazy's gonna happen."

KERRI HARROP (Sub Pop Records sales and retail employee) I can even remember what I was wearing, the show was that significant. First of all, Bumbershoot's this family-friendly event—it's out on the open lawn in the shadow of the Space Needle—and you have these complete weirdos out on this stage.

CHARLIE RYAN It's sunny and nice out, and we're all in black leather and top hats and dark shades and being as menacing as we could be. Our freak show only appeared at night, in dark places, but here we are, in broad daylight. My mom was there—the end of the show wasn't her proudest moment.

LARRY REID At the end of the set, the sun was just going down. Mike Tucker and myself walked out to the edge of the stage, and we're each pouring what appeared to be a gallon of vodka into the pond. And Bigley comes out—they're doing this song called "They," which at that point was the standard last song.

JIM TILLMAN The last song was "Green Trumpet," though I could be wrong. There were 2,000 or 3,000 people there. A couple of our friends, this guy Mike, who was sort of a roadie, and this other guy Tommy Bonehead—his real name was Tom Simpson, but he was called Bonehead because it didn't matter how hard you'd hit him, he'd always fight—are pouring lighter fluid on either side of the stage.

TOM PRICE (U-Men/Cat Butt/Gas Huffer guitarist) We were playing a song called "10 After 1." And John ducked behind an amp, because we didn't want the authorities to see what was going on.

JOHN BIGLEY (U-Men/the Crows singer) I had gotten a broom and cut off the bristles, so it was just a nub where the bristles joined the handle, and wrapped it in a T-shirt soaked in lighter fluid. I ran back behind the drums, lit the broom with my lighter, and waited until the song "They" kicked into gear.

CHARLIE RYAN And John comes out, doing this insane tribal voodoo dance with a lit broom, menacing the crowd. And then he chucks it into the water.

MIKE TUCKER When John dipped his torch into the moat, it didn't immediately ignite. It was like, "Oh, fuck, it didn't work." The second time he dipped it in, suddenly this wall of fire went up.

JOHN BIGLEY I throw the broom in and there was a giant fireball, 20 to 30 feet high, easy. It was gigantic and it made a sound, this *whoosh* of oxygen.

LARRY REID The pond fuckin' exploded, man! I mean, it made the bathroom look like child's play. It went up, oh, 10, 12, 15 feet.

JOE NEWTON (Gas Huffer drummer) My recollection was that it was over in the blink of an eye. It burned fast, it burned hugely high and bright, but it just lasted a second. I knew they were going to do it, and it was like, "That's it?" Other people totally remember it being this huge wall of fire.

DENNIS R. WHITE (Pravda Productions partner; *Desperate Times* zine cofounder) In a lot of cases, people remember things being much bigger than they were. In this case, they don't. It looked like the band was engulfed in flames.

JOHN BIGLEY And with the supercharged rock-and-roll music, that's when the vast majority of the folks started jumping around and dancing. It was a crazy primal deal.

JAMES BURDYSHAW (Cat Butt guitarist; 64 Spiders guitarist/singer) The U-Men were into bones and skulls and black clothes and witch-doctor sort of imagery. The whole voodoo tribal thing became real 'cause the sun went down right when the flames happened. You felt like there was something dangerous going on but you couldn't look away. The crowd was screaming, but it wasn't out of fear. It was like, *Yes! Yes!* It was elation.

It was like, *Fuck the Man, we're the most dangerous voodoo band—and we're gonna do a human sacrifice next.* It felt like that was gonna happen.

LARRY REID It was perfect, except we'd failed to take into consideration that the stage was built out over the pond. There was creosote and tar underneath the stage, so there was just black smoke billowing long after the flames had died down. And the soundman freaked out, thinking the stage was on fire, and he's running up, trying to get his sound equipment off the stage. The audience is now going apeshit crazy. Cops being cops, they started wading into the audience and beating people with their billy clubs!

CHARLES PETERSON (photographer) The thing I remember most is that we all just went fuckin' bonkers, and started slam-dancing into each other. And there were these Seattle Center security guards who thought we were getting into fights and were trying to separate us. This 60-year-old security guard was just freaking out, and some of us were like, "Dude, they're just dancing!" I recall somebody grabbed a security guard's hat and danced around. It was mayhem.

JOHN BIGLEY We finished the song, definitely. Someone, it might have been Larry, grabbed me and threw me towards the drums: *"Get the fuck out! Load the shit!"* It was very chaotic—people running and screaming and kids holding their eyes and arrests and that whole thing.

TRACEY ROWLAND (co-owner of Roscoe Louie/Graven Image galleries; Larry Reid's wife) Norman Langill, who was running Bumbershoot, was yelling and screaming and freaking out and jumping up and down. He was furious.

JIM TILLMAN I'd parked our tour bus—it was a 1960s Chevy city school bus that said TACOMA HILLBILLIES on the side, though I have absolutely no idea why—in this spot next to the stage.

JOHN BIGLEY *"Load the shit, load the shit!"* We got loaded up and drove off before the police had gotten their act together to approach us.

CHARLIE RYAN I'll never forget driving our bus out of the Seattle Center grounds—all of these nice, normal people looking up at us, these freaks in a school bus who had just set the moat on fire.

KERRI HARROP I was blown away by the audacity of it. I'm sure if there was a panoramic shot of the crowd, virtually everyone who ended up in a band or who was in a band at the time was at that show. I think that if you were in a band and you saw that, it made you step up your game.

MARK ARM (né Mark McLaughlin; Mudhoney singer/guitarist; Green River singer; Mr. Epp and the Calculations guitarist/singer; the Thrown Ups drummer) I don't know if it was necessarily the best U-Men show I ever saw, but that was the coolest event at a U-Men show. They really made something happen.

LARRY REID The U-Men were banned from Bumbershoot, and I wasn't the most popular guy around there for a while. The year after that, they started draining the pond. And now they've filled it in with cement.

The day after the show, I met the Everly Brothers at the hotel and brought them to the venue—I was working at Bumbershoot, operating as an informal chaperone for the bigger acts—and the first person I ran into was Norm Langill, the producer of the festival. He just came unglued. He said, *"What are you trying to do to me?!"*

Phil Everly was really kinda sweet and came to my defense. He told this great anecdote, which was possibly apocryphal, about a show they had played with Jerry Lee Lewis. Jerry Lee was squirting lighter fluid on the 88s and pounding out "Great Balls of Fire." And the next thing you know . . . accidents happen. Apparently Jerry Lee was dancing on the piano, which was an impromptu addition to his normal routine, and caught his pants on fire.

That story got me off the hook. That calmed everything down, because Norm held the Everly Brothers in real high regard. Phil told him, "Leave the kid alone. That's rock and roll."

* * *

TOM PRICE The U-Men started in late '81. My family had moved to Seattle in 1965. I started playing music, believe it or not, mostly through the church. They called it "guitar mass"—it was the acoustic-guitar-strumming, long-haired Christians. Very *Jesus Christ Superstar*. In my early teens, my older brother was turning me on to all this weird music, like Captain Beefheart and Lou Reed. And so when punk came along, that was a natural jump. The U-Men was probably my first band that made any records.

Me and Charlie had both dropped out of high school together and moved into a crash pad in the University District. Charlie was a really funny character. He's an Irishman, his dad was a bookie, and he had his own apartment downtown, just this whole weird style that was pretty unfamiliar to kids like me from tree-lined residential neighborhoods.

CHARLIE RYAN I was born and raised in Seattle, and grew up pretty much downtown. Bookmaking was the family business. My father was a bartender for years, and he was given this little business by someone who was retiring. Which afforded him a lifestyle of going out and dining and drinking on a nightly basis. Later on, in the '80s, I started taking bets over the phone for him so he didn't have to do anything except go collect the money.

I met Tom at Roosevelt High School. We were all standing outside smoking pot all the time. Nobody went to class. It was a little hotbed of soon-to-become-punk activity: The Mentors went to school there, Duff McKagan was there, Chris Utting. I moved into this house in the U District with Tom Price and Rob Morgan. Rob had a lot of weird, punky bands—the Pudz, the Fishsticks—that he put together over the years. He was older and had this huge record collection. He was very influential on us.

The entire idea of the band was Tom's. We stole our name right off of this Pere Ubu bootleg called *The U-Men*. We weren't working—we were playing records and drinking a lot and coming up with funny ideas. Tom said, "I think we should start a band, Charlie." And I said, "Okay."

And he said, "You'll be the drummer."

And I said, "But we don't know how to play."

He goes, "That's okay, we'll learn."

I go, "Okay. We don't have any equipment."

He goes, "Don't worry about that."

Tom was very resourceful, and he would obtain things that we needed all the time. I'm not trying to imply that anything against the law happened, but things just got done, things appeared. I don't know how he did it.

TOM PRICE We'd have one pair of drumsticks, and if Charlie broke a drumstick, that's it, we'd have to rummage around and see if we could find some wooden soup spoons or something. We played in the basement of this house and had cymbals hanging from the ceiling, since we didn't have enough cymbal stands, just playing through these crappy little amps on crappy little guitars.

CHARLIE RYAN Tom says, "There's this girl I know from Alaska, and she's going to run away from home. I'm going to pick her up at the airport, and she's going to be our bass player."

ROBIN BUCHAN (U-Men bassist) I went to Roosevelt High School. My home life was not good, and as a 13- and 14-year-old, I was really withdrawn and depressed. My one outlet was music, 'cause I played the string bass in our school's chamber orchestra and the youth symphony. I got into the punk scene, which was my chance to bust out completely. My parents were scandalized by the change and were worried that I was drinking and doing drugs, which I was.

When I was 15, things in my life kind of blew up. My mom over-reacted, and she asked my dad to take me away. They were divorced and my dad was remarried. He was in the Air Force and he was on his way up to Elmendorf Air Force Base outside of Anchorage. They knew I didn't want to go, so they tricked me into it: "Oh, you're just gonna go for the summer." Once I got up there they were like, "Nope. You're staying here."

I'd met Tom Price in Seattle, but I didn't know him very well. We wrote letters back and forth when I was in Alaska, and somehow it was determined that I was going to play bass for the U-Men. I had a friend in Seattle whose mom worked for Alaska Airlines, so we told her mom this crazy story—actually, it was only a small stretch of the truth—that my dad had kidnapped me and I just wanted to come home and be with my mom, which was completely not true. And her mom went for that; I sent them my money, and they sent me a plane ticket. I got really, really drunk at a party in Alaska, then got on a plane and threw up and passed out. I woke up, and I was in Seattle.

CHARLIE RYAN Oh, Robbie was gorgeous. Gorgeous woman. She had a classic Marilyn Monroe figure. She never talked about much; she was a very private person. All I ever heard was some muttering about parents, having to get away. It was always mysterious.

TOM PRICE Robbie would play super-loud and way too many notes, but she seemed weird enough that it was cool.

ROBIN BUCHAN Tom became my boyfriend shortly thereafter; he was my first real boyfriend. Tom was like this island of sweetness. And being a teenage runaway, there wasn't much sweetness in the world for me in those days.

CHARLIE RYAN When Robbie played onstage, she used a bass whose strings were not where they should've been—they were much too high. She was so tough, she could just hammer those strings down. She would drink a ton of gin before going onstage, and she had boobs out to *here*. Guys would come up to her, and they'd try to get a little bit too close, and she would just bat people in the face with the end of the guitar. Just like, Stay back, man. She was ferocious. Just ferocious.

TOM PRICE One of the first times I ever met John was when I was at a party at some punk-rock crash house. I don't know what happened—he basically fell through a window and landed on the yard outside and got up with a stunned look on his face, like, Who pushed me? I think he was just drunk and high and fell down some stairs and went through the window.

He's a big guy, like six-three. Charlie and I had seen him around and saw him fall through the window and thought, Man, what a weird dude, we should get him to be our singer. We had no idea if he could actually sing or not, but of course, in those days that was just a complete nonissue.

CHARLIE RYAN We were intrigued by and also quite scared of John. He had a Jim Morrison kind of thing. He was gorgeous: short hair, Beatle boots, tight black jeans, a crazy look in his eye, like he was ready for anything. You didn't know if he was going to kiss you, kill you, fuck ya. We'd seen him get into a fight or two at parties.

We wanted him to be the singer for the U-Men, but we were too scared to approach him. So we asked Robbie, the girl, to do it. She laughed and called us wimps, and then the next chance she got, she went and talked to John.

JOHN BIGLEY I was at a Johnny Thunders show at the Mountaineers club. Robbie came up to me and talked for a while; she was definitely acting funny. And finally: "Do—do you. Want to. Be in. A band—our band? Try out. For it?"

ROBIN BUCHAN Really? I don't remember that at all. When we met John, he was so outrageous. One time we got drunk and went swimming in the middle of the night, just him and me in the canal under the Fremont Bridge, which was dangerous because it's a shipping lane. He would do anything. He would take any drug. He was a wild man.

JOHN BIGLEY I said, "I'm not sure. I never sang, never really thought about it much." Finally, I said, "You know, sure."

I remember the first practice. The third Clash album had just come out, so we did "Brand New Cadillac." We were in a laundry room and there was a shelf full of paint and paint thinner and all this stuff. So they'd run through songs they'd been writing and I'd just rant off of the backs of found objects—hyphenated chemical-compound names and silly brand names.

CHARLIE RYAN John showed up to our first rehearsal, and he was wearing a short-sleeve T-shirt and had a leather bag over his shoulder. He was just so bohemian. We're all excited and nervous. He pulls out a bottle of wine. "Anybody want a glass of wine?" "Yeah, I'd love some wine!" We'd drank nothing but beer our whole lives, and here comes John with a bottle of wine.

Yeah, he sang directions on how to bleach your laundry. His voice was ferocious. It was unpolished. It sounded like an animal. He was just wailing away, and we were thrilled: *This is it! This is it!*

TOM PRICE John went to the University of Washington, and he was in a frat house of all things, but it was this real low-rent frat house that everybody hated. John had a good baritone voice, but at the early shows he was almost more like a performance artist than a singer. A lot of the time he would just stand there and glare at the audience. It took him a while before he started really singing and getting comfortable with that. He was really into the Birthday Party, the Gun Club, the Cramps, and the Germs. Public Image Ltd. and Captain Beefheart were huge influences on me. Me and Charlie in particular were getting into rockabilly and surf music, and the Sonics and the Wailers, all that great Northwest '60s garage rock.

Our first show? That's pretty much impossible to say. Sometime in 1981 or '82. Somewhere in there we started doing some shows at parties and basements and garages. There were no clubs happening. There was nowhere to play. There were a couple taverns, but none of us was 21. Sometimes you'd get a bunch of people together and rent a hall yourself and hope the cops wouldn't shut it down.

JOHN BIGLEY Someone gave this to me—it's the Laurelhurst Community Club newsletter from January 1982. Laurelhurst is a quite wealthy enclave down on Lake Washington. The headline is VANDALISM AT THE RECREATION CENTER:

What were all the police cars doing at the recreation center early last month? Well . . . it was rented out to a group called the U-MEN for a youth dance with certain restrictions (no liquor or Punk Rock) that got violated. The evening (Nov. 6th) turned into a mild ruckus involving fists, broken windows, and beer bottles. The police were called twice; the last time it was out you go with much resistance. Fortunately someone turned on all the lights which proved the turning point for all the varied night creatures, who snuck away muttering. Later that evening and on two successive weekends the building sustained broken windows, a smashed door, broken bottles, and sprayed on graffiti . . . pure coincidence??

That show was with the Fastbacks and Aaiiee!! The Bopo Boys, who were a gang, using the term loosely, were there to see us play. They were omnipresent back then—drinkin' beer, skateboarding, hustlin' chicks, a street fight here and there. They were tight with us and the Fastbacks. Then all these locals started showing up. Back then we would call them jocks; I guess you still would. They started driving around the parking lot of the community center and burning rubber and yelling "Faggot!" A couple fights happened, people rode off and found phone booths, and all of a sudden a bunch of our brothers and sisters from the Ave—University Way, where all the panhandling punk rockers hung out—and elsewhere showed up and there was a turf war.

ROBIN BUCHAN The only thing I remember about our shows is getting shut down by the cops over and over and over again. We had the dubious honor of having 13 shows in a row shut down by the Seattle police. I was really amazingly good at disappearing when the cops came.

LARRY REID The U-Men were quite a bit younger than I was, but I went to a couple of their shows, which would just always go south for whatever reason. The P.A. would go out, the cops would show up. There was something about the energy and the atmosphere of a U-Men show that was right on the edge of complete chaos, which immediately appealed to me.

I saw them at the Funhole, probably about 1981. The P.A. had gone out, and it didn't stop 'em a bit. The singer of course couldn't sing, but the show went on, and Bigley is pantomiming and doing this crazy absurdist theater to this wall of dissonant noise, in front of about 20 people with their jaws all dropped. I thought he was some kind of bent genius.

I had just done a really successful record-release party for the Fastbacks at Roscoe Louie, the art gallery that my wife and I ran, and Bigley approached me and said, "We need some help." And it was serendipitous, because at that particular point we had made the decision to close Roscoe Louie.

TOM PRICE Larry was maybe 25, which when you're 18 is a massive difference. What was amazing about him is that he never cared about money. He'd get a thousand people crammed into some tiny space, and he never cared whether he made any money or not. He just likes creating a scene, I guess.

LARRY REID I became their formal manager, and at some point I started taking 10 percent of nothing. What we primarily did was save all the money for recording. Later, after Robin left, we got into a 16-track studio called Crow, with a guy named John Nelson, and we recorded some great stuff there and had a long relationship with them. The U-Men put out an EP in 1984 on Bombshelter, which was nominally Bruce Pavitt.

CLAUDIA GEHRKE (the Vogue club booker) Larry Reid? Larry Greed, as we always called him. I remember at one U-Men show he goes, "I'm going to sit across from you with a clicker and count how many people come in to make sure you don't rip me off," and I said, "You go right ahead." We got to the end of it, and I'd taken in more money than he was expecting. He'd been drinking beers while clicking. I was like, "See? I don't know why you had to play me like that."

LARRY REID I would get away with murder. We pushed it to the limit, but their shows never got shut down. I remember one show counterfeiting an occupancy permit for the fire department. You know—this is before computers—photocopy it, use some Wite-Out, type in all manner of misinformation, photocopy it another three or four times. Wad it up and stuff it in an envelope, and when the fire department showed up, it's like, "Here it is." Well, they know it's not right, but they can't prove it.

We had a show at the Meatlockers—it was exactly what it sounds like—and had a complete bar setup in a freight elevator, so when the cops did show up, we just raised the freight elevator up, shut the doors, and, "What bar? There's no bar here."

In fairly short order, the U-Men built up an audience. I started 'em out opening on three-band bills and pretty soon they're in the second slot and then they're headlining. Probably the turning point was the last show that the Blackouts played here before they moved to Boston; the U-Men were the second on that bill. And it was a big show. The Blackouts were *the* band at that time—they opened for all the touring bands. They were really rhythm-heavy; they had a sax. You can't write the history of grunge without kudos to the Blackouts. The U-Men get a lot of credit as being the proto-grunge band, but the Blackouts leaving put the U-Men on the top of a very small heap.

MARK ARM In the '70s to mid-'80s, people didn't stick around Seattle if they were tryin' to get somewhere. Duff McKagan went to L.A. The Blackouts moved to Boston. The guys in the Tupperwares moved to L.A. and formed the Screamers.

A lot of touring bands totally skipped Portland and Seattle because it was 14 hours north of San Francisco and 32 hours west of Minneapolis. People in the Northwest had to make up their own entertainment.

JACK ENDINO (producer; Skin Yard guitarist; Dawn Anderson's ex-husband) Nobody thought there was any chance of having any success, so no decisions were made with that in mind. People made records entirely to please themselves because there was nobody else to please, there was no one paying attention to Seattle. It was like a little, isolated germ culture.

ROBIN BUCHAN The first time I broke up with Tom, I was struggling with a lot of emotional issues and I wasn't experienced enough to realize that there wasn't a problem with the relationship, there was a problem with me. The second time, we were starting to grow apart musically. I didn't really like the nascent grunge scene very much. It's just not my style. I was getting more into Siouxsie and the Banshees and Magazine.

Also, I was really tired of being so fuckin' poor. Tom and I were sharing this moldy, leaky basement apartment on frat row, which was a horrible place to live if you're a punk rocker. So I broke up with him and left the band at the same time. I sold everything and disappeared to Europe.

TOM PRICE Robbie was still in the band after she and I broke up; I think she left more because she wanted a lifestyle change. She wanted to go back and graduate high school and go to college. It took a while to find our new bass player, Jim Tillman, who was actually the ex-boyfriend of my girlfriend at the time, Kim Stratton.

JIM TILLMAN I was still friendly with Kim, and she had suggested to Tom that they talk to me. I had been playing guitar for a band called the Horrible Truth, and we kinda petered out. When I practiced with the U-Men it was the first time I picked up a bass. The band was really cool. One song might be kind of swampy, another one would be full-on rockabilly with a twist, and something else would be really moody and dark.

TOM PRICE Jim was a great musician, which was a huge turning point. It encouraged the rest of us to get it together and start playing more real music.

We forced Jim to do a makeover. He had long hair and glasses, and we made him get contacts and cut his hair. At that point, our look was kind of a Cramps rip-off: big, scraggly hair, just all kinds of garbage tied around your neck, vests, no shirts, studded belts, steel-toed boots. Really cracks me up when I look at pictures of myself back in those days because, oh man, I looked almost too skinny to support all that hair.

LARRY REID We opened the Graven Image Gallery about eight months after Roscoe Louie closed. Roscoe Louie was a visual-art space that had some music and performance elements, while Graven Image was exactly the opposite—it was more to provide a rehearsal space for the U-Men.

TOM PRICE Upstairs, Larry was trying to pass the Graven Image off as a for-real art gallery. It was all clean and brightly lit up there, and then you'd go down the stairs at the back to the basement, and it was pretty much a dungeon. Yeah, total firetrap.

TRACEY ROWLAND Did Larry tell you about the time he got arrested for posing a "significant menace to human life" or something? About nine months after we opened, the fire department showed up and took note of the fact that there were way too many people in the basement. We were a block and a half away from the fire department—it surprises me that it took 'em that long to figure it out.

LARRY REID One time, the Butthole Surfers ended up getting stuck in Seattle. I let them rehearse in the basement, but after a while I said, "Man, you guys gotta get outta here." I mean, nice enough guys, but they were just underfoot and they were dusted. And on Christmas Day of 1983, I put on a show with them at Graven Image and the deal was, "I'll give you all the money, but you have to leave."

JIM TILLMAN The Butthole Surfers were playing so loud that one of the speaker columns actually caught fire. Everybody came, and we got them like $250 at the door so they could make their way back home to Texas.

MARK ARM The first time the Butthole Surfers came to Seattle, Gibby Haynes came out with clothespins in his hair. Later on during the set, he shook his head and they just went flying. Everyone's like, "That was weird." Bands were always trying to think up crazy stunts.

TOM HANSEN (the Refuzors/the Fartz guitarist; heroin dealer) There was a lot of gimmickry in the scene, but it was mostly improv because we couldn't afford flame pots and sparklers and bombs.

On the way to a show at Danceland in '81, the Refuzors stopped at Benson's Grocery on the corner of Pike and Bellevue to get some beer, and there it was: There was this cat that had just been run over on the street. Its head was twisted around a little bit; its tongue was hanging out. We had this song called "Splat Goes the Cat," so when we saw the cat, the lightbulb goes off. We put it in a cardboard box and brought it to the show.

We had this friend of ours, Jeff House, a notorious troublemaker, bring out the cat during that song and just frickin' swing it around his head by the tail and throw it into the crowd. And it ended up getting thrown back up onstage and thrown back out and thrown over here and there. Eventually, it ended up back behind the equipment somewhere. *(Laughs.)* It didn't look too messy to me, but of course it got exaggerated in the paper. They interviewed some girl who said, "I got totally splattered with blood, *ehhh.*"

The Humane Society was looking for us, because they thought we had killed the cat in some satanic ritual.

CHARLIE RYAN A couple of times we played at the Meatlockers, and we would not have an opening band. This is something I learned from a Refuzors show: We'd put on the poster SHOW STARTS AT 9:00. We would have kegs of beer and for a $2 or $3 admission, you could drink yourself silly. We'd have a DJ, and we would not play until midnight. We would push it until we thought that if we waited any longer, the crowd would actually be passed out on the ground. At this point, people thought they saw God that night.

DAVE DEDERER (the Presidents of the United States of America "guitbassist"/ singer) I'll never forget seeing the U-Men at the Meatlockers, a sweaty, hundred-capacity former meat locker in the industrial part of town.

Tom and Jim are plugging in, and Charlie takes three or four minutes to get ready. He takes off his vintage blazer, very deliberately, and neatly folds it up so that it doesn't get creased, and not in a "watch me" kind of way. This was just his thing. Puts the jacket down next to him on a milk crate, takes off his hat, snaps the brim up so it doesn't get creased, places it gently on top of his blazer, and lights a cigarette.

And then they proceed to just rip the shit out of the place.

CHARLIE RYAN We weren't stylish from the outset. Then John and I thought, We're goin' onstage; we might as well look like something. The lime-green tuxes were my doing. An old family friend owned a formalwear shop, Brocklind's, on Capitol Hill. I discovered them there, and I said, "Would you outfit four of us in these tuxes?" They were a sight. A sight. We wore those when we opened for the Cramps at the Golden Crown.

We started thinking about more and more outlandish things to do—and themes. Night of the Living U-Men was good. We handed out barf bags that said, "A registered nurse will be on hand at all times in case you're overcome by the sheer terror of this."

LARRY REID We also did wrestling at U-Men shows. I was the Assassin, a Mexican wrestler with a mask and body leotard. I wrestled a local punk-rock guy named Slam Hate.

CHAD BLAKE (a.k.a. Slam Hate; concertgoer; posterer) Larry was a scrawny little guy, and I was a beefy kind of guy, so he was a little scared at times. I would get a little out of control, basically.

LARRY REID He'd smash a breakaway bottle over my head. And then he'd go off script and start jabbing me with it. Yeah, it cut me. Was I bleeding? Hell, yes!

TOM PRICE Some of the stuff John would do—you know, he'd show up wearing hip waders and a Speedo. Sometimes he'd wind up underneath the stage curled up in a ball just screaming. I think that was part of our appeal.

LARRY REID They were strapping, handsome young men, and there were lots of girls. As the result of all the girls coming, the boys would come. Later, I experienced that same phenomenon myself with Nirvana. Like, "Let's go see Nirvana and look at the girls!"

NILS BERNSTEIN (Sub Pop Records publicist) The U-Men were all good-looking, in very different ways: Jim was young, very beautiful, perfect skin. Tom's just a very handsome man, very cool. Charlie's kinda mod, and girls love mods, especially then. And then John was just larger-than-life, kinda mysterious. It's funny, because people probably look at a picture of the U-Men now and they're like, *"They* were the hot guys at the time?" But no question, anybody who was around then is like, "God, of course those guys were."

CHARLIE RYAN I felt that we were really too weird to attract any kind of women. But everybody has a different experience. Tom was quite the ladies' man—that's what I heard for a while. John was with the same gal, Valerie, through most of it. But girls liked John because he was out there, putting it out.

KERRI HARROP As a teenage girl, it was like, Oh, my God, how can I make out with John Bigley? He has got a swagger about him that is unparalleled. One thing about Bigley is, especially after enough beers, he almost has this kind of cigar-store-Indian demeanor about him, where he'll just size up the situation and then weigh in with, "Uh-huh. Yep. Uh-huh." He always seemed like such a mystery.

JIM TILLMAN John was a bit cryptic and a bit brooding. There was always a sense that he was tolerating talking to you, whether it was me or somebody else. But I remember a time when we were doing acid at Charlie's apartment. And at one point, John and I were like, "We gotta get out of here." And so we walked downstairs, and I remember this clear as day, it's just bizarre—we're in the hallway, walking toward the foyer of the apartment, and we're just laughing hysterically. I don't know what the hell we were talking about. I just said, "Times these days," and he started laughing at that phrase, and he picked me up and gave me a huge bear hug. He's a big guy. And we stumbled out on the street and started repeating, "Times these days! Times these days!" And we're laughing. That particular phrase became lyrics in one of our songs.

So if he didn't feel like he had to cultivate that sense of cool, I think John was a warm and caring person. My sense is that he's a decent person who decided years ago that he had to have a big wall up. The reasoning for that I'd never be able to say, but I might hazard a guess that it's because, I think, he was adopted.

JOHN BIGLEY I grew up knowing. I'm sure it did affect me, not knowing your dad or knowing you never will. You know, Do I look like him? I'm so used to it, I don't really think about it too terribly much. That could have fueled my trip a little differently than someone else.

DANIEL HOUSE (Skin Yard/10 Minute Warning bassist; C/Z Records owner) There was just something about John Bigley, like you never knew what was gonna happen. Even if nothing happened, there was just that slight glimmer of insanity. Something I loved was that he went to the DMV to get his license one year and had makeup lines around his eyes and at the ends of his mouth. They actually took his picture that way! So for many years he looked like a demented, evil clown on his driver's license.

JOHN BIGLEY I had a lot of personal issues that would have probably fueled some of my attitudes and behaviors. No deep, dark secrets—just big, corny, Reagan era, state-of-the-world, teen angst, existential stuff. The band was a big deal. It wasn't a *yahoo-let's-have-fun-TGIF-rock-and-roll* experience for me. I was really uncomfortable in front of people, so it was move around or break shit or lash out. It was very intense.

Every show, that was the real me.

CHAPTER 2
THE GOSPEL ACCORDING TO BUZZ

BUZZ OSBORNE (a.k.a. King Buzzo; Melvins singer/guitarist) I never hipped my parents that much to what I was doing musically. But that's okay—they had their own shit going on. They dealt with being parents with the tools that their parents had given them, which was none. My father was born in a West Virginia hovel with no power or running water, and his father was a coal miner. My grandfather left home when he was 12 years old because his father couldn't feed him anymore. He was a hobo. My mom was 15 years old when she had me. My parents never would have fucking gotten married if it wasn't for that.

My parents did exceptionally well with what they had, which was nothing, and their parents had nothing, they came from nowhere. That's the way that lots of families are: death and destruction and every bad thing that you can imagine.

I have a distrust of humanity. I lost my faith in all those kinds of things a long time ago, probably as a teenager. But that's okay. I understand I'm not normal. I'm just a weirdo walking around like Bozo the Clown.

MATT LUKIN (Melvins/Mudhoney bassist) I was born in Aberdeen, but I grew up in Montesano. It was pretty redneckish and just simpleminded.

BUZZ OSBORNE I was born in a town called Morton, Washington, which is approximately an hour and a half from Aberdeen and Montesano. Middle of nowhere. My parents were poor people, lower-middle-class at best. My dad worked in the timber industry.

When I was about 12, we moved to Montesano. Around then, I started buying *Creem* magazine. This was about '76, '77. I got interested in the Sex Pistols solely because of the way they looked in those magazines. At the same time, I was getting into David Bowie.

MIKE DILLARD (Melvins drummer) I was a sophomore when I met Buzz. He was a year ahead of me in school. I can distinctly remember being in his bedroom. He had this big console stereo system that his mom and dad had given him, and he put the Sex Pistols' *Never Mind the Bollocks* on the turntable. At that time, he'd already completely worn the record out—it was all scratched and staticky and popping. I was going, "Oh, my God, this is the greatest thing I've ever heard!"

MATT LUKIN I met Buzz in high school. He was just this freaky guy that played guitar. He was different from everybody else as far as his attitude—and his hair. He had a big Afro. Another good friend of mine that I knew since first or third grade, this guy Mike Dillard, just happened to be friends with Buzz, and they'd get together and jam. Mike had a drum set, Buzz had a guitar, and then Dillard's cousin had a bass. They tried to recruit me as a second guitar player 'cause I had a Les Paul and a guitar amp. But Dillard's cousin didn't show up very often, so they let me play bass.

BUZZ OSBORNE Matt Lukin had a guitar at school, which was an oddity. He was from certainly more of the jock element. And more established. I was an outsider, because I moved there when I was in seventh grade. You gotta understand, you're going to school with kids whose parents went to school together, who dated each other, who give each other jobs. You can just forget it, you know? I might as well have been from fucking Mars.

MIKE DILLARD Buzz and I both worked at the Thriftway. We bagged groceries and brought 'em out to the cars for the old ladies. We'd always close up the store at night, and we'd have to take these big boxes of garbage out back. So we'd toss a couple cases of beer in the boxes, cover them up with garbage, and throw them in the dumpster. When we got off, we'd drive around back, grab the beer out of the dumpster, and take off.

When we started out, we were playing some Who covers and some Hendrix covers and Cream, a bunch of classic-rock stuff. I remember Lukin coming to Buzz and me about two weeks after he started jamming with us. He goes, "Holy shit, you guys are insane! I've smoked more pot and drank more booze in the last two weeks than I have my entire life!" We were probably responsible for him going down the road of drugs and alcohol.

BUZZ OSBORNE Alcohol was really amazing. In a hopeless situation, it makes you feel like you've got something to live for. If I'd have been left there and hadn't discovered music, I'd have blown my brains out. No doubt. I would have killed somebody or killed myself. But I stopped drinking in the '80s. I thought it was better for me and everybody around me if I didn't do it. When I drank, I'd break out in felonies or break out in bandages, one of the two.

TIM HAYES (Fallout Records store owner) I was working at a chain record store called DJ Sound City back in Aberdeen, at the Wishkah Mall. I was about as fringy as you could get—I had a pompadour at the time. Cats would come in and buy their Doobie Brothers or Styx or Rush or Skynyrd. A lot of bad music. Buzz and Matt would come in and hang out, and I'd turn 'em on: "Hey, man, you gotta check out this Cramps record or this Black Flag record." One day they came in and said they'd started a band.

BUZZ OSBORNE We named the band after this guy who worked at the Thriftway. Melvin was a fucking asshole. He was an adult and was in a position to give you orders. He was the kind of guy who would yell at you in front of somebody else to try to impress them. Horseshit. We wanted to call ourselves that because it sounded stupid. We liked the inside joke.

MIKE DILLARD Right behind the Thriftway, there was a park-and-ride place where you could park your car and catch the bus. We found this outdoor plug from a building next to the parking lot. We just drug a big extension cord over there and plugged all the amps and stuff in and set up at about seven o'clock on a Saturday night.

KURT COBAIN (late Nirvana singer/guitarist; Courtney Love's husband; Frances Bean Cobain's father; from his journals) I remember hanging out at Montesano, Washington's Thriftway, when this short-haired employee box-boy who kinda looked like the guy in Air Supply handed me a flyer that read: "The Them Festival. Tomorrow night in the parking lot behind Thriftway. Free live rock music."

Montesano, Washington, a place not accustomed to having live rock acts in their little village. A population of a few thousand loggers and their subservient wives. I showed up with stoner friends in a van. . . . There stood the Air Supply box-boy holding a Les Paul with a picture from a magazine of Kool Cigarettes laminated on it, a mechanic redheaded biker boy, and that tall Lukin guy . . .

They played faster than I ever imagined music could be played and with more energy than my Iron Maiden records could provide. This was what I was looking for.

BUZZ OSBORNE We did a bunch of stuff like that; it wasn't really a show. What I consider our first show was in Olympia, Washington. That was in '84 at a place called the Tropicana. We practiced our heads off for a long time, and we played all original material. A few weeks later, we played a show there with the Fastbacks, and all the kids who came up to see us play the first show came up to see us play again. So at that moment was when I knew, Okay, we did it. We pulled it off.

KURT BLOCH The Melvins were unlike any other band. They had this absurd sound, which was just pummeling, but at the same time it wasn't like hardcore where you're telling everyone how much you hate your parents and school and stuff like that. The lyrics didn't make any literal sort of sense, but they're yelling them like they mean them. They were very pretentious but without any pretense. They didn't have that whole antigovernment and "kill rock stars" attitude.

DONNA DRESCH (Screaming Trees bassist; Team Dresch guitarist/bassist; Chainsaw Records founder) The Melvins were the guys that would come to our parties in Olympia and be crazy obnoxious and kick holes in the walls. I totally remember that sinking feeling you got when they came into your house. Still, you'd go to every one of their shows and know every single weird word that they made up and just mosh your head off.

MIKE DILLARD It was a big step to actually leave town and go play somewhere. We start hanging out with this band March of Crimes. We'd go up there and stay overnight at their place. Ben Shepherd, who was in Soundgarden later, was the guitarist. And this kid named Munkeyseeker was the singer. They lived on Bainbridge Island; they were closer to the scene, so they were hooking shows up for us.

JONATHAN EVISON (a.k.a. Munkeyseeker; March of Crimes singer) We quickly befriended the Melvins and stopped by to stay with them in Montesano. Just got totally baked in their practice space. They played for us and we were like, "Unhh!" It took the air out of us, they were so fast and so tight. We were rolling on the floor, stoned out of our wits, just like, "Oh, my God!" I told somebody about them at the Grey Door, where they used to pay us in pot—we got an eighth of weed for a show—and that was the first place they played in Seattle.

BUZZ OSBORNE We did a lot of fun shows there. We were the last band to play the Grey Door when the lease was up. When we were done playing, the owner handed out half a dozen sledgehammers, and we just fucking destroyed the place.

MATT LUKIN Dillard got kicked out a year or two after we were out of high school. He had a girlfriend that was your typical bitch of a girlfriend: "You don't spend enough time with me, blah blah blah." He was like, "I can't practice. I'm with my girlfriend. I gotta go to a movie." What the fuck is that?

Buzz had me tell Dillard, "Buzz is quitting the band. He's going to start another band with Krist Novoselic and somebody else, this guy Crover. He might call one of us if that doesn't work." Well, apparently, Novoselic didn't work out on bass, so he calls me back. And he didn't call Dillard back. That was his spineless way of kicking people out of the band so he didn't have to face them. He made me do the dirty work.

BUZZ OSBORNE We went and found another drummer and just never talked about it. That might have been a mistake on my part, but when you're passionately involved in what you're doing, you don't always make the right decisions.

MIKE DILLARD I had a girlfriend, and I'm sure my lack of interest in the band was showing. If I remember right, it was Buzz goin', "I'm not gonna do this anymore. I'm done." And I remember thinking, Fine with me, I didn't really want to do it anymore, anyway. I think at that point they'd already gotten things squared away with Crover. It was no big deal. And they couldn't have found anybody better than Crover. He's the bee's knees, man.

BUZZ OSBORNE I met Krist Novoselic through a friend of mine who was thrown out of the Aberdeen public school system for lighting up a pipe bomb in the school, this guy named Bill Hull. At the time he was known as the Aberdeen Bomber. And I became friends with him when he came to my school. I thought Bill was exceptionally intelligent, an underachiever with a high degree of ability. Unrecognized genius, certainly. He was working at a Taco Bell in Aberdeen with Krist. Bill had told me that Krist played guitar.

MATT LUKIN Me and Buzz stopped by the Taco Bell. And as we're saying hi to Bill, there's this tall freaky guy in the back, singing along to Muzak Christmas carols—it was right around Christmastime. We're like, "What's up with the freak back there?" "Oh, that's my friend, Krist."

BUZZ OSBORNE I played Krist some music, and he was one of the few people who actually got it.

KRIST NOVOSELIC (Nirvana bassist; Shelli Novoselic's ex-husband) It was like a revelation. It changed my whole approach to life. Buzz was the preacher, and his gospel was punk rock.

MATT LUKIN After a while, we were like, "We need to find another drummer. Do you know anybody?" So Krist took us around and introduced us to a couple of friends of his who played drums.

Actually, the first guy he introduced us to was Aaron Burckhard—later he played drums for Nirvana—and within two minutes of meeting him, we realized, That guy isn't going to work out. It was just his personality. And what was going on in the back house—there were a bunch of "Hey, dude!"s partying: "Hey, dude!" Plus, he had a mustache. Having a big, bushy Tom Selleck mustache just meant you were trying to be something you weren't.

BUZZ OSBORNE What I wanted was a heavy-metal drummer. I wanted somebody who was going to push the band beyond belief. Like a freight train, a combination of Keith Moon and the guy from Iron Maiden.

MATT LUKIN Then Krist took us over to meet Dale. He was just some freaky high school kid who was a great drummer. He looked like a long-haired metal dude.

DALE CROVER (Melvins/Nirvana drummer) Before the Melvins, I played in a band called Rampage. Even though they liked other rock stuff that I liked, it was kind of like, "Oh, we have to play this Eddie Money song. We have to play ballads."

Rampage got this opportunity to play on a Christmas benefit radio program for this group of mentally handicapped adults called the Sunshine Kids. So we go down there, at the Elks Hall in downtown Aberdeen, and this band's already playing. They were the Melvins. The other guys in my band were going, "What the fuck is this shit?" And I was like, "I don't know, it's kind of cool. And they're playing their own songs." They played super-fast, they're loud as shit, and they just blasted one song into another.

BUZZ OSBORNE I had seen Crover play in a cover band—Loverboy stuff, crap, garbage—and I thought that he was a good drummer. When Krist mentioned him, I went, "Oh, yeah," so we went to talk to him. When Crover joined the band, he was a do-nothing stiff. I think he quit high school after doing 11th grade for the second time.

DALE CROVER The guidance counselor said, "It looks like you know what you want to do already." Basically I'd started touring with the Melvins—we'd been doing shows on weekends. He was like, "My advice is to drop out, because you're gone all the time, so you're just going to fail anyway."

DAN PETERS (Mudhoney/Nirvana/Screaming Trees/Feast/Bundle of Hiss drummer) Dale was this kid with a furry-lined Levi's jacket and long scraggly hair. His drum sets were always cobbled together with these odd-shaped and -sized drums. Everything was a different make and model, held together with baling wire. He'd just pound the shit out of the skins.

MATT LUKIN Dale was really into speed metal at the time. Which was kind of funny, in the sense that the Melvins were slowing down: "Everyone's playing a hundred miles an hour, let's slow things down. Freak people out."

DALE CROVER The idea to slow down came pretty much from Black Flag's *My War*, side two. Side two of that record is all of these slow songs, which their fanbase didn't like because they wanted faster stuff to mosh to.

BUZZ OSBORNE We certainly liked *My War*, but I don't know if it's the one that made us decide to slow down. I actually saw Black Flag on that same tour with this band Saccharine Trust, and they were every bit as slow, and weirder. They were hugely influential as far as atmosphere.

We slowed down, but I always thought that was just another thing that we were doing. We always played fast—*always*. People get hung up on us playing slow. Whenever I see journalists writing "sludgecore . . . Melvins"—yeah, that's true, if you listen to about 20 percent of our stuff. That means that they don't have any concept of what we're really doing.

DALE CROVER I'd also played with this guitar player named Larry Kallenbach in a band called Special Forces. He had an influence on the Melvins for sure, because he taught Buzz how to tune down to D. That was the Black Sabbath trick. "Into the Void" was tuned down to D.

JEFF GILBERT (journalist; KZOK DJ; concert organizer) Seattle isn't a glamorous town at all. It was pretty pathetic. Very depressing. That's where this music came out of. I've made this comment before: Grunge isn't a music style. It's complaining set to a drop D tuning.

DAN RAYMOND (Melvins "hanger-on") Buzz and I went to junior high and high school together. I went off to college, and when I came back on break, he was playing really slowed down. Before I actually heard it, I asked him, "What are you doing now that's different?" He said, "I call it 'twisted Sabbath.' "

TRACY SIMMONS (a.k.a. T-Man; Blood Circus bassist) I went and saw the Melvins at this little warehouse in the Fremont area in Seattle and was totally blown away. I was like, Oh, my God, that's the heaviest music I've ever heard. I gotta tell you, that really influenced Blood Circus a lot. Melvins were *the* band that inspired the grunge sound more than anybody.

MATT LUKIN Dale was dealing weed for a while in $5 grams. It got to the point where we had to lock the door to the practice room, because every five minutes someone would show up to buy weed from Dale.

DALE CROVER Dealing pot? I will not confirm or deny that. No, I did not sell anybody pot from my parents' house—I'll put it that way. But there probably was some kind of pot smoking going on on my back porch at some point. We were kids.

Whoever says we called the people who hung out with us the "Cling-Ons" is completely full of shit, because I never heard anybody described as Cling-Ons.

BUZZ OSBORNE I had nothing to do with those people, other than the fact that they were hanging out at Crover's parents' house, in Aberdeen. Aberdeen is a shithole. I didn't like any of these people. They were just a bunch of redneck fucking dumbass kids with this white-trash arrogance. Have you seen that Larry Clark photo book *Tulsa*? That's a good example of it. They were pot-smoking, alcoholic, thieving little bastards.

We were actually friends with Krist and Kurt. They understood what we were doing, liked what we were doing. We trusted Krist right away, went on all kinds of adventures with Krist. Went into Seattle and freaked out. It wasn't so much making trouble as discovering the world, like Mickey Mantle showing up in New York City for the first time.

MATT LUKIN I knew Cobain from junior high. When we were 14, 15 we were on the same baseball team in Babe Ruth. Sat on the bench. He was a quiet, skinny guy. We talked about our favorite rock bands. Didn't pay attention to baseball. At the time, we were both really into Cheap Trick.

BUZZ OSBORNE I was about 12 when I met Kurt. I really started to know him when we were in an art class together in school. He was a really good artist, so he would do things like draw a picture of the teacher with his head cut off, and it looked exactly like the teacher, or draw a picture of some girl getting raped, and it was a girl from the class. Eighth-grade bullshit. Lynchings, dark humor. I still like that stuff.

MATT LUKIN I remember not seeing Kurt for a few years, and one day he showed up at a Melvins practice with a guy who lived next door. They were both really drunk at the time. We were just playing Clash covers and stuff upstairs in Dillard's garage. I remember him going off: "Whoa, you guys were great!" He just started hanging around, and we started seeing more of him.

BUZZ OSBORNE One time, Kurt got popped by the cops, but the rest of us got away, luckily. Me, him, and Lukin and I don't know who else were walking around, spray-painting stupid shit, my favorite being FUCK YOU in big letters. I think I spray-painted GOD IS GAY or something. We were always getting rousted by the cops one way or another. But that was the only time that one of us actually went to jail. Who bailed Kurt out? Not me. If I went down there, I would have been put in the same jail as him. Fuck that, he was on his own.

DALE CROVER Is the story that Kurt slept on my porch in a cardboard box true? My mom gets all bent out of shape about that for some reason: "He slept on my porch, and I didn't even know about it?!" You know what, he probably slept on the porch when he was drunk once, and that was it.

All that stuff has just been so overstated, but nobody ever wants to know the truth. Like the stories that are written about Kurt sleeping under the bridge. It's just not true! I know that he did once, but it's not like he said, that he spent hours and days down there, becoming this tortured artist. That's the biggest myth, right there: Kurt Cobain, the tortured artist. People don't realize that guy was a funny motherfucker.

MATT LUKIN Yeah, Kurt did try out for the Melvins, and it fuckin' sounded great! And a couple of days later, I was asking Buzz, "Hey, what's up? That sounded great when Cobain was playing with us." And he's like, "Yeah, I don't think it's going to work."

DALE CROVER We thought about having Kurt in the band, but he didn't have any gear. It was like, "How's he going to play if he doesn't have an amp?" It's not like he passed or failed, it was just that he didn't have any money and didn't have his shit together.

BUZZ OSBORNE As far as Kurt trying out for us, that's not true, absolutely not. We jammed with him on numerous occasions, same with Krist. We never tried anyone out for the band, ever. I've always just thought of somebody who we wanted to play with and made that decision long before we tried it.

SLIM MOON (Earth guitarist; solo artist; Kill Rock Stars label founder) Krist Novoselic had a zebra-striped van that he drove the Melvins to their shows in. He was really tall and always really drunk. There was one party where he set off the fire extinguisher and another where he started dancing on top of a table and the entire table collapsed. Yeah, that was Krist in those days. He reminded me of Shaggy from *Scooby Doo*.

MATT LUKIN I don't know if I'd say Krist was a roadie, but we started using his van, and he'd drive with us to Seattle and help load our equipment. So, yeah, I guess he was a roadie. Cobain took that role after a while.

BUZZ OSBORNE We never had any roadies—that's bullshit. They were just friends. Sometimes Krist would drive us places. I always laugh at that: Kurt Cobain was our roadie. Look at him—he could barely lift himself out of bed. A roadie? For what, a flea circus?

CHAPTER 3
HELLO, SEATTLE!

BEN SHEPHERD (March of Crimes guitarist; Soundgarden bassist; Hater singer/guitarist) The first time I met Andy Wood? It was on the way to the first March of Crimes house-party gig, in Bainbridge. There was a car wreck right in front of me and our bass player. We pulled over, and these kids we knew in one car had come down the hill and nailed this other car. Everyone involved was headed to the same party.

Everybody was fine. We're all outside talking, and I look over at the other car, and I go, "Who's in there? What's going on?" They're like, "Oh, that's Landrew."

All of the sudden, Landrew piles out of the back of the car wearing this really long kimono-type thing, and his hair is all wild. Total character.

He'd been sleeping in the car. He's like, "Whoa. Hey, Shepherd, how are you doing?" We'd never met, but I stuck out like a motherfucker, man. He knew who I was.

"Hey, Landrew, how's it going? Are you okay?"

"Yeah. I was having the weirdest dream."

DAVE REES (Malfunkshun bassist) When he was in sixth grade, Andy won a listener contest on KZOK. He got to host the radio show—it was a program called *Your Mother Won't Like It*, from six to nine on a Sunday night—and he was brilliant. I remember him playing a lot of Kiss. He told stories, and he did little comedy bits. He had one Mister Rogers bit, I remember. You know, a "Can you say that?" type of thing. His brother Kevin was the show's engineer or producer.

It was great, but I remember talking to Andy after that and he seemed a little disappointed. Because he had wanted to be a DJ, but he realized that there was no immediate feedback. There was no audience there. And that really bummed him out. He actually told me, "Well, now I'm gonna have to be a rock star."

KEVIN WOOD (Malfunkshun guitarist; brother of Andrew and Brian Wood) I was still in high school and Andy was probably in middle school when we went to see Cheap Trick opening for Kiss. It's at that show, after Cheap Trick played, that Andy told me he wanted to be a rock star.

REGAN HAGAR (Malfunkshun/Brad/Satchel drummer) When I was about 10 or 11—which seems crazy to me now—I saw Kiss. It was the same show Andy and Kevin were at, although we did not know each other at that point. I remember being totally blown away, and for some reason it clicked in my mind that these were people and that they were getting paid to do what I was watching.

KEVIN WOOD We were a pretty close-knit family because we moved around a lot. We moved to Bainbridge Island from San Antonio, Texas, around '76, when I was about 14. Bainbridge is kind of a bedroom community for Seattle. Back then, it was rural and there were more eclectic-type people there—more alternative-lifestyle mentalities. My parents weren't hippies, but my mom was more open-minded about vegetarianism and self-awareness and enjoying the country. My dad was in the military—he was a recruiter in Seattle—but he was a very open-minded guy. I'm the oldest. I've got a brother, Brian, who's a year younger than me. And Andy, who's four years younger than me.

ROBERT SCOTT CRANE (Soundhouse Recording Studio owner; Michelle Ahern's ex-husband; son of *Hogan's Heroes* cast member Sigrid Valdis and murdered

Hogan's Heroes star Bob Crane) My parents were well-known actors, and when my father passed away, there was a lot of media interest in our family, so we moved from L.A. to Bainbridge Island to go somewhere where nobody knew who we were. Of course, people found out really quickly who we were. It was a real gossip-fest on that island.

Very shortly after moving there, while riding the school bus, was when I met Andy. I was probably in eighth grade and he was maybe in ninth. I noticed him on the bus being a total class clown, commanding a lot of attention. We got off at the same bus stop, and it was, "Oh, *you* live here? *I* live here." Somehow pot came up, and three seconds later, we were in the woods across the street from our house smoking.

KEVIN WOOD I think Andy was still in elementary school when he started smoking pot. I probably started drinking when I was about 10, but not like every day.

ROBERT SCOTT CRANE Andy and I really bonded in that when we smoked pot, we liked to obliterate ourselves with it. It was insane how much pot Andy could smoke. Looking back now, he was really just trying to block things out. Which is the same thing I was trying to do.

Bainbridge was a weird place because there were quite a few kids like this, in that they didn't take a half a hit of acid or a hit of acid—they took *eight* hits of acid. It wasn't like, "Let's smoke a joint and sit on the beach," it was, "Let's make it so we literally don't remember our own names."

KEVIN WOOD In 1980, we were toying around with the idea of putting something together, and we had invited this kid Dave Hunt to come over and drum, without realizing it was Easter Sunday. We were supposed to go out to dinner with our grandparents for Easter, but we stayed home and formed a band instead.

The band was called Report Malfunction at first. I was working in a restaurant, and there was a sign above the dishwasher that said REPORT MALFUNCTION, and I thought that'd be a cool band name. I came up with the image of a guy on a phone with a mushroom-cloud explosion behind him, and he was reporting the malfunction. One thing me and my brothers always shared was a dark sense of humor. The name got trimmed down immediately to Malfunction, and then the different spelling came about.

DAVE REES I was best friends with Brian Wood, the middle Wood brother, in high school. So the Woods were starting a band, but they didn't have a bass or a bass player. One of my buddies had a bass and a bass amp, so I brought it over to their house and they said, "Great, you're our bass player." I had never even played before.

REGAN HAGAR I grew up in Seattle in a neighborhood called Ravenna, and then in eighth grade we moved to Bainbridge. I was super-upset about leaving the city. So I'd save my lunch money Monday through Friday, and use it to take the ferry to Seattle. I got a job at the Showbox when I was probably 14. We didn't get paid money, but we—there was a group of kids between 14 and 19—cleaned up and hung posters and tore tickets and behaved as security during the shows. Blaine Cook, who was in the band the Fartz, worked there.

BLAINE COOK (the Fartz/10 Minute Warning/the Accüsed singer) We did security, cleaned up, hung flyers, worked the door. We didn't get paid, but you got to hang out and see the shows. Regan and I had a bit of a side business where we let people into sold-out shows, and the money would find its way into our pockets.

REGAN HAGAR I think all the Fartz worked there. Also, Kyle Nixon, who was the singer of the band Solger, worked there. Duff McKagan was just another kid around. John Bigley was at the Showbox with us at the beginning. Bigley goes all the way back.

JOHN BIGLEY I was 18 when I started working at the Showbox, before it became official—back then it was a rental place, the Talmud Torah, a Jewish bingo hall. The best job there, which I started getting quite a bit, was standing with a flashlight by the backstage area where the equipment would be set up, where you could just sit and watch everybody onstage. And back then it was such a treat. Paul Weller, Captain Beefheart, James Brown—they were doing shows like that.

I'd come home at five, six in the morning, go to sleep, and wake up two hours after class. *Oops.* Hence, crash and burn at school. I got a 0.00 my first two semesters at the University of Washington and stopped.

The area around the Showbox then was dipping into old Seattle. Extremely pre-Microsoft.

MARK ARM Seattle was a lot sleazier then, in all the best possible ways. You could go down to Third Avenue, and there'd be storefronts with women in lingerie in them. There was no actual prostitution going on there. They were kind of skirting the law, suckering people in—drunk sailors and whatnot—trying to separate them from their money.

JOHN BIGLEY There were a lot of sailors coming in from Bremerton, with the white bell bottoms. And there were long-haired street-guy hustler drug-dealer types dukin' it out with the sailors. And then the punk-rock weirdos dukin' it out with the bikers at the Indian bar—they were called Indian bars, open at six in the morning. Right there was probably as rough as Seattle was. I was a lover not a fighter, but you'd have to learn techniques like the throw-the-garbage-can-in-the-person's-face trick.

REGAN HAGAR Most of the fights I remember were between punks and what we called Donut Holers. Only a parking lot separated the Showbox and this donut store that stayed open late, where all the homeless kids who were prostitutes and thieves would be.

DAWN ANDERSON (journalist; *Backlash* zine publisher; Jack Endino's ex-wife) I spent a lot of time at the Showbox. I was a suburban girl with Farrah Fawcett hair. To me, it was this place where you could go and check out all the freaks and weirdos. There was a pornographic bookstore next door, and the guy who owned it used to go outside and glower at these punk rockers that were lining up and ruining his neighborhood.

REGAN HAGAR I sort of met Andy at the Showbox. He and Kevin were in line for Devo, I think. We acknowledged each other, like, You look familiar to me from the halls of our eighth-grade school, Commodore. Andy approached me at school the following day and said, "I have a band. Are you interested in playing?" And I said, "Sure, let's do it." This guy Dave Hunt was quitting. We would practice in Andy's parents' basement or my mother's garage. We would get pushed from house to house. I remember getting letters in my mother's mailbox asking us to make it stop because we sucked. I've kept the letters—they're pretty great.

KEVIN WOOD Andy and Regan were like Laurel and Hardy. It was always lots of smiles, lots of joking. Regan was more of a straight man; Andy was the funny guy.

JONATHAN EVISON The Woods lived on Miller Road, which is two blocks from the road that I grew up on. Andy I knew before punk rock; we were kind of the resident Elton John freaks. Andy could tease, he could be a pain in people's asses, but there was always a playful good nature under it. He just had genuine goodwill status wherever he went.

DAVE REES Dave Hunt lived in a trailer in the woods on Bainbridge and he had a home CB unit. Andy would get on that thing, and he had these handles, like Ratchet Jaw Penis Snatcher. And he had these truckers laughin' their asses off to the point where one of them said, "Hey, tone it down or I'm gonna drive off the road."

He made you laugh all the time, in any forum. I loved goin' over to the Woods' house. There was this crazy energy there—of music, of fun.

ROBERT SCOTT CRANE There was kind of a cold, dark feeling in that house. The story that I know is that Kevin would often get into physical conflicts with his father and his brother Brian, trying to protect Andy, the baby of the family. Andy couldn't physically defend himself, so he tried to be the court jester. And I remember the final straw for their mom, Toni, leaving the house when they were my neighbors was that Brian came home drunk, and she told Brian that he either had to stop drinking or cut his hair. So he came back a few hours later drunk and bald. And she moved out. And disappeared for I think a couple of months.

DAVE REES There *was* tension. I was there when there was infighting amongst the Wood family that wasn't pleasant. But, like I said, I loved goin' over there. Mr. Wood's stereo system was the loudest thing I'd ever heard; they'd crank Judas Priest and Kiss and Sabbath at concert volume.

And their parents supported and encouraged their music. His folks took Andy and my brother to meet Van Halen as they went into the radio station in town, KISW. My brother got Eddie Van Halen's autograph, and Andy went right to David Lee Roth—David Lee Roth and Freddie Mercury were huge influences on him.

Everyone else was asking for autographs, and Andy said to David Lee Roth, "I just wanna shake your hand." David Lee Roth shook his hand and said, "I'm on a schedule, son." Andy loved it.

REGAN HAGAR During our high school years, the Woods probably switched houses just about every year, which was good for the band because we could move the noise around. Seems like both our houses were always just for us, because our parents were always working. Andy's parents got separated around the time we were finishing high school. It started with a separation, followed by divorce. And that was a super-bummer for Andy.

DAVE REES Our first show was on a stage built on the side of a hill with strawberry fields around it. Andy named it the Strawberry Jam. When we were driving there, I had all the equipment loaded in my 1970 Buick Estate wagon, and there wasn't enough room for the guys in the band. So Andy and Regan rode on the luggage rack up top. And when we get there, Andy's long hair was gone. Regan had shaved Andy's head on the way there. There always had to be something going on.

At that show, Andy wore a shirt with a swastika with a circle around it and the red line through it. It was more antihate; he hadn't figured out Love Rock yet. But he was always thinking that way. Even then, his marketing ability was just amazing. When you walked off the ferry boat from Bainbridge into Seattle, there were these big metal panels overhead, and on every panel Andy wrote a saying. At the end, it came to the punch line: ROCK AND ROLL'S ONLY CHANCE: MALFUNKSHUN.

That was my one official show with Malfunkshun. I went to Seattle to go to college, and when I came back, Andy was playing my bass and he was quite a bit better than me. I ended up taking Dave Hunt and this other friend of ours and forming a band called Skindiver. So it was amicable. Skindiver played shows with Malfunkshun, but these guys did not compete with my band or with any other local band. They were going right after Led Zeppelin and Aerosmith. They had these wild conceptual songs. And the characters that they developed . . .

REGAN HAGAR Andy had the band on paper. He had notebooks full of drawings, descriptions, histories, all made up. In the beginning, my character was Thundar. My last name's Hagar, I'm Nordic. I have this love of Vikings, and I was thunderous. Andy got his name, Landrew the Love God, from an episode of *Star Trek*—there was a character who spread love and was this omnipresent love person. Kevin's identity was a little built by Andy, as well: Kevin Stein, like he was this dead guy.

KEVIN WOOD I originally was calling myself Ded Springsteen, as a protest against Bruce Springsteen, because he was so dorky and stupid. And then I changed into Kevin Stein. No, not like Frankenstein. I just wanted to have a different last name. Actually, the Stein thing came from a kid who was really popular in high school when we lived down in Texas. It was a 70 percent Chicano high school. This guy Stein drove a convertible; he always had a girlfriend. He was white and had blond hair, but he was bigger than most of the other kids—maybe he got set back a few grades—and so all these Mexicans just worshiped this guy. They always called him by his last name: "Stein! Hey, Stein!" He was the big man on campus. So that's why I adopted that as my last name.

But these nicknames I generated for myself didn't last long. It was just easier to go with my real name, because it's what everyone knew me as.

REGAN HAGAR Around '81, Andy would wear a big, long choir robe, with whiteface. Nobody else back then changed for the stage. It was uncool. But he went through the whole process, preshow. I only wore makeup for a short period of time—more Alice Coopery stuff, like black around my eyes with lines that came down. It was kind of a drag to deal with, and Andy was full-bore and up-front, so I didn't need to do it later.

Andy would have girls who would do his makeup. Girls were just all over him; they would love to come back and help him get ready.

ROBERT SCOTT CRANE Women loved Andy. I mean, he was, fuck, maybe five-six and overweight, but he was so charming. I knew two or three of Andy's girlfriends after he was with them. And since then, I've met one or two women who just randomly had a one-night stand with Andy, and they all have basically the same feeling: They'd love him. One-night stands in high school can be a bad thing, especially for the girl, but they all were like, "He was an angel. He treated me so sweet. He was so loving."

REGAN HAGAR When Andy was probably 15, he was rejected by a girl that he had gone out with for a while. End-of-the-world stuff for him at that time, I'm sure. I don't know what he used to do it, but he carved her name across his chest. Not terribly deeply, but it never went away, which was a point of a little jeering 10 years later. Her name was Ruth, but when the scar settled in, it looked like it said RUSH. When you'd see it, the joke was, "Wow, you're *really* into Rush."

DAVE REES Andy really became a character. Even in his picture in his senior annual, he's in whiteface makeup and has a Malfunkshun quote. He was a star in his own mind already.

REGAN HAGAR Back then, 666 was huge—black-metal stuff was going on. Andy came up with the opposite, 333: "This is going to represent our band, and we're gonna call it Love Rock." We had a roll of stickers that were black with a white *3* on them, and we put 'em on shit. It was a big spindle that lasted for years. It was just a Love Rock thing. Three is a magic number.

DAMON STEWART (KISW DJ; Sony Music regional A&R scout) Andy had such a big-arena-rock-show presence. Even a little club like the Vogue, which seemed like it could barely hold a hundred people, he treated the crowd like it was a hundred thousand.

REGAN HAGAR He'd regularly speak to the balcony—and there wouldn't be a balcony. He'd do typical rock banter: "How you doin' tonight?" "Let me hear ya in the balcony!" Lots of "Hello, Seattle!"s. It sounds almost too cheeky, but the way he delivered it was just great. He brought big rock to a small-punk ethic.

KEVIN WOOD He'd mention that the band came down from Olympus to play the show. We were gods, right?

ALEX SHUMWAY (a.k.a. Alex Vincent; Green River/Spluii Numa drummer) The first time I saw Malfunkshun was at the Metropolis. We were waiting for them to play. Regan's behind his drum set, and Kevin's up there with his guitar on. And all of a sudden, you hear this real heavy, grinding bass. We're going, "Where the hell is that coming from?" We're all looking around, and when we turned around, there was Andy walking across the bar, with a wireless on. He had on white makeup with purple eye shadow and really red lipstick, and he was wearing purple spandex pants. And he had this peacock stride. Everybody's going, "Oh, this is fuckin' awesome!"

TOM PRICE The thing that always cracked me up about Malfunkshun— and the thing I loved about them—was that they would come to the end of the song and Andrew or Kevin would jump in the air to signal, Okay, the song ends here. *Boom!* But nobody would stop playing—the band would just keep going and going and going. Every show they did was one big, long song with a monster guitar solo all over it.

REGAN HAGAR We would get heckled for doing guitar solos. I feel like—and of course, I probably romanticize things—Malfunkshun changed the sound of the city by putting metal into the punk, which was such a taboo for a band like the Fartz, who would never, ever have a guitar solo.

MARK ARM I saw Malfunkshun open for Whitehouse, that neofascist industrial band, and Malfunkshun fuckin' destroyed them. Whitehouse was a stale joke by that point: this guy in jackboots and a black leather trench coat coming through the crowd going, *"I'm going to rape you!"* I was like, "No, you're not." They weren't the least bit threatening or real.

It was posturing, whereas I just saw a really unhinged performance on the part of Kevin Wood, who was on his knees the whole time with his eyes rolling back in his head, just playing the craziest shit.

JOHN BIGLEY One of the first things I remember about Andrew was him telling me, "If you're ever on Bainbridge Island, let me know and

I'll show you my Kiss shrine." I go, "Kiss shrine?" He was deadpan, not clowning around. "Oh, you're not kidding." And he starts describing this shrine: "There's two red bongs and a signed Kiss *Destroyer* jacket"—and he just went on—"and I'd like you to see it."

No, I never saw it—they were still living at their mom's.

REGAN HAGAR When we moved out of our parents' houses, Andy and I moved into a house together in West Seattle with Blaine Cook and two other guys from our circle. The place was a total shithole. There were parties, and all we ate was cereal. Because we were fresh out of our parents' houses, and what does any kid want? Sweet cereal. We would cut the fronts off of all of the cereal boxes and cover the kitchen walls with them.

Andy started dating these two girls called Tiger and Jane. They were kind of like a lesbian couple. They were strippers—they took their clothes off and did their bit together in a club on the same street as the Showbox. I would get nervous when they were at our house because if you walked by Andy's room and they heard you coming, they would literally come and try and grab you to bring you into their circus freak show.

BLAINE COOK Andy was just a regular Joe around the house. If anything, he liked to spend his time playing that little handheld football game.

REGAN HAGAR It was the Mattel Electronics football game. Our friend Paul and Andy and I had teams. Andy kept stats, and we had this thing called the World Bowl, which is like the Super Bowl, at the end of a season. My team, the Hawaiian Angels, beat his team, the Dallas Cowboys—he was always the Dallas Cowboys—and he cried.

ERIC JOHNSON (Soundgarden/Pearl Jam tour manager) It was either during the Malfunkshun days or right after, and Stone Gossard was working at this little bakery in Pioneer Square. I was talking to Stone when Andy came in wearing a white fur coat, makeup, white gloves. His look was amazing—and this was just walking around. He came in looking like that and started talking about the Dallas Cowboys and football.

That's why it was hard to take anything in Seattle really seriously.

CHAPTER 4
THE MOST BEAUTIFUL DANCE

SUSAN SILVER (Soundgarden/Alice in Chains/Screaming Trees/U-Men manager; Chris Cornell's ex-wife) Alex Shumway and Mark Arm were, far and away, the two people who caught my attention at the Metropolis. They just spun with the most incredible, youthful, vibrant energy I had ever seen. Them stage-diving was the most beautiful dance to watch. They were so graceful and fearless. It was mesmerizing.

ALEX SHUMWAY Okay, here it is—this is the embarrassing part: I was a ballet dancer. This was when I lived in Sacramento, when I was 14, 15.

The best part of being a ballet dancer was that as a straight guy, you get the pick of the litter. I went out with two or three of the girls. After shows there would be a huge party, and everybody would get totally shitfaced; people would be smoking up and maybe do a little coke. It's like you have to be really prim, proper, and prissy, and then it's like, Oh, Jesus Christ, you have to let go some other way. I would give it a shot, and I would end up puking or just being like, "This isn't good. I don't like this." So I went straight edge pretty early on.

Once I got into punk more and more, I got tired of ballet. I got involved in the music scene in Seattle pretty soon after I moved there with my mother and my sister in '82.

STEVE TURNER (Mudhoney/Green River/Mr. Epp and the Calculations/the Thrown Ups guitarist) I started going to a private school in Seattle called Northwest School of the Arts, Humanities and Environment for my senior year. Both Alex Shumway and Stone Gossard went there. They were both a year younger than me. Alex, we befriended each other right off the bat 'cause when he first started going there he had a dyed-black mohawk and wore a kilt over his jeans—he was the Circle Jerks skanking guy come to life—and I was a skate punk and we both loved Minor Threat.

ALEX SHUMWAY I met Mark Arm at a show—I think it was the U-Men—at the Metropolis. We were both on the floor and I saw the back of his shirt, which said STRAIGHT EDGE. I was probably one of three people at that time who I knew in town was straight edge. So I was like, "Hey, dude, that's cool!" But I think the shirt was ironic. I could be remembering incorrectly, but I recall him telling me long, long after that, "Dude, I was on acid that night!"

MARK ARM Wow, his memory is off. I never had a STRAIGHT EDGE T-shirt. I was kinda into it in my own way, I suppose. At the time, I thought weed and alcohol dulled the senses, and psychedelics enhanced them. I wasn't on acid that night, but I was into Minor Threat.

STEVE MACK (singer for the U.K.'s That Petrol Emotion) I remember in particular one night at the Metropolis. I was always right in the middle of the pit, because I loved slam-dancing, and that night I felt this tap on my shoulder. I turned around, and there's this skinny, wiry kid and he's telling me, "Link your fingers together. Give me a boost." So I lock my fingers together, and he plants one foot firmly on my hand and leaps over me onto the stage.

He jumps back out in the crowd, and I went over to him and tapped him on the shoulder and said, "Okay, my turn. You link your fingers together." So he did that and threw me onstage. And that was the first time I ever met Mark Arm.

MARK ARM I was born on Vandenberg Air Force Base in California. I was too young to really remember living there, but I do remember living in Germany after that. My dad was in the Air Force in World War Two. Met my mom after the war; she was German. They were engaged for like 10 years while he was in the Pacific and she remained in Germany. And then they got married and had me in the early '60s. We came to the States and ended up in Seattle in '66.

My mom was an opera singer. Her career got interrupted by World War Two. She tried to get it going again after the war, and she apparently got some good reviews, but she was by this point a little too old. She was strictly into classical, and any other kind of music was a lesser form of music. Rock music was everywhere—except in my house.

MAIRE MASCO (Pravda Productions partner; *Desperate Times* zine cofounder) It's kind of hard to imagine now, but a lot of people in the scene didn't even have telephones. In order to get a phone you had to put down a deposit of like $75 to $125. That was a lot of money! So the way you communicated with people was flyers, not only to promote bands and events, but sometimes to express political beliefs or public commentary.

This band started putting up posters that were just hilarious. One was MR. EPP AND THE CALCULATIONS: GREATER, BIGGER, LOUDER THAN THE GRATEFUL DEAD. Some of their other great taglines were LOUSIER THAN BOB DYLAN and LESS CREATIVE THAN JOHN CAGE.

Dennis White and I were watching these flyers go up and we're like, "We gotta figure out who these guys are." But there was no phone number on the flyers, no dates. And one day we were walking down First Avenue, and we saw some kids putting up a flyer, and we ran up to the flyer and realized it was for Mr. Epp and the Calculations. And we're like, "Oh, my God, we found them!" They were a block or so ahead of us, so we ran down the street chasing them. They, of course, thought we were gonna beat them up or arrest them or something.

Finally we caught up to them and we said, "So are you guys Mr. Epp and the Calculations?" And it was Mark Arm and Jeff Smitty, and they kinda looked at their feet and shuffled around and said, "Yeah, I guess," like they were guilty of something. I said, "Well, I'm Maire Masco, this is Dennis White. We're with Pravda Productions and we'd really like to book you."

They just started laughing, and I think it was Mark Arm who said, "Oh, my God, that means we have to get instruments!"

MARK ARM Mr. Epp was a fake band for a number of years, as retarded as that sounds. It was named after a math teacher in our little private Christian high school. One of our friends, Darren Morey, was actually a good drummer, but the rest of us didn't know how to play anything. I was forced to play piano as a kid, but I quit in seventh grade and did my best to forget about it. We made these weird tapes with shit that was at hand in the house, appliances and whatnot. We didn't think we were being avant-garde; we were just a bunch of kids dicking around.

After high school, we decided to make the band a little more real, and my friend Smitty and I went in on a guitar and an amp. At that time, Darren was still in high school. And Todd was like 16. He was Darren's brother and the baby of the band.

How'd I get the name Mark Arm? My friends and I were into non sequitur humor. One day, Smitty and I had this fake argument using non-offensive body parts in place of normal swear words, like "nose face" or "ear elbow." It culminated in Smitty calling me "arm arm," which made us all just double over in laughter.

DENNIS R. WHITE They were snotty, self-important 16-year-olds. I may have been as old as 24 or 25 at the time, and they saw us as completely old and useless. There's no doubt there was a certain sense of fun and novelty, but there was something else that we heard—they took it one step beyond the typical DIY ethic. There was such a sense of mission in what they were doing. And they would've just sneered at that: "What do you mean, 'mission'?"

STEVE TURNER I met Mark in October of '82, right when my senior year started. He'd come back from one year at college in McMinnville, Oregon, when I met him—we could never really decide if it was the Public Image Ltd. show or the TSOL show where I met him in line. We had a lot in common: Snarky sense of humor, some amount of disdain for the punk rockers. One of Mr. Epp's jobs was definitely to piss off the punks, 'cause they were so easy to rile up.

JEFF SMITH (a.k.a. Jo Smitty; Mr. Epp and the Calculations singer/guitarist) The DJ Rodney Bingenheimer started playing our song "Mohawk Man" on the radio in L.A. and people liked it. We were always amazed that anyone liked what we did at all. A lot of people hated us, just because we didn't have the right signifiers, like mohawks or songs about Reagan. Which is what "Mohawk Man" is making fun of.

TOM NIEMEYER (the Accüsed/Gruntruck guitarist) The Metropolis kinda forced different social scenes into hanging with each other. Like Duff McKagan, all those cats. Duff was part of the leather-jacket-wearin', spiky-haired *real* punks. And the Accüsed were "gosh, I wish we could be like real punks" from Whidbey Island, which is way outside of Seattle.

ROISIN DUNNE (now Roisin Ross; 7 Year Bitch guitarist) I'm from the suburbs, in Edmonds. Live music typically meant high school dances or AC/DC at the Tacoma Dome. Discovering the Metropolis opened a whole world for me. The fact that there was no separation between the audience and the bands totally resonated with me—you could always get up front or sit on the edge of the stage. I would go by myself and didn't know anyone for a long time, but I didn't care.

The Fastbacks played there, and it was inspiring. Kim and Lulu from the Fastbacks seemed cool, and after a while we became friends. They definitely had an influence on me, but in many more ways than just wanting to play guitar. Through them, I met so many amazing women in that scene.

MARK ARM It wasn't an anomaly to have women in Seattle bands. There were the Fastbacks, who were around forever. There were plenty of local bands with women in them earlier, post-punk bands like Little Bears from Bangkok, which was three women and a guy singer. The Visible Targets were three sisters and a drummer; in the early '80s, they were one of the bands that was on their way to making it—they got a record produced by Mick Ronson. There just didn't happen to be women in the bands that got huge in the '90s.

TOM NIEMEYER And then there was Mark Arm and Mr. Epp—they were part of the University Avenue crowd of punks. They were fuckin' smart-asses all the time. You never even tried to compete with being wittier or funnier.

MARK ARM To the people of my generation, the Metropolis was immensely important. The bands that played there actually got paid. When Mr. Epp played there, it was the first time ever we made any money. "We got paid $100! That's crazy!"

HUGO PIOTTIN (now known as Poki Piottin; Metropolis club owner) I was born in Lyon, France. Came to the U.S. in '78. I ended up in Seattle, where I connected right away with a group of young folks dabbling with video production. They were in their early twenties, so I was a little older. We thought, Okay, we need a studio to create these videos. I had about 50 grand in the bank from fishing in Alaska, so I was the one financing everything. We found this place in Pioneer Square that had been an old tavern, probably built in the '20s or '30s. It was a gay bar for a while and then for a while it was a place called the Love Canal. It may have been that the gay bar was called the Love Canal, but I'm not sure.

GORDON DOUCETTE (Metropolis partner; Red Masque singer/guitarist) Hugo had the biggest heart in the world, and he also had a pretty short-fused temper, which made for an interesting combination. The big-hearted side of him recognized that there were all these kids on the street with absolutely nothing to do, and an all-ages live music club just wasn't around at all; you could see pockets of kids gathered outside clubs to hear the music coming from the inside. So Metropolis was his dream. I just wanted to be a part of it.

SUSAN SILVER I ran the juice bar, and next to me at the end of this beautiful bar was Bruce Pavitt spinning discs. Hugo's idea was the Factory West Coast, a place for people to come and express themselves in any way: hear music, see films, and make art projects together. And then commercial needs took over, so it morphed into a showplace. There were lots of shows: You could have Jah Wobble one night and TSOL the next. GBH and the Violent Femmes.

I met Gordon in Belltown, during an evening out. We were together a few years. He was quiet, mysterious, enigmatic, creative. Hugo and Gordon were polar opposites in terms of personalities, which made for a really well-rounded experience as far as what the place looked like, what the programming was like. One was outspoken and passionate and wanting to connect people, and Gordon was more reserved and protective.

GORDON DOUCETTE Susan's involvement in Metropolis was just monumental. She had a great business savvy. She's a woman with a huge heart. There's a lot of clubs where the owners are never present—they're shrewd businessmen counting cash in the office—but Susan, Hugo, and myself were always out there; we were part of the crowd and directly involved. So 95 percent of the people who walked through the doors of Metropolis knew us by name.

SUSAN SILVER We had the Replacements there, and the three of us went through a lot of effort to make the place look nice. We had a group of young people who really cared about it. And after the Replacements left, we went into the dressing room and they had just trashed it. They pissed in there and graffitied all over the walls—they drew a caricature of Fred Flintstone with somebody shitting in his mouth. It was juvenile, it was imbecilic, but beyond all that, it was disrespectful. I was gutted.

Later, knowing what that felt like, that sort of thing was a "no discussion" issue between me and my clients. I had to walk Mike Starr from Alice in Chains out of a couple of places by his ear. We were at a pub in England and he was peeing on the wall and I said, "You know what, dude, somebody just like your mom or your grandma is going to have to get down there and clean that up. So stop now."

MAIRE MASCO Susan and Gordon did some bookings. I did some booking. Hugo did booking. It was kind of a communal effort. I'll probably get in trouble for saying this, but Gordon really was kind of Susan's arm candy. Susan was gorgeous; she didn't need arm candy. One time Gordon would show up with like a poofy shirt, and then next week it was something else.

LARRY REID She had bad taste in men, that's what I remember about Susan. Oh, man, she went out with Gordon Doucette from Red Masque. He had a wandering eye, to say the very least.

SUSAN SILVER I learned that much later, after the third year. It was infidelity. He was a general scallywag.

GORDON DOUCETTE Believe me, I've given her many apologies over the years. It was a horrible ending between us. That's pretty much when I took my exit from Metropolis.

STEVE TURNER Some hardcore friends of mine, Alex Shumway included, started a band called Spluii Numa and I rehearsed with them a few times. It wasn't my scene, so that's when Mark said, "Quit them and join Mr. Epp on second guitar instead." So I did, and we played two shows and broke up.

JEFF SMITH Mr. Epp's last show was at the Metropolis. Darren and I got all the hair and dirt that we cleaned out of his dad's hair salon, and then we threw it on the audience. People ran away. The club was super-pissed. They were like, "You'll never be able to play here again!" And we were like, "Well, we're done with the band. . . . And we'll sweep up."

HUGO PIOTTIN The life of the Metropolis was about a year and a half. They let us have the place on the condition that we'd pay month to month. Next door was a building that was being turned into a fancy condo. And they didn't want to have that kind of crowd on the weekend—people sitting on the sidewalk, drinking, making noise.

GORDON DOUCETTE The people who I know who remember Metropolis remember it like they do a family member. They tell me, "I can't say this about any other club, but I really, really miss Metropolis."

MARK ARM After Mr. Epp, Steve and I decided that we wanted to keep playing. We got Alex Shumway, who'd already been drumming with Spluii Numa, to start a band with us.

ALEX SHUMWAY The origin of Spluii Numa's name? Somebody at our school wrote on the wall JOHN LENNON LIVES! And somebody else had marked out LIVES and wrote WENT SPLUII NUMA! Meaning got his head blown off, blood splattered all over the place. We thought it was hilarious.

MARK ARM We just needed a bass player. We thought Jeff Ament would be a good guy to get in the band; in Deranged Diction, he jumped really high and played bass through a distortion box.

JEFF AMENT (Pearl Jam/Temple of the Dog/Mother Love Bone/Green River/ Deranged Diction bassist) There were fifty to a hundred kids that hung out at Metropolis, and that's where I met Mark and Steve and Stone. I met Alex the year before at an X show. I met Mark when I was DJing there one night. I was playing Black Flag and Aerosmith and Minor Threat and SSD and Kiss. We both had a common interest in a lot of the same bands.

MARK ARM But we didn't know Jeff very well. He and his band had recently moved out to Seattle from Montana. Steve got a job at the same place that Jeff did, basically just to get to know the guy. That's probably one of the weirder things we've ever done—stalking a bass player.

STEVE TURNER I had Jeff help me get a job at the coffee shop Raison d'Être that he worked at as a dishwasher, so I worked there to kind of infiltrate and convince him that me and Mark could do a real band where we actually write songs and practice.

MARK ARM Jeff was not a fan of Mr. Epp, but apparently Deranged Diction was running out of momentum, so he was open to practicing with us. The first Green River practice was the four of us.

It was a very auspicious day when I came up with the idea for that name and Steve came up with the idea for that name. We met up and were both excitedly going, "I think I got a name for the band!" We both thought of Green River. When does that happen?

Steve was shopping at a thrift store and saw something for Green River Community College Track or something. I don't remember exactly what my lightning bolt was—probably the Creedence song. The Green River Killer was in the headlines at that time. Kind of awesome and dark.

ALICE WHEELER (photographer) There's always been this sort of hovering darkness over the Northwest, and a lot of it was about the Green River Killer, 'cause that was going on when I first moved to town. One of my best friends, who has since passed away, his cousin was victim number 14. There's always been this element of danger for women in the Northwest, and I think part of what influences grunge is that element and a sort of depressed somberness.

ALEX SHUMWAY Some people I'd run into would ask, "What's the name of your band?" "Green River." "Oh, that's just sick and wrong."

MARK ARM We opened for the Dead Kennedys and the Crucifucks. I didn't see any evidence of it, but apparently there was a group outside picketing based on our name. Okay, it's the *Dead Kennedys* and the *Crucifucks,* and you're picketing Green River?

The very first show we played was at a party in a storefront-slash-house that a friend of mine was living at with his band called PMA. Before the show, Jeff was joking around a little at practice like, "Maybe I'll put on some whiteface." Landrew from Malfunkshun was doing that regularly. I was like, "Yeah, that'd be funny," and he showed up at the show with complete whiteface on. "Wow, okay, I guess he wasn't kidding." But that only happened once.

Stone Gossard had joined the band before that show, but he didn't feel comfortable enough to play it. Stone got on board through Steve and Alex—they all went to high school together. Steve and Alex were the kids that went to punk-rock shows, and Stone hung out with kids that went to metal shows more. But somewhere in there, the scenes converged a little.

MATT WRIGHT (Gas Huffer singer) One thing I remember about seeing Green River is a lot of times they'd take the stage and the percentage of females in the audience grew exponentially. It was like a bunch of models all of a sudden appeared, as if on cue. I'm exaggerating, but they had some tall, long-haired dudes in their band. They were also kind of the cool band for a lot of people.

CHRIS HANZSEK (C/Z Records label/Reciprocal Recording studio cofounder; producer) When Green River came into the studio to record, they were all pretty young. I remember Stone Gossard wasn't in the band initially, but they added him. And when they brought him over and introduced him, I was worried that he was skipping high school to be there. With those demos, they were able to get their deal with Homestead Records, and then they invited me to help produce their *Come on Down* record.

BRUCE PAVITT (Sub Pop Records cofounder) I was working at Fallout Records, and I got a phone call from Gerard Cosloy at Homestead, and he asked, "What are the happening bands in Seattle?" I said, "You want to check out the U-Men and Green River."

MARK ARM Green River had three offers, believe it or not. We'd played with Fang in Seattle, and Tom Flynn, the guitar player, had a record label called Boner. And we'd also gotten an offer from Enigma somehow, which is kind of baffling to me. I remember the contract from Homestead was like seven pages and the contract from Enigma was like 60. And we were like, "Well, this one is smaller and easier to understand." And at that time Homestead seemed like the coolest record label on the planet, next to SST. They put out Foetus and Nick Cave and Sonic Youth and Volcano Suns.

STEVE TURNER My tastes were changing. I was discovering more of the '60s garage punk. My hair was gettin' longer and then I shaved my head, got a buzz cut, as an act of rebellion against the Green River thing—right before Jeff wanted to get some band photos taken. So I was kinda being a dick.

MARK ARM Steve stopped playing with any kind of distortion, and during at least one show, he played sitting down on a chair in passive-aggressive protest.

STEVE TURNER I didn't want to go on tour when they wanted to, and I felt like I was kind of holdin' them back. As soon as I quit, they got Bruce Fairweather in on guitar and they got so much better so quick.

BRUCE FAIRWEATHER (Green River/Mother Love Bone/Deranged Diction guitarist; Love Battery bassist) I was born in Hawaii and lived there until I was 18. I was interested in going to forestry school, and the University of

Montana had a good forestry program. And the catalog they sent me had this area in the quad that looked totally skateable. So I decided, I'm going there!

The first thing I did when my parents dropped me off at college was find that spot. And that's when I met Jeff Ament, who was skateboarding there. He had on these shorts with 999 and Sex Pistols and the Germs and Black Flag and stuff, and I was like, Whoa! Who's that guy? So I started talking to him, and we became really good friends and started Deranged Diction five months later.

SLIM MOON I saw the first show after Steve Turner quit, and it was much more of a hard-rock set. They did a bunch of Led Zeppelin covers, which Mark Arm kept joking about. I think Steve was the advocate of a sort of punk simplicity, which was against what the other guys in the band wanted, which was bombast. When he left, it was just bombast. The glam influence really came in.

There were a lot of different moments where you could say, "It's the birth of grunge," but I like to mark it as that moment: when Steve Turner left Green River.

CHAPTER 5
SCREAMING LIFE

KIM THAYIL (Soundgarden guitarist) In 1981, I cashed out my bank account in Chicago—I had very little money—and Hiro and I loaded up the Datsun B210 with suitcases and threw in our guitars, mandolins, portable amps. I played guitar. Hiro played mandolin; he didn't play bass yet. And we drove the 2,000 miles to Seattle.

The people our age in Seattle seemed to be easily five years—in some ways, 10 years—behind Chicago in terms of fashion. A lot of people with mullets and '70s-style stuff. Those big combs they shove in their rear pockets. People weren't wearing Levi's, they were wearing Jessie Jeans or Britannia. We thought, Wait a minute, we're in America still, and nobody looks the way they do in Chicago or New York or Minnesota. This is weird.

HIRO YAMAMOTO (Soundgarden/Truly bassist) Seattle was a cowboy town back then. When we got there, people still wore cowboy hats and cowboy boots.

I was born in Park Forest, Illinois, a southern suburb of Chicago. It was a planned community, with winding streets and a lot of parks. I met Kim when I was a senior in high school; he had already graduated. We both went to this place called Rich Township High School, but we were in a program called ALPS—Alternative Learning Process School. Bruce Pavitt had also gone there. At ALPS, you kind of didn't have classrooms, you didn't really get grades. We played a lot of Frisbee.

CHRIS CORNELL (Soundgarden singer/guitarist; Temple of the Dog singer; solo artist; Susan Silver's ex-husband) At the time I was growing up, it was the tail end of the baby boom, so there were tons of kids in the neighborhood. Tons of boys, young and old. So there was tons of drugs. The definitive Seattle neighborhood. . . . I never went to high school. I never really finished eighth grade. . . . From the time that I started playing drums at 16, I was already out of school.

HIRO YAMAMOTO The first time I left Park Forest was after high school, when I moved with my friend Stuart Hallerman to Olympia. I had a job, but I got laid off and moved back home.

KIM THAYIL I was best friends throughout high school with Bruce Pavitt's middle brother, and his youngest brother was in a band with me called Identity Crisis. In 1981, Hiro and I were both in bands, both had girlfriends, but then our bands broke up, the relationships with our girlfriends ended, and there was no real reason for us to stay. We came out to Seattle for an adventure. Bruce was out here, Stuart was out here. Bruce is sending us records and tapes from bands in Seattle and Olympia that we were really into—the Blackouts, the Beakers.

MATT DENTINO (the Shemps guitarist) I've known Kim Thayil since '72. We went to an alternative high school in Park Forest together. It was an alternative to the traditional high school, which I got kicked out of because I was too alternative—all I did was play guitar and study Jimi Hendrix.

In 1980, Reagan got elected and I was more of a left-wing Democrat back then. I said, "I'm outta here, because I'm 20 and this guy's gonna shave my head and put me in the Marines, and I gotta go fight a war."

The day Reagan was elected, I went to Seattle on a Greyhound bus, 'cause my brother was out there goin' to med school, to play rock and roll and party, and chase chicks—which I wasn't very good at, by the way.

When Kim and Hiro came to Seattle, we eventually hooked up and started hanging out a little bit. All of '84, I spent building the Shemps. Kim would play bass, and sometimes Hiro would play bass. Sometimes I was the lead guitarist, and I think a few gigs Kim played guitar with us, too. And what we were doin' was lots of classic rock. And the reason that we did lots of classic rock was, number one, it was easy to learn. And there was lots of old hippie gigs that we could play right away, and I needed to work. I was starving; I was living in Kim's closet.

STUART HALLERMAN (Soundgarden soundman; Avast! Recording studio owner/ operator) I get a call from Hiro saying, "Guess what? I joined a butt-rock band!" That was the Shemps. I was kinda surprised, because this had nothing to do with his tastes prior to that. In school his nickname was Bean because he was the brains of the school; he played viola and listened to bluegrass music, classical music, some jazz. His entire rock collection consisted of one Grateful Dead record and one ELP record.

MATT DENTINO I put an ad in *The Rocket,* saying the Shemps were forming and we're a "combination of the Three Stooges and Jimi Hendrix." Chris Cornell answered the ad, and everything changed.

SCOTT McCULLUM (a.k.a. Norman Scott; Skin Yard/Gruntruck/64 Spiders drummer) My dad and I moved to West Seattle when I was nine. In high school, a friend of mine, Eric Garcia, and his buddy you might've heard of, Chris Cornell, we'd just get together and jam. At that time Chris was playing drums and I was playing guitar, just doing covers and messing around. He wasn't singing yet. Chris was pretty quiet, reserved. People took that as some sort of aloof rock star thing later on, but it wasn't that. He just didn't really have attitude or ego back then.

CHRIS CORNELL I went from being a daily drug user at 13 to having bad drug experiences and quitting drugs by the time I was 14 and then not having any friends until the time I was 16. There was about two years where I was more or less agoraphobic and didn't deal with anybody, didn't talk to anybody, didn't have any friends at all.

SCOTT MCCULLUM I remember heading down to Bumbershoot with Eric Garcia and another friend to see George Thorogood play. We were in Chris's car, and he's driving, and he's like, "Guys, you know what? I'm gonna try singing." He starts singing "Bad to the Bone" at the top of his lungs, and we all just fuckin' cracked up. Because we were just bullshitting with each other, and he was so serious about it. It sounded pretty good, but we were like, "Yeah, whatever."

MATT DENTINO He was 18 years old and he had very short hair, as I recall. He was a cook. And he just blew my backside away when he started singin', you know? He just was a very mellow, deep-thinking dude all the time. I'm a mouth-runner. I just speak, speak, speak. But he was just kind of sitting there, collecting everything.

Suddenly I had what I believed was one of the best singers on the planet. The first song I did with Chris was "White Wedding" by Billy Idol. And I was like, "Man! You know, dude, you're hired." And he could be Morrison-like, he could blow it out of the water.

I've read stuff like the Shemps was a "cheesy cover band." But we weren't doin', like, Foreigner hits. We were doin' Jimi Hendrix and Doors and Allman Brothers and good blues.

KIM THAYIL The Shemps was a bunch of nonsense. And I don't mean nonsense in an endearing way, but nonsense, like nothing. It has nothing to do with the lineage of the Seattle scene. It was influenced by nothing in the Seattle scene and influenced nothing in the Seattle scene. The only claim it has to the Seattle scene was that I played in the band and Hiro played in the band. I never thought I was even *in* the band—I thought I was helping out my friend, who had some gigs lined up. And I forgot what might be Matt's biggest claim to fame: He introduced Chris to me.

MARK ARM Kim was in my philosophy class at the University of Washington. He would always come into class five or 10 minutes late, and then proceed to monopolize the class. He would just take the class on tangents. You could almost see the professor roll his eyes every time Kim came in. Kim came up to me at a TSOL show at the Showbox and was like, "Hey, I think you're in my philosophy class," and we struck up a friendship. He had long hair and a scrub mustache. He looked like a hesher—I wouldn't have guessed for a minute that he was into punk rock.

I saw them before they were Soundgarden. That cover band. I don't even know exactly what songs they played, but my impression of it was that whatever they played, Chris sounded exactly like the singer of the original song. If they did a Doors song, he sounded exactly like Jim Morrison. It was like, "Wow, this kid can really sing."

MATT DENTINO Chris moved in with Hiro, and upstairs was an A-frame, and we'd jam up there. Hiro was also in a band called the Altered, where they did a lot of original stuff, and it was New Wavy and jangly. He wanted me to not play with distortion and not play lead—he saw what I was doing as old-school, dinosaur. Well, I might as well cut off my testicles!

But being broke and not wanting to lose this thing, I complied. We played till the end of the year, and I was just hatin' life, and doin' a lot of drugs—almost died. And finally, I was so hurt I cried out to God. And his name is Jesus. I got touched by God and I'm like, I need to get out of here. And I told those guys, "I've gotta go. I'm leavin' you for Jesus, so to speak."

HIRO YAMAMOTO Chris was living with me, so me and Chris would play together, just us two, bass and drums. That was right around the time Kim was in his senior year of college. Me and Kim, we would sit around and drink beer and talk all night. Chris would do it a little bit, but then he'd just head off into his room and disappear.

KIM THAYIL So Hiro's playing with Chris. They audition and jam with various guitarists. Hiro called me up and asked me to come by and jam. The first time we jammed, we wrote three songs. The very next day, we wrote two more songs. Everyone was just glowing, smiling ear to ear. We were like, "This is the coolest experience any of us has had." It was so natural and spontaneous. Then Hiro kept calling me, "Dude, did you have fun jamming?" I was like, "Yes, that's better than any band I've been in before! It was so natural."

"Well, don't you want to come back and play?" "Dude, I got a test. I have to see my girlfriend this weekend. I'm DJing Thursday nights. I'm working Monday and Saturday. . . ." They were getting ready to think about other options, but I came back and played, and more material came out. It was just too jaw-dropping. Things went so easily.

MATT DENTINO About three months later, Chris called me: "Dude, we're goin' on. Come to our first show." So I played hooky from church, and I went to their first gig. Lo and behold, Kim's using distortion, playing lead, and sounds like Zeppelin. I'm like, Hey, wait a minute, stop that! I thought we weren't supposed to be doin' this. Yet that's exactly what made them powerful.

KIM THAYIL The name Soundgarden was evocative, and it was among a list of names we were thinking of. *A Sound Garden* was a three-word name for a metal sound-sculpture on a beach here in Seattle. We derived the name from there, but we never were paying homage to the sculpture, never. Just liked the word *garden* as an element in a name. It's visually evocative and it's not overtly metal or punk or anything. It doesn't type us. A year later, we thought maybe we should change Soundgarden to Sungarden or Stonegarden, but then Soundgarden just kind of stuck.

STUART HALLERMAN There weren't too many other bands with a makeup like Soundgarden's. Hiro's a Japanese guy; Kim's an Indian guy. The transition for the three of us, goin' from a very mixed Chicago area to the very whitewashed Northwest, was kinda weird. It took me years to kinda deal with, Is this a real city? Where are the other people?

HIRO YAMAMOTO Race is very pivotal when you're young and trying to figure out, Who am I? How do I fit into this world? Kim and I would talk about that a lot. The rock scene was pretty much all white. There were a couple of black guys who played, but they were few and far between.

KEVIN WHITWORTH (Love Battery guitarist) I consider myself African-American, but I'm just one of your first multiculti babies—now everyone's got one. Basically black, but Peruvian and Cherokee Indian and a bit of German, I guess. I don't really think in terms of race, mostly because I grew up in a middle- to upper-class black family and we had the biggest house in our town in New Hampshire. I've always been treated like a white person, basically.

But there was one night that made me feel a little bit weird; it might've been when Love Battery played one of those packaged shows—a "nine for the '90s" show—at the Paramount. The Paramount's pretty big, and out of all those people I was the *only* one, besides maybe some janitor in the back *(laughs)*, who was somebody of color. It was something I never revisited again, because that's just the way it is. I do recall that we did have a black fan who followed us to a couple of shows. I kept wondering, Is this for real? Does this guy really like us? Even *I* couldn't believe it.

* * *

SUSAN SILVER I met Chris at the end of '85 at a Halloween party, at an artist studio in Belltown, and I was out on the town that night with my dear friend Chuck, a.k.a. Upchuck from the Fags. And Chuck dressed me up as him in drag—he was in drag most of the time—so I had a long blond fright wig and a kimono and pancake makeup.

Soundgarden was playing the party, as a three-piece, with Chris on drums and vocals. They were amazing. I'd worked with Ben McMillan in a vintage clothing store in town called Tootsie's. And Chris came in to talk to him, and the story that Chris told me is that I caught his eye. So he kept coming in and trying to get my attention, but I paid him no mind. Partly because I had just broken up with Gordon earlier that year, so I was in a pretty dark space.

After the band played, Chris came up to me and *recognized* me, which he got huge points for because I was in full drag-queen regalia. He said the band were trying to get a show in Vancouver, so I told him that I was going up there to a show in the next week, and if he wanted to meet, I would take a tape for them.

So we met, and he gave me that tape, and we saw each other a week later at the Vogue. After that, we went to a 24-hour diner. We tried to go back to my house, but I'd lost my keys. We made out for a while, and then he took me to my mom's in West Seattle, and it was just on from there. At the time, it was healing for me.

SCOTT SUNDQUIST (Soundgarden drummer) I worked as a carpenter at a seafood restaurant in Ballard called Ray's Boathouse, building tables for them and repairing things. That's where I met Chris Cornell. He was a line cook, a teenager—maybe 19. When I met him, I was about 31. Chris and I hit it off because we're both sort of loners.

Before I joined, I saw Soundgarden open for Hüsker Dü at an all-ages place called Gorilla Gardens. Because Chris was playing drums and singing, his energy was really confined. That had something to do with them pushing him forward to become more of a front man and to have a drummer, which became me.

CHRIS CORNELL The beginning of me thinking maybe I should get out there in front of the drums was seeing Matt [Cameron] play in the band Feedback. They were at a club where the back of the stage was actually the venue's storefront, and I was standing outside on the sidewalk, watching Matt play. I'd never met Matt, but I knew who he was. Other than seeing Elvin Jones on film, this hadn't happened to me before, where I'm watching what he's doing and I'm hearing what it sounds like and I couldn't really make the connection. And I thought, Oh, that's what a good drummer is supposed to play like. Maybe my talent lies elsewhere.

TOMIE O'NEIL (soundman; RKCNDY club co-owner/comanager) There were two rooms in the Gorilla Gardens, and I did sound in both. I was there the night Cornell came out from behind the drums and said, "I'm the singer now." That was amazing.

KERRI HARROP Gorilla Gardens was this shitty old all-ages place down in Chinatown, so it always seemed really sketchy to go there. And you would just see these insane bills of bands—I saw Hüsker Dü there, I saw the Melvins there. Gorilla Gardens is also the first place I ever saw people having sex in public. It was that kind of place.

MICHELLE AHERN (concertgoer; Robert Scott Crane's ex-wife) Andy Wood took me to my first punk-rock show, at the Gorilla Gardens. My girl-friends and I went with Andy and Regan and this guy Chewy from the Accüsed. It was Andy's 18th birthday. I sort of ended up being his date. I don't know what started it, but at the show a huge fight broke out between the rockers and skinheads. Somebody picked Andy up by his white fur coat and flung him into a chain-link fence. We jumped into a cab and sped off into the night. I ended up spending the night with Andy at his house. I guess you could say I was his 18th-birthday present. *(Laughs.)*

TOM NIEMEYER I think the mix of punk and metal was single-handedly because of Gorilla Gardens. It was an old theater that had two stages, a metal side and a punk or alternative side. So in the lobby, these people listening to very metal stuff had to be mixed in with people being very punk rock. And they had to use the same bathrooms. That's what made the crossover happen. Right, at the urinals! Exactly!

SLIM MOON It would be lovely to make a big, dramatic punks versus rockers thing out of it, but it was a punk club. It always had some hard-rock shows because the guy who ran Gorilla Gardens, Tony Chu, wanted to make money any way he could.

TOM NIEMEYER Sometimes we would get paid at the Gorilla Gardens, sometimes we wouldn't. "There's a shitload of people here, Tony, where'd the money go?"

"Oh, you know, blah blah blah . . . the electric bill."

"For the night? Three hundred dollars for the night? For electricity? Jesus! I know we got big amps, but my God!"

ART CHANTRY (*The Rocket* newspaper art director; Sub Pop Records freelancer; album/poster designer) There was one famous show at Gorilla Gardens—I think it was a Red Rockers show, some people say it was a Butthole Surfers show. The fire department came in and tried to close it down because they didn't have enough fire exits. Everybody was getting really pissed off, so somebody took a chain saw and literally cut a hole in the wall to the alley outside, and the shit went back on. They had a fire exit now, didn't they?

TOMIE O'NEIL There were a bunch of legendary shows there. Guns N' Roses played in the small room. That night, we're also havin' a great Violent Femmes show—maybe 400 or 500 people in there. And my friends were like, "Dude, you gotta go in the other room, there's this metal band that's just fuckin' outta hand—and Duff's in it." Duff had lived in Seattle and went, "Fuck you guys, I'm movin' to L.A. and I'm gonna be the hugest fuckin' rock star!" And I remember walking in the other room and goin', "Man, these guys are fuckin' great!"

DUFF MCKAGAN (bassist for Los Angeles's Guns N' Roses; played various instruments in Fastbacks, the Fartz, the Living, 10 Minute Warning, the Vains, many more) We were horrible. We had a car with a trailer, which broke down in Bakersfield—that's a long way from Seattle. So we hitchhiked with our guitars and used the Fastbacks' gear. But it was great for me coming back to Seattle. That was our first real gig. Well, I think we played a gig the night before we left, at Madame Wong's East or something, to three people. In Seattle, we played to 12. There's been thousands that said they were at that gig, but actually there were 12, and four of them were the Fastbacks.

TOM NIEMEYER When the Gorilla Gardens building was no more, Tony Chu opened another Gorilla Gardens, but it wasn't the same—it was just one room, over in another spot across town. There were some famous clashes with police that happened there that were of note. The big snowy, midwinter Circle Jerks riot with the cops. The Accüsed were supposed to play that show. The cops showed up before anyone played because there was no permit to have a show there. There were a good amount of people who had literally walked through the snow for miles to get to this thing, so people were pissed off. Some skater-punk kids got the idea to hurl some nearby loose bricks at the cop cars. I left, and it got ugly—as I was walkin' up the hill, I remember seein' cop cars startin' to catch fire and shit like that. *(Laughs.)* It was pretty epic.

Then parents started sayin', "We don't want our kids at these things." I think that led to the Teen Dance Ordinance. It made all-ages shows impossible to get—you had to have like a million-dollar insurance bond to allow kids to see live music, period. Unbelievably fucked, you know? So we had to play bars and stuff just to fuckin' survive here in town. It sucked.

KRISHA AUGEROT (Kelly Curtis's assistant; Green Apple Quick Step comanager) When I was probably 14, I got into going to the Monastery downtown, which was a gay nightclub that ended up soliciting kids on the Ave and on Broadway and giving them free passes. I'd go there with

Stone Gossard and Regan Hagar. We'd stay there all night long and then go hang out downtown in the morning and have coffee. Basically, it housed a lot of hardcore, homeless street kids. It was just a lot of crazy shit going on with minors and drugs. It was like the ultimate bad place for children to go if they were out. I think parents and the city decided that was not a good option for kids and created the Teen Dance Ordinance to shut it down.

MARK ARM Of course, I was totally against the Teen Dance Ordinance; it made it impossible for legit all-ages shows to happen. This may not be the most popular thing to say, but there was some good in it, because we had to go looking for different kind of venues, mostly bars. So we found places like the Ditto Tavern, which was a tiny place on Fifth Avenue, and we got the Vogue to let us play on Tuesday and Wednesday nights—they wouldn't even have bands on the weekends because they made more money off of DJs playing New Wave dance tunes.

It also drove things into more underground spaces, like house parties. And when Seattle promoters wanted to do bigger all-ages shows, they would have to go out of town. There was Natasha's in Bremerton, and the Crescent Ballroom in Tacoma, where we played a great show with Redd Kross.

BRUCE FAIRWEATHER Green River opened for Redd Kross in Tacoma, along with Soundgarden and Malfunkshun. And a label person was coming up to see us play. Soundgarden played first, and we found out after the show that Susan Silver had snuck them out of the building during our set, so whoever the A&R person was didn't see us play. She did what a manager would do, and got them out of the building. Back then, they weren't signing bands left and right. Jeff was furious with Susan for a long time about that.

It was a really awesome show, too, so we were totally bummed out. Mark had on his silver pants and the black negligee that he used to wear. He might've been on drugs that night.

MARK ARM I was out of my mind on MDA that show and thought it would be a really great idea to climb to the top of the P.A. and, from there, jump onto a fluorescent light that was hanging by two chains from the ceiling and try to swing on it like it was a kid's swing.

TOMIE O'NEIL Mark Arm, wantin' to do something crazy there, climbs up on top of the P.A. It was a pretty tall building, and they had four-foot fluorescent lights hanging on chains down from the ceiling. With the mic in his hand, he jumps on top of that thing like a swing, and the minute he hit it, it pulled down about six to eight inches, and we thought, He's done. It looked like that thing was gonna come down. He's like 15 feet off the ground, and he fuckin' sang a verse up there.

BRUCE FAIRWEATHER Mark was up there. His head was 20 feet in the air. He was swinging and he was able to jump—he hit the stage and rolled with the microphone. It was pretty cool. I fell to my knees and split my pants open, and I didn't have underwear on. I think I was more concerned about that. I was like, "Whoops!" That was a fun show.

CHAPTER 6
LEAVING HOME

JACK ENDINO I was born in Connecticut. Lived in a town called Salisbury. Moved to Bainbridge when I was 17, that was in the '70s. I had two half-brothers who were much older than I am, because they were from my mother's previous marriage. Effectively, I was an only child.

Ended up working at the naval shipyard in Bremerton for two and a half years. Civilian electrical engineer. It was a pretty soul-destroying job. Walked out of that job in 1983, and resolved that I was going to do something else with my life. Specifically, something with music. And that was the last day job I ever had.

I played the drums a little bit, I played a little bit of guitar. After I left the navy yard, I rented a single-wide mobile home at a place called Tiger Lake, which is out in Belfair, Washington—middle of nowhere. Set up my drums, my four-track recording machine, some amps and speakers, some guitars, and spent the winter of '83 teaching myself how to record, using myself as the guinea pig.

The ensuing five years of my life played out just as I had imagined: moved to Seattle, joined a band, started working in a recording studio. It all came to pass. I visualized it quite strongly.

DANIEL HOUSE My first band was Death of Marat, which I affection-ately refer to as the worst band in Seattle. Not too long after, there was a three-piece band called Bam Bam, and I remember being really im-pressed by their drummer, a guy named Matt Cameron.

MATT CAMERON (Skin Yard/Soundgarden/Temple of the Dog/Pearl Jam/Hater drummer) I grew up in San Diego, and I started drumming when I was about nine years old. I started playing in rock bands when I was about 13, 14, just with the neighborhood kids. When I was 14, my neighbor John De Bello did this low-budget film that became a cult classic, *Attack of the Killer Tomatoes,* and he had me sing the song "Puberty Love" that killed the tomatoes at the end of the movie—my voice was so horrible that it just vaporized them.

I moved to Seattle in 1983 with a friend of mine. I was 19 at the time and looking for a new adventure, and boy, did I ever find it.

DANIEL HOUSE Matt didn't stay very long with Bam Bam, but somehow I managed to find him. The guitar player was a guy named Tom Herring, who went by the moniker Nerm—I have no idea why. Together we cre-ated Feedback, which was a very cerebral, very mannered prog-rock instrumental three-piece.

For a lot of that year I was actually in both Feedback and 10 Minute Warning, which is largely known as the band that Duff McKagan was in before he moved to L.A. When Duff quit, so did their bass player, so I joined playing bass.

JOHN CONTE (the Living/the Blunt Objects singer) Duff was the youngest of like eight in a Catholic family where every person is musical. He was the type of guy that you could shut in the room with a new instrument, and within 15 minutes he would've learned a song and come out and played it for you. Everywhere you went people would just come up to him because they knew his brothers and sisters, and he always had tons and tons of girls. I mean, just flocking to him, just to be around him.

DUFF MCKAGAN When I was 14, a friend of mine who was a drummer and I formed a band with Chris Utting called the Vains—it was my first punk-rock band. My first gig ever was opening up for Black Flag at the Washington Hall in '79. Later, the Fastbacks asked me to play drums because Kurt Bloch was initially playing the drums and he's really a guitar player; Kim Warnick became my musical mentor. By '82, I was playing drums with the Fartz, which was a hardcore band. I was in a million bands and really having fun, starting to tour down the West Coast and play Vancouver all the time. I was writing music with Paul Solger of the Fartz, and these songs were really dirgy and slow and weird and long. We got Greg Gilmore to come in and play drums and we got a different singer, Steve Verwolf, and that was 10 Minute Warning.

BRUCE PAVITT When I first moved to Seattle, I got a job in a yuppie restaurant called the Lake Union Cafe, working as a prep cook, and Duff was working as a baker's assistant. I'd be chopping carrots, and he'd be next to me putting pecans on cakes. I very distinctly remember him saying, "I'm gonna move to L.A. and try to have a career as a musician." It was indicative of just how impossible it was to make music a career in Seattle.

RICK FRIEL (Shadow singer/bassist) Duff and Mike McCready were really good friends. Mike, my brother Chris, and I were hanging out at my parents' house, and Duff came by with this guy named Chris Utting, who went by Criss Crass, and Duff had his SG guitar over his shoulder. He was like, "I'm moving to L.A., and I wanted to say good-bye to you." And we're like, "No way! That's so cool." And he was like, "Yeah, I'm gonna go for it. I'm gonna drive down there and live in my car if I have to." We were speechless. Somebody's actually doing something.

DUFF MCKAGAN I've heard people quote me as saying, "I'm gonna move to L.A. and become a rock star." Then they add, *"And he did."* Everybody says they knew me in 1984, when they actually didn't. It wasn't any of that. I wanted to be a musician, and the people I was playing with in Seattle, everybody was doing heroin, and I wasn't. Heroin decimated 10 Minute Warning. A friend of mine who was strung out said, "Man, if you don't get out now, it's going to pass you by. You're the guy, you're our hope."

JOHN CONTE Duff was a no-drug guy. Just beer and cigarettes or booze and cigarettes. And the Living even had an antidrug song called "No Thanks," which he wrote. For a lot of us, when he gets introduced to the hardcore drug scene down in L.A., it was sort of like, *Geez*, Duff. Someone really worked on you. That was too bad.

DUFF MCKAGAN Becoming a famous rock guy was never really my intention; I wanted to be in a band that felt amazing and go tour, because that's what I do. It was between going to New York and L.A., and I had this old piece-of-shit car, and I knew it wouldn't make it to New York.

DANIEL HOUSE After 10 Minute Warning finally disintegrated, the drummer, Greg Gilmore, moved down to L.A. and moved in with Duff. And from what I understand, Greg actually had the opportunity to join Guns N' Roses, but passed.

GREG GILMORE (Mother Love Bone/10 Minute Warning/the Living drummer) I had nothing else going on at that time, and Duff came to me one day and said, "We gotta get outta here."

We lived right in the middle of Hollywood, right behind the Chinese Theatre, and we were real close to the Musicians Institute. You'd see these guys walking up and down Hollywood Boulevard on their way to and from school with their guitars on, just playing because they are *so dedicated* to making it. They are fully regaled, fully groomed hair dudes. You never know when you're going to be discovered. It could be standing right here on the corner of Hollywood and Vine, so be ready.

KURT BLOCH One day I got a call from Duff in L.A. He's like, "You should come down here and play with my new band. We need a guitar player, and there's a Marshall stack here waiting for you." The band was Guns N' Roses, and they didn't have a lead guitar player. I was like, "Ah, I don't know if I want to go down to Los Angeles. I'd have to quit my job." And he was like, "Come on, man, it'll be great!" I could've gone down there and played with them. Whether I would've got the job or not, who knows?

GREG GILMORE We met Slash and Steven Adler through an ad in *The Recycler*. Slash and I, just the two of us, went and jammed one evening, and that was cool. But by that time I was not really digging it. Those guys all drank quite a bit, and I did not really. I couldn't hang. But the

Guns N' Roses that we all came to know was two years later. All those wild tales of debauchery and excess weren't happening yet.

I wasn't asked to join Guns N' Roses. Not explicitly, anyway. I remember being there when they were brainstorming about vocalists and Slash brings up his buddy Axl.

But that's the same time that I was already winding down there. There was just a lot of emphasis on the business of making it. Not that I had a problem with that. I just didn't really get it. I came back up to Seattle for the holidays, and I decided that was it for me.

JACK ENDINO As soon as I moved back to Seattle, there was my friend Tom Herring, jamming with Daniel and Matt. Their band was kind of falling apart. I played Daniel some solo recordings that I'd done out by the lake, and he liked those. He said to me, "Do you want to join Feedback?" But then he decided, "No, I think Feedback is over with, let's just start a band with you." So I ended up inheriting Tom's rhythm section.

DANIEL HOUSE We knew we wanted a singer, and we had no idea who that singer was going to be. We didn't have a name. And we started playing house parties and the basements of various places, instrumentally. We played two or three parties where we had people just grab a mic and wing it. And our stuff was not easy to sing to. It wasn't three-chord rock, and we played a lot with time signatures and we did a lot of stuff with counterpoint. We were a little too arty to really fit in with the whole grunge scene, and yet way too heavy to really fit in comfortably with a lot of the art-rock bands.

Ben McMillan ended up being at one of those parties. It was at 14th and Spring, a block away from my house, and it was in the basement. He grabbed the mic, and he was the first one who seemed kind of comfortable and did something that resonated with us.

JACK ENDINO Matt made it very easy to write difficult music. You could throw anything at him, and he could play it. I rather enjoyed it, but Ben had a hard time singing on some of the quirkier stuff we were doing in the early days. It was a bit prog, actually.

Ben had no history with music whatsoever. He was just a guy with a rich baritone voice who wanted to give it a try. Completely unschooled, no natural sense of melody at all. I basically had to teach him how to sing.

We discovered quickly that Ben was good with lyrics, and he had the pipes, and it was an issue of, "We need melodies now." He developed a knack for coming up with these melodies and these cadences that would work. But you couldn't say, "Try it in a different key," because he didn't know what a key was. He wasn't a musician, he was an artist—a very talented artist, actually.

JASON FINN (later Skin Yard drummer; the Presidents of the United States of America/Love Battery/Fastbacks/Feast drummer) When I met Ben, he made more money than anybody I'd ever known before in my life. He sold airbrushed shirts at the Pike Place Market, mainly for tourists. They'd have cat's eyes and New Wave girls and stuff on them. He made $150 a day, which was incredible. I was like, This guy has really got it figured out, because he's doing his own thing and it's creative, and he's obviously wealthy. *(Laughs.)*

JACK ENDINO Ben lived in this cooperative, low-rent apartment building called SCUD—Subterranean Cooperative of Urban Dreamers. He was extremely creative, extremely unreliable. Missing practices. Being late. Not coming up with words until literally right when you're about to record the song in the studio. Always bumming $20 from you. "Ben, you made more money than I did last year. What are you bumming $20 from me for?"

CAM GARRETT (photographer; SCUD cofounder; Ben McMillan's first cousin) Pretty much anybody that lived in SCUD was some type of artist. We would have regular meetings. Ben was having trouble getting his rent together all the time and making it to the meetings, and we were wondering what to do about him—we didn't want to kick him out. So we made him president. Then he not only came to every meeting, but he had to chair the meetings, he had to get everybody else there, and he was really good at that. He really blossomed.

DANIEL HOUSE Ben was very gregarious. He was very funny, and he tended not to take things particularly seriously, and I think that's part of why we clashed. I felt like I would do a lot of work, and I could never get him to really contribute. Then he'd have this attitude of, "Hey dude, whatever. Lighten up." It's like, "Uh, you need to show up at practice." Though I probably *did* need to lighten up, for what it's worth.

JAIME ROBERT JOHNSON (a.k.a. Crunchbird; singer/guitarist) Ben used to have this joke he would tell onstage. I got out of treatment once and Skin Yard were playing at the OK Hotel, and I showed up. And he tells the audience, "We're gonna dedicate this set to Jaime, who's clean and sober now. We have this box at the end of the stage, so if you have any drugs, put 'em in the box and we'll dispose of them later." That made my day.

DANIEL HOUSE Ben worked out a lot, so he was kind of pumped. Lifting weights or going to the gym wasn't something that people did back then. And then here's Ben, who's very dashing and just cut, very trim.

ROBERT SCOTT CRANE Chris Cornell, when he was young—when you look at him on the cover of *Screaming Life* and in some of those other Charles Peterson photos—he was a boy. He was a very pretty boy. Ben was a *man.* And I remember young girls were kind of like, Oh, that's a sexual force up there. He's like a lumberjack. Ben was this big, muscular guy—and not in a gross, Danzig way.

KERRI HARROP So much of that music has a dude edge to it—there aren't a whole lot of love songs in the Skin Yard catalog. I don't get intimidated very easily, but I felt intimidated at shows back then because there were so many dudes. It just seemed so cool, plus they were a couple years older than me, which made it even more daunting. And shows would get wild! With stage-diving and the pit, it's like, Jesus, something could happen to you.

DAWN ANDERSON A lot of people I knew didn't really like Skin Yard that much, but I just loved them. I used to ask people, "Why don't you like Skin Yard?" "Oh, they're just so arty, they're too complex." I guess they were a little too intricate and didn't just "rock out with a cock out." And some people thought Ben's voice was kinda weird—he was doing more of a spacey David Bowie thing. And then someone suggested that it was because they weren't cute, but I disagree with that. After all, I married the guitarist.

JACK ENDINO I proposed naming the band Skin Effect because I'm an electrical engineer, and *skin effect* is a particular electrical phenomenon related to high voltages. Then we discovered there was a band in town called Cause/Effect, so that was out the window. Matt said, "Why don't we call it Skin Yard?" None of us were particularly happy with it as a band name, but nobody actually vetoed it.

DANIEL HOUSE Our first show was June 7, 1985: the U-Men Leave Home show. The U-Men were *the* band in underground Seattle. And it was a big deal that they were going on tour.

JACK ENDINO We were the first out of five bands: U-Men, Baba Yaga, Girl Trouble, the F-Holes, and there was a performance artist called Function Disorder. The MC was Slam Hate. It was in a hall called the Odd Fellows Hall. It was a big show by any standard.

Larry Reid put the show on. He tossed us the opening slot just to be nice to us. Well, just to get Daniel to stop calling him. Daniel was very persistent about promoting the band. Probably got on a lot of people's nerves, but then a lot of things happened that wouldn't have happened otherwise.

JULIANNE ANDERSEN (Supersuckers/Gas Huffer booking agent) Daniel House was a player. A player in a scene that didn't have players. Daniel House in L.A. makes sense. Daniel House in Seattle did not.

DANIEL HOUSE I'm *that guy*. I'm the guy who is gonna make the shit happen if everybody else is sitting around with their thumb up their ass. I was the one hustling for gigs. I networked in that scene and knew a lot of people. I was the de facto manager of the band.

I remember being kind of pissed off that we opened that show, which goes back to the arrogance of youth. It's like, dude, it's your first show, and it's a big-deal show.

LARRY REID The U-Men going on tour was another watershed moment, because it was the first local punk-rock band that really went on a legitimate tour.

GILLIAN G. GAAR (journalist/author) I can't remember who said this first, but he put it well: "It seemed more amazing that the U-Men put a record out and went on tour than it did that Nirvana went to number one." I mean, how could people get on a record and how did records get out there? It seemed totally unattainable, and you had no idea how to do it. Like nuclear physics or something.

MIKE TUCKER The U-Men toured in a 1963 Chevrolet Viking school bus. It was pink, so it was kind of phallic-looking. And it barely ran. We built plywood boxes in the back for their equipment, and we had a couple sleeping spaces on top of the equipment. When I went with them on their maiden trip to San Francisco and Los Angeles, and then on to Austin, in the summer of '85, the whole ceiling of the bus was pasted with pornography; primarily straight, hardcore pornography. We also had all these Uzi posters, which Larry and I had gotten at a gun show that we got kicked out of.

So we get pulled over in Los Angeles, the cop came on board this bus with the pornography and gun posters—and at the time, the band looked like complete freaks—and he just shook his head, like, Just get out of here. I'm not even gonna bother with you.

TOM PRICE The first one was called the Doomed Faggots tour. Because we were doomed—we knew we were gonna be miserable and starve.

JIM TILLMAN In a sense we were doomed because there really weren't many places to play. And we were discovering that.

JOHN BIGLEY We went down the West Coast, and everything between Los Angeles and El Paso either got canceled or fucked up. We went to the Woodshock festival in Texas, which was our excuse for touring, and wound up staying in Austin for a month. Woodshock was held on this ranch in Dripping Springs. Naked cliff-diving, eatin' mushrooms, bathtubs full of marinated beef ribs. It was a mind-blower. Made some pretty strong friendships through it, with bands like the Butthole Surfers and Scratch Acid.

DAVID DUET (Cat Butt/Girl Trouble singer; U-Men roadie) The first U-Men tour, I flew down and met them at Woodshock. I'd moved from Austin to Seattle Thanksgiving of '83 with my girlfriend Lisa. I met John and Tom on the bus home, and that pretty much instantly blossomed into a cool friendship.

When we got to Austin for Woodshock, the base point for Tales of Terror, Tex and the Horseheads, the U-Men, and all the other assorted musicians that were hanging about was Chris Gates from Poison 13's house. It was quite the rowdy party scene. The morning after we all hooked up, I remember being woken up by a cop knocking on my knee with his billy club. A majority of us were passed out across the street from Chris Gates's house—in a funeral home parking lot, with various tarps and blankets thrown over us. A funeral procession was trying to get into the lot.

JOHN BIGLEY The plan was to tour out of Austin, but the only other show we did was Houston. All the other shows got canceled. That happened a lot in the mid-'80s: The venue would cease to be before you got there.

TOM PRICE You could barely call it a tour. It was more like a migration for the summer. A couple weeks after Woodshock, we'd have a show somewhere in Austin, so we'd just hang out until then. We'd find jobs and shoplift food from the 7-Eleven. We'd stay with other musicians, like the guys from Poison 13. That was a huge influence, seeing all these cool bands, which were Texas rock and roll but punk, too, definitely not fitting the hardcore mold.

CHARLIE RYAN In Austin, these people let us stay on their couches for weeks. They fed us and put us up, and it was a monthlong party for us—until they got sick of us. "When you goin' home?" "Well, we're broke, so we ain't goin' anywhere." That was our excuse.

Finally, a few of them said, "We gotta get 'em out of town." So some of the bands actually put on a show and gave us the money so we could put gas in the bus and leave.

TRACEY ROWLAND When the U-Men were in L.A. at the beginning of the tour, Larry couldn't make it, so he talked me into going down—to keep 'em out of jail, I guess. So John's girlfriend Val and I drove down in my 1964 Volkswagen Bug. The band's bus was such a wreck that everywhere we went in L.A. during that week and a half, we went in this Bug.

So the band, Mike T., Val, and me are all crammed into this Volkswagen Bug, and we pulled into this gas station to get gas, and we all piled out of this Volkswagen. And there's Duff McKagan!

DUFF MCKAGAN I was coming home from work, and I ran into them. I was living in a cockroach-infested single-room apartment. L.A. at the time was Quiet Riot, Ratt, some really terrible bands. In L.A., Guns N' Roses was considered a punk-rock band. We were huddled in this corner of Hollywood, snapping viciously at any gig we could get.

JOHN BIGLEY Tom goes, "That's fucking Duff!" There's this fuckin' wanker wearing a bullet belt, with his pants tucked into his cowboy boots. His hair is all teased out and long and crazy. You know, Hollywood butt-rocker guy. "Duff, what's goin' on? Look at you, man!"

He goes, "Got this band goin'. It's goin' really well."

"What's it called?"

He sighs. "It's the singer's name . . ." He whispered it: "It's called Guns N' Roses." Yeah, he was embarrassed. He used to be in a band called *the Vains,* man. Guns N' Roses?! "The singer is calling himself Axl."

Guns N' Roses. Axl. We're all laughin'. "Wow, how *magnificent!*" I go, "That sounds like *fuckin' shit.* Good luck with that, you freak." But he was super good-natured about it.

The band laughed about it for a couple of days. "Duff's doing metal!" Then, fuck, two years later: *"Welcome to the jungle!"*

CHAPTER 7
A THIRD SOUND

CHRIS HANZSEK We tried to make *Deep Six* a post-hippie, communal "Let's make a record we all love" compilation. The compilation was inspired mostly by Jeff and Mark in Green River. I think they might've even first mentioned it to me, like, "Hey, what do you think of this idea?" And then right away I loved the idea, and my girlfriend Tina agreed to be the general financier.

TINA CASALE (C/Z Records label/Reciprocal Recording studio cofounder) I first met Chris at Penn State in '78. He turned me on to all these crazy bands: Television and Patti Smith and the Sex Pistols. I immediately shaved the top of my head; there used to be a hairstyle—it wasn't a mullet—where you shaved the top of your head and left the rest long.

CHRIS HANZSEK We lived in Boston for two years, where I got my technical start in recording. A couple of college roommates wrote me a letter that said, "We're living in Seattle now, and you ought to check it out." My friends sent me compilations called the *Seattle Syndrome*, parts one and two, a record by the Blackouts, a record by the 3 Swimmers, and a single by the Fartz. I went, "Seattle looks like it's got a bunch of crazy people doing crazy stuff." So that sealed the deal.

We moved there in '83 and on the first day of 1984, Tina and I opened a studio, the original Reciprocal. I did some sessions with the Accüsed; I did Green River's first demo. When you're recording for 10 bucks an hour, you can be remarkably popular. But after our one-year lease was up, the landlord saw to it that we didn't want to continue. It was the loss of the studio that made me think, Geez, what else could I do while I'm hot to trot here?

KIM THAYIL Originally, Chris and Tina wanted to finance a record with Green River, and they came out to see a show we were opening for them. They were really impressed and wanted to make a flip-sided record: Green River on one side, Soundgarden on the other. We could've just left it at that, but Mark Arm and I thought it'd be important to include the Melvins and Malfunkshun and the U-Men.

We struggled with whether we should ask the guys in Skin Yard to be on it. So we debated it for a while: "They're a little bit different, they're a little bit younger, but they're kind of like us, and we like Jack Endino. Maybe make it six bands, everyone contribute a couple of songs."

CHRIS HANZSEK The label's name, C/Z, was Tina's idea. She told me that I was the Z, and she was the C. I said, "But my name doesn't begin with Z," and she said, "That's okay, it's in the middle."

DANIEL HOUSE Back then people in the Seattle underground weren't putting out records, and for the most part, when you did, you'd put out a single or maybe a four-song EP. Then suddenly, there's this guy, Chris, who was recording a bunch of bands. He kind of came out of nowhere. I remember feeling that I had to talk Chris into including Skin Yard on *Deep Six*.

KIM THAYIL Chris Hanzsek was pretty confident that we could make the record without the U-Men, and I had to keep pushing Chris, saying, "Getting the U-Men would be very important to help get attention for the record."

LARRY REID I remember us being completely on the fence about it. It was just that we were leaving on a big fucking tour, to play with the

Minutemen and Nick Cave and the Bad Seeds. It just wasn't fitting into our schedule. We had to get to fucking Idaho that night. But Daniel was bugging me about it. We recorded "They" in one take—used whatever kit was there, didn't unload amps, just guitars. It was 10 minutes from the time we pulled up to the time we left.

TOM PRICE All I remember is it was recorded at Ironwood Studios. I don't remember actually recording the song—at that point I was kinda whacked out on drugs—but I've heard people say that there was some problem with getting us to do the record in the first place because we thought the other bands on it were too heavy metal.

TINA CASALE I had minimal input in the whole thing. I helped clean the studio up and put the tape on the machine, but Chris was the recording person. When we set up the mix-down, we said to the bands, "You can have two members come in and help with the mix-down." Allowing the whole band to come in would've just been chaos.

REGAN HAGAR Each band was allowed one band member to come back to mix, and Andy and I both went. 'Cause we were like one, in our minds. We'd say, "These rules are set up, but we are excluded because we're in Malfunkshun." Our egos were really, really healthy.

When we were mixing the songs, we had Kevin really loud and all this guitar stuff going on, but when the record came out, it wasn't that way. I was told that Tina decided that ours wasn't good enough. So they remixed it without us, which was frustrating.

TINA CASALE Many years later, I heard that Stoney Gossard said that I was kinda controlling. Well, maybe to a point I was, because I can be a little bit overpowering.

CHRIS HANZSEK Part of any conflict that arose with Green River or anybody else was they were suddenly in a relationship with Tina, and they hadn't learned yet to appreciate her matter-of-factness and East Coast directness. She was kind of like a pit bull for a girlfriend.

I just remember there was yelling and there were tears. And Stone wasn't the one who was crying. Tina had another side to her, too.

KIM THAYIL Our mix might've ended up suffering the most because Chris and Tina were arguing during our mix session. They had a certain mix of "Tears to Forget" that sounded muddy, and I was trying to get it brighter. This argument started between Tina and Chris about how they should mix, and then some personal stuff started coming out.

CHRIS HANZSEK Tina and I split up during the mixing stage. Yeah, the breakup was my present for doing *Deep Six*. Let's say you're already having a hard time getting along with your tough-as-nails girlfriend you've been with for about five years. And then some giant pressure-cooker struggle of "Let's make six bands happy and put out a record" thing comes along.

TINA CASALE No, it didn't have anything to do with the record. We were together for seven years and by that time we were just separating. I ended up moving back to Pittsburgh, back to where I grew up.

CHRIS HANZSEK The record came out around late February of '86. We pressed 2,000. This is the part that for years made me a not-so-happy camper: I quickly picked up on the buzz that I wasn't promoting the record enough. I felt dumped on. And I also heard some feedback that the record wasn't well produced. A lot of that democratic process—all those conversations and having the artists there for mix-downs—showed up on the record itself in terms of its sound.

KURT BLOCH I remember being excited for Soundgarden, but their songs on that sound pretty crappy. It could've been a really exciting introduction to those sort of bands, but it just sounded like it was recorded on a cassette recorder.

CHRIS HANZSEK There are all sorts of rookie issues going on with the recording. Let's just call it "muddled." But I think *Deep Six* did its job in the sense that it was a signal flare that there was something afoot, that there was life on this planet here in Seattle.

DANIEL HOUSE It didn't sell for shit. Nobody cared about Seattle or the music coming from Seattle. And at the time there weren't really bands playing music like this. What was big was synth-based New Wave.

Everything that the bands on *Deep Six* were doing was basically a "fuck you" to the popular music of the time.

But locally, it was a big deal. After that record came out, we had no problem getting shows at all. *Deep Six* got a lot of play on KCMU and acted as a beacon for more people to begin starting bands, ones that were a lot more guitar-heavy and maybe dark or angry.

JACK ENDINO My then–future wife, Dawn, actually wrote the review in *The Rocket*. She called attention to the fact that we needed a name for this music: "What do we call this? It's not metal, and it's not punk."

DAWN ANDERSON (reviewing *Deep Six* in *The Rocket,* June 1986) The fact that none of these bands could open for Metallica or the Exploited without suffering abuse merely proves how thoroughly the underground's absorbed certain influences, resulting in music that isn't punk-metal but a third sound distinct from either.

Some of these influences are apparent visually; blatant posing on stage is acceptable again. I've seen all but one of these bands live at least once and a few of the musicians, along with many of their fans, could pass for members of Ratt. Some people find this distracting, as it seems to have little to do with the style of their music. I personally don't mind boys in makeup. If bands today can get by with rifling rock history for any cheap thrill they can find, I say that's great, because it serves to further break down divisions and discourage snobbery and purism, the worst enemies of rock 'n' roll.

*   *   *

TOM PRICE The second of the U-Men's three tours was called the Miserable Sinners tour. Every night, something weird would happen. One night, we all took some very powerful LSD in Indianapolis, Indiana, and boy, things got really out of hand. A couple windows on the tour bus got broken out, one of us wound up flailing around in the mud in the rain outside. People screaming, minimal clothing. It's all a little hazy.

JIM TILLMAN The goal of that tour was opening for Nick Cave and the Bad Seeds at Danceteria in New York. Some people compared us to Nick Cave's old band, the Birthday Party, but I think the comparisons are more due to people's ignorance. If you listened to everything we did, it would be harder to compartmentalize us.

CHARLIE RYAN We'd get paid $75, and we'd want to run to the liquor store, and Jim would be like, "You know, we should go buy some gas. Buy some food, maybe?" We'd say, "Fuck you! No money goes to food! Absolutely not!" That was our rule. Jim wasn't as much of a raging alcoholic as the rest of us.

JIM TILLMAN I was not a teetotaler by any stretch, but when everyone else was getting really loaded, I wasn't. Somebody had to drive. When I was in the U-Men and later in Love Battery, I was the mom and the cop. And it's not the most enviable position to be in.

MIKE TUCKER I remember arriving in New York for the Nick Cave and the Bad Seeds show and parking on Eighth Avenue near 14th Street. John was the first one to go off the bus, as if we had landed on the moon or something. It was like he was Captain Kirk, and he went to go check it out. Came back and reported that everything was good, and it was exciting.

That was the big-deal show, because they definitely worshipped Nick Cave. I remember being on some steps near the stage, and Blixa Bargeld from the Bad Seeds stepped on me. I was thrilled: "Blixa Bargeld stepped on me!"

JIM TILLMAN So we're standing outside the club. All of the sudden, we look up and my mom is standing there with John's parents. And we're all, "What the fuck?" She had elected to call John's parents, unbeknownst to me, and said, "Let's go to New York and see our kids play." Immediately, everybody looked at me and said, "Dude, what are they doing here?"

John actually came from a little bit of money, but he never wanted that to be known. And being the singer and the center of attention, he was even more mortified when his parents showed up. It was all on me that our parents showed up. It certainly seemed like a nail in the coffin of my relationship with the band.

JOHN BIGLEY Jim's mom invited them? Oh, really? I never figured out how the fuck my parents knew. We were on our bus, power-drinking, and they showed up with a bottle of champagne. It's the first time to my knowledge that they had seen the band. They were taken aback. Blown away that that many people would want to see the show and by the life forms there, as well—all the fuckers crawling from Alphabet City to go to Danceteria to see Nick Cave.

JIM TILLMAN John was so nervous that he got wasted beforehand. I recall Larry elbowing him, saying, "Dude, wake up, you're sitting next to Lydia Lunch!" And John's like, "Huh?" He was so wasted he didn't even realize he was sitting next to her.

LARRY REID The craziest thing was the U-Men playing in front of 1,500 people in New York City at a sold-out show with Nick Cave and the Bad Seeds and the audience knowing the lyrics to the U-Men's songs. And singing along with the band—what the fuck?

CHARLIE RYAN The show was unbelievable. The place was huge, four floors, and it was absolutely packed. That was one of the highlights of the band. That was as big as it got for us.

• • •

BRUCE FAIRWEATHER We went out on our first tour in October 1985, and if anything should've broken up Green River, it should've been that tour. We went in Stone's piece-of-shit station wagon, which we called the Shled, and attached a U-Haul trailer.

ALEX SHUMWAY I like to call it the Prema-Tour, because it was premature for us to go out. Our record, *Come on Down*, was supposed to come out about a month before we went on tour. Then it was supposed to come out three weeks before the tour. Then it was supposed to come out a week before the tour . . .

STONE GOSSARD (Green River/Pearl Jam/Mother Love Bone/Temple of the Dog/ Brad/Satchel/March of Crimes guitarist) We put up our own money to go out to tour in New York. We played six shows in frickin' six weeks, which is a joke. We were just pretending. Or we were doing it, but it was like we were making three or four fans. Someone behind the bar would go, "Hey, you guys are pretty good." Or not.

ALEX SHUMWAY We played Cincinnati, opening for Big Black, and across town the Red Hot Chili Peppers were playing that night, which meant we weren't going to draw anybody. In the middle of our set—*boom!*—all the power went out onstage. We thought they had cut our power. And Mark was like, "Fuckers! Motherfucker!" and he went over and grabbed every mic off the stand and threw them into the audience.

MARK ARM Actually the show was in Newport, Kentucky, across the river. I can't even recall what my motivation would have been for acting so stupidly, but I just decided for some reason to take the microphone and throw it as far as I could.

BRUCE FAIRWEATHER It turns out that the club had just blown a fuse. The guys in Big Black said, "You guys should leave," because somebody called the soundman and he was probably coming to kick our asses.

STEVE ALBINI (singer/guitarist for Chicago's Big Black; recording engineer) I was looking forward to playing with Green River because I was into a cassette of them I'd gotten. But they were acting like fucking rock stars. They were kind of petulant.

I remember the singer, Mark, smashing a couple of microphones, getting pissed at the monitor or something like that. And there were just 10 people there at that point. He was being a total crybaby, and it really bothered me. Everyone I had grown up admiring in the punk scene thought of all that rock-star behavior as stupid and offensive. I don't know how to describe it, except maybe like going to a vegetarian restaurant and seeing them slaughtering hogs in the lobby.

MARK ARM They were threatening not to pay us, and I remember Steve Albini going, " 'Course they don't want to pay you—you just fucking destroyed a mic," and me feeling admonished, and rightfully so. What I did wasn't calculated. Maybe I was spoiled by being able to get away with really stupid shit in Seattle.

BRUCE FAIRWEATHER When we made it to Detroit, we played this place called the Greystone, out in a sketchy part of town. The show was on November 1, after Hell Night.

MARK ARM We were driving into Detroit, we put in the Stooges tape, and we're like, "Fuck, this is gonna be so great. Detroit." But everywhere you looked were these buildings with the windows smashed out, just totally desolate. You'd see a lone figure huddled near a fire.

ALEX SHUMWAY Buildings were burning. It looked like a war had been through there.

MARK ARM The next morning we went to eat breakfast somewhere. The waitress, who was probably about our age, finally just asks if we're all gay. We're like, "What?" It could've been the way some of us were dressed, sure. Jeff's hair was a little big at that point. And Bruce Fairweather, his jeans had holes in them and he'd wear his girlfriend's fishnets. But the waitress's reaction was a signifier of what Detroit was gonna be like: If you're not totally tough, you're gonna be considered gay.

ALEX SHUMWAY We were opening for Samhain, one of Danzig's bands. Everybody there was *grrr-grrr, ruff-ruff* kind of fans. People were calling us fags, throwing shit at us. I remember Jeff came onstage and he was wearing Capezio dance shoes and a T-shirt that said SAN FRANCISCO in pink letters.

MARK ARM Jeff is wearing a pink tank top that says SAN FRANCISCO in purple cursive writing. Why would he do that? Because he has *giant balls*. I remember there was this particular girl in the front row that kept spitting at Jeff, like she was really offended by him. At one point Jeff stuck his foot up in her face, like, Knock it off.

JEFF AMENT And her boyfriend, from behind, grabbed me, pulled me off the stage, into the crowd, and I got pummeled! . . . I'm just getting like beat to death. It was horrible.

MARK ARM I'd gotten pulled into the crowd before, when we opened for Black Flag, and Jeff had thrown his bass off and jumped in after me and saved my ass, so I'm like, Oh, great, it's my turn. I gotta save Jeff's ass.

ALEX SHUMWAY I wasn't gonna jump in a crowd of 700 people! Screw this crap!

BRUCE FAIRWEATHER All I remember is Stone and I look at each other, and we just backed up. I was like, They're on their own, man. I thought they were going to get *killed*.

MARK ARM We're about to get pummeled by the angry crowd that surrounded us. But a security guard, who was an off-duty cop with a gun, stepped in and saved our asses.

JEFF AMENT Went up to get paid afterwards, after probably the most humbling experience ever. And Corey Rusk, who was in the Necros at that point—I was really excited to meet him, 'cause I loved the Necros—and he runs Touch and Go now, he was the promoter for the show. We were supposed to make like a hundred bucks, which was a huge payday for us at that point. He's paying Danzig like $12,000 or whatever he's making that show. And I put my hand out, and he goes, "Man, I thought you guys *sucked*. I'm only giving you $25."

BRUCE FAIRWEATHER The reason for this whole tour was that we were supposed to open for the U.K. Subs in Boston. Gerard Cosloy from Homestead had booked the show, so we drove all the way to Boston to find out that the U.K. Subs didn't make it into the country. So that show didn't happen.

ALEX SHUMWAY Gerard said, "Okay, I can get you guys a show on Wednesday at CBGB's in New York." We were going, "Fuckin' awesome! CBGB's!"

MARK ARM Of course, we played last, which is cleanup—it wasn't the headlining slot. The place cleared out, and we played in front of the staff and a couple of Japanese tourists.

ALEX SHUMWAY On the way back, we were driving through some part of North Dakota or South Dakota, and it was pitch-black out and snowing lightly. We were all just wiped out. Mark was driving. I was laying in the way back of the station wagon, and we were all talking about lighting farts on fire. "Oh, you can't light a fart on fire." "Sure you can."

And Stoney goes, "Yes, you can," and he puts his legs up, takes a lighter, puts it between his legs and just rips one out. And the flame goes *boom!* Everybody was like, *"Fuck! Oh, my God!"* thinking he was gonna blow the place apart. And it scared Mark so bad that he yanked the steering wheel and hit black ice, and we go flying off into this ditch.

MARK ARM Fart-lighting? *(Laughs.)* I don't recall anything like that happening at all in Green River. It wasn't like a frat house. Also, the sun was just starting to come up, and everyone was pretty much asleep when that happened. We were driving through a snowstorm and had to get gas. So I started taking an exit and the exit was basically a sheet of ice, and we ended up going off the edge of the road.

BRUCE FAIRWEATHER Me and Jeff and Stone were in the back sleeping. All I remember is waking up, with Alex going, *"Oh, my God, oh, my God! No!"* And looking up and seeing the trailer bouncing and snow flying everywhere. I just wrapped my head in the pillow and went, "Oh, let it happen."

Mark was never the greatest driver, and he took an exit on black ice going 60 miles an hour. We just went off down this hill, totally out of control, through a ditch and . . . ended up right at a gas station.

We were fine. We were all just terrified.

CHAPTER 8
THE FOUR WEIRDEST GUYS IN ELLENSBURG

MARK PICKEREL (Screaming Trees/Truly drummer) Ellensburg, Washington, was definitely a sleepy little town. It was mostly a farming community, a little rodeo city, but there was also a university there that saved it from being a total backwards hillbilly town. It was a strange juxtaposition of farmers and some very radical thinkers. I would say that the Screaming Trees were, if anything, influenced more by the university than by the farmers.

Van Conner and I met when I was a high school freshman, in fall 1981. It was a school-sanctioned band trip to Walla Walla, and I had my Walkman and was running low on options for listening. I happened to be passing Van as he was going through his cassettes and I asked him if I could glance at what he had. I didn't think he would have anything good, because Van was kind of a square kid back then—his clothing did nothing to indicate that he was into, you know, good music. He had everything from standard stuff like Cream and Jimi Hendrix to a lot of groups I hadn't heard before, like Echo and the Bunnymen, XTC, Siouxsie and the Banshees. He told me, "Most of these cassettes my brother made for me." His brother being Gary Lee Conner, who had already graduated from high school but still lived at home.

Van told me his brother played guitar and was looking for somebody to jam. So I brought my drums over and set up shop in Lee's bedroom, which was in a garage that had been converted into a rehearsal space. Lee was obsessed with the 1960s, everything from the Monkees to the 13th Floor Elevators.

Van was the original singer. At that point, our name was Him and Those Guys. Later, we became the Explosive Generation. Shortly after we formed, Gary Lee Conner Sr. booked us at Lincoln Elementary School, where he was the principal. We played the Sex Pistols and Dead Kennedys and Rolling Stones and Cream at this third-grade assembly. It was the most awkward experience of my life up until then. These third-graders were just completely terrified by us. Not only were we playing pretty edgy material, but it was really loud and out of tune.

VAN CONNER (Screaming Trees bassist) My dad got in trouble for that. A bunch of teachers complained officially because he was bringing "satanic" music into the school.

MARK PICKEREL Later on, Van started telling me about this guy Mark Lanegan, who he shared a drama class with. It turned out that Lanegan was a big fan of the Damned and Black Flag and Motörhead and all these bands that we thought belonged exclusively to our weird little group of art-fag friends.

Lanegan came from a circle that we were all afraid of. It was a crew of guys that were hillbillies and some jocks and stoners—but the edgier side of each one of those cliques. I think Mark spent maybe a season playing football. Back in those years, he was a stoner and did a lot of drinking, so it's hard for me to imagine that he attended practices religiously.

I was kind of afraid of Mark because he was quite large in high school—he had to have been a good 60 to 80 pounds heavier than he is now. He was wearing a beard and looked like a logger. The jobs he had were usually manual labor, so he dressed the part. He was flying the flannel, as Mike Watt would say, a good eight years before it was in *Vogue* and all the fashion magazines.

VAN CONNER I met Mark Lanegan in detention when I was a sopho-more. He saw that I had a Jimi Hendrix button on my coat, and peo-ple in Ellensburg didn't even listen to Jimi Hendrix back then. So we started talking and he told me about this band the Stranglers, who I didn't know. And then we started trading records.

Lanegan wasn't really intimidating to me, but I could see how he could be. Him and his friends all looked like they were out of that movie *Over the Edge*, with Matt Dillon. Jeans jacket, stringy hair, tough guy.

MARK LANEGAN (Screaming Trees singer; solo artist) When I was a kid, I got caught shoplifting by a store security guard in Ellensburg. The next time I saw that store guard was when I got thrown in jail again—this time for not paying court fees. The guy happened to be in jail, too, right next to me. And the third time I saw him was when I got off the bus to play the Gorge years later. This guy was now head of security at the Gorge. That's what Eastern Washington is like—you never get too far away from anybody.

MARK PICKEREL A lot of people were afraid of Mark because if he was at a party and he was drinking, once fighting was on his mind or once somebody pissed him off, that was it. But he was also a very loving individual and cared about all of us deeply. Any time there was any shit-talking going on around town, if anybody crossed any of us, he was always the first to come to our defense.

ERIC JOHNSON I lived in this great little building in Ellensburg that happened to be across the street from this apartment where Lanegan lived, so I met him and he turned me onto John Fante and all these dif-ferent, weird L.A. Depression-era writers that I had never read before. He is probably one of the most well-read people I've met.

VAN CONNER After Mark Lanegan graduated, I hadn't seen him in about six months. We ended up running into each other at a party and he was like, "Hey man, let's start a band." Our first practice was around '84. At first it was just the three of us—me, Pickerel, and Lanegan. I don't know why Lee would want to be in a band together, because we fought all the time. In our previous band, the Explosive

Generation—with Pickerel, David Frazini, and Dan Harper—there was too much violence.

GARY LEE CONNER (Screaming Trees guitarist) When Van was really little, he used to tag along with me, and my friends would get real upset. But in high school, I became reclusive and stopped having friends. So I started hanging around with his friends, which is how our early bands came about. Even though I was four and a half years older than Van, it was like he was the older brother.

MARK PICKEREL My impression was that Lee was jealous that we had this social life that was thriving outside of the band. We were in high school and he'd dropped out of college and was living at home, so his entire focus was the band. And Van and I were doing things like canceling practices to go to a friend's place or a dance or a party.

Their mom, Cathy, was always really paranoid that Van and I would fall in with the wrong crowd and start doing drugs. At that time we were pretty straitlaced—we actually were going to youth group and church. But Lee was constantly telling his mom that he thought he smelled marijuana in the house or on our clothes. So we decided to punish him by starting a new band that he wouldn't be allowed to play in. The problem was that our rehearsals were going to take place in his bedroom.

We end up having this band practice with Lanegan, myself, and Van. I think we made an attempt at some classic-rock standard, but Lanegan was trying to play drums and was having a really difficult time holding down the fort. I made my best attempt to sing something like "Sunshine of Your Love," and we might've made one more attempt at another song when Cathy Conner came barging into Lee's room and demanded that Lee be in our band: "Goddammit, you guys! If you think you can practice here, in Lee's room, you've got another thing coming!"

Until finally, Lee snuck behind Cathy, plugged in his guitar, and started messing around. And during the argument, Lanegan got off the drums—as big and intimidating as Mark could be, I think the whole thing scared the hell out of him—and ended up standing there, totally perplexed. I was used to it by this time and was doing my best not to laugh out loud.

Next thing I know, I'm back at the drum set, and we started playing with Lee in the band. We segued into a fast, punk-rock version of the Doors' "The End," with Mark singing. All of us were totally taken aback by Lanegan's voice. He sounded just like Jim Morrison! I mean, it was uncanny. It was obvious that he was the singer and that it would be ridiculous for me to approach the mic again, just as much as it would be for him to decide to play the drums. We'd stumbled ass-backwards into something good.

After a couple rehearsals like that, Lee presented us with some demo recordings that he'd been making on a four-track. He'd written six or seven of these psychedelic pop gems. They were amazing.

GRANT ALDEN (*The Rocket* newspaper managing editor) The Conner boys were large and not athletic, and Mark Pickerel was sort of sallow and small, and Mark Lanegan was a professor's kid, I think, but he was this brooding, big, scary guy. They were the four weirdest guys in Ellensburg, Washington, and they ended up in a band together because who the hell else was gonna hang out with them?

VAN CONNER The Screaming Trees' first show was at—it's kinda silly, but we saw this video of the Cramps playing at an insane asylum, so our big thing was to get a show at an insane asylum. I think Mark Pickerel's mom lived right next to the Eastern State mental institution in Spokane, and I had her talk to somebody, but it didn't work out. Instead, we played at this group hall in Ellensburg for people who were mentally challenged.

MARK PICKEREL The place was called Elmview. And I don't remember how we ended up playing there—we had a couple friends that worked there, I think. On one level we were doing it as community service, but obviously we were very well aware of the Cramps video of them performing at a mental institution. So it was partly for our own sick amusement.

Oh, the show was incredible, as you can imagine. Early in the Screaming Trees days, Lanegan could be kind of a performer. When it was time for a guitar solo, his body would go into convulsions and he'd kick his legs around. But on this particular night, one of the guys in the audience was mirroring back every one of Lanegan's movements. It was just too much for him. It seemed like that was the beginning of Lanegan refining his movements onstage. He seemed more selective with his body language. His stage presence, especially as the years went by, became very still and detached.

GARY LEE CONNER When we played our first club show, at GESSCO in Olympia, I kind of went nuts for some reason. I really got into it, jumping around, doing windmills and stuff. I was like, "Whoa, that was fun!" Eventually, having to go nuts onstage became a burden, because I was sacrificing my playing.

VAN CONNER My parents ran a video store in Ellensburg called New World Video. We had a huge back room there, which we made into a practice space. Lee decked it out. It was like that episode of *The Brady Bunch* where Greg gets his own room. It was totally psychedelic.

STEVE FISK (producer; keyboardist for Berkeley, California's Pell Mell; solo artist) Mark Pickerel had sent me a fan letter because he'd bought my first 45 and told me that he really liked it. So when I moved to Ellensburg from San Francisco in the winter of '85, I looked up Mark, who was working at the video store that the Conner family owned. So I got to be friends with Mark. I was working at Velvetone Studios in Ellensburg, which was started by Sam Albright, my old friend from college.

I didn't see the band perform until they came to record at the studio. They thought that recording was doing something very much like a live show. Me and Sam Albright were in the control room and the Screaming Trees are out in the studio, facing us like we're the audience. They had an extreme, jumping, crazy kind of physicality, reminiscent of the Who. It was the most uninhibited thing I'd seen in the recording studio up until that point, and probably for some time since then. Those recordings became the *Other Worlds* cassette that we distributed on Velvetone Records.

GARY LEE CONNER Me and Lanegan were driving over to the video store or something one day, and we were talking about naming the band the Screaming Freaks. That was something we thought about for 30 seconds. And that name sounded like the Screaming Trees, and we just decided, "What about Screaming Trees?" It was appropriate, because even though we didn't live right next to a forest—Ellensburg is where the desert starts—outside the town there's a whole bunch of forests.

I didn't even know about the Screaming Tree guitar pedal until later. But Van kept saying in interviews that we named ourselves after it, so people were like, "That sounds good."

SAM ALBRIGHT (Velvetone studio/label owner) They were a young band, but they had a pretty specific idea of what they were after. It was this psychedelic, grungy sound—they didn't want it too slick. They were big guys, and they played big.

Later on, Shawn O'Neill, who's a musician and a writer, and Steve and I made a movie, a B-grade—a C-grade black-and-white sci-fi movie, *The Fertilichrome Cheerleader Massacre,* and the members of the Screaming Trees are in it. They played the gang under the evil Dr. Stimson, played by Steve Fisk, who—this is after the Great Apocalypse—creates a chemical called Fertilichrome to repopulate the earth. The evil Dr. Stimson ends up experimenting on Mark Pickerel's character; he shoots him full of Fertilichrome, causing him to explode. We cast latex parts and organs and filmed Mark's chest exploding, with fluids squirting out. It looked great!

STEVE FISK Their first album, *Clairvoyance,* was on Velvetone. I sent the record out to radio and booked a tour for them. It was impossible. No one returned your phone calls—no one wanted to hear about a band from Eastern Washington, let alone a small town that no one had ever heard of. I would have to thank Ray Farrell for hooking up the Screaming Trees with all kinds of interesting connections.

RAY FARRELL (SST Records promotion department head; Geffen Records/DGC A&R and marketing executive) There was something unique about them that was reminiscent of '60s punk records, like the *Nuggets* compilations. There were elements of Lanegan's baritone, of the songwriting that they did, that hearkened back to that time period.

Steve Fisk, who I knew from his instrumental band Pell Mell, asked me if I could help book some Screaming Trees shows along the West Coast. I think that the only thing I was able to get was an in-store show at the Texas Record Store, in Santa Monica, and it had a really good crowd. And it was right around that time that some tapes of them got to Greg Ginn at SST, and Greg really liked them. And it was as simple as that: They were signed to SST.

MARK PICKEREL Steve had sent Ray Farrell at SST some music, and he presented that music to Greg, who was also the guitarist in Black Flag. Maybe half a year earlier, Van and Lee and I had gone to see Black Flag play in Seattle. Somehow I managed to get through the pit and leave a cassette in front of Greg's monitor. He picked it up in between songs and put it on his amplifier, and I remember wondering if he'd actually give it a listen. Sure enough, he did.

GARY LEE CONNER We were in the video store, where we always hung out and worked, too, and we got a call from Greg Ginn. Mark Lanegan talked to him. Greg asked, "Would you be on SST?" Hüsker Dü, Dinosaur Jr., Black Flag, Minutemen—all those bands that we idolized were on that label. I remember being like, Whoa! It was hard to believe.

Signing to Epic later on was sort of anticlimactic—the typical major-label kind of crap. But signing to SST was the coolest and most amazing thing that happened in our entire career. It felt like we were a real band.

CHAPTER 9
GOING OUT OF BUSINESS SINCE 1988

LARRY REID I remember this conversation—this is in that period between Roscoe Louie and Graven Image, in 1983. The U-Men are playing at a punk-rock party in the little, tiny room of a basement of this house. And Bruce Pavitt was there, and he told me, "The Seattle music scene is gonna take over the world."

And I just fuckin' laughed. Here we are, with what at that point was arguably the biggest punk-rock band in Seattle playing in front of 30 people in the basement of this house. But goddamn, guy was right.

BRUCE PAVITT Sub Pop started with a $20 investment. Fifteen years later, the company received a check for $20 million from Time Warner.

In 1979, I arrived at Evergreen State College in Olympia, from the Chicago area, and was deeply interested in punk. Coincidentally, upon arriving at Evergreen, I found that the radio station there, KAOS FM, had probably the most inclusive collection of independently produced music in the United States.

And in meeting up with some of the folks who worked there, specifically John Foster, who was the editor of *Op Magazine*, I started to look at punk through a different lens. John's philosophy was that punk was a folk music and that what was radical about it was that anybody could put out music and put out their own records. From that position, I started to dig deeper into regional music scenes, specifically into more of what was going on on the West Coast and in the Northwest.

I got to a point where I felt that I wanted to share some of the information with people, so I put out *Subterranean Pop* fanzine. The first issue came out in spring 1980. Had a budget of about $20—I had an X-Acto knife, a glue stick, and a box of crayons. I invited friends over, and we all individually colored a lot of the pages. Put 'em all in a box and shipped them to a distributor in San Francisco. I just said, "Here's 200 copies of my fanzine. I know you're gonna want to distribute this." They hadn't ordered any, so I took a risk there. But I got some good feedback and things kept building from there.

CALVIN JOHNSON (K Records cofounder; Beat Happening singer/guitarist) We met in September of 1980, but I'd been hearing about Bruce for about a year before, through people at *Op Magazine*. I grew up in Olympia, but my senior year of high school I moved away just for one year, and that was right about the time Bruce moved to Olympia. He actually took over my time slot on KAOS and did the first issue of the *Sub Pop* fanzine while I was gone. I started working on the fanzine with the second issue.

Most of the fanzines that existed in 1980 were very Anglophile. They were oriented toward whatever the latest flavor-of-the-month, major-label New Wave band was: XTC or Gang of Four or whatever. But Bruce was writing about bands that no one had ever freakin' heard of. And he was concentrating on Northwest bands like the Beakers and the Blackouts. That was exciting.

BRUCE PAVITT I called it *Subterranean Pop* because my theory was that there was a tremendous amount of music happening in America that had the potential to be very popular. But because the distribution channels and the media channels were shut off, those acts had to work their way out of the ghetto. So it was an underground culture that had the potential to be very popular. Nirvana was the ultimate example of that.

The name changed from *Subterranean Pop* to *Sub Pop* on the second issue. I proceeded to put out more, and a couple years later we put out a cassette compilation, *Sub Pop 5,* which featured tracks by a group from Lawrence, Kansas, called the Embarrassment and tracks by the producer Steve Fisk and one by myself. The big "hit" was a novelty piece by an artist named Doug Kahn, and it was a montage cut-up of a Ronald Reagan speech. The cassette did very well—I sold like 2,000 copies, which at that time, for cassettes being duped out of your bedroom, was huge. At that point I began alternating between cassette versions and written publications. We put out nine issues—three of them cassettes—and that was kind of it.

STEVE FISK To me, the idea that a bunch of little know-nothings in Olympia, Washington, can make a bunch of cassette tapes and get them reviewed in Australia, get them sold in Japan, get John Peel's attention—that's radical. That was a radical thing to do in '81.

CHRIS PUGH (Swallow guitarist/singer) I met Bruce in Olympia. There were only one or two places to play in Olympia back then, but there was a bubbling undercurrent of things going on. People were having dance parties at their apartments. All kinds of people were starting bands, getting their ideas out. It was a DIY kind of thing. People weren't terribly concerned with musical ability.

DONNA DRESCH I remember the first show I ever went to in Olympia. I was just wandering around with some other teenage friends of mine downtown. We heard people say, "There's a show in the alley!" So we went in the alley and the whole place is lit with candles, and at the very end of the alley, which is like another miniature alley, Beat Happening was playing. And it was just a guitar and two drums, like a floor tom and a snare. And Calvin was dancing and singing in this totally surreal, almost a cappella–style punk show. Everybody was slam-dancing in this little alcove in the alley.

I thought it was amazing. I remember having heard Beat Happening on the radio and thinking, These guys can't even play their instruments! But then I understood it.

GARY LEE CONNER You know the scene in *A Charlie Brown Christmas,* where they're all dancing and Schroeder's playing the piano? That's what the Olympia scene was like. It was really innocent, and it wasn't about anything except having fun and playing music.

MEGAN JASPER (Sub Pop Records receptionist-turned–executive vice president; Dickless singer) If you watched Bruce dance, he always did Calvin-esque kind of moves. You could tell they were close. It was like this weird Olympia thing. They would do almost like disco moves, but then they would freeze and stay frozen for 20 beats or so, and then start moving again. They'd be shaking their arms around. It was just a really funny, unique style of dancing. It was also really fun to imitate.

MARK PICKEREL We thought it was unusual that Calvin took such an interest in the Screaming Trees. He talked about us being his favorite band. And his actions backed that up—I mean, he was booking little tours with us and distributing our cassette right away, and he wrote a really great review of our music in a publication.

But musically, it didn't seem like we had anything in common. I was surprised when Beat Happening wanted to collaborate on an EP with us and it turned out pretty good. It was a little bit awkward just because none of those guys knew how to play their instruments the way we did. Not that we were super-accomplished.

ALICE WHEELER In Olympia, the cool thing was to sit around and talk about ideas and the meaning of life. Less so in Seattle, where people were like, "I wanna be cool." Kurt lived in Olympia—that was the place he moved after he left Aberdeen—and that's why Nirvana was so political. He lived with his girlfriend, Tracy Marander, in Olympia, and then got his own apartment there without Tracy. And he was really good friends with Kathleen Hanna, the woman who started Riot Grrrl.

BLAG DAHLIA (singer for San Francisco's Dwarves) The grunge scene eventually came to have a P.C. cast to it, and I think a lot of that has to do with that Olympia influence, which kind of turned into that Riot Grrrl thing, a movement that had almost no music attached to it but had a lot of instructions for how you're supposed to live your life. Whereas the not-famous Kurt Cobain might've chuckled at the Dwarves album cover with naked girls covered in blood, the famous Kurt Cobain felt he had to make a stand against those kind of things.

BRUCE PAVITT I moved to Seattle in 1983, and for five years wrote a monthly column called Sub Pop that was in *The Rocket*. Like Duff, I'd made a break for the big city. A lot of my philosophy was you should be able to make a scene happen where you are, so for me to actually leave Olympia for the big city of Seattle was seen as a hypocritical gesture by Calvin and other such luminaries from the region. But it wasn't like I was moving to New York or L.A.

MAIRE MASCO Bruce Pavitt, we were involved for a while romantically. When I met him, he was a stoner from Evergreen. He had just moved up from Olympia, and I think I met him at the Metropolis. He definitely had a great ear. He was very creative, he knew a lot of people, though not really in Seattle. There's the old story of how he started Sub Pop with my Rolodex. I certainly gave him a lot of contacts. And then he got back together with his old girlfriend from Evergreen and dumped me! *(Laughs.)*

JONATHAN PONEMAN (Sub Pop Records cofounder) I'd met Bruce informally at Bombshelter, a record store he had owned, but he wouldn't remember it because I was kind of "anonymous guy" then. Bruce gave one of my bands, the Treeclimbers, a tip of the hat in his Sub Pop column in *The Rocket*. But the first time I'd had an extended conversation with him was when *Sub Pop 100* came out and he went on *Audioasis,* the program I hosted on KCMU, which was a publicly funded college-based radio station.

BRUCE PAVITT In '86, I decided to try and do a vinyl version of what I'd done with the cassettes. And by that time we had more of a name. *Sub Pop 100* had Sonic Youth from New York and the Wipers from Portland and the U-Men from Seattle. And that sold like 5,000 copies, which at the time was like having a gold record in the indie scene. I used the money to go to Amsterdam and party for two weeks.

After *Sub Pop 100*, I put out the Green River *Dry as a Bone* EP, and at that time, around '87, I became convinced, as did Jonathan, that there was kind of a unique sound happening in Seattle, and although I'd spent a lot of my time networking regional scenes, I got to a point where I wanted to focus my attention on Seattle and help the scene out, and Jon was doing the same thing with his show. We were both philosophically in the same place: We wanted to help Seattle blow up.

CHRIS CORNELL I had never really thought of Seattle, or even necessarily my own band, as being something that could become a worldwide phenomenon. I remember running into Bruce outside a show at the Moore around 1988, and I made some comment to him about how there just suddenly seemed to be so much talent in Seattle and that Sub Pop seemed to be putting out all these amazing records.

And he just put his arm around me and he had this funny look of confidence in his eyes, and he said, "Seattle's gonna take over the world!" It was a little bit tongue-in-cheek, but it wasn't really—it was like he was serious about it. And that was the first time that I actually believed it and felt like someone did have a vision.

JONATHAN PONEMAN There are few times where you can say, "This is an event that literally changed the course of my life." But the first time I saw Soundgarden, in 1985, really was one of those times.

I saw them at the suggestion of Ben McMillan, who had a radio show right before mine. He knew that I had started booking these nights at the Rainbow, and he suggested that I put his band Skin Yard and this other band, Soundgarden, on the bill.

Soundgarden had this intensity—the best bands to me just *are*, you know? I don't mean to sound metaphysical or anything like that. I thought, I would love to be in a band like this, but I just never will be. I continued to play in bands for a couple years after seeing Soundgarden, but in seeing them I thought, The die is cast. This is a band that's gonna take over the world. Because even at that show, where there were maybe 40 people, you could tell there was a chemistry and a sense of inevitability.

DANIEL HOUSE Kim Thayil and I would just drink and drink and get fucked up together and spew for hours about everything and anything, philosophy and ideas. Before Soundgarden signed to A&M later on, invariably we would bandy about who was the bigger band, Skin Yard or Soundgarden: "Well, you know, *we've* played more shows." "Yeah, well, *we've* been together longer."

But in the end, the reality was that we always opened for them; they never opened for us. And history pretty much tells the whole story. The fact is, they had Chris. We didn't have Chris.

JEFF GILBERT Back in the day, I would say Chris was more shy than anything, 'cause when they would play, Chris would sing with his back to the audience, or off to the side, for a good portion of the show. It took a while for him to get his confidence level up. But when he started to get into it, it was like that picture of him on the back of *Screaming Life*, where he's on the club floor. That's where you saw Chris mostly: either he was on his back or on the floor.

JAMES BURDYSHAW I remember one Soundgarden show where this girl was so enthralled with Chris that she was dancing like crazy and rubbin' her rear end against me, all while staring at him. Did she know who she was rubbing up against? Probably not. I might as well have been a pole to her.

MARK ARM This might be coming from a place of jealousy, but the shirt-lessness seemed contrived. Chris would wear tear-away shirts—clearly someone had done some damage to the seams before he would go on-stage, because he would grab the shirt right in the middle and then pull it straight off him. I think I might have respected it more if he just came out onstage without a shirt at all.

HIRO YAMAMOTO It bugged me a lot. "Do you have to take off the shirt? Do you have to break a mic stand every show?" It was one of those things that kind of made me quit eventually, to tell you the truth. "Could you not take off your shirt tonight?" He wouldn't even answer. Or he'd walk out of the room. That became this real tense thing.

SUSAN SILVER The shirtlessness? I never even thought about it. Honest to God, it's just what he does. Love is blind, I suppose.

The female attention never ruffled me. I felt we had such security in our relationship then that it never occurred to me. I remember a show in Philadelphia in the early '90s, some girl got on her boyfriend's shoulders and was screaming, *"Chris, I wanna fuck you!"* or some other equally poetic phrase. Come on. You're embarrassing our entire sisterhood here.

So when the show was over, I found her and was like, "Excuse me, can I talk to you for a second? I have a message for you from Chris."

Her eyes light up. *"Really?* What?"

"He heard you in the audience, and he was wondering if you would stop embarrassing yourself that way."

KIM THAYIL Competition with Skin Yard? There was only one person really participating in that, and it was Daniel House. It's the strangest thing. We thought they were our buddies, and they'd run ads for Skin Yard like, FAR LESS DOOM AND GLOOM THAN SOUNDGARDEN.

Ever see those old Bugs Bunny and Daffy Duck cartoons? Bugs Bunny never really advanced the competition. It was Daffy who was advancing it. He was the one who was more competitive, bitter, jealous. We never had to compete with Skin Yard—we always drew far more than they did, were far more successful, both critically and commercially.

They were our friends. I was very close with Jack. Matt Cameron ended up quitting their band to join us when he found out that we were looking for a drummer.

SCOTT SUNDQUIST When it became time to have to tour, it was hard for me, with my son, who was seven. My wife and I had an on-again, off-again relationship, so single parenting was sometimes a part of it. I was older than them and was unsure about money. In the end, I stepped aside so that those guys could tour. It was very emotional for all of us. We were really close, and to this day still are. I think of them as younger brothers.

SCOTT McCULLUM I was in the band 64 Spiders when Chris asked me to try out for Soundgarden. I actually got the gig. Everybody was excited. I remember sitting on the front porch and Chris sat down next to me and went, "Hey dude, you're in the band! We got a show in two weeks, so you gotta start fittin' in our practice schedule!"

So two days pass, and I don't hear from anybody, right? And somehow I found out that Matt Cameron had tried out for Soundgarden. He was the preeminent drummer in Seattle at that time, and, of course, they're like, "Shit!" So Chris reluctantly called me up and told me that they decided to go with Matt. It totally sucked. I loved Soundgarden.

MATT CAMERON I was in Skin Yard for about a year and a half. I quit because I was ready for something new. I told the Skin Yard guys I wanted to pursue jazz, which wasn't totally untrue. But it turned out that I was just searching for that right rock band to play in. It was a coincidence that, once word got out that I was out of Skin Yard, I called Kim or Kim called me, and they were at a crossroads with Scott Sundquist. My first practice with Soundgarden, in Chris's living room up in Capitol Hill, it was pretty instantaneous. I remember after I played like one song, Chris said, "Hey, man, you're playing it perfect."

JONATHAN PONEMAN I wanted to do a record with Soundgarden. But the thing is, I didn't really know anything about record-making. I had like $15,000—savings bonds from when I was a little kid—which at the time was a lot of money.

Soundgarden had a meeting with Bruce at the Oxford Tavern that I had walked in on towards the end of. I saw them meeting with Bruce, and I was freaking out—I thought, Here is Bruce Pavitt muscling in on my turf.

BRUCE PAVITT I had known Kim since he was probably 11. He used to hang out at my house quite a bit in Park Forest. We went to the same alternative high school together. He was a longtime friend of the family. Soundgarden were probably at the time a little too metal for my taste, but I still thought they were pretty interesting and I think they ultimately became a great band.

KIM THAYIL Bruce had an established brand, with a cool little logo, and contacts throughout the country within the indie network. But Bruce is in debt to his dad at this point. Jonathan *did* have money, and was ready to put out the record then.

JONATHAN PONEMAN Kim Thayil said, "Look, we wanna work with both of you. I've known Bruce since I was a kid back in Park Forest, Illinois. Have you guys ever considered doing something together?" And for some reason I hadn't ever thought of approaching Bruce. But then it just made all the sense in the world.

KIM THAYIL I called Jon a couple of times and said, "You need to talk to Bruce," and he said, "I don't need Bruce." I called Bruce and said, "You need to talk to Jon." "I don't really need Jon." It was something that I pushed very aggressively, because there wouldn't have been a Soundgarden record otherwise. Eventually they called each other.

JONATHAN PONEMAN So I was just gonna be an investor in the Soundgarden record. We did a limited-edition single, which was "Hunted Down" backed with "Nothing to Say," and then the *Screaming Life* EP. And while working on that project, we both kinda had the same idea at the same time, which is: Let's make Sub Pop an ongoing concern and let's document the happening scene that's going on in Seattle.

GRANT ALDEN You can reduce this to a handful of people who made Seattle happen. Bruce and Jon are clearly on that list. Susan Silver is on that list. Art Chantry is on that list. And without Charles Peterson's camera and his visuals, I don't think it would have happened. I don't think it would have been a cohesive, coherent movement in the way that it was perceived by the outside world.

BRUCE PAVITT The moment that I began envisioning a record label that focused on Seattle bands was when I stepped into a house in the U District called the Room Nine House. The band Room Nine lived there. Charles Peterson lived there, too, and he had printed up photos that he had done of local bands that were literally life-size. Instantly, I was like, Oh, my God, these photos so perfectly capture the energy of the shows.

RON RUDZITIS (a.k.a. Ron Nine; Room Nine/Love Battery singer/guitarist) We lived behind the Rainbow Tavern, which was pretty convenient. My girlfriend at the time knew Charles Peterson, so that's how I met him. He became my roommate, and all of the sudden, Charles's friends started coming to hang out. Mark Arm was Charles's best friend, so Mark was over there all the time. People like Ed Fotheringham, who did everybody's album covers and was the lead singer for the Thrown Ups. Right around the time Charles moved in, we got to be known as quite the party house.

LILLY MILIC (Top Hat Records store owner; Garrett Shavlik's wife) The parties were always the same group of people, the same soundtrack. Scratch Acid, Butthole Surfers, the Kinks, Bad Brains—and you would hear that for a whole year. Same party, different place. One thing we would always laugh about is everybody at these parties would immediately stash their beer somewhere—you would have hiding places at each house. When the junkie scene started taking over in Seattle by '88, '89, I noticed people weren't trying to steal my beer as often 'cause they were nodding out.

RON RUDZITIS When Charles first moved in, he goes, "Hey, I want to throw a party!" It turned into one of those out-of-hand things where our next-door neighbor had a water hose and was spraying all the people on the front lawn. I was worried about the house getting burned down—people were blowing up eggs in the microwave. We had instruments set up, and a bunch of bands got up and played. It's pretty hazy, but I think the Melvins might've done a couple of songs. Maybe Green River.

CHARLES PETERSON At the time, none of the indie labels were really using photography; it was more about illustration. So Bruce was like, "Let's use photography," because you can use photography to make something look larger-than-life. It was a small scene—at any given show, there were maybe 50 to 150 people, max—but by using a wide-angle lens and just getting right in the face of the performer and maybe including a slice of the audience or the performer interacting with the audience, it looked like, Oh, my God, this is so exciting!

BRUCE PAVITT Both Charles and Jack Endino captured the energy of the bands. And they were perfect complements for one another. Jack became, in effect, Sub Pop's house producer.

CHRIS HANZSEK I didn't have the time for C/Z, or the money for it, because I was now a studio owner. I rekindled Reciprocal in early '86 with Jack Endino, in Ballard. It was in a classic wooden building in the shape of a triangle that had previously been a studio called, imaginatively enough, Triangle Recording. A month or two into our partnership, Jack decided that he wanted to pursue being a producer, and asked me if I wouldn't mind being the studio owner, so I bought out his contribution.

Plus, I was feeling a little bit bitter still about everybody heaping on me with the *Deep Six* thing, so believe it or not, I had a little bit of a distaste for running the label. At one point, Bruce and Jon actually called me up and invited me down to their office. Bruce was sitting on the floor, laying out some artwork for the Green River record, and Jonathan said, "Sit down, we want to talk to you." They said, "Are you still going to release records on C/Z?" And I said, "No, I've decided not to go forward with it."

They just kind of looked at each other and smiled and went, "Okay. That's good." They wanted to make sure I wasn't still competing with them.

DANIEL HOUSE Chris and Tina had done *Deep Six*, and they had done the first Melvins single, which was a six-song seven-inch. He'd told me that he had no interest in doing this anymore. He had a futon bed underneath which was all his unsold inventory. And so I offered to basically take over the ownership of the label and buy his inventory from him.

Skin Yard had recorded enough material for a full album and no record labels were biting. So taking over C/Z was basically me just going, Well, how hard can it be to put out a record? I can do this. So I took over C/Z in '87 and my first release was CZ003, the first Skin Yard record. I was pretty connected with all the bands in town, so I started putting out records by my friends' bands, like Coffin Break and My Eye.

JACK ENDINO At first, Daniel and I were going to do C/Z together. CZ003 was the first Skin Yard record. CZ006 was a compilation record called *Secretions* that someone else put together, but I ended up being the guy who got it dumped in his lap. And that was the last thing I did for C/Z in an organizational sense. From then on, it was just Daniel's. He was actually working for Sub Pop then, but pretty soon, he started getting more and more serious about C/Z.

CHAPTER 10
SOUNDS LIKE THROW UP LOOKS

STEVE MACK My college roommate at the University of Washington and I were looking for another place to live. And in the student union building there was this ad posted on a piece of paper, with all these things cut out of different magazines and collaged together. Scrawled in black Magic Marker, it said: DOGS FUCK THE POPE, NO FAULT OF MINE—that's a Hunter S. Thompson quote. CHANCE KILLS US ALL, EVENTUALLY, WITH NO CHOICE. We thought, This is the guy for us.

So we called the guy, Todd Chandler, and went over to look at his place. He had the Misfits cranked at full volume, and we thought, Okay, this is going to work. We lived in that house for three months before we had to move out, at which point we all moved to a much larger house. That's when Leighton and a number of other people moved in with us.

JOHN LEIGHTON BEEZER (the Thrown Ups bassist; the Blunt Objects guitarist) Todd was hemophiliac, and when kids were born with hemophilia, they used to wrap them up in cotton, like they were fine china. And at a certain point, his mom got fed up with this and said, "Even if he has to die young, he's gonna live like a normal kid." So this was a guy who basically expected to die at any time.

Todd was the drummer in our band the Blunt Objects, which also featured Jim Sangster, who ended up playing bass in the Young Fresh Fellows, and John Conte, who went on to a band called the Living, which featured Duff McKagan and Greg Gilmore. Todd's drum set was literally speckled in blood; any little cut would just bleed continuously, and he'd have to get a transfusion after every practice. His attitude was, Fuck, we're only here so long, so let's have some fun. I think that's where the attitude of the Blunt Objects came from. And the irony was that Todd did survive well into adulthood, and he didn't die from hemophilia—he died in '96 from AIDS he got from a blood transfusion.

STEVE MACK The word got out that we had these crazy punk-rock parties. We started intersecting with a couple of other large party houses: There was one house full of women, and then there was another house full of guys, where people like Mark Arm lived and hung out. It was like this golden triangle.

But at the same time, there was a nasty streak amongst the sort of Seattle street punk rockers, the Bopo Boys. Here we were, these nice, middle-class suburban kids who just dug this crazy punk rock, and all of the sudden, these street kids came in, and they had speed and heroin and liked to get into fights and trash our house. I remember one night in particular, I found my television in the fireplace—on fire.

We had a party on New Year's '84—by this time, we were in our third house—and after, my friend Mike Faulhaber said, "I got an idea. Let's just stay up until our first class," which would've been another two days away. "We'll make music."

"That sounds fantastic!"

"Okay, but we're going to need a lot more drugs."

So Mike and I were in my bedroom, just making all this music, and at some point, I believe at two in the morning, Leighton walks in with his eyes as big as basketballs. He had decided to try a little experiment: "I'm going to try to megadose myself on psychotropes tonight." He said, "What are you guys doing?"

"We're on an epic quest. We're going to play music until our first class, in 51 hours. We're just going to keep playing." So Leighton joins us and we just kept going and going and going. We made it until about 4 o'clock in the morning before my first class, which was at 9:30. By this point, Leighton had collapsed. Mike and I, we both looked at each other and I said, "I can't go any further!" He's like, "I can't, either!" At that point, we both collapsed.

Leighton came back a couple of days later, and he was like, "I really think we're on to something. We're going to play, but we're never going to rehearse." Leighton kept asking me to sing, and I just wasn't feeling it. So I let them carry on with it, and it was at one of those parties that one of our drinking buddies, Ed Fotheringham—he was the crazy Australian—stepped up to the mic, and a match was made.

JOHN LEIGHTON BEEZER After that party, I remember we were leaving the basement and Ed said, "You know, that sounded like throw up looks."

So I said, "Well, I guess that makes us the Thrown Ups." And the name stuck. That was when it became me and Ed and Mike, and we recruited a drummer from a band called the Limp Richerds, Scott Schickler. A year later, in the winter of '85, we played our first show, opening for Hüsker Dü at the Gorilla Gardens. We had a jar of oysters, and I threw the oysters at people in the crowd. Ed always came up with the ideas for the shows.

Mike left the band, and right after Steve quit Green River, he joined the Thrown Ups. And then Mark joined, too, replacing Scott. That was Mark and Steve's way of staying together musically.

MARK ARM We did one show where we all played in our boxers and the four members of the band were wearing flower heads. Apparently, the whole time Steve's ball sac was hanging out of his boxers.

STEVE TURNER Yeah, apparently my underwear was too short.

MARK ARM The most brilliant thing was when Ed came up with the zit pants.

ED FOTHERINGHAM (the Thrown Ups singer; illustrator) It was a suit that I made out of black garbage bags turned inside out, seamed with duct tape and with about 30 Ziploc bags filled with Barbasol shaving cream on the inside. It just looked like a puffy leather suit. I had a sharpened chopstick, and at the end of the show, I would pop these things and squeeze them. And to my glee and surprise, they worked so well—this stream of white liquid went out like 30 feet into the audience and actually hit the bar. It was just a mess. We got kicked out of the Ditto Tavern for that.

TOM HAZELMYER (Amphetamine Reptile Records founder; U-Men bassist) Turner was always twistin' my arm, like, "You gotta listen to this tape! We need someone to put the record out. It's me, and Mark Arm on drums and Ed Fotheringham on vocals and Leighton on bass, and we just make everything up as we go." I was like, "That sounds fucking *horrible.*" Somehow he got me to listen to it, and I was like, "Fuck. This actually sounds great!" I ended up putting out all their albums on AmRep.

JACK ENDINO The Thrown Ups? Probably the best band ever. Steve and Mark and Leighton and Ed would make the most ridiculous list of song titles you could think of, and pick from the list. "Okay, 'Sloppy Pud Love.' What would that sound like?" They'd start jamming, and they'd look at me and go, "Okay. We got it. Roll it." And I would just roll tape, and they'd come back, listen to it, everybody'd have a good laugh, and then they'd go down the list again. "Okay, 'Elephant Crack.' What would that sound like?" Ed would literally make up lyrics on the spot. We're not talking Hemingway here, but it was always funny as shit.

* * *

MIKE LARSON (Green River manager) When I became the manager for Green River, there was a little notice in the gossip column of *The Rocket*: "Michael Larson is now the manager of Green River, who are working with Joe Perry of Aerosmith fame in the studio." I think Jeff actually put that in there. My sense is that he made up this rumor to create buzz.

I don't think they ever met Joe Perry. But that rumor had a life of its own. And the funny thing is, if you look at the "Together We'll Never"/"Ain't Nothing to Do" single that we released, it says, "Produced by J. Perry." For the next couple of years, every once in a while someone would go, "Hey, so have you guys been working with Aerosmith?"

BRUCE FAIRWEATHER Green River got to open for Public Image Ltd., at the Paramount Theatre in '86. When I showed up, Andy Wood and Regan Hagar are hanging out backstage, and they're totally out of control. I was like, "You guys seem hammered."

They're like, "Yeah, we've been going upstairs to PIL's dressing room and stealing their beer." So I was like, "Hell, I'm going to have some." Grabbed a couple of beers, and kept going up and taking a couple more. Finally, we just went up there and took everything.

STEVE TURNER I snuck in the back with Andrew and Regan from Malfunkshun. We were throwing lunch meat onto the roof of PIL's tour bus. We were yelling back and forth at their dirtbag roadies, telling each other to fuck off. And finally, this voice from the sky says, *"Would you like to be silenced?!"* And that was John Lydon. Yeah, it's fucking Johnny Rotten. And this shut us all up.

MARK ARM Our room was just down the hall and we could hear John Lydon fucking raising a hissy fit about the fact that there isn't a La-Z-Boy recliner in his room. You're supposed to be punk rock! By the time we played, we'd worked ourselves up into a tizzy about this outrageous behavior. It fed into my anger and made me want to fuck shit up.

MIKE LARSON Here's the founder of punk, and he's getting pissed off and irritated, so we'll just see how irritating we can be. We just start yelling back at him, and Mark starts yelling back in a faux British voice. We didn't hear anything from them after that, and then the band went onstage.

MARK ARM (from the stage at the Paramount Theatre, June 28, 1986) Hey, if you ever wanna know what it's like to become what you hated, ask the next band.

BRUCE FAIRWEATHER Four or five songs into the set, Mike comes out on my side of the stage, starts saying something in my ear, like, "Bruce, you know, you guys have to quit playing." I'm like, "Get the fuck offstage." And then they shut the power down on us. Apparently, John Lydon was running around backstage saying, "I want them out of the building right now!"

MIKE LARSON After about the eighth song, I remember the promoter coming to me and saying, "You gotta tell your band that this is the last song." I remember those guys looking at me going, "What the fuck? We're not stopping." They did about four or five songs after that, and the promoter just went mad. We were able to get them off just in time, so they didn't have to cut the power.

BRUCE FAIRWEATHER The fish incident? I remember it being Mike's idea to do the fish. We were opening for Agent Orange at the Washington Performance Hall. Mike tells Mark, "I think for this show, you should put a fish down your pants." Mark used to wear these silver lamé Iggy Pop tight trousers. And so Mike went down to the Pike Place Market, and found this horrible, stinky trout.

MARK ARM The only problem was the fins were really spiny. It was worth it for the art, though.

BRUCE FAIRWEATHER About halfway through, Mark pulls the fish out of his pants and throws it out into the crowd. Sure enough, it comes back in pieces on stage. Alex had borrowed the Agent Orange drummer's drum carpet, and it got all over the drum carpet. The Agent Orange guys were furious.

ALEX SHUMWAY The smell was just terrible. I'm almost positive that we got banned from there. We were banned from almost every place that we played at least once. And then they would ask us to come back 'cause we made them money.

BRUCE FAIRWEATHER Years later, when I was in Love Battery, we played with Agent Orange, and I reminded the singer about the fish. I was like, "It was great, right?" He didn't say anything. He just shook his head and walked away.

DAWN ANDERSON After a while, the Green River fans knew when to step back, because there might be green Jell-O coming at you.

JULIANNE ANDERSEN That was at the Central. I looked at my friends and all of a sudden they were taking six, seven, eight steps back. I didn't know what the hell was happening, and I got the worst of it. My hair was bleached blond at the time, so I had green hair for a week. I still fuckin' hate Mark Arm for that.

ALEX SHUMWAY Mark wanted to keep the band more down to earth, and the other guys wanted it to become something bigger. There was even talk at one point, "Hey, let's move down to L.A. and make it down there." That was Jeff and Stone's idea. It was more something that was thrown against the wall to see if it would stick. Mark was like, "Hell, no," but I was a whore—I'd have gone anywhere.

JEFF AMENT There was some shit-talking afterward, some things about me and Stone being careerists—which is basically what Cobain adopted later. I was the only guy in the band who didn't have a trust fund. I guess if not wanting to work in a restaurant for the rest of my life made me a careerist, then that was probably true.

BRUCE FAIRWEATHER Trust fund? God, no. I had girlfriends whose places I'd be crashing at.

MARK ARM To be truthful, I would have been perfectly happy being in a successful band.

The idea that I should get singing lessons was in the mix. I'm not the greatest singer. My reaction was, "I don't want to learn the 'right way' to do something. I want to try to figure out something that's uniquely mine."

It's kind of unfair to characterize it as me against Jeff and Stone. By that point, it was probably me against the rest of the band. Also, to be fair, I wasn't hanging out with those guys so much at this point. I was starting to dabble with heroin. It was partly curiosity. There was some arrogance: I can handle it. I'm smart enough. I knew I could not do this every day, and I managed to keep it on that level for a couple of years, where it was just like any other recreational drug, no different than MDA or LSD.

ALEX SHUMWAY A couple of months before Green River broke up, Jeff, Stone, and Bruce were playing in Lords of the Wasteland, a cover band with Andy and Regan. I later learned that their side project was actually the beginning of Mother Love Bone. I didn't really pay attention to it. I had blinders on.

STEVE TURNER Mark did a one-night joke cover band with some friends from work called the Wasted Landlords. I thought that was hilarious, 'cause if they were thinking about using Lords of the Wasteland for real, they couldn't anymore. That's the way I looked at it: They just shut down that name.

MIKE LARSON I quit right before Green River broke up. Partly because I got a real job in San Francisco. I remember thinking, This is such a waste of time. How can this ever turn into something bigger than what it is now?

MARK ARM A night or two before our last show, we played in San Francisco at the Chatterbox. It was a great show, and we finished our set and people wanted more and we just kept playing and playing and—here's where singing lessons might have helped out—at the end of the night, I'd just totally blown out my voice.

Our last show was in L.A., playing with Junkyard and Jane's Addiction. I was not a fan of Jane's Addiction. At the time, I was really opposed to high-pitched vocals—to me that was just like fingernails on a chalkboard. Junkyard were this AC/DC-ish, Southern rock–ish, L.A. glam-metal band, but they had Brian Baker from Minor Threat and Chris Gates from the Big Boys and Poison 13. I thought, I don't want to just be another ex-punk who plays in some shitty glam band.

And there was the guest list issue. Jeff had put a bunch of A&R people on the list. He's trying to make something happen, while my point at the time was, "Why can't we get our friends in?" We ran into Anna Statman, who at the time worked at Slash, and I think she was the only A&R person on the list that showed up.

We sucked. I sucked, in particular. I couldn't hit half the notes. The rest of the band was probably glad the A&R people didn't show.

JEFF AMENT Stone and I were on the side of the stage when Jane's was playing, totally mesmerized by the interaction between the band and the crowd. . . . It was the first time I had seen an alternative-music show where it was like the most reverential hard-rock crowd. That night

Jane's Addiction showed us that you could do something totally different and make it work, which basically caused Green River to break up since the other guys didn't dig it as much as Stone and I did. Our drummer hated them. When we got back to Seattle we just knew we wanted to do something else, something with less limitations, something that had endless possibilities . . .

ALEX SHUMWAY On Halloween of 1987, me and Mark were there waiting for practice. Jeff, Stone, and Bruce walked into the practice space and said, "We don't want to do this anymore." And Mark was like, "Okay."

I was a bit devastated. Stoney said something that I wanted to punch him in the nose for at the time. He said he felt that I didn't want to practice. Stone's like, "I'm practicing at home." I've got a *fucking drum set.* What, am I gonna lug this back to my apartment? I think they were trying to make as clean a break as possible. And that was his way of doing it.

JEFF AMENT Sub Pop was right upstairs from the coffee shop I worked at. Stone and I had decided we were gonna quit, and I remember Jonathan coming down and saying, "Yeah, we're gonna buy a van for Sub Pop. You guys can tour on this record in the van." And for me that was all I ever wanted, to tour and see the world playing music. It was tough at that point to say, "No, we're not that psyched creatively, and we want to do something else."

MARK ARM I felt relief. I was tired of fighting to be heard.

DAN PETERS I was at a show at the OK Hotel. Mark came running up to me, completely hammered, while I was standing in line at the bathroom. He's like, "Green River broke up!" And he was totally psyched. He's like, "Can I cut in front of you to use the bathroom?"

When he comes out, he goes, "All right, see you later." I walk in, and he had puked all over the place. Obviously he had been celebrating the fact that Green River broke up, couldn't handle it, and blew it all over the bathroom.

CHAPTER 11
WE'RE RIPPING YOU OFF BIG TIME!

KURT DANIELSON (TAD/Bundle of Hiss bassist) I grew up in a small town called Stanwood, an hour north of Seattle. My dad was a journalist, and he owned and ran the town newspaper, the *Stanwood/Camano News,* and he was a respected pillar of the community. He found himself having to publish stories about certain acts of vandalism that were occurring around the city—he didn't know who was responsible, but he could make a pretty educated guess judging from the style and the handwriting. When I was 15, I got kicked out of school for having pot and had to go to school in a different town.

I started playing bass at 17. My dad had a pressman, Gene Fleming, working for him who used to play bass with Loretta Lynn years ago. According to Gene, *Coal Miner's Daughter* was fairly accurate, except that his character was completely expunged from the movie. I talked him into selling me his bass, and I began to learn how to play it. And then I formed a band with friends called Bundle of Hiss, which went through many moves and permutations. The constants were myself and Jeff Hopper, the guitar player, and Russ Bartlett, the original drummer who'd become the singer. I eventually ended up in Seattle, where I was a student at the University of Washington, and that's where I graduated in '86 with a degree in English.

When we moved to Seattle, around '83, we were introduced to a drummer by a mutual friend, and he was just a little kid, 15 years old. I remember going to his house wearing clothes I'd bought at Value Village—psychedelic flares that were high-water, and these high-heel Elton John kind of shoes. I'm wearing a red, white, and blue sweater. I had a shaved head with weird chunks of hair growing out. I wanted to look like I'd been kicked in the head so many times I was brain damaged. And Dan opens the door and he took a look at me and wanted to slam the door in my face, but I wouldn't let him. And from that point onward he was in the band.

DAN PETERS Kurt's from Stanwood, which was separated from where I'm from, Camano Island, by a one-block bridge. It was absolute hell. Just total hillbilly action. I was probably around five when I got my first pair of drumsticks. I would sit around in my bedroom and act like I had a drum set and was the drummer for various bands. I'd practice every day in my make-believe world until I got a drum set when I was 14 or 15.

When my evil stepdad found out about the drum set, he threatened me with violence if he was anywhere around the house and heard it. Things got out of hand at my house, so I made the great escape and moved to Seattle to be with my dad. Then I got a call from Kurt, and he came down, gave me a tape. He had big, crazy, curly hair, and a big ol' sweater with an American flag pattern.

KURT DANIELSON At some point, Russ quit and we were a three-piece, with my friend Jamie Lane doing vocals and guitar, me on bass and a bit of backup vocals, and then Dan on drums. At about this time, we learned of a new band that'd moved to town from Boise, called H-Hour. And that was Tad Doyle's band. We did some gigs with those guys, and Tad was perhaps the most powerful drummer I'd seen play, ever. He'd have this look on his face—staring straight at the crowd, as if he had literally killed, stopped the heart of everybody in the room with one hit of his drumstick against the snare.

DAN PETERS I was way underaged. I couldn't be in the club until it was time for us to play, and then I was allowed in the club to play, and then I was immediately booted out. Of course, I tried to hide out somewhere, but I was always found—usually with a beer in my hand. But there was this one club called the Ditto, which was a haven for all of us. We could do weekend shows there and they had a pretty lax ID man.

While I was playing with Bundle of Hiss, I joined another band called Feast, which was quite a popular band in town in that era. Feast's singer, Tom Mick, was a wild man, divin' on tables and swingin' from the curtains and whatnot. There was two females in the band, a female bass player and a female singer, and they tried to get me to wear poofy shirts and stuff. I was like, "No." The closest I came to accessorizing was when they bought me some concho belt. I think I put it on.

KURT DANIELSON At some point, H-Hour broke up, mainly because Tad wanted to play guitar and not drums anymore, and so he joined Bundle of Hiss, though he also played drums in Bundle of Hiss. So we had two drummers or two guitarists, depending on the song. Bundle of Hiss had been more of an art band, but at this point we started to put more humor into the music and lyrics, partly because of the influence of Tad.

DAN PETERS By the time Bundle of Hiss recorded, we went into the studio with Jack Endino. I knew Jack because Bundle of Hiss and Skin Yard played together all the time. When Jack started working at Reciprocal, anybody who could pony up $100 could probably go in and record with him.

JACK ENDINO I was making about five bucks an hour working at this little studio. Bands tend to trust people that they know from other bands, as opposed to producers they've never met, and so as a peer I had an advantage.

In January 1988, Kurt Cobain called me up at the studio and said, "I don't have a band name, but I've got the Melvins' drummer helping me out. We just want to come up and record some songs." I'd already been a Melvins fan for years, and thought, This is a no-brainer. Let's do it.

Between noon and 5 p.m., we recorded and mixed 10 songs. I thought Kurt had a really good scream and a really good melodic approach. And I thought it was good enough that I insisted they let me keep a cassette of it, and said, "Hey, can I play this for some people?"

DALE CROVER When I first played with them, they weren't even called Nirvana. They were in between names; they couldn't decide. One show we did as Pen Cap Chew. Next week, we'd be Skid Row. I named the band Ted Ed Fred for a show. I recorded their first demo with them with Jack Endino at Reciprocal studios. They wanted to have their stuff on tape so they could shop it around and find a drummer. They got a record deal instead.

JONATHAN PONEMAN I got the tape from Jack and I listened to half of the first song, "If You Must," which later ended up being part of the box set, and I went, "Oh, my God." I went to Muzak, where Bruce was working, and I lent him the tape.

RON RUDZITIS I was working at Muzak at the time, and I remember Bruce playing the demo for the people who worked there. We all stood around the little blaster in the cart room. It was a little too metal-ish for my taste. I really liked Kurt's vocals, but nothing really grabbed me. There was kind of a collective "Hmmm . . ." in the room.

JACK ENDINO Frankly, to those guys, I think it was a little too metal. It wasn't indie rock enough sounding, because Nirvana basically started as a heavy-riff rock band.

DAWN ANDERSON I was there when Jack first called Jonathan and asked, "What did you think of the tape I gave you?" Jonathan was saying that he loved it, but that Bruce thought it was a little too arty. And Jack thought that was just incredible. I remember he got mad. He said, "He's into mediocrity!"

JONATHAN PONEMAN But Bruce did me a solid and joined me in seeing Nirvana play at the Central Tavern. I remember they were pretty good, but the room was practically empty. Tracy Marander, Kurt's girlfriend at the time, was there. There was a bartender, a sound guy, and maybe like one other person. I remember when they played "Love Buzz," which was not on the tape, Bruce looks at me and says, "That's the single."

DALE CROVER I was friends with the Nirvana guys, but I'd already invested all the time in playing with Buzz, and I liked the Melvins better. I probably could've done both bands, but I was moving away.

BUZZ OSBORNE We played with that band Clown Alley, and their guitar player, Mark Deutrom, asked us to be on Alchemy, the label he was starting with this guy named Victor Hayden. And we said, "Sure, why not?" We had nothing else going on. So they gave us barely enough money to get down to San Francisco and record, and paid for the recording of that first record, *Gluey Porch Treatments*.

MARK DEUTROM (Alchemy Records cofounder; producer; later Melvins bassist/ soundman) One of the things that Buzz and Dale used to joke about is the fact that they were gonna do this recording without drinking any beer. They did it stone-cold sober. That got laughed about frequently in the future, how they just white-knuckled their way through the whole experience. I think that contributed to the intensity of it.

BUZZ OSBORNE And that's where I met Lori Black. She was always a weirdo, which is what attracted me to her. And I knew, within the next year, when she became my girlfriend, that I wanted to move to San Francisco.

MATT LUKIN When we recorded *Gluey Porch Treatments*, we stayed at this house in San Francisco where Lori and her boyfriend Mark Deutrom lived. I think that's when Lori and Buzz kind of hit it off. Then she started to come visit Buzz, and then they started dating. Buzz had Dale tell me, "Buzz is moving out to San Francisco, quitting the band, going to live with Lori in San Francisco." And I'm like, Okay, that sounds familiar, that's exactly the same story he had me tell Dillard when we kicked him out.

I called Buzz and I go, "So you're moving to San Francisco to be with Lori, huh? I think you're moving to San Francisco, and Lori's going to be your new bass player and Dale's going to follow you." A month later, they're down in San Francisco playing shows, Dale's living in the house with them—everything that I accused him of. Fucking spineless asshole.

BUZZ OSBORNE I didn't really want to go with Matt Lukin—it wouldn't have worked. He didn't want to leave. I think he stayed in Montesano for a really long time after he started playing with Mudhoney. I told him, "I'm moving to San Francisco. I'm either starting a new band or I'm starting this band up again."

MARK DEUTROM Lori and I were together for about 10 years. We split up, Lori and Buzz got together, Lori joined the band, and I moved to London at that point. Then Buzz called me up and said, "Hey, want to produce our next record?" So I came out from London, and we recorded *Ozma*. That was, of course, pretty much the Fleetwood Mac scenario.

FRANK KOZIK (poster artist; video director) I remember when I got ahold of the Melvins' *Ozma* record, and I was like, "This band is fucking brutal!" And they came to play at this tiny club in Austin called Cave Club, and I did this little shitty black-and-white Xerox for it. I'd never even seen a picture of them. Buzz comes out, and he had his huge hairdo, and I was like, "What the fuck, who is this faggot-looking dude? What is this, the opening band?" He looks like some reject guy from the Cure or something. But it was him, and they rocked, and I was just blown away.

DALE CROVER Lori was a really solid bass player. She had really good meter and would bust me for speeding up, which helped me become a more solid player. I really liked her. She was really into spirituality and things like that. She really had a tough time because she assumed people wouldn't accept her being in the band. One, being a female, and two, replacing Matt Lukin. People definitely liked Matt Lukin. We were like, "Don't worry about that."

BUZZ OSBORNE When I went to San Francisco, I moved directly into Lori's house. Now, bear in mind, I started going out with her long before I ever knew who her mom was. Months and months later, she said, "My mom is somebody famous." I was like, "What are you fucking talking about?" It was crazy. I couldn't believe that her mom was Shirley Temple.

Lori's dad was Charles Black, who came from oil money, I think. And Shirley is a self-made woman. Shirley's parents squandered every dime she ever made as a child before she had a chance to spend any of it. She got nothing. Zero. So she's a pretty tough broad, you know? She'll rip your head off and eat you for breakfast. She was the ambassador to Czechoslovakia at that point, after being the ambassador to Ghana.

Their house was unbelievable. Lots of stuff from the Hearst collection. Amazing shit—they had really great taste. And there was an Oscar sitting there. Shirley talked about her acting a lot. At one point they had her playing drums, and she had a recording of her playing drums when she was a kid, and she sounded like fucking Buddy Rich. And then she showed us how tap dancing is really just drumming. She tap-danced for us, and she was fucking amazing.

DALE CROVER Shirley was like, "Yeah, my mom made me give away my drum set because it wasn't ladylike to play drums." I was like, "Oh, you couldn't spread your legs with a dress to play drums. I get it." She was sad about it.

The family was kind of weird and straight and conservative. Proper. I remember we'd line up outside the dining room and all kind of walk in together for some reason. I didn't really understand it. But they were nice to me.

BUZZ OSBORNE They probably thought that I was some leeching weirdo and that their daughter went out with me just to screw with them. Her dad was never nice to me. Shirley was nice to me to some degree, but they're very guarded people. I'm sure they thought I was going to write some book or something. And believe me, without going into any graphic details, there are massive skeletons in that closet.

One thing that Shirley said to me was, "Working in the government, you can always get somebody audited." I took that to heart. They never did anything to me personally, or even threatened me, but they didn't need to. You don't need a weatherman to know which way the wind blows. They were über-right-wing. Now, I'm not talking about Rush Limbaugh; I'm talking about the people who make life-and-death decisions. And it's not necessarily evil; it's more realistic. Charles was ex-CIA. It's weirder than you can possibly imagine. I certainly never got the truth.

Since then, everything that's happened—from Nirvana going crazy and on and on and on—none of that holds a candle to how weird that situation was. That's David Lynch weird.

• • •

DAWN ANDERSON I lived with three other girls in North Seattle, and we had this big housewarming party. The Melvins had just broken up, and Matt was just wanting to really get drunk. And he got really drunk. He kept spilling orange juice and licking it off my rug, down on all fours.

I had this huge stick of dynamite that someone had given me—I used to go out with a weird, demented nerd that liked to build explosives—and I remember this as if it was in slow-motion: Matt Lukin picking up the stick of dynamite, lighting a lighter, and moving it toward the thing. I remember, again in slow-motion, running across the room, grabbing it from him, and going, *"N-o-o-o-o-o-o!!"*

I got it away from him, and he looked at me completely innocently: "Oh, that was real?"

DAN BLOSSOM (Feast guitarist) It was really kind of strange—everyone split up the same month: Feast split up, Green River split up. The Melvins split up, sort of. And that's when all the new bands started forming.

DAN PETERS Steve Turner came up to me at a party and said, "Do you want to get together with me and Ed Fotheringham and do something?" I totally liked Steve's guitar playing in the Thrown Ups, even though that band was a complete train wreck. The three of us got together at this practice space called the Dutchman and Steve started playing the riff which would eventually be Mudhoney's "You Got It," which he and Ed had used for a Thrown Ups song called "Bucking Retards." We mucked around for a while, and I think that was the one and only time that Ed was involved. After that, Mark came into the picture.

STEVE TURNER Ed didn't wanna do a real band. He was like, "Practice? The *same songs*?!"

MARK ARM Steve and Dan and I had been working things out as early as November. But the first practice with Matt is when we marked the birth of the band: New Year's Day of 1988.

MATT LUKIN I got a call from Mark Arm, asking if I wanted to come over and jam. I'd never met Dan Peters before the first Mudhoney practice. We just drank a lot of beer, jammed, hung out, had a good time.

Something I'd learned was that you can't drink beer and play Melvins stuff. It just isn't going to work out. What was so great about the first Mudhoney practice was that I downed a 12-pack and was still able to play through the songs. I'm like, Oh, this is easy! Although it wasn't as easy as I thought, because I remember at one point Mark was complaining, "How can you and Dan not get this? It's the simplest thing, and you both come from bands that play intricate stuff."

MARK ARM When I was in Green River, the Neptune movie house did a night of Russ Meyer movies. The first one was *Up,* the second was *Mudhoney,* and the third was, of course, *Faster, Pussycat.* I decided to get something to eat when *Mudhoney* was playing but thought, Mudhoney, that's a really good name, and tucked that away.

DAN PETERS I found out we were called Mudhoney when I read something in *The Rocket* saying this band was forming with such-and-such people in it, and they're called Mudhoney.

MARK ARM I was working with Bruce Pavitt at Muzak, and I brought in a recording of one of Mudhoney's practices. I said, "Hey, Bruce, this is what we sound like." It was recorded on a boom box, so it sounded muffled and staticky; it was just an indistinguishable roar. So he's like, "I can't tell what's going on. Why don't you just go in to record with Jack Endino? We'll pay for it."

BRUCE PAVITT Obviously it was an extremely ironic situation that the break room at Muzak would become kind of the testing grounds for underground Seattle music. Bands would come in with their demos, play them, and we'd all critique them. Mark Arm and Chris Pugh worked there. Tom from Feast and Chris from the Walkabouts. That's where I first heard Mudhoney's "Touch Me I'm Sick." It's where I first heard the Nirvana demo that Jack Endino had passed on to Jon Poneman.

RON RUDZITIS I worked with Tad at Muzak, and he gives me credit for getting Bruce to put out his first single. Tad had gone into Reciprocal to record some of his songs. He did all the instruments. He played me the cassette in the cart room, and I go, "I've never heard such a good drum sound on a recording out of Seattle." Tad still really didn't know

Bruce that well. I marched right out of the room and said, "Hey, Bruce, you gotta listen to this. This is Tad's—you know, cart room Tad—and I think you would like it." So he listens to it, and that's how Tad got going with Sub Pop.

TAD DOYLE (TAD singer/guitarist; Bundle of Hiss guitarist/drummer; H-Hour drummer) We were playing my demo in the department where I worked, and Bruce walked in and says, "What is this?" He was really excited about it and he asks, "Is this the new Butthole Surfers?" And I just started grinning from ear to ear.

. . .

BRUCE PAVITT April 1, 1988, is when we quit our day jobs and moved into our tiny, original office, in the Terminal Sales Building downtown. It's the first day of Sub Pop, with a big asterisk next to it: *Except for the previous eight years.*

MARK ARM I think they got a good deal on it because the elevator stopped at the 10th floor. They were on the 11th floor, so you had to take an extra set of steps to get up there. It was a pauper's penthouse.

CHARLES PETERSON I was office boy for quite a while in the early days. Prior to that I was working evenings developing film for *Auto Trader,* the little news magazine for used cars and trucks. I was filching film from *Auto Trader* to shoot Sub Pop bands. But that got tiresome, so Bruce and Jon offered me a job, essentially as an office manager.

The "warehouse" was the toilet, so you literally had to slide sideways through these stacks of record boxes, like Green River's *Dry as a Bone,* to take a leak. Since Jonathan was more on the business side of things, he got his own office with a big glass window and a door so he could sit in there and make deals. Bruce didn't really need a desk, because Bruce was always in motion—probably residual effects of MDA.

MARK PICKEREL I moved to Seattle a few months after Lanegan did and started working for Sub Pop early on. My impressions of Bruce and Jonathan were pretty popular in the office. Bruce would come in with some outrageous story about a band expecting this or their attorney expecting that. Every time he got excited, he would pace back and forth in the room, kinda like a caged elephant. He had his hands on his forehead and his eyes were bulging out and he would hold his breath so his cheeks would do this Dizzy Gillespie thing. And then Jonathan would go into this very focused, eloquent speech that would calm Bruce down and assure him that the problem at hand was an outrage, but with proper strategy they could turn the whole thing around. This exchange would happen two or three times a week.

GILLIAN G. GAAR Bruce had these dark, intense eyes and looked very striking because he shaved his head. For a while he had that huge beard—he had the Fidel Castro look. He had an intensity about him that I think made people feel he was more intimidating than he was, whereas Jon seemed more approachable and laid-back.

JONATHAN PONEMAN When I worked at Yesco, which was sold to Muzak, and Bruce worked at Muzak about a year and a half later, we both were sickened by what we thought was a *Bonfire of the Vanities*–type yuppie culture. At the time, you had the managerial class working upstairs and you had the workers in what was called the dupe room, the duplication room. So we parodied the corporate culture through grotesque overstatement. Instead of making *Sub Pop 200* a cheap vinyl record, let's make it an overstated, bloated box set!

BRUCE PAVITT Part of our shtick was that we were this huge player on the West Coast, and a lot of people bought into that. In the *Sub Pop 200* compilation there was a picture of the building, and it said SUB POP WORLD HEADQUARTERS. And so people looked at the picture and were like, "Wow, they've got this 11-floor office building!" When in actuality we had maybe 50 square feet.

In the *Sub Pop 200* booklet, my title was listed as supervisory chairman of executive management, and Jon's was executive chairman of supervisory management. We felt there was at that time a lack of humor and a forced modesty in the punk/indie scene, and we were really going against the grain. We were ironically undermining corporate culture.

CHARLES PETERSON When we got paid, we would literally run down to the bank *that very minute*. If you were last in line, your check might bounce.

CHRIS HANSZEK Jack did a lot of the early records for Sub Pop at Reciprocal, but ultimately when the recordings got done, I was in charge of making sure they got paid for. So I ended up being the guy on the phone with Jonathan Poneman every couple of months, going, "Where the hell's my fucking money?"

JONATHAN PONEMAN We had ever-changing mottos, like "Going Out of Business Since 1988." And the mottos keep coming. Later, we did the LOSER shirts, which was an idea that was cribbed from Bob Whittaker, who quipped, "Why don't you just make a bunch of shirts that say LOSER on them?" They became very popular. I remember getting lectured by a band member's parent or something who got angry at me, saying, "That's not very good for the self-esteem of the wearers of the shirt." It's like, "I don't give a shit." *(Laughs.)*

KURT DANIELSON At the same time, I had this idea for a song called "Loser." As I once said, it seemed to me like the existential heroes of the '90s were the losers. TAD needed an extra song in the studio working on *Salt Lick* with Steve Albini, so I wrote it really quickly and I thought, This'll be excellent because there's already gonna be T-shirts that say LOSER on them, they'll be promoting the song, it'll be just magical.

THURSTON MOORE (singer/guitarist for New York's Sonic Youth; Kim Gordon's husband) Sub Pop turned the tables a little bit: We're geeks, we're record collectors, we're losers, we're pathetic. People like Mark Arm and Kurt Cobain and Tad, these guys embodied this in such a great way. They were not your typical good-looking punk-rock stars. They were kinda skinny, nose-picking nerds. Except for Tad, who was a fat, burger-burping geek. They were also lovable, and you sort of wanted to be part of that gang.

BLAG DAHLIA I would never wear a shirt that said LOSER. I felt like, Hey, I'm reasonably good-looking and cool, why would I label myself a loser? I never really identified with that side of rock and roll—"Oh, I'm such a loser" or "I'm so put upon by the jocks." That's sort of the essence of grunge, and part of why I never really identified with that very much. I was like a little Charles Manson in high school; I had girls following me around, I dealt drugs, and I didn't feel like a big loser.

Ultimately, all the symbols of grunge came to be these cute, young, skinny guys. They didn't really seem like losers to me, although I guess if they did enough dope it made them losers.

BUZZ OSBORNE Cobain had the wounded-junkie look that for some reason women watching MTV think is really cool. I've said this before: If Kurt Cobain looked like Fat Albert—same songs, everything—it wouldn't have worked. Same with Soundgarden. If Chris Cornell looked like Fat Albert, a 500-pound black guy, nobody would have given a shit.

TRACY SIMMONS Being on Sub Pop would help sometimes. They were getting notoriety, and they definitely had collectors in some towns. And in some places it didn't help us much at all. Here comes a bunch of long-haired guys from Seattle wearing lime-green Doc Martens and motorcycle jackets, and you get up onstage in front of a bunch of farmers from Omaha, Nebraska, and they're like, "What in the hell is this?" And they start chanting, "Play 'Freebird'!"

BLAG DAHLIA I've said that being on Sub Pop was like starving to death in a really cool suit. It was fun to be able to say that you were on Sub Pop, and it was nice to show up in Boise, Idaho, and have a little Sub Pop logo in the newspaper next to your name—that was your nice suit—but you just weren't making any money from the label.

GRANT ALDEN Sub Pop was in your face: WE'RE RIPPING YOU OFF BIG TIME!—that's what their ad said. This is a record label that managed to finance itself on that Singles Club.

MARK ARM One of the label's biggest tricks was selling itself so that people would want to get *anything* on Sub Pop, whether it was good or not, because of the packaging and the label identity. They came up with the Singles Club, getting people to pay [$35 a year] up front without knowing what they were getting. That helped them stay afloat.

THURSTON MOORE The Singles Club was completely brilliant. These guys had a real sense of design, which appealed to the record geek. The singles became almost like trading cards.

ART CHANTRY I have no idea who actually physically designed the black bar with the band's name and the Sub Pop logo at the top of the singles—probably Lisa Orth or Linda Owens. Bruce liked to change things up periodically, but I talked him into continuing to use the black bar when he wanted to dump it: "This is your identity here. Make sure people know it has that Good Housekeeping Seal of approval."

JACK ENDINO There was a little bit of weirdness with Sub Pop, because Skin Yard was not a band that they felt was appropriate for the label, and it wasn't hard to see why—we were a little too metal. But strangely enough, our bass player, Daniel, wound up working for them for a couple years. It used to drive Daniel nuts that he couldn't get his own band onto the label, but I stayed the hell out of this because I was still recording all the records for Sub Pop.

DANIEL HOUSE When I first started working there, it was Bruce, Jon, and me. Charles Peterson had been there earlier and a couple people would come and go. Bruce seemed to have almost contempt for Skin Yard. He hated Ben's singing. Too melodramatic. He felt like there were elements of our music, the prog-rock elements, that were anti-everything that his label was trying to establish. Jon liked our band. And he actually tried to push Bruce to put us out, but Bruce wouldn't budge. They eventually put out a Skin Yard seven-inch to just shut everybody up, or at least that's how I saw it.

JASON FINN Daniel asked me to join Skin Yard at a gig I was playing with a band called Paisley Sin. Matt had quit to join Soundgarden; Steve Wied had played a couple shows with Skin Yard, and Greg Gilmore had maybe played one.

We did our first-ever West Coast tour together, traveling in Jack's truck. Jack and Daniel would sit in the front, and Ben and I sat in the back with all the gear, and then we put a mattress down. This is with the cab on. And we would just kind of scrunch into the other side there, and Ben and I were doing a lot of crystal and smoking. Jack was pretty much a teetotaler, but I don't remember him ever saying, "Hey, guys, get your shit together." I have to assume he was irritated by our antics more than once, but Jack is a born record producer, and more than anything in the ears, it takes a boundless patience.

After like 10 months, my girlfriend, who I was sure I was going to be with forever, moved to Europe. She was calling the shots, so I moved to Europe. And by the time I got back, Skin Yard had definitely moved on; they had Scott McCullum drumming for them by then.

Skin Yard was more of the working band. We didn't have a Stonesy swagger—it was more of a Yes kind of swagger. Which is not really what rock and roll is about. The U-Men were definitely the übercool band. Back then, if Tom from the U-Men said hi to me, which he did a couple of times, that made my week.

CHARLIE RYAN Jonathan and Bruce begged the U-Men to record for them and be on their label. John and I drank in this bar called the Virginia Inn, which was right across the street from the Sub Pop head-quarters. We'd run into Jonathan and Bruce quite often. They'd say, "You guys gotta get on our label! Would ya?" And we'd say, "No, I don't think so." Because they wanted it so bad, it was just more fun saying no to them.

CHAPTER 12
TOUCH ME I'M SICK

SUSAN SILVER Larry Reid got a job as the director of COCA [Center on Contemporary Art] and needed to let the U-Men go. So I inherited them for a year or so. The difficulty was not having that much experience. How do I get them shows? I remember booking them a tour across the U.S. from my bedroom, using a phonebook, 411, and fanzines.

CHARLIE RYAN Susan tried. We weren't very interested. Susan would offer us a show, and I'd go, "Oh, I'm not playing with them. I have no respect for them." We were rather shortsighted.

TOM PRICE We'd wanted to kick Jim out for a while. I liked Jim personally, and I thought he was a great bass player, but the problem for me was I always got stuck having to mediate between him on the one hand and John and Charlie on the other hand. We made Susan fire Jim, because all of us were too cowardly to do it ourselves.

SUSAN SILVER That sucked. It was horrible. It was very sad to see, because Jim was the workhorse. He was the one who went and got 'em money; he was the one whose parents funded everything. One time, the bus broke down in the middle of the night coming home from Bellingham. We were there on the side of the highway until Jim's parents came to bail the band out, like they did every single time.

JIM TILLMAN Nobody said one word to me. That's Seattle—it's very passive-aggressive. I first found out that something was amiss when I saw a poster advertising a show for Scratch Acid and the U-Men at the Central Tavern. I'm like, Oh, I didn't know about that. I called Susan Silver and asked her what the hell was going on. She said, "They didn't talk to you?"

"No, what do you mean? What's going on?"

And she said, "They're having Tom Hazelmyer play bass for that show." She was sympathetic, though she was a little surprised that they hadn't said anything. I asked her what was going on and she said, "I know they're having a band meeting tonight at Charlie's apartment." Susan told me that they were scared of me.

I went over to Charlie's apartment that night, and I wanted to totally surprise them, so I basically broke into the building by climbing up the fire escape. I went up to his door and knocked on it. Charlie answered, and I think he was pretty drunk at the time. He said, "Oh, is this the blond we're supposed to fuck?"

And I said, "Well, evidently you already are." And I walked into the room, and John and Larry Reid were there, and Susan was there, as well, I think. Tom was out getting beer. I said, "What the hell is going on?"

Charlie said, "Well, uh, uh, uh . . . What are you talking about?"

And I said, "Fine. Fuck you, I quit."

LARRY REID I just remember it being really tense. I was there to support the band. I don't remember too much about the specifics, except Jim protesting. I was against firing him, because I thought there was a pretty good musical chemistry. But the decision was personality-driven. Jim was the most genteel member of the band. These other guys at the time were almost like Ave rats, not real far removed from street-urchin punks.

JAMES BURDYSHAW Jim Tillman was out of the band, so the U-Men all of a sudden had some free time. David Duet had gone out on that last tour with them, and he did a good job of getting Charlie interested in doing a kind of Stones garage rock-and-roll band. And Tom agreed to play bass. They needed somebody to play guitar, and David got his friend, this guy named Mike Hutchins, who went by John Michael Amerika and was like 12 years older than him.

CHARLIE RYAN Tom and I accepted our friend David Duet's invitation to be rhythm section in his band Cat Butt until he got something more permanent. One of the guitar players was John Michael Amerika. He was a real fringe guy. As fringe as we were, I still felt like I had a foot based in reality at all times. I could always go to the old man if I ever needed to get bailed out. I could always get back into working in a restaurant. But man, a lot of the guys that you met would never be going back and entering normal society.

DAVID DUET My girlfriend and I used to do this thing where we'd braid our hair and then rub black dye in it, and then rebraid it and rub bleach in it, and rebraid it and rub different colors in it, and then cut the braids off. We called them calico cat–butt hairdos, 'cause it looked like a calico cat's butt. That's where the initial spark for the band name came from. But in radio interviews, I always told a half-true story about my great-grandparents, who at one time were wealthy and had a maid named Sally. She was an old black woman with two fake legs who had a lot of cats and grew her own vegetables and sustained herself very modestly. Somehow in my mind what transpired was that she would shave a thin layer of meat off each cat's ass—allowing the other cats time to heal—and then cook it like bacon.

JAMES BURDYSHAW I was playing in 64 Spiders, and Tom was workin' at Fallout Records, and when I saw him there, he nonchalantly brought up Cat Butt. He's like, "Hey, we're lookin' for another guitar player. Are you interested?" I was like, "Yeah!" The notoriety of having two guys from the U-Men, plus David's charisma, meant all of our shows were crowded, and girls were comin' up to me like they'd never come up to me before.

TOM PRICE Cat Butt was the kind of band that something always went wrong. David would either break a bone, or an amp would blow up.

Almost every show I did with them, and every show I saw them do afterwards, there would be at least one member of the band that was totally out of it and didn't even seem to know which song the rest of the band was playing. That was a good part of their charm.

JAMES BURDYSHAW Tom and Charlie did seven shows with us. The last show we played with them before they finally left to concentrate on the U-Men again, Michael's leg was in a cast, and he made up this story about falling down the stairs at his apartment trying to catch the cat or some nonsense. The truth of the matter is, he broke his foot jumping out of a second-story window of a pharmacy he was rippin' off. He was a total drugstore cowboy, before that movie ever came out.

DAVID DUET We're waiting to play a skateboard contest, and eventually John Michael shows up, and he's wearing his Zorro hat and his leather overcoat and he's got a brand-new cast on each leg. He played the show sitting in a chair. We were kind of wasted and I was in a long blond wig and black leather miniskirt and fishnet hose. On the first song, I split my knuckle open on my tambourine and blood squirts all over these little kids in the front row. *(Laughs.)* It was a Sunday afternoon and there were a lot of parents there that were just appalled at what they saw, 'cause we were the biggest freak show on earth.

JAMES BURDYSHAW Cat Butt played the Vogue and most of the band took LSD a half-hour before we played. The opening band was this supergroup that Mark Arm, Ron Rudzitis, Tad, and Chris Pugh were in called the Wasted Landlords, as a joke on Lords of the Wasteland.

RON RUDZITIS I was playing bass, and Tad had an inflatable doll, which he bought for the show. The doll was wrapped around his waist, and he pulled out a can of whipped cream and shot it out—like come, basically. I think he emptied the whole damn can. I felt really bad for Cat Butt, 'cause the stage was covered in whipped cream after we were done.

JAMES BURDYSHAW I was so high that I just saw a big swirl on stage. Dean Gunderson, my friend who we got in the band, was wearing a toga, walkin' around barefoot. We would just giggle and giggle and giggle until it would become like this comedy routine. Onstage, Dean steps on some broken glass with bare feet and he's bleeding and he comes over to me in the middle of a song and stops playing and says, "Hey, James, my foot's bloody, ha ha ha ha."

DEAN GUNDERSON (Cat Butt bassist) I remember looking down and there was a broken pint glass there and a big pool of blood. I remember everybody looking at each other confused and forgetting what song we're on, and the distance between my frets and the strings looked like it was a quarter-mile long. The next day, we were just like, "Oh, God, what the fuck did we just do?" But a lot of people say it was the favorite show they ever saw.

JAMES BURDYSHAW Tom Price was lecturing us the next day, in a fatherly way: "Now what was it that made you think it would be cool to take acid right before the show?"

TOM PRICE We'd wanted Hiro to play bass for the U-Men, but at that point he couldn't do it. So we got Tom Hazelmyer, a friend of ours stationed out here in the Marines.

TOM HAZELMYER I think there was one other guy on the same base who was into punk-rock stuff. It was "don't ask, don't tell." I started Amphetamine Reptile in the barracks—the whole label fit in an ammo crate that I put under the bed. By the time I took up with the U-Men, they had honed it down to just rock action, gettin' away from the postpunk kind of theatric thing they had been doin'. I played three awesome shows with those guys, but figured out pretty quickly that me bein' in the service was pretty restrictive as far as practicing or hitting the road.

TOM PRICE And then we got Tony Ransom on bass. Like our first bass player, he was a refugee from Alaska. He was younger than the rest of us and sort of a Sid Vicious kind of guy.

TONY RANSOM (a.k.a. Tone Deaf; U-Men bassist) I was 18 when I joined the band in July of '87; the rest of the U-Men were a good seven or eight years older than me. Unfortunately, they were already on their downward trajectory.

CHARLIE RYAN Tom wanted to play faster stuff. Sometimes I wish I had more patience and let Tom do what he wanted at that point, and let the band evolve more. John and I had different ideas of what we wanted to do musically; we went on to do the Crows, which was slower, boozy, bluesy, creepy kind of stuff.

TONY RANSOM The last time the band performed live was Halloween 1988, at somebody's loft in Pioneer Square. John's girlfriend, Val, had made these superhero costumes for us. We got through the first three songs fine, but somebody's guitar string broke and in the time it took to replace the string and get back in tune and start the next song, the MD 20/20 we'd been drinking really started to have an effect. It really hit John, because at some point during the break, he fell backwards into the drums. And he just laid there.

JOHN BIGLEY The U-Men got together and did it and it happened and it was over and then you start getting told you're a "bridge builder" and a "gate opener." It's great. I'd seen press stuff saying that here and there, and back in the day, I'd be out getting tea and: "Hey, all right, Mr. Grunge Blueprint!" That's better than a lot of aspects of the music deal that other people experienced. I'm happy with that.

• • •

DAN PETERS Mudhoney's first show was at the Vogue, opening for Das Damen. The scene was pretty small back then, so when the dudes from Green River and Melvins are forming a new band, people are going to come and check it out. I remember it being a sloppy, drunk affair.

STEVE MANNING (later Sub Pop Records publicist) I went specifically to see Das Damen, who were from New Jersey. I didn't know who Mudhoney was; I didn't know who Mark Arm. But when I saw Mudhoney, everything shifted for me. There was something about them that made me feel, This is the band that I've always wanted to see or hear.

All three—Steve, Mark, and Matt—were really flying, launching themselves around the stage. They were unhinged.

I had a man crush on Mark Arm. He was the coolest rock guy and had a gorgeous girlfriend at the time. I wanted to be friends with him *so bad*. I would see him play and afterwards tell him, "Good show," and I'd be sweating, my heart would be racing.

BOB WHITTAKER (Mudhoney manager) Steve Turner gave me their first single downtown one night. When I got home, it was late and my girlfriend was asleep and I put my headphones on and put it on the turntable, and I just sat there on my knees listening to "Sweet Young Thing Ain't Sweet No More" over and over again. It just blew my socks off. It had so much texture to it and felt kind of tossed off, but beautiful. The other song, "Touch Me I'm Sick," was neat, too, but it didn't really strike me. Maybe "Sweet Young Thing Ain't Sweet No More" was too dark, because it was "Touch Me I'm Sick" that struck the chord nationally and internationally.

MARK ARM I have no idea where the phrase "Touch me I'm sick" came from. I know I thought it was funny. It was like, "I came up with a phrase; now I gotta build a song around it." When we recorded that first single, in my mind "Sweet Young Thing" was the A-side, though we didn't put A or B on either side.

BRUCE PAVITT When "Touch Me I'm Sick" came out and got such an incredible response, that was a magic moment where Jack Endino really established himself as a producer. The song was funny and timely. I think there was a lot of energy around the AIDS epidemic, and in a way that song kind of touched on that, but over and above that it sounded very Stooges-inspired. It was punk without sounding like punk rock from that era. It didn't sound like Black Flag.

MARK ARM If it was a song about AIDS, I think I would have said something about AIDS in there. It's about a creepy character, a jerk. It's summed up in the first two lines of the song.

KURT BLOCH "Touch Me I'm Sick" is a perfect single. Great song, it's super-funny, you can play it over and over and over again. That, along with Nirvana's "Love Buzz" single, pretty much encapsulated what grunge was all about.

KURT DANIELSON Bundle of Hiss and Mudhoney coexisted for about six months or a year. Then Bundle of Hiss fell apart. Our guitarist, Jamie, made this announcement out of the blue one night: He'd decided to get married and go to grad school back at Syracuse. Then Dan said, "Well, I'm playing in Mudhoney already, so why don't we break up the band?" And then he suggested, "Why don't you and Tad just play together, Kurt?" Because Tad had already started recording the first single for Sub Pop anyway. And so TAD became sort of a partnership between me and Tad.

Sub Pop was gonna put out a Bundle of Hiss record, but when we broke up they scrapped that idea and just put it all behind TAD. Pavitt, being the impresario that he is, felt that he could market the guy very easily. He could see that Tad was a born ham and loved the limelight.

BRUCE FAIRWEATHER My favorite Tad story that I love telling is when Mudhoney was playing a show at the Motor Sports Garage. My wife and I were sitting on top of Mudhoney's cooler onstage, behind the P.A. Mudhoney are playing, and all of the sudden, I see this shadow go by me, and I look up, and it was Tad. And this is when he was in top form, man—he was probably 400-and-something pounds. He was just running, and he dives into the audience. He took out 20 people. Everyone gets up, and they're just going, "Holy crap!" It was amazing that nobody got killed.

KURT DANIELSON Jonathan said, "You guys need to get a drummer and another guitar player so you can record and hit the road." So I got hold of Gary Thorstensen, who used to play guitar in a band with Jonathan called the Treeclimbers. Tad knew Steve Wied, because H-Hour had played some shows with Steve's former band, Death and Taxes. Both these guys came down to practice, and it clicked, so we said, "We're going into the studio in two weeks. And then we got a whole bunch of shows coming up, so we gotta get ready for those, too." And they just looked at us like, What? Because in those days, usually it took forever to get your first gig and then forever to get the record out, and even then nothing ever happened. But here everything was set up and ready to go, and boom boom boom, it went.

GARRETT SHAVLIK (drummer for Denver's the Fluid; Lilly Milic's husband) We were from Denver, and our first shows in Seattle were probably fall of '88. We get into town and we visit the Sub Pop office, and Bruce and Jonathan and Daniel House and Charles Peterson were the only guys who were hanging out. We get an offer immediately. They felt like kindred spirits.

So we play the Vogue—I think we played with TAD that night—and we didn't know what to expect. "We're here, we got a label, but do you think anybody will be at the show?" We walk in, and the guy that owns the Vogue, his name is Monny. He was a badass. Monny dressed like a dominatrix, but sexier—not so hardcore-leather-prostitute—and he's burlier than shit, like he could snap your fuckin' neck. So we're loading in, and he's wearing this outfit and says in this gruff voice, "Yeah, boys, just put the stuff in the back." We're thinkin', This is one of the coolest fuckin' transsexuals we've ever met, and then his girlfriend shows up and she's dressed to the nines, too, with the platforms and dominatrix look. They're just totally cool-lookin' together.

BENJAMIN REW (musician; TAD roadie) Monny, the cross-dressing bartender that ran and owned the place, and his wife were always super-sweet to me. I remember when I first got in the Vogue, it was like, Man, you have arrived. All the people I knew had kinda moved up a level from hanging out on Broadway to having an actual place that was our own.

All the cool, older people were there: Mudhoney, Soundgarden, Green River, guys from Love Battery, Gruntruck, the metal bands like Forced Entry and Sanctuary. Andy Wood was always at the Vogue; he had his seat there. Everyone smoked pot in the back room, behind where the stage was. I met Tad in the back room of the Vogue in probably '89. There were *tons* of hot girls, and they were mostly all strippers. It was heaven.

GARRET SHAVLIK During that trip, we met all of our new friends—the new family. Seattle was so cool in the fact that the bands cared about each other and they hung out, where Denver was very self-defeatist.

When other Denver bands that we loved and respected would find out that we had been on the road and are putting out records with a legitimate label, they got pissed off and thought we were rock stars.

DANNY BLAND (Cat Butt guitarist; Best Kissers in the World/Dwarves bassist; Sub Pop Records booking agent) In Arizona, I was in a punk-rock band called the Nova Boys and in '85 or '86, we did a West Coast tour. We went to Seattle, and I remember it was August first and I could wear my leather jacket. So I decided I was going to move there. It was the complete and total opposite of Phoenix, which is what I was looking for. It took a couple of years, but I eventually moved there with my band, the Best Kissers in the World, in '88. Once we got there, a lot of people followed us up. A lot of friends who would go on to form bands, like Kelly Canary, who became the singer of Dickless, and Kerry Green, who was in Dickless, too. And Supersuckers came up from Tucson.

EDDIE SPAGHETTI (Supersuckers singer/bassist) We didn't want to be cliché and go to L.A., and Danny, who was a friend of ours, was saying, "You guys should come up here. There's like three bars to play at here and there's only one to play at in Tucson, and you can wear your leather jacket well into May." And we were thinking that sounded pretty dynamite because it's so hot that it kills cattle in Tucson.

RON HEATHMAN (Supersuckers guitarist) Everything was stronger up there, too: the booze, the pot, the dope. You get enough of anything in you, and it all seems pretty glorious.

EDDIE SPAGHETTI We thought we were totally awesome and that we were going to be the best band that Seattle had ever seen. How wrong we were. This whole Sub Pop scene was just starting up, and we were super-stoked to see the aggressive music that we liked was popular in Seattle.

KURT DANIELSON Tad had read somewhere about the "brown note," this frequency that supposedly could induce spontaneous voiding of the bowels of anybody standing within close range. So at live shows and in interviews, Tad would refer to this frequency, and claim that one of the goals of the band was to achieve it so that all the audience members would spontaneously shit their pants.

JACK ENDINO TAD were a pretty scary band—I say that as a compliment. TAD went into the studio with me in late '88, and we started recording the *God's Balls* album.

KURT DANIELSON *God's Balls* is a cry from the heart. It's primal, it's primitive. There's a lot of screaming. We wanted to manufacture a kind of demented white-trash vision of America. Tad and I were fascinated with Ed Gein. There was the song "Nipple Belt" that was directly inspired by him.

There was also a song "Behemoth" that was about being attacked and beat up. Tad and I and a few other friends had taken acid, and we were walking down a street in the U District in Seattle, and we got jumped and attacked by a bunch of guys. These guys were Samoan, some of them were black, and they were all wearing these weightlifting belts, walking on the street looking for frat boys to beat up. But what they found was just a bunch of drunk punk-rock-type dudes with long hair. They took Dan Peters and threw him through a glass door.

DAN PETERS We were out celebrating my 21st birthday. One of the Samoan guys pulled off his weightlifting belt and hit Tad with it, and I just remember Tad goin' down. We all ran in different directions, and I ran to the door of Kurt's apartment building, which was kind of an enclosed area. And the next thing you know, there's about three of them standing in front of me.

I woke up on the sidewalk with a bunch of paramedics around me asking me my name. Apparently the guys were goin' to town on me, and a couple cops across the street eating at IHOP came over and pulled these guys off me and arrested them all. It didn't sound like they were gonna stop beating me. I had a concussion and a separated shoulder. I got my clock cleaned.

KURT DANIELSON The album title? At a bachelor party that was being given for Jamie from Bundle of Hiss, we had some porn films. I think Tad was there, too. In this one particular film, there was a priest. He was wearing his priestly robes and he was getting a blow job. And he kept screaming, "God's balls, that feels good! *God's balls!*" And that phrase stuck with me.

TAD DOYLE I remember my mom, when I showed her the record . . . She saw the picture and she saw me smiling, and she goes, "Oh, you look so good." And then she saw the title, and she says, "Oh, Tad, how could you? *Why?* Why did you name the record that?" It was disappointing for her. But then she'd go back and, "Well, you're smiling. That looks good. That's nice. Nice boy."

CHAPTER 13
HE WHO RIDES THE PONY

REGAN HAGAR I saw Xana working in this used-clothing store on the same block as the Showbox. She looked like Cher: big nose, kind of Greek features, long dark hair. And Andy loved Cher. So I brought him to the store, and he was crazy about Xana. She was getting off work, so we followed her for a couple blocks to the bus stop. She stopped and said, "Why are you following me?" I remained silent, and Andy went and talked to her and they exchanged numbers. And, I mean, within days they were living together.

XANA LA FUENTE (Andrew Wood's fiancée) I'd never even been with a blond. I wasn't really attracted to Andrew at first. I'm six feet tall—I used to carry him around on my back—but it was his personality. I mean, he had me laughing constantly. He would do Joe Cocker imitations onstage, he wasn't afraid to make a fool out of himself. He had tattoos, he had his ears pierced, he wore a Cowboys baseball hat and his hair up in a bun, and he would wear my skirts around the house.

JACK ENDINO Andrew was the only heavy-metal stand-up comic in Seattle grunge history. Always had me rolling on the floor, laughing the whole time.

MATT LUKIN I remember one time the Melvins were playing with Malfunkshun in Olympia. They were setting up the sound check and Andy didn't have a cord to plug his bass in. I lent him one and said, "You came all the way down here, you got your amp and your guitar, but you didn't have a cord?" He goes, "We used to be musicians dabbling in drugs. Now we're druggies dabbling in music."

XANA LA FUENTE At the time I met him, he had been in rehab, he was clean. I know he had hepatitis, he had gotten yellow. I was 16 when I met him. I had no idea about addiction. It was not a concern at all. I was so naive.

REGAN HAGAR Chris Cornell opened the door to Andy, and let him in as a roommate when he needed to find a place away from the drugs. Chris was straight at that time, so it was thought of as a good thing.

CHRIS CORNELL He was going to live on the island with his parents, where he grew up. I thought that would be harder for him. Most of the time it was me watching him struggle not to shoot up, not to drink. It wasn't like observing Andy's high; it was more like experiencing him squirming.

XANA LA FUENTE I moved in about a week later. I told Chris, "I'll be Mom." I remember the day I moved out, I told Chris, "You never washed a single dish." And he's like, "Well, you said you wanted to be Mom."

Around the time I moved in, Chris had just got laid off from being a fish cook at Ray's Boathouse, and he was going through a depressed time. He would sit there and drink Jack Daniel's and black coffee and stare out this picture window—you could see all downtown. Then he started writing music on his own, doing his solo stuff, and he would lock himself in this little boiler room off of the kitchen.

LANCE MERCER (photographer) When I was leaving high school, I finally got a photo shoot with Malfunkshun. Unfortunately, Kevin didn't show up. So we used Xana for Kevin, which, looking back, was not a good idea. Kevin was pissed. But at the same time, I just wanted to photograph Andy. I was so used to taking pictures of musicians that pretended not to want to have their photo taken. Bands like Skin Yard, where it was four guys against a brick wall. Andy would come into this character of Landrew, and he was all about getting his photo taken.

Later, I shot just Andy and Xana together. It was more subdued. He was with this woman that he loved, and it was definitely a lot more emotional because he wasn't being Landrew. Andy loved Xana; he was totally infatuated with her. There's a shot I took where she's sitting on a stool behind him, and he's on the floor and her legs kind of tower over him, kind of spider-legged around him. That photo, for me, embodies what their relationship was like. She was definitely the stronger one of the two. I think he looked to her to take care of him.

REGAN HAGAR Andy and Xana always fought, and there was blood. It was just part of how he liked his women. The fighting was always behind closed doors. But I'd see the aftermath. He would be physically beaten. Like black eyes, bloody noses. Now, in my older wisdom, I would say, "There's a problem, and I should be getting involved."

XANA LA FUENTE I used to slap him around because I'm pretty big and he's small. And then one time, he started fighting back, and I was like, Damn, he's pretty strong. And I was like, Never mind. I stopped. It would be more like wrestling—it wasn't serious. I never felt like a victim of domestic violence.

KEVIN WOOD It was very weird having two grown people clawing each other's skin and screaming at each other and fighting violently. Weird. . . . Come to think of it, maybe I didn't see them actually exchanging blows, but I did see scratch marks and evidence of physical fighting.

RODERICK ROMERO (Sky Cries Mary singer) I was working at Raison d'Être, which was the first pretentious restaurant/café in all of Seattle.

Andy Wood was a dishwasher guy, and Jeff Ament was the espresso dude. We all had to be there early in the morning to get that place up and running. It was awesome. We'd fight over what music to play before we had to open up, 'cause then we had to play jazz. Andy would want to play Kiss or Elton John, and Jeff would want to play Aerosmith, and I would want to listen to Bauhaus. Usually, we all settled on one thing we were all fine with, which was Southern Death Cult, before they became the Cult. But Jeff ran the scene. In the end, whatever he wanted to listen to, we listened to. He'd just look over at you and smile, and you're like, "Okay, you're right, let's do that." He has this way, this charisma that is undeniable.

JEFF AMENT Stone and I had known Andy a long time before we were in a band with him. . . . But I kind of saw a lot about his personal life and what was going on with it, and so when Stone first said, "Hey, you know, maybe we should try to start a band around Andy," I was like, "No way." It's like, "I don't want to be in a band where I'm gonna have to babysit anybody."

And then I went and saw Stone play an acoustic show with Andy at this gay bar that was like three blocks down the street, and he was just so frickin' great at the show. I could totally hear a couple of the songs that they played that night kind of over the top of a rock band. And so we gave it a go . . .

GREG GILMORE I had split—went to Southeast Asia with a one-way ticket and a pocketful of traveler's checks—for about five months. The very day I came back to town, I was walking on Broadway and ran into Stone, who I didn't really know well, and he asked me if I wanted to come down and play sometime.

REGAN HAGAR Green River and Malfunkshun shared practice spaces for a few years. Andy and I started playing with Jeff and Stone a lot for fun, doing covers. We did a few shows together as Lords of the Wasteland, which was essentially Mother Love Bone. When Green River came back from tour, they called Andy and me and said, "Green River's breaking up. We're parting with Mark and Alex, and we need a new singer and drummer. You guys wanna make a go at it?" And so we're like, "Sweet, let's do it." But we didn't break Malfunkshun up; it just was never even a thought to me.

We still had the same practice space, so Malfunkshun—Andy and Kevin and I—were going there on what was supposedly a day off for Mother Love Bone or Lords of the Wasteland or whatever the band was called then. The three of us walk in and there's Stone and Jeff, and they're playing with Greg Gilmore, who I knew from 10 Minute Warning and always kind of worshipped.

It was like, Whoa. Everyone looked at everyone else. We didn't say anything, and we turned around and left.

KEVIN WOOD I remember that quite vividly. Me and Regan were heading over to meet Andy to do a Malfunkshun rehearsal. Andy was up on the bandstand, playing with all those guys—the Green River guys, plus Greg. Absolutely nothing was said. Regan appeared visibly shaken. At that point, I knew Regan was on the outs, too. I was already on the outs with them. I'd kept saying, "Hey, why don't you pull me into this mix? I could play some guitar with you guys."

We waited for them to stop, then it was our turn to play. So we got up and did our set, but I don't really remember much more about it.

GREG GILMORE I had no idea what was going on because I did not know that they had been playing with Regan. Yes, it was awkward.

BRUCE FAIRWEATHER It was around Christmas, and I was gone. When I came back, Jeff and Stone were like, "Hey, we practiced with Greg Gilmore." I was like, "Really. Did you talk to Regan?" They were like, "Well, he walked in when we were practicing." I guess it didn't go down real well.

REGAN HAGAR I went home and within an hour or two the phone rang, and it was Stone. He was apologizing: "This isn't how I wanted this to happen, but we're gonna start playing with Greg now." At that point, Stone and I were always together. Andy and I used to be that way, but by then Andy had a live-in girlfriend and I didn't see him as much. Stone was very good with me on the phone. He's a Spock-type personality. He helped you remove emotion from your decisions and really think logically about what's going on. He let me know that I was loved, and this was probably the best thing for this group of guys.

KEVIN WOOD When what turned into Mother Love Bone became real, people were coming up to me, "Hey man, sorry to hear about your band breaking up." And that was news to me.

REGAN HAGAR I didn't believe that Malfunkshun was ending, so it wasn't a huge thing. I honestly thought, and I still carry with me, this feeling that we were the greatest band ever. We were the loudest, best band Seattle had to offer.

At the last Malfunkshun show, which we didn't necessarily know to be our last, Kurt Cobain approached Kevin and asked him to join Nirvana, which Kevin laughed off: "Who are these kids?"

KEVIN WOOD Kurt was at Malfunkshun's last show, in Tacoma. Chad Channing was a buddy of mine, and Chad asked if I wanted to jam with Nirvana. It wasn't an invitation to join the band, just to jam, because Kurt was looking for other guitar players to join and make it easier for him. I said I wasn't really interested because I was planning some different things, a different direction. Nirvana at the time was playing an old-school punk kind of thing that I felt like I had grown out of already.

• • •

KELLY CURTIS (Mother Love Bone/Pearl Jam manager; Heart tour manager; Ken Deans's business partner) I saw the Beatles in Seattle on my 10th birthday. I met Nancy Wilson shortly after that. I wanted to get guitar lessons after seeing the Beatles; our parents went to the same church, and they hooked me up with her to get lessons. She was like 12. I'd never met a girl that could sing and play guitar and was cool. We became fast friends.

When I was 17, Nancy asked me to go with her as a roadie for Heart. So I dropped out of high school and went with her. I started off driving a truck for them and hauling gear around. I was with them for eight or nine years, and I worked my way up to being their tour manager. I quit

Heart in '84, then tour-managed a Japanese heavy-metal band called
Loudness and lived in L.A. for a bit before coming back to Seattle
in 1987.

KEN DEANS (production manager; Kelly Curtis's business partner) Kelly and I
started a production company with the explicit purpose of not managing bands. After Kelly left Heart, we managed a New Wave band called
Maurice and the Clichés and spent stupid amounts of money trying to
get them signed, to no avail.

We set up an office in Pioneer Square, and we would eat lunch oftentimes across the street at the Grand Central Bakery, where Stone
Gossard worked. One day, Stone handed me a tape. It was a very poorly
recorded tape, but I took it back and I listened to it and went, "Wow,
there's some really great songs." So I played it for Kelly, and he goes,
"You know what, I don't hear it. It sounds like crap. We're not into
management."

ANNA STATMAN (Geffen Records/Slash Records A&R representative) I thought
Green River was just fantastic. I met them at a show in L.A. when I was
at Slash. When I got to Geffen, Jeff called me up and said, "I've got this
new band!" And I said, "Okay, let's do a demo." I liked it and thought
we should sign them. And they were still technically under a demo deal
with me when Kelly Curtis—whom I introduced to the band via my
secretary Rose, who used to be in a band that Kelly managed—shopped
the deal behind our backs.

KEN DEANS Why did we change our minds about management? Geffen
had started talking about a real record deal. So now it's starting to look
like maybe we could do this. Maybe there's enough money to do this.
And then the rest of the interest started happening. We decided Kelly
would handle the management side of the company, and I would handle the production side of the company.

NANCY WILSON (Heart/the Lovemongers singer/guitarist; Ann Wilson's sister;
Cameron Crowe's ex-wife) One of our very oldest, dearest friends, Kelly
Curtis, was working with Mother Love Bone. We were like, "Hey, this
is authentic stuff," outside of the MTV kind of disposable, flaked-
and-formed thing that we were wrapped up in at the time. The record

labels were pressuring us to do other people's songs as our singles or they wouldn't promote the album. The image had to be bigger, bigger, bigger. More hairspray.

JEFF GILBERT Ann and Nancy Wilson were nothing but huge supporters of the local music scene. Kelly brought Ann down to the Central to see Andy play. Andy got a can of beer, took a big swig out of it, and just shook it up and threw it on Ann. Doused her in beer. She got this horrifically shocked look on her face, and looked up as if to say, "What the hell?" And Andy just smiled at her and winked. She got the biggest grin on her face.

REGAN HAGAR Andy did a show at the Ditto. I think he did it without Malfunkshun, where he was just master of ceremonies. He poured himself some Cocoa Puffs, added the milk, had a couple bites, and then he turned the bowl and just threw it on the audience. In celebration of the cereal. People applauded and cheered. Andy could throw anything on anybody—and they would be happy to have it on them.

NILS BERNSTEIN In Malfunkshun, Andy was very clearly being a character. And with Mother Love Bone it was like, Oh, wait a minute, this is a commercial rock band with aspirations. They're doing the Landrew rock-star shtick, but it didn't have the cool, underground feeling of Malfunkshun. It was like instead of playing a rock star, he was *being* a rock star.

ANNA STATMAN I really don't know why it took Geffen so long to try to sign Mother Love Bone. By then, it was already out of my hands because I had turned the project over to Tom Zutaut, who was A&R.

BRUCE FAIRWEATHER Tom Zutaut was the guy who signed Guns N' Roses. We met him in the lobby at the Four Seasons in Seattle. When I went to take a leak, he followed me into the bathroom. He was trying to find the ins and outs of the band, but in a creepy kind of way. Like, "So, Andy's into drugs, huh?" Or "Jeff's into drugs, huh?" He was just throwing it out to see if it would stick. He was trying to go to everybody to find out dirt about everybody else, and we were like, "That was a bad meeting. Man, screw that guy."

KEN DEANS We actually backed off of Geffen because there was so much interest from the other labels starting to happen. So we end up at a point where we're going to have a showcase at the Central Tavern, which was down the street from our offices at the time. There's five or six labels that are coming to see Mother Love Bone. I remember standing in front of the door to our office, and all these record executives are coming out of the Central and coming up to Kelly and making offers on the street: "Okay, we'll do a two-record guarantee, $500,000 advance," and back and forth. And it's really getting kind of crazy. We were actually laughing.

And after two or three hours of this kind of circus event going on, we went back up to the office with Michael Goldstone from PolyGram. It was really more about the quality of the deal, rather than the financials. Who was going to champion the band? Who was going to really stick by the band? And really, Michael just laid it out. So it was pretty much decided that night that we were going to go with PolyGram. I'm pretty sure it was Kelly, myself, Stone, Jeff, Greg, maybe Bruce there. I pretty much know Andy *wasn't* hanging out.

BRUCE FAIRWEATHER The day we had the final meeting with Michael Goldstone where we said we were going to sign with them, Andy didn't show up. The meeting was down at the Market, and we ran into Xana there, and she had a black eye. And we're like, "Oh, God, what's Andy going to look like?" I think Kelly took Xana aside, and I don't know if Michael ever saw what was going on.

DAN PETERS Me and Andy were messengers together at this company called ABC Messengers. Xana didn't want him being around any bad influences, and I think she looked at me as one, since I was a musician. I lived in an apartment close to work, so me and Andy would bug off during lunchtime and smoke pot. Xana would come by and meet him after work so he'd go directly home. She was just really protective, for obviously good reasons. I didn't know Andy all that well, but I could tell he was a man with not a whole lot of self-control.

XANA LA FUENTE When he was a messenger, Andy would try to write on his breaks but he knew he had another calling and he felt like it was really taking away from that. So I told him, "I can pay for everything. Your job is just going to be to stay home and write music."

He wasn't allowed to write about drugs. I used to go through Andrew's notebooks with a red pen and cross stuff out: "No. . . . No. . . . No. . . ." He let me do it.

KEVIN WOOD When Mother Love Bone was taking off, I had some resentment, sure. No, I never talked to Andy about it. He lived in Seattle and was doing his own thing. I was doing my own thing on Bainbridge. So I never saw the guy. And there was no reason to hang out, either, because we weren't in a band anymore. And when I did see him at a family gathering, it was always the Andy Show, and he would be his normal jocular self. There was no room to get serious and say, "What the fuck?"

XANA LA FUENTE We went to Andy's dad's every weekend in Bremerton. It was his dad, his stepmom, his little brother, who was maybe six years old. All they wanted to hear about was the record deal. I had a bruise on my neck from a fight about drugs, and I was like, "See this? He's not gonna have a deal if he's dead." We were close—I was closer to him than my own dad—but he just would ignore it. I guess they were in denial.

GREG GILMORE We would be in the studio and Xana would come around and she's got Andy off in the corner and they're bickering. "Oh, fuck, what is she doing here?" There always seemed to be a lot of drama when Xana would be around. Probably because of that it was tough to hear the part of her message that was real, that Andy has a problem. It was just, *Ugh*, be gone.

BRUCE FAIRWEATHER The only time we toured, we were opening for the Dogs D'Amour. We were in Toronto, and the guys from the Cult, Ian Astbury and Billy Duffy, were there in the crowd. During the show, Andy went running around in the crowd and came back onstage totally smiling. And he just went to all of us, holding the microphone down, saying, "The Cult's here! The Cult's here!" Afterwards, we met those guys, and Andy's running around behind them, jumping up and down, smiling. He was super-excited about stuff like that.

MICHAEL GOLDSTONE (PolyGram Records/Epic Records A&R executive) When Andy got to a city, he would pick up a newspaper before he got onstage and try to find the most outlandish thing that he could come up with just to catch the crowd off guard. In Boston, he came onstage one night, and at the time, Michael Dukakis was running for president. Andy did the classic, "How ya doin', Boston?" Followed with, "I was just out drinking shots with Kitty!" And people didn't even know how to respond, since Kitty Dukakis obviously had an alcohol problem.

DAVE REES I was at a Mother Love Bone show at the Central Tavern before they recorded *Apple,* and Andy had a little ladder that he used to get his piano that was stashed up in the rafters. He sat down at the piano and started singing "Crown of Thorns." And I actually called him after the gig and asked him about some of the lyrics, like "He who rides the pony must someday fall." He said the lyrics were plain as day if you listened to the song. I tried going deeper, but he wasn't really willing to go there with me. He had told me that he'd gone to rehab and how hard it was to stop. But he said he was doin' good.

KEVIN WOOD I did rat Andy out once, just because I was concerned. Actually, my mother was giving me a hard time about drinking, and she always worshipped Andy as this perfect golden boy. So I blurted it out: "Why don't you quit ragging on me about my drinking? Andy is shooting fuckin' heroin!" And then I realized, Oh, shit. But it felt good, because somebody had to know.

XANA LA FUENTE Andrew and Kevin took acid one night, and Andrew cried in the bathroom on the floor in a fetal position for about eight hours. His eyes were swollen like he had been beaten. And that's the night that Kevin quit drinking. It was one of their birthdays. Kevin didn't freak out, but Andrew was like, "I'm gonna die, I'm gonna die. I saw my future. I know I'm gonna die."

Every time he used he would come and tell me. He would cry. I never saw tracks on his arm, I never saw him dope sick. He never took money from me to use.

BRUCE FAIRWEATHER I didn't realize how involved he was in it until he went into treatment. He was definitely doing some bonehead things.

He was sleeping in parks when he and his girlfriend were fighting. But when we were recording *Apple* down in San Francisco—that was when that huge earthquake hit—he was super-present. In the downtime between recording and getting ready to do the tour, I think he may have got more heavily into doing drugs.

XANA LA FUENTE The rehab place was an hour or two away. I used to drive out there every night and sneak him food. I'd be outside the window handing him pizza through the window, bringing him salads with feta cheese and sun-dried tomatoes.

BRUCE FAIRWEATHER When he was going through treatment, the band went and visited him, and that's when I started realizing that this is serious. We had meetings with him and his counselor. Andy would go, "I can't be around you guys if you're drinking or smoking or doing anything." We were planning on going on a tour, and we were like, "...Okay." It was hard. Not what you want to hear when you're 26 or 27.

REGAN HAGAR He was really trying to be good, and I was a dumbshit about it. He'd come out of rehab, and I'd ask him if he wanted to smoke pot. Talk about insensitive and stupid. I feel like an asshole because I didn't get it.

XANA LA FUENTE After a while, he said the pink cloud that he felt when he got out was gone. He was what you call "dry drunk," when you're still acting out these behaviors even though you're not drinking. He refused to go to meetings. He was kind of being a little asshole. He was just different about it—he wasn't all kind and apologetic anymore. He was like, *"This is what I am."* Just being kind of mean about it. I was crying a lot.

CHAPTER 14
BANDS THAT WILL MAKE MONEY

KIM THAYIL Mark Arm, myself, and Buzz Osborne were hanging out at Mark Arm's apartment in the U District, listening to records and BS'ing about bands, around late '86. Buzz mentioned that on a number of Black Sabbath songs, Tony Iommi used a tuning called drop D, where the low-E string was tuned down a whole step. It makes things a little bit lower, a little bit heavier. After that, I went ahead and wrote a number of songs in drop D tuning—the first song I wrote with it was "Nothing to Say"—and then we experimented with other drop tunings. People started comparing us to Zeppelin or Black Sabbath, but we weren't listening to those bands then—we were listening to Bauhaus and Killing Joke.

DAN PETERS I always thought it was ballsy and funny that Soundgarden put out that song "Incessant Mace" that *was* Led Zeppelin. It sounds just like "Dazed and Confused"!

FAITH HENSCHEL-VENTRELLO (KCMU music director) I was the music director at KCMU, so I talked to people from all around the country and in Europe, and I keep trying to tell them that there was amazing stuff going on in Seattle, and people would be like, "Yeah, yeah, yeah," 'cause nobody visited. So I did the *Bands That Will Make Money* tape, which had a piggy bank on the cover, to send to A&R people. I didn't know if they would make money or not; I was just trying to get the A&R guys' attention. It was like Soundgarden, H-Hour, Chemistry Set, Skin Yard—because Jack Endino is the one who helped me put it together.

I sent Brian Huttenhower, who was Aaron Jacoves's assistant at A&M, the tape. They listened to it, and they wanted to come up and see H-Hour. H-Hour was about to implode, and so I said, "Oh, you've really gotta check out Soundgarden. They're playing at the Vogue" on this day. So Brian came up and saw them, and he ended up going back to L.A., saying, "You gotta check this band out."

AARON JACOVES (A&M Records West Coast director of A&R) The band I showed interest in was Soundgarden. What struck me was the energy. The rawness. And Chris Cornell's voice. I got hold of Chris and said, "Here's 600 bucks, do more songs." Later, Chris called me and told me about this label up in Seattle that I didn't know about. He said, "They're friends of ours. We wanna put out a record through them. Do you mind if we use these recordings?" And it was my thought at the time, Hey, anything we could do to build an underground swell would make it easier for me to get them signed. And that was the Sub Pop record.

As far as what was used on the Sub Pop records, I can't fully say for sure. I know Chris recalls it differently. I know others are gonna argue, but the truth is, we were the first onto the Seattle scene.

KIM THAYIL Sub Pop did not have the money to make another record for us. They wanted us to stay with them, and we would've loved to stay with them, but we were ready to make another record. The Sub Pop single came out in '87, and at that point there was some interest expressed by Bob Pfeifer at Epic. SST had the money and wanted to put us in the studio, so we recorded *Ultramega OK* for them. It was a one-record deal. And at that time, we were also getting interest from Geffen, Slash, Capitol, and A&M.

AARON JACOVES Brian and I flew up to see Soundgarden. There was a show in Vancouver, at a club called Graceland. The show was like this

acid trip. The club was dark, there was a lot of smoke. Chris was un-
dressing onstage. Girls were lapping it up.

When Susan was driving us back to the airport, she asked me about
managers and I remember kinda biting my tongue and saying, "I would
never recommend this to anybody, to have a girlfriend manage a group,
but I think you're doin' a great job. You should do it." And I think that
was fully her intention anyhow.

SUSAN SILVER I'd had some managerial experience with this band called
the First Thought and with the U-Men, so it just sort of segued into
managing Soundgarden. I wasn't necessarily interested in being the real
enactment of Spiñal Tap, but it just happened.

CHRIS CORNELL It put the other three guys in the position where maybe
when you want to call your manager and say, "Fuck you," they don't feel
like they could do that. And there was often what felt to me like an as-
sumption that I should know everything that's going on in the business
side of it 'cause I'm married to the manager. Most of the time I didn't
'cause I didn't have that kind of communication with her. It created a
situation that was more difficult than what other bands might have had,
but I always felt proud of the four of us individually and how we dealt
with that.

AARON JACOVES Later on, Susan came over to my parents' house and
said the band had reached a decision: "We wanna sign with A&M."
And the next thing I know, I hear that Bob Pfeifer from Epic was meeting with them, and it kinda ticked me off. There was a moment where
I almost said, "Fuck it all."

BOB PFEIFER (Epic Records senior vice president A&R; Hollywood Records president) A bidding war ensued. It was very emotional and intense. At one
point I felt like throwing my stereo out of the window! I was nuts about
that band. I thought I saw God. That was very early in my career. I
didn't have a lot of hits, so I didn't have a lot of power.

KIM THAYIL Geffen already had a stable of what they considered
hard-rock bands, many of which they weren't working or promoting. We had no interest in being lost in that. Epic had a few hard-

rock acts. We liked Bob Pfeifer, but they were also a very large label. A&M wasn't quite as big and didn't really have any bands at all that were comparable to us, so we figured we could get their undivided attention.

MATT CAMERON We met Herb Alpert—he was the *A* in A&M—and he was painting oils in his office and drinking wine and there was a hint of pot smell around. It was kind of a cool boho vibe, and we decided to try to plug in with that.

AARON JACOVES Between the Sub Pop record and the A&M record, there was the SST record, *Ultramega OK*. We had them signed by that time to A&M, and we licensed them to SST for that record. It was all part of the process. A fanbase is helpful, and I was tryin' to build it. We don't wanna fuck this up.

STUART HALLERMAN Every summer, Slim Moon—who later had the Kill Rock Stars label going on—worked with the Olympia parks department and police department to put on a punk-rock show on an August afternoon in Capitol Park. The state capitol is above, the water's right behind you, and they'd play on a flatbed truck. He'd hire me because I had my own P.A. system. My Name, Nirvana, and Soundgarden were the three bands in '88. Soundgarden had just done the *Fopp* EP, so they played all the stuff that was on that.

BEN SHEPHERD Soundgarden played a show in downtown Olympia, a signing party. I remember it was outside. I met Chris for the first time that day, right before they played. Kim introduced me to him. That was the first time I got to see Matt with them. It was like, Oh, now they have a real drummer, and it's over the top. It was all golden, the sun was going down behind Matt's blond hair, and all the hardcore kids, like our generation of musicians and fans of music, were there. And the cops were there, and they were allowing it to happen. Olympia cops used to be total fucking pricks. They were definitely scared of punk rockers. They tried to arrest March of Crimes a couple of times for playing there, just for being around: "What are you guys doing? Punker!" At this show, it was like, Wow, even the adults are all right with this. But they're scared of us still.

STUART HALLERMAN I stepped back from the mixing board to see what it sounded like there. And on the sides of me are these parks department and police sponsors, these uniformed cops. I said to 'em, "How do you like the show?" And one of the cops goes, "You know, I just thought this was gonna be awful music, but this band in particular"—and he'd liked Nirvana—"but this band in particular I thought it was all gonna be dirty lyrics, but it's really clean, and they're talented guys!" And we look back at the stage with smiles on our faces, and at the end of "Fopp," Chris—instead of singing "Fopp and rock!"—is going, "SUCK MY COCK! SUCK MY COCK!" So much for being clean.

After that show, Chris is like, "You know, we're going on our second tour in about a month. You wanna be our soundman on the road with us?" I'm thinking, Drive all over the country with these beer-soaked punk rockers? "Yeah, sure, I'll go!"

We get in a van, and in the first hour on the road I realize, These guys get along so great. They're friends, they're having fun! They're not arguing, they're not talking behind each other's backs trying to get a new bass player or something like that. That's part of their success. It made being on tour with them really fun. It was the second tour for their tour manager, this guy Eric Johnson. Gunny Junk. He had this whole L.A. rock-and-roll persona, Gunny Junk—junk being a heroin reference—with the cape and the screaming that went along with it.

ERIC JOHNSON I met the Soundgarden guys when I booked them for a show in Ellensburg, in '86 or '87. I remember I took this class on George Orwell in college, and his world is all about the proletarian, the worker guy, and he just describes dirt and grime and these heavy working situations. Then these guys showed up and they're kind of these strange Orwellian creatures. Matt had a red Volkswagen van and they were all working on the clutch or something, so all of them were under this car working. They all had work pants on and boots rolled up, and Chris looked like he just got done workin' in a steel yard. I thought they looked so cool.

The first tour I ever did with them was on the West Coast. Gunny Junk came about on a trip to L.A. It was when Guns N' Roses was huge and we all made up our own little names as we were going to do a show at the Club Lingerie, I think it was. We were all laughing and making up names and the next thing I knew, I was answering to Gunny Junk.

STUART HALLERMAN Kim would say, "We're all about sex and drugs and rock and roll! Except minus the sex and drugs." They were saints on the road. They each had their girlfriends at home, so there was no road head or bitches or anything like that.

And they weren't big partiers. Especially in those early years. I brought a little bag of weed on the road with me once, and nobody would smoke it. It should've been gone three days out, but I still had this little bud weeks later. And then I got busted for it in Louisiana. Got searched for hours on the side of the road, but didn't get arrested. That's why the Louisiana DEA appears in the credits of *Louder Than Love*.

ART CHANTRY When Soundgarden were doing their first major-label record, we were all in my design studio. Susan and Chris were kind of mumbling among themselves 'cause they were like a unit that worked independently of the rest of the band. Whenever Chris spoke, he'd mumble into Susan's ear, and then Susan would turn and talk to the band, and if the band ever wanted to talk to Chris, they'd talk to Susan and Susan would mumble in Chris's ear.

I said, "What's the title of the record?" They said, "Well, we don't even have one yet." And I said, "Why don't you call it *Louder Than Shit*?" I always wanted to see a band call its album that. Someone, maybe Kim, goes, "No, no, we'll call it *Louder Than Fuck*!" The band thought that was great. And then Susan stepped up and said something to the effect of, "No band I'm involved with is gonna have *fuck* in the title of their record." And so when the record came out it was *Louder Than Love*. It was such a huge-sounding band that when I saw that, I kinda groaned.

*   *   *

MARK PICKEREL When I was in the Screaming Trees, it was really just Van and I that were experimenting with anything at all, and I kept it strictly to booze and pot. Lanegan was totally clean during that period, because after an accident with some farm equipment in '86 or '87—he almost lost his leg—the doctor was like, "With this injury, if you keep drinking, you're not gonna make it." So he had to go cold turkey when he was only about 22.

MARK LANEGAN [The tractor] was coming right for my balls. The thing about the wheels is they're so big, by the time one foot would get loose and I would roll over trying to get away, the other one would already be caught under the tire. Man, to this day it seems like it took a million years to get all the way over me, but it really must have just took a couple of seconds. It crushed my legs, fucked them up pretty good.

MARK PICKEREL Van liked to tease and terrorize Lee, even though Lee was his older brother. Van would make up all these little songs that ended with Lee being sexually molested by a trucker or something like that. Lanegan would join in on the chorus and come up with his own lyrics to support this story, and next thing you know the whole band would be singing along and making up a verse. That would be the kind of thing that would continue on for an entire hour.

VAN CONNER Around the time my son Ulysses was going to be born, we'd been touring a lot. To be honest, it was hard stinking work, and I thought maybe I could get out of it. Plus I didn't want to be gone from home with a baby. I knew we had more touring coming up, so I quit.

GARY LEE CONNER One of the people called us up at the time was Krist Novoselic. He was like, "Oh, I hear you need a bass player." And this was when Nirvana was first starting out. To them, we were like "big band with records on SST." Actually, if we hadn't got Donna Dresch, we would've gotten him. I joked with Krist years later about that: "It's probably a good thing you didn't join the Screaming Trees."

DONNA DRESCH They called me, and I was like, "Yeah!" We went to L.A. and recorded a double album, and then we went on a tour of the States for two months. We started listening to Mudhoney's *Superfuzz Bigmuff* on tour, and they were like, "We want our record to sound like this." So when we came back, they said, "We don't want to put out this double album."

On tour, we'd get a hotel with two beds in it, and me and Mark Pickerel would always share the bed. It was never romantic, but we were always super-cuddly, which I think is hilarious now, because I'm a gold-star lesbian—never had a boyfriend or anything. I found out a couple of years ago that Lanegan has this druggy, crazy-guy reputation, but I don't know that about him. I knew him as being really funny and caring and thoughtful.

Lee would just go bananas onstage. At one show, he was rolling around in glass—I don't know if he broke the bottle on purpose or if it was an accident or if someone threw it onstage—and when he stands up he's all covered in blood. He rubs the blood on his face, sticks his tongue out, and goes *"Aaayeahhhhhh!"* and then continues on with his perfect guitar solo.

VAN CONNER The guys said Lee acted even weirder without me there. I wasn't there to control him, I guess. We hadn't been apart for more than like two days our whole lives, probably. I don't know if you ever saw that movie *Strange Brew,* but there's that part where the brothers are separated for 10 minutes for the first time ever? Maybe he had a Bob and Doug McKenzie–type withdrawal. I spent more time with him until I was 30 years old than probably any human being has spent with another. That's probably why we couldn't stand each other by the end of the band.

When they came back, they said, "We were wondering if you wanted to be back in the band again?" At the time, I was getting a divorce from my wife—we were super-young and didn't know what the hell we were doing—so I was like, "Okay!"

MARK LANEGAN We didn't have a damn thing in common except insanity. So we fought a lot. . . . And when [Van] came back, the very first show back, I was walking off while the show was still going, like I usually did, and I heard a commotion that sounded not like your usual applause. I came back out and there he was beating the shit out of Lee Conner, onstage. *(Sighs.)* It was like prison. Without the sex.

VAN CONNER When we on tour for our album *Buzz Factory,* SST told us it was going to come out every day of the tour, and it didn't come out until the last day. Finally, we all talked and we're like, "Fuck this, we're gonna get a fuckin' manager to deal with the fuckin' record label." So we called Susan Silver and we said, "Hey, you want to do it?" She was like, "Yeah, sure."

We did a record on Sub Pop and then went on another European tour. When we got back, Soundgarden had just signed to A&M, so

Susan was like, "Do you want to be on a bigger label?" We'd never even thought about it before Soundgarden got signed.

MARK PICKEREL Susan took on a fairly motherly role in our lives. When we were working on *Buzz Factory*, it was so sweet, she came down to the studio with a bunch of groceries for us. If it hadn't been for Susan, I don't know that we would've ever been signed. A lot of labels turned us down before Epic signed us.

VAN CONNER At Epic, we met this guy Bob Pfeifer, who had been in this band from Cleveland called Human Switchboard, so he was a musician who was working the system from the inside. He had a fuckin' credit card and he was charging it up, buying us all drinks. So we kind of related to him, and he didn't give us any bullshit.

MARK PICKEREL There were labels that thought we were just too physically unattractive to sign. A friend who worked at A&M told me that was one of the reasons A&M passed on us. Back then, the music that was driving record sales was Warrant and Poison and White Lion and Guns N' Roses, bands with a lot of sex appeal.

BOB PFEIFER I recall getting an argument from a superior saying, "Look at the two fat guys in the group. How could that be successful?" So I actually turned that around into an argument: why they're unique. It was that ludicrous at points.

I probably spent more time with Mark than any member of the band. We would go on a lot of walks and talk. About his songs, about life, a lot of stuff. He'd send me his lyrics, we'd go through them, talk about them. Having said that, I would always let the Trees pretty much do what they wanted. They're brilliant. You just let brilliance go, you know what I mean? There's certain artists that you work with where you push them in certain ways. There's others—I remember when Ornette Coleman called me up and played a line over the phone to me, and I go, "Why are you doing this? You're a genius. I have nothing I could possibly contribute other than to say it's great." The Trees were kind of in that league.

CHAPTER 15
THE MUSIC BANK

JOHNNY BACOLAS (Alice N' Chains/Second Coming bassist) I grew up in Shoreline, Washington—Richmond Beach was what it was called then. It's a North Seattle suburb. I got my first guitar at 12, and James Bergstrom and I started a group around 1982. We practiced at his mom's house, and then at my mom's house. Back and forth during those early years. We ended up getting some guys together, and by 13, 14, we had a group called Sleze. We were into heavy rock: Slayer, Venom, Mercyful Fate. We were also into some of the glam rock. When Mötley Crüe came out with *Shout at the Devil,* we thought that was the coolest record and started wearing more makeup.

There was a guy Ken Elmer, who went with us to Shoreline High School. Ken told us that he had a stepbrother who went to Meadowvale High School. He said, "You know, my stepbrother is a drummer, but he really wants to be a singer. He's got peroxide-blond hair." We thought that was really cool, right out of the gate. So we called him up, and his mom drove him out to James's house—I still remember that day, vividly. We met him for the first time, started playing Armored Saint songs and Slayer songs and Mötley Crüe songs. He was into the exact same stuff we were into. It was literally a match made in heaven. Layne was the new singer.

Ultimately, when we switched the band name to Alice N' Chains, it was me, Nick Pollock, James Bergstrom, and Layne Staley. The name? What I recall was we were at a party in North Seattle, probably about 16 years old. I was outside having a cigarette with a guy named Russ Klatt, who was a vocalist. Sleze had made these backstage passes months prior. Again, we're kids—there was no real backstage. We just thought it was cool to have our own backstage passes. We'd go to Kinko's and get 'em laminated, so they looked really legit. One of the passes said WEL-COME TO WONDERLAND. Somehow we started talking about that being an Alice in Wonderland–type thing. Russ started saying, "What about Alice in Chains? Put her in bondage and stuff like that." I remember thinking, Wow, that has a cool ring to it.

We'd outgrown the name Sleze, and we didn't like it anymore. I brought up that name, Alice in Chains, and everyone liked it. But we changed the name to Alice N' Chains, because three members of the group had really Christian mothers. Alice N' Chains made it not sound like a bondage name—we would lose our jamming room, we'd lose all of our rights if we did that.

NICK POLLOCK (Alice N' Chains guitarist; My Sister's Machine singer/guitarist) Layne was totally cocky and ended up being my best friend really quick, and he and I were inseparable. We worked together at a place that made radiation-containment devices. It was a crap job that longhairs could get at the time, out in Kirkland. He and I partied all the time. We would go to parties, we would make parties happen at people's houses.

One night, me and Layne and a few other friends were in West Seattle, and we'd imbibed quite a bit that evening. We ended up going down California Avenue, and *A Clockwork Orange* comes to mind—we were kicking over garbage cans and someone broke a window or the antenna off of a car. The cops got involved. The rest of us got away, but they were chasing Layne. Like I said, Layne was cocky, and he was a smart-ass to the wrong cop, who actually sicced his dogs on him. They chewed up Layne's legs a little bit. When the rest of us were driving away, by 7-Eleven, there he was, handcuffed in the back of the car, nodding to us. We picked him up from jail the next day.

MATT VAUGHAN (Gruntruck manager; East Street Records stores owner) My mom was the manager of Queensrÿche their first three records, so that would have been from like '81 to '86 or so, right before *Operation: Mindcrime*. I had a stepdad at the time that was a record collector. They managed Queensrÿche together. My folks would take three months off at a time to go on tour and leave us at the house with a maid or housekeeper. Sometimes that was pretty fun—I lost my virginity to my housekeeper.

My sister and I were super-tight. She was a good-looking girl, and she was friends with Layne Staley. I remember him comin' to our house, and he wanted to talk to my mom because he wanted to be a rock star. He was standing in front of the mirror doing his hair and he had his Capezios on, and he was trying to show how he'd make his stage entrance. And I remember him pointing at my mom and saying, "I *will* be the biggest rock star in town." My mom just kinda laughed. She walked away and said, "Goddamn, he might just have it, but he's an egomaniac."

JEFF GILBERT The metal guys were very business-savvy, whereas the grunge guys—we didn't call them grunge, we'd call them "Sub Pop guys"—they clearly weren't, because Sub Pop didn't have any money back then. The Sub Pop guys would rely on playing a little circuit of downtown dive shithole clubs. Where the metal guys, they knew where their fanbase was, so they were renting out large grange halls, bingo halls, VFW halls, and putting on their own shows. And doing very well.

RICK FRIEL Shadow went from playing high schools to these huge shows that were packed with people you didn't know, and we instantly became really well-known. Some of the attention was because we were so young; my brother Chris was this little kid with a mouthful of braces, playing a giant drum set.

CHRIS FRIEL (Shadow/Goodness drummer) We were like 14, 15 years old, just tearing the place up with total abandon. Shadow was a five-piece group then: my brother and myself, Mike McCready, Danny Newcomb, and Rob Webber.

RICK FRIEL There weren't really a lot of places to play back in '82, but they were doing concerts at Lake Hills Roller Rink. What was genius about it was they had a stage on each end of the rink. The minute one band would be done, all the kids ran down to the other end, so there was no downtime.

We were pretty much the only band there from Seattle; all the other bands were from the Eastside. There was a band called Myth, which eventually became Queensrÿche. There was Wild Dogs from Portland, and Overlord and Culprit, who we became really good friends with. Everyone was super into metal and dressing up in spandex.

CHRIS FRIEL Eventually, we became a three-piece—just Rick and Mike and myself—and we started practicing at this rehearsal space called the Music Bank, where we met Sleze, who became Alice N' Chains.

JEFF GILBERT "Queen of the Rodeo" was one of Alice N' Chains' glam hits, about a gay rodeo guy. It's actually a very good song. It's funny as hell. They looked like Seattle's answer to Poison, to be real honest. Just Aqua Netted hair, eyeliner, rouge on the cheeks. But it was all very tongue-in-cheek. They'd bring a mirror out onstage and primp in between songs. So funny. I remember they did a show at the University of Washington. Sold out. The first 30 rows were nothing but women.

JOHNNY BACOLAS The mirror? I'd totally forgotten about that. There was a movie that Prince came out with, *Purple Rain*. And the guy, Jerome, would hold up a mirror so Morris Day could fix his hair. When we did it, I think it was one of our roadies that would come out on cue and hold up a mirror for us. Between each song, we had little skits. Layne would come out on a tricycle or we'd do "Queen of the Rodeo" and he'd put his cowboy hat on and tuck his jeans into his cowboy boots and play the part of the cowboy. We really planned this stuff, almost like a Las Vegas production.

NICK POLLOCK Layne's mom kicked him out of the house. Let's just say that he and his mother did not see eye to eye. I was trying to get Layne to come live at my house, but my folks wouldn't do it, so he ended up living down at the Music Bank.

TIM BRANOM (Gypsy Rose singer) I had nowhere to go, too, so that's how Layne and I ended up sharing a room at the Music Bank, which was a warehouse with 60 band rooms. He was so quiet, he wouldn't really tell you what was going on in his mind at all. He would sleep on the couch, and I would sleep on the floor in a sleeping bag. Right above the couch, he had a picture of his family, but apparently he wasn't able to make the family photo session so they had superimposed Layne into the photo—they'd taken a picture of Layne, put it on top, and took a picture of that. It was hilarious, because he was too big and he looks like this giant in the photo, like this super-Layne.

MIKE STARR (Alice in Chains bassist) I moved to Seattle, from Florida, when I was in the fourth grade. I got a job at IHOP as a dishwasher when I was 11, 12, and I saved up my money and I bought a bass off of the brother of this drummer named Dave Jensen for 50 bucks. Yeah, I was 12 years old and working at IHOP. When I was 12 or 13, I was going into bars in Atlantic City, because I had a start of a mustache and my dad was the bartender. I spent the summers in Atlantic City with my dad. I swear to God, I looked 18, and you only had to be 18 to drink in Atlantic City.

By the time I was 13, I had that drummer Dave Jensen in my band. It was called Cyprus; I found the name in the Bible. All I wanted to do 24 hours a day was play music. Eventually we needed a new drummer, so we found this guy Sean Kinney, who'd put an ad in the paper. He was cool as hell, and he was a smart-ass. Then me and Sean got kicked out of the band because we were too young. I didn't see Sean again until I was 18.

Six months or a year later, I had rejoined that band, and when I was like 16, we won the Battle of the Bands at the Crossroads Skate Center in Bellevue. We were called Sato then, after an Ozzy song. Because we won, we got to record one of our songs called "Leather Warrior" for this album called *Northwest Metalfest.* "Leather Warrior," man, gayest freakin' song in the world, but it's a song. And then I got kicked out of that band for some reason. I don't know why.

I saw Sean again at the Southcenter mall. He said, "Man, I've been keeping up on you. You're Mike Starr. Remember me? Sean? We were jamming when we were young?" He had just gotten kicked out of his house. I don't know why. He came over to my house, and he started living there with my mom and my sister Melinda. He started going out with my sister and became part of the family.

TIM BRANOM I played in a band called Gypsy Rose. For about six months, Mike Starr played in the band. Jerry Cantrell played in the band for about three weeks. Jerry had a little bit different style; we were kind of going for the metal speed-demon, Yngwie Malmsteen–type players, and he was more song-oriented, so it didn't work out. Mike Starr got kicked out of the band because he and the drummer were fighting over a girl. Then Jerry called up Mike Starr and started a new band.

JERRY CANTRELL (Alice in Chains guitarist/singer; solo artist) I wasn't really close to my dad, so that affected me heavily. I lived with my grandmother and my mother until they died. Right after my grandmother died—and that was a big enough shock—my mom came home one day and told me that she had about six months to live. And that was so heavy. My mother died of pancreatic cancer at 43.

NICK POLLOCK I introduced Layne to Jerry. I'd met Jerry out in Tacoma. Alice N' Chains played a show at the Tacoma Little Theatre. I remember I was out in the back of the place and he came out and said hi and was a really enthusiastic guy. We traded numbers and he started coming up into my neck of the woods and started hangin' out with me. Since Layne and I went out all the time, we'd all go out and go to parties.

DAVE HILLIS (producer/engineer/mixer; Mace guitarist) When I first met him, Jerry was just moody and always ready to start a fight. I got to know Jerry quite well over the years, but at that time he was just a dude I didn't really want to know. He had a hard upbringing, I think. He had a chip on his shoulder, but he was incredibly determined.

JERRY CANTRELL I never had a whole lot of money and stuff. But when my mom passed away, I got a little money that she left to keep me jamming. So I just totally went crazy. I bought a bunch of amps, did a lot of drugs, and was an idiot, but fortunately it turned out okay.

I met Layne again at a house party right after [Gypsy Rose]. . . . I didn't have a place to live, so he invited me up to Ballard, where he lived at this place called the Music Bank, which was *fucking* awesome for a bunch of young kids.

SOUNDGARDEN'S CHRIS CORNELL at the Apocalypse Club, Toronto, November 4, 1989. © DEREK VON ESSEN

THE U-MEN in front of their tour bus, Seattle, 1985. Clockwise from left: Jim Tillman, Tom Price, roadie Mike Tucker, John Bigley, and Charlie Ryan. © MEGAN SULLIVAN

THE MELVINS on the road, circa 1986. From left: Buzz Osborne, Dale Crover, and Matt Lukin. ©MATT LUKIN

(left) GREEN RIVER at SCUD Studio, Seattle, July 1986. From left: Bruce Fairweather, Mark Arm, Jeff Ament, Alex Shumway, and Stone Gossard.

© CAM GARRETT

(below) MALFUNKSHUN at the Serbian Hall, Seattle, 1982. From left: Regan Hagar and Andrew Wood.

BESTROCKPHOTOS.COM

SOUNDGARDEN at Myrtle Edwards Park, Seattle, June 1987. Clockwise from left: Matt Cameron, Kim Thayil, Hiro Yamamoto, and Chris Cornell. © CAM GARRETT

(above) SKIN YARD play Gorilla Gardens, Seattle, July 1985. From left: Jack Endino, Matt Cameron, Ben McMillan, and Daniel House. © CAM GARRETT

(left) SUB POP cofounders Jonathan Poneman (left) and Bruce Pavitt at the label's Seattle office, 1988. © JIM BERRY

(left) THE FLUID play the Garage at 23 Parish, in their hometown of Denver, circa 1990. From left: Ricky Kulwicki, John Robinson, and Matt Bischoff. © 1990 JOEL DALLENBACH

(below) SCREAMING TREES in their hometown of Ellensburg, Washington, May 1988. From left: Mark Lanegan, Mark Pickerel, Van Conner, and Gary Lee Conner. © JAMES BUSH

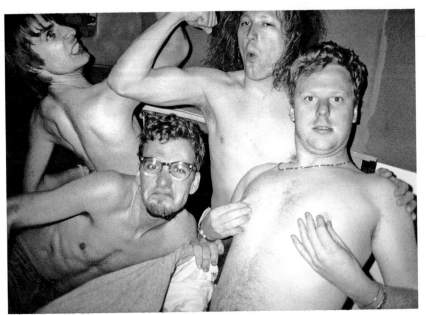

MUDHONEY on a European ferry (after a few drinks), August 1990. Clockwise from left: Steve Turner, Mark Arm, Matt Lukin, and Dan Peters. © BOB WHITTAKER

CAT BUTT in Ballard, Seattle, fall 1988. From left: Erik "Erok" Peterson, David Duet, James Burdyshaw, and Dean Gunderson. © JAMES BUSH

NIRVANA, *Bleach* photo shoot
in Belltown, Seattle, February 25,
1989. From left: Krist Novoselic,
Jason Everman, Kurt Cobain,
and Chad Channing.
© ALICE WHEELER

TAD in New York, summer 1989. Clockwise from lower left: Tad Doyle, Gary Thorstensen, Kurt Danielson, and Steve Wiederhold. © IAN TILTON

JEFF GILBERT The Music Bank—a hideous place. Underneath the Ballard Bridge. You'd constantly hear those damn Alaskan fishing boats coming through there, and you'd hear the winches and the cranks of the drawbridge just grinding all the time. Those guys could make as much noise as they wanted, and it was just a monstrous party pad.

There was just one bathroom in the whole building. You know those public bathrooms in bus stations and seedier parts of downtown? Multiply that by a hundred rock-star wannabes and, yup, pretty disgusting. Most of the time people who slept there just pissed in the corner, because when you're that drunk, and you get up in the dark in the middle of the night to try and find the door to go to the bathroom, trippin' over band gear, you end up givin' up.

JOHNNY BACOLAS The Music Bank was open 24 hours. You could go there and knock on the door at 3 in the morning and the guy that was working the keys would come, look through a peephole, let you in if you had a room there, walk you to your room, unlock it with the key—he had a huge key ring with probably 150 keys on it—and you were good to go. Layne was one of the key guys, and he usually worked the graveyard shift.

Jerry was living in our jam room, so in the middle of the night, Jerry would be in the office with Layne, watching TV with his guitar in his hand saying, "Hey, dude, check out this riff. I got this idea." That's quite a big catalyst to that incredible connection those two had.

NICK POLLOCK Alice N' Chains went our separate ways, but it was very amicable. I could see where things were going with Layne with drugs. All of us did. That did have a certain amount to do with why we parted company as a band. He had never put a needle in his arm or tried heroin at the time, but he was doing other things to excess that could be quite startling. And it wasn't gonna stop, and we all knew it.

James and I went and made a band together called the Society, which was more of a funk band with all different music styles. It didn't last very long, about nine months, and James went his way and I started My Sister's Machine. By that time, the new Alice in Chains was formed. Actually, it was called Diamond Lie.

SEAN KINNEY (Alice in Chains drummer) I first met Layne around 1985 when his band was playing at Alki Beach. . . . When Layne and Jerry hooked up, they were looking to put together a band. Jerry knew Mike Starr from playing with him in Gypsy Rose. Layne said that he knew this drummer, so he gave Jerry my number. He called me up, and I went to the rehearsal studio with my girlfriend to listen to some demos. I thought he was pretty cool, and then he told me that they were playing with Mike Starr. My girlfriend and I laughed, and Jerry asked why we were laughing. My girlfriend told him that she was Mike's sister, and I had been playing music with Mike since we were 12.

MIKE STARR I guess I had met Layne a couple years before, but I don't remember it. I was on acid at the time. I was so high I couldn't even dress myself, so I wore my bathrobe, with underwear on, and my sunglasses and my cowboy boots and rode on my Honda motorcycle to the beach. I heard Layne saying on a New York radio station one time, "When I met Mike Starr, he was on a Honda motorcycle in his bathrobe and his sunglasses. I said to myself right there, 'That's the kind of guy I want to be in a band with.'"

JERRY CANTRELL Layne was playin' with another band, but he came in to jam with us after we'd been playin' together. . . . He was just such a cool fuckin' guy and his voice was just amazing, and we knew we wanted to be in a band with him right off the bat. So it was just a period of time of waitin' him out. And then that didn't seem to work, so we told him, "We're gonna get a new singer," and we started auditioning singers in his rehearsal room, and we just brought in the shittiest guys we could find. *(Laughs.)* We auditioned a redheaded male stripper who was just terrible, and that was it. And [Layne] was like, "Fuck it. I can't let you guys play with these fuckin' clowns. I'll fuckin' join the band."

KEN DEANS I was approached by a guy named Randy Hauser. He was a convicted drug dealer that was on parole, and liked to hang out in the rock scene. He came to me and he goes, "Hey, here's a band that I think is really special." So he took me out to see Diamond Lie, and I agreed. They were definitely a full-on rock band. They were great players, they partied beyond their capacities, had sex with every woman that looked at them, and didn't have a pot to piss in.

I talked to Randy and I said, "Look, we need to take these guys into the studio and make a demo so we can shop it." Nick Terzo was there 10 minutes after me.

NICK TERZO (Columbia Records/Maverick Records A&R executive) I was hired by ASCAP [American Society of Composers, Authors and Publishers] to be a membership rep, and the first trip I did was go up to Seattle. We came across something called the Music Bank, which had 50 or 60 rehearsal rooms, all full. It was kind of odd because I was thinking, Where did this come from? It was surreal to me, to see this much activity, this many rooms, a multitude of different genres. I was coming from L.A., thinking that's the only music scene at the time.

MIKE STARR I was at the Music Bank all night, and it was after 2, and we had no beer left. And these two guys walked in with a case of beer. I was like, "Hey, where are you going with that beer?" And they go, "We're going to see this band"—I don't even remember the name of the band. I go, "They suck. Come into our room, and bring that beer." And within 10 minutes, they were in our room with the beer and we were jamming, and we were playing good that night. One was Nick Terzo, from Columbia Records, and one was Ron Sobel from ASCAP.

NICK TERZO At the Music Bank, I went and saw a band play called Diamond Lie. The room was so small that the musicians had to stay in one room and their lead singer had to sing in the hallway because there just wasn't room. It was a rough, crude situation, but I was pretty impressed with the lead singer. Just his voice. And he had a wicked sense of humor.

MIKE STARR We had a show at Kent Skate King, and we decided we needed a new name because we were getting pretty popular. Layne was like, "Well, I made up the name Alice N' Chains for my old band." I'm the one who came up with the idea to put the *i* in Alice in Chains, so it wasn't like Guns N' Roses.

NICK POLLOCK I remember James and I were at a show they played at Skate King. He was like, "Layne called me today, and he said they're gonna change their name, and he was wondering if I minded that." I think at the time, both James and I were thinkin', That's shitty. That was our band. Come up with your own name. But ultimately, Layne was our pal, our brother, so we were like, "Okay, whatever you wanna do."

MIKE STARR For the show, we put a white sheet up in front of the stage and our manager came up and said, "Ladies and gentlemen, Diamond Lie won't be here tonight, but we have for you . . . Alice in Chains!" You could just see our silhouettes through the sheet, and by the first quarter of the song, the sheet dropped and it was us. And we had a backdrop that said ALICE IN CHAINS.

It was Halloween, and we were all dressed in these bad '70s dresses. Layne had a brown dress on, I had a flowery dress on. It was a killer show. I had a threesome that night with two girls.

ROB SKINNER (Coffin Break bassist/singer) Coffin Break shared a room in the Music Bank with Alice in Chains for about a year. Every room there was a party. The girls loved the Alice in Chains guys, so the band would always have these South End or Eastside girls show up with their friends and hang out. They definitely rehearsed and did their thing, but the suburban metal background is a lot different than the punk-rock background. There are no girls watching you practice when you're a punk-rock band, let's put it that way.

DAVID DUET Cat Butt rehearsed at the Music Bank. Alice in Chains had a giant rehearsal room, one of the biggest there, that had mirrors all the way around. We'd walk by, and they were doing high kicks. One time when I went by they had flash pots, another time they had a whole P.A. system set up in the hallway.

ROB SKINNER They were working on stagecraft, which we thought was kind of strange because nobody else did that. Everyone else was drinking beer and playing and honing the set. Being more concerned with the music than the look.

The Alice guys took me to a strip club for the first time, and that was a lot of fun. I think I was the first person to take them to the Vogue, because they were more from the metal scene from the suburbs. They loved it, and actually they played their first club show there at the Vogue.

JAMES BURDYSHAW At first we thought their band, which was Diamond Lie at that point, was awful. They sounded like Poison. For us, that was disgusting. We even made fun of them, but Layne was such a sweetheart that he won us over. He'd come up to us, like, "You guys need anything, just let me know. You want pot, you want beer, whatever you need, I can do it. You want me to square you some coke? No problem." We're all like, "Whoa, this guy is pretty cool." And him and David started to get close.

DAVID DUET Alice in Chains didn't know what to think of Cat Butt; no one did at that time. We'd practice with the lights off, with black lights and strobe lights. We'd bring smoke machines in our practice room. We had crazy papier-mâché artwork hanging everywhere that we used to have onstage with us—a big, psychedelic biker voodoo trip. So they'd always walk by and look in our door. At one point, one of the managers of the place said, "Look, I know this is ridiculous, but Alice in Chains is telling us that they walked in the bathroom here and all of Cat Butt is shooting up and sucking each other off at the time same." *(Laughs.)* Which, actually, I loved. I thought that was great! They probably did walk in on Michael in the bathroom, and it got exaggerated.

Layne's girlfriend, Demri [Parrott], was the one who made the connection between our bands. Demri, who was the cutest, most beautiful thing in the world, came up to me one night and lifted up her shirt. She showed me her belly button, and she goes, "Look, I can make a cat's butt!"

REED HUTCHINSON (Feast guitarist) Before Layne was going out with Demri, I got to know her through my girlfriend Angela. Demri was super-funny and very forward. I was probably 18 and super-shy and I remember her asking me super-direct questions like, "So, how's the sex between you and Angela?" And I was like, "Oh, my God, you can't talk about this!"

XANA LA FUENTE "Innocent yet provocative." That's how Andrew described Demri when he first saw her. She kind of reminded me of Brooke Shields in the movie *Pretty Baby*. Young, but very sexy. She was really frisky; she was all over everybody. But not in a slutty way.

PONY MAURICE (Feast singer) I kind of fell in love with Xana and Demri for a while. Yes, I like both men and women. We would all just hang out and go to shows and play around. They were both so beautiful in their own weird way. Demri was five feet tall and tiny, and Xana was six feet tall and, like, Amazon. I just was smitten with Xana. She had this really cool, big Roman nose. I knew Andy before her, but I started getting a lot closer to Xana than I ever had with him. He knew that I liked her, and I think she would sometimes use me to make him jealous.

DAVID DUET At our next rehearsal, Demri and Layne walked in together, and within a month I was doing guest appearances with Alice in Chains, singin' Bowie songs and stuff. And then shortly after that, their whole sound changed 'cause they got introduced to the scene and Susan Silver. They changed into this dark, brooding, heavy thing.

ROB SKINNER There was this huge pot operation that nobody knew about next door to the Music Bank. Came home from a show to load our gear back in and there was cops everywhere, and one guy who lived there had a gun pointed at his head by the cops. Now, had we known that all that pot was next door, we would've tunneled into it. 'Cause we spent a lot of time trying to find what was just six inches away from us without even knowing. The Music Bank ended up shutting down, we went our way, and the Alice in Chains guys went their way.

SOOZY BRIDGES (intern for Kelly Curtis/Ken Deans; club booker) The band all lived together in a house a little south of Seattle. I'd keep their gig money and make them buy groceries because they had no food. They'd eat Grape-Nuts with water in it, or crackers and ketchup.

MIKE STARR There were girls there all the time. I'd wake up, and there'd be girls sitting on the couch just waiting for us to get up so they could hang out. One time, for Layne's birthday, there was this girl and I handcuffed her to my chin-up bar—she let me—and I go, "Layne, happy birthday!" and I pushed him in my room. It was funny.

KEN DEANS I'm talking to Atlantic and Island, and Nick is still at ASCAP. So as it starts to heat up, Kelly goes, "I'm going to shop the band." Then it's decided that Nick's going to go to Columbia, and the band's going to go with Nick. At this time, Kelly and I are separating; I did some things that probably weren't smart, and Kelly did some things that I didn't agree with. Around then, we had extra space in our office, and we offered Susan Silver a place to work out of.

The band was problematical from the start. And whether it was drug use, whether it was alcohol abuse—it was really all of the above—it just seemed like a time bomb waiting to happen. So Kelly had trepidation going forward with it. At that point, I approached Susan and said, "Kelly and I are done, but he's going to fuck this thing up—he's going to walk away from it—so you need to partner on this band with Kelly. They've got a chance and, yes, they've got their problems."

SUSAN SILVER Ken gave me a cassette tape of some of the songs that Alice had done, and they were *so* catchy and *so* wonderful. I went to see them live and thought they were great fun and very energetic and entertaining and spent a little time with them and they were *hilarious.* In a matter of time, the fellow that they called their manager, who was a hairstylist-slash–coke dealer, took a second vacation to prison. Ken asked Kelly and I if we both wanted to work on the project together, so we said we'd give that a try.

MIKE STARR We had a manager, and one day Kelly and Susan sat us down and said, "Your manager is gonna get busted by the cops for selling coke." I don't know how they knew that, but they did. They said, "We'd like to manage you," and so we thought about it, and we said yeah. Went over to our old manager's house one night, and he opened up his safe and he had this acid from the '60s. He gave it to us, and right when we were peaking we said, "Yeah, we're gonna go with new management," and we walked out. It must have been a bad trip for him.

KEN DEANS Overall, the guys were terrific human beings. The biggest problem was Mike Starr, who did anything he could for himself. This is a guy who would sell spots on the guest list, and get people to buy him drugs and beer because he was Mike Starr from Alice in Chains. You never knew what problem Mike was going to cause next. You knew what was up with Sean; if he got drunk, there was a chance that he might end up in jail. Jerry, you just had to keep him pacified because he would get frustrated with it all. Layne was doing his job and was one of the nicest guys you could ever deal with.

MIKE STARR And when we went with that management company, with Susan, Kelly, and Ken Deans, we started playing with Mother Love Bone and Soundgarden.

TIM BRANOM Alice in Chains played with Mother Love Bone August 1988 at the Central, and that was a really odd pairing because they weren't the same type of bands. Yet they were growing together as friends. I think that started people meshing styles together.

MIKE STARR When I saw Jeff Ament in Mother Love Bone, I was like, Wow. They just looked different, man, wearing shorts over their long johns, with combat boots. I remember we started dressing like that. We started wearing Value Village clothes and not showering for a while. We were trying to have our big hair and everything at the beginning, and then Layne got dreadlocks. We just kind of molded into whatever they call grunge now.

KIM THAYIL When they were Alice N' Chains, their first demo probably owed a little bit more to Poison than the huge monster they became. That really changed when they heard us. *(Laughs.)* Jerry Cantrell and I were at some show, I think it was DOA playing at a venue called the Hall of Fame in the U District. Jerry asked me how to play songs like "Nothing to Say" and "Beyond the Wheel" and was there some kind of weird tuning thing? And I said, "Hey, there's this thing called drop D tuning." And a short time later, they recorded a demo that contained many of the songs that you hear on *Facelift* and they had drop D tuning on them.

NICK TERZO On that same visit to Seattle, I'd also met Susan Silver and Chris Cornell. I stayed in touch with everyone, and actually when Mother Love Bone did their demo, I helped shop it. Alice would send me a demo when they did a demo. I had committed to ASCAP for one year. I stayed there for one year and two weeks and got a job as director of A&R on the West Coast at Columbia Records in spring 1989. I signed Alice in Chains that summer.

CHAPTER 16
WHERE'S THE GROG?

BOB WHITTAKER My father, Jim Whittaker, is a bit of a Pacific Northwest icon in that he and his twin brother became famous mountaineers, and he was the first American to summit Mount Everest. My father was really good friends with the Kennedy family and with Bobby Kennedy. In fact, I'm named after Bobby. After Bobby was shot, my father was a pallbearer at his funeral. I was never allowed to have squirt guns or toy guns as a kid because of that.

When I was in high school in the '80s, I'll never forget my dad walking into my room, where I'm listening to Wasted Youth or whatever, and there on top of the stack was the Dead Kennedys record. I felt horrible. Here I am—Bobby Kennedy is my namesake—and I have this sacrilegious record. That was a tough one to explain away.

Stone Gossard and I hung out as very young kids. We were from the same neighborhood. My mother, Blanche, didn't tell me about this until much later, but apparently Stone's dad had been keen on her. She was working at the concession stand at Paradise, the lodge at Mount Rainier National Park. Stone's dad either had taken her on a ski trip or invited her on one. He drove up there at one point with flowers and champagne, and she said, "I can't see you anymore. I'm seeing Jim Whittaker." And then she ended up marrying my dad. I told Stone that story, and he and I got a big yuck out of it.

MEGAN JASPER My first New Year's Eve in Seattle, I went with J Mascis from Dinosaur Jr. to a party at Bob's house. J had a Jim Whittaker–brand jacket and thought Jim was cool, but we didn't know he was Bob's dad. So we walk into Bob's house and see pictures of Bob and his dad on the refrigerator. J looked at me and goes, "No fuckin' way." That was kind of a trip, but then an extra trip was that it looked like someone had OD'd on the floor, and people are just walking over this person. I just had this moment, like, Welcome to Seattle: mountain climbers and heroin addicts.

JOHN LEIGHTON BEEZER Bob Whittaker had this skin condition—I think it was a combination of growing up in a sunny climate and acne, so he had pits—which is not the kind of thing I would ordinarily mention. But when we were recording *Melancholy Girl Hole,* Ed told Bob, "I'm going to record the new Thrown Ups." And Bob goes, "Well, do a song about me." So Ed did a song about Bob's skin condition. And just to make it clear he's singing about Bob, at the very end, he goes, "Bob Whittaker!"

BOB WHITTAKER And thus was born "Hairy Crater Man." He basically just slanders me in the song, wonders why girls like me.

JOHN LEIGHTON BEEZER It did cross a line for me. I thought, That needs to just go to the bottom of the ocean. But I was overruled by everybody else in the band. Three or four months later, Bob comes up to me. "Hey, I hear you didn't want to put out that song. How come?"

I was like, "Well, gee, Bob, I don't know, I thought it really was cruel to you." I mean, I'm the only guy that had enough decency to say, "Maybe we shouldn't do this," and now he's trying to embarrass me, putting me on the spot: "What's your problem? This is my song!" And that's why Bob was the ideal guy for Mudhoney. They were incredibly cruel to Bob, but he could take it, so he belonged in that club.

MARK ARM On our first tour, we just brought Bob along. I'm not even sure why. He didn't know how to run sound. He's much more outgoing than any of us, so his job was essentially to find us a place to crash every night. At first, he was just kind of a mascot.

STEVE TURNER Bob didn't give a rat's ass about equipment or any of that stuff. He was like, "It's your own damn amp—you carry it!"

MARK ARM That first tour we went from Seattle to the East Coast and back. Then we played with Sonic Youth and the Screaming Trees in Seattle, and just went down the West Coast and over to Texas with Sonic Youth. Sonic Youth had played with Green River almost every time they came here. We ended up becoming pretty good friends on that level. Like, "Hey, you guys again." It was a great opportunity. Sonic Youth and the Butthole Surfers were the biggest underground bands at the time, at least in my mind.

JAMES BURDYSHAW We were watchin' Mudhoney just skyrocket past us, and then TAD. These are both bands that started after Cat Butt had been together for more than a year. Mudhoney went from playin' a sloppy show in Pioneer Square with Blood Circus to like three or four months later goin' on tour with Sonic Youth. It was like, What the fuck? Even with Mark's cachet, to just instantly have this big push, it seemed like, Whoa, wait a minute. Besides being jealous, we felt like we were gonna be left out if we didn't do something, so we went out on a tour and then got Sub Pop to green-light doing our record.

DAVID DUET On the record's jacket spine, we thanked the girlfriends of Mudhoney, TAD, and Nirvana. I said it as a joke, and Bruce Pavitt insisted that we put it in there. It was very much based on reality, though, except for Nirvana. Kurt's girlfriend came up to me at one of our shows and said, "Why did you guys put that on the record? None of you have ever done me." *(Laughs.)* I said, "It was just to balance it out, honestly." It sounded better with Nirvana in there.

BOB WHITTAKER Mudhoney and myself would sheepishly sneak into Sonic Youth's dressing room to make off with the beer on their rider because they were almost teetotalers. Sonic Youth would get to a city and want to go to a bookstore and the thrift store, and Mudhoney were like, "Where's the grog?"

THURSTON MOORE Mark used to try to mythologize Sonic Youth's profile. I remember him being in my hotel room on tour and calling up different bands staying in the same hotel at 3 in the morning, saying he was me, asking people to come up and hang out. They'd be asleep, not very into it, and he'd be yelling into the phone, "Don't you know who I am? I'm Thurston Fucking Moore from Sonic Fucking Youth, and I demand that you come up here and hang out with me!" And then hang up the phone. I'd be like, "Mark, please don't do that!"

MATT LUKIN I got into all kinds of trouble that tour. A few running-around-naked nights. There's nothing funnier than a drunk naked guy, if you're the drunk guy. But it is kind of sad, thinking back. I do remember one night, playing in the L.A. area with Sonic Youth, and the Redd Kross guys were there. We all came out onstage and played "I Wanna Be Your Dog" with Sonic Youth, and I had my pants around my ankles while playing Kim Gordon's bass.

The next night, Kim's doing sound check with that bass, and I pointed to it and said, "Hey, Kim, my penis was touching the back of that bass last night!" And she's all, "Really?" She took it off, and I don't think she ever played it again. I'm like, Damn, am I that repulsive?

MARK ARM I can pinpoint when Matt became a cartoon character, like Yosemite Sam or something. It was when we were on this short West Coast tour in 1989. We played a show with Cat Butt in Davis, California, and afterward we all went to someone's condo or apartment where everyone crashed. It seemed like *A Midsummer Night's Dream*, but with boozed-up punks instead of fairies and wood nymphs. There was lots of craziness and a complete lack of reason.

DANNY BLAND It was kind of a funny, fundamental difference between the two bands: Mudhoney were all on the pull-out couch trying to get some sleep, and we were just raging and keeping them awake.

Dean Gunderson, the bass player, was disgusted by this brand-new, white Camaro in the parking lot. He's a giant, like six-seven, and he came crawling up on the hood of the car, dropped his pants, and actually laid a turd on the hood of this white Camaro. He's a big man, it's a big turd, and it was quite amazing.

DEAN GUNDERSON That was another LSD night. The car offended me, I don't know. The guy actually came out, and we watched him try and get it off: He backed the car up and slammed on his brakes so it would roll off the hood, but it ended up rolling back towards the windshield wipers. It got stuck in there, and he drove off.

MARK ARM The next morning, everyone was in the place's pool for a while. Matt stayed in the pool by himself, and he wouldn't leave. He started hovering his hands above the water, and he's totally mesmerized and focused, going, "It's like glass. It's like glass." He was trapped in glass. *(Laughs.)* Some fuckin' switch went off in his head, and it hasn't flipped back yet.

. . .

EDDIE SPAGHETTI Early on, I remember being at Sub Pop—I was stuffing some singles for them for some spare change—and they put in the cassette of *Bleach,* and I was like, "Oh, my God, this is a local band? This is so fucking good." I couldn't believe all these bands were from the same town that we were now living in.

JACK ENDINO Some of the biggest records I made on Sub Pop were when I'd only been an engineer for one or two years. Mudhoney's *Superfuzz Bigmuff,* the first Soundgarden EP; *Bleach* was recorded in '88.

Nirvana came in for *Bleach,* and they weren't sure they wanted to put it on Sub Pop, frankly. Sub Pop was such a new label that they were still thinking, Maybe we can get on Touch and Go or SST or some other label. Kurt was basically thinking, I'm gonna shop it to some other people, so we're gonna have our friend Jason here pay for it. So Jason paid the $600 and change.

JASON EVERMAN (Nirvana guitarist; Soundgarden bassist) I grew up on the Kitsap Peninsula, which bisects the Puget Sound. I met Chad Channing in my homeroom class in sixth grade. To me and my friends, Chad was this mysterious guy. We perceived him as mature and sophisticated and exotic. His family moved twice a year. He had a mustache in sixth grade. And he had long hair. I didn't have long hair, none of my friends really did. We ended up playing together in a thrash-metal band called Stone Crow.

KERRY GREEN (Dickless guitarist) Chad Channing was this odd little pixie guy. He was always really lighthearted and sweet. I heard that once when Nirvana were out on tour, Krist woke up and saw Chad driving with his teeth, with his hands behind his back. Krist decided to take over driving at that point.

JASON EVERMAN Around '88, Chad was like, "You should check out this band that I'm playing with." I don't even know if they were called Nirvana at this point. I went to see them at the Community World Theater in Tacoma, I'm guessing, and they were great. Even then it was pretty evident.

Through Chad, I started hanging out with Kurt and Krist socially. I liked Kurt. There was a point in time where I considered us friends. It was probably Kurt who asked me for the loan. I had money from working in Alaska as a commercial fisherman. No, they never repaid it, but I'm not going to go crazy over $500. I've lost more money than that to friends, so whatever.

JACK ENDINO *Bleach* was just another album. I thought it was a very good other album, but I thought, Here's another great record that nobody's ever gonna hear.

ALICE WHEELER My first band shoot was Nirvana in 1988. I usually got the jobs Charles Peterson didn't want. Which is why I got Nirvana's first single, because everybody in Seattle thought Mudhoney was gonna be the big band and they didn't pay any attention to Nirvana.

KIM THAYIL Nirvana's influences were certainly the Melvins and us. I saw Kurt at a Melvins show and I told him how much I loved *Bleach*, and he said, "Well, you should consider yourselves our biggest influence." When they got going, Nirvana were huge fans of Soundgarden 'cause we kind of came out of the punk scene, but were doing heavy rock without being idiots about it. We weren't doing songs about cars and parties and chicks.

RON RUDZITIS When they released *Bleach*, I heard "About a Girl" and I became a fan. All of the sudden, there was another side to Nirvana. It totally reminded me of the Beatles. I'm just going, "Holy shit, this guy can write a hell of a song!" "About a Girl" wasn't on that first demo Bruce played for us at Muzak. If it had been, I know I would've freaked out, like, "Gee, sign these guys!"

BRUCE PAVITT I was at a party next door to my house when I got this intuitive feeling, like, I really gotta go over to my house. Right as I did that, Krist Novoselic was walking up my stairway. He's inebriated and he's intimidating and he's demanding a contract. It was very scary. He's a very big guy. I called up Poneman and said, "Look, I know we don't have contracts with any bands and I know we don't have the money to hire an attorney to write a contract, but we need to get this guy one."

JONATHAN PONEMAN I said, "The contract's coming." Krist wasn't in a friendly, jolly mood. He seemed like he could go off. He didn't really know who we were, and stories about corrupt record-label people are legion. He wanted to be protected. I sat up for a couple nights and composed a contract, which was largely taken from various music-industry books. We later discovered that the contract was, as you might imagine, very much the product of somebody who didn't really know what he was talking about.

BRUCE PAVITT I didn't really believe in contracts, and indie labels didn't really do contracts. You did handshake deals. So it was like, "What the fuck? Why are we signing this three-record contract?" It seemed ridiculous to me, but it's that contract that ultimately allowed the label to stay in business. So Krist coming to my house to kick my ass was the biggest blessing of my life.

JASON EVERMAN I can't remember when Kurt suggested that I play with them, but the first time I did play with them was a party in K Dorm at Evergreen State College. After the party, Kurt was like, "Do you want to join the band?"

ALICE WHEELER Oh, yeah, Jason fit in. He was the prettiest one of them all. He was a good-looking guy. Most of the punk kids were more nerdy.

Kurt is extremely photogenic—and after he got to be a star, he learned how to play it up—but he was kind of slouchy, he was really skinny, his hair was kinda stringy.

KELLY CANARY (Dickless singer) Dickless shared a practice space with Nirvana for a while. We were all starstruck by Kurt even before he was famous because you could tell that he was so gifted. Plus, you kind of just wanted to take him home and take care of him, he just looked so sad and lost at the same time.

GARRETT SHAVLIK Kurt was very sweet and very young, and he would confide in me: "How do I deal with Jonathan and Bruce? Who do I need to believe?" After my meeting would be done with Jonathan and Bruce, I'd talk to Kurt at the Sub Pop offices. I'm like, "Go to Bruce. Jonathan will tell you you're gonna ride the fame train and fuckin' be beaten by 20 virgins. But Bruce is the real guy."

With Sub Pop, we'd talk about things like, "What should we do about Europe?" Bruce said, "I don't think it's pragmatic for you guys to go right now, and I don't think we can afford it." "That's funny, because Poneman just said, 'Yeah, it will be all good.'" Jonathan could bullshit you. It wasn't intentional. It was just that he was a positive cat: "It's gonna be great, man!" Well, sometimes it isn't fuckin' great.

BRUCE PAVITT There is a story that is true, and it's kind of embarrassing: I called Kurt up and said, "Can I borrow your money to put out your album?" Which sounds absolutely insane, but that's where we were at financially. You have to be really shameless. He said no. We ended up borrowing $5,000 from a friend to put it out.

DANNY BLAND I mostly dealt with Krist, and he was a bright guy. Ambitious for what we were dealing with at the time. Not the kind of ambitious that said, "We're going to be on the cover of *Rolling Stone* someday." But he definitely seemed to be sort of career-oriented, like he wanted to do this for his job.

I had a semicircuit of clubs that was interested in Sub Pop bands and we would put Nirvana into all those places. At the Sun Club in Tempe, Arizona, they were supposed to get 50 bucks and a case of beer, and

I don't think they got either. But sure enough, when I walk into the club years later, the photo that someone took of Nirvana playing on the stage is proudly displayed over the cash register. So I went to the owner and gave him some shit: "Oh, are you ever going to pay us for that show?"

CHAPTER 17
CREATE YOUR OWN MYTH

ANTON BROOKES (U.K. music publicist) I was working for a British distribution company called SRD, and Sub Pop was just one of the new labels that we had taken on. I was trying to find some journalist to champion Mudhoney and the label, and already there was a little buzz about Sub Pop here because on the radio the DJ John Peel had been playing the hell out of *Sub Pop 200* and any piece of Sub Pop vinyl.

The legendary Stud Brothers at the *Melody Maker*—they weren't actual brothers, just two friends who wrote together—wanted to write about Mudhoney. Over here, it's usually the labels that have to pay for the journalists to travel. Obviously Sub Pop didn't have a lot of money, so in the end Everett True got to go out because it was cheaper to send him and a photographer than two writers and a photographer.

JONATHAN PONEMAN Anton said, "Would you guys consider flying over a journalist and a photographer from the *Melody Maker,* put them up, and introduce them to Mudhoney? In exchange, Mudhoney will get a cover and they'll throw in a story about Sub Pop on top of it."

That was a paradigm: exporting American talent, letting the British hype it up, and then reimporting it back over here. It's popular lore that Jimi Hendrix started off as a local musician in Seattle, went into the military, came out, went to England, and became a pop star there. And then the music was exported back here.

BRUCE PAVITT There was a genuine chemistry between Everett True, Jonathan, and I. We supplied him with lots of alcohol, I remember that. *Spin* later listed flying Everett over as one of the Top 100 sleaziest moments in rock and roll. Whatever.

EVERETT TRUE (*Melody Maker* newspaper writer; Nirvana biographer) The only purpose I had in my writing was to make people jealous of me. So I would talk myself up and talk up the people around me any way I could. And that's why it was a stroke of genius getting me over, because I totally bought into the hype.

Bruce Pavitt and Jonathan Poneman were some of the most charming, eloquent liars that I ever met. I just thought it was hilarious that everybody lied. Like Krist Novoselic, when you first met him, would say he was a competitive tree climber. And I printed it because that's funny. If they wanted to portray Tad Doyle as some kind of chain saw–toting, dope-smoking, backwoods redneck who didn't wash and used to be a butcher—I met him, and he was clearly an incredibly intelligent, witty fellow—that was cool by me, because why the hell not?

TAD DOYLE I *was* a journeyman butcher for a number of years. It was fun to play on and effective, but at the same time the lumberjack, 300-pound ex-butcher image painted my band into a corner.

KURT DANIELSON Here we are, trying to make music that we really believe in, and on the other hand, we're being marketed as these redneck lumberjacks who live in the woods and eat raw meat and drink and do God knows what, emulate Ed Gein and other serial killers.

At some point, people began to come see the band play for the freak-show factor—to see the fat man cavorting on stage, to see the crazed bearded rednecks—rather than to listen to the music. Now, who was responsible for this? It was all of us, really. We were trying to be as obnoxious as possible in flaunting the fact that we were not your average, everyday chicks with dicks, like in Poison. We heard that somebody at MTV had rejected our "Wood Goblins" video on the basis that the band was considered too ugly.

KIM THAYIL Have you seen the first TAD single? It has a photo of Tad on it, and the text looks like he wrote it all with the wrong hand: "Hi, my name is Tad. I like make music." It was 'tardo grammar and punctuation—and I'm not saying that to offend people of intellectual diminishment. Like this guy is musically a savant but had some kind of social or intellectual impairment that made him this brilliant folk artist. I was upset in that the way he was presented diminished the talents of a friend of mine.

BRUCE PAVITT I found out that when Tad was a teenager he played jazz drums at the White House for President Nixon. We didn't want people to think that maybe he was a refined intellectual and a jazz prodigy, so we tried to put a lid on that story.

BOB WHITTAKER When the London press first got ahold of it, Mudhoney was presented as a blue-collar thing. When the press found out Mark and Steve went to college, it was a real letdown for them.

MARK ARM The U.K. was so fuckin' class-oriented. Like if rock is going to be authentic it's gotta come from the lower class, which is crazy. I mean, Mick Jagger went to the London School of Economics.

BRUCE PAVITT It was my contention that people in Europe would get excited about American music if, from their perspective, the bands actually looked or felt more authentically "American." And Europeans don't see Americans as refined. They see them as spirited, but somewhat unmannered.

   When I told people I was going to the Seattle area to go to college, they were like, "Oh, my God, there's still cowboys and Indians out there." And it was seen as extremely backwoods. This is prior to Microsoft and Starbucks and everything else. In addition, Seattle had very little music history, so it essentially had a clean slate. It didn't have the baggage of San Francisco or New Orleans or Kansas City. So we got to create our own myth.

JOHN ROBINSON (singer for Denver's the Fluid) We came to Seattle for a show, and Sub Pop had posters made that said MEAN MOUNTAIN ROCK FROM DENVER. And we were just, "What the hell are you talking about? 'Mountain rock'?" We actually got mad at Bruce and Jon for saying that. They just thought it was funny.

LORI BARBERO (drummer for Minneapolis's Babes in Toyland) In the late '80s, we played at the OK Hotel with someone from Sub Pop, and I remember clearly the poster said BABES IN TOYLAND: PREMENSTRUAL GRUNGE FROM MINNEAPOLIS. I was like, "Holy shit!" I thought that was so fucking badass.

CHARLES R. CROSS (*The Rocket* newspaper owner/editor in chief; Kurt Cobain biographer) Kurt Cobain hated that he was presented as an inbred logger. Though Kurt himself occasionally played into that; he wrote these mythical bios for Sub Pop that they circulated, claiming he met Novoselic at a woodworking class, so he did some of this stuff to himself. That's not Sub Pop's fault, but it certainly is true that the way they were marketed made them look like hicks.

Then you have bozos like Everett True who play into that, and the press pumped that up. It almost doesn't matter what the case was. It's like that John Ford quote: "When the legend becomes fact, print the legend."

EVERETT TRUE Charles absolutely misses the entire point. The whole point about Sub Pop early on was it was a lot of fun; that's why we made up all those stories. You might as well create your own myth, because if you don't, somebody like Charles Cross is gonna come along and create his own myth, and it's gonna be a lot more tedious. That book he did on Kurt, that's way more about mythologizing than anything I've ever written in my life, anything Sub Pop ever did. What's that whole chapter detailing what Kurt was thinking when he killed himself? What's that if not mythologizing?

JONATHAN PONEMAN Kurt Cobain protested vigorously later on in his career, saying, "Those guys portrayed us as a bunch of dumb rednecks." That we were turning them into cartoon characters. The Beatles *literally* became cartoons in their marketing. I'm putting way more thought into my explanation than we ever did back then, because it was all intuitive.

EVERETT TRUE There's a quote of mine from the Sub Pop article that has been used more than anything else I've written, which is the earliest description of Nirvana in a British music paper—how "They're four working-class guys from Aberdeen, blah blah blah." What's really kind of annoying about seeing that description everywhere is, although it's attributed to me, they're not my words. I was on serious deadline, and I wasn't an experienced writer by any stretch of the imagination back then. So I was on the phone to Jonathan Poneman in Seattle and I was copying down word-for-word what he was telling me about these artists. That's quite dreadful, really, but what the hell.

DANIEL HOUSE I was at Sub Pop during that time, and I understood what they were doing, but I was kind of appalled. Because they were basically providing Everett True the Sub Pop version of the scene, as if Sub Pop were the whole thing. They booked a whole bunch of shows with all the Sub Pop bands and promoted the hell out of them, so they made sure that his entire experience was like, "Wow! Look at the Seattle scene! I saw TAD this night, I saw Blood Circus that night, I saw Nirvana this night." It wasn't like all those bands would normally be playing during the same two-week period.

STEVE TURNER Seeing the article on us was like, Whoa! That was a big fucking article. Being in those magazines shifted things for us, and it made some of the straight press in Seattle pay attention. Patrick MacDonald, who was a clueless *Seattle Times* music critic, was dismissive of anything that was valid about Seattle music until people like Everett True and foreign magazines gave us the thumbs-up. Then he said, "Oh, great stuff here in town that I've been ignoring for years and saying was crap!"

AL LARSEN (Some Velvet Sidewalk singer/guitarist) I remember traveling in '89 across the country with Mecca Normal and the Go Team and staying every night in some kid's apartment. It's March of '89 and we're in, I don't know, Kansas. And the kid has the Sub Pop Flaming Lips seven-inch next to the stereo. And then we drive for 10 hours and we go to some other kid's house, and he has the Sub Pop Flaming Lips seven-inch next to the stereo. We broke down in Pittsburgh, and we're staying at some kid's house, and their kind of hard-rock roommate lets us into his room and there he's got the *Melody Maker* with the spread on Sub Pop. And I just remember being like, Whoa. We're traveling around playing to no one and this other thing—grunge—has totally caught the world on fire.

BRUCE PAVITT Everett's articles had a lot of impact. Also, John Peel was playing *Sub Pop 200* right around the same time. And John Peel, in *The Times* of London, circulation two million, stated that Sub Pop had the most distinctive American regional sound since Tamla Motown. Now that's a piece of hype.

EVERETT TRUE In my original articles, I'm supposed to have used the word *grunge* to describe the music. Lester Bangs certainly used to use the word. I used the word myself in the '80s to describe the Happy Mondays. You know, "They got grungy guitars." It was a description that was in the rock-journalist lexicon. I guess one of my subeditors at the *Melody Maker* picked up on the word and used it in a headline or something and all of a sudden the word started sticking.

JONATHAN PONEMAN I read the expression *grunge* many, many times in music journalism before Everett True used it. Everett took the word from the Sub Pop mail-order catalog description of Green River's *Dry as a Bone* that Bruce wrote: "ultra-loose GRUNGE that destroyed the morals of a generation."

FAITH HENSCHEL-VENTRELLO I worked in radio promo at Sub Pop. I remember Jon and Bruce looking through the thesaurus and coming up with *grunge*. I believe Bruce was the one who took it out of the thesaurus, who said, "Grunge! *That* word."

BRUCE PAVITT I believe that's the first time the word was used more as a marketing description. As with any adjective, you can go back and say, "Well, this was used in such-and-such zine," but that came to me intuitively when we opened the office and were piecing together our first catalog. We were trying to emphasize the grittiness of the music and the energy. I just remember thinking that it sounded right at the time. Like, "Nailed it. All right, let's move on."

EVERETT TRUE It's kind of ironic that this music I absolutely despised and is anathema to everything I love about music, that is the one music I'm credited with inventing! To me, grunge is another crap musical form that MTV invented. The original grunge, the Sub Pop grunge, had nothing to do with the grunge that became popular, like Silverchair and Puddle of Mudd.

JACK ENDINO None of us is entirely sure about who used the word first. I saw it in a Lester Bangs record review in *Rolling Stone* in the '70s. Mark Arm had used the word in the early '80s.

MAIRE MASCO *Desperate Times* had letters to the editor, and Mark Arm wrote this letter complaining about his own band, Mr. Epp and the Calculations, being "pure grunge." Before that, the word had been *grungy*, an adjective. Mark basically turned it into a noun.

MARK ARM (writing in to *Desperate Times*, July 22, 1981) I hate Mr. Epp & the Calculations! Pure grunge! Pure noise! Pure shit! Everyone I know loves them, I don't know why. They don't even wear chains and mohawks! They all look different, yuk! And they have no sense of humor. In fact, they have no sense. They're all pretentious, older than the Grateful Dead, and love Emerson Lake & Palmer (my mother's fave).

I love Philip Glass! While my friends listen to Mr. Epp & the Calculations, I listen to Mr. Glass. His music is repetitious, redundant, and repetitive. Pure art! It's sooooooo intellectual, like me. I love to listen to Philip Glass over and over and over and over again etc. ad infinitum.

Mark McLaughlin
Mark McLaughlin
Mark McLaughlin
Mark McLaughlin

(Ed. note: Mark McLaughlin does guitar & vocals in Mr. Epp and the Calculations.)

MAIRE MASCO I actually remember when we got his letter, I said to Daina Darzin, the editor, "I don't think *grunge* is a word." And she said, "It doesn't matter, it sounds cool."

MARK ARM Am I the person responsible for coining the word *grunge*? I don't think so. In 1981, I wrote a fanzine a fake letter from the perspective of a disgruntled person who happened to stumble upon my shitty band at the time, Mr. Epp. It was fake hate mail. You know, this publicity stuff is very tricky!

The word *grunge* was tossed around a little bit here and there well before I ever used it. Steve Turner picked up this '70s reissue of a Rock 'n' Roll Trio album, and the liner notes talk about Paul Burlison's "grungy guitar sound." That was written in the '70s about a '50s guitar player.

Grunge was an adjective; it was never meant to be a noun. If I was using it, it was never meant to coin a movement, it was just to describe raw rock and roll. Then that term got applied to major-label bands putting out slick-sounding records. It's an ill fit.

RICKY KULWICKI (guitarist for Denver's the Fluid) The first time I heard the word *grunge*? We had just started the Fluid, and we were opening for the Dead Kennedys at the Blue Note in Boulder, Colorado. Jello Biafra from the Dead Kennedys is from Boulder, and he knew us from when we were in punk-rock bands. Afterwards, while we were loading out, he comes up to me and he's like, "Hey, Ricky, it's good to see you guys are continuing the legacy of Denver grunge." I'd never heard that word before in association with music. But I knew that it was a compliment. I was like, "Thanks, man." This was in 1985.

DAVID DUET People keep saying I was the first one to say *grunge* in that scene. I know we were definitely the first ones to use it in anything. I've gotten a lot of hell for that.

The first thing I came up with was *grungedelic,* which is from a lyric for our single "64 Funny Cars." We wrote the song in '86, '87. It was just stuff that came out of my mind while we were playin'. After that, I came up with Moto Grunge, which appeared on one of the early Cat Butt flyers. I was fascinated by biker patches, like Moto Guzzi. I was tryin' to come up with a Cat Butt logo and I started messing around with the

Harley image, and I was tryin' to think of words to go in there. I tend to talk to myself and that slipped out one day. And it fit in the logo: Moto on top, Cat Butt in the center, and Grunge on the bottom.

BEN SHEPHERD I hate that word *grunge*. It has nothing to do with anything. It's fuckin' concocted bullshit.

JACK ENDINO Sometime around '87, '88, the word *grunge* started getting thrown around. It might've been Everett. I hate to say it, but it might've been me. At one of my high school reunions, someone told me, "You used to use that word all the time!" I'm like, "*What?* Don't tell me that!"

   No one fucking knows, and frankly I don't think anyone really wants to take credit for it. So let's leave it at that, all right?

•   •   •

MARK ARM Everett's article on us came out just before we went to the U.K. with Sonic Youth. Those shows were at the start of a nine-week European tour. We did a couple more shows with Sonic Youth in northern Europe, but most of the tour was us going around by ourselves before ending up back in the U.K. for a couple shows.

RON RUDZITIS I'll never forget Mark's last day of work at Muzak and just being so fucking jealous. He was leaving to go open for Sonic Youth in England. Fuck! That is my dream come true. It was a huge inspiration for me to work really hard. I got really focused, and I bugged the hell out of Bruce, and eventually not only got the Love Battery single out, but convinced Sub Pop to put out our albums.

DAN PETERS Toward the end of the tour, we played at the School of Oriental and African Studies in London. We were being supported by Soundgarden then—my, how times changed. The show was in what appeared to be a cafeteria, so they got this haphazard stage set up. It was sold out, and there's probably a thousand people there.

STEVE TURNER The stage was really rickety, and after the first few bars Mark headed into the crowd. I headed into the crowd. Everything became unplugged, the stage started falling over, everyone's trying to hold up the stage and the speaker columns.

MARK ARM The kids had the fever. The band was totally apeshit wild. I made a joke, saying, "Okay, everybody get onstage," thinking there's no way everyone can get onstage. The crowd took that at face value, and they pushed us back all the way to the wall. And people who were normally observers—writers like Keith Cameron and Everett True and our publicist at the time, Anton—were rolling up their sleeves, pushing people back.

ANTON BROOKES The stage was built on loads of school desks, so it wasn't the most stable setting. It felt like *Zulu*—it's an old English film, with Michael Caine, where there's a couple British soldiers against 10,000 Zulu warriors. They just keep coming and coming and coming and coming.

DAN PETERS I remember looking over, and the monitor guy starts unplugging stuff and taking equipment away. One of the English journalists gets up and screams into the microphone, *"This is nonsensical! This is nonsensical! Everybody get off the stage!"* The stage starts to fall apart, and I just go, "Well, that was interesting," and walk to the backstage room where Matt Cameron's sitting. He goes, "Jesus Christ, does this happen every night with you guys?"

I was thinking, The show's over. There's no way in hell it's going to go on. That's when people are like, "You guys got to go back out there and play or shit's going to happen."

STUART HALLERMAN I'm scoping out the exits, totally planning my escape. I was worried for my life.

MARK ARM We played a little more, and to illustrate how stupid that whole scenario was, I said, "Okay, let's get everybody on top of the P.A." I didn't learn my lesson the first time. I turned around and the security guy was fuckin' coming right at me. Anton and Keith had to hold him back.

STUART HALLERMAN Hours afterward, a guy got stabbed within a quarter mile of the place. It doesn't seem to have had anything to do with the show, but the newspaper blamed it on the mayhem: RIOT AT THE MUDHONEY SHOW! DEATH RESULTS!

MARK ARM To call it a riot is so out of proportion to what happened. It wasn't like people were smashing chairs because they were affected adversely by the music. It wasn't Stravinsky playing *The Rite of Spring* for the first time.

. . .

JAMES BURDYSHAW By '89, things had reached critical mass, 'cause that's when Lamefest happened—all of a sudden, Mudhoney and TAD and Nirvana played the Moore Theatre, and it was sold out. Over a thousand people were there. It was clear to me that the Seattle bands that my friends and acquaintances were in were getting really, really big. In my mind, a really big band had always been a band that would come in from out of town. The U-Men couldn't headline the Moore Theatre, as big as they were.

BRUCE PAVITT The first Lamefest—that was the moment when grunge blew up. That was the defining moment. That was the record release party for Nirvana's first record, which a lot of people don't realize.

STEVE TURNER It was like, "Wow, who are these people, and where were they a year ago?"

CHAD CHANNING (Nirvana drummer) The one show of this tour that really sticks in my mind was the Lamefest at the Moore Theatre because Jason put on this Mickey Mouse outfit just because he wanted to. It was pretty comical, actually. There's the band, and then there's Jason as Mickey Mouse with all this long hair.

JASON EVERMAN I made the Mickey Mouse shorts I wore onstage. It was kind of absurd, the red pants with the big yellow buttons. I got the idea from this *Calvin and Hobbes* story, which I thought was really funny. In the comic, Hobbes is telling Calvin, "Check out my Mickey Mouse pants." And Calvin is like, "I don't know."

BRUCE PAVITT The manager of the Moore Theatre had actually sent most of his security guys home because he was convinced that nobody was gonna show up. So when the local youth went off at the show, stage-diving and everything else, the security staff on hand was overwhelmed. Mark Arm very famously kicked a security guard and knocked him right off the stage.

That show ignited the city's youth and put Seattle on the map.

CHAPTER 18
INCOMPATIBLE INDIVIDUALS

JANET BILLIG (Hole manager via Gold Mountain Entertainment) I was working at Caroline and living in a 300-square-foot apartment on Seventh Street and Avenue C in New York. Tons of people crashed there on tour. Mudhoney and TAD were there a lot. Hole, Nirvana, Screaming Trees, Soundgarden, Skin Yard. L7 once stayed at my house and called Alaska and ran up my phone bill; there was blood all over my sheets—I have no idea what they did up there.

I had a part-time job at a foot doctor's office on Fifth Avenue and Ninth Street. He was closed on weekends, so I had Mudhoney sleep there one night in the waiting room. I told them, "You have to be out by 9 on Monday morning. That's when the appointments start." Once Mudhoney had a box of merch stolen, and urban myth is that for months after that, all the homeless people in the neighborhood were wearing Mudhoney shirts.

The first time Nirvana came to New York, they drove from Chicago or something, and when they showed up, I was like, "My friend is moving from Queens to Manhattan, I need you guys to move her." Kurt was like, "No way, I'm not moving your friend," but Krist and Chad went and moved her. She worked for *CMJ* at the time, so I think they got a lot of extra coverage out of that.

JASON EVERMAN We were staying in Alphabet City. I confided in Chad that I was done, and Chad had in turn confided in Kurt and Krist. I was becoming frustrated because I came to the realization that my role in the band was essentially going to be the rhythm-guitar player. I had the desire and inclination to write, as well. Same thing with Chad. It became obvious that wasn't going to happen. Also, we were broke and burned out from touring. I think in some ways it was a convenient excuse to go back to Washington.

CRAIG MONTGOMERY (Nirvana/TAD soundman) Jason was a nice kid. I don't really know much about the dynamic between him and the rest of the band, but the main thing I noticed was that all the guitar sounds that sounded like Nirvana were coming from Kurt. Jason's guitar sound just didn't sound right to me, so I never used very much of it. It was just kinda tinny, white-noisy, buzzy, whereas Kurt, even then, had this big, beefy guitar tone that was musical. Having Jason seemed redundant to me.

JANET BILLIG They kicked Jason out literally at my house. It was awful. They talked about leaving him there. I was like, "You gotta take him back home."

CHAD CHANNING We just decided to drive straight home and bag the rest of the shows. . . . There wasn't any discussion about it. We did not say anything about it the entire trip home. We got home, dropped him off, said, "All right man, we'll see you later." And we parted there . . .

JASON EVERMAN That's the last time I spoke to Kurt. I quit Nirvana, though I guess it's a matter of perspective. You can believe what you want to believe.

ROBERT ROTH (Truly singer/guitarist) I met Kurt in summer of '89. My band Storybook Krooks had just released our cassette. But we broke up, and I remember being on a bus going downtown from Queen Anne and seeing Jonathan Poneman. He liked the Storybook Krooks, and I told him, "We just broke up last week." And he goes, "Keep this under your hat, but Nirvana's looking for a second guitar player. And they want somebody who can write." So I gave a cassette to Justin Williams, who was a friend of Lanegan's, and Lanegan passed it to Kurt.

A week or two later, I went down to the Vogue to a TAD show and ran into Kurt, and was like, "Hey, I'm the guy with the tape." He was like, "Oh, yeah, Lanegan said he really liked it. I haven't checked it out yet, and we're gonna go on tour in about two weeks and we're not gonna try anybody out until we get back. We're gonna see how it goes as a three-piece." And I told Kurt, "I'm gonna be busy by the time you get back, so if you want to play with me, now is the time."

Kurt and I really hit it off. I learned some of Nirvana's songs, and they dragged all their gear up to my rehearsal space. We probably played about four, four and a half hours. When Krist took Chad back to Bainbridge, Kurt and I just hung out and shared the last couple of cigarettes we had between us and talked about drummers. No offense to Chad, but it was just kind of obvious to me and Kurt that if we were gonna do this band thing, that we might need to think about another drummer, and he was describing the type of drummer that he would want to have ideally, and it was a John Bonham-esque type drummer.

They apparently got back to Justin and told him that it was looking pretty good with me, but they just wanted to hang out one more time. But after their tour, Kurt just said, "Yeah, we decided to stay a three-piece." And then a week later, I met up with Mark Pickerel, and then our band Truly got rolling.

It was kind of an odd summer, because Jason is half quitting, half getting kicked out of Nirvana; meanwhile, Hiro is leaving Soundgarden, and then Jason tries out for Soundgarden; and I'm trying out for Nirvana. And at the same time, Pickerel and Lanegan and Kurt and Krist had a band doing all Leadbelly covers. So there was a weird musical chairs thing going on.

JASON EVERMAN After Nirvana, it's not like I had a Plan B; it's not even like being in a rock band was a Plan A. It just kind of happened. I had money in the bank from fishing at the time, so I was planning on traveling. Then Kim Thayil called me and told me, "Hiro's quitting. We're auditioning people. Do you want to audition?"

SUSAN SILVER It's not an easy life, sleeping on strangers' floors. And Hiro just didn't like it, and he really appreciated the indie scene, it seemed like. He wasn't as interested in growing when the band signed to a major label.

I know it was very inconvenient when he left in the middle of touring Europe. I was on the tour with them, and I remember having to cancel the rest of the tour, get everybody home, and figure out how we were going to pay for it, which was usually on my mom's credit card. Sorry, Mom, ruined your credit there for a while.

HIRO YAMAMOTO We're getting bigger and the pressures were mounting. A&M is telling us, "We want you to tour like 10 months. You gotta go out and hit the road." That was more than I wanted, but I told the guys, "Look, we got to where we are by making our own choices, and now we're on this major label and they're tellin' us this stuff. We don't have to do what they tell us." I didn't want to live on the road. But they wanted to do it.

I liked Terry Date, who did *Louder Than Love,* but he was a metal producer. The label wanted to sell us to heavy-metal stations. I thought we were different than that. Sure, I'd like to sell a million records and live in a castle and not have to work, but at the same time, I want to be able to say, "This is me. I'm not just part of a mass-marketing machine." Maybe I'm being naive, but when we got to that point where we're on the major label, you're a product. You might as well be Ivory Snow or Clorox bleach. We were just another product for the heavy-metal market. I like metal and all. It's way more complex than "Hiro didn't like metal."

It affected my friendships with everyone in the band a lot. It really hurt Kim that I would leave.

KIM THAYIL His reasons for leaving would probably be different from what we saw. The band and friends of Hiro's perceived that he was very heavily involved in this relationship with his girlfriend at the time, who he later married and had a couple of kids with. He really hated touring. That kind of discomfort with being with a bunch of beer-drinking, guitar-wielding guys in a van when he'd rather be with his girlfriend was sometimes expressed in an agitated manner, which caused friction with the band.

I didn't want him to quit. Chris didn't, Matt didn't. He had been threatening it enough: "I want to quit, I want to go home." Eventually, Chris said, "Fine. You keep voicing your dissatisfaction. I'm tired of hearing it. Just leave." But Chris didn't want him to leave at all. Chris just wanted him to stop complaining. We didn't take what Hiro was saying too seriously. Hiro liked to bitch. But Chris calling him on it forced his hand. I think everyone was bummed out, but I might've been the most bummed out, because I moved out to Seattle with the guy.

> ✱ ✱ ✱

DANIEL HOUSE Ben was definitely the resident alcoholic in Skin Yard, and that was a point of contention between he and I. Maybe for me, that tied back to the fact that my father had been an alcoholic, so I had limited capacity for that sort of thing. On any tour that we ever went on, the first order of business was stop by 7-Eleven and get a six-pack or a half case of beer. So within the first half hour of any trip, Ben was drinking. Initially we'd have to stop every 30 minutes so he could go piss. Eventually we said, "If you're going to drink, you need to arrange something different." So he'd pee in in a Big Gulp cup, and every couple hours, he'd either throw it or dump it out the window.

One time we were in Chicago, after our last show on a tour, and we decided we were gonna make a straight-shot drive home. It was a 42-hour drive, and it was like 2 or 3 in the morning and I agreed to take the first shift of driving, and Ben had managed to get some meth. So I did a little line of crystal, and he did some crystal because he was gonna stay awake with me. And he was all excited because he got a half case of beer from the bar. It was like 35 degrees out or something and our heater didn't work, so me and Ben are both wrapped in our sleeping bags as best we can.

Maybe an hour into the drive, Ben unrolls the window to throw out his cup and this blast of cold, cold air comes rushing into the van and everyone's like, "Roll up the fuckin' window, Ben!" He throws the cup out and the next bit is basically one of those slow-motion moments where I remember looking over and seeing the cup do like two 360s out of the window. The top comes off, the entire contents of this Big Gulp cup come rushing in through the window, hitting Ben squarely in his face, completely drenching his hair and the top quarter of his sleeping bag. And there was nothing he could do because it was freezing so he couldn't take his pee-soaked sleeping bag off, and now he's wet in his own piss.

And so everybody is howling with laughter because after dealing with an entire fucking tour or two of him peeing in cups and the inconvenience of it all, and the cup getting spilled every so often, it just felt like he finally got his due. Karma's a bitch, motherfucker.

JACK ENDINO Daniel will never let that story go. I remember it because Ben was reading one of my paperbacks at the time. My paperback had this yellow stain on it afterwards. I was like, "Uh, thanks."

DANIEL HOUSE Then there was the Tour from Hell. It was just one of those tours that I can't imagine things possibly being worse. Our then-drummer, Scott McCullum . . . how to be polite about this? He was beyond difficult that tour. He was not playing very well, he was constantly missing cues and coming in at the wrong places. The main reason was he was drinking excessively.

SCOTT McCULLUM Oh, yeah, Ben and I were just fucking blotto on that tour all the time. I don't remember it being that out of control, not like the way it was later on in Gruntruck—we used to call ourselves Drunktruck. No, I don't think it affected my playing. I play rather well when I'm drunk.

DANIEL HOUSE Scott and I had one physical altercation, but it was actually on another tour. As idiotic as it seems now, looking back, it was over a girl. There was this woman that I had hooked up with kind of on and off over the course of probably a couple years. And when I'd been with her, it had been before I was with my son's mother, and I have to admit, also after I was with my son's mother. And I had just gotten into a place where I was like, I can't keep doing this. This is wrong.

So I was in San Francisco and this woman wanted to get together, and I just said, "I can't." And rather than just accept that, she started flirting really heavily with Scott right in front of me. I confronted them both and he totally fuckin' blew up. He basically had me pinned against the wall, with his fist cocked back, on the verge of punching me in the face.

SCOTT MCCULLUM I didn't really know the history between Daniel and this woman other than that they knew each other. So I get there, and we end up hooking up, so to speak—you know, hanging out and stuff. I can't remember what words I exchanged with Daniel, but I finally got so angry I pushed him into the street, and he almost got hit by a car. Not a smart move, but it was just in the moment.

JACK ENDINO Scott lasted for two years. We did have one more album in the can at the time—it's a very angry record, *Fist Sized Chunks.* Bruise Records put it out, and for about 14 months there were no Skin Yard shows.

SCOTT MCCULLUM The tour definitely took its toll. But ultimately, it was the songwriting. It got to the point where I saw a different vision. I think Ben did, too. And this is when we started to collaborate on songs. Ben and I were staying down in Arizona, and we had written that song "Paint." We meant it to be a Skin Yard song, but we thought, They're going to fucking destroy this thing. It's not going to come out how we want it. And that's how Gruntruck started to form.

JACK ENDINO During the 14 months when Skin Yard weren't a band, I tried out for Soundgarden. I just pestered them about it: "Come on. I can play bass." I went over to jam with 'em one night. It was pleasant, but it was like, "Thanks, but no thanks." I come to find out later that Daniel had tried out, too. *(Laughs.)*

BEN SHEPHERD What's funny is that the Soundgarden guys asked me to try out the day after Nirvana had asked me. "Well, Nirvana asked me to try out before you did, so I have to try out for them first."

I had no way of learning Soundgarden's songs, really. I had a cassette, but I didn't have anywhere to play music. I even had to borrow a bass to play; I'd never really played bass before. We didn't talk at the tryout. I just walked up and turned the amp up and we jammed for two hours instead of learning the songs from *Louder Than Love,* which we should've been doing. I came back again, more earnestly this time—tried to learn the songs with them—and then they chose Jason.

I found out while walking to a show with my then-girlfriend. I see Stuart Hallerman, Soundgarden's sound guy, and he told me. It was pretty logical. Jason looked the part—he had long, curly hair—and he somehow knew some of their songs. And he could drink. I was 20 and couldn't, legally.

"Yeah, that figures," I go. "Watch, in six months they'll come back and get me." And almost six months to the day, they did. Why did I think he wouldn't last? Because I knew Jason. I went through junior high and high school with him. He just didn't seem to be cut out for touring and being part of a group. He's more of an incompatible individual. Plus, when I said that, I was being a smart-ass. Because everyone always treated me like that. I was always the second choice.

JASON EVERMAN All those guys were about five years older than me, which when you're 19 and they're 25 is a big difference. So I wasn't hanging out with them socially then. I kind of had 'em on a pedestal, as well, because they were my favorite Seattle band. There was definitely a little bit of a feeling of being an outsider.

The energy of the band? God, how do I put this? The band was being managed by Chris's girlfriend or wife. Nice woman. So there's Chris's gig, and the rest of the band's. There was definitely a two-tier system going. In retrospect, I understand it. Chris, he was the star. For me, there was a sense of inequity.

BEN SHEPHERD Kurt and Krist had asked me to try out. Chad never told them I even played guitar. That's why Kurt was like, "Man, we would've never messed around with Jason had we known you played guitar!" So I went on an American tour with them, but I never played with them, because they only performed *Bleach* and I'd only rehearsed the songs that were going to be on *Nevermind*. Why? Because that's what they wanted to practice.

Was it frustrating? Of course. I like playing music. But it was cool with me to be able to watch my friends knock people over. I was helping them load in and out, trying to sell shirts for them. I always thought they should be a three-piece anyway.

CHAPTER 19
ALL ABOUT KICKS

TAD DOYLE When we were touring with Nirvana in Europe in '89, we had a 48-day schedule, of which we played 45 days. We had three days off, and they were travel days. It was during the winter, and I wasn't the only one that was having problems with barfing and other gastrointestinal difficulties. It was probably a combination of dehydration, too much smoking, drinking, poor health, and bad water.

Kurt Cobain would hold a bucket or a garbage can for me to vomit in. We'd rate it, by chunk size and what the velocity was, what the color was, what the consistency was. "Oh, that was a good one." He laughed a lot; he loved it. When your insides are just wrenching, it takes a lot out of you. But I was laughing my ass off, too, in between blowing chunks.

CRAIG MONTGOMERY There were nine of us packed in this small van, so we're sitting shoulder to shoulder, all cramped on these long drives. It was the band members and me and Edwin Heath, who was our tour manager from the Dutch agency Paperclip.

The main thing about that tour was just laughing. It was always, "What could we do that would be funny?" Like somehow they got hold of some Arnold Schwarzenegger exercise video, and Kurt Cobain made a cassette tape of Arnold Schwarzenegger saying things like "Sexy, slim waist" over and over. During some of the shows, my instructions were that whenever there was a gap between songs, I would bring this cassette in, so between Nirvana songs you'd hear Arnold Schwarzenegger going, "Sexy, slim waist."

KURT DANIELSON I grew up in a small town, and my whole thing was to get away from there, not just the physical limits of the town but the psychological limits, the mind-set of the place. And so I went to school and got my degree. And then I turn around and find myself in a band projecting this image of precisely what I tried to escape. So this white-trash aesthetic was very ironic for me. Later, as I studied it from an intellectual standpoint, I began to be fascinated by certain aspects of it, especially all the characters that I knew in my hometown.

The best conversation I had on the subject was in Europe with Kurt Cobain, because he had the very same experience in his small town. I would tell him about the freaks that I knew, and then he would tell me about the freaks he knew, and we'd go back and forth, talking for hours. For instance, there was this short, drunk guy I knew named Freaky Freddy who wore a purple-felt 10-gallon hat. One time when I was about 16, I was driving at night looking for him, because he would buy booze for you. I would've run over him had I not seen him passed out, spread-eagle, in the middle of the road. I pulled him into my car, revived him, brought him to the liquor store. He bought me booze, I let him go, and then he passed out again in the liquor store parking lot.

STEVE WIEDERHOLD (a.k.a. Steve Wied; TAD drummer) I shared a room with Kurt Cobain, just the two of us, toward the end of the tour, and he didn't talk to me. Seemed like he had a stomachache all the time, like he was suffering.

I shared a lot of rooms with Chad Channing, laughing all night about the stupidest stuff we could think of. And I'll tell you one thing: Me and Chad came up with this story about selling kids for food. We were joking about it: "We came up with this really funny story last night, and it was about selling kids for food!" And it's probably because of us that line ended up in a Nirvana song.

CRAIG MONTGOMERY The guy you didn't want to room with was Tad because he snored really loud. So people were like, "*Ohh*, I roomed with Tad *last night*."

KURT DANIELSON When we took the ferry over from England, we used that opportunity to get blind drunk, at least Krist and I did. When we got to the hotel in Holland, Krist was just lying there on the floor of their lobby; he wouldn't move. He said something like, "Hey, you faggots!" to the proprietors. He didn't mean it personally. Nobody knew the proprietors were gay, but they were, and they kicked us out.

STEVE WIEDERHOLD Krist would drink a whole big bottle of wine every single night. But that night was the only time he was ever really out of control. Something snapped. He ran out of the van and got up on this rooftop right above one of those canals that's only about a foot deep, and he was gonna jump. And we're out there for like half an hour trying to talk him down. And he's yelling at God and the world, and he's pissed off at everything. I'm like, "This is getting to be a headache. This guy is a lot of work!"

But by later that same night, Krist seemed to be normal again. That's when I shared a room with Krist and Kurt. They said, "Wow, we wish we had a drummer like you." Hinting. Hinting. It was already out that Chad wasn't working out, you know. I said, "I can't hear anything that Kurt Danielson's playing on bass anyway." That was kind of a way to say, "I wish I could play with a bass player like you." But I didn't say it right. They liked my drumming, so I don't know. It could've happened.

KURT DANIELSON The day the Berlin Wall went down, we drove into East Berlin. The line of Trabant cars leaving East Germany was 40 kilometers long, and most of them were broken down. And the West Germans were rewarding the East Germans with baskets of fruits and bottles of champagne.

KRIST NOVOSELIC We played another show in the West, then ended up in Hamburg the next night. Hamburg is known for its entertainment district, the Reeperbahn: full of strip clubs, porno stores, and brothels. Now it was packed with little Trabants and their newly liberated owners. Oh yes, the freedoms of the West! The TAD dudes dragged me into a porno shop to show me the most disgusting porno ever. The photos had people smeared with feces having sex. I literally ran out of the shop screaming!

KURT DANIELSON I remember one night in Germany, we were staying in an old hostel that obviously had been an officers' barracks at some point in its past. And for that reason, Krist had nightmares that he was in a Nazi concentration camp. Krist sleepwalks, and he was sharing a room that night with Kurt. He actually punched Kurt, thinking he was a Nazi!

JONATHAN PONEMAN Bruce and I flew to Europe, the idea being that we were hoping to provide some kind of support as they were entering the last week of their tour, which was going to climax with a big Sub Pop Lamefest, with Nirvana, TAD, and Mudhoney, at the Astoria in London.

MEGAN JASPER Bruce and Jonathan went to Europe to see TAD and Nirvana, and as soon as we knew they were gone, we took every bit of furniture in the Sub Pop office and pushed it aside and made a big dance floor. We'd blast music and do dance-offs and gymnastics. We did cartwheels, flips, somersaults, all of us acting like three-year-olds.

JONATHAN PONEMAN We arrived in Rome and went to the show. TAD and Nirvana were obviously worn out. Kurt had broken and repaired his guitar so many times that it was the second or third song into his set that his guitar just completely came apart. He smashed his guitar once and for all and climbed up on the mains, and he looked like he was ready to jump off, which would've been disastrous both for the people he would've landed on and for him.

BRUCE PAVITT The guy had a nervous breakdown right in front of everybody, and it was really scary. Everybody was freaking out, but they managed to talk him down.

I remember going to the guitar shop with Kurt and Jon and coming up with $150 or whatever for another guitar. And it was $150 that we barely had. And instead of him driving up to England, we all took a train together. People would oftentimes give us a hard time about being so broke, but what they also have to realize is that a lot of our money was spent on bailing bands out like that.

ANTON BROOKES Sub Pop had flown into Italy to see them play, and they must have come business-class or something. I just remember that there was a big hoo-ha about it because the bands thought they were suffering on the road to make Sub Pop money and that Sub Pop was squandering it. That was probably the first sign of any discontent within the label.

BRUCE PAVITT Did we need to go to Rome? No. Did we need to go to England? Yes, I do think so, because there's a lot of media and press there. The U.K. Lamefest really broke the scene internationally—our bands got on the cover of the *NME*—just like the first Lamefest broke the scene in Seattle.

EVERETT TRUE I've spoken to quite a few people who were at Lamefest, and everyone's got a different opinion. Some people thought, That's the worst concert I've ever seen Nirvana play, and other people thought, That was the greatest show I ever saw them play. I'm not sure musically Nirvana were up to anything at all that night, but they realized that, so they just trashed the stage, absolutely left it completely wiped clean of anything: amplifiers, guitars, drums.

ANTON BROOKES Nirvana stole the show, basically. Kurt threw himself around the stage like a man possessed. Afterwards his knees would be all cut and bruised. I always remember thinking, We're going to have to get him some knee pads. Looking back on it, it was obviously one of the key points in Nirvana's history. That was the gauntlet that they laid down to everybody: Take us seriously; we can play.

KURT DANIELSON By the time Mudhoney played, I was really totaled. Billy, the drummer for the Cosmic Psychos, and I decided to try to rip Lukin's pants off, but Lukin had these really tight black jeans on and his belt was fastened in some really arcane manner. So we're onstage, like a couple of deer in some headlights, and we decide to throw him into the crowd instead. Then we went in after him. At the same time,

Tad came out and threw Dan way out into the crowd. Mark was hiding under the drum riser. Or was that Steve? It was Tad, Bill, Dan, Lukin, me out there.

I remember that crowd was so dense. You didn't sink down to the floor for a long time. We were lucky none of us got killed or ended up with a broken neck. It was thrilling; it was all about kicks. Those were the days.

CHAPTER 20
SMELL THE MAGIC

MEGAN JASPER I moved from Northampton, Massachusetts, to Seattle in 1989. I had been on tour with Dinosaur Jr., selling their merch and doing random stuff. I came on as Sub Pop's first receptionist. In the morning when we got in, there would be all these messages from Courtney Love from the night before: *"Where the fuck are you? Fucking call me back, it's Courtney,"* and all different variations of that. She would call constantly, whether we were in the office or not. She wanted a record out on Sub Pop, and we eventually did a seven-inch with Hole. I have to give it to her—her drive and her ambition were so intense.

COURTNEY LOVE (singer/guitarist for Los Angeles's Hole; Kurt Cobain's widow; Frances Bean Cobain's mother; actress) In any scene I've been in, whether it's Minneapolis or Liverpool or Seattle or Portland or L.A. or New York, I've always been the fucking most ambitious one in some weird way. And I've always been the one that didn't really fit in with what everyone else was doing, and I'm pretty proud of that. We were not grunge. The bands that were labeled that were Mudhoney and Nirvana, Soundgarden, TAD, that shit. Sometimes, when it was all "grunge this" and "grunge that," I wished we were a grunge band, because we would maybe sell more. At the same time, the name was always retarded and I knew it would date, and that's the last thing a prodigious person needs.

But Hole wasn't grunge. I wasn't allowed to be then, why should I be ghettoized now? No, I'm asking you, it's not a rhetorical question. You find me one fuckin' article that says that Hole was a grunge band in 1991, '92, '93, '94, or '95 and I'll give you a hundred bucks.

ERIC ERLANDSON (guitarist for Los Angeles's Hole) First we were called "foxcore" by Thurston Moore, and then we started to be lumped into Riot Grrrl. With the grunge thing, I always thought we weren't really a part of it, but the press wanted a label, so eventually you'd start seeing in a magazine, like, "Grunge Rock: Hole."

MEGAN JASPER Courtney would call all the time, and I would try not to talk to her all the time. There was nobody who wanted to talk to Courtney for the 48th time. Except we had this kid Rob who started at Sub Pop and had worked at Doctor Dream Records in Southern California. So we called him Doctor Dream, because he was kind of a nerdy kid. He was more than happy to talk to Courtney.

COURTNEY LOVE The two times I went to Seattle previous to being successful as a musician were really frightening. The first time there was a guy named Vinny up on Capitol Hill with a huge abscess in his leg, and then when I came down from Alaska, after I went up there to gather my thoughts, because I was 24 and if I hadn't succeeded by the time I was 25 I was pretty much gonna jump off a roof. I spent three fuckin' months in Alaska in the dark, in a trailer writing lyrics and working a fuckin' six-hour shift at PJ's, a strip club that fishermen go to.

I got off the bus in Seattle and saw a U-Men poster and a Mudhoney poster, and I got one block from the Greyhound station and went, "No way. They will throw me out of town or I will die." So I got back on that bus. Why? Just instinct, man. Just instinct. I felt like it was a dangerous place. It's got death in it. For someone like you, it probably appears to be a nice town. Like it's all holistic and trees and arboretums. Bullshit! What I know about Seattle is dark, dark drug stuff, dark, dark money stuff. Fuckin' lumber, fuckin' corruption, fuckin' heroin, fuckin' scary!

MEGAN JASPER We told Courtney that Bruce and Jon weren't doing A&R anymore, that Doctor Dream was doing it, and we would just direct her calls to him. I really got the sense that he enjoyed chatting with her. She *is* bright and funny. It's not like she was horrible and screaming at us. That came afterwards, when thankfully I wasn't there.

NILS BERNSTEIN The heart of Sub Pop was always the receptionist. It was Megan for a while, and then it was Kim Warnick from the Fastbacks. When I think of Sub Pop back then, I think of Megan. Megan and Kim have similar styles, as far as talking back to people on the phone or playing practical jokes. To me, they really set the tone of the label as much as any fuckin' marketing plan.

MEGAN JASPER I was in the poor man's version of Dickless. When Kelly Canary left, the other girls didn't want to stop, so they must have hit a level of desperation and they asked me. The funnest shows were when you could provoke someone in the audience and they would get really upset. My sister had made me this wand, which I called the Herpes Wand; if I touched someone with it, they got the herpes. So at shows, I kept giving people wand herpes. Some people loved it, and some people thought it was the worst thing in the entire world. Mark Arm didn't seem to mind; Krist Novoselic didn't seem to mind. The funny thing was, all the girls made a mental note of everyone who bitched about it: Don't kiss that guy, because you know he just had a herpes outbreak.

COURTNEY LOVE I moved to L.A., and I had about six months left ticking on my 25-year-old clock, so I was hurrying as fast as I could to put songs together and to put a band together. I became acquainted with the ins and outs of the grotesque L.A. scene: the Bordello and Taime Downe and girls named Marilyn that Axl bought pink Corvettes for. Just the Strip. Strip culture.

I remember being in Portland once and looking at a "Love Buzz" seven-inch and a Cat Butt single. I still don't like that Kurt's wearing a Harley-Davidson shirt on the cover of "Love Buzz." It was just so part of the Strip, and it signified to me that he was trying to fit in, like that guy Jason in his band who had long hair and was doin' whatever the fuck he could to make it. I didn't like that Kurt was wearing a Harley-Davidson shirt, so I bought the Cat Butt single instead.

MEGAN JASPER When I moved to Seattle, I used to go to this bar called the Comet Tavern on Capitol Hill. I was in there with the Dickless girls and a bunch of other people who were giving me the scoop on Seattle, and one of the first pieces of advice I got was, "Whatever you do, don't fuck anybody in Cat Butt. They just went on tour with L7." Apparently L7 liked to enjoy themselves with a lot of men, and it was implied that if you went on tour with them you had some skanky experience.

STEVE TURNER That trip with L7 was legendary for Cat Butt. I remember getting the heebie-jeebies hearing about it. Like, Ughhh!

JAMES BURDYSHAW I was the first person from Cat Butt that L7 met, so the whole L7–Cat Butt connection happened because of me. It was on Cat Butt's first tour, in January/February of '89, and a lot of crazy shit happened—sex, drugs, debauchery, acid, weirdness. In L.A., we went to the NoMeansNo show at Raji's. Our drummer Erik ["Erok" Peterson] and Dean and I got super-fuckin' drunk and started flippin' the singer shit, even though we love NoMeansNo. All of a sudden, this real cute girl keeps comin' up to me and goin', "Hey. Hey. Hey. Who are you?"

It turns out it's Jennifer Finch from L7. So I go to where she's staying, with her bandmate Dee [Plakas], and this guy who Dee was dating or friends with. I'm waitin' for them to go to bed so I can make out with Jennifer. And this dude sits in the chair and waits for me to fall asleep. He won't leave me alone with her. I can't remember his name, but I'll always fuckin' be pissed at that bastard, 'cause that was my one chance to hook up with Finch.

The *only* reason why that connection was created was because Jennifer was flirtin' with me. Though Jennifer might deny the whole episode even happened.

JENNIFER FINCH (bassist for Los Angeles's L7) I had just met a girl whose mom was dating Bruce Pavitt, so she gave me the phone number for her mom. This is kind of how it went when L7 would book shows—you just get a phone number and call. Danny Bland, who was in Cat Butt, answered the phone at Sub Pop, and we started talking and I sent him a promo pack with a cassette, and he set up a show with Cat Butt.

DANNY BLAND Shortly after I moved there, Dave Duet got in touch with me and wanted me to join Cat Butt. I replaced John Michael Amerika. Dave and I had met in Phoenix, when the U-Men had come through; he was their roadie or driver or whatever. We were thick as thieves right away. I've always been fond of lunatics, and he's quite obviously one from the get-go.

DAVID DUET Mike was a sweetheart and the greatest guy in the world, but he had a drug problem. We were gonna play Squid Row, and I wasn't living with Lisa anymore; she was still at the Blaine House, which became a notorious house and was constantly being watched by cops. I was over and there was a knock at the front door, and there are two cops asking for Mike, using a fake name he used. And we're like, "Uh, I think he left town." And they were like, "Oh, really?" and lift up a Cat Butt flyer for Squid Row. They're like, "We'll just catch him at the next show then." So not only did they know him, they knew I was the singer.

So Tom Price agreed to play Squid Row and the next Vogue show. And after that, people were comin' up to me after shows saying stuff like, "He owes me 60 bucks, can I get it from you?" I had to kick Mike out of the band. It was one of the hardest things I ever did.

DANNY BLAND Every band that I ever was in, my main thing was to go on tour. So Cat Butt was doing West Coast runs and going into Texas and all that. That got the attention of Bruce and Jonathan, because a lot of other bands were not touring, and we were the biggest fuckups around, and for some reason we could get it together enough to go on tour. One day they just sat me down and asked, "How?" I explained that I had this Rolodex of phone numbers, people that I knew, and I'd just call and set up shows. So they asked me to do booking for Sub Pop.

JAMES BURDYSHAW I get back from that tour and all of a sudden I'm at a party in Seattle and guess who's with Danny? Jennifer. I was like, "What the fuck are you doin' up here?"

"Oh, I'm just visiting. I'm hangin' out with Danny." I put two and two together and realized that they'd shacked up, and I was like, "Oh man, how come he gets her?" I didn't realize at the time how entrepreneurial, shall we say, she can be. She was basically trying to find out, What's happening in Seattle and how can I get L7 involved?

JENNIFER FINCH We were received incredibly well in Seattle. Sub Pop gave us the single of the month. Sub Pop as the tastemakers declared this was the next thing. Eventually we went up to Seattle so much that people in Los Angeles thought we were from Seattle.

DANNY BLAND Before that tour with L7, we did shows together in California. Yeah, somewhere along the road, I woke up on top of Jennifer one morning, I guess. *(Laughs.)* My girlfriend, Kerry Green, who was in Dickless at the time, found out. Yes, that was awkward. Awkward, disastrous, all that good stuff.

L7 were badasses. They were guys. They were an all-male female rock-and-roll band. They fuckin' smelled as bad as we did.

MEGAN JASPER L7 came into the Sub Pop office, and I think I told you how we would rate bands on how much they smelled? No? It wasn't an official list, but our accountant, Geoff Kirk, would make jokes and write it down. L7 were on the list, but Babes in Toyland were the smelliest. Geoff actually followed them around one time with a Glade air-freshener, spraying them.

Nirvana was also on the list. Those were the three biggies. It was mostly the drummer, Chad. One time it smelled so bad in the office when Nirvana was there—it was beyond a human smell; it smelled like yeast or something—and everyone was trying to open the windows. Because I didn't think it was a person, I said, "What is that smell?!" And Chad said, "Oh, I think it's me."

JAMES BURDYSHAW Donita named our big tour together Swapping Fluids Across America. Why? Guess. Donita was with Dean, and Danny was with Jennifer. It lasted about seven weeks, across the entire country. It was five of us, four of them, plus a roadie, all in the same vehicle. It was like the fuckin' Partridge Family. We had this Aeroporter bus, which we painted metallic gray. It looked like a big bullet, but Donita called it the Poon Tank. L7 loved crackin' sex jokes.

Donita was very down-to-earth and really interested in me as a friend. I would have liked it to be more, but that's not what ended up happening. She and Dean had a relationship for a while that started from that mini-tour. I was really bummed. Dean always got the girls. He was very confident, he's tall as fuck, and he had a mane of flowing red hair. I mean, I was a redhead, but you couldn't even notice that I was, being in a band with him.

DEAN GUNDERSON Donita was a pretty amazing character. Real excitable, really intuitive. We liked each other a lot.

JENNIFER FINCH There were lots of fluids being swapped. A few members of L7 were dating a few members of Cat Butt. There was a lot of alcohol. There was a lot of vomiting. James had terrible intestinal trauma on that tour.

JAMES BURDYSHAW I ended up having stomach flu really bad. I kept shitting my pants. The first show of the tour was in Kansas City, and Donita took me to a drugstore, and we bought some fuckin' Depends. I was humiliated. The show where I was wearing the Depends, everything seemed fine until right at the end, literally the last fuckin' chord. That's when I said, "Oh, shit," which is hilarious because I just shit. Nobody knew except for David, and he was laughin'.

DANNY BLAND I remember thinking, I'll probably never be on a tour that's this fucking crazy ever again. Because it was not only the regular disasters that go along with a tour on that level, like the van breaking down. Cat Butt were a roving gang, and anybody who fuckin' looked sideways at the girls fuckin' risked a pummeling.

JAMES BURDYSHAW We go to this place called the Bar of Soap, a laundromat and bar in Dallas. Some Chuck Norris–lookin' fucker was talkin' to our friend Kathy Kowgirl from Houston, and he must've said something that was really rude 'cause she threw her drink at him, and the next thing I know, this drunken dumbass with blond feathered hair and a mustache punched her right in the face. I just jumped on him, grabbed him around the neck, and he flew to the ground, then everybody else ran up on him and started punching him and kicking him. David grabbed him and threw him outside. Danny and David were just fuckin' him up. Fuckin' bashed his face in. The guy was so drunk he didn't even know what hit him.

DAVID DUET When we were in New York, L7 were walking up ahead of us, and all of a sudden the girls were being harassed by a group of Puerto Rican teenagers, all carrying backpacks. So Danny and I step up to be the gentlemen and the protectors, and the kids whip hatchets out of their backpacks! One of the kids swings at Danny and breaks the bottom of his beer off. We were tripping on psychedelics, and at that point all the Cat Butt guys just started dying laughing. And then the girls started laughing. And then the guys with the hatchets started laughing. They put away their hatchets and walked away, laughing their heads off.

DANNY BLAND Where does someone all of the sudden pull out a hatchet in New York? We were magnets for trouble, and we liked it that way.

JENNIFER FINCH Donita got stabbed in New York, where we were staying at Janet Billig's house. Donita was in the bus and some gal from that neighborhood who didn't really want a big bus with people like us in it—weird rockers or junkies or white people, I'm not even sure—just reached into the van and stabbed her through the window and then came into the van to continue trying to assault her.

DAVID DUET That same night with the kids with the hatchets, I get back to the bus and I see a Latin couple, very tough and streetwise, walking past our bus, and one of the windows was slit open. Donita had been climbing into her bunk in her leopard-skin underwear and the girl starts screaming at Donita, "You bitch! You bitch!" Accusing Donita of trying to seduce her man. Erik, Dean, and our roadie are on the bus, and the guy comes onto the bus first, screaming. They jump up and start wrestling with the guy. Donita runs up behind them to see what's going on and the woman whips out a straight razor, goes in between the guy's legs, and slashes Donita's knee open. She was going for Donita's crotch, but Donita sees it coming, jumps backwards, and it slashes her knee.

At the same time this is going down, a couple of car spaces up, two guys gangland-assassinate another guy right on the street, in the back of the head. *Bam!*

DEAN GUNDERSON Donita waved down the ambulance that came by. They were like, "We're looking for some guy that got shot in the head, but we'll take you." In the hospital waiting room, there was a woman who was not mentally completely there crying the entire time right next to me. She had some snot dripping from her nose, and it kept getting longer and longer and longer and longer. I was on LSD the entire time, but it wasn't the drugs. It was actually happening. It got to like a foot and a half long, just dangling there. At that point, I was like hypnotized. It was swinging around and it hit her mouth and she sucked it up.

Donita had a limp the rest of the tour, but she had a pretty good sense of humor. She was always saying, "Wait up for the gimp!"

DANNY BLAND Several of us were indulging in hardcore narcotics. I remember walking around Detroit looking for heroin in a neighborhood where cars were literally on fire, and there were no firemen or police even *thinking* about coming into that neighborhood. The person we were staying with was an assistant to a veterinarian or something, so she had all of these needles, but they were these giant fucking horse needles or something. I don't know if they were made for basting a turkey or what, but those needles were quite ineffective.

DAVID DUET There was an agreement amongst the L7 camp that there would be no hard-drug use, but not everybody participated in that. There was no agreement in Cat Butt about that. *(Laughs.)* Danny and I were dabblers. Jennifer was a little more ahead of the game. She was kind of an instigator. It really didn't come into play until Detroit. Crazy night in Detroit. If I'm not mistaken, we saw a pimp shot that night. We saw a lot of gunplay. I'm not clear on the events of that night, but I know that was the beginning of the rest of L7 being not so happy with Jennifer.

JENNIFER FINCH I barely remember the tour. I was on so much heroin. Actually not when I was on the tour. I used maybe twice, when I was in larger cities, so you'd think I'd remember more.

DAVID DUET Actually, there wasn't that much hard-drug use on the tour. When we were in the band, there was the image that we were doing all these drugs, but we actually weren't. We put that image out in interviews and stuff and tried to seem like the craziest people alive, but we're actually not. We were quite un-drug-involved then. Especially considering our peers at the time. Our peers just kept it on the down low.

JAMES BURDYSHAW I'd quit doin' hard needle drugs in spring of '88. I never was addicted 'cause I couldn't shoot myself up—I'd have a friend do it for me—and I couldn't afford it and it was scary to me. I liked the high, but I didn't like the process. I was afraid of death and still am. I quit after my roommate shot me up with a speedball and I started hyperventilating. When I came down, I thought about John Michael and all the people he had ripped off and how brown his teeth were and how he used to scratch himself all the time, and I was like, I'm not gonna do this drug anymore.

DANNY BLAND One of the most amazing things is that Suzi Gardner from L7 was clean and sober that whole time. At the time, I had never heard of anybody being sober. I was like, "Explain this to me." She kind of did, and it still didn't compute. Goddamn, that girl really loves playing music, or else she would've ran screaming from that van.

DEAN GUNDERSON About two-thirds of the way through, Donita and I broke up. I was young and dumb and having someone like me that much freaked me out. I was pretty much a 20-year-old bimbo.

DANNY BLAND I always thought that Cat Butt should've been documented more on film than on record. Our M.O. was just to get as annihilated as possible and rock out. It was a very volatile situation, and often there were fistfights on stage between band members. If I recall, the fights were between James and David, in some fake struggle for fake leadership of some completely retarded and dysfunctional rock-and-roll band.

JAMES BURDYSHAW We get to L.A., and by this time I was not getting along with David. We were getting into shouting matches and fights. He liked to pick on me a lot. My bandmates would tease me all the time, talk shit about me. When Donita told me, "I've never seen a lead guitar player treated with so much disrespect," that's when it really started to make me feel like I couldn't take it anymore.

In my mind, David and me were supposed to be the leaders of the band, and instead it was David and Danny. Danny was the newest member of the band and he could barely play the guitar, and I was writing all of the songs, everything on that Cat Butt record except for a few little bits.

We finally get back to Seattle and played a welcome-home show that nobody came to. It was like the worst attendance we've ever had. *This* is welcome home?

Then the Babes in Toyland come to town, and I started a mini-fling with the bass player, Michelle Leon. Beautiful girl. We were hanging out, and they played a Halloween show with Lubricated Goat. Somebody had some fuckin' mushrooms and I got really high, and we were all in the Babes in Toyland van headin' to this party. I'm trying to give directions, but I'm really wasted, and David and Dean are also in the van, and David says, "Don't listen to him, he doesn't know a goddamn thing" to the girl that I'm trying to impress, and I just went off. I started yelling, "Fuck you!" All of a sudden David punched me in the face.

I got out of the van, and I told Dean, "I'm quittin' this band!" We were so high. Michelle and Guy Maddison from Lubricated Goat run up to me, "Are you okay?" Michelle told me, "Don't play with that asshole. Fuckin' quit his band." And I did.

DAVID DUET How can I put this delicately? It's no secret that James can be a very hard person to work with, and I really made strong efforts. Tried to be very diplomatic. But at times I couldn't handle it. It was Halloween night, and I punched him. James was bein' a prick. I was drunk. I think there were psychedelics involved.

Then things started getting weird. Drugs were becoming more prevalent in the Seattle scene. I decided to get away from Seattle 'cause everybody was getting incredibly strung out. I checked myself into a five-day-detox wino hospital. Stayed there about three days. L7 was playing down the street, and I convinced the nurse to let me out, that it would be better for me to go play rock and roll, and she did. It was amazing. I hobbled down the street, got on stage with L7, did a Frank Sinatra version of "Strychnine" 'cause I was so looped out from all the medications they had me on, jumped in the van with L7, went to Canada. Came back from Canada, packed up all my stuff. Flew down to Texas for what was gonna be a month visit and ended up staying for four years.

CHAPTER 21
RAISE YOUR CANDLE HIGH

KEVIN WOOD The last time I saw Andy alive? I remember that distinctly because it happened to fall on the third day of the third month, 1990. He'd set up a deal where he was gonna get a solo album, and he invited me to do preproduction rough mixes for it. So he was pulling me back in and rectifying things.

After working on preproduction that day, we were heading downtown when we ran into Regan just by chance. We mentioned that it was a 3/3 day, that's about it. It wasn't a long meeting. And that was the last time me and Regan and Andy were together.

XANA LA FUENTE Andy and I had gone to see Aerosmith Wednesday night, but we didn't go backstage and meet them. We were with all the other kids that buy the book at the show with pictures of the band. On Friday, all the members of the band except Steven Tyler and Joe Perry came into my store. And I said, "We came to your show. What are you guys still doing here?" They spend about $3,000, and I gave them a Mother Love Bone tape. I said, "We're touring with you in a few weeks in Europe," and they were like, "Yeah, we're really excited."

That's the day I came home and found him.

DAVID DUET I saw Andy that day, at the Denny Street House. There was a drug dealer that lived there. I saw him copping. That was really weird. He was one of those people you did not expect.

MIKE STARR That day I walked into Kelly Curtis's basement, and Andy was there. I said, "What's up Andy? How ya doin'?"

"I got 40 days clean, man."

I was like, "What the fuck does that mean?"

"Clean off heroin."

I was like, "What?" Back then, I didn't know anybody that ever did heroin. Then he goes, "Can you give me a ride home?" I gave him a ride, and we passed his apartment by about three blocks and he goes, "Just drop me off right here." I dropped him off, and he went up to this Mexican guy when he got out.

GREG GILMORE Jeff and I and Kelly were out to dinner with a prospective tour manager. Kelly had called Andy about coming, but Andy, apparently with a froggy voice, said he wasn't feeling very well.

XANA LA FUENTE Andrew was supposed to meet that night with the guy that was supposed to be his chaperone on the road. He called Kelly and said, "I'm sick," and he said, "Xana is going to think I did drugs." And Kelly said, "Did you?" He said, "No." Well, he was lying.

KELLY CURTIS We had just had dinner with the tour manager that we were gonna hire. I went home and there was a note on my door from my then-wife Peggy that said, "Andy's in trouble. He's at Harborview." I had just left Jeff, and I knew where he was, at a bar downtown, so I drove back down there and yelled at him, and he got a couple of the guys, and we all showed up at Harborview, and Andy was in a fuckin' coma.

XANA LA FUENTE I just happened to have a work meeting that night, and my boss was really pissed off at everybody; there was stealing going on at the store. Two coworkers asked me if I could drive them home, and I had to take them way past my apartment.

When I got home, Andy was on the bed facedown unconscious, so I called 911 and they were trying to tell me how to give CPR. I tried, but they got there pretty fast. When they got there, they had me sign this paper. They pronounced him dead at the scene, but they told me to go to the hospital, so I went to the hospital—and then he was alive again. He was in a coma, and he immediately looked totally different. He was swelled up like a balloon, unrecognizable, and all his organs just started to shut down, his brain wouldn't stop swelling.

That work meeting was about 30 or 40 minutes, and then taking my coworkers home was probably another 30 to 40 minutes. The nurse at the hospital said if I would have been home 10 minutes sooner . . .

GREG GILMORE When me and Jeff went in to see him, it was brutal. Andy had not been on the respirator very long. If you have ever seen someone on a respirator, in the beginning it's very unnatural. After a while your body seems to relax into the rhythm of it so it doesn't look so freakish, but at that point it was still very mechanical. It just makes someone look more dead.

REGAN HAGAR I went down immediately with my girlfriend, now my wife. Andy looked really bad. His hair was really messy. My wife had a brush, and we brushed his hair out because there was a lot of people gathering and people coming in, and I remember being mad at people for letting him look like this. It seems so stupid now. I was concerned about Andy and how people perceived him.

There were a bunch of people there that were friends of friends. It wasn't very family to me. I remember going down a hall and finding Brian Wood, who was going through the same kind of thing. He was very angry. It was frustrating. Actually, like three people had overdosed that weekend, so there were hangers-on around for other people, too. It was a total scene.

BENJAMIN REW My keyboard player from my band at the time, Sleepy Hollow, had also OD'd that same night, potentially off the same stuff. It was the first time that Billy had ever shot up heroin; he ended up being in a coma for four and a half months at Harborview, but he eventually recovered. So we were all waiting in the hospital together. All the guys from Mother Love Bone and Alice in Chains, Soundgarden and us.

I think Jerry Cantrell thought I was there to pretend that I was cool, because there were a lot of people that were there that shouldn't have been there. There'd be like random chicks. So I think it got confused that I was there for the wrong reasons, and Jerry brought it up. He asked me why the fuck I was there. It was as simple as, "My fucking keyboard player is dying in there, asshole!" That normally will spark some confrontation. Basically, I think I lunged at him. And I think Jeff and some other guys and my guitar player Rick got in between us. I was pretty stoned at the time.

XANA LA FUENTE I had this thought recently: Sometimes I wish I would have never called anyone and told them he was there. Because of that scene there. A lot of people didn't deserve to be part of that. There were a lot of groupies showing up.

BRUCE FAIRWEATHER It happened on a Friday night, before cell phones. I was on Orcas Island with some friends of mine and didn't find out what happened until I got back on Sunday. I went over to Kelly's, and everyone else was there. I said, "What's going to happen to the band? What's going to happen to the band?" and "Andy's going to be all right. He's going to pull through."

But when I saw him at the hospital the next day, I was like, "Fuck. Who cares about the band?"

XANA LA FUENTE I knew he was gone. His mom kept saying, "When he wakes up, we're going to kick his butt." I'm like, "You don't get it. He's not waking up."

KEVIN WOOD They had to do some tests to see if he could possibly come back—a brain scan after his brain stopped swelling. But he was deprived of oxygen too long for him to have any hope of recovery.

STUART HALLERMAN Soundgarden was at L'Amour in Brooklyn, and somehow the tour manager was on the phone talking to Andrew's girl-friend. He's like, "I'm not gonna tell Chris till after the show, because I don't want to ruin the show for him, but Andrew's in a coma." We did tell them after the show, and Susan was out with us, and she started plying herself and Chris with liquor to dull the pain a bit. Driving back to Manhattan, Susan was like mumbling and falling over in the van. It was maybe the only time I've seen Susan drunk. The band played the last show of the tour in Hoboken the next night, and Chris and Susan flew out and got to the hospital.

XANA LA FUENTE I wouldn't let them unplug him until Chris Cornell got there. Andy's parents were getting pissed at me. They kept going in and saying their good-byes, and they wanted it over with. I was like, "We gotta wait for Chris," and Soundgarden had been on tour, so we were waiting for him to fly from like Chicago or something. I kind of threw that at Chris: "I got a lot of shit for keeping him on life support when everyone already said good-bye, waiting for you." It wasn't right of me. I was just mad at the world.

I made Andy's hair into three braids because that was the Malfunkshun number, three. I made it into three braids, and I cut it off. I still have it. Me and Brian were the last ones in there.

KEVIN WOOD When they pulled the plug, me and my brother Brian were there, and that's about all I remember. It was such a traumatic experience. We stood by his bed and watched the heart meter slowly stop, and then, boom, it was over.

DAVE REES I went over Regan's the day Andy died. We decided we'd make a tape for the service, so we drove down to Stone Gossard's parents' house and got the tape deck that we'd use to make it, and in the deck was the rough mix of *Apple*. So that was an emotional listen, to hear that for the first time on the day he died. It was so bittersweet. I was amazed at Andy's vocals and his songwriting ability. It was Regan and I think Mara West, one of Andy's old friends. We basically just sat there and cried and no one said a word for the entire day.

KELLY CANARY When Andy died, everybody was like, "I'm gonna get my shit together." People had their come-to-Jesus moment, which lasted a good hour or so—and then went away.

DANNY BLAND At the time I was like, "Man, what kind of idiot would overdose?" That was me in my cockiest, most delusional period, as an "indestructible" twentysomething-year-old guy in the grips of addiction. The fact is, we never know exactly what we're shooting in our arm.

TOM HANSEN By that time, selling drugs had completely taken over my life. I'd started in '85, when I was done with the Fartz and the Refuzors. I sold to Andy a few times. I was a little bit surprised by his death, too. I didn't know he was into it that much. But then again, it's those part-timers that get nailed, because they don't have any type of tolerance.

EDDIE SPAGHETTI I was using then, but I never really did it that much. For me, it was a weekend-only sort of a thing, and then it became weekends and Wednesdays. When Andy died, mainly people wanted to know where he got it. People thought it must have been really good, and that he'd obviously just done too much. "Where did he score that good shit from?" People were sick and twisted with that drug. It really fucks you up.

JEFF SMITH Andy Wood seemed like he wanted to die. My then-girlfriend Nancy and I saw him at QFC, the grocery store, a few days before he died, and he just seemed so bloaty and spacey. I said, "It seems like he's already gone." And then he died a few days later, and people were like, "How could you say that?" I guess because that's in bad form, to acknowledge that people sometimes don't want to live.

REGAN HAGAR I do know who the guy who sold it to Andy is; he is still around the city. And then there's the guy who supposedly was there with him doing it, panicked and ditched, who I got more upset with. I wrestled with that stuff in my mind, and then I realized that I couldn't put blame on either of those people. Andy did what he did, which ended him, and no one forced anything on him.

DAVE REES Andy's memorial service was the strangest funeral I've ever been to. First of all, it was at the Paramount Theatre. Regan and I both laughed beforehand that Andy would have dug this, because there was his name up on the marquee of the Paramount: ANDREW WOOD, and then the years that he was born and died. All of Soundgarden was there, Alice in Chains. Andy's nephews were there and they had Mother Love Bone T-shirts on that he had signed. It was this weird mix of rock and roll and extreme sorrow.

TOMIE O'NEIL I did sound, and we played a bunch of Andy's music. Andy had hours and hours and hours of music, him playing piano and guitar, that he recorded at home, with tons of reverb. His voice was big as a building.

GREG GILMORE It was a weird thing—there were fucking druids there. People in hooded robes. It was like out of the movies. What is this? Why the costumes?

TOMIE O'NEIL We did this candle thing where they lit one candle and everybody lit a candle off that candle and they blew the candle out. The preacher guy was my guy. I think he was like a Universal Life minister.

REGAN HAGAR There was some religious group there that Xana had hired. All these people were holding candles and this guy was asking people to blow out their candles, which represented him being gone, and said that "Andy's going down in the elevator."

I was like, "What do you mean he's going down in the elevator?" I was shaking mad about it and so was another close friend of Andy's, Mara West, who was Malfunkshun's number-one fan. We were like, "We cannot allow this to happen." So we went up to the podium in front of everyone and I said, "I don't know what this guy is saying, but Andy spread his wings and flew. He went *up*, if anything; he didn't go down. Raise your candle high for Andy."

BRUCE FAIRWEATHER What Regan said was great. Everyone was just like, *Yes!*

REGAN HAGAR Also, what Andy's dad said really bugged me: "My son was a junkie." He was trying to encourage the crowd to not do drugs. I just didn't agree with him. I saw Andy as someone who would take drugs but was fully a musician and a busy person. He wasn't laying around being a junkie. It's just semantics, but the term bothered me.

XANA LA FUENTE Andy's dad said, "Xana, thank you for keeping him alive all these years. We're sorry we didn't listen to you, we're sorry we didn't understand." I kept trying to tell them and tell them and tell them, and all they wanted to hear about was the record deal.

ROBERT SCOTT CRANE Regan was sitting behind me and Chad "Slam"— "Chadwick" is what Andy called him—who was a big supporter of the scene. At the service, Chad held up the Mother Love Bone EP *Shine* and a lighter. And he yelled, and he doesn't have the greatest-sounding concert yell—it's somewhat like a wounded animal. Right after a lot of serious speeches about drug addiction! We had just lost the angel of Seattle!

CHAD BLAKE I was holding the *Shine* EP that Andy autographed for me before he went bye-bye. The lighter? I thought it was a good thing to do. It was spontaneous.

ROBERT SCOTT CRANE It's like, *that's* where Andy is. Because this is *fucked*. This whole thing is so morose and dark, and the opposite of Andy. And Regan yelled out something like, "This is a memorial! Put that down!" Shunned him. *This is serious. This is a memorial.* To hear Regan tell him to stop—oh, I just wanted to leave. Social convention's not Chad's forte. That's how he's expressing his pain. Andy was alive in that one moment where Chad held up that lighter. It makes me cry thinking about it, because Andy would've fuckin' loved that.

KEVIN WOOD We had our own private ceremony afterwards, with just family, at the gravesite. Most of the people were at the Paramount because it was a big event. They didn't even know Andy, although I'm sure everybody felt like they knew him. It seemed kind of tacky.

SCOTT SUNDQUIST After a while, Chris and I just wanted to get out of there. We grabbed a handful of helium balloons from inside the venue and took them outside. We let them go, as if we were letting go of Andy.

Chris and I had a lot of unspoken moments, a connection to each other as friends. That was one of those moments where it was just a glance, and we knew where the other was at. And then we went on to a house somewhere with other musicians for a bit of a wake.

NANCY WILSON There was such an amazing community that only gelled further from Andy's memorial. 'Cause everybody came to Kelly Curtis's house that night. I had three springer spaniels and I decided to bring those dogs to the house, and everybody at the place took turns getting down on the ground and hugging the dogs because it was really comforting. There's such a family aspect to the Seattle music scene. We just felt really completely honored to be included because we figured they'd written Heart off a long time ago as just some dinosaur.

CAMERON CROWE I loved Mother Love Bone, so when I was writing the movie that would end up being *Singles*, I wanted to interview Jeff and Stone to explore the whole coffee-culture, "two or three jobs, one of which is your band" lifestyle. The terrible turn of events that took place was that Andy died. And everybody just instinctively showed up at Kelly's house that night. For me it was the first real feeling of what it was like to have a hometown—everybody pulling together for some people they really loved. That was a pivotal moment, I think, for a lot of people there. It made me want to do *Singles* as a love letter to the community that I was really moved by. . . .

CHRIS CORNELL We were crammed in a smallish living room with people sitting on every available surface. . . . I remember Andy's girlfriend looking at everyone and saying, "This is just like *La Bamba*," then suddenly I heard slapping footsteps growing louder and louder as they reached the front door and Layne flew in, completely breaking down and crying so deeply that he looked truly frightened and lost. Very childlike. He looked up at everyone at once, and I had this sudden urge to run over and grab him and give him a big hug and tell him everything was going to be okay. . . . I didn't get up in front of the room and offer that and I still regret it. No one else did, either. I don't know why.

MIKE STARR I made an ass out of myself for a second there, because I was in my thoughts and I walked into this room and I said, "Who wants to smoke a joint?" All of a sudden, I realized that Chris Cornell was sitting there looking at this photo album of Andy and crying. And I was like, Fuck. Why did I fuckin' say that shit?

XANA LA FUENTE I had all these Mexican prayer candles and put them on the headboard of the bed in this small room in Kelly's house. Somebody came up with this idea that everybody leave something for Andy. Chris Cornell left a pin of a silhouette of a girl—like on the back of truckers' mud flaps—that was on his hat. Ann Wilson left her hoop earrings. Some drunk guy left his cowboy boots. Poems and letters. Unfortunately that became the bedroom where I stayed, so I had to sleep with all that stuff. At one point, I laid down and when I woke up I couldn't find Andy's hair, and I was freaking out. I'm like, *"Where's his hair?! Where's his hair?!"*

GREG GILMORE After Andy died, it was "What do we do now?" Despair, confusion, discussions, meetings. The bottom line was whether to go on, and to go on means finding another singer. I was in favor of that at the time, but I don't remember if anybody else really was.

MICHAEL GOLDSTONE *Apple* was supposed to be released in March, but was pushed back to July. The possibility of trying to find a new singer was brought up at PolyGram, in marketing meetings. It was in the context of "How do we want to promote this record?" I don't remember who exactly said it. It was obvious that they didn't really understand the personality and the aesthetic of the band to think that replacing Andy was even a remote possibility.

ROBERT SCOTT CRANE Seattle absolutely lost its soul when Andy Wood died. But I feel like the soul started to get sucked out of Seattle with the signing of Mother Love Bone. Because although I was really excited for my friend getting signed to a major label, I knew that essentially Mother Love Bone was a sellout that just wanted to be Guns N' Roses. Coming from Green River and Malfunkshun, they took a huge shift to be a major-label band. They just absolutely sold their souls.

Andy still kept his soul as a person. He was the light, fun part of Seattle, as opposed to the other side, like the Jerry Cantrells—and I would even put Chris Cornell into this—the brooding, quiet, angry types.

XANA LA FUENTE If people think bad stuff about me now, it's because they knew I started using after that—although I've been clean for a long time now. So I lost respect there. After Andy died, I just didn't care anymore. I wanted to try it right away, but I couldn't find it. No one would give it to me. I wanted to know what the shit is that's so great that he had to throw everything away for it.

They knew that I remarried pretty quickly after that, so they felt like . . . You know, I don't know how long I was supposed to mourn. Did you know sex is a part of grieving? You become really sexual? I didn't know that. It's like a psychological effect, I guess, of grieving. They saw me with some other guys.

Andy dying feels like yesterday. I don't think it's ever going to not feel like yesterday. I've had my surgeon; I had the cute Spanish model; I had the millionaire in Hollywood, and he spoiled me. And I've had a couple other flings. I had Mickey Rourke for a while; he was so young and delicious back then.

But every guy is just playing second fiddle to a dead guy.

KEVIN WOOD For a long time after Andy died, I spent a lot of my time driving a taxi, and I would have conversations with him, in my mind, and I'd dream about him. Once when I was driving the cab, I picked up these Japanese tourists who wanted to go see Andy's grave. They had no idea I was his brother. I picked them up in Winslow, at the ferry terminal in our hometown, and Andy was buried out in Bremerton, so it was kind of a weird trip. It was a decent fare, too, like $150. These two girls—they were probably in their teens, early twenties—could barely speak English, so they had a hard time telling me where they wanted to go and what they wanted to see. I did get across the fact that I knew where it was and that I was his brother, and they were freaking out.

We took pictures by the grave—typical Japanese tourist kind of thing. I posed for a couple pictures; we all took turns taking pictures of each other. They were just nice girls who were fans and who happened to jump in the right cab in the wrong town. We were all freaking out because it was just such a strange experience. I was probably as blown away by it as they were.

CHAPTER 22
A BRIGHT, CLEAR SOUND

JOHN ROBINSON The Fluid were lumped into grunge. We were trying to do something that was a lot different than the bands in the Northwest that Jack Endino was working for were trying to do. What I always heard in the early days of Seattle was a Black Sabbath influence. There was a dirgelike sound that came creeping out of every band up there, with the exception of one or two. There wasn't 10 ounces of that in what the Fluid were trying to do. We didn't want a muddy guitar sound. We wanted a crisp, clean, chiming, super-loud Gibson guitar sound.

We made *Roadmouth* in '89 with Jack Endino, and a lot of people who were into the Fluid really loved that record. But everybody in the Fluid can hardly even listen to it. It had such a muddy sound. Jack had many recording successes in that time period with various acts. That was not one of them.

BUTCH VIG (producer; drummer for Madison, Wisconsin's Garbage) I had done a lot of local punk bands in the Midwest circuit, and I did a lot of records for Touch and Go. One of the bands was Killdozer; I did three or four records with them. I did their album *Twelve Point Buck*, which got a lot of press. After it had been out maybe a couple months, I got a call from Jonathan at Sub Pop.

JOHN ROBINSON When it came time for us to make another record, the Sub Pop guys suggested this producer out in the Midwest named Butch Vig. We said, "Never heard of him. Can you get us some music that he's done?" So they sent us a cassette, and it had a lot of noise bands from that region, like Killdozer. We were like, "Okay, we don't like any of this music specifically, but the sounds are really good."

So we went to Madison, Wisconsin, and recorded with Butch, at his studio, Smart Studios. Came back to Seattle with the record, which had a bright, clear sound. Everybody heard it and said, "Holy shit, who is this guy?"

BUTCH VIG The first Sub Pop band I did was the Fluid, then TAD. One of the things Jonathan told me on the phone was, "Tad is this big guy, but also there's a sensitive side to him. He pretty much bellows. See if you can get him to sing." Tad tried it, and there's a handful of songs on that record where he sings, and I think his voice is really cool.

They were super-cool guys. I remember Tad would get sort of withdrawn. It seemed like he was sort of depressed. An interesting thing is that, thinking about it now, it's sort of a precursor to working with Kurt Cobain, because Kurt was like that times a hundred.

That was one of those records that got a lot of press. One of the reasons why is because of the cover art.

TAD DOYLE The first legal problem we had was with a release called *8-Way Santa*. A friend found a photo of a couple in a photo album that they got at a thrift store or a garage sale. The photo was of a guy that looked like he was in Nazareth—with a big mustache and sideburns, long hair—and a woman. They both looked cooked, totally stoned and glassy-eyed and grinning ear to ear. Looked like they'd just had some good sex or something.

KURT DANIELSON And then he's holding the girl's breast with his hand in sort of an irreverent, shocking way. She is wearing just a bandanna on her breasts, which is totally white trash. Bruce Pavitt had the photograph color-enhanced, so all the colors look really phosphorescent.

So you have this sort of white-trash snapshot taken from a delirious LSD vision, and that's in keeping with the title of the record: 8-Way Santa is a kind of blotter acid that Tad had taken in Boise when he was growing up. And at the time it seemed like, Who cares if anyone objects, including the couple in the photograph, because this is artistically right, symmetrical, beautiful, and who'd want to interfere with that?

ART CHANTRY I remember when Kurt Danielson called me and said, "We want to use this photo on a record cover. We found it at a thrift store, and we bought the entire album of photos, therefore we own it and we can do whatever we want." I said, "No, don't fuckin' do that." They went and did it anyway, and then the guy who was on the cover had a friend who worked in a record store and saw the photo and said, "Hey, Bob, your photo is on this record cover, isn't that cool?" And he went and showed it to his ex-wife, the woman on the cover, who had become a Christian singer. And she got pretty pissed off.

JEFF GILBERT I was working for KZOK, which is Seattle's still-reigning classic-rock station. *8-Way Santa* came in, and I had the album sitting there in the station. One of the station managers comes over and says, "Oh, my God! That's my buddy!" So he brings in the guy who had his hand on the chick's tit in the picture, and I said, "Dude, check it out, you're famous!" And he goes, "Aw, where the hell did they get that?" I said, "I think somebody found it at a garage sale."

And here it goes, the fateful move: I said, "Man, can I get you to autograph this for me?" He loved it, and he goes, "Sure, man!" And he signed it. The woman in the picture had turned into some religious freak and wanted to sue, and I said, "Wait just a second there," when I heard that. "The guy who's in the picture, he liked it so much, he autographed it!" And there's your evidence right there.

KURT DANIELSON That really damaged their case. Between us and Sub Pop, we had to pay a certain amount of money, but I don't think it was more than what they had to spend on legal fees. So if they got anything out of it it was more of a moral victory, in that they were able to get this thing yanked off the shelves. But it destroyed the momentum we'd built up the couple of years before. We never really recovered from that.

ART CHANTRY So they had to pull the cover and replace it with a generic band shot. TAD was a monstrously talented band and that was
the record everybody thought was gonna be the next big one. Then
they put it back out there, and Bruce thought, in his marketing genius
(laughs), that this record really needed a kick in the ass. He wanted to
try and get free publicity, because they had no money. There was a song
on the record that was called "Jack Pepsi," which was about getting
drunk drinking Jack Daniel's and Pepsi-Cola and wrecking your monster truck in a swamp or something like that. Bruce decided that what
he was gonna do was put this on a CD single and do the Pepsi logo on
the front with the word TAD inserted where Pepsi was, then send it to
Pepsi-Cola corporate headquarters with the hopes of actually getting
sued, as I understand it.

GRANT ALDEN I remember the guys at Sub Pop had really planned to lose
a battle with Pepsi over "Jack Pepsi." I can remember being at their office
and seeing the artwork or the album and having Bruce or Jonathan say,
"We're probably gonna have to reprint this." My memory is that they had
budgeted a certain amount of money: "We're gonna lose some legal fees
on this, but we'll make it up on the backside with publicity."

BRUCE PAVITT We didn't have a lot of money to pay for advertising, so
you try to stir up some controversy. Did I think we were gonna get sued?
No. I thought that we were under the radar enough, but it's the kind of
thing that I felt people could look at and think, Oh, fuck, these guys are
gonna get sued. Geez, maybe I should buy this thing. That was more
my intention. There was a disgruntled ex-employee who notified Pepsi.

TAD DOYLE The name [Pepsi] I haven't spoken in many years. It's not a
sore subject; it's just financially prudent for me to leave it alone.

KURT DANIELSON Bruce wasn't afraid to court controversy, but I don't
think he notified P——. Because that record was intended to break
the band, and I don't think Bruce would have deliberately fucked
with it in that way. I know for a fact that there was such a disgruntled
ex-employee, who I believe is responsible for it.
    The story of "Jack P——" is kind of funny because it has a couple
different layers to it. When we were in the studio with Steve Albini

doing *Salt Lick,* Tad was asking Steve for songwriting advice. Steve said, "Well, just write about some real things that have happened to you." And then Tad told him this story about Tad and a buddy borrowing the buddy's father's brand-new pickup, driving it out onto Lake Lowell, this frozen lake outside Boise, Idaho, doing 360s and 180s all over, and then hitting a weak spot on the ice. The truck fell through, sinking to the bottom, and those guys barely got out alive. Steve said, "Shit, man, write about that one! I'm surprised you haven't already." And so, subsequently, Tad did write about it.

How the song got its title and how that fits in is a different story. When we were on tour with Nirvana in San Francisco, I had a bottle of P—— and a bottle of Jack Daniel's. It was just Krist, Kurt, and myself. Kurt back in those days hardly ever drank, but on this particular night he decided he wanted to get drunk. Krist always liked to drink, so he was all for it. So we started mixing up drinks and I came up with this idea of this character Jack P——. I put a stupid hat on and I started talking with an accent: "I'm Jack P——. I do this, I do that, blah blah blah."

Tad walks into the room, thinks that's hilarious, and later on we say, "Let's incorporate that into this song that we're writing, and we can say that Jack P—— is this deity that we pray to save us when we're about to drown." The refrain is, "Help me Jack P——!/Help me Jack P——!"

A lot of times, either I would write the body of a song or Tad would, but we'd need something else to make it really work, and then the other guy would come to the rescue. I still miss working with Tad.

STEVE WIEDERHOLD I quit right after we recorded *8-Way Santa.* I wasn't getting enough say. On one particular song, "Stumblin' Man," we had a really big problem, because I had a whole different kind of drum thing for one part going, and that wasn't gonna fly. Tad was like, "You have to play it this way, or else." So we had a *big* problem with that, and I decided then that I'm quitting.

BUTCH VIG Jonathan called me up and said, "Butch, I really like what you did with TAD. I got this band Nirvana, they're amazing. They could be as big as the Beatles." I sort of laughed when he said that, because I never heard anybody say something that sort of pretentious. He said,

"They're gonna be doing a tour." He wanted to bring them out here to do an album; it wasn't going to be demos at the time.

Nirvana show up maybe two or three weeks later at Smart. They definitely seemed a little bit like misfits. Krist was super-nice. Kurt walked in and sat down in the back of the control room and didn't say anything. Kurt would go sit in the lounge and the second time he did that, Krist said to me, "Kurt gets like that. He's fine. He'll come out of it." Chad was a nice guy, but while we were setting up, Kurt was critical of where Chad was putting the drums or something—there was a little bit of friction going on.

They had booked like five or six days, and they played a show in Madison on like the fourth day. There's this club called Bunky's, and downstairs there was this Italian restaurant, where they played in the back corner, which held maybe 75 people. It's the first time I got a sense that there was a buzz about the band, because it was jammed in there and people were freaking out when they started playing.

Kurt was singing so fuckin' loud, probably 'cause there were no monitors, he kind of lost his voice about 10 songs into the set. It fell apart at the end, and he threw his guitar and walked off the stage. He came in to sing the next day, and he couldn't. At that point, we'd recorded like six or seven songs. I think we recorded one more basic track, and then they had to take off.

Jonathan called me and said, "Maybe you could come out to Seattle for a week to finish the songs or maybe we could get them back out for another week in a month or two." Until I heard otherwise, I thought it was going to be a Sub Pop album.

JONATHAN PONEMAN Kurt got frustrated, came home, and soon after they started shopping for a new label. He said many times with regard to *Bleach*, "This record should be selling millions of copies." And I'm explaining to him what, in retrospect, seems foolish and condescending on my part, that the idea of a band like Nirvana selling between 30,000 and 50,000 records then was amazing.

BUZZ OSBORNE When Nirvana started doing better, we played a show with them in Portland, and that was when the worm had turned. That was before Dave Grohl was ever in the band. We just assumed that we were going to play last, and they said that they thought that they should headline, because things were really taking off for them, and then they were really weird about splitting up the money. That was when I knew that things were not the same with these guys. They had become exactly what I had always tried to avoid.

This was *way* before they got popular—that's what people don't get. They lined up for this shit. They put themselves in line to be aligned with horrible people. I blamed them for the whole thing. They got in line to be involved with horrible management, horrible booking agents, horrible everything. They didn't need to do it, but they did it.

CHAD CHANNING I was looking forward to being able to write some stuff for the band, and when Kurt said that he'd appreciate some input and help, that was one thing I was looking forward to. And after a while I realized that that really wasn't going to happen. . . . I started feeling more like a drum machine than anything else. Somewhere along the line I started losing my inspiration, and of course, when you do that, it's gonna show.

Krist and Kurt made the long drive up and came up to my place. That was a weird drive for them. I remember talking about it with Krist years down the road. He was like, "Yeah, that was a really horrible drive. Me and Kurt were not looking forward to that at all." 'Cause the thing was, we were always good friends. So to say it was for "musical differences" would be exact, because it really was.

*　　*　　*

JEFF GILBERT Jason Everman was a nice guy, but not the right guy for Soundgarden. Painfully obvious. I went to New York with them for my second Soundgarden cover story for *The Rocket,* and Jason never hung with the band. Onstage, he played well, thrashed his hair around, did what he was supposed to. But he was always very moody. It was like putting on wet shoes: They fit, but they're just not comfortable.

KIM THAYIL What we ended up learning on the road with Jason was that losing Hiro caused a huge wound to the band. This was a very fragile time for us, and Jason was new, he was spending less time trying to establish and maintain these relationships with us, especially with Chris and Matt. He was just trying to get his footing. And Jason's presence wasn't helping to remedy these fragile and wounded relationships between us all.

CHRIS CORNELL When we were auditioning [Jason], he was really shy, withdrawn, and really intimidated by the whole thing. I figured that, given a few months, he was gonna roar. It never worked out. Things never gelled, and rather than let them fester, we fired him.

JASON EVERMAN I guess I was fired because I wasn't getting along with Chris. No fights; it was just tension. We're on tour in Europe, and Matt got sick in Italy. He went to a hospital, but I think it turned out to be a G.I. problem, food poisoning. It wasn't anything serious. We went back to Washington, home for a couple of days, had a band meeting at Matt's house. The meeting was like two minutes long. Chris did the talking. It went something along the lines of, "We've been talking. We don't think you're working out, so we want to try some other people out."

KIM THAYIL Something else that was influential in this decision was Andy Wood's death. I think during that period of time, Chris wasn't fucking around anymore. He became more prolific—he ended up writing *Temple of the Dog*—and I got the sense that he felt he needed to honor Andy and champion that kind of unique personality.

So after we parted ways with Jason, Chris said, "You know, I keep thinking about Ben. He's from Bainbridge, like Andy. They knew each other. There's nobody like Ben." Ben's not a regular guy; he's an intense, creative person. I thought Chris's reasons were fantastic.

JASON EVERMAN Oh, I was destroyed. I stayed in my room for three days, brooding. It was like being dumped by this woman that you're totally in love with. It was probably one of the defining experiences of my life, for sure. It put me into a definite sink-or-swim situation, existentially. Was I going to stay in Seattle and start my revenge band, or was I going to travel? The decision I came to was to move to New York. I joined some other bands.

BEN SHEPHERD The phone rings, and it's Kim: "Hey, Ben, we're back in town from tour. You want to hang out and get a beer or something?" By then I'd turned 21. We went and hung out, and the next day we all went over Chris and Susan's house to meet Chris's new Pomeranian. And that's when they asked me to join.

I spat on the ground and said, "Fuck, yeah!"

KIM THAYIL The fit with Ben was immediately a little bit better. He was certainly more outgoing and willing to contribute creatively. Now, I'm not going to say that Ben healed the wound that was left when Hiro left the band. But the band regained some of the spirit that it had in the good days of Hiro, as well as transformed the band into what it became on *Badmotorfinger*.

BEN SHEPHERD The first tour I did with them was in Europe. Played Roskilde Festival as my first show. I remember going on stage to the chants of "Hiro! Hiro!" I don't think they knew that Hiro left the band. It's probably the only performance where I ever stood still. When I joined Soundgarden, I was thinking, I gotta do this exactly like Hiro. I gotta do this exactly right. Had no fun the first show. That's bullshit. So I decided to change that and the next day, go for it.

JEFF GILBERT Ben is a *punk rocker*. When he played his bass, he looked like he was trying to murder it. He has a very aggressive spirit, which is what I think Soundgarden really needed after Jason Everman.

JANET BILLIG I understood why Jason couldn't be in Nirvana. He just didn't quite fit in. He really fit in way more with Soundgarden. I was surprised that didn't work out. I got him a plane ticket to come out to stay at my place in New York so he could recover from the madness of it. He was a buddy. I had a lot of love for Jason Everman. He's an intense dude. He was a guy who was like, "I want to know what it feels like to kill people," and he went and joined the Army and has been in Iraq.

JASON EVERMAN After I quit the band Mindfunk in '93, I did two periods of service, starting in 1994. Joining the military was one of the most punk-rock things I've ever done, this "Fuck everyone, this is what I'm going to do" type of ethos. Becoming a warrior is huge.

Did I join the Army to find out "what it feels like to kill people"? No. There's nothing cool about being in a gunfight. This notion that it's some kind of sociopathic desire to kill people is absurd. I don't know where that came from. People project whatever they want to project, you know? I have no problem with the notion of destroying the enemy, but . . . no. I would like to think I'm a gentle soul, and for the most part, I am.

CHAPTER 23
GOOD LUCK IN YOUR FUTURE ENDEAVORS

JENNIE BODDY (Sub Pop Records publicist) Steve Turner was always going back to college, supposedly. Mudhoney was really on the road to breakup, because Steve was so nervous going back to college, and at a certain point, even as their publicist, sometimes I didn't know what was true and not true. Was he going back to college, or did they just keep saying that because it became so funny?

STEVE TURNER I went back to school a lot. *(Laughs.)* I didn't see a straight line through college, but I told my parents I was hoping to be done with college when I was 30. When I hit 30, I was like, Fuck, man. I gave myself 12 years, and I failed.

Was going back to school a reaction to our success? Probably. I don't know what I was afraid of. I didn't think I was meant to be a rock star, so I was fighting it.

MATT LUKIN Steve's like, "I'm taking the year off, I'm going to school." And I'm like, "Well, fuck it, then. I gotta go back to work. I can't sit around for a year and do nothing." So I went back to work as a carpenter, and it kind of took the wind out of my sails as far as being in the band.

DAN PETERS I ran into Kurt's and Krist's girlfriends, Tracy and Shelli, at the Vogue one night, and they told me that Nirvana was looking for another drummer. Steve was back in school, so I'm like, "I got some time. Let 'em know that I'm interested." Next thing I knew, I get a call from Kurt, and I start jamming with those guys. But the practices weren't fun, like in Mudhoney, where we were drinking beer and having a good time. But I was glad I was able to record that one song, "Sliver," with them.

The one show I played with them was at the Motor Sports International Garage. You could tell there was a lot of momentum building for those guys. They were already planning on leaving Sub Pop at the time.

JONATHAN PONEMAN That was a huge show, with the Melvins and the Dwarves and the Derelicts on the bill. I was on the side of the stage, and I remember Kurt looking at me from the stage and saying in front of probably fifteen hundred people in the audience, "Jon, we're not signing to Capitol." That was the rumor that had spread around.

JULIANNE ANDERSEN The Motor Sports show? That was the moment. That's when I knew. This little kid from Aberdeen that's obviously a little bit shy, a little bit overwhelmed by everything that's happened, and there's so many cameras in his face.

I remember watching Charles Peterson have to jostle for space; that was his deal, and that guy had to fight for physical space on that stage. It just wasn't right. I had photo passes, but I walked off that stage, because I knew right then and there that quiet kid from Aberdeen was in for a long and rough ride, and at the time, I felt like the best thing anyone could do for him was back the fuck off.

SALTPETER (bassist for San Francisco's Dwarves) That was an all right show, until some little cunt in the audience threw a 7-Up bottle and split my forehead open during "Let's Fuck." I did finish the song before I went to the emergency room and got my head sewn up. The other thing I remember was that the Dwarves had like a $100 guarantee. And I think Nirvana had like $1,000. And I remember Blag haggling with Krist over money before the show, like, "Could you kick us another hundred bucks for gas money?" And Krist was not having any of it, until I went to the emergency room. When the Dwarves came to pick me up after the show, they said, "Hey, we got another hundred bucks out of Nirvana because you got hit with a bottle." I guess that was worth it.

DAN PETERS The day after that show, they had an interview and BBQ scheduled at Krist's place in Tacoma. And I was like, "Let me see if I can borrow my wife's car." And they were like, "Nah, don't worry about it." And I'm like, "I'll make it." And they didn't say anything.

I go down to Tacoma the next day and do the interview and the photo shoot. And this guy Dave, he's the drummer for Scream, is hanging in the background, having hamburgers and whatnot, and nobody says anything.

Kurt and Krist were going off to L.A. to talk to labels, and there was talk of the band going off and doing a U.K. tour after that.

BRUCE PAVITT There were rumors that Nirvana were shopping themselves around. Jon had asked me to go down to Olympia to talk to Kurt to try to convince him to stay with the label, to have a heart-to-heart. It was more of an act of diplomacy. I brought down a couple of records that I thought he would really appreciate, *Philosophy of the World* by the Shaggs and *Hi, How Are You* by Daniel Johnston, two of the freakiest, most obscure records I had in my collection. My intention was to essentially communicate to him that at the end of the day, Sub Pop was going to support unusual points of view. To this day, I take great pride in turning Kurt on to Daniel Johnston; I saw Kurt wearing his T-shirt in *Rolling Stone*. It was about six hours of just getting to know each other and talking philosophy.

He was quiet and not very confrontational and very reclusive, so you'd hear things through the grapevine and interviews, but one thing I knew he was upset about was that we were not buying a lot of advertising for Nirvana in particular. We tended to run group advertisements, and we were really pushing Sub Pop more as a label. It was a more cost-effective way of advertising, and I felt that he was truly missing the big picture, because we were so effective at garnering press. Literally a year and a half after he was sleeping under bridges, he was on the front cover of *Melody Maker* in England. I'd say that's pretty effective label promotion.

DANNY GOLDBERG (Gold Mountain Entertainment founder/president; Nirvana/Hole manager; Atlantic Records president; Warner Bros. Records chairman/CEO; Rosemary Carroll's husband) The first meeting I had with Nirvana, Krist did most of the talking. Kurt didn't do much talking, and Dave Grohl did no talking. I asked at one point if they wanted to stay on Sub Pop. Kurt, who had been quiet up until then, just said, "*No*, definitely not!" He wanted to be big. They committed to us after the first meeting.

DAN PETERS They go down to L.A. and come back, and Kurt calls me up, and I go, "Hey, what's up with the U.K. tour?" He goes, "Yeah, that's why I'm calling. Well, we got another drummer. That guy Dave, from Scream."

"Ah, all right," I go. "That's cool." I was kind of taken aback, but really relieved, because, like I said, Mudhoney had this unique bond, and I felt nothing like that playing with Nirvana. But in hindsight, I'm like, *Aww, Jesus.*

MATT LUKIN Crover kind of spoiled Nirvana. Dan's more *tippy-tap*—we always used to make fun of Dan and call him Tippy Tap—while Dale's more *thunk-thunk-thunk.* Grohl's more of a beater, like Dale.

DAN PETERS What I was bummed about was that all they had to do was just be honest—don't be pussies. Communication on those guys' part was not all that happening. I found out that Dave had been up there in Tacoma practicing with those guys for a while. He was probably more prepared to do that show I played than I was.

SLIM MOON Scream's show at Gorilla Gardens in 1984 or 1985 was one of the best shows I ever saw. Years later, I convinced Kurt to go up to Tacoma to go see Scream. I was tapping my foot because I was so anxious to get to Tacoma and see this awesome band Scream. I was talking them up, and when we got there, they were this really bad Van Halen. It was not at all the same band I had seen. They were just awful.

Kurt went on this crazy tirade all the way home about how much he hated Telecasters. Scream's choice of guitar became symbolic of everything he hated about them. We didn't even talk about the drummer. So it was funny that we lambasted Scream and just talked about how much we hated them, and a year later or something, Scream's drummer was his new drummer.

BUZZ OSBORNE I was friends with Dave Grohl when he was in Scream. Dave has a really good sense of humor. Really severe black humor. Actually, he had some pretty great stories about Scream's black bass player. I think that those stories would have been good regardless of what color he was.

Dave called me when I lived in San Francisco. The Nirvana guys were in town, so we went and saw Scream play. It's been written that I took them there to see Dave Grohl play, but that's not true. I was going to go anyway.

CRAIG MONTGOMERY We had Dale play drums on a tour, the tour with Sonic Youth. And the Melvins let us stay at their house in San Francisco for a couple days before the tour started. We went and saw Scream at the I-Beam. Kurt saw Dave play and he said, "That's the kind of drummer we need."

BUZZ OSBORNE A couple of weeks later, I got a call from Dave, and he was in L.A., stranded. The bassist of Scream had sold all their gear. And I said, "Well, you know, Nirvana's looking for a drummer." And I didn't know at that time that they'd already hired Danny Peters. And Dave said, "Really?," because he was looking for anything he could do. And so I called the Nirvana guys and said, "Remember that drummer that you saw play for Scream? Well, he's looking for something to do. Call him up."

. . .

SLIM MOON Me and Dylan Carlson moved to Seattle in '90, and we moved in with these two guys from Ellensburg—Nate Hill, who was in a band called King Krab, and Lanegan, from Screaming Trees. While I was living with Lanegan, he was recording his first solo album. I think Dylan and Kurt were using drugs together at that point, though Dylan wasn't deep into drugs yet. But I started to feel unsafe around Dylan, because he was so into guns.

There was this one scary time when Krist Novoselic came to our house. The front door was locked, which was unusual, and it was late at night, and he needed a place to crash because he was wasted. So he crawled up onto the roof in the back and was trying to open the upstairs back window. He finally widgets the window open, looks up, and he's staring at a double-barreled shotgun right in his face.

It turned out that Dylan had not heard him knocking on the front door, and had woken up to hear somebody trying to break in, so he had gotten the gun from under his bed. Dylan, despite all his bravado about how quick he'd be to shoot an intruder, waited long enough to figure out who it was. The world very narrowly escaped Dylan blowing Krist's brains out, years before Nirvana got famous.

It scared the crap out of me, but Krist and Dylan just thought it was hilarious. It was just another good story. It was one of the events that led to me quitting Earth and moving back to Olympia.

DAVE GROHL (Nirvana drummer; drummer for Washington, D.C., area's Scream; Foo Fighters singer/guitarist) The first phone call that I had with Kurt was really funny, 'cause we had played Olympia, Washington, where he lived, maybe like four weeks beforehand. . . .

SLIM MOON The next time Scream went on tour, they had a show in Olympia, but I didn't go because I had already planned a party and plus, they had sucked before. But after the show, somebody told them, "There's a party going on," so they showed up in my apartment and walked in while Tobi Vail—who Kurt was with at some point after Tracy—was playing solo on electric guitar.

DAVE GROHL This girl sits down and she plays the most saddest, depressing fuckin' [song]. And there's all these people who look like they're fuckin' *Scooby Doo*, with the glasses, and they're just sad, and hot chocolate party shit and all of that crap. And we're there with our beers like, "What the *fuck* is going on? This place is screwed, man. This is horrible."

So the first phone call I had with Kurt . . . I'm like, "Man, afterwards we fuckin' went to this party at someone's apartment, and it was kinda fucked, man, 'cause we showed up and we had all our beer and shit. And then this fuckin' girl starts playing this *shitty* fuckin' depressing fuckin' *bullshit*."

He's like, "Yeah, that's my girlfriend." *(Laughs.)* I'm like, "Ohhh . . . Whoops. Whoopsie daisy."

COURTNEY LOVE Dave performed a really great service for Kurt. He made him make hot dogs and get over chicks that were pounding on pots and pans singing about their vaginas. "We're goin' to a strip club, motherfucker!" That's good. I don't know if that's in the history books. They didn't have a lot of money for strip clubs, but Dave was very much a heterosexual red-blooded young man who did not understand why Kurt was mooning over some pudgy girl.

DANNY GOLDBERG I think there were six labels that were interested in Nirvana, and my partner, John Silva, was excited about meeting the labels. But I thought it was pretty obvious that Geffen would be the best place. They had staffed up in the alternative world in a way that the other labels hadn't. They had Ray Farrell, who had come out of SST and who really knew the retail scene, and Mark Kates, who was very much on the cutting edge of dealing with this burgeoning alternative-radio format. And Geffen had a huge advantage because we had just been through this experience with Sonic Youth, who had a lot of the same concerns that Nirvana had about protecting their image, and Geffen had not screwed up. So it was kind of theirs to lose, and they didn't lose it.

NICK TERZO My biggest problem trying to sign Nirvana to Columbia was I didn't have Sonic Youth. Kurt cared about Sonic Youth and being where Sonic Youth was. I remember getting the call at Christmas that they had signed to somebody else. That was not a good Christmas gift.

DAN PETERS After I played with Nirvana, Jonathan told me that Mark Pickerel was quitting the Screaming Trees. And I was like, "Well, hell, I got some time. I love the Screaming Trees."

MARK PICKEREL The band dynamics had just become so complicated. My then-girlfriend Jana, who was in Dickless, was equally complicated and demanding of my time and energy, and she wasn't happy about all the touring. I wasn't happy about all the touring. I was having a harder time finding my place in the band because it was already hard enough as a drummer to exert much creativity in the group. And when we got signed to Sony, I found that it wasn't just band members that I was having debates with anymore, it was management, it was people at Sony.

I'm only just starting to admit that now, that I left the band partly because of a relationship. Although the band may have suspected it, at the time I told them that it was for other reasons.

DAN PETERS Then I got a call: "Hey, I hear you might be interested in playing with us." And I was like, "Yeah." And he just kind of laughs, and I'm like, "Well, who the fuck is this? Are you fuckin' with me?" I had to ask him a couple of times. And eventually he's like, "It's Lanegan." Mark's a funny guy. He was probably flippin' me shit.

GARY LEE CONNER Then we had the tour with Dan Peters, which started off with the big wreck. We had two vans instead of one, so it was slightly more luxurious. Mark and our two road guys were in the equipment van because Mark wanted to be by himself. We did one or two shows, we're driving through Wyoming, and it was early spring, but there was black ice on the road. We were ahead of him, and the van flipped over a bunch of times, all the way from one side of the freeway, through the median, to the other side.

We thought they were gone, all dead. Considering how bad it looked, it was a miracle no one got seriously injured. The van was history, but everyone came out fairly unscathed. Mark did not get injured, but he sure was traumatized, apparently.

I think the band kept him sober, because he had something to keep him going, as a distraction or whatever. On the surface, it looked like the crash changed that. We got to Chicago a couple of days later, and apparently Mark started drinking, and that lasted for I don't know how many years.

DAN PETERS But by the time we hit Chicago, Lanegan started drinking again. I went to the store with Van and Mark, and Mark walks over to the beer cooler and pulls out three Foster's oilcan beers. I kind of laughed, and he was like, "What?" And I'm like, "What are you doing?"

He goes, "I'm going to drink these." I'm like, "Really? Well, I'll get some, as well." We went back to the hotel and drank some Foster's.

GARRETT SHAVLIK The Fluid were playing in Chicago at Lounge Ax, and I went to see the Trees, who were playing a matinee show at the

Cubby Bear. Mark got notorious for this shit—he'd get onstage and sing like two songs and throw the mic down and walk off.

GARY LEE CONNER Das Damen was opening for us. We played one or two songs, and Mark, I don't know if he just freaked out, but he said his voice went out. He left the stage, and we ended up playing the rest of the show jamming with the guys from Das Damen. So that was the beginning of a little bit of nastiness.

GARRETT SHAVLIK I followed Lanegan and said, "What the fuck is wrong with you, man? These guys are bleeding without you."

"My throat's fucked up, Tidbit." He'd call me Tidbit. I don't know why.

"Your throat is not fucked up."

"Give me some of that Bushmills. Pour me some of that stuff."

"Fuck you, you're not fuckin' Morrison, dude. Come up here and look at what's going on."

He's like, "They got it." They're doing horrible covers, just trying to make the fuckin' set so they can get paid.

"You're a fuckin' asshole for fuckin' leaving them high and dry."

He loved the fact that I'd call him on that shit. We got to be good friends that way.

DAN PETERS The tour got canceled in Florida. Mark decided the tour was done. He caught a flight home, and we all drove from Pensacola, Florida, back to Seattle.

VAN CONNER We used to do that all the time. We'd have such intense tours; it would be like a month, and then we'd have a week left and Mark would be like, "Let's just fuckin' go home." After burning the candle at both ends for a month, I would not argue.

DAN PETERS Mudhoney had recorded *Every Good Boy Deserves Fudge* while Steve was going to school, so that record's getting ready to come out. Meanwhile, the Screaming Trees are getting ready to go into the studio to record, so I demoed some stuff with them. Then I realized that I was going to have to make a decision.

I'm like, "Steve, what's the deal? Do you want to tour, or are you going to school?" And he's like, "I think we should tour." To me, that was all I needed. As much as I was having a gas with the Screaming Trees, Mudhoney was my band. There was nothing like a Mudhoney show at that point.

          ·   ·   ·

DANIEL HOUSE I left Skin Yard in early '91. The primary reason was that my son was born in 1989, in March. And I actually left to go on tour when he was two weeks old, and when I came back he was two months old. So I was miserable, but I did it because it was something that I understood was necessary to develop awareness and a fanbase for the band. But I wanted to be a responsible and present parent, so I couldn't justify that in my own mind.

During that same time, C/Z had begun seeing a fair bit of success on its own, even though it was a side hobby. Sub Pop believed, very incorrectly, that I was using Sub Pop time to do Skin Yard business or C/Z business, and nothing could've been further from the truth. I had far too much pride about the quality of my work to ever mix the two. When they actually let me go, it was pretty hurtful and I was pretty angry. I worked so hard; I was earning them $30,000 a month at that point, personally. And it was that piece of the business that was pretty much keeping Sub Pop afloat at that point. I'm convinced to this day that they decided to get rid of me because they got somebody to do my job for cheaper.

Suddenly, two of the things I identified myself as being—the bass player/songwriter in Skin Yard and the sales/distribution guy at Sub Pop—were not there, and the only thing I really had left was C/Z. So either I had to get a real job or make a go at C/Z, so it seemed like a no-brainer. In retrospect, I have to thank Sub Pop for the opportunity to take a leap forward and take a chance on the label, which would basically carry me through the next many years.

PETER LITWIN (Coffin Break guitarist/singer) Coffin Break started in '87. Originally, Sub Pop was going to put out our first seven-inch, and then they backed out at the last minute because they didn't feel like we fit their label totally. We were a little more punk rock; we weren't quite as grungy. We went with C/Z, where it wasn't one type of sound. Daniel signed people he liked, and that could be grungy or more punk or metal or whatever—where Sub Pop had a pretty clear garage/grunge sound.

We did end up putting out a seven-inch on Sub Pop years later, but there was some jealousy. Like all their bands were doing amazing and we weren't getting as much notoriety. So I wrote this song "Pop Fanatic." One of the lines is about how I felt Sub Pop was on the way out: "People don't care 'cause you're on the descent/Don't think you'll go far 'cause your energy's spent."

STEPHANIE DORGAN (the Crocodile club owner; Peter Buck's ex-wife) The Crocodile opened April 30, 1991. Jonathan Poneman and Bruce Pavitt would come to the club's restaurant for lunch all the time because Sub Pop's offices were pretty close, and I remember at the beginning they'd trade CDs for lunch sometimes. They were on the verge of being broke.

RICH JENSEN (Sub Pop Records general manager; musician) The first job I had at Sub Pop, in '91, was to go into the previous bookkeeper's office, which was completely strewn with paper, and determine what was a bill. And I put them in a big stack, organized them, and then typed everything into a spreadsheet, which those guys had apparently never heard of. That was my great talent: I knew what a spreadsheet was.

I printed it out on an old-fashioned, dot-matrix printer, and it was a six-foot-long list that I hung up on the window in Bruce's office. At the bottom it said we owed $250,000. We had $5,000 in the bank. That was probably May. Megan was let go that summer. Most of the staff was. We were reduced to a core group of like five people.

SALTPETER The original Sub Pop office was pretty much a free-for-all. I remember looking in this closet once there and finding the master tapes to stuff, including our album *Blood Guts & Pussy*. If I'd had the foresight, I would have just stuck 'em in my underwear and walked out. At the time you could pretty much do whatever you wanted. I remember finding a can of spray paint and thinking, This makes sense. I spray-painted on the office floor YOU OWE DWARVES $.

KIM WARNICK (Fastbacks singer/bassist; Sub Pop Records receptionist) And that stayed there forever. I thought it was fuckin' hilarious.

JONATHAN PONEMAN We were lying to bands, but we were lying to ourselves, as well, by being overly optimistic about when money would come in.

Bands would see records being sold and they'd go, "Where are my royalties?" Never mind the fact that we had bought them a van, we'd flown them to Europe, advanced them rent. We didn't have even rudimentary bookkeeping knowledge. What we did was definitely fiscally irresponsible. But it's not like we were being criminals.

THURSTON MOORE When I first saw Nirvana play at Maxwell's in Hoboken, Sub Pop had helped them out with a van. They had this van, but they had no money. And I remember them just completely destroying all their amps and equipment onstage, and I was like, "How are you gonna finish your tour?" Bruce was figuring out how to get their shit fixed every night.

MARK ARM Every once in a while, I'd go, "Bruce, I really need some money." And he would cut me a check. Sometimes he'd go, "I really shouldn't do this," because by this point I was doing a lot of drugs.

STEVE TURNER I'd been told about Mark dabbling with heroin here and there right after I quit Green River. My attitude was always, and still remains: He's a big boy, everybody is. It's not my place to tell someone not to do something like that. That wasn't anywhere in my scene, and I was not comfortable around people doin' that stuff, and he knew that. So we weren't hanging out like we had a few years before. I think for him it's something he had to go through because so many of his heroes, like Iggy, went through it.

MATT LUKIN I wasn't aware of it until Mark was knee-deep in it. I remember him scolding me one time because I was spouting off to my friends about him OD'ing. And I go, "But dude, really, are you okay? I don't want you to be strung out and fuckin' OD'ing and dying. Let's deal with it." But at the same time, I really didn't want to deal with some junkie dragging me down.

STEVE TURNER Mark wouldn't do drugs on tour, generally. We would start tours, and he'd be a wreck. I remember a few tours where we stored him like a sack of potatoes in the back of the van. Kinda throw him up on the loft and drive to Minneapolis. And by the time we get there, he's in better shape.

BRUCE PAVITT Mark says, "You used to give me money for drugs," and the reality is, Mark would come in and say, "I need money for rent." So if you have a musician who might get kicked out of his apartment, what are you gonna do? What he does with that money is his choice.

This used to happen a lot: A band would come in and say, "Hey, we want some money," and Jon would say, "Sure, you can have your money. Come in tomorrow." Oftentimes, we simply would not have the money.

When Steve Turner of Mudhoney came in saying, "Jon said I could get my check for $5,000 today," I started laughing, kind of a nervous laughter, because we had maybe $20 in the bank. I think Steve just felt like he was being jacked around and that I was disrespecting him by laughing in his face and telling him I didn't have the money, when in actuality I was barely able to hold it together. Based on that conversation, Steve said, "Well, fuck you, we're going to a major label." I remember breaking down and crying in front of him.

STEVE TURNER Bruce is a very emotional guy; he wears it all on his sleeve. I wanted to get out of there before we weren't friends anymore. We were afraid they were for-real gonna go out of business, owing us a lot of money. It was like a bad breakup, a vote of no-confidence from us. The way I remember it is that we decided we would look around for another label after Sub Pop released *Every Good Boy Deserves Fudge*. But I didn't have any desire to go to a major label at the time. None of us really did.

MARK ARM Sub Pop flew the Afghan Whigs out and put them up in a hotel room and had them record at I think Bear Creek Studio, which is a really expensive studio, and we weren't getting paid? At one point, instead of payment they offered us stock in the company. We were like, "What?!" We didn't know anything about stocks, but it just seemed like it would've been empty paper.

BRUCE PAVITT Mudhoney were our biggest band and they decided to walk because we couldn't pay them, and not only couldn't we pay them, we were lying to them about paying them! That's just really fucked up. What can I say?

CHARLES R. CROSS Seattle was a small enough world where *The Rocket* did typesetting for Sub Pop, we ran advertisements for them, so we knew they owed us money and we knew the record-pressing plant and Jack Endino and everyone else, and we knew they owed *them* money, so it wasn't exactly like a *Wall Street Journal* investigative report to figure out that they owed $20,000, $30,000 around town and that they had very little revenue. We basically wrote this piece saying there's some questions on whether they'll be able to continue. They were quite angry and they felt that our piece affected their ability to get credit.

GRANT ALDEN The inception of the "Sub Plop?" cover story I wrote was that they were not paying their bills and there were all sorts of rumors they were gonna collapse. I knew that they were in trouble. I also knew that if they were allowed to hold on for six months, they were gonna be fine. Because there was the Nirvana record coming out on a major label, which I knew would be enough to get them out of the kind of hole they'd dug—though I had no idea the extent to how well it would do. Also, they had a Mudhoney record coming out, and I knew roughly what numbers that was likely to sell, and that again would be enough.

What I did was slightly unethical, and I'm still troubled by it. I wrote that story as fairly as I could, but with the intent to diffuse the bomb. I said they had problems, but here's how they're gonna fix it. It said, "Don't worry." It was "Sub Plop" with a question mark. It was not, "They're about to crash."

Bruce and Jon cooperated with that story, and they were honest. I felt at the time if we had allowed the rumors to fester, if we had not addressed it head-on, that Sub Pop would've collapsed and that would've been the end. I don't think that's really what my job as a journalist is. But I felt the article was as close to what was true as I could get, and I felt it was necessary.

JONATHAN PONEMAN We ended up putting out Mudhoney's *Every Good Boy Deserves Fudge* late that summer. That sold 100,000 copies and got us back on our feet.

JENNIE BODDY Right before the electricity was about to get turned off, it was always a Mudhoney release that would save us. They kept the lights on, Mudhoney did.

GARRETT SHAVLIK There were times near the end of the Fluid's being on Sub Pop where we'd do interviews, and some jackass is saying, "Hey, must be killer to be on the ol' Sub Pop! 'World Domination'!" I'm like, "Dude, I work for Mr. Mark Arm. Have you seen the sales on *Every Good Boy Deserves Fudge*? He's basically paying my fuckin' bills."

MARK ARM We agonized over our decision greatly. If we had known that there was even a slight chance that Sub Pop would've been financially flush in a year, we wouldn't have felt the need to look elsewhere.

JOSH SINDER (the Accüsed/TAD/Gruntruck drummer) I wanted the Accüsed to get management and push it further. So I quit, made a demo tape, and took it to Susan Silver. And then TAD was looking for a drummer—Rey Washam was right before me, and I don't know why they got rid of him or why he quit—and they called Susan asking if she knew anybody, and she said, "I've got this demo tape from this guy in the Accüsed." So I tried out, and Tad called me and said, "Do you want to play drums for us?"

  We did a lot of practices, and we smoked a lot of pot. Literally, we wouldn't practice unless we could smoke pot. We would get in Tad's little car—he had this Datsun B210—and we would drive around West Seattle trying to find the different people who were selling weed. And if we couldn't find pot, we would just go, "Well, I guess there's no practice today."

  I did their last record on Sub Pop, the "Salem/Leper/Welt" EP. Everybody was waiting in line to get their major-record-label deal, and we were like the last ones to get a major deal.

KURT DANIELSON All we could see from our vantage point at that time was continued strife and financial instability at Sub Pop, and we thought that if we went to a bigger label, we would not have that problem. We also assumed that going to a major label, we would be understood and marketed correctly, and on top of that, have financial stability. In fact, when we moved to a major label we were not understood, we were not properly marketed, and we were lost in the shuffle.

ROBERT ROTH Mark Pickerel and I set up a meeting with Sub Pop and went there with four-track demos of some Truly songs. Nirvana had just left Sub Pop that day, and Jonathan was fuming about Nirvana, just fuming. It was great timing for us, because how much more of a receptive audience can you have than a label guy who just lost his best band? He really gave our songs a good listen and said, "Yeah, I love it. Let's do an EP." So we were off and running.

JONATHAN PONEMAN When all the bands left it was hurtful. Back at the beginning, I remember having a very poignant conversation with Susan Silver, the manager of Soundgarden. She was saying basically, "Sorry, guys, we've gotta go on without you." The die was cast early on with Soundgarden; we all understood what was going on. But still, having the conversation somehow made it even more hurtful. The thing that I always took as the subtext of that conversation is, "We're leaving and moving on, and good luck in your future endeavors—if there are any future endeavors."

CHAPTER 24
SICK OF CRYING

CHRIS FRIEL I was 17 when Shadow moved to L.A. My parents have always been just incredibly supportive. They were into it 100 percent. Mike's parents were not into it at all. They were right, my parents were probably the ones that were sort of crazy.

Duff came to our very first show down there, which we played before we moved. We were in L.A. for well over a year. It was kind of humbling because we had come from Seattle, where we were a pretty big band, to down there, where you're totally starting over and also really feeling like we didn't fit in. We just really weren't partiers. There was drugs, girls, all this stuff that you read about in the rock books. I think we were probably a little scared.

RICK FRIEL You'd be around people who were wasted all the time. You'd be at the Cathouse and see Slash get thrown down a flight of stairs. The whole thing was so foreign to us. But I loved everything about L.A. and Hollywood. I had this burning desire to make it, and I loved seeing all these shows and driving around seeing palm trees. I thought, I'm never moving home.

We were basically living on Top Ramen and generic beer and pancake mix. I believed that it was gonna happen, but Mike and Chris were like, "We gotta move home." I think Mike was getting frustrated with the life. He just started partying hard and getting wasted. It wasn't our thing, so he was doing it on his own. I'd be tryin' to write lyrics; my focus was completely on the band. We never discussed this with him, but it probably was a reaction to, What the hell's happening to my body? 'Cause he didn't know he had Crohn's disease at the time—that's when it kinda started.

CHRIS FRIEL I was working at a record store, and I remember hearing the first Soundgarden EP and thinking, There's definitely some cool stuff going on in Seattle. People were saying things were starting to happen there, and I was thinking, Did we move at the wrong time?

RICK FRIEL I was very sad when we moved home. Once we did, that was the end of the band. Mike fell off the face of the earth, and then he came over and gave me his guitar and said, "That's it, I quit. I'm never playing music again."

Mike became a hardcore Republican. He got a weird haircut and started wearing Hush Puppies and corduroy and big sweaters and started raving about Barry Goldwater. We were like, "What the hell?" But that wasn't gonna last, 'cause every time we'd get together at people's houses, we'd have these jams and we'd *always* hand him the acoustic guitar 'cause we were really upset he wasn't playing anymore. He was like, "No, I don't wanna play. I'm done." But we would say, "C'mon, just play one song!" And it would turn into three, four, six songs. Eventually he formed a really cool band called Love Chile. It was a Stevie Ray Vaughan/Double Trouble, Jimi Hendrix Experience–type band.

MIKE McCREADY (Pearl Jam/Temple of the Dog/Mad Season/Shadow guitarist) I was sitting around at a party with Pete Droge, an old friend of mine. I had my guitar and I was just jamming to a Stevie Ray Vaughan record when Stone, whom I'd known for a few years, walked up and said, "Wow, you're really good!" At the time Stone's band, Mother Love Bone, was happening, so I was really pleased that he liked my playing. About three months later, Stone called asking if I wanted to jam. So we got together and everything clicked.

A short while after we played together, Stone called and asked whether I'd be interested in joining his new band.

JEFF AMENT I was going through a major identity crisis at that point; I'd put my heart and soul into Mother Love Bone, gave up school, and to have it be snuffed out so quickly. All summer, Stone and I would meet up, mountain bike, and just talk. We aired our grievances with one another. He told me that I needed to lighten up a bit and I told him that he needed to take it more seriously.

CHRIS FRIEL Matt Cameron did most of the playing on the demos, and I did the rest. They had Matt play the stuff that was a little bit more like Mother Love Bone and a little more complicated. And with me, they knew they would get a pretty straight, really nice feel, a lot of space. I know that they were very keen on not letting too many people know that this was like a band—I think there was some legal wrangling going on—so it was called *Stone Gossard Demos*.

MICHAEL GOLDSTONE I knew Jack Irons from his band What Is This. He was always around L.A., and I ran into him at a party. Stone and Jeff had sent demos specifically for me to get to him. When I ran into Jack, I handed him the CD with the instrumental tracks on it.

JACK IRONS (Red Hot Chili Peppers/Eleven/later Pearl Jam drummer) I was in the Red Hot Chili Peppers in 1983. We were the original guys that started the band, and that lasted about nine months or a year. I stayed with my band What Is This, and I rejoined the Chili Peppers in '86. We went through a pretty laborious process to get the material together for *The Uplift Mofo Party Plan*. We did a lot of touring, and that, along with the band's drug use, started to wear on me. I was not ever participating in the drug use, but it's very stressful to be around your friends when they're doing it.

After our guitarist, Hillel Slovak, died of a heroin overdose in June of '88, I was really struggling with my mental health. I was having a nervous breakdown, and that went on for a long time. Eventually that was diagnosed as bipolar disorder and I was hospitalized. It became a lifelong commitment to treat it and live with it.

When I met Eddie, I was on tour with Joe Strummer. It was a very significant tour for me, because prior to meeting Joe Strummer, I was not going to do music anymore. I'd been traumatized, and I just couldn't see that life again. But Joe offered me a gig and got me out again, because I love Joe, and I love the Clash. During that tour, I met my wife-to-be, and the next night, I met Eddie.

I remember the club, the Bacchanal in San Diego. Eddie was backstage—he may have been there to help out. He knew the people at the club, and he wanted to meet Joe and he wanted to meet me, because he knew that I had been in the Chili Peppers. As I recall, all the power went out in the building, and we were just sitting there in the dark. Eddie had the lighter, so he kept the room lit.

After that, we kept in touch and started to hang out and play basketball together. Like every weekend he would drive up from San Diego to where I was living in L.A. He and my wife were probably the two main people in my life at the time, and then, of course, my band Eleven.

MARCO COLLINS (KNDD DJ) My first major radio job was at a station called 91X in San Diego. I was doing a local music show, and I was relegated to Sunday nights after 10. Eddie Vedder was in a band called Bad Radio that I used to play. We never met in San Diego, we just knew each other on the phone, because he would call my show all the time and request that I play his band. He was the guy doing all the work in the band, in terms of promoting it.

He wrote that song "Better Man" in '88. It took a different shape when Pearl Jam recorded it. Bad Radio were a little bit more funky; they had that Chili Peppers thing going on a little.

JACK IRONS In August of 1990, Stone and Jeff were rebuilding from Mother Love Bone and they were looking for a drummer and a singer. They were familiar with my work from the Chili Peppers, and they wanted me to check out what they were doing. I met them at a hotel where they were staying in L.A., and they said, "We'd like you to come play with us."

At the time, my wife was pregnant, I didn't have any money, and the requirement was that I would have to move to Seattle. I had committed to touring with Redd Kross as their drummer for three months and I needed to work. With my son coming at the time, I told them that I wasn't ready to move to Seattle and that I was going on this tour. They were like, "Well, if you know any singers . . ."

EDDIE VEDDER (Pearl Jam/Temple of the Dog singer; Hovercraft drummer) Jack sent me three of their songs. I had them in my head from the night before at work, and I went surfing and had this amazing day. The whole time I was out there surfing, I had this stuff going through my head—the music—and the words going at the same time. I put them down on tape and sent it off.

BENJAMIN REW I was at a bookstore/coffee shop down in Pioneer Square right after Andy died. And Kelly Curtis was having a meeting with Jeff and Stone about what they were gonna do. I overheard them talking about all their options for getting another singer. I wanted to try out for them, and then I talked to a mutual friend, and she said I looked too much like Andy, they wanted to go with a different look.

DAN BLOSSOM I was in a band called Hippie Big Buckle, and our singer disappeared. This was right after Andy died. We put ads up, and there'd be all these Andrew Wood wannabes coming to the audition. There was one person in particular, you'd try to have a conversation with him and he'd be doing Andy's stage shtick, acting like an arena rocker from another world where the gods lived. We were just rolling our eyes, like, Get the fuck outta here!

BENJAMIN REW But I kinda threw my name into the hat for Jeff and Stone's band anyway and got subsequently denied. I thought Tal Goettling, the singer from a band called Son of Man, would get it, because Tal was just an amazing singer, but he was also blond and blue-eyed.

DAVE KRUSEN (Pearl Jam/Hovercraft/Candlebox drummer) I'm originally from Gig Harbor, Washington, which is about 45 minutes outside of Seattle. I had just moved to Seattle, and I got a call from a guy that I played with in a band when I was 13—Tal Goettling. He said that Jeff and Stone were looking for drummers to play with. I called Jeff up and he said, "We'll jam and see what happens." And it kinda went from there.

Because I just had such low self-esteem, I didn't feel deserving. There was a lot of weird squirreliness with some people because they were like, "Who's this guy? He came out of nowhere." So many people wanted that gig. And I just happened into it.

KELLY CURTIS Jeff played me the tape at my office one day and said, "I think we found our singer." It was pretty apparent that there was something special going on. It was pretty immediate. We were all real excited, and then I met Eddie a few weeks later. He was super-shy, super-polite, and super-quiet.

MIKE MCCREADY I'd never been in a situation where it clicks. It all happened in seven days. We had worked up all the music a month prior to that with Krusen. When Eddie came up he had "Footsteps," "Alive," and "Black." And out of that week came so many other things. It was very punk rock. Eddie would stay there in the rehearsal studio, writing all night. We'd show up and there was another one. And then he had to get back. I remember giving him a ride back, at about 5 in the morning, to Sea-Tac Airport. I remember him saying "Don't be late!" He had to get back to work.

JEFF AMENT The minute we started rehearsing and Ed started singing— which was within an hour of him landing in Seattle—was the first time I was like, "Wow, this is a band that I'd play at home on my stereo." What he was writing about was the space Stone and I were in. We'd just lost one of our friends to a dark and evil addiction, and he was putting that feeling to words. I saw him as a brother. That's what pulled me back in [to making music]. It's like when you read a book and there's something describing something you've felt all your life.

DAVE KRUSEN I could tell that Eddie was definitely the real deal, very artistic. He wasn't trying to come across as deeper than he really was. He was a very interesting person and had been through a lot.

EDDIE VEDDER I never knew my real dad. I had another father that I didn't get along with, a guy I thought was my father. There were fights and bad, bad scenes. I was kind of on my own at a pretty young age. I never finished high school.

[My mother] came out [to San Diego] with the specific purpose to tell me that this guy wasn't my father. . . . At first I was pretty happy about it, then she told me who my real dad was. I had met the guy three or four times, he was a friend of the family, kind of a distant friend. He died of multiple sclerosis. So when I met him, he was in the hospital. . . .

I had to deal with the fact that he was dead. My real father was not on this earth. I had to deal with the anger of not being told sooner, not being told while he was alive.

DAVE KRUSEN A week later, we played a show. It was at a place called the Off Ramp, and we were called Mookie Blaylock. I didn't know anything about basketball, so I did not know who Mookie Blaylock was. I remember somebody asking, "Why Mookie Blaylock?" And Jeff answered, "Michael Jordan is just not very cool-sounding."

NANCY WILSON I saw the first time they played, as Mookie Blaylock. Eddie was quite shy. He was kind of studying his boots onstage. He was a really amazing singer, but being in Seattle with this whole tight community of people that loved Andy Wood before him, he was probably a little bit nervous.

LANCE MERCER I photographed them at their first show, at the Off Ramp. I had to walk out for a while. Because the last time I had seen Jeff and Stone play was with Andy. I just kept seeing Andy, and I got really sad.

SCOTT MCCULLUM I remember Chris being really pissed at Andy, shortly after he died. I was really surprised by that, actually. He'd be, "Fuckin' idiot! Fuckin' motherfucker!" Really just mad, and upset, that he had done what he did. He was really hurt. Of course, obviously he came to terms with it; the Temple of the Dog thing happened, and he wrote some amazing songs and got a great album out of the whole thing.

XANA LA FUENTE With Temple of the Dog, Chris handed me a cassette and said, "These are songs I wrote about Andrew for you. This is just for you." Stoney and Jeff heard me playing that cassette at Kelly Curtis's house, where I was living upstairs at the time. They flipped and were like, "What is that?" I said, "It's Chris's, songs that he made for me." They rode his ass and they were like, "We gotta do that."

CHRIS CORNELL I had written "Say Hello to Heaven" and "Reach Down," and I had recorded them by myself at home. My initial thought was I could record them with the ex-members of Mother Love Bone as a tribute single to Andy. And I got a phone call from Jeff, saying he just thought the songs were amazing and let's make a whole record. When we started rehearsing the songs, I had pulled out "Hunger Strike" and I had this feeling it was just kind of gonna be filler, it didn't feel like a real song. Eddie was sitting there kind of waiting for a [Mookie Blaylock] rehearsal and I was singing parts, and he kind of humbly—but with some balls—walked up to the mic and started singing the low parts for me because he saw it was kind of hard. We got through a couple cho- ruses of him doing that and suddenly the lightbulb came on in my head, this guy's voice is amazing for these low parts. History wrote itself after that, that became the single. . . .

XANA LA FUENTE By the time Andy died, I was sick of crying. That's why Chris wrote "poor stargazer/she's got no tears in her eyes." Everyone was just waiting for me to flip out because I never cried.

KIM THAYIL The initial purpose of Temple of the Dog, to be a tribute to Andy Wood, was not the concluding purpose. I think to be a tribute to Andy Wood, there were a lot of people who were close to Andy, like his brothers, who probably should've been involved. It became something else; it became a Chris solo record, with some of his friends, the survi- vors of Mother Love Bone, playing with him.

KEVIN WOOD I fully expected to be included in that project, although they never called me. I was pretty pissed off at the time that I didn't get to play on that, or wasn't even considered to be asked.

GRANT ALDEN I happened to be in L.A., on the A&M lot. I was friends with a publicist at A&M named Rick Gershon. Rick came back to his office and the publicity photos for Temple of the Dog were sitting by his desk, and I remember Rick looking up, looking at me, and looking down at the photo and saying, "Who the fuck is Eddie Vedder, and why is he in my picture?"

SCOTT VANDERPOOL (KXRX/KCMU DJ; Room Nine drummer) I did an on-air interview with Eddie Vedder at KXRX when he was pretty new to the area. The one thing that I remember about it was that when we were listening to songs and talking in between, he said he didn't want me mentioning on the air that he'd been hanging out with Chris Cornell. He didn't want to be seen as some kind of rock star.

NANCY WILSON The next time I saw those guys, probably just a few months later at the Moore Theatre, Eddie was climbing off the P.A. speakers up the side of the wall and jumping headlong into the audience off the balcony. He had acquired his wings. The next show I saw him at, I waded through the people and found him and said, "Hey, Eddie, I hear you can fly!" He just got this big sunshine grin.

KELLY CURTIS PolyGram had let everybody go from Mother Love Bone except for Jeff and Stone and said, "We retain the rights to you guys." In the meantime, both Michael Goldstone and Michele Anthony, who was Alice in Chains' lawyer, went to Sony. We kept trying to get money from PolyGram to make a demo, and they kept saying, "Fine," but they didn't do anything.

We realized that we needed to get off PolyGram. We wanted to be on Sony, and they wanted us, so we figured out who the attorney was that had gotten Rick Dobbis, the new president of PolyGram, his gig and we hired him as our attorney. We asked the attorney, "Will you please help us get off PolyGram? Our singer died, we don't have a future." We didn't tell him about our demos or anything. The attorney goes, "If you meet him face-to-face, he'll let you go." So we went back to New York, and me, Jeff, and Stone went to PolyGram, and Rick Dobbis said, "I release you."

We had already set up a secret meeting downtown with Michele and Michael, and we get there to have dinner with them. We already knew we had Eddie. We had the demo. So we go to meet Michael and Michele for dinner, and Rick Dobbis just happens to walk in right before we're gonna meet them. We're going, "Oh, shit, if he sees Michele and Michael here, we're gonna be screwed." So Rick Dobbis asks us,

"How was dinner?" He thought we had already eaten. We said, "Great," and we got up and left and cut off Michael and Michele down the road a bit. If he would have seen us meeting with Michael and Michele, he might have known that we weren't being truthful. Yeah, close call.

* * *

JERRY CANTRELL Within our own community, there was always a little bit of nose snubbing. When we were coming up, it gave us more impetus. We were inspired by all of those bands, especially by Soundgarden, but we have our own voice. Seattle wasn't like a lot of musical communities I've seen where everybody is doing what's hot. We were all rocking, and it was hot, but nobody was trying to cop someone else's thing. It was a respectful competition.

GRANT ALDEN There were a series of bands who saw what was working and began to try to do that. I think Alice in Chains was one of them. It doesn't mean they were without talent, but it meant in some ways that they were without heart or without soul.

It's indicative of my impotence as a rock critic that Alice in Chains had a career, because I did my level best not to do anything on them at *The Rocket*, to squash them. I've always said this as a joke—it is somewhat true, nevertheless—my mother's name is Alice, so their band name always pissed me off. Beyond that, they were a suburban metal band and decided that they would be Soundgarden Jr. We called them Kindergarden.

MARK ARM Everyone came from different backgrounds. There's no kind of purity test. I think that's retarded. Alice in Chains were definitely better than some of the punk bands that were happening in town.

DAVE HILLIS I think Alice in Chains' change in sound was natural. I don't think they jumped on a bandwagon. I remember the first demo they did with Rick Parashar at London Bridge, before I worked there, sounded so good; it sounded like a record. They weren't hair metal, and they weren't quite the Alice you know.

NICK TERZO As a singer, Layne just had power. Combine that with the unusual sweetness of Jerry's voice laying down melody, and that was unusual at the time. Most of those vocal parts were contrasting each other—there was give-and-take between the two of them—while every other band at that point was just singing choruses together.

DAVE HILLIS The most drastic change with Alice really came when they started using Dave Jerden as a producer. When they recorded with him at London Bridge, I was able to be there sometimes. What I noticed was that Dave Jerden slowed their tempos down, which made it sound heavier, and that's what they're most known for.

DAVE JERDEN (producer) For *Facelift*, they got me a condo down by Puget Sound, and we did all the basic tracks at London Bridge. I was just amazed how great Jerry was and Layne was. Sean's arm was broken, so I tried to use the drummer from Mother Love Bone, but he couldn't play the backbeat parts, so Sean ended up playing the drums with a broken arm, and it came out good. Mike Starr was great; I liked Mike Starr a lot.

SUSAN SILVER With Alice, it was just balls-to-the-wall enthusiasm. I had to bring it down a little bit because Alice didn't have straight jobs and didn't have a sense of budget, and Dave came along and said, "Just go buy what you need," which is like telling a kid in a candy store that there's no limit. So I said, "Look, Dave, we've got X amount of dollars to spend on this record. We don't need to blow it on a bunch of equipment that they're going to use once to get the sound that you want. Let's capture the sound that they have and get only what we need."

Three of the guys understood that really well, and Mike Starr, he understood ultimately, it just took a little more conversation with him, because in his mind he was already a huge rock star.

DAVE JERDEN Jerry and I just saw eye to eye about everything. He was in control of the band. I just spent all my time with Jerry up there. We'd go to the Vogue every night, and after the Vogue, the party would usually end up at my place and then we'd stay up all night and then go fishing for salmon in Puget Sound and then go to the studio.

NICK TERZO I was vegetarian at the time, and I had this long discussion with the band at dinner once about how veal is actually produced, how these calves are put in the boxes. That was kind of the genesis for the song "Man in the Box."

Dave Jerden was my number-one pick to produce. I just thought the Jane's Addiction record he did sounded amazing. I wanted it to sound like that. He had very good chemistry with the band. Dave's a tough guy—he's a bit of a taskmaster—but he's got a very good sense of humor.

DAVE JERDEN Then we went to Los Angeles, and they got an apartment at the Oakwood Apartments. They wanted to know where the local strip bar was. So they went to the Tropicana, and all the strippers ended up hanging out at their apartment. They had a calendar with all the Tropicana strippers on it, and they put X's on the ones that they fucked. They had 'em all X'd out.

ERIC JOHNSON Mookie Blaylock's first tour was with Alice in Chains, down the West Coast. There was the Alice in Chains minivan and the Mookie Blaylock minivan, and my best friend Keith was driving the Alice in Chains minivan and being an all-around roadie/tech/lighting guy. I was in the van with Mookie Blaylock, and we would have food fights between the minivans at 80 miles an hour on I-5.

Mookie Blaylock and Alice in Chains were different on every level. Why they would fit together I didn't know, but they almost seemed like one big band then.

DAVE KRUSEN One night on that tour, we went to see Ozzy, because Alice in Chains were playing his Children of the Night benefit show in Long Beach. They sent a limo for me and Mike to go to the show. We got all excited, and I brought my bong. The limo was fully stocked with booze, so we were pretty torn up by the time we got there.

MIKE INEZ (Ozzy Osbourne band bassist; later Alice in Chains bassist) The first time I saw Alice in Chains play was when I was in the Ozzy band and we did a benefit concert at Long Beach Arena. Alice was the first band on, and as I'm walking in, they were playing to basically an empty arena. But I'm like, Wow, this band is really cool. I went and stood on the side of the stage and watched them play. I gotta tell ya, Layne was, and still to this day is, one of the most compelling front men I've ever seen. He was so cool and creepy and just a badass dude.

DAVE KRUSEN By the time we left the show, everybody was in the limo with us, including Alice in Chains. We were sitting in the limo, and some girl came up and she said, "Who's in the car?" and Sean Kinney goes, "It's Ozzy," and points to me. She's looking right at me, and I looked like a little kid. She was like, "Oh, my God! Ozzy!" So Sean goes, "Let him sign your tits." Someone gave me a Sharpie, and I wrote OZZY really big.

At one point on that ride back, McCready was taking a leak out the window as we were going down the freeway and Kelly Curtis was holding him by his belt. That was entertaining. The bill for the limo, with all the burn marks and the trashing that happened, was huge. The whole tour was like that for me, Mike, Mike Starr, Sean Kinney, and Layne.

ERIC JOHNSON Alice in Chains weren't that decadent yet, but they were learning how to be. There was a lot of beer drunk and probably a lot of weed smoked, and a lot of laughing. It was still pretty pure.

DAVE KRUSEN We played a show in Seattle, and the cast from *Singles* came—Matt Dillon and Bridget Fonda, Kyra Sedgwick. I remember Jeff saying, "When we're done playing, we're gonna take pictures with Matt Dillon and some of the other people from the movie."

KELLY CURTIS I knew Cameron Crowe's roommate, this photographer Neal Preston. When Cameron was working on *Fast Times at Ridgemont High,* we'd go hang out on the set. And just knowing Nancy, I knew she and Cameron would be a perfect couple. I think Neal felt the same way. So we just brought them together, and it happened.

How'd I become the associate producer of *Singles*? I think Cameron was really feeling sorry for me, plus he was making a movie about the Seattle scene, so he gave us a bunch of money. He gave me a flat fee for *Singles*. We got 30 grand or 50 grand. That money helped get the demo made.

CAMERON CROWE I was trying out the camp counselor thing: "Let's all go to the club and check out these bands." . . . It was so packed and people were throwing beer bottles, and after a little bit, Kyra Sedgwick says, "I really get the wonderful scene going on here. I'm going to go home now." Then the costume girl goes, "Great. This is great. Bye!" It ended up being Matt Dillon and Campbell Scott hanging until the very end, slam dancing.

DAVE KRUSEN I had a lot of friends there, and when we got done playing, I took off with them and was partying and kinda forgot about it. McCready did the same thing with some of his friends. And the next day, Jeff was like, "It's too bad you guys took off, because you could've been in the band that we're playing in the movie."

We were like, "What?!"

"Hey, I told you to stick around."

And we were like, "Awww."

Jeff would do things like that—be real subtle about things that would turn out to be something huge. I think he'd downplay things so people wouldn't get wigged out and nervous.

JOSH TAFT (video director) I shot the making-of-the-movie thing for *Singles*. The best moment was the day that Matt Dillon was trying on his Eddie Vedder wig. He was assuming the role of a hybrid Eddie Vedder/Chris Cornell. We all had to go and give our opinions on 120 wigs that they pulled. I remember Matt being very insecure. You know, Matt Dillon is Matt Dillon. He doesn't wear a wig. If anything, the guy plays himself, so he seemed super-uneasy with it.

NILS BERNSTEIN In retrospect, it's amazing that there's a Matt Dillon movie about grunge, but at the time so many weird things would happen every day that it just seemed almost expected, you know?

STEVE MORIARTY (the Gits drummer; OK Hotel club booker) I remember seeing fake posters on the poles for a show that the band in the movie was supposed to be playing. They'd filmed them, then left the posters up. We were like, "Is that show really going on at the OK Hotel? I don't remember booking that." I was like, "Who the fuck are Citizen Dick?"

DANNY BRAMSON (*Singles* music supervisor) Jeff Ament was in the movie's art department. He crafted the cover artwork and the logo for the now-legendary Citizen Dick album. I remember Cameron sitting around on set and writing these fictitious song titles that were almost hilariously sensitive: "Seasons," "Nowhere but You," "Flutter Girl." Jeff included them on the cassette Matt Dillon's character, Cliff Poncier, sold for loose change next to his guitar case.

At one point, Chris Cornell calls: "Danny, will you send me over the song titles from the Citizen Dick album?" And he goes, "It's a secret. Don't tell anyone." When we wrapped the movie, he gave us a tape of songs he'd recorded with those titles. When we first looked at it, we went, "God, is this a joke?" But his delivery of those songs was so heartfelt. We just could not get "Seasons" out of our heads, and thankfully, with Susan's deft hand, she secured it from A&M Records, which was extremely proprietary, for the movie and for the soundtrack.

NANCY WILSON Jeff Ament had his big line in the movie, and everybody was like, "Wow, that sounded kinda like he was reading." The delivery was kinda self-conscious. Cameron always gave him a hard time about it.

JEFF AMENT Acting was really uncomfortable. There's one part where I'm trying to get someone to leave an apartment and I say, "C'mon, while we're young." I felt like I really didn't pull it off, and the next day, all the people from the Lollapalooza tour who saw it with me kept going up to me and saying, "While we're young," and I knew then it came off as bad as I thought.

JASON FINN I was an extra in *Singles*. I was part of the infamous French café scene. If you read about that movie—there's a Cameron Crowe diary—he's like, "That scene was a huge pain in my ass," and he finally cuts it. It was just a couple of the principals talking, and we all had to smoke constantly to make it smoky. The crew was coming through wearing masks, going, "Keep smoking! Keep smoking!" I was sitting with Roderick of Sky Cries Mary and his wife. I was a heavy smoker at the time, but we were there for four or five hours and finally we couldn't take the smoke anymore. We said, "Fuck it," and went over to the Pioneer Square Saloon and got some beers.

BEN SHEPHERD My fingers were so sore from doing so many takes for the movie. You have to get all the different camera angles and performances of the actors and stuff. We're in the background, playing "Birth Ritual," and that song, if you play it enough—that sliding stuff, whoo, my fingers were so sore by the end. Big, nasty blisters from that. And they edited me out. All you can see is part of my elbow.

ROBERT ROTH I was at the OK Hotel the night that Nirvana debuted "Smells Like Teen Spirit," and across the street there was a private thing where they were filming Alice in Chains for *Singles*. At the time, there was the punk-rock side of the street, which I was on—I was more of a Mudhoney, Sonic Youth, Nirvana kind of grunge fan. Then there was another side, which was more connected to that late-'80s metal scene.

KURT BLOCH That show at the OK Hotel was legendary! There were a few genre-defining shows, and certainly that was one of them. I remember standing next to Nils Bernstein, and then, "Hey, here's a new song, blah blah blah." They started playing "Teen Spirit," and Nils and I looked at each other like, Holy fuck! This song is unbelievable.

STEVE MORIARTY Nirvana needed gas money to drive down to L.A. to record *Nevermind,* so they played a last-minute show at the OK Hotel, which my partner Robin booked. The band walked away with a few hundred bucks, drove down to L.A., and the rest is history.

NICK TERZO Alice in Chains were the first band to have radio success in that movement, and that's a fact. It's been revised since, but the fact of the matter is, "Man in the Box" broke down tons of doors. The album came out in August 1990, but radio started playing "Man in the Box" in early 1991. And after that, their song "Would?" broke down doors on alternative radio—and then Nirvana went right through.

RICK KRIM (MTV director of musical talent) MTV used to have this thing, for a while it was called Hip Clip of the Week and then it was called Buzz Bin. I remember discussing in a meeting whether we took Alice in Chains or this band Thunder, which was a hair band that sounded like Whitesnake. There was a whole big discussion, and I'm pretty sure we all picked Alice in Chains.

The video for "Man in the Box" was pretty dark. Sort of the antithesis of a lot of stuff on the channel. Alice in Chains felt like it was something new, and Thunder felt like it was something old. That was the first sign: When MTV opts for this Alice in Chains band over a hair band, that was starting the tides turning.

NICK TERZO The "Man in the Box" video definitely reflected a certain intensity. There was man with his eyes sewn shut in it. On radio, they had plenty of problems with the song. That lyric, "Jesus Christ, deny your maker," caused a lot of stations to drop the song once they got into the lyrics. Some stations were playing it only at night. You had some stations playing it in the day, some stations sticking with it for six months, which was kind of unheard-of back then, and some stations dropping it after three months, then putting it back again. It was an anomaly, 'cause no one really knew how to deal with this music, or what it was. No one knew what grunge was then.

* * *

DAVE HILLIS I became Rick Parashar's assistant at London Bridge toward the very end of his work on Temple of the Dog. Then we did the Mookie Blaylock demos, which was interesting because they were all friends and cohorts of mine. When we started working on *Ten,* they didn't have the Pearl Jam name yet; it was still Mookie Blaylock.

A lot of people ask me, "What was it like working on the Pearl Jam record? It must have been magical." And honestly, it really wasn't. The music was great and everything, but nobody knew—they weren't famous yet and they were developing as a band in the studio. Eddie really wasn't Eddie yet. Eddie drove a yellow low-rider pickup, tinted windows; very San Diego Beach, which you don't see in rainy Seattle. He just had a different personality. He wasn't brooding and serious, the way people imagine him.

At the beginning, Eddie was kind of struggling getting vocals done, and people were getting a little nervous. He wasn't fully nailing it. Think about it: He was in the shadow of Andy Wood, brand-new band, he's still trying to figure out the sound. Plus the weight of, Wow, I'm on a major label. Then he started staying the night in the studio. We would leave blank tracks that he could record himself singing on, and then pick the good parts from there. He'd watch Bukowski videos and all these different types of things to influence him. Over the making of that record, the Eddie Vedder persona seemed to take shape.

MIKE MCCREADY Recording *Ten*, we probably did "Even Flow" 30 times. [B-side] "Yellow Ledbetter" was probably the second take; when we did that song, Ed just started going for it. But [*Ten*] was mostly Stone and Jeff; me and Eddie were along for the ride at that time.

DAVE HILLIS I know Rick and Stone butted heads a little. Rick had a very different way of producing. He's not one of those guys that sits behind the desk, jumping up and down and really getting into the music. He had a very traditional East Indian background and had a very different demeanor than you would think of someone producing a rock record. Stone wanted him to get into it more. I remember listening to them talk, and Stone would say, "Just act like you like us." Rick would be like, "I'm not there to do that. I'm there to make your record good."

DAVE KRUSEN It got to the point where we need to pick a new name, because obviously we can't call it Mookie Blaylock. I remember sitting down in the practice room and everybody writing down names, and it went on for a while. *Pearl* came out of one category, and *jam* came out of another.

JEFF AMENT The first time I mentioned Pearl Jam [as a band name] was when Ed, Stone, and I were watching Sonic Youth play with Crazy Horse. In the middle of Crazy Horse, I turned to Stone and said, "What about 'Pearl Jam'?" A couple of years later, the first time that we played [Neil Young's] Bridge School [benefit], I saw Neil's big black, must have been a '55 Chevy, and the license plate says PEARL 10. I think I'm in a dream. I asked Neil how long he'd had those plates, and he said 15 years.

DAVE KRUSEN I used to do a lot of psychedelics, so I really like the story behind the name that they came up with: that Eddie's grandmother Pearl had a hallucinogenic jam.

I remember Eddie made each of us in the band a little artwork that said PEARL JAM. It was some glittery, purple goop on a clear CD tray. It looked a little like sperm the way that it was written, like a liquidy thing that had dried. People I knew were like, "Oh, I see what that's about!" And I was like, "No, dude, it was just two words that came together!"

DAVE HILLIS Dave I just always loved. What's weird is I never even knew he drank. I never saw him party once in my life.

DAVE KRUSEN I just wanted to party and get fucked up. When we did the photo shoot for the album, I got some beer, and halfway through the shoot, I started to fall asleep. Afterward, they were showing pictures and going, "You remember that?" "Hmmm, no. And I didn't think I had sunglasses on." They were like, "You didn't. Your eyes were shut, so we had to put sunglasses on you." I was sitting down, propped up against the wall.

The *Singles* wrap party was the last gig I played with them. At the time, I had a lot going on in my personal life. I wasn't really dealing with anything, because I just drank all the time. I remember Mike going, "I'm not gonna drink until after the show." And I said, "Oh, that's a good idea." Well, I didn't hold out, and that ended up being the night that things got really bad.

By the time I got to the big party at the hotel—it was at Cameron Crowe's room or whatever—I was just really bad off. I got into an argument with my kind-of girlfriend at the time. In a nutshell, I'd gotten together with this girl, she got pregnant, so I tried to do the right thing and stick around, but I was miserable. My son was born a day after we went in to record *Ten,* which only made things more intense in my life. It's been written about that night that I beat up my girlfriend and put her in the hospital, but that is not true.

Some guy jumped in who didn't know who I was, and I got in a fight with him. It turned into a huge melee, and the cops end up coming. Everybody talked them out of arresting me. I left and passed out for a couple of days. They couldn't find me, and when I woke up and finally called them, they were like, "We gotta go to England to mix the album, and you can't go because you need to get straightened out."

I remember getting off the phone knowing I had to go to rehab, and I did. But it didn't take, and it took me another two years to finally get to the point where I wanted to stop, and in '94 I got sober.

MATT CHAMBERLAIN (Pearl Jam drummer) I was originally in a band with Edie Brickell, the New Bohemians. I was living in Dallas, and I had been in that band for three or four years. I'd met G.E. Smith, and he said, "Hey, if the New Bos ever break up, give me a call," because he was doing the house band for *Saturday Night Live*. We broke up at the end of that tour, and I called G.E. up and said, "Man, I'm so into moving to New York City and doing this gig."

Probably two weeks after I had gotten all that sorted out, I get a call from Tony Berg, who was the producer on the second New Bohemians record. He said, "Hey, my pal Michael Goldstone, who's this A&R guy at Epic, has this new band called Pearl Jam. They are doing a tour, and they need a drummer. It's a really short commitment." It was for that last part of the summer before I started the *SNL* gig, and I thought, Perfect.

Everywhere we played, we were the opening band, but people were just flipping out. Eddie wore army shorts, white Doc Martens, and a Butthole Surfers *Locust Abortion Technician* T-shirt every fucking day for the whole tour. He washed his clothes in the hotel room sink. He had a hole in the ass of his shorts, which he gaffer-taped. After every gig, he was shell-shocked because he was giving it his all. The tour culminated with a gig at RKCNDY in Seattle, which is where they filmed the video for "Alive."

All the industry people that I ran into were saying, "This is going to be huge." I remember the guys in the band saying, "We don't know what's going to happen. We'd be really happy if this sold 100,000 copies, and we could just continue doing this."

They were looking for someone to join and be on the road forever. They had offered the position to me, and it was an issue at one point: "Are you going to join the band or are you not going to join the band?" It felt like a prearranged marriage, like somebody saying, "Hey, you should marry this person—there'll be a lot of money in it for you." But I just didn't feel any connection to it. I thought, I'd rather just live in New York City.

I recommended Dave, who was a pal of mine in Dallas who'd been playing around in some local bands. I think he was working at 7-Eleven.

He was not doing so hot, but I always thought he was a great drummer, so I called him up.

DAVE ABBRUZZESE (Pearl Jam drummer) When Matt called, I was in a funk band in Dallas called Dr. Tongue, and I was working at a head shop. My expertise was in the grow department, so if people would come in saying that they wanted to grow lettuce hydroponically in their closet—wink, wink—I would help them get set up.

I had a show on community radio with a friend of mine called *Chris and Dave's "Music We Like" Show.* People would call and request music; if we didn't like it, we'd just play something else. I dug through the CDs and found Mother Love Bone and Pearl Jam's sampler CD. We put the Mother Love Bone stuff on-air and I was like, "Eek," and turned it off and put on Pearl Jam, and I think I made it through about 25 seconds of the first couple of songs. They just didn't hit me right.

I said, "What do you think, Chris?"

He said, "It's a free trip to Seattle."

KRISHA AUGEROT I was *shocked* to see Dave Abbruzzese in the lobby of Curtis Management when they were trying out drummers. Because he was such a rocker. Super-long hair, wearing a track suit. He's from Texas, so it's a totally different vibe. But a very skilled drummer, and I really liked him. Visually, it just was not what I was expecting. I could see him in Alice in Chains, not in Pearl Jam.

DAVE ABBRUZZESE The first day I got to Seattle, I actually met them all an hour before their first video shoot, for "Alive," at RKCNDY. I just stood back and took it in. The show was cool. I was watching it think-ing, I wish I was playing right now. Dallas was a place where people were standing back, with their arms folded, watching, whereas at that show, everyone was excited.

After we played our second show together, at the RKCNDY, I was in the Curtis office. That show just felt good and the music was great, and all of a sudden I felt like I was a part of that same energy that I experienced witnessing that show the first day I got there. I came across one of Jeff's drawings, and one of the images was that stick-man figure; it's tribal art of a man standing, arms outstretched, surrendering to the sky or whatever. That image really resonated with me, so the next day, I got it tattooed on my left shoulder. It wasn't necessarily a statement of camaraderie; it was to document that personal feeling that I had then. The way I felt at the show that night, if I would have stopped playing right after that—if my car would've flipped over and I lost my arms or something—I would have felt gratified musically.

CHAPTER 25
THE FINAL COUNTDOWN

KATHLEEN HANNA (Bikini Kill singer) In August of 1990, I found myself laying on my stomach, in the woods, with a pair of binoculars, a bottle of Canadian Club, and my friend Kurt Cobain. The reason why I had the binoculars was because I was the lookout while he ran across the street to a teen pregnancy center that had just opened in our town. And it really wasn't a teen pregnancy center. It was a right-wing con where they got teenage girls to go in there and then told them they were gonna go to hell if they had abortions. Since Kurt and I were angry young feminists in the '90s, we decided that we were gonna do a little public service that night. We drank our Canadian Club, and he watched out while I went across the street and wrote FAKE ABORTION CLINIC, EVERYONE, 'cause I was kinda like the pragmatic one. And he was more creative, so he went over, and in six-foot-tall red letters he wrote GOD IS GAY. He was kinda cool like that.

So, after that, we polished off the Canadian Club. And we lived in Olympia, Washington; we walked down the hill, we went to the bar, we got some more Canadian Club. Then we went to my apartment, we got some 40-ouncers, we got a little more drunk. And apparently I insulted just about everybody in my whole entire town, and I threw up on someone's legs. It was one of those nights that like later on, whenever anybody mentions it you don't want to think about it. So, ended up at Kurt's apartment, and I smashed up a bunch of shit. And I took out a Sharpie marker and I wrote a bunch of shit all over his bedroom wall. . . . Then I passed out, with the marker in my hand. And I woke up, and I had one of those hangovers where you think that if you walk in the next room there could be a dead body in there. So I wasn't that happy when six months later, Kurt called me up and said, "Hey, do you remember that night?" I was like, "*Ehhhh . . .*"

Then Kurt is like, "Well, there's this thing that you wrote on my wall and it was actually kinda cool and I want to use it as a lyric in one of my songs." And I was like, as long as I can get out of the conversation and not think about [that night] anymore, you can use whatever you want. So I hung up and thought, How the fuck is he gonna use "Kurt smells like teen spirit" as a lyric?

BUTCH VIG The first thing Nirvana played, on the first day of rehearsals for *Nevermind,* was "Smells Like Teen Spirit," and I was just completely floored. It sounded huge and crushing loud. I just was pacing around 'cause it sounded so fuckin' cool. I was like, "Play it again, play it again." I made them play it like three or four times, and I went, "Wow, this is really, really good." I knew at that point that just the power of them playing together was like a hundred times what it was when they had come to the Smart session, and a lot of that was because of Dave.

In the big room next to where we were, Lenny Kravitz was rehearsing for a tour. On the third or fourth day of rehearsals, Gary Gersh, their A&R guy, was supposed to come by at a certain time. A couple hours went by, and the band didn't want to just play, so Krist went out and got a bottle of Jack Daniel's and drank. Then he went into the office and got on the intercom: "Paging Lenny Kravitz!" I think he started going off: "Where's Gary Gersh, that fuckin'-ass record company . . ."—you know, that kind of thing. And I had to run down there and persuade him, "Okay, maybe we should go back in. Let's go and talk about your bass sound."

We went up to Sound City up in the Valley in Los Angeles to record. We only spent like 16 days in the studio. The band was staying at the

Oakwood Apartments, which they completely trashed. It looked like an atom bomb went off. Junk food and beer and records laying around and cassettes and guitars and guitar strings and sticks, and Kurt had drawn a bunch of pictures and written lyrics on the walls.

That band Europe that had a big hit with that song "The Final Countdown" was staying next to them. So there's these blond Scando guys with their girlfriends out by the pool, and Kurt would take his guitar out there, and the Nirvana guys would sit out by the pool and make up songs about them. They were definitely punks. They were fuckin' around as much as they could.

There was this BBQ place called Dr. Hogly Wogly's near the studio, and one night I had the runner at the studio just get a huge meat slaughter, basically. The girls from L7 were there, and I was trying to finish an edit or something, and when I came back out they'd had a food fight. I think L7 had spurred it on. They'd just completely taken the sausages and BBQ sauce and stuff and thrown it all over each other. There was a huge, ugly mess all over the walls of the studio lounge.

JENNIFER FINCH I was going out with Dave then, so we were around all the time. We started going out when L7 did a tour in England with Nirvana. I was friends with his first band, Scream, because when I was a promoter I did a Scream show in Los Angeles. Dave and I kind of shared the role of being the youngest in both of the bands. Also, we had a very similar past with hardcore that none of the other members had shared. He was very lighthearted and very kind and considerate.

I had this problem with a stalker. I have a good memory of this because I had to keep these letters that this guy wrote me. In one of the letters, he put a newspaper photograph of Dave and I and X'd him out and threatened to kill him and do all this kind of weird stuff. Our management hired a private detective to keep tabs on that person. I think that that person eventually went away. He worked for the postal service.

BUZZ OSBORNE Everything that Nirvana did that people consider good was clouded by some horrible thing. Everything. The happiest I ever saw them was the time that we stayed with them in L.A., when they were recording *Nevermind*. They had rented some condo, and I think Krist had just gotten a DUI.

BUTCH VIG One night we went to see L7 play, and I didn't know this, but Kurt and Krist took mushrooms, and Krist was driving. He had also drank like half a bottle of whiskey by the time we got there. After the show, they disappeared.

The next morning I went in at noon, and at 1 or 2, no band. I kept calling, "Where's the band?" Finally, I got a call from Silva at 4 or 5, and he said, "Krist was driving the van on one of the canyon roads, drunk and tripping." And when he got pulled over, there was still like a quarter of a bottle of Jack Daniel's, and Krist was like, "I don't want him to fuckin' catch me with it," so he chugged the rest literally in the 30 seconds it takes the cop to walk up to the van. So he was completely out of his mind. Of course, they arrested him and took him to the slammer.

KRIST NOVOSELIC You open the cell door and boom—the heat hits you from all the people in there. . . . There's like 50 guys in there with these cigarettes and nobody has a fuckin' match! It was totally quiet, except when somebody would walk in and [this] little guy would say, "Yougotanymatches?" Finally this guy walked in with matches and they all just lit up like crazy, smoke is filling the room.

BUTCH VIG Kurt, still trippin' his brains out, got out and walked from wherever they were, back like seven miles, and this is like at 2 in the morning. They had to go bail Krist out, and needless to say, they were pretty fried when they came in.

BUZZ OSBORNE They were in good spirits, laughing, having fun. We went down to the studio with them one or two of the days that they were recording. Really relaxed. And it was just good. We were playing a show in San Diego, and Dave went with us down there, rode along. We had a blast. That was it, that one little window, where I was able to put all my bad feelings aside, and none of that negative stuff came up.

BUTCH VIG The afternoon we tried to track "Lithium," we had done a few passes, and for whatever reason Dave kept speeding up and it didn't feel good. Like halfway through the fourth take Kurt says, "Stop! Stop!" He started playing "Endless, Nameless," and I just kept the tape rolling. Kurt was singing so hard I thought he was gonna kill somebody. The veins in his neck were bulging out, he just was pouring sweat, strangling his vocal chords, and at the end of song, he started smashing his guitar. I was in the control room and didn't even know what to say. I went out and asked, "Are you okay?" He just got up and walked in the other room, and Krist sort of looked at me like, Whoa!

I've never seen so much rage in someone in the studio that came out that instantaneously. It was scary to watch him play that song. I'm not kidding.

BARRETT JONES (Nirvana drum tech; Laundry Room Studio owner/operator) When they were recording *Nevermind* in L.A., I flew out and stayed with them for a week. I remember they were trying to figure out that song "Stay Away." The original lyric was "pay to play," and they didn't like that. And I suggested "stay away." Not that they would remember that. After listening to playbacks of most of the stuff, I told Kurt, "Man, this is amazing. You're going to be on the cover of *Rolling Stone* within a year." Oh, I totally believed it, and I was totally right.

BUTCH VIG We went to Devonshire Studios and I started mixing some songs. I had spent three or four days mixing and wasn't particularly happy because the band was there all the time. Anytime I tried to make stuff sound better to me, Kurt would go, "No, no, turn all the treble off the guitars. Make it sound more like Black Sabbath," or whatever.

DAVE GROHL "More low end! I want it to sound like the Melvins!" "It has to be heavier, heavier, heavier!" Butch was doing his best to do what Kurt wanted, and it just wasn't turning out.

BUTCH VIG The mixes were sounding kind of muffly, and Gary Gersh and Silva came by and listened and they were like, "Let's just get a good mix guy in, and we'll try and keep the band away from the studio a little bit and let him do his thing." I was like, "Cool."

So they sent over a list of all these mix guys. I showed the list to Kurt and at the bottom was Andy Wallace, and it listed Slayer first on his credits. He said, "Call that guy." If he'd looked further on Andy's credits, it had Madonna. If Madonna's name had been first, Andy wouldn't have gotten the call.

BEN SHEPHERD First time I heard anything off of *Nevermind,* I thought, Wow, these guys are going for number one. We heard some songs that somebody snuck out of the studio down to our studio. Chris is in the other room mixing "Slaves & Bulldozers." Matt and Kim are in this room listening to *Nevermind.* I think it was the song "Come as You Are." And I stood in the hallway and I could hear my friends listening to my friends and watched my other friend work on a song that me and my friends had put together. So it was really intense.

I stood there watching these two different worlds going on. Then I walked towards Chris, towards the music we were working on, instead of listening to someone else.

GRANT ALDEN We had advance cassettes of both *Nevermind* and the Soundgarden record, *Badmotorfinger,* in *The Rocket* office. It was a good Soundgarden record, but there was something special about that Nirvana record. People would come in and go, "Can I make a copy?," and it was probably three-to-one, four-to-one they wanted to borrow or copy the Nirvana tape over the Soundgarden tape.

SUSIE TENNANT (DGC Records Northwest promotion representative) Being in Seattle, there were advance copies of *Nevermind* around. People made copies for other people, and that whole summer and fall, you couldn't go anywhere in Seattle without hearing it. You'd pull up at a stoplight and hear it from the car next to you. You'd be walking on the street and hear it blaring out of stores.

JONATHAN PONEMAN Bruce and I had gone to the Off Ramp and we ran into Susie Tennant, and she said, "Have you heard the new Nirvana record yet?" So we went into her car and she had a cassette tape and I remember listening to it—I was sitting in the backseat and Bruce and Susie were in the front seat—and it started off with a song that I remember hearing them play live. It was like crescendo after crescendo after crescendo. I mean it was orgasmic—probably more female orgasmic than male orgasmic—and, of course, it was "Smells Like Teen Spirit." Bruce and I just looked at each other and said, "This is going to be huge."

JEFF GILBERT I actually hold the distinction of being the first person in Seattle to play "Smells Like Teen Spirit" on the radio. Three of us got the record. I was working over at KZOK, an AM station. Cathy Faulkner over at KISW got it, and there was somebody else. They said, "Not until noon. We're gonna be listening." Well, I just went up to the clock and advanced it five minutes ahead of time, because as the guy on the low end of the dial on AM, I thought, This is how I say "Fuck you" to the rest of 'em. So I played it first.

Something changed in the week or two following: That song never left the radio. It just kept getting more and more requests. Suddenly, it just felt different around town. It's like, you're on the very top of the roller coaster and you're about to go into that big, spinning dive. That anticipation, it was in the air.

CRAIG MONTGOMERY We drove down to L.A. from Seattle to film the "Teen Spirit" video and do some shows. And I remember being in the van, and Kurt was in the back and he played me "Teen Spirit" on the boom box. And he asked me, "Do you think it sounds too much like the Pixies?"

SAMUEL BAYER ("Smells Like Teen Spirit" video director) I had come out to Los Angeles in the summer of 1991 hoping to get my big break directing videos. I knew Robin Sloane, who commissioned videos at Geffen Records. Took her out to lunch, begged her for some work, and she was nice enough to send me an advance of some songs from the Nirvana album. I've said this before, but I think that they picked me because I had the worst reel. It was a bunch of artsy, pretend videos. I think one of them was set to Muddy Waters music and one of them was for a stockbroker that had hired me to do a video for his band in New York. *(Laughs.)* Maybe it was a punk thing to do, to pick the guy with the really bad reel.

CRAIG MONTGOMERY The "Teen Spirit" director wanted to do all this story, narrative stuff, and Kurt just wanted to have the band playing and kids going nuts. Krist wanted booze and sent me out to liquor stores to get it. Did that cause things to disintegrate? The thing was never integrated enough to disintegrate.

SAMUEL BAYER It was completely out of control. I was a very hungry, angry young man that wanted to make the greatest video of all time, and they were a band that had never made a video before—or at least, a corporate video—and we clashed like oil and water from the get-go. It was an all-day shoot from 10 in the morning to 11 at night. I pulled in every favor I possibly could: The janitor was the janitor from my apartment complex in Venice; the cheerleaders were strippers recruited from some strip club in L.A.

DAVE GROHL Originally we wanted L7 to be the cheerleaders, that was our idea. So instead I think they got porn stars. Which kinda wasn't really the vibe we were going for.

KRIST NOVOSELIC I go, "Well, why don't we have the cheerleaders, they'll be cheerleaders, but they'll have anarchy A's on their shirts." So that's a whole nod to the punk-rock sensibility.

SAMUEL BAYER The kids were recruited from a Nirvana show on the Sunset Strip, and they were egging on the band, so it was kind of me versus them—and I was losing. Kurt absolutely hated me by the end. He didn't want to lip-synch the song. And I always believed that maybe his anger with me added a whole level of intensity to his performance. I always had a vision for something destructive at the end of the video, but truth be told, I was so beat up by the end of the day I just couldn't take any more. I was sitting on the dolly and somebody came up to me and said, "Kurt wants to invite the kids down to destroy the set." And I'm like, "Great. Destroy the set. What do I care?" And the kids came down, and it was this beautiful display of anarchy and destruction; I just flipped the camera on and shot 400 feet of film, and that was the end of the video.

Kurt wasn't happy with the edit. He sat with me in the editing bay to finalize it. He took out a bunch of conceptual shots that in retrospect absolutely should have been removed, and he switched some performance stuff around, purposefully putting in a shot where you can tell he's not playing the proper chords. It was very uncomfortable—we weren't real friendly with each other—and I was just happy when the whole thing was over. That was the last time I saw him: disheveled, looking like he just woke up on the sidewalk, walking out into the sunlight.

AMY FINNERTY (MTV director of music programming and talent relations) The "Smells Like Teen Spirit" video came in at the same time the new Guns N' Roses video came in, and at this point I hadn't worked at MTV for very long. I went to Abbey Konowitch, the head of the programming department at that point, and said, "Look, I love this place. I'm having a great time. That being said, this place doesn't really represent my generation. We really aren't playing videos from bands that I'm passionate about. We have something that's come in that I'm extremely passionate about. I'm just saying to you that if we don't play this, I don't feel like there's a place for me here." I put my job on the line, basically. I believed in it that much.

The video world-premiered on *120 Minutes*. Within a week or two, we got it in heavy rotation, and within less than a month, the face of MTV had started to make a major transition.

SAMUEL BAYER In the fall of 1991, that video was getting a lot of airplay on MTV, and I would spend hours at my girlfriend's house just laying in bed waiting for it to come on, 'cause it was really exciting, really like nothing else out there. At the time, I think my competition was a million-dollar Guns N' Roses video and Michael Jackson doing something with Eddie Murphy or MC Hammer. The "Teen Spirit" video was nasty, brown-colored—it looked dirty, it really stood out.

Within a year of that, there were a lot of different-looking videos: Pearl Jam, Stone Temple Pilots, Soundgarden. It seemed like all the videos now had this angry, dark vibe to them.

CHAPTER 26
PUNK BREAKS

COURTNEY LOVE I met Kurt in Portland in 1989. Nirvana played with a band called the Dharma Bums—they were very big in Portland. I met Kurt there and everyone knows that story, and it's pretty true as is told. I just read a first draft of the biopic film, and it's deadly accurate. He was with Tracy, and then Kurt and I got into a wrestling thing. But in the first draft of this script it says Living Colour was on the jukebox. No, for fuck's sake, it was a song called "Dear Friend" by *Flying* Color from San Francisco.

We started wrestling because I told him he had a fat girlfriend. I was just being a dick. But then he gave me a sticker—a little sticker with Chim Chim [the monkey] on it that had Nirvana in his hand.

EVERETT TRUE Did I tell you the story of me introducing Kurt to Courtney? No, there's not that much debate about it. The only debate that exists is the fact that Courtney made up a story that she met Kurt a couple of years earlier in Portland and Kurt backed it up—with my full approval, because we didn't want her to be seen as a gold digger. I went along with it because I thought it was funny.

ERIC ERLANDSON Courtney and I saw Nirvana together in L.A. a couple times. They were playing some weird club in a strip mall. L7 were raving about them, and we were like, "Uhhh." We left early, I think. We were both into the Mudhoney thing still at that point, not Nirvana. It wasn't until the next year, in the spring of '91, when Courtney actually met Kurt, when Everett True was here. Courtney and I were dating then; we were still living together.

EVERETT TRUE Courtney, how should we say, had a talent for being slightly liberal with the truth. That was one of the things I loved about her, and so did Kurt. Kurt had a talent for being liberal with the truth, too. All of us did. If you go back and do the research, there's a cover story in *Sassy* magazine in '92, where Kurt and Courtney refer to the first time they ever met, and it's at a Butthole Surfers show.

It was my first time in L.A. The next night there was a show down at the Hollywood Palladium—the Butthole Surfers, Redd Kross, and L7—and I went down there early to make sure I could get in. The first person I bumped into was John Silva, who had just started managing Nirvana at the time. I said, "John, do you know anything about this girl Courtney Love? I want to meet her; her band is playing in town in a few days' time."

He said, "I do know who she is, and actually I can introduce you to her right now, because she's here and she lives in L.A." So he introduces me and we got along ferociously well, because as excited as I was to meet her, she was even more excited to meet me, because Courtney obviously wanted more than anything else at that point in time for the media to pay attention to her and here was this hotshot British music journalist—probably the best known at the time, certainly in America—paying attention to her.

We started going around stealing other people's drinks, because neither of us had much money, and she's not really much of a drinker. I think somebody slipped acid into my whiskey and at some point we started physically fighting because, I'm only guessing here, I was getting really annoyed because I felt she was flirting with me. I said, "Man, you don't need to do that with me, because I already like your music." So we started punching each other and rolling around, kicking, screaming, on the floor.

All of a sudden, Nirvana show up on the scene, and Kurt didn't know who the blond woman I was fighting was—or maybe he recognized her,

I don't know. But he certainly knew who I was, and it was also equally apparent that the two of us were having more fun than the rest of the audience combined, so the most natural thing in the world was for him to race over to where we were fighting on the floor, jump on top of her, and join in the fight. And that's how they met.

I had a blackout of about nine or 10 hours. About a year later, I was speaking to Kurt on the phone and he told me, "We were back at the apartment, it was about 2 or 3 in the morning, you just turned up, talking all about this woman Courtney Love: 'Courtney Love! I'm gonna marry Courtney Love!'" I was saying that because I was so off my head. He said he ringed her up right there and then and asked her out on a date. I was like, "You did?" He's like, "Yeah, I never showed up to it. I only did it to show off in front of you."

That whole evening was incredibly complicated. I'm not sure that all of the stories have come out of it yet. I just remember waking up completely naked underneath a glass coffee table in Nirvana's apartment in the Hills the next morning about 7 a.m.

MARK ARM My view towards Courtney changed when all those made-up stories about how they hooked up started coming out, like they met each other in Portland at the Satyricon. What's the point of this fake backstory? I remember on that tour we did with Hole in '91 she was asking about him; it seemed like she had her sights set on Kurt even then. Maybe she's trying to make herself seem like she wasn't a gold digger, and I don't think she needed to do that. Because, clearly, they liked each other. Who cares when you met?

LORI BARBERO Kurt and Courtney? I pretty much introduced them. In 1991, when we did the movie *The Year Punk Broke,* I had already known them each at that point for like five years, and then I had known Dave when he was in Scream. Courtney showed up at that Reading Festival and she's like, "Can you introduce me to Kurt?" Courtney was there because she was dating Billy Corgan from Smashing Pumpkins, and Nirvana was there, too. And she kept saying, "You need to introduce me to Kurt." I'm like, "Okay, okay, whatever."

DAVE MARKEY (*1991: The Year Punk Broke* documentary director) After Reading, in Rotterdam, Courtney came backstage and brought Billy Corgan to meet everybody. I specifically remember Sonic Youth and Nirvana and me in this sort of classroom that was doubling as a backstage room. The Smashing Pumpkins were getting huge at that time, and in walks Courtney with Billy Corgan, arm in arm.

I remember they left the room, and everyone was cracking jokes at Billy Corgan's expense, like, "Oh, yeah, we met the rock star." Cobain went up to the wall and wrote in Magic Marker, COURTNEY + GISH, *Gish* being the Smashing Pumpkins album at the time. I think that was pretty telling of where people's attitudes were at that time. Everyone was making fun of the fact that Billy Corgan was already known as sort of an alternative-rock star. This is right before Nirvana would become the real rock stars that we were parodying in the film.

KAT BJELLAND (singer/guitarist for Minneapolis's Babes in Toyland) I didn't really know Nirvana when we played Reading. Courtney kept trying to introduce me to Kurt. She's like, "You gotta meet him! You gotta meet him!" Of course, Courtney tried to get the limelight out of anything. When Babes in Toyland were doing interviews for MTV, she was jumping up and down in the back screaming, like a really weird little kid who can't get enough attention.

PETER DAVIS (tour booker; *Your Flesh* zine editor in chief/publisher) Hole was a nightmare. Courtney Love. Really driven and brilliant in a lot of ways, but also very much a crazy person. Bookin' tour dates and havin' her disappear so that she could go and schmooze with Billy Corgan one weekend in Chicago and then turn around a week later and she's doing the same thing, same venue but with Nirvana. It was very peculiar.

LORI BARBERO Later on, Courtney called me in Minneapolis. She's like, "You need to meet me in Chicago because Nirvana's playing," and so I went to Chicago, and then I introduced them at the Metro. She was dating Billy, and she broke up with Billy that night.

COURTNEY LOVE I didn't dump Billy to go out with Kurt. If anything, later on Billy dumped me because I had something with Trent Reznor, and that was past grunge. Dating Billy was rough. He loves me. I guess I love him, too. He's a good guy. He saved my life a few times. You can't ever forget that. We had this very romantic relationship, almost like girlfriends. We wrote letters to each other. We didn't "do it" a lot, you know what I mean? I know that's a bad visual, I'm sorry. We were like girlfriends. Girlfriends that loved each other very much.

DANNY GOLDBERG I first met Courtney in Chicago after *Nevermind* came out. The band did a tour of clubs to show they were still connected to their punk roots before they went on to play bigger places, and one such club was the Metro in Chicago. My wife, Rosemary Carroll, had already told me about Courtney because she had been Courtney's lawyer for a while and had negotiated the Hole deal with Caroline. Rosemary told me she was really intense.

Lori Barbero from Babes in Toyland was there also, and I guess she wanted to see Dave Grohl. Courtney disingenuously told me she was just there to keep Lori company. But I noticed in the dressing room about 15 minutes later—this was after the show—that she was sitting on Kurt's lap. I guess they had met sometime before. From that night on, they were always together.

CRAIG MONTGOMERY I remember that night Dave, who was rooming with Kurt, had to come over and sleep in my room. Because I'm sure Kurt and Courtney needed some privacy.

DANNY GOLDBERG There was this benefit coming up for Rock for Choice that Dave Grohl had wanted the band to do, and the band was happy to do it. There was Nirvana, I think Sister Double Happiness, L7, and Hole. Courtney thought she should go higher on the bill, which gave me the sense that this was somebody who was a strong-minded person.

JENNIFER FINCH I knew Kurt completely separate from Courtney when L7 were putting together Rock for Choice. We called Kurt directly, and when Courtney found out that Kurt was on that show she was just like rambling off every good excuse . . . When Courtney wanted to go out with him, I was verbally against it, although I introduced them because she just would not shut up. Because I come from a place where if you're gonna do music, don't date who you want to be.

Dave and I broke up after going to the first Lollapalooza together. Dave and I and Kurt went. We had two seating tickets and a third ticket in the back. It seemed at that moment that Dave had no problem with giving me that third ticket to go sit in the back. . . . I'm telling you, I'm psycho, okay? His intentions were of no harm whatsoever; he just felt like he needed to bond with Kurt—they had just been going through this recording process. So I went and sat in the back totally resentful. I hung out with my friends there for the rest of the evening and got a different ride home.

After that, we were just hanging out one day, and Dave was playing guitar and video games, and I was like, I don't want to be with somebody who plays guitar, because I play guitar. It was jealousy, absolutely. He had his sights on what he is today the second he was in Nirvana. Central figure, songwriter. When he was the new guy in the band, the A&R people would come around and he'd slip them his demo. Songs that he wrote. I knew myself well enough that that would get in the way of any future planning. But I didn't have the words to explain it to him. It was just out-of-control emotions, and probably someday I owe him an apology.

ERIC ERLANDSON I was actually relieved a little bit when Courtney started dating Kurt, because Nirvana was more our world than the Smashing Pumpkins, and we all got along. When she started out going with Billy, the main problem was that she started treating our band on tour like Billy treats his band. She was putting people down more, and with the group, she started to become more like, "This is *my* thing." That was harder than our breakup.

JENNIFER FINCH I know Kurt and Courtney were a couple pretty soon after that show, but it was really when she got pregnant later that I actually accepted it. It just seemed really transitory. They're both such heated freakin' people, I can't even believe they could be in the same room together. Yes, Kurt was heated. They had times when they were very loving and very sweet together and times where there was just a lot of someone not getting their way and the other person being kind of nasty. It wasn't always Courtney being nasty, like some people might think.

* * *

BUZZ OSBORNE Nirvana management was never nice to us. Outright fucking asshole bastards. Right when *Nevermind* came out, we played a show with Nirvana in New York. Their manager, John Silva, said to me, "If you were a real band, on a real tour you'd understand that this is just fine." Meaning them fucking us over in one form or another: T-shirts, money, everything. That's the defining moment for me with Nirvana management. Somebody can only say that to me once, and then I hate their guts forever.

Nirvana had surrounded themselves with regular rock-and-roll people by then. The same rock-and-roll road crew that now does Nine Inch Nails–type tours. I generally don't get along with those types of people, for good reason, mostly because they're a bunch of human turds. I've never met a group of people who hate music more than rock-and-roll professionals.

After John Silva gave me that speech, I walked out into the lobby of the club, the Marquee, where there were huge, floor-to-ceiling Nirvana *Nevermind* posters up. Right under the baby on the Nirvana record cover, I wrote in huge letters THE MELVINS SAY NIRVANA SUX for everybody to see when they came in. And Silva went out there and tore it all down. That was pretty funny.

DANNY GOLDBERG I remember when Nirvana played a headlining show in L.A. right after *Nevermind* came out. Eddie Rosenblatt, the president of Geffen Records, was there with Axl Rose. Guns N' Roses was the biggest act on Geffen, and Nirvana were the second-biggest act. And he came up to me and said that Axl wanted to come by Nirvana's dressing room. I knew Eddie was on the spot—he had to look empowered to his star—but I had a pretty good idea of what Kurt was gonna think. I told Kurt about it, and he just made a face. Kurt just didn't like the idea of Axl.

I said, "Look, man, why don't you and I just duck out of the dressing room? You won't have to talk to him because you won't be there." Kurt and I went and sat on the stairs, and I gave Eddie all the passes so at least he could walk Axl into the dressing room and maybe say hello to the other guys.

EDDIE ROESER (a.k.a. King Roeser; singer/bassist/guitarist for Chicago's Urge Overkill) Cleveland was our first show with Nirvana, and they hadn't really quite hit it really huge there, and like within a week, by the time we were in St. Louis, it was the most insane crowd I've ever seen. Kurt could obviously see that there were a lot of frat kids with baseball hats in the audience who would have literally been the kids beating the shit out of him a couple years before, so Nirvana were like, "This music is not for you." There was also a metal-crossover crowd. But you can't choose your audience.

MARK KATES (Geffen Records/DGC head of alternative promotion) I went to the show at First Avenue in Minneapolis in October of '91, which was amazing. One of the topics that night was them going on tour with Guns N' Roses and Metallica, which I had been asked to bring up to them. They had a hard time taking it seriously. Nor should they have, really. It was a very preposterous idea.

BRYN BRIDENTHAL (Geffen Records publicity head) Axl wanted Nirvana to open for Guns because he, too, heard in the music something really, really special, and he wanted to do whatever he could to help, figuring they were this new young band and not realizing that they were at the front of a movement. He just didn't understand why they didn't want to, and Amy—his sister, who worked for him—called me one day and said, "Why won't they take our help?"

I said, "Because you represent everything that they're against. You're a big, successful, corporate million-dollar rock band. That's the antithesis of Nirvana." But Axl didn't think of Guns in that way.

RIKI RACHTMAN (host of MTV's *Headbangers Ball*) I was bummed when Nirvana came on *Headbangers Ball* because I liked Nirvana a lot. I was listening to *Bleach* all the time, and I knew this band had a buzz. I was all excited, I couldn't wait to meet them, and then here comes Kurt Cobain, and he's in the greenroom, facedown, passed out. It was dope. Unless he was suffering what everyone else seems to suffer from: "exhaustion."

When he comes onto the set, he's got this big yellow gown on, with a huge collar on it. If he was like, "Hey, check it out!" there'd be a way to have fun with it. The whole joke was that he wore a ball gown because it was the *Headbangers Ball*. It took me years before I even got that joke. So when he did it and was like, "Uhhh," and wasn't answering any of the questions very well—maybe he didn't want to be on *Headbangers Ball*. Then stand by your own rules and don't be on *Headbangers Ball*. Don't go on and act like you don't want to do the show. Just don't do it.

BUTCH VIG After *Nevermind* came out, I got solicited with tons of projects, and most of them were not appropriate. Like they'd be sending me, say, a woman blues singer and going, "Can you make her sound like Nirvana? Can you give it that 'grunge sound'?" Like I invented the sound of Nirvana. Also, some of the hair-metal bands' managers were contacting me. I got a sense of desperation from them, like, Wow, we need to change our sound a little bit to be hip with the kids.

When we started Garbage, all of our crew guys had come out of that metal scene, working with bands like Skid Row or White Lion. They'd be like, "Butch Vig, fuck that guy, man. He ruined the career of the band I was with." They'd joke about it with me over a beer. But then they ended up working with us for a long time.

JEFF GILBERT With Nirvana's success, all of the sudden, heavy-metal chicks who'd been dressing in spandex and fishnets and stiletto boots, now they started showing up to shows and they had washed all the Aqua Net out of their hair and they started to look as ratty as some of the guys. I thought, Oh no, the beginning of the end.

BRET MICHAELS (singer of Los Angeles's Poison) Most of the bands of our genre changed a little. When I started in my career, I would buy my spandex pants at the Sunoco gas station on Route 83 in fucking York, Pennsylvania, just 'cause I thought that was cool. When grunge hit, it definitely affected the look of bands. I never set out to stay in spandex my whole career. I thought it was great for the day.

RIKI RACHTMAN What happened is, fashion and times change. If there was no Nirvana or no Soundgarden or no grunge era, those hair bands still would have died. We still wouldn't be listening to Slaughter and Warrant today.

BLAG DAHLIA The glam guys' lyrics tended to be more obvious and more prosaic and not as allegorical. With something like Warrant's

"Cherry Pie," everything's right on the surface. I think Nirvana wrote abstract lyrics well; then you get to somebody like Pearl Jam and the allegorical shit is so horrible it looks like a 15-year-old's notebook. And it's like, Wow, these lyrics are really terrible, but they're abstract, therefore people can feel that they're intelligent.

BRET MICHAELS When I heard "Smells Like Teen Spirit," I'm goin', "Well, goddamn, what a great song." Someone forgot to send me the memo that I'm supposed to be hating this or threatened by it. My career didn't end with grunge. My career with the media ended with grunge. Most bands get a couple-year window to slowly die down. The media didn't kinda shut us off. They *completely* shut us off. But there were three bands in our genre that stayed in the arena: Def Leppard, Bon Jovi, Poison.

In '91, I got Alice in Chains to play a bunch of Northwest dates with us. All I knew was they were starting to break out big. I had a little studio at my house in Malibu, and in probably '93, Jerry and those guys came out and we sang, wrote music, partied, had a good time. I was talkin' to Jerry, and we both addressed how now there was supposed to be this anger and hatred between us. I said, "We don't hate each other, right?" We both laughed, and he goes, "I grew up on Sabbath and Kiss." And I said, "Me, too."

And he said, "I know we're supposed to not like each other, but you're a cool dude." We were laughing about the media portraying us as such enemies. If you like somebody, you like somebody.

CHRIS CORNELL In 1990, *RIP* magazine comes out and there's an article on Soundgarden and you turn the page and it's Poison. We were confronted with: Now, does that make us Poison? If we go on tour with Skid Row, are we Skid Row? We're not playing Skid Row songs. We're not changing our clothes. All we could really do is just stay who we were. Touring with Skid Row turned out to be a good thing, because we took all their fans, and they went away.

AARON JACOVES I'll tell you what kicked Soundgarden into gear. It was when Axl, at the height of Guns N' Roses' career, started speaking about the group in interviews.

SUSAN SILVER After I got the call about the Guns N' Roses tour, I went to where they were, at Stuart Hallerman's studio, Avast! I remember walking in, I had a box of T-shirts, some new designs. And I was *so excited*. Oh, my God, I was so excited: "Hey, guys! I have something to tell you! We got an offer today ... *to go ... on tour* ... WITH GUNS N' ROSES!"

They didn't say a word. After about 30 seconds—it felt like an eternity—one of them said, "What's in the box?"

BEN SHEPHERD Our tour with Guns N' Roses? Yeah, not my fault. I don't like that kind of music—and don't fuckin' make something out of nothing by me saying that. They're all really nice guys, don't get me wrong. But still, let me finish. I'm a punk rocker, man. I like Black Flag and way more hardcore stuff. That kind of butt rock, I don't like. I want nothing to do with that kind of world. I'm not a rock star, I don't like rock stars, and I don't want to be around them. That word *rock star* is really derogatory to me. There seems to be a malicious factor in calling someone that. It's a put-down.

The Guns N' Roses tour was a full-on metal-circus extravaganza. It was insane. I never wanted to play stadiums. It's so far removed from your fans and the feeling, and the sound is like crap. So there we are, getting exposed to all these butt rockers, the same kind of people who would try to beat me up when I was a punk rocker. So I had a massive animosity towards those fans.

MATT CAMERON We were metal. We definitely had a metal edge. I'm proud of that fact. I always thought it was funny that all the P.C. punkers were completely dismissing us because we did one tour with Guns N' Roses.

The Guns N' Roses tour was kind of a nightmare backstage, but it was sort of fun to be a part of it. It was an eye-opening lesson as far as how not to tour if you become successful. Like each guy had a bodyguard, and they were just completely wasted all the time. Axl would make the band wait an hour or two before they went on, so they always had to pay out these exorbitant late fees at the venues. One gig I remember, Axl was threatening to go out and actually break up the band onstage. There were a couple of occasions like that where we had to clear the fuck out because people were predicting a riot was going to happen.

CHRIS CORNELL [Axl] was always hidden somewhere having a personal crisis—always. One time I was in the room when he was talking to his manager, Doug Goldstein, about wanting the Goodyear blimp for the show. I said this as a joke—even though it was true—that the Fuji blimp was the largest blimp in the world. Axl was like, "That's it! It's gonna be the Fuji blimp!"

ERIC JOHNSON At that point I was working for Pearl Jam. I drove out there with Jeff Ament to see them in Las Vegas, I think. To be perfectly honest, it wasn't the Soundgarden I knew. They looked bored and unhappy. They were playing to a mostly empty house. I remember Kim did a beard solo that lasted about two minutes. You shoulda seen it: He played with his beard, and then he hung up his guitar and left it making feedback. Then he kind of moseyed off stage. That was kind of sad.

SLASH (guitarist for Los Angeles's Guns N' Roses) February 1, 1992, was our last show with Soundgarden, at Compton Terrace, Arizona, and we decided to commemorate it with a little prank. We got ourselves a few inflatable sex dolls, and Matt and Duff and I took our clothes off and went onstage with them. Come to think of it, I was the only one of us completely naked. In any case, Soundgarden was touring the *Badmotorfinger* album, and they came from a place where there was no fun to be had while rocking, so they were mortified. They looked around and there we were screwing blow-up dolls all around them; I was drunk and I fell. I got separated from my doll, and at that point I was totally naked—it was a scene.

SUSAN SILVER It was Soundgarden's nature to never be enthusiastic about anything, to the point where the Guns N' Roses crew referred to them as Frowngarden.

BEN SHEPHERD Why'd we get called Frowngarden? Because we weren't party monsters. We weren't motherfucking rock stars. We were not like that. We were there to play music. We weren't there for the models and the cocaine. We were there to blow your doors off.

CHAPTER 27
ON THE CORNER OF DOPEY AND GOOFY

JACK ENDINO After Daniel bowed out of Skin Yard, we got our friend Pat Pederson to play bass. We all had a pretty good year in '91, because we were all getting along at that point. Our fourth album, *1000 Smiling Knuckles,* which was Barrett Martin's debut as our drummer, came out around that time. It sold 14,000 copies or something, which was really good for an indie record then.

During our September tour in the U.S. was when we started hearing *Nevermind.* I was amazed. We thought, This is really slick sounding, but at the same time, the vocals are really raw, which is good. It was difficult to recognize that this was the same band that I had worked with on the *Bleach* record two years before, until you heard the singing. And also, the very pop direction they had gone, with "In Bloom" and some of the other tunes. The Melvins' influence on Nirvana was definitely on the wane. They had found their own voice.

We went to Europe in October '91. We ended up being added to a show in Vienna opening for Nirvana, of all people. Prior to that gig, Nirvana had always opened for us. We knew what was going on. We would call our friends back home in Seattle, and they'd say, "Yeah, it's climbing the album charts. It just sold another hundred thousand copies." We were getting these sales numbers from people back home, because they were following them like it was a sports team.

GREG DULLI (singer/guitarist for Cincinnati's the Afghan Whigs) When it came time for us to make the Afghan Whigs' second record, *Congregation,* Sub Pop gave us the then-unheard-of bloated advance of $15,000. We started making the record in Seattle and then moved down to L.A. to continue working on it.

Everybody else in the band finished their parts and flew back home, but I stayed to sing and overdub and mix, and then Sub Pop ran out of money. And that was about the time that they had those T-shirts that said WHAT PART OF "WE HAVE NO MONEY" DON'T YOU UNDERSTAND? Which I'm sure was pretty funny, but I got stranded in L.A. and had to get a job. *(Laughs.)*

The record got delayed; the studio wasn't gonna let me keep working when no one was paying the bills. Sub Pop eventually paid them, but I didn't know if *Congregation* was gonna come out because I didn't know if the record company had the money to put out records anymore. They went fucking broke, dude.

Then *Nevermind* came out, and Nirvana saved the whole fuckin' label, man.

BRUCE PAVITT The success of *Nevermind* was miraculous, to say the least. By Christmas of '91, *Nevermind* had sold two million.

JONATHAN PONEMAN We had a participation in the *Nevermind* sales, plus we were getting a lot of money from *Bleach* sales, when people wanted to find out about Nirvana's first record.

BRUCE PAVITT I was in a state of disbelief that we went from not being able to pay our phone bill to getting a check for half a million bucks. Of course, after that, we were so happy they went to Geffen.

GREG DULLI If every Sub Pop band did not send a fruit basket to Kurt Cobain, then I certainly did. Well, I figuratively sent him one. I went to Nirvana's show at the Palace in L.A. and hugged Kurt and said, "Good one, bro. Congratulations. And thank you—now I can go home."

STEVE WIEDERHOLD Everywhere you go people are cranking up fuckin' *Nevermind,* everywhere. That really fucked with my head. I didn't expect it, I didn't think this would happen. I was always like, "Nobody cares." People were actually interested, I guess. It was on TV, on the radio. I'm out of TAD, I'm working at Sears, Roebuck and Co. doing shipping and receiving, and I don't want anybody to know that I know Nirvana. I just want to concentrate on my work, you know.

BILLBOARD ("Nirvana Achieves Chart Perfection," by Paul Grein, January 11, 1992) Nirvana pulls off an astonishing palace coup by dethroning King of Pop Michael Jackson from the top spot on the Billboard 200 Top Albums chart. The Seattle-area alternative band's "Nevermind" surges from No. 6 to No. 1; Jackson's "Dangerous" drops from No. 1 to No. 5.

MARK KATES By the time the Michael Jackson thing happened, we were ready for it. He represented the old business, which involved the ability to pay for chart positions. The *Billboard* chart, prior to the [May 1991] introduction of SoundScan, was comprised of store reports. Theoretically, the stores reported what they sold. However, that wasn't always the case. There were companies that you could hire whose job it was to get the best possible store reports. This might not be fair to Michael Jackson or Epic Records, but it really was seen as a changing of the guard. We knew that what we had going on couldn't be bought.

AARON STAUFFER (Seaweed singer) I was working at Sub Pop when they found out that the Nirvana record went to the top of the charts. Pavitt did some insane Elvis-looking maneuver in elation. He swung his arm in a circle, got down on one knee—with one fist in the air, head down—and went, *"Yesss!"*

MARCO COLLINS One of the landmark moments for me was going over to Nils Bernstein's house for a party when Nirvana first played *Saturday Night Live.* There were 15 or 20 people over there; I think Rusty Willoughby, Kurt Bloch, and maybe Dan Peters from Mudhoney were there. Everybody is drinking a shitload of beer, and there's just an obnoxious, fun attitude in the room.

When Nirvana launched into their song, the room just got quiet, and when they were done and *Saturday Night Live* cut away to commercials, the room was still dead silent. It was like everybody in that roomful of drunk people realized at that moment how big it actually was. I'm getting chills even talking about it right now.

AMY FINNERTY I remember that when Nirvana played *Saturday Night Live,* I was in the greenroom. Somebody, I'm guessing Janet, told Kurt that I was the person that had gotten their video played, and he pulled me aside and was like, "I just wanted to say thank you," and then he said, "I never knew what you did over there. We always thought you were like the VP of Post-it Notes"—I don't know what that meant. "We just liked you and thought you were cool to hang around with."

BRUCE PAVITT I spent some time with Kurt backstage after Nirvana's *Saturday Night Live* show. That was a real good heart-to-heart rap session. He talked about signing autographs for some young kids, and I think that made him feel really good. He was a sensitive guy who really liked kids and animals. I remember the first time I visited his apartment, he had like three different cages of gerbils. I got the impression he liked animals more than a lot of people.

He talked about maybe starting a petting zoo. He was just kind of musing. The energy I was getting was kind of magical: *I can pretty much do anything I want. I'd like to start a petting zoo.*

That week, Nirvana had knocked Michael Jackson off the charts. In a lot of ways, Kurt reminded me of Michael Jackson. Think about it: Neverland . . . having a passion for kids and animals. I found it somewhat ironic. If I'd heard those same words coming out of Michael Jackson, I wouldn't have been surprised at all.

Later, I read that Kurt OD'd that night.

DANNY GOLDBERG That time when they were in New York, it was clear that Kurt and Courtney were doing drugs and probably heroin. They looked so stoned, and she wanted thousands of dollars in cash to quote-unquote go shopping. Kurt is so amazing that on camera he was fine, but afterwards he just looked really wasted and you had to really be blind or totally inexperienced with seeing people on drugs to not see that.

DAVE GROHL I remember walking into their hotel room and, for the first time, really realizing that these two are fucked up. They were just nodding out in bed, just wasted. It was disgusting and gross.

DANNY GOLDBERG Right after that, there was an article published in *Bay Area Music*; this guy had been with them a couple of weeks earlier and said that Kurt was on drugs. That's probably true, but it wasn't yet in my head until *Saturday Night Live*. But with the combination of *Saturday Night Live* and the article coming out, we just knew we had a huge problem on our hands and that we had to do something.

JANET BILLIG Right when it started coming out that Kurt was doing drugs, I remember Steven Tyler called and wanted to help. I told Kurt, "Holy shit, Steven Tyler called my office and he wants to help you. Can I give him your number?" And he was like, "Steven Tyler got to be a junkie for *18 fuckin' years*. I've only been doing drugs for an hour." Lots of stars called. Kirstie Alley called a lot for Courtney to try and make her become a Scientologist.

DANNY GOLDBERG So within a day or two of them getting back to Los Angeles, which is where they were now living, we did an intervention. I'd never done an intervention before, and I think I called David Geffen and he put me in touch with somebody that had been involved with Aerosmith. And that also was around the time that Courtney found out she was pregnant. The two of them, for the rest of their lives—certainly for the rest of Kurt's life—were in and out of rehab, in and out of treatment.

JANET BILLIG The biggest misconception about them as a couple? That Courtney was the puppet master. That she stuck a needle in his arm and made him do drugs. It couldn't be further from the truth. Kurt had done drugs well before he met her. They weren't good for each other habit-wise, but I do think she kept him alive. I think he would have killed himself way before he did, otherwise.

CRAIG MONTGOMERY Then we went to Australia and Japan. I know that Krist and Dave enjoyed that a lot. We went out to beaches and went boogie boarding and stuff together. Kurt and Courtney did not. They stayed in Sydney and tried to get drugs and were sick, and so Alex MacLeod, our poor tour manager, had to stay behind and deal with them while the rest of us had fun. There was definitely tension within the band for various reasons, drugs being one of them and royalties being another one. The royalties thing really started coming to a head on the European leg after that.

During the Australian trip, the whole band was pretty fractured. There was Kurt and Courtney, and then there was everybody else. And I was always very studious about staying neutral and not getting in the middle of anything. 'Cause if you start taking one side over the other, then you're probably gonna get fired by the side that you didn't take.

BARRETT JONES We went to Australia and New Zealand and Hawaii and Japan. The Australia thing was so much fun, but Kurt was pretty frail for those shows. He was in pain; he had a stomach problem. Then when Courtney came around about two weeks into the tour, it started to get worse. She doesn't like me at all. I never kissed her ass, is what it was. I never really understood the allure; she just seemed like a total snake to me. She used to try to get me fired. We were out somewhere, and she was like, "Kurt, fire him!" I don't even remember what it was about.

It all really came down to me telling Courtney—I told her to her face—that I thought it was not a good idea to be doing drugs while you're pregnant. And she didn't appreciate that. I didn't expect to go to their wedding in Hawaii anyway—it wasn't a big deal. Krist's wife at the time, Shelli, and my girlfriend had been talking about Courtney apparently—and I didn't even know that—so she disinvited them. And that was really hurtful, because Shelli and Kurt had been friends since they were kids. So then Krist didn't go, and Dave was really the only one that went.

■ ■ ■

MIKE MCCREADY I remember after the New Year's Eve 1991 show, somebody running onto the bus and saying Nirvana had just hit number one. I remember thinking, Wow; it's on now. It changed something. We had something to prove—that our band was as good as I thought it was.

EDDIE VEDDER In San Diego we were playing with Nirvana and the Chili Peppers. I had climbed an I-beam that you could kind of wrap your hand around. So I got to the top, and I thought, Well, how do I get down? I either just give it up and look like an idiot, or I go for it. So I decided to try it, and it was really ridiculously high, like 100 feet, something mortal. I was thinking that my mother was there, and I didn't want her to see me die. So somehow I finally got back onstage, finished the song, and went to the side and threw up. I knew that was really stupid, beyond ridiculous. But to be honest, we were playing before Nirvana. You had to do something. Our first record was good, but their first record was better.

KELLY CURTIS Our record came out almost the same time as Nirvana's, and all the hype was around Nirvana. Nirvana happened immediately, and it took us like six months. The record label didn't know what format we were—if we were rock or alternative, they didn't know what the fuck it was—so it was just having a hard time.

Nirvana probably opened the door for us at radio, for sure, but once that happened, it was kind of all over. It was within a few months of the release of the record that you could sense that something major was happening.

MARK KATES At least among those of us who were professionally involved, it was pretty safe to say there was a rivalry between Nirvana and Pearl Jam. And from our standpoint, it was based on a record that we didn't really believe was musically related, even though they were from the same city and the same scene. To be fair, those guys in Pearl Jam were at it before the guys in Nirvana were on a significant level, because they were in Green River and Mother Love Bone. But we were frustrated that this other career was launched off the back of our band.

Alternative rock had a lot of rules. The biggest accomplishment of this era, and Pearl Jam deserves as much credit as Nirvana does, was breaking the rules those of us who were alt-rock lifers had. Pearl Jam broke them musically, and Jeff Ament's haircut kind of broke the rules, too. All that band did was prove how stupid all those rules were. You can sing any way you want to. You want strings in your record, go ahead.

JEFF AMENT Kurt was talking shit about us, and we talked a little shit back. In retrospect, I think it was that when we got interviewed, the second or third question was about Nirvana. And I'm sure they were getting the same questions about us. After about a hundred of those interviews you're like, You know what? Fuck those guys.

Michael Azerrad was the guy who wound the whole thing up by printing some stuff that Kurt said and stuff that I said in *Rolling Stone*. My point was: Fuck, man, we were putting out records on Homestead Records while Kurt was going to Sammy Hagar concerts. At that point I was like, If you want to talk punk-rock credibility, I can back it up. I was there when it was going down.

A couple of times I went up and introduced myself to Kurt and tried to have a conversation with him, but he didn't want to have any part of it. I had conversations with Krist about it, and Krist, who I always got along with, just rolled his eyes and was like, "Whatever. It's just a bunch of crap."

DAVE ABBRUZZESE When Nirvana were going on stage at Cow Palace, I said "Have a good night" to Kurt and he growled at me. I was just not in the mood, so I reacted by saying, "Hey, fuck you," and I grabbed him, got into his face, and our tour manager, Eric, said, "Hey, hey, hey." I wasn't about to take that from the little guy.

STEVE ISAACS (MTV VJ) When I was hired at MTV, in August of '91, I was "musician guy." I had long hair, and I was a singer-songwriter. And then the next month, *Nevermind* hit. It was the most perfect time to have an experience like this. I became the silly MTV grunge poster boy. I was wearing flannel a lot. I loved Nirvana, I loved Pearl Jam, I loved Alice in Chains, I loved Soundgarden, I loved Screaming Trees. When I talked about Whitney Houston on-air you could see me die in my eyes a little bit.

Kurt went off in the press about Pearl Jam, about how they were false and they were jumping on this bandwagon that Nirvana wasn't trying to start. Pick on the shitty bands, don't pick on each other! I guess when Pearl Jam came out, they felt a little underdoggy. So I wrote a letter to *Rolling Stone* after their first Nirvana cover story, the one where Kurt was wearing the CORPORATE MAGAZINES STILL SUCK T-shirt. The letter in essence said it was pretentious to call anything false. My 22-year-old self was like, "Come on, don't fight. Just back off those guys."

Apparently Kurt got pissed off by my letter, which I don't blame him for. When I went to Madrid to film some stuff for MTV, I was supposed to interview Nirvana. And then we get a fax from them, and it said, "Anybody but Steve can interview us."

STEVE TURNER We knew Jeff, and for Kurt to say anything about Pearl Jam not having roots in punk rock—are you fuckin' stupid? *(Laughs.)* Hello? Jeff was there from day one of the Seattle thing.

STONE GOSSARD It was painful at times. All those words that were used to describe Pearl Jam—as posers, as somebody who's getting a hand up from the label, as someone who is more manipulative than talented, not the real thing compared to Nirvana—all it did was raise the bar for Pearl Jam. I think we took them as challenges, and we had to discover whether we were being real to the situation, or am I a jerk?

TOM NIEMEYER Gruntruck opened that show at the Moore where Pearl Jam filmed the "Even Flow" video. I really wanted to thank Jeff, because I thought he had something to do with Gruntruck opening. After our set, I saw him in the hall and it was a weird exchange—there was almost no exchange. Maybe he was just focused, I don't know. But I saw him a couple times after that, too, and it was like we didn't even know each other. I was bummed because we slept on the guy's floor in Montana and we went skateboardin' and shit together. I thought we were buds!

JOSH TAFT The night I was shooting the "Even Flow" video, Eddie told me to make sure we could see the crowd in the video. The only way to do that is to turn up the venue lights. When he saw how bright they were, he yelled at me to turn them down. Then the dimmer board malfunctioned and we couldn't turn them off. So I physically smashed the board, and the hall went black. Long story short, I ended up turning in the cut of the video to MTV with that bit—him screaming at me—in there. And I wasn't looking to call him out. It was just like, That wasn't my fucking fault. I needed to turn all the lights up.

And then I called him out about it on a personal level, and I said, "Listen, that wasn't cool." We were friends at that point, and I said, "I'm not turning into your employee, and if that's the case, I'm not cool with it." That was the moment his personality changed. Ever since then, he's been a different guy, in my opinion. He was feeling his own power and his own potential, and was willing to do anything to maintain it.

JONATHAN PLUM (producer/engineer; now London Bridge Studio co-owner) I started working at London Bridge after *Ten* came out. Pearl Jam came back a few times—they came back to do some soundtrack work on *Singles* and to rerecord "Even Flow" for the video.

I was 19 or 20 and nervous and excited. Mike McCready was a very friendly guy and he was able to say, "Hey, dude, what's going on?" and be normal. I had conversations with Eddie Vedder and thought he was very weird and complicated. We'd sit and have breakfast together, and I'd ask how his day was going and his answers sounded like he was getting interviewed for a magazine. He was very careful about what he was saying, and he was always making these big, blanket political statements. Where I just was like, "Hey, man, how are the waffles?"

I sensed that he was not comfortable being himself. It's like he needed to project something, rather than just relax and have a normal conversation. I remember Jeff and Stone talking about wanting to do certain PR things and Eddie being kind of pissed off and uncomfortable because he was pushing for more of this punk, Fugazi approach. It seemed like every argument the band was having, he would always ask, "Well, what would Fugazi do?"

* * *

MARK ARM You want to hear a little bit about our label search? Sub Pop at the time was distributed by Caroline, and we thought that we would cut out the middleman and go straight to Caroline. So the president of Caroline, Keith Wood, met with us. At our little business lunch, he said, "We'd love to work with you guys but there's just a couple things. You're gonna have to tour for nine months out of the year." We'd just done a nine-*week* tour of Europe, which drove us fucking crazy. And then he was like, "You gotta sweeten up your guitar sound." It's like, "Fuck, if we sweeten up our guitar sound, what do we have?" And then he says, "You can't do any side projects." Steve and I had just done the Monkeywrench record.

And we're like, "If this is the kind of shit we're gonna get from an independent label, we might as well start talking to the majors."

BOB WHITTAKER When they were leaving Sub Pop, I told the band, "Listen, I know we're not really fans of management companies and managers and big powerful lawyers." But we had a couple of good, relatively connected lawyers who weren't too obnoxious, and I said, "With those two lawyers, I could easily step in and be the hub of communication and help you guys, be your manager and see to it that you are all very involved in the decisions."

DON BLACKSTONE (Gas Huffer bassist) Gas Huffer toured with Mudhoney in '91. Certainly Bob was the type of guy who would put a couple of holes in a can of tuna fish and hide it under the seat of your van—or worse. I thought he was a hilarious guy, but I gained some respect for Bob on that tour when I saw what he actually did.

GARRETT SHAVLIK Bob taught me how to road manage. I remember at the 9:30 Club, me and Lukin and Bob and Peters are wrestling all over the place, doing body slams, and the promoter walks up and says, "Hey, you guys wanna get paid?" And Bob just snapped out of his whacked-out Warner Bros. cartoon persona and grabbed me by the scruff of the neck and went right into full-on business mode.

BOB WHITTAKER The guys agreed to it, and then we shopped independent. Then we went to majors and did the obligatory fly to New York and L.A. and meet with people, to varying degrees of disgust.

MARK ARM We had this meeting with John Silva about potentially signing to Geffen through Sonic Youth. We were in this restaurant, and he positioned himself so that he could see this TV screen showing MTV. He's telling us that by signing to Geffen through Sonic Youth, he would essentially be our A&R man. Our backs were to the TV, and he kept his eyes up there—he wouldn't even look at us and focus—and then, all of a sudden, the "Smells Like Teen Spirit" video comes on and he just starts laughing maniacally and is like, "Look at that!" You could see the dollar signs rolling in his eyes. That's why we didn't want to be on Geffen. Get us as far away from this guy as possible.

DAVID KATZNELSON (Warner Bros. Records A&R vice president) When I found out Mudhoney were looking for another label, I immediately flew up to Seattle. I was this little schmo 21-year-old kid who is the biggest fan ever. I got thrown into the real chaos of the Mudhoney world that night. The first person I see is this raggedy, crazy-looking guy named Bob Whittaker who has hair everywhere and is wearing this big, thick green sweater. He told me, "The guys will see you soon. Come with me." He takes me to his house in West Seattle where he has these crazy roommates—the kind of guys who'd shoot holes in walls with guns—and they start plying me with alcohol and throwing on single after single of all the Seattle bands.

Then I met the band. The only one who was kind of off-putting to me was Steve, and I think that's because of his sarcastic, cynical wit. He'd be like, "Hey, where's your American Express card? Aren't you gonna buy us dinner?" And, "Are you gonna make us wear the prune suit?"—like the Electric Prunes, who the label forced to wear purple suits at one point in time.

GARRETT SHAVLIK The Fluid left Sub Pop about the same time Mudhoney left. We were getting hustled by Virgin and by Warner Bros., and then we went with Hollywood Records. We went on the road with Love Battery and toured for fuckin' 14 weeks straight. Somewhere on the road coming back, some Hollywood execs flew in. They're like, "What we'd love you to do is rent a house down in the Dallas/Fort Worth area, because that's where *Nevermind* totally broke open on the radio. Go down there and just work that club circuit for a while, three or four months." I went, "Fuck you, man. We've been fuckin' touring since fuckin' '86." They thought Dallas/Fort Worth was the pocket, man.

The Hollywood Records guys didn't know about rock and roll. They knew about soundtracks for fuckin' cartoons, Disney. Hollywood Records was in the Disney complex studio area, and all the boulevards are named after characters. They were on the corner of Dopey and Goofy boulevards. *Really.* Could this be a fuckin' sign?

JACK ENDINO Major labels didn't want to have anything to do with me. I was not the one who did the record that broke Nirvana. I was the guy who did the Nirvana record that said it was done for $600. That probably did not help my career. Most people didn't even *listen* to the record because it said "made for $600." They'd go, "Ha ha, next!"

PETER BUCK (guitarist of Athens, Georgia's R.E.M.; Stephanie Dorgan's ex-husband) I did an R.E.M. record in Seattle in '92, *Automatic for the People,* and moved there in '93. As an outsider, it seemed like things got really intense really quickly. Except for the B-52s and R.E.M., nobody from Athens got hugely successful, and there weren't really bidding wars. It wasn't seen that any band from Athens was gonna make a million dollars, but Seattle was like a gold rush.

RUSTY WILLOUGHBY (Flop/Pure Joy singer/guitarist) I'm sure if Flop were from Birmingham, Sony wouldn't have touched us with a 10-foot pole. We were from Seattle, and we were doing relatively well on Frontier, an indie label. I think they thought we were grunge, and us being from Seattle is why they pulled the trigger. We would tell them that we weren't grunge: "Don't expect us to be Mudhoney." But as much as they said, "Oh, yeah, sure," they saw dollar signs. Even if they knew in their hearts that we weren't grunge, they were going to market us like we were. It was always "Flop *from Seattle.*" Once they realized we weren't grunge, they were more than happy to get rid of us, after just one record.

PETER BUCK Everyone was kind of conscious that the world was looking at them. Everyone felt embattled. The one thing I remember with a lot of pleasure is seeing that impromptu Nirvana show at the Crocodile, where they opened for Mudhoney. Everyone seemed really clearheaded, and it was really loose and fun. It was the last great experience I had of that era. Everything after that seemed kind of dark. It seemed like everyone stayed home, except for the people who'd just moved to town.

CLAUDIA GEHRKE What I found the most annoying was people all of the sudden flocking to Seattle thinking they were going to get a gig. They'd be like, "Oh, I'm from Seattle." And it's like, "No, you're not. You're from L.A."

DANIEL HOUSE Suddenly there were all these bands that you had never heard of, out of nowhere, that embraced that sound. At C/Z, we used to get demos all the time, and we used to say, "Oh, it's a Pearl Jam demo," "Oh, it's a Soundgarden demo," "Oh, it's a Nirvana demo." Those were the templates.

RAY FARRELL At Geffen, whenever we were trying to go to do any Nirvana business, you couldn't get a flight from L.A. to Seattle because every flight was filled with major-label guys looking for the next big thing after Nirvana. I'm serious. If you crashed every one of those planes you could've killed the record business singlehandedly.

DANIEL HOUSE I was angry at what the major-label music industry was doing to our scene, because it changed a lot of people's motivations for why they were in bands. Some of the bands on C/Z actually yelled at me because they blamed *me* for them not getting signed to a major label.

TOM HAZELMYER Every band thought they could be Nirvana, and that was insufferable. The attitude was "Why aren't I big yet?" It's like, "Have you listened to your own fuckin' record? It's just like fuckin' frog noises with a distorted guitar being smashed up. Are you kidding me?"

TOM NIEMEYER People wanting to be the next Nirvana, I saw it every *fuckin'* day, dude. It was disgusting! I *will* rattle off names if I can remember them. But they're all gone now. They had demos out, maybe got signed to EMI for a record or whatever.

And the record-label people moving here, having offices here, it poisoned the clear waters of Puget Sound. All of a sudden, there was this weird oil slick over all this shit. You didn't wanna be from Seattle.

CHARLIE RYAN Early on, when you went to a club, there were no drinks, there were no snacks, there were no televisions, there was no paint on the walls. You took the bus for an hour to go to a club and stand there for three hours and watch a band. It was solely people wanting to see people play music. I was constantly reminded of that years later, when I was in the Crows. We played at the Crocodile, and nobody even cared what was onstage.

RUSTY WILLOUGHBY All of the sudden, Seattle was becoming this thing that was kind of gross. Around mid-'93, Drew Barrymore started hanging around in town a lot; she was going out with Eric from Hole. Oh, no, I think Drew Barrymore's great. It was just that people would go to the Crocodile just to see if Drew Barrymore was there.

CHARLIE RYAN I had a theory that on any Friday or Saturday night, you could take the lids off of all these clubs and you could snatch the bands out and swap 'em and nobody would give a shit. They were there to chase girls and to dress up and have cocktails and get drunk and catch up with friends. And that's fine. But it was just such a complete turn-around from early on.

CHAPTER 28
WILD OUTBURSTS IN PUBLIC PLACES

BEN LONDON (Alcohol Funnycar singer/guitarist) I went to a little liberal arts college in central Ohio called Antioch College that's historically been a very left-leaning school. My roommate in my first quarter was a guy named Steve Moriarty, who ended up being the drummer in the Gits, and the room next to us was Matt Dresdner, who ended up being the bass player in the Gits, and a guy named Adrian Garver, who went on to be in a band called the D.C. Beggars out here in Seattle.

We formed this band with Steve, myself, Adrian Garver, and this guy Roger Garufi that was called Brothers Voodoo, and that morphed into what became Big Brown House. The Gits started the second year. Andy Kessler, or Joe Spleen as he's known in the Gits, was a year ahead of us. Part of Antioch's thing was cooperative education, so you worked for six months and studied for six months out of every year, and at one point, Andy and Matt and Mia Zapata ended up doing a co-op in San Francisco at a place called the Farm—which was some sort of urban farm that did a bunch of punk-rock shows—where they formed an early version of the Gits. When they came back, the Gits and Big Brown House coexisted, sharing a drummer, Steve.

As we got closer to graduation, we were all like, "We want to keep playing music." When we discussed where we wanted to go, four cities came up. The general discussion in this group—it became more of a collective later—was that New York and San Francisco were too expensive, Chicago was too close to where we already were, and Seattle just seemed like this great place. I was mildly aware of Soundgarden, but we didn't really know that it was going to be a good place for music at all.

We arrived as an army of people, in August of 1989. It was not only the core members of the Gits and Big Brown House, but others, including Valerie Agnew, who ended up being the drummer in 7 Year Bitch.

MATT DRESDNER (the Gits bassist) When we first moved out here, Valerie was dating Steve, our drummer. And I ended up dating Stefanie Sargent. They were interested in starting a band, and we helped them. They started in our practice space at the Rathouse on our equipment. We helped teach them, Stefanie and Valerie specifically, how to play their instruments.

BEN LONDON Rathouse was the name of our collective, which was a combination of Big Brown House and the Gits' original name, the Sniveling Little Rat Faced Gits, which comes from a Monty Python skit. And that's what we called the group house that the bulk of these people lived in, on 19th and Denny in Capitol Hill. Steve Moriarty and Valerie Agnew; Julian Gibson and Carla Sindle from D.C. Beggars; Andy Kessler and Mia Zapata were the primary people living there. That's where we practiced in the basement. It was very much like the community center for our social scene.

STEVE MORIARTY Why was it called Rathouse? Don't remember. Oh, oh, the guy that owned it was a warlock, and he said there had been rats in the house but he caught one and cooked it and ate it and then all the other rats knew that they had to leave the house. I think that's where it came from. The place was disgusting when we moved in.

ELIZABETH DAVIS-SIMPSON (7 Year Bitch bassist) I came over from Eastern Washington. Walla Walla. My parents wrote contemporary Christian music and performed music. My dad—he just died a couple years ago—was a musician since the '20s. All my oldest siblings played guitar and sang and did a lot of music in church. In third grade, I had an aha moment when I got punished for innocently asking my teacher a question about original sin, and I realized I was not going to be a Christian.

After graduating from Walla Walla University, I was working on a fishing boat in Alaska with my boyfriend, and the boat ported in Seattle. My boyfriend was a guitar player, and he thought, Oh, I'll buy my girlfriend a bass and she can play along with me. I played with him one time and then I was like, "I don't want to play that kind of music," which was introspective and sensitive and complicated, so I just started playing along with AC/DC and Stooges records, and it came real fast for me.

SELENE VIGIL-WILK (7 Year Bitch singer) We were in a band called Barbie's Dream Car for a minute. Elizabeth, who also worked at Pike Place Market, ended up being the bass player and then the other girl left, and Stefanie Sargent joined. Me and Stefanie knew each other; she stayed with me off and on and we used to see each other around at shows.

ELIZABETH DAVIS-SIMPSON I worked in the Pike Place Market, upstairs from the health-food store where Valerie and Selene worked. I used to go down there and get snacks, and I would see Valerie and Selene there, and I thought, These girls are the hottest and coolest chicks in Seattle. I kind of idolized them. Then I saw Valerie walking up the street with cymbals and I said, "Hey, I just started playing bass." She said, "We're playing in a band but our bass player is going to Germany so why don't you come and play with us?"

So I started playing with Valerie, Lisa Orth, Selene, and Stefanie in Barbie's Dream Car. I was intimidated by everybody. The only people I'd really hung out with before were Seventh-day Adventists. Lisa left, so we moved our sessions from Lisa's loft to the Rathouse basement. We started from scratch and had three songs but no band name.

Our first show was opening up for the Gits for a books-for-prisoners benefit at the OK Hotel. We needed a name for the flyer, and Ben London came up with 7 Year Bitch, which I did not like, but then it stuck.

SELENE VIGIL-WILK We played a house party at a professional snow-boarder guy's place, and that's when I met Eddie Vedder and his girlfriend at the time, Beth. She really liked our band. Eddie became a friend.

VALERIE AGNEW (7 Year Bitch drummer) Pearl Jam couldn't open some shows for the Chili Peppers, so the Peppers' management asked who Pearl Jam would want to replace them, and Eddie said that they should call us. And I will never forget the day that they called. Selene and I were living together in this little house, and we got home and there was this message on our machine, and we literally fell down on the floor, just screaming and laughing. "No way! The manager from the Red Hot Chili Peppers is calling us? What's going on? This is crazy!"

ELIZABETH DAVIS-SIMPSON I don't think I related to the Gits as much as the other girls did. Those guys were hard-drinking intellectual liberals, and I really admired them and thought they were awesome, but I didn't really fit in or relate necessarily. Mia was the one that I related to the most. She was really encouraging of 7 Year Bitch, and she would come down when we were rehearsing and say, "Keep doing it. Keep playing, keep writing music. You guys are doing really good."

BEN LONDON 7 Year Bitch were not well-skilled musicians at that point, but there was the delivery and the intent, and everything was very charming, and you had some really attractive women that were part of it. And so I think Daniel saw . . . One thing I'll give Daniel House is, I don't think he ever saw a dollar sign he didn't like. So he put a seven-inch out with them on C/Z.

DANIEL HOUSE For me, the 7 Year Bitch song title alone that is undeniably confrontational, without knowing any of the lyrics, is "Dead Men Don't Rape." That sort of militant attitude was so shocking. I had a girlfriend who had in fact been raped in her own apartment, and I had previous experience with my mother having been raped when I was a kid and being aware of it, and so for me, those lyrics alone, that song title alone, brought me to a place where I'm going, "Fuck, yeah! That's right."

STEVE MORIARTY C/Z wasn't a good experience 'cause Daniel couldn't really understand where we were coming from artistically or personally. We would say, "We don't wanna do this show that you have us lined up to play with these bands that have a poster with a bunch of references to pussy on it. Mia doesn't wanna be objectified as a female singer." He wouldn't get that, and he would do it anyway.

We held our nose and signed to C/Z because he had enough money to put out our record, and that's what we were looking for right then. We decided with 7 Year Bitch to do it, thinking we would be the main bands on his label and anything that he tried to throw at us we could boycott if we didn't like it.

DANIEL HOUSE The Gits were, from the day I first started talking to them, innately paranoid and mistrustful. They were of the opinion, it seemed, that everybody was out to take advantage of them, everybody was out to fuck 'em over. They almost seemed to resent that we as a label, as a business entity, were going to be making a profit off of them if they saw success. At one point, I had to say, "I don't know if I can do this if you are just going to be so paranoid and mistrustful of our relationship before we've even started."

MATT DRESDNER Daniel seemed friendly enough, but he had a reputation for being out for himself more than for the bands—and whether or not that was deserved, it gave us pause. There was a lot of internal conflict within the band about whether or not to go with C/Z, and some of us were very distrustful. They came to us with this nine-page contract, and we were like, "*Nine pages?!* What the hell is that?" 'Cause we had done everything with a handshake before that.

ELIZABETH DAVIS-SIMPSON I felt like Sub Pop was the shit and everyone else was trying to be as good as Sub Pop. Rathouse was really sub-sub-sub-Sub Pop. What I'm trying to say is, that to some people, Sub Pop was really establishment.

STEVE MORIARTY We felt separated from the Sub Pop scene because we were kind of punk purists. We felt more like we belonged in England or in Europe, and we found that people were more welcoming of our sound in Europe. The Gits represented more of the underbelly of Seattle. More of the homeless teenagers—as opposed to the college frat boys and young upwardly mobile cool kids in nice, cool clothes—because we played a lot of all-ages shows. Mudhoney were glamorized in such a way by Sub Pop that a lot of our fans hated them, hated those other bands, and were looking for something different.

SELENE VIGIL-WILK We were constantly called grunge or Riot Grrrl, because that's what was going on in Seattle at the time. It's hard to put yourself into a category or perceive yourself as that, 'cause it's like, "Well, yeah, maybe a little bit, but not totally. Kinda, sorta . . . but not." We made aggressive, punky, in-your-face music. They gotta call you something. I get it now.

VALERIE AGNEW We never got labeled grunge that I can remember. That would have been a nice relief. We definitely were considered Riot Grrrl, which was really frustrating for us at the time. Not because we had anything against Riot Grrrl, but we didn't have anything to do with them. We certainly had feminist ideals and ideologies. We knew those people, loved their bands. Allison from Bratmobile did our very first interview in one of her zines, and I think that's probably where it started.

DANIEL HOUSE The Gits also didn't seem to trust the press. There were a lot of opportunities they just said no to. 7 Year Bitch were incredibly friendly and very willing and very eager to talk to the press. They got their asses out there, they did the work, they went to radio interviews.

STEVE MORIARTY 7 Year Bitch were sort of socialites. That's what you have to do to get popular in music. We were the opposite. Mia would hide in her room and write poetry and songs and was more like Patti Smith than Madonna. Matt was into motorcycles, and Andy was into books. We were more into music for music's sake; they were into music for the love of the scene. We hated the scene in a lot of ways. Our bands were very different, but we complemented each other. That's why I think we ended up being such good friends.

DANIEL HOUSE I remember when 7 Year Bitch was on the cover of *The Rocket*, Steve came to the office and was rather upset with me. He in all seriousness asked me why the Gits hadn't been on the cover of *The Rocket*, and I had to explain to him that we try to get all our bands on *The Rocket*. I had pushed really hard and our publicist had pushed really hard to get *The Rocket* to pay attention to the Gits, and they just wouldn't.

COURTNEY MILLER (*The Rocket* newspaper advertising manager) Whoever got the cover of *The Rocket* was a big deal in those days. *The Rocket*'s office, when it moved to Fifth Avenue, was down the hall from C/Z Records and I was good friends with Daniel, so I would get earfuls all the time. Of course, Daniel always thought that Sub Pop got everything and he got nothing. He was like the redheaded stepchild—no pun intended, because he's got red hair.

DANIEL HOUSE The Gits felt that we were just giving all our attention to 7 Year Bitch and completely ignoring the Gits, which could not have been further from the truth, 'cause within the offices of C/Z not everyone was a 7 Year Bitch fan. But within the offices of C/Z *everybody* was a Gits fan.

MATT DRESDNER We were always really tight with 7 Year Bitch and very supportive, and when all of a sudden they started getting a lot of attention, we were absolutely thrilled for them. I felt like they felt a little bit guilty because we had sort of been their mentors. And they went out of their way for us. When the documentary *Hype!* came out here to film, *Hype!* wasn't gonna include us, and those girls said, "You guys are blowin' it if you don't get the Gits on film." So it was a very supportive, very collaborative, loving relationship between those two bands.

STEVE MORIARTY Stefanie and Mia were great friends and drinking buddies. They both had tempers. They both liked to get fucked up and cause havoc. They both were total misfits. They were both lovely people, and they were both really kind of naive and accepting, almost to a fault. Mia was often taken advantage of by people. They'd go, "Oh, it's so cool, I'm hanging out with the lead singer of the Gits. Let's get her wasted and see what she does." And the same went for Stefanie.

SELENE VIGIL-WILK I remember a boyfriend of Stefanie's started dating another girl and she just lost it. She grabbed him off of his chair at the

Crocodile and punched him. Crazy stuff, throwing beers on people. Wild outbursts in public places. But she was a sincere, good friend to people.

VALERIE AGNEW Stefanie had a shitload of charisma. She could talk you out of your pants, man. When we first started playing shows, she would get guys to come up and tune her guitar. I was like, "Stefanie, you know how to tune your guitar." She was like, "I know, I don't care. He's cute." We would be out on some road trip and she'd manage to get someone to carry all her gear for her or give her a ride really far away. We were so deep into our feminist all-girls-playing-rock thing at that time that we were like, "Stefanie! You're fucking with our image!" *(Laughs.)* She didn't give a shit.

If she was missing at a show we'd find her with some boy in the back of a van. Some would say she was a little bit reckless. She referred to herself as the punk-rock Marilyn Monroe. She was a huge Marilyn Monroe fan, and she identified with her. I never asked her why. I didn't get to know her long enough.

LORI BARBERO Everyone always said, "You need to meet Stefanie Sargent. You two are identical. Both of you look similar, both of you have dreadlocks and you both blah blah blah." It just so happened we both had a salamander tattooed on our forearm even. We shared our energy and our passion for music. And we love people. We met in Seattle when 7 Year Bitch played, and we got along famously.

I was dating a gentleman named Chris at the time, and she was dating . . . what was his name? From Young Fresh Fellows, I think it was. She worked at Piecora's, a pizza place on the Hill, and we ended up getting "married" there. She gave me a ring. I gave her a ring. I still have the ring. "Let's get married!" I have no idea why we decided to do that. I mean, it wasn't like any kind of lesbian love affair, it was just best friends. Our boyfriends gave us away, and it was at Piecora's upstairs, and it was just really funny.

JAMES BURDYSHAW When I was in 64 Spiders, Stefanie and I dated for a little while. It wasn't like we were a couple and people would see us together all the time. It was more like she had a big crush on me, and I hung out with her. This was back in the day when you didn't really have a girlfriend. You'd go to shows, go over to somebody's place late at night after drinking, and end up in their bed or they'd end up in your bed.

Stefanie had always been a girl who was like the groupie chick. Like she was Soul Asylum's little groupie—not sleeping with them, just hanging on. She loved to follow bands. She was a real tomboy, but she was a real soft girl, too, and she didn't like being called Sarge.

ROISIN DUNNE I knew Stefanie from hanging out on the Ave, goin' to the Grey Door and the Gorilla Gardens; I maybe even met her as early as the Metropolis. Whenever we found each other at shows, we would hang out, watch the band together. Right up front.

I'd moved to L.A., but once when I was visiting Seattle, I saw Stefanie at a party. I hadn't seen her in years. She was like, "You gotta come see my band! I'm doing great!" And she put me on the guest list at RKCNDY. It was a really fun night. Stefanie gave me the single for "Lorna," and I recall being really happy for her.

ELIZABETH DAVIS-SIMPSON There was something about Stefanie where there was a lot of fun and a lot of smiles and a lot of laughter, but there was also some kind of a cloud. She seemed to have had a really troubled past. She moved to Seattle from San Francisco, oddly enough, to get away from dope. Seattle seems like a ridiculous place to go if you're try-ing to avoid heroin.

It's hard for me to imagine Stefanie being a middle-aged woman.

JAMES BURDYSHAW I rejected her because I thought she was doing too much dope, and I thought she was too obnoxious, but I stayed her friend. She was workin' the pizza places and I'd show up and she'd feed me, and then we'd talk and we always would kiss, and we were very close. I shoulda been her boyfriend, because she was a wonderful girl.

MATT DRESDNER I hated heroin usage. I hated junkies. I was very, very, very anti, and while Stefanie and I were dating, part of the platform of our relationship was she could not be involved in any of that stuff or I was gone. And as far as I know, she was clean during that time. It made it all the more painful for me that that's how Stefanie finally did herself in, because she had been doing so well.

VALERIE AGNEW We had been looking for her that weekend. We were supposed to have a meeting at the OK Hotel about going on tour. It was really weird that she was MIA, but we weren't terribly worried at that point. I remember Selene and I going by her house and looking up at her apartment window, and her light was on and she had a red lightbulb in it. I remember having this premonition. I was like, "Oh, shit." I had a really bad feeling because it was in the middle of the day and the sun was shining, and I started freaking out. Then we got a call the next day saying she hadn't shown up for work, which was really unlike her.

When we got home to our apartment, we got a call from her room-mate, who'd gotten back from her camping trip at the end of the week-end and found Stefanie.

SELENE VIGIL-WILK It was devastating because I'd never experienced that before. Stefanie's roommate called me, and Valerie and I just jumped in the van, and we actually hit a parked car while driving up to her house on Capitol Hill.

VALERIE AGNEW We got there, and Stefanie was still in her room. Selene and I both went into her room and sat there with her for a little while, and I remember surveying the scene and trying to piece it together. We didn't suspect foul play, but it didn't make any sense. She was supposed to meet us that night at the OK Hotel. Why was she alone? Was some-body here and they left? Those kinds of questions were going through our head. I just remember it being really hard to think. You feel like you're underwater.

ELIZABETH DAVIS-SIMPSON Valerie called me and I just got in a cab. I went up to Stef's place and met Valerie and Selene there and it really seemed fake. Have you ever had a friend die? It really feels like you're sleepwalking, like you're in a dream and you just want to wake up.

STEVE MORIARTY I took a cab up to Stefanie's house, and she was dead in her bedroom. What do you do when somebody dies? You have all this energy and horror and there's nothing you can do about it except wait for them to come and take her.

ELIZABETH DAVIS-SIMPSON When the coroner or the EMT or whoever took her away, they had her in a body bag on a stretcher and one of her dreads came out of the bag as they walked past us. And seeing that was like, Okay, that was really *real*, this is Stefanie's shell. She's not here anymore.

DON BLACKSTONE I was a really good friend of Stefanie's. She introduced me to my first wife. I talked to our booking agent Julianne Andersen on the phone and she said, "Stefanie OD'd." And I didn't put OD'ing and dying together. I thought, Okay, so she's in the hospital. And I called my friend Lisa, who'd found Stefanie, and she was like, "She's dead." And I just lost it. I was standing at a pay phone in a parking lot in the QFC or some shit, and for the first time somebody that was really close to me died, and it just bowled me over. Stupid misadventure death. Just a waste. Makes you mad at them to a large degree, like, What the fuck were you doing?

ELIZABETH DAVIS-SIMPSON I remember Andy from the Gits telling us, "Don't be mad at Stefanie." That was really wise, because I never would have thought, I'm going to be angry at this person, but then you do reach a point where there is some anger. I tried to take his advice and fight that anger.

JAMES BURDYSHAW I was pissed at her. Two months before Stefanie died, I spent the night at her place. I was just gonna sleep on the couch, and she asked me to come in her room. At that point, I had given up everything except beer and pot. That night she swore up and down that she wasn't using and she was through with it. She even picked up a copy of *Rolling Stone* and said, "That motherfucker lied! He's a liar!" Talking about Kurt Cobain saying he wasn't using. She knew. Probably 'cause she was gettin' it from the same fuckin' source.

After that conversation, I saw her at the Off Ramp and she wouldn't talk to me. I said, "Hey," and she looked at me and then she looked away. Then she was talkin' to somebody who I knew was into drugs. I was like, Oh, my fucking God.

SELENE VIGIL-WILK Stefanie had been drinking, and if you're on your back and throw up and you're so fucking out of it . . . Yeah, she choked.

It wasn't like, *bam,* she shot heroin and OD'd, but that was part of what killed her. I learned not to judge people around situations like that. People who didn't know us assumed things. They'd say things they had no business saying. Stefanie wasn't a junkie.

RON RUDZITIS Love Battery and 7 Year Bitch were close friends. Stefanie wasn't really known as a druggie. I think she was on the fringes, messing with stuff. It's usually those people who OD 'cause they don't have a big resistance. I think I was into it at that point, but I'd never done it with her. Everyone was pretty damn private about it. It was pretty taboo back then, especially after Andy Wood passed away.

LORI BARBERO It was sad, too, that when she died, we were on tour. I didn't get back to go to the funeral.

Her drug issues? We never really talked about it. It was kinda like, What can I do? We don't even live in the same city, and that's when we were touring hard. And I was trying to take care of Kat 24/7. I was fightin' demons in my own band. Kat was a demon. A demon with a demon. Taking care of one is more than enough. I don't know how many times we had to go to the consulate to get a new passport for Kat. I had to keep an eye on her 'cause she liked to kinda get screwed up at night and she'd do this thing where she'd shriek at the top of her voice and smash a glass so she could get attention. Between her and Courtney, it was kinda like, Who can get the most attention all the time? They were both exotic dancers. I don't know where the hell "exotic" comes from, but you know, they both had a need for attention.

BARBARA DOLLARHIDE PRITCHARD (C/Z Records public relations and marketing director) Before Stefanie passed, I wasn't dealing with the major media. They didn't care that much about us. But when that happened, all of the sudden they did. To have media zero in because of that kind of an incident—that was a frustrating period.

ROISIN DUNNE I was furious when I read that *Rolling Stone* article. The first line was about Stefanie, but it wasn't about her, it was about her death. I was like, You've never written about this woman in the entire existence of this magazine and now all of a sudden you choose to put her name in there based on her heroin overdose?

MATT DRESDNER Once Stefanie died, there was one less personality to rally around. With these clone bands trying to get signed and what seemed like an influx of thousands of musicians, the cohesiveness of the scene was really fracturing and the loss of people like Stefanie precipitated an even faster fracturing.

ELIZABETH DAVIS-SIMPSON That whole time following Stefanie's death is really hazy to me. I remember the three of us going from place to place to place, hanging out with different people and drinking and being really, really sad. I don't even remember, was I going to my job? What was I doing? I can't even remember it.

SELENE VIGIL-WILK After Stefanie died, Eddie Vedder really helped me through it. One night, when I was really distraught, I was at the pier downtown with him and I was way too drunk, and I either fell or I slipped off the dock. And I was so drunk I would've just drowned. It's a blurry recollection, but I remember sliding into the water and him grabbing me and pulling me up. I was drinking Crown Royal, and I don't normally drink whiskey like that. I was gone. I was crazy.

VALERIE AGNEW I lived in a studio apartment by myself, and I kept this altar up of Stefanie for a really long time. I'd set up candles and photographs of her and things that she'd cared about. The rest of the band was like, "You have to take that down. It's not healthy anymore."

We only had six or eight songs recorded for our first album when Stefanie passed away. So the CD ended up being this weird mishmash of recordings. Stuff we wouldn't have put on there had she still been there to rerecord some songs or write new ones.

The decision to go on was like a survival instinct. To not would have been like a whole other loss. I don't even remember us having a doubt. It was never "Should we?" It was "When will we?" or "How will we?"

ROISIN DUNNE I was friends with Kim Warnick, and she recommended me to the band. I showed up for an audition, and I remember I went into it feeling very nervous and awkward and weird out of respect for their loss. They were like, "You can plug in to that." And it was Stefanie's amp. They had clearly done a lot of processing together. It was time for them to play again.

They had sent me a tape of the songs ahead of time. So I pulled out my guitar, and we played. They were great. Then Selene said, "Okay, let's go to the Comet." And that was the audition.

CHAPTER 29 BILE HOG!

BARRETT MARTIN (Screaming Trees/Mad Season/Skin Yard drummer) The irony was, by the time that the whole Seattle thing was catching on and major labels were starting to call us, Skin Yard had run its course. When Dan Peters went back to Mudhoney, Van Conner called me and said, "Hey, I heard Skin Yard broke up, do you want to come audition?" They offered me the job when I hadn't even met Lanegan yet, 'cause Lanegan told them, "Well, if he's good and you like him, then just offer him the gig."

The first time I met Lanegan, I remember he was kinda being surly with me, and I just sort of laughed it off, because he's a big guy, but so am I, and I wasn't physically intimidated by him. And I didn't know what his reputation was, because I can't say that I was reading the fanzines and gossip columns about the band.

KIM WHITE (Screaming Trees manager) I was at the Gorge for Lollapalooza and a couple different people had come up to me and said, "Mark Lanegan wants to have a meeting with you." At that point, they were being managed by Susan Silver, but she really wasn't doing anything for them; Soundgarden and Alice in Chains were the priority.

I went to Mark's apartment, and we talked for about three hours and by the end of it he asked me to be their manager, and I said yes. They had the reputation of being a little wild, but I had worked with some of the most difficult bands out there, including the Chili Peppers. This is the funny part: He said, "You have to say it out loud in order for it to be real. I want you to say, 'I am the new manager of the Screaming Trees.' "

I said, "Okay. I am the new manager of the Screaming Trees." When I said those words out loud, I kind of felt like, My life is over.

BARRETT MARTIN Once the bands all started to get on major labels and were touring around the world, we would see each other more commonly backstage at some gigantic festival in Europe or Australia than we would see each other in Seattle.

GARY LEE CONNER Roskilde was the biggest show we'd ever played; there were probably 70,000 people there. We had a great time hanging around with the other bands. Nirvana's playing, Pearl Jam's playing.

KIM WHITE I think everybody in the band was intimidated by the crowd, so everybody continued to drink all day. Denmark was playing the World Cup and they were showing the game on the big screen. When Denmark won, the crowd was going crazy. Right after, Pearl Jam played.

BRETT ELIASON (Pearl Jam soundman; producer/mixer) Ed went into the crowd, and security had been facing away from the stage, so when he went to climb back up onto the stage, they didn't recognize him and one of them grabbed him and was manhandling him pretty good. Our tour manager at the time, Eric Johnson, went down there, got Ed behind him, and was just swinging at security guards. All the other band members jumped down and had a tussle until they finally got things worked out and the show could go on.

JEFF AMENT It made us feel like playing those huge shows maybe wasn't as important as we thought it was. We packed our bags, and we left the next morning.

VAN CONNER That was the first time I ever hung out with Mike McCready. He came in our dressing room after Pearl Jam played, and he was pretty drunk. And we were like, "We're gonna teach you how to drink, McCready!"

KIM WHITE Because Kurt and Mark were best friends, Kurt's like, "I want you guys to headline the show." And we were like, "That's not a good idea." Kurt's like, "No, I really want to help you out. I think it would be great if you guys played after us and close the show."

And we were like, "No, no, no, that's really not a good idea." But for some reason, it ended up happening. So, picture this: Denmark wins the World Cup, the crowd is going crazy. Pearl Jam plays, the crowd is going crazy. Then Nirvana plays, and the crowd goes crazy.

DAVE ABBRUZZESE Courtney was near the stage, yelling to security, "Don't let those Pearl Jam fuckers up here!" And then she saw me and said, "Except him." For some reason we got along. We watched Nirvana together.

VAN CONNER We had Jägermeister, vodka, and beer. Our dressing room was very fancy, but by the time we were set to go on, because of McCready and Lanegan—and I might have had a hand in it, too—there was literally nothing left to the room except for a pile of rubble two feet deep. Everything that could be broken was broken into little pieces. Lanegan was super-hammered.

KIM WHITE And then: "Ladies and gentlemen, the Screaming Trees!" And you hear crickets. You can hear the band's footsteps as they walked onto the stage. That's how quiet the crowd was.

GARY LEE CONNER We started playing a normal set. At one point, I heard Krist Novoselic, who was off to the side of the stage, say, "Play the one about the devil!" I said, "They're all about the devil!" And then all hell broke loose.

BARRETT MARTIN We're playing "Change Has Come" and Mark's trying to sing, and it's not coming out right, so he throws the mic stand down and then he sits on the drum riser, just sits in front of my hi-hat stand, and keeps drinking. We just keep playing the riff and wait for him to go back to singing.

KIM WHITE The two brothers came and sat down by his side and were like, "Come on, Mark, you can't do this to us." They got him a new mic and a new stand, and he got up to sing "Ivy." And again, the mic wasn't working, and the monitors weren't working. He knocked one monitor over successfully and then the stage crew came to try to get him.

BARRETT MARTIN He runs to this corner of the stage and throws one of those big TV video cameras—destroyed a $50,000 camera. The security came after him, and they were throwing punches, but not landing any.

KIM WHITE The last monitor that Mark threw over landed on top of one of the Denmark television station's cameras and broke it. One of the mic stands hit a guy in the audience wearing glasses, broke his glasses. Afterwards, I had to call our insurance company in the States and say, "We just broke a $100,000 camera, and this guy got hit in the head and his glasses are broken, he's bleeding."

GARY LEE CONNER We saw he was going nuts, so everybody else just went nuts. I smashed my guitar. I'd never purposely smashed a guitar before. Barrett smashed up his drums. Then Mark had to go run and hide . . .

DAVE GROHL We had to hide him in the dressing room. But you don't wanna mess with that dude. Give him a microphone, let him sing, then get the fuck out of his way.

KIM WHITE The promoter said, "You gotta get Mark out of here, because if these guys get their hands on him they're gonna beat the shit out of him." So we took Mark back to the hotel and said, "You gotta stay, because they want blood." But Mark put a disguise on—a wool cap and a different jacket—and went back to the festival anyway.

The promoter was like, "Oh, my God, this is fucking great! It's like the Who in '69, but theirs was staged. This was real." The Screaming Trees really did make a name for themselves at that show. They walked out to crickets and when they left the stage, there were probably 60,000 people thinking that was one of the best fucking things they've ever seen.

BARRETT MARTIN I think the Screaming Trees corrupted me. I didn't really start drinking until I was in the band. After Roskilde, something shifted in the way we were perceived: as being real brutish, tough, beating people up, looking for fights, fighting amongst ourselves. But it was a distortion of reality. I'm not saying that it didn't happen on a small scale from time to time, but you wouldn't have the energy to keep going if you did that all the time.

We didn't go around trashing the backstage at our shows. We didn't get in fights, unless we were in a bar. There was one brawl, later that year, in Asbury Park, New Jersey, in front of the Stone Pony. We were walking out, and we got jumped by about 10 guys.

VAN CONNER We were all so drunk that whole week. I wasn't there for the actual fisticuffs, but how I remember it was that the fight was between Mark and Barrett and the club security guys, who were huge and looked like they were on *The Sopranos*.

BARRETT MARTIN It was the four of us—Van and I and Mark and one of our roadies—against the 10 of them, these New Jersey hoods. They had no idea who we were. It was full-on. We're big guys; we can take a punch, and we can throw a punch. At a certain point, the bouncers came out and the thugs realized they weren't gonna be able to take us, so they just walked away.

The next day, we were on *Letterman*, and Lanegan's got this huge black eye. My arm was in a sling, so they had Steve Farrone play drums instead.

VAN CONNER Letterman was all excited because he likes to make jokes about fat people, apparently. So during the food segment he held up a giant ham and was like, "This is trail mix for the Screaming Trees." Actually, for a band that's good publicity.

KIM WHITE Letterman said, "I think I'm scared of you guys." They got a nice shot of Mark's shiner, too.

• • •

JIM ROSE (founder of the Seattle-based Jim Rose Circus Sideshow) Lollapalooza felt a lot like a Seattle coming-out party. That was the year everybody felt this whole "alternative" thing. So I quickly read a *Spin* magazine and watched an hour of MTV and said, "Okay, they want it fast, with the F-word." That's what I delivered.

MARC GEIGER (Lollapalooza festival cofounder; talent agent) The way the first Lollapalooza formed was organic. Each of the seven of us—meaning the four Jane's Addiction members, myself, Don Muller, Ted Gardner—we picked the bands ourselves. The next year, it was much more Don and myself, along with the Red Hot Chili Peppers.

Don represented both Soundgarden and Pearl Jam, and more. Soundgarden was a band we wanted to get on the year before, but we couldn't, because they were out of cycle. I was a huge fan of theirs. And then Don said, "We gotta put Pearl Jam on." I said, "It's the same thing as Soundgarden." And he said, "No, it's not. You're an idiot." Perry Farrell didn't want *either* of 'em. Yeah, Perry had broken up Jane's Addiction, he was completely out of his mind on worse drugs than he had been before, and he wanted to do a rave.

I didn't want two Seattle bands on the bill. But Don was a hundred million percent right, and I realized it quickly. I remember going to the first show, and Don's standing next to me as Pearl Jam's playing. Eddie's climbing up on the scaffolding, people are going fucking bananas. Don's like, "In your face, bitch!"

KELLY CURTIS Around Lollapalooza, it was just starting to blow up for us and there were a lot of arguments about placement on the bill or how big our backdrop was. And the band decided collectively that we should go on as early as possible. Because at the top it was so heavy with Soundgarden and Ice Cube and the Chili Peppers, we just thought, Let's not even worry about our position, let's just make it early. And it paid off really well for us.

MARC GEIGER Lollapalooza was the tour that catapulted Pearl Jam, because it showcased them in a way that they could just kill everybody else. They were sandwiched between Lush and the Jesus and Mary Chain, so it wasn't exactly a fair fight, from a rock standpoint.

BEN SHEPHERD After their MTV hit, the fans were just—*whoosh*—storming the stadium once the gates opened to see Pearl Jam.

MARK PELLINGTON (video director) The "Jeremy" video just became this monster. As a viewer, you were saying, "Fuck, it's on all the time."

I had maybe an hour-long phone call with Eddie about what the real story was behind it, about him reading this article about a kid in Texas who shot himself in front of his class. The vision tapped into my own childhood pain and my parents arguing, and an eight-page treatment came pouring out of me.

Eddie wanted this to be a story. "Okay, but let's have Eddie sing." Embedded still in my skull is the memory of walking behind the camera with a little handheld monitor. Eddie was sitting, we were moving around him, so I'm keeping an eye on him and an eye on the monitor. And I still can feel the chill when we come around and Eddie's head was down, but his eyes were up. Just watching his catharsis, his performance, gave me shivers.

In the original version, the kid comes in, tosses the apple, puts the gun in his mouth, shoots, it flashes to three, taking it back to the beginning—the time, the weather, and the place—and the whole last shot is just his blood on the kids' frozen faces. But MTV wouldn't show the gun in the mouth.

RICK KRIM Pearl Jam didn't want to edit the video. I don't remember what the final straw was that made them relent, maybe it was label pressure, but I recall many a conversation back and forth with management and the label. Having the shot where the kid sticks the gun in his mouth was just too graphic. You saw the aftermath anyway, so that it wasn't necessary to have that little extra shock value.

MARK PELLINGTON People misinterpreted the edited video and thought, because of the blood on his classmates, that he killed the kids in the classroom. He didn't point the gun at them. You'd have to be kind of stupid to misinterpret this, especially if you read the lyrics.

SAMUEL BAYER I think Mark Pellington is a really talented guy; Pearl Jam's an amazing band. I just thought my Nirvana video was more interesting. I never liked seeing lyrics brought to life literally. I don't wanna see children frozen, covered in blood. I don't wanna picture who Jeremy is. I was too much of an ambitious, jealous, competitive guy to see any merit in that video.

AMY FINNERTY When grunge was in full swing, I went to one of my bosses in the programming department, Rick Krim, and said, "Hey, Rick, I don't know if you know about this Temple of the Dog record—it's about a year old or so—but two of the guys in this band are Chris Cornell and Eddie Vedder. I think we should revisit this." And he fell in love with it and called the record company and basically said, "Let's make this happen." They rereleased the record and resubmitted the video, which we put into heavy rotation.

KIM THAYIL When Pearl Jam started going through the roof, the record company, in a very cynical move, decided to rerelease *Temple of the Dog* to capture and hang on to the success of Pearl Jam. They released "Hunger Strike," which featured Eddie's vocals prominently. Of course, as a record company guy, you *should* do that.

Chris doing Temple of the Dog ultimately helped Soundgarden, in that it got him to exercise some of his creativity muscles and bring that back to Soundgarden. It was bad in that at some point, I think *Temple of the Dog* was outselling *Badmotorfinger*.

HIRO YAMAMOTO I didn't play for like two years after I left Soundgarden, and then Pickerel called me up and I joined Truly. Truly ended up playing this Lollapalooza over on Bainbridge Island. We were playing on a side stage at 12 noon, and Kim was like, "You should come over." We went over there, and Scott Sundquist, our first drummer, was there, too, and they were saying, "You guys are gonna come up onstage and we're gonna do 'Circle of Power' and 'Tears to Forget' together."

We're standing on the side of the stage, and I couldn't believe how many people were out in the audience. There were like 60,000 people, and the stage is so huge. I'm like, "Wow, we're supposed to go out *there*?" We got to that point where we were supposed to go out—and Chris kept on singing, and they kept on going. I think he didn't want us to do it. That's Chris. I was kind of pissed, but I was actually relieved. I hadn't played those songs in three years.

At the same time, I was lookin' at those guys, and I was watching the way Ben was spittin' on the crowd, and I was like, I am so glad I'm not that. What an ass. Ben is definitely a different personality than I am. He has a more metal attitude. I like Ben and all, but he likes bein' a jerk to people.

JIM ROSE I went from being unknown to literally needing security within a 48-hour period. MTV punched it hard, and *USA Today* said the sideshow was the "word of mouth" act of Lollapalooza. I offered the audience a chance to come up and drink a sideshow member's vomit—*bile* is what we called it to soften it up. You'd take a big clear cylinder pump, with a long, clear tube attached to it, thread the tube into your nose down into your stomach, pull out the contents from your stomach, and then shoot it into a glass.

One day, Eddie Vedder drinks it and the crowd went nuts and it was all over MTV. Then Al Jourgensen from Ministry started coming up, and Al and Eddie got into a battle of who could drink the most of it, and MTV followed it every day. Finally, at the end of the tour, Eddie was slightly ahead. But Al said, "I'm gonna win because I'll just make my own vomit."

EDDIE VEDDER Just looking for attention, I guess. Every city there'd be some old friend or my wife's parents, and I'd get to gross everyone out.

JEFF GILBERT Around that time, I went to a live taping of Jim Rose's show at the Crocodile Café that was being shown live in England. Jim came up to me earlier and said, "Look, we're gonna do the 'drink the bile' shtick, and I want to make sure that, since we're on live TV, when we ask for a volunteer, somebody jumps up there right away." And I said, "I'll do it."

During the show they do the "drink the bile" shtick with Matt "The Tube," and Jim goes, "Who gets to drink the bile?" And at that point, the crowd normally goes, "Oh, no way!" So I jumped up there. Well, Eddie was in the crowd, too, and he jumped up, edged me out of the way, took the glass right out of my hand, just slugged it right down.

In the footage, you can see me wrapping myself around him from behind—I was gonna squeeze him and make it come right out his nose—and I'm whispering in his ear, "You bile hog!"

CHAPTER 30
THE EMPEROR'S NEW FLANNEL

JENNIE BODDY Every local paper would call up like they had some unique idea: "Oh, I want to do a story on this hot topic: the Seattle scene." I'd tell them not to, that it's been done too much already. What a great publicist! Nobody wanted to talk about it anymore. That was before Pearl Jam hit, and it was already tiresome.

It was a sorry day when Bruce and Jonathan had to get their publicity shots taken. Because you shouldn't have the owners of the label doing publicity shots. You really want to read a story on Eminem and see Jimmy Iovine pictures? This is about music. It was just ridiculous. But they were so quotable and funny and irreverent that it worked.

BRUCE PAVITT Our philosophy was never to turn down an interview no matter what, so we were in everything from *Maximumrocknroll* to *Fortune*. Part of the game is that to become truly popular you have to infiltrate every nook and cranny of the popular system.

CONRAD UNO (Popllama Records founder; Egg Studios owner; producer/engineer) The media was everywhere, and it was sort of aggravating and weird. The light was bright and it was kinda gettin' in your eyes. Kinda wanted to go back into the basement, where the studio is, and have fun. But honestly, it was exciting, too.

ART CHANTRY During the height of the mania, there was one crazy-ass day where we had five media crews come in to the *Rocket* offices to interview everything that walked. It was like *The Christian Science Monitor,* some Italian fashion magazine, somebody that spoke Japanese, *Rolling Stone, The New York Times,* all taking pictures. Now we look back on it as this real event that happened, but at the time we thought it was the funniest goddamn joke in the world.

JENNIE BODDY When Tabitha Soren from MTV News came to do this special report from Seattle, it was ridiculous. All the girls around her were kissing her ass and calling her Tabby. I took her for some Mudhoney interviews, and Mark Arm was trying to claim the origin of *grunge* was the sour curd in the bottom of the milk carton.

And then I took her to a Seaweed show—even though they're not grunge, it didn't matter. She liked the young boys at the Seaweed show. She's like, "Where can we get more of that?" And I was saying, "Well, that doesn't really capture it." She was a little disgusted that the rock stars weren't so cute. She wanted them to all be Chris Cornell or something. I took her to meet TAD, and she was just very rude. TAD was a huge part of what grunge was, but she didn't want any of it. She just wanted the cute boys.

KURT DANIELSON When Tabitha Soren came to Seattle, they filmed us playing the song "Pansy," which is about a serial killer that gives young girls candy, abducts them, and then murders them. I don't think she found any redeeming qualities in our music. She interviewed us, they filmed us playing the song, and then they left. I think she spent most of the time out in the van, shocked and disgusted.

JENNIE BODDY After that, I took Tabitha to go see Earth, Dylan Carlson's band. That was my last stop, because I couldn't stand her anymore, and I knew the music was just so *slowww.* It looked like she was going to crawl out of her skin. I was so happy.

STEVE TURNER Ron Reagan Jr. interviewed us for some stupid TV show. Nice guy. We went bowling with him, gettin' drunk, and I'm flipping him shit: "Do you realize how many hardcore bands write songs about your dad?" I started rattling them off. He wanted to shut down that conversation in a hurry.

But it was the bait-and-switch thing that pissed me off with some of that mainstream press. Ron Reagan Jr. wanted to talk to us about the music scene, but when it finally came on TV it was like, "Oh, the music scene in Seattle" and then immediately: "*There is, however . . .* A DARK SIDE." And they paid some fuckin' junkie to shoot up on camera. That had nothing to do with the music scene—just some Seattle junkie, some young kid. As if musicians doing drugs was a new story and somehow unique to the Seattle explosion that was happening.

JEFF GILBERT We always used to laugh, because the national media made such a big deal out of heroin in Seattle. We were looking around, going, "Really?" There's like three or four high-profile people that did it, we lost a couple from it. There were a lot of dabblers—it seemed chic at the moment—but it was alcohol that was doing the most damage. *God,* the alcohol. It's almost inhuman how much beer was gone through. But that's not a glamorous rock-and-roll tale. That's the standard.

DOUG PRAY (*Hype!* documentary director) When I started the movie *Hype!,* it seemed like the worst idea in the world because I was just late. I had just come out of UCLA film school, and I had done music videos for the Young Fresh Fellows and Flop, who had nothing to do with grunge but were pretty respected Seattle bands. A producer from the UCLA Producers Program, Steve Helvey, came to me in 1992 and was like, "Look, we have to do a documentary film about the Seattle music scene." And I was like, "It's just too late."

It was just embarrassing starting out. You could not have possibly put together a more cynical and media-wary—not just wary, but willing to fuck with the media—group of people than that group of bands and musicians and publicists. For example, Steve called Charles Peterson, and Charles was so incensed that a movie was gonna be made about the Seattle music scene at this point, when there had been so many journalists overrunning the town, that Steve's response was, "These people are so fucking pissed off, we *have* to do this movie."

(above) MOTHER LOVE BONE play the Vogue in Seattle, January 1990. From left: Jeff Ament and Andrew Wood. © PAUL HERNANDEZ

PEARL JAM, first publicity shoot, Seattle, 1991. From left: Stone Gossard, Jeff Ament, Mike McCready, Eddie Vedder, and Dave Krusen. © LANCE MERCER

THE GITS at Venice Beach, January 1993. From left: Andy Kessler, Steve Moriarty, Mia Zapata, and Matt Dresdner.
© MICHAEL GALEN NICHOLS

7 YEAR BITCH at the Satyricon in Portland, Oregon, 1992. From left: Elizabeth Davis-Simpson, Valerie Agnew (obscured), Selene Vigil-Wilk, and Stefanie Sargent. © DAVID C. ACKERMAN

THE MELVINS AND L7 on tour together, October 1994. From left: Buzz Osborne, Jennifer Finch, Suzi Gardner, Dee Plakas, Dale Crover, Donita Sparks, and Mark Deutrom. © 1994 JENNIFER FINCH

NIRVANA at the U.K.'s Reading Festival, August 23, 1991. From left: Kurt Cobain, Krist Novoselic, and Dave Grohl. © ED SIRRS

(left) BABES IN TOYLAND at the Waterloo Village, New Jersey, Lollapalooza stop, July 1993. From left: Lori Barbero, Kat Bjelland, and Maureen Herman.
© DANNY CLINCH

HOLE in Seattle, early 1994. From left: Kristen Pfaff, Eric Erlandson, Courtney Love, and Patty Schemel.
© KAREN MOSKOWITZ

SINGLES STAR MATT DILLON (left) and director Cameron Crowe on set, 1991.

(left) ALICE IN CHAINS
in Capitol Hill, Seattle,
late 1993 or early 1994.
From left: Sean Kinney,
Layne Staley, Jerry Cantrell,
and Mike Inez.
© KAREN MOSKOWITZ

(bottom of facing page)
PEARL JAM AND
PRESIDENT CLINTON
meet at the White House,
April 9, 1994. From left: Jeff
Ament, Mike McCready,
Stone Gossard, President
Clinton, and Eddie Vedder.
WILLIAM J. CLINTON
PRESIDENTIAL LIBRARY

(above) SCREAMING TREES at Myrtle Edwards Park, Seattle, 1996. From left: Mark Lanegan, Gary Lee Conner, Barrett Martin, and Van Conner.
© ALICE WHEELER

(right) GRUNTRUCK at the Georgetown Steam Plant, Seattle, 1990. Clockwise from bottom left: Scott McCollum, Tom Niemeyer, Ben McMillan, and Tim Paul.
© LORI GARNES

SOUNDGARDEN in Seattle, January 1994. From left: Matt Cameron, Kim Thayil, Ben Shepherd, and Chris Cornell. © ED SIRRS

CANDLEBOX impersonating Courtney Love in a 1995 *Rocket* cover shoot outtake. From left: Peter Klett, Kevin Martin, Scott Mercado, and Bardi Martin. © KAREN MOSKOWITZ

MEGAN JASPER Shortly after I got laid off from Sub Pop, there was a U.K. magazine called *Sky* that called up saying, "Maybe you can give us some words people in Seattle use?" So I threw out some lies to them, and they published this lexicon that they thought was real. The Mudhoney guys got their hands on that publication while they were over there touring and started using those words as jokes in interviews.

Somehow someone at *The New York Times* heard there was a lexicon that existed. So they called Sub Pop. Jonathan knew I'd have fun with it, so he redirected them to me, and the reporter called. At that point, I was working out of my apartment for Caroline Records. I'd had three pots of coffee and I was flying out of my fucking skin. I was thrilled I had a distraction I could have fun with. I said, "Why don't you give me words, and I'll just give you the grunge translation?"

The reporter, Rick Marin, was super-sweet on the phone. I kept escalating the craziness of the translations because anyone in their right mind would go, "Oh, come on, this is bullshit." I thought we would have a hearty laugh, and he would have to write it off as 15 minutes wasted, but it never happened, because he was concentrating so hard on getting the information right. My favorite was "swingin' on the flippity-flop," which meant "hanging out." That came from a crazy guy from Northampton, Massachusetts, who used to work at the Red Lion Diner and wore a T-shirt that said CATCH YOU ON THE FLIPPY-FLOP or something.

When I hung up, I was like, Oh, it will be edited out in the end. And a few days later, it was a huge thing on the front page of the Style section.

THE NEW YORK TIMES ("Lexicon of Grunge: Breaking the Code," by Rick Marin, November 15, 1992) All subcultures speak in code; grunge is no exception. Megan Jasper, a 25-year-old sales representative at Caroline Records in Seattle, provided this lexicon of grunge speak, coming soon to a high school or mall near you:

WACK SLACKS: Old ripped jeans
FUZZ: Heavy wool sweaters
PLATS: Platform shoes
KICKERS: Heavy boots
SWINGIN' ON THE FLIPPITY-FLOP: Hanging out

BOUND-AND-HAGGED: Staying home on Friday or
  Saturday night
SCORE: Great
HARSH REALM: Bummer
COB NOBBLER: Loser
DISH: Desirable guy
BLOATED, BIG BAG OF BLOATATION: Drunk
LAMESTAIN: Uncool person
TOM-TOM CLUB: Uncool outsiders
ROCK ON: A happy goodbye

DANIEL HOUSE Oh, people were in hysterics. It just showed how desperate everybody had gotten to do a piece on Seattle, that they'd print anything and wouldn't even bother to see if it was true. So C/Z printed up two different T-shirts with the "Lexicon of Grunge" on the back, both with a different word on the front, one being HARSH REALM, the other being LAMESTAIN.

The shirts sold pretty well. Not as good as BRUCE PAVITT GAVE ME HEAD, though. That was the single most popular C/Z shirt. It came out while I was still working at Sub Pop. What did he think of it? If Bruce didn't like it, I never would've known it.

MEGAN JASPER Tom Frank, the editor of *The Baffler*, called me, laughing: "Do you know that all the publications are talking about this, because the *Times* is such a prestigious paper?" No one could believe it happened.

Once *The Baffler* got the word out, that created another shitstorm, which *The New York Times* caught wind of. So the editor of the Style section called and yelled at me. She's like, "It caused a lot of problems here, and it's irresponsible of you to lie to our reporter." And then she asked me where she could buy the LAMESTAIN T-shirts from. She was obviously pissed off, but she wanted me to think that she was in on the joke.

SCOTT MCCAUGHEY (Young Fresh Fellows singer/bassist/guitarist; Popllama Records/Egg Studios employee) I'm working at Popllama, and *Rolling Stone* wants to come and interview me and shoot me for a story. So they come and I happen to be wearing a flannel shirt; it's cool sometimes there in the basement when you're packing records. But they've got this entire rack of other flannel shirts that they wheel in. And I'm like, "Why can't I just wear the one I'm wearing?"

They put some other flannel shirt on me and they take pictures of me boxing records. The shirt wasn't that different from what I was wearing. I think when they had the picture of me in the article, it said, "Wearing such-and-such shirt, $89" or whatever. Which is probably why they had me wear it, because otherwise it would've said, "Wearing his shitty old shirt that cost $1."

BOB WHITTAKER Someone, I think it was Charles Peterson, jokingly attributed grunge clothing to my dad, because he was the first full-time employee and later the CEO of REI, Recreational Equipment Inc. At the old shows at the Metropolis, you'd see guys in ski jackets. Everyone was wearing their parents' beat-up mountaineering clothing, their crappy down parkas, and flannel and stuff like that.

JEFF AMENT . . . I wore shorts year round. I rode bikes everywhere, didn't have a car, and if I was going to practice I had to carry my bass on my bicycle, so I couldn't wear jeans. I'm not sure what defined what grunge was or wasn't. I never ever wore a flannel shirt. I had a few hats, for sure. That started off when I was in Green River and had a girlfriend who made hats. At the time, I don't think I looked like a rocker, I looked like a dumbass. It was partly function and partly what was laying around.

ROB SKINNER As far as the grunge look, that was all Eric Johnson. Eric worked at the Espresso Roma on Broadway, and that's when I met him. He was the first guy that I ever saw with cut-off shorts with long johns underneath, and I thought that was totally badass. Maybe he got it from Chris Cornell, or Chris got it from him, but once those guys started sporting it, it spread, because Eric was kinda high-profile—long hair, cool guy, smoking-hot girlfriend, working at the coffee shop on Broadway. And he worked for Soundgarden. And Soundgarden were the alpha dog, always.

ERIC JOHNSON I could never really say if I was the first to do it. I just know that I wore it. Where I went to school, in Ellensburg, you wore long johns. I think one day I ended up puttin' a pair of shorts on over a pair of long johns and then wearing a pair of boots. I thought, This is pretty comfortable. The big thing when I was a little kid was you wore your shorts over your sweat pants; that look was huge. Also, I grew up skateboarding, and people into skateboarding would put their skate shorts on over jeans.

Do I take credit for the look? *No.* I'm sure people have been wearing shorts over anything for a million years.

TAD DOYLE People were wearing flannel here long before grunge came out. It's cold here. It's a cheap and effective clothing apparatus for living in the Northwest. I don't even associate it with a fashion statement or the lack thereof. I thought Eddie Vedder did more for flannel than anybody.

KURT DANIELSON The loser ethic is an anti-ethic, and grunge fashion is an antifashion. It's basically taking all things and putting them on their heads and pretending they're cool, like the emperor's wearing no clothes. In this case, we're saying that the emperor is wearing a flannel shirt.

ROBERT ROTH The flannel and the long hair and the Doc Martens, that kinda was passé in Seattle when all of a sudden it hit in late '91, early '92. It was like watching it happen all over again.

JONATHAN PONEMAN I got a call from an editor at *Vogue* magazine who wanted me to write a piece about grunge fashion, which I did. Some people said, "Why are you doing that?" And I said, "Are you kidding me?" It was like performance art—just the idea that I, who is as much of a fashion spaz as anybody that I've ever known, would be writing something for *Vogue* magazine.

Plus it was a couple thousand bucks, and it was a kick. I wrote it hours before my final deadline, and they threw it in there practically unedited, just to fill space. It was a really poorly written piece of tripe. But it was, "Hey, look, Mom, I'm writing for *Vogue.*"

LINDA DERSCHANG (Linda's Tavern/Basic clothing store owner) Jonathan called me up and told me he was writing an article about grunge fashion for *Vogue.* He asked me for a quote. "Are you kidding me? Really?"

I owned a store, Basic, that carried the stuff that people wanted to wear—the purple hair dye and Doc Martens.

Sometimes 16-year-old boys might be trying on a pair of Doc Martens, and one of our salespeople, Tammy Watson, would say, "Yeah, Chris Cornell from Soundgarden, do you know who he is?" The boys' eyes would light up, and they'd say, "Yeah?"

"Well, he was in here last week and bought that exact same pair of cherry-red Doc Martens." *"Really?"* "Oh, yeah."

I'd just roll my eyes going, "Oh, God. He was not!"

Kurt Cobain *did* used to buy hair dye there. Some kid would come in and ask, "Do you know what color Kurt bought recently?" And if we had a lot of, say, cherry red, we'd go, "Cherry red!" It was probably a bit awful, but they didn't know the difference!

KIM THAYIL The height of absurdity? Gosh, one of the first things that comes to mind is the *Vogue* spread about grunge fashion. Having models walking the runways in Milan in some kind of flannel skirts—I embraced it, on some level, because there's an element of parody in it.

ROBERT SCOTT CRANE I dated some models back then. It was really kind of a tragic thing—girls in their young twenties were suddenly doing heroin because that's what was cool to do. All of a sudden, at the Crocodile you saw all of these really pretty girls, instead of just the grunge girls, and they were all fucking high. These people are here because this music is on MTV, and Kate Moss is on the cover of the magazine looking like she's from Auschwitz.

PETER BAGGE (*Hate* cartoonist) I'm so out of it, I didn't even realize how prevalent heroin use was in the grunge scene. I drew the band the character Stinky managed, and I was trying to think of the most absurd lyrics I could think of, so I had the singer scream, "I scream, you scream, we all scream for heroin!" I picked heroin to be "out there"—you know, freak out the parents. Then I was informed that heroin was a scourge. (*Laughs.*) A lot of people in the music scene were very upset. But then I found out there were people I knew who were heroin addicts and who thought it was hilarious! Like Mark Arm. He thought it was a riot.

Pavitt and Poneman also thought it was hilarious, and a couple of times they asked me to do variations on that for them for T-shirts or posters or ads. They had me do "I scream, you scream, we all scream for a fashion spread in *Vogue!*"

KELLY CURTIS Marc Jacobs approached me about Eddie, probably for a fashion layout or something. A bunch of people did. There's so many crazy offers that have come our way over the last 20 years. You name it—every corporation or advertisement or reality-TV show or starring vehicle or pajama company. Ninety-nine percent of it, I just say no.

LINDA DERSCHANG In a way, "grunge fashion" was a nonfashion. That's why it was so funny that it turned into a Marc Jacobs line for Perry Ellis. Marc Jacobs was fired from Perry Ellis after that line came out. Which was, in a way, also pretty funny.

MARC JACOBS (fashion designer) We were fired from Perry Ellis. I think there were a lot of reasons. People love to attribute it to the fact that this grunge collection was so controversial and outrageous and whatever, but . . . very often the designer collection isn't really the moneymaking thing, it's really the icing on the cake, and it's something that promotes the image of the company. But that part was financed by Perry Ellis, the company itself, whereas all the other things, like Perry Ellis shirts, the menswear, the jeans, those were all licensed, so the expenses were taken care of outside. So, of course we did this grunge collection, and it *was* very controversial. Anyway, somewhere just after that, they decided they didn't want to continue with the whole idea of a woman's collection on that level or on that scale.

COURTNEY LOVE Marc sent me and Kurt his Perry Ellis grunge collection. Do you know what we did with it? *We burned it.* We were punkers—we didn't like that kind of thing.

NEAL KARLEN (journalist; Babes in Toyland biographer) "Kinderwhore" fashion was personified by the babydoll dress, clothes that would look very Lolita-ish on 25-year-old women. Kat Bjelland from Babes in Toyland took that fashion on as this sort of symbol of her music and who she was. And it became a big deal when Courtney became so big and claimed this look as her own. She ripped off Kat's act.

For a short time, Courtney Love was in the band that evolved into Babes in Toyland; there's debate between her and Kat about whether it was even called Babes in Toyland at that point. And Kat, who was the leader, kicked Courtney out of the band. I think that word *frenemy* was invented for those two.

MICHELLE LEON (bassist for Minneapolis's Babes in Toyland) It got blown totally out of proportion by making this big rivalry. I'm not saying that there wasn't tension and that they didn't have falling-outs, but even I don't know all the details, and I was there.

MAUREEN HERMAN (later Babes in Toyland bassist) We're getting interviewed every fucking week and somebody's asking us which Hole songs inspired us and, "Why did Kat copy Courtney's look?"

KAT BJELLAND The media did that, and it was really hurtful to me for a long time. They'd say it's some kind of battle. Which it wasn't. We were friends. And then someone started believing the press. But if you really do the research of when I started my band and got onstage looking how I look, they would see who the originator is.

COURTNEY LOVE It's not about a dress thing. I'm about to hang up on you! Go read some old copies of *Ms. Magazine,* and *Backlash,* and get back to me. Seriously, like, dresses? *What?* No, it was about a Rickenbacker, if you really want to know the truth. The fuckin' Rickenbacker I bought at Captain Whizeagle's. And she stole my gear, and I was really pissed about it. The dress thing was kind of part and parcel of it, but obviously that was way, way, way back in the day.

LORI BARBERO Who won? I think Courtney won because she sold more records, she was the richer person, and she had a longer career. But who cares? In all of the hundreds and thousands of hours that we were in vans and airports and everywhere, we never talked about our attire. Except once, in Providence, Rhode Island, or somewhere up that way, Kat was walking on the street in her big, black clunky shoes that went with her knee-highs and her little dress with the big collar. Someone yelled out to Kat, "Nice polio shoes!" She screamed back, *"They're not* *polio shoes!*" She never wore those shoes ever again, and I was so glad because I thought they were so ugly. Oh, and one time Michelle had to leave a really important meeting to go buy some cow-print pants she wanted before the secondhand store closed, and we still laugh about how ugly those fuckin' things were.

I think those are the only two times we really talked about clothes: the polio shoes and the cow pants.

CHAPTER 31
THE OLD IMMIGRANTS HATE THE NEW IMMIGRANTS

KEVIN MARTIN (Candlebox singer) The Seattle scene? We were the redheaded stepchild. We were in the right place at the right time. Fortunately, our music had its own voice. Unfortunately, everybody believed that we had moved there to steal the sound.

Does talking about it stir up bad feelings? Not at all. It's easy to talk about. It was a scene that was fuckin' groundbreaking.

I moved to Seattle when I was 14, in 1984, after my father took a job up there. We lived on Mercer Island, where I stood out like a sore thumb. I was a skateboarder, with white, short spiky hair and Converse and ripped-up jeans. I got beat up by jocks the first week of school.

San Antonio, Texas, where I moved from, was worlds apart, musically. San Antonio was predominantly punk rock. My first concert was Dead Kennedys, Black Flag, Butthole Surfers, the Big Boys, so when I moved to Seattle, it was a culture shock. I come from this warm-weather punk-rock attitude. In Seattle, it's rain, there's not a lot of punk rock, there's what I call dirgy rock—slow, down-tuned, heavy—which is what everybody named grunge.

Susan Silver was the manager of the John Fluevog shoe store I worked at, around '87. It was cool working for her, man. I was underage, and she was getting me into all these great shows, and I was meeting incredibly talented musicians. I was playing drums in a couple of punk bands; I wasn't singing yet. I became friendly with Chris Cornell and Andy Wood. They'd come into the store: "Hey, Kevin, what's goin' on? How's the band?" Shit like that.

I was 17, they were 21, 22. So it's not like we were going and having beers together at the Vogue or Linda's Tavern. I was just standing on the side watching this great shit happen and enjoying it.

SCOTT MERCADO (Candlebox/Sky Cries Mary drummer) I'm a little bit older than the other guys in Candlebox. I was born in San Francisco and at the age of one I moved to Kirkland, which is a suburb about five miles outside Seattle. Even though I was ingrained a bit in the Seattle scene, I never thought it would be anything. My thoughts, having studied jazz and having gone to school for music in L.A., were, This is cool, it's interesting, but it will never go anywhere.

Susan Silver managed a band I was in, First Thought, which was a Simple Minds wannabe kind of band. I was also in Sky Cries Mary, who were kind of a grunge band—very alternative, some electronica involved, too. I knew Stone, and I was also jamming here and there with Shawn Smith. I met Tad. In fact, I auditioned for his band, but I just wasn't really into it at that time.

I was also friends with Jonathan Poneman. I never met anybody so enthusiastic about the music scene here. Like, "Scott, you'd like this drummer. His name is Matt Cameron, he plays for a band called Soundgarden." "Oh, come on, Jonathan, you talked about that band last week." So I did go and see them, and sure enough, that was probably the first band that I saw and I said to myself, This band's gonna go somewhere. There were only a couple other bands that I thought were equal to Candlebox, if not better, music-wise, and one of those was Soundgarden.

BARDI MARTIN (Candlebox bassist) I was born in Olympia, Washington, and moved to Seattle when I was a few weeks old. I went to Mercer Island High School with Kevin. He had a different haircut every week. I can vaguely remember him having one-inch-long bleached dreads.

He was trying pretty hard at it. He was always kind of a fast talker, but a good guy.

PETER KLETT (Candlebox guitarist) I grew up outside of Seattle, in what they call Bellevue. People considered it Bellevue, which was very rich and yuppie, but it was actually more the Eastgate area, which was a little less pretentious.

I got out of high school and joined some goofy band called Toxxl'rae. The singer was real into fucking Def Leppard and Aerosmith. The poser-type shit. I did some shows around town, and the '90s thing hit. I saw Mookie Blaylock. I saw Soundgarden at the Off Ramp and Alice in Chains at the Central. Just before it really exploded. Me and the drummer of Toxxl'rae really liked that kind of music, so the group basically disbanded.

SCOTT MERCADO I knew Kevin because I crashed his 16th birthday party with the lead singer of First Thought, Joshua Pierce. His 16th birthday party—how funny is that? I was probably 20. Yeah, it was a little weird—it was my friend Joshua's idea. I think he was 19. Even though I was a little older, you hear about these huge parties that you need to go to. We all got drinking and there were lots of girls there, lots of people hanging out. But it wasn't like a high school party.

I hung out with one of Kevin's future girlfriends, Angie, who came up to me after I left Sky Cries Mary and said, "Remember Kevin Martin? He wants to start a band; he's thinking about calling you."

I'm like, "He plays drums. We're not going to have two drummers in the band."

She said, "No, he's singing now." He wasn't a great drummer, but he had a lot of charisma and was very outgoing, so being a singer is definitely more his personality.

KELLY GRAY (producer; Queensrÿche/Myth guitarist) I've known Scott Mercado, geez, since I was 16. He was in a band called Realms, who had played with Myth and Shadow. Then the guitar player, Peter, I knew from a band he was in with another buddy of mine, which was called Toxxl'rae—it was the '80s, you know. And the way that Candlebox came together is that Kevin Martin and Scott Mercado had a project called

Uncle Duke. And I'm at the Vogue, I'm hanging out with Pete, and Scott Mercado came over and told me they didn't have a guitar player.

PETER KLETT Kelly introduced me to Scott, and I was like, "Cool. Let's do it." As I was walking out of the Vogue, I met Kevin. So that was my introduction to what was Uncle Duke.

BARDI MARTIN I had been in a string of shitty bands, and I was over at a friend of mine's, Adam, who was the singer for Sweet Water, and Sarah his girlfriend, venting about just how frustrated I was. I hadn't seen Kevin since high school, and they mentioned that Kevin is looking for a bass player.

I was the last person to join. What ended up being "You," which was one of the songs that did really well, happened when we were improvising, the first hour we were together. I had a rough song idea that became "Far Behind," and I think we worked on that that night, too. It felt pretty magical early on.

At one point, I left town for a few days, and when I came back the band was called Candlebox. I always thought it was a shitty name.

KELLY GRAY I get a call about needing to get some demos for these guys, so we go in to Robert Lang and record basically a full-length demo. When Kevin was singing "Far Behind" at the studio, I looked at their then-manager and I said, "These guys are gonna make us rich." It was obvious.

And then things started really changing. They were playing the Weathered Wall, which was basically the next club down from the Crocodile Café. It probably held about 600 people stuffed. They want me to run sound on this show, and I walk into this club—and it's literally like their fourth gig—and there are so many people in this thing, and outside the door people can't get in. I'm just like, "What the fuck is this?"

KEVIN MARTIN Spring of '92 is when we did our demo tape and changed the name to Candlebox. We hadn't been thinking, We're gonna get rich doing this, until *Nevermind* went through the fuckin' roof.

Candlebox took the most heat as a young band. Because nobody knew who we were, and we had kind of come out of obscurity.

BARDI MARTIN Things happened really fast for us. There were a lot of people that were really happy for things going well, but at the same time, musicians are some of the shittiest, most insecure people on the planet. There were people that were trying to make it that thought of us as unworthy. It seemed a lot like high school.

JEFF GILBERT Seattle never liked them—let me back up . . . Seattle fans *loved* them. But they were sneered at by the local rock journalists, and even the established grunge bands. They came on the tail end of grunge, and it looked like they were just trying to copy everything else before it. But, you know, they could knock out a good set of songs.

KELLY GRAY People just loved the band so much. They weren't as crazy-serious as those "integrity-driven" bands like Pearl Jam and Soundgarden and Nirvana. Candlebox was doing a more normal, middle-of-the-road type of rock.

KEVIN MARTIN We got thrown on a BMI [Broadcast Music Inc.] show-case at the Off Ramp at the last minute. They said, "We need one more band. We'll give you the 7 o'clock slot." It was us, Sweet Water, Green Apple Quick Step, the Fire Ants—which was Kevin Wood's band—and Blood Circus. Maybe one other band.

BARDI MARTIN It was like a "find the next Nirvana" sort of thing. The industry people descended on Seattle like flies on shit, and so there were just a ton of people from L.A. and New York there.

KEVIN MARTIN EMI saw us there, and they flew us down to Los Angeles in October of '92. We played a show at Club Lingerie. We were supposed to meet with Fred Davis, who was the president of EMI at the time, but he never showed up.

Guy Oseary, who did A&R for Maverick, was there, and Guy saw us and called Freddy DeMann and said, "I want to meet this band." Guy was 19 at the time; he went to school with Freddy's daughter. Freddy was the president and owner of Maverick and Madonna's manager at the time. Madonna was the money.

GUY OSEARY (Maverick Records A&R scout–turned–partner) It's by luck, really, how it all came together. I had heard about Candlebox a few nights earlier—there's this band from Seattle and they're playing at Club Lingerie. I actually attended a party a few blocks away the same night, and luckily for me, it was a terrible party. I said, "You know what, why don't we go check out that band that's a few blocks away at Club Lingerie? This place sucks." So I went over there, and as soon as they started, I was just in love.

KEVIN MARTIN Now, everybody knew that Madonna was looking for a band from Seattle. They weren't looking at us specifically. She's not stupid. She knew that she could find something from Seattle that would give her a great opportunity to start her label.

GUY OSEARY That's absolutely one million percent not true. She never told me what she was looking for. I was there, I was a young kid at the company, and this is what I liked. I gave you the story: I walked into the club, and if the party around the corner was great, I would've never made it over. It was one of those fortuitous moments.

KEVIN MARTIN And this is where it got really fucked up. Green Apple Quick Step was being managed by Kelly Curtis. Green Apple had been flown down by Maverick. We were staying at the Holiday Inn Regent Plaza Suites, which was right on Hollywood Boulevard. Green Apple was staying there, as well. We ran into them and said, "Hey, what are you guys doing?" They're like, "We came to do a showcase for Maverick."

We had just gotten a phone call that Guy and Abbey Konowitch are on their way to come meet us to talk to us about signing to Maverick and we're like, "That can't happen. These are our friends." They were flown down by Maverick, that's just not going to work. They're gonna fuckin' think that we're trying to take the deal from them, which wasn't our thing.

We knew what was going to happen, and it sure as shit did. Kelly Curtis called up Maverick and said, "How fuckin' dare you? You can't have both bands. Who the fuck is Candlebox, dah dah dah?"

GUY OSEARY I was looking at Green Apple Quick Step, and they were meeting with a lot of people at the time, as well. We were given an ultimatum, if I recall, from someone in the Green Apple Quick Step camp. An "us or them" sort of thing.

I'd been lucky to spend some time with Jeff and Stone from Pearl Jam, and I thought, These are two of the nicest people I've ever met. Candlebox reminded me of that vibe. Good, quality people. Candlebox knew we were looking at Green Apple Quick Step, and they didn't give us an ultimatum. I wanted calm, easygoing guys who don't care that we may sign two bands from Seattle. It just felt right.

KRISHA AUGEROT We were just not down with having them sign two bands from Seattle. Green Apple Quick Step wanted their own thing, and found that more with Kevin Patrick at Medicine, which was part of Columbia Records. In our minds, it was more of a decision based on Guy or Kevin. Maverick was a really new label at that time. Guy was super-young. He couldn't even drink. There were pros and cons for both. Madonna was really the pro for going over there, 'cause she had so much muscle. But we felt like Columbia was tried and true, and Kevin Patrick's a real music-head. So I think our decision was based more on that than on Candlebox.

PATTY SCHEMEL (drummer for Los Angeles's Hole) I moved from Seattle to San Francisco in '91. I was there for a bit, and I got a call from Dylan Carlson, who said, "Hey, Kurt's wife is looking for a drummer, and I suggested you." So I went to L.A. and tried out and Courtney called me and said, "We want you to play drums in the band."

When I moved back up to Seattle, it was totally different. It just seemed like everybody had a record deal. Even the smallest bands. No offense to this band, but there was a band called Green Apple Quick Step, which is the dumbest name I've ever heard, and they have a record deal.

GUY OSEARY The first artist that I ever tried to sign was Hole. I was 17, 18 years old. The second band I tried to sign was Rage Against the Machine, and the third group I tried to sign was Candlebox. Both Rage and Hole were down to the wire—both didn't sign with us—and here comes Candlebox, who had other people interested and signed with us.

KEVIN MARTIN We got a ton of shit for being on Madonna's label. Everybody thinks that you sleep with her. She had just released her *Sex* book. It's like, "Did you fuck her?" We didn't meet Madonna until a year and a half after we signed. No one had sex with her.

PETER KLETT There was the perception that we got it fuckin' easy, man. "Madonna's label—oh, dude." But Madonna didn't have shit to do with breaking the band.

KEN STRINGFELLOW (the Posies singer/guitarist) Candlebox suddenly appeared in our practice place, and they're already signed to Maverick. First I just saw in the loading area of our rehearsal complex like 57,000 road cases stenciled CANDLEBOX. I was like, *Candlebox?* Geez, Louise. Not that our band has a great name, either.

I don't even know if they'd played a show. They had gotten their deal straight out of the rehearsal room, more or less. That's the kind of frenzy that was ensuing at that point. I knew the drummer, Scott, from another band, but I was like, "Where the hell did these guys come from?"

It was like "the old immigrants always hate the new immigrants" kind of thing.

JONATHAN PLUM I worked on the first two Candlebox records, and the band was very kind to me. I was still the house engineer guy—clean the toilets in the morning—but they actually gave me a coproduction credit on a song 'cause I'd gotten so involved in it.

The very first conversation I remember in the studio was people in the band bitching about them being compared to Pearl Jam and how much of a drag that was. And I remember the moment Kevin got on the microphone to warm up he started singing Pearl Jam songs. It was like, Dude, no wonder why!

KEVIN MARTIN The big misconception is that we had moved from Los Angeles to Seattle to get signed. I, to this day, don't know how that came about. I think it had something to do with our CD saying our management was in Los Angeles.

KELLY GRAY Courtney Love kept saying Candlebox were from L.A. She didn't know where the fuck the band was from. People like her were saying that just because Nirvana was huge, Candlebox should've just never been a band. They should've just quit. It's fucking ridiculous.

BARDI MARTIN It's kind of funny because we were probably one of the most *Seattle* Seattle bands around. Pete, Scotty, and myself were all born and raised in Seattle. Kevin moved to Seattle when he was like in 10th grade, and that must have been a good five years before Nirvana formed. We were supposed to have been from L.A. and moved up to Seattle to cash in. That was the kind of shit-talking I'd hear second- or thirdhand.

SCOTT MERCADO There was a rumor going around that Mommy and Daddy gave us a loan to go into the studio. I wish we could've said that, but the fact is we sold almost everything we owned to get the $1,500 to get in the studio. I'm like, "Why are people saying this stuff?" A lot of people were jealous that we became successful and they didn't.

DAVE KRUSEN People thought that Candlebox were a put-together band. Back then, I was in a new version of Son of Man, and we were doing demos for Epic. But the band never got signed. My bandmates were bitter towards a lot of bands. Especially a band like Candlebox, who came out of nowhere as far as they were concerned, when Son of Man had been playing all these shows with Soundgarden and Mother Love Bone. The attitude was, "Who are these guys? Rich kids from the Eastside."

What was a really cool, tight-knit scene, changed to a lot of back-stabbing and shit-talking because some people were getting signed and some people weren't.

KEVIN MARTIN We'd been a band for a year and a half. And some people felt that wasn't long enough, which never made sense to me. The biggest detractors? The young bands that weren't successful. Not Alice or Soundgarden—none of those guys were talking shit about us. It was Sweet Water, Green Apple Quick Step, Easy, Satchel. They felt like we didn't really deserve it.

We took a lot of shit in the city, and nobody ever fuckin' stood up for us.

CHAPTER 32
STRANGE LOVE

LOS ANGELES TIMES ("POP MUSIC: The Ruckus over the Vanity Fair Profile," by Steve Hochman, August 16, 1992) The 20 words that shook the record business are found near the end of *Vanity Fair* magazine's eight-page profile this month on rock provocateur Courtney Love.

Talking about a day last January when her husband Kurt Cobain's band, Nirvana, appeared on *Saturday Night Live*, the 26-year-old singer is quoted as saying, "Then, we got high and went to *SNL*. After that, I did heroin for a couple of months."

The shocker is that Love, the lead singer of the group Hole, was pregnant at the time.

Could she have knowingly put her future child at risk by taking drugs, especially heroin?

EVERETT TRUE Courtney would phone me up and tell me all this stuff she was telling Lynn Hirschberg from *Vanity Fair*. I'd be like, "I'm not sure this is a good idea. You can tell me that. I'm a music critic. This woman isn't a music critic; she's a professional journalist, and there's a very big difference."

JANET BILLIG I don't want blame it on my age, but I didn't have experience in this, I didn't know. *Vanity Fair* is doing a feature article, it might be a cover—she has music, she has movies, she's pregnant, and she's married to this big rock star. All is good, why would it be bad? Courtney of all people is always so good at the spin, I never thought twice about, Should we or shouldn't we?

COURTNEY LOVE Janet said to me, "You may never get another shot at *Vanity Fair*," when I knew I'd get all the *Vanity Fair* covers I fuckin' wanted. I'm gonna get 20 fuckin' *Vanity Fair* covers if I want. But there was this haunting voice in my head: "You'll never have this chance again."

DANNY GOLDBERG Why even be in *Vanity Fair*? You're a punk-rock singer. Courtney had this yearning for mass-culture acceptability and just couldn't say no to something like that. I had a sense of foreboding about it, but I had no idea it was gonna be as bad as it was.

Courtney's done a lot of stupid, self-destructive things, but I don't believe that she screwed around with her pregnancy. All those allegations were anonymous. They were "Sources say . . ." and "Friends say . . ."

SUSAN SILVER Danny Goldberg called me at one point, saying, "I'm just calling on Kurt and Courtney's behalf. They really want you to stop talking to people." He didn't specifically say *Vanity Fair*. Somebody else told me that I was supposedly a quote-unquote source, which I wasn't.

There was one time when I spoke to an English female journalist that had come to Seattle. I can't remember her name, Victoria something. She was so lovely and disarming that it felt like I was just talking to a girlfriend, saying, "I've seen some crazy shit that doesn't make any sense to me." After Courtney hooked up with Kurt, it was the first time that anyone had ever publicly trash-talked anybody in the community. It was really awful to have somebody with this addict behavior of conquer-and-divide. We had this really lovely, cohesive, supportive community, and this tornado came and started blowin' things apart.

LOS ANGELES TIMES ("POP MUSIC: The Ruckus over the Vanity Fair Profile," by Steve Hochman, August 16, 1992) In a statement by Love and Cobain that was released through the couple's management company, they declare:

"The *Vanity Fair* article . . . contains many inaccuracies and distortions, and generally gives a false picture of both of us, including our attitude about . . . drugs."

Addressing the allegation that she was using heroin after knowing she was pregnant, they continue, "We unequivocally deny this. . . . As soon as Courtney found out she was pregnant, she immediately contacted an obstetrician and a doctor specializing in chemical dependency and has been under their care since then and has been assured that she can expect to have a healthy baby."

ERIC ERLANDSON I was known as a "chipper" for 10 years. Not all heroin—I was never a big fan of heroin—but just a bunch of different things. I was just dabbling. I was the guy who didn't get strung out. Unfortunately, people around me didn't have that capability. So that's why I was more like the glue, the stable person in that craziness.

I was there at the hospital when Courtney was giving birth. It was an intense time. I was the only one around. I was the caretaker. Courtney's there and they're inducing labor, and then Kurt's upstairs in another room, for his stomach problems, and I'm running between the two.

DANNY GOLDBERG I remember visiting Courtney in the hospital after Frances was born, and the article had just come out. She was sobbing. She said, "Things will never be the same, this is terrible. Don't give me your optimistic shit!"

The social services got involved and there was a question of whether they were fit parents, and Courtney had to go to the welfare office a few times and show that she wasn't on drugs. Her sister had to be flown down to temporarily help look after the baby. It was three or four weeks of tremendous anxiety.

JANET BILLIG Courtney never shared drugs with me; I never saw her doing drugs. I don't know. She was pregnant, she had her baby. I have no idea. I know she smoked in front of people when she was pregnant.

When Franny was like two and three and developing, whenever she dropped a pencil, we were like, "Oh, my God, was Courtney doing drugs?!" You'd question. But Franny's fine. She's smart. She's a great kid.

AMY FINNERTY The Lynn Hirschberg article came out, and the MTV News department was going to run a piece on it. I took it to John Cannelli, who at that point was my boss, and I said, "We can't run this. You have to bury this. This is not a story about music, it's a gossip story, and this is gonna be detrimental to the relationship between us and this band." He said he would talk to Dave Sirulnick, who was running the news department at that point, and see what he could do. The story ran, and it made them mad. MTV just rereported what was in the *Vanity Fair* piece, but it was on MTV, which all the band's fans watched, so it made the story bigger than it initially would have been.

Now I look back and realize that, of course, my position was skewed by my personal relationship with the subject, but at the same time, my position was always, "This isn't a music-based story." If we decided not to run it, it's not like we were gonna miss the biggest music story in the world. At that point, I don't think that Kurt Cobain understood that Kurt Loder didn't really make those decisions, and so he placed the blame on Kurt Loder.

KURT LODER (MTV News anchor) I read somewhere that Kurt hated Lynn Hirschberg and *me* more than anyone else in the world, and I got that book, his notebooks, and I just didn't find that in there. I know Lynn Hirschberg. She's a really good reporter, and maybe it's true, maybe it's not, but Lynn Hirschberg's not some hack. You can't just say, "I'm not gonna cover this because Nirvana might be mad." And, you know, it could have happened—let's be honest.

COURTNEY LOVE It's not about the paragraph about the heroin. I don't give a fuck. Forget that I did heroin in the first trimester of my pregnancy, because I did, that's no big deal. I didn't do it knowingly, of course. That would be a pretty vile thing to do. I don't think I'd be capable of it. I did it within the first trimester, until I took a pregnancy test. After that, I did not do it again. It's that simple.

I don't give a fuck, but the rest of it involves fucking my child, it involved fucking my husband. The tone of it was irresponsible, that tone was incorrect, and that tone emasculated a man. Read it. It makes Kurt look like a fucking two-foot-tall, small-cocked beta male. I would have never married a beta male. Do I sound like the kind of bitch that would fuckin' marry a beta male? I don't like somebody that I can boss around. If I'm gonna fuck you, throw me around the fuckin' room. If you can't do that, then sorry, son, you're out.

I don't know what would happen if I ran into Lynn Hirschberg in polite society. I'm very, very good under pressure and in polite society, and generally I can't even remember who I hate. I don't hate that many people. But I mean, I'd knuckle-sandwich her if I saw her. She wouldn't be able to walk.

. . .

EVERETT TRUE Reading '92 was a very big deal. Sunday was Grunge Day. It was one of grunge's high points for sure. It probably started to spiral downhill after that, when MTV took over. Nirvana picked all the bands to play with them. It was a great lineup; Mudhoney were playing, L7, Teenage Fanclub, Björn Again.

DAN PETERS The cool thing was that this day in a major festival in the United Kingdom is taken over by the equivalent of a bunch of friends: Melvins, Screaming Trees, Mudhoney.

BARRETT MARTIN I wouldn't say it was like, "We've arrived," because we'd already kind of arrived. It was like, "Wow, we're all from Seattle, we all used to play these grimy little club shows together, and now here we are, playing essentially to a world audience."

JEFF SMITH I was there, filming the Melvins and Mudhoney playing. The whole weekend was just nuts. It was like *Apocalypse Now*. It was so cold and wet, even though it was August. There was so much mud.

MARK DEUTROM I was doing sound for the Melvins. There were some issues with Lori that tour, so they got Joe Preston in to play bass. It was one of those deals where I think the Melvins were . . . *resentful* would be too strong a word, but it was like pulling back the curtain when they finally get to Oz. Your big rock-star buddies invite you to play on this day of the festival, which they get to pick the lineup for, and then you get to start playing at 10:30 in the morning. You get to play below Teenage

Fanclub and a bunch of other crappy bands. People get to wake up with terrible hangovers and hate you. Stand in the mud and the rain and the wind and just flip you off.

BUZZ OSBORNE We opened for an ABBA cover band, so there you have it.

MARK DEUTROM People were standing next to me going, "What is this shit?" in the sound booth. And the Melvins are playing their hearts out, with 400 people standing there, maybe 75 people liking them. The booking agency relayed the message, from whoever was in charge of talent at the festival, that "You're the worst band that ever played this festival."

DAN PETERS When your name is Mudhoney, you tend to get things like mud thrown at you when it's raining out. Onstage, Mark was pelted in the face with a big mud ball by somebody who he had taunted and teased: "You guys don't play baseball—you throw like a bunch of pussies." Got hit squarely in the face. Good times.

JENNIFER FINCH People were throwing mud at us when we were playing. Donita was like, "Fuck this!" and went behind her amp and pulled out her tampon and threw it into the audience. It was hysterical. That's something we used to do, growing up: drive around and pull our tampons out and throw them at people that made comments. It's the ultimate kind of "fuck you." I always thought Donita was a bit of a reactionary, but thank God, she just expressed how angry and upset she was at that moment.

DONITA SPARKS (singer/guitarist for Los Angeles's L7) What I wanted to do was drop my pants and pull it out, so everyone could see what I was doing. I had on these baggy shorts and didn't have a belt so I used duct tape, double-knotted, so I'm like, shit, I can't get these pants down. I turn around, and I look at Dee, and she sees my hands go down in there while I try to pull out this tampon. I swung it around my head, threw it out into the audience, and all these kids are yelling—they think I'm throwing out a lighter or something—and someone caught it, realized what it was and threw it back up onstage.

JEFF SMITH When L7 threw the tampon into the crowd, people ran away. Tough English people seemed to be pretty scared of a little pussy blood.

VAN CONNER At Reading, I went to walk down the stairs, which were all wet and muddy, and I had a beer in one hand and a mixed drink in the other. Dan Peters and I think Krist Novoselic and Dave Grohl were down at the bottom of what was probably a 12-foot stairway. I go, "Hey, wait a minute, I'm comin'." And somehow my feet went out from under me, and I landed on my back at the bottom of the stairs. It was a crazy fall. I almost blacked out. I couldn't feel my back, and I thought, Okay, I'm dead. Everything is over.

And all of a sudden the feeling starts to come back and I look up at Dan Peters standing over me, and he says, "Hey, man, you saved your drinks." And I looked down, and I hadn't spilled either drink. I guess that was the most important thing to me at the time.

EVERETT TRUE It was just around the time Frances Bean was born. Everybody's saying the kid's been born a freak, it was deformed. Also, there's all these rumors that Nirvana weren't gonna show and Kurt had OD'd. I was slumped against one of the walls of Nirvana's trailer with a bottle of vodka, and then, all of a sudden it must be getting close to the time, and somebody was yelling, "Where's the wheelchair?"

Kurt came over to me, and he's like, "It's gonna be a burn on all those people who say I'm in the hospital and I've OD'd. I'm gonna wheel myself on in a wheelchair and pretend I've just come from the hospital, and we got this smock here." I'm like, "That's a great idea! Why don't you get me to push you on the stage? That will be even funnier."

I can remember pushing him on the stage, and it was around 9 o'clock at night. You can just hear this massive roar and feel all this steam and sweat coming from the front and the lights blinding you. I was trying to walk in a straight line, and so I start pushing Kurt towards the mic, and he reaches up and grabs me. I thought, Oh cool, he wants to have a mock fight onstage like we always used to have. So I start kind of punching him, and he's saying, "No, you asshole, you're pushing me to the wrong microphone."

CRAIG MONTGOMERY More so in the early days than in the very late days, but a Nirvana show was the most hilarious thing you ever saw.

They went onstage thinking, What could we do that would be funny? When talking about Nirvana, it pretty quickly devolved into, "Oh, how was Kurt feeling? What were his drug problems like?" But when Nirvana was onstage, that was not what it was about. It was not about drugs and depression and angst and death. It was about rock and roll as a great big joke.

JEFF SMITH It sounds hokey, but you could tell you were witnessing some epic moment. It's 60,000 people, it's 10 o'clock at night, everyone had been standing there for three days in the mud, and people are singing along almost louder than the band. Nirvana were firing on all 12 cylinders that night. The best time I ever saw them.

DAVE GROHL [Reading] was a pretty strange experience. Kurt had been in and out of rehab, communication in the band was beginning to be strained. Kurt was living in L.A., Krist and I were in Seattle. People weren't even sure if we were going to show up. We rehearsed once, the night before, and it wasn't good. I really thought, This will be a disaster, this will be the end of our career for sure. And then it turned out to be a wonderful show, and it healed us for a little while.

*   *   *

AMY FINNERTY Nirvana was booked to play at the MTV Video Music Awards. They were booked on like a Monday or something, and coincidentally I went to Reading with them the following weekend. I remember telling them, "Hey, we booked you on this Video Music Awards," and they didn't even know about it. I felt a little bit uncomfortable about that. I was so young, and I was just getting my feet wet in terms of how all this business got done, yet here I was, involved with the biggest band on the planet.

DANNY GOLDBERG MTV was very pushy. The award shows were big ratings things for them. They were in the business of selling advertising and not worrying about the feelings of rock stars, selling records, or anything else. They had a virtual monopoly on the music video world at that time and said, "We'll really be upset if you don't do it," and I felt obligated to tell Kurt this. I believe they knew he was in rehab then. It was near the end of his time there, and so he left a day or two early to do the show.

Ethically, I couldn't have kept it from him; I had to tell him, and it was his choice. He was an incredibly strong-minded, strong-willed guy that didn't do things just because I told him to do them or not to do them. He wasn't a child. Nonetheless, I feel creepy about it in retrospect.

AMY FINNERTY Somebody told the band that if they didn't play "Smells Like Teen Spirit" that I was gonna lose my job. It actually took me a couple of years to get any sort of answer out of Dave Grohl about who it was, and I don't really want to say—it was someone within their world, but outside of MTV. The band wanted to play a new song, "Rape Me," and at that point at MTV, no artist had ever come out on the Video Music Awards and played anything except for the hits.

I went with Courtney and saw Kurt at Exodus, and Kurt and I sat in the backyard and had a conversation about it. It was intense because my bosses kind of sent me over there. I was like, "Look, I'm the VP of Post-it Notes, remember? If I lose my job, you can take me on the road and I'll sell T-shirts. I want you guys to do what you want to do. Don't worry about my job."

In the end, the executives made an agreement that the band could play "Lithium" instead of "Smells Like Teen Spirit." At the last rehearsal, when we were walking from the dressing room out to the stage, Kurt grabs my hand and walked with me all the way up the stage, to make a point to the executives, like, Fuck you. I'm gonna do what I want, but you can't mess with her.

RICK KRIM Pearl Jam really wanted not to perform "Jeremy" on the VMAs; they wanted to perform "Sonic Reducer" by the Dead Boys. Interestingly, there was a simultaneous conversation going on with the Nirvana camp about them wanting to perform "Rape Me."

How'd we convince Pearl Jam otherwise? It was probably a bunch of us explaining, "This is our Super Bowl. 'Jeremy' has got all these nominations, there's all these expectations, it's a very mainstream TV show, and to come out and do a song that no one in our audience is going to know is not what we intended when we booked the band." They got it. I don't recall it being too contentious.

AMY FINNERTY During the show, I was standing right next to Judy McGrath, the president of the network and my mentor and idol. She really was behind me, and she was behind Nirvana. The agreement was that if they played the wrong song, then they were gonna go to a commercial break. We were standing next to the guy who'd potentially push the button, and they started playing "Rape Me."

We're all lookin' at each other like, Are we gonna press this button or not? And Judy said, "No, let them play," and then after 30 seconds they went into "Lithium," and we just got big huge smiles on our faces and cracked up, and everything was great from then on.

KRIST NOVOSELIC Nirvana gets introduced, and we start playing our prank, then switch into "Lithium." I'm plugged into some awful bass rig that's distorting terribly. I can barely hear what I'm playing, and the tone deteriorates into an inaudible mess. Fuck it—time for the bass-toss shtick. Up it goes!!!!! I always try to get good air—I bet I hit over 25 feet, easy! But . . . I was not on my game—the only time I've ever dropped it was then in front of 300 million people. Ouch! I was fine [when it hit my forehead], but I faked like I was knocked out . . .

RICK KRIM "Jeremy" went on to become Video of the Year and blew the band up, and made them not want to make videos anymore. I have a Pearl Jam "Choices" poster in my office with a little girl, that was actually Kelly Curtis's daughter when she was two years old, kneeling with a gun and a bunch of crayons in front of her. Choices. The band signed the poster back then, and Eddie wrote right underneath the gun, "This is the gun we couldn't show in the video, but we ended up showing too much anyway." Meaning exposure-wise, I think.

MIKE MCCREADY It was at that time that Eddie took it over. Benevolent dictatorship: That's kind of the theory. Jeff and Stone running things from one angle, but with Eddie, it was all about pulling back.

ROSS HALFIN (photographer) When I first shot Pearl Jam, they were easy. They were quite fun to hang out with and shoot, and Eddie Vedder I always got along great with because I shot the Who a lot and I could tell him about it. In the early '90s, a magazine called *RIP* did a special issue and called it *Grunge* and stuck a group shot of mine of Pearl Jam on the cover. Pearl Jam went mental, and that's when they literally, seriously overnight banned everyone from shooting them, because they ended up on the cover of a magazine that they didn't want to be on. By the second album they became fairly impossible to deal with.

I was with the Who a couple of years ago in Seattle and I ended up getting really drunk and I ran into Eddie in the Who's hotel bar and I said, "You're the people's band, right?" He goes, "Kind of." I said, "Then why do you have more rules than the fuckin' Army? It would be easier to get into the Pentagon than take pictures of your band."

EDDIE VEDDER I felt that with any more popularity we were going to be crushed, or our heads were going to pop like grapes. I went through this fucking yearlong period where I wore helmets all the time. . . . It was this kind of analogy, like I need a helmet . . .

KELLY CURTIS As Eddie puts it, he was sick of seeing his face everywhere. That's when everything stopped. It wasn't like we called up Epic and said, "We're never doing a video again," it was more like, Let's just stop everything now: interviews, photo shoots, videos. There were some great people at the label that were really supportive, and then there were people that didn't understand. Tommy Mottola, the CEO of Sony Music, told me at Sony's MTV Awards after-party that if we didn't release "Black" as the next single, it would be the single hugest mistake I've ever made in my life and my career. But the band was done. They just said it was too big: "We're not gonna go out with some freakin' power ballad."

AMY FINNERTY Earlier that day at the VMAs, we were sitting in a green-room tent outside. Kurt was sitting next to me, Janet, Courtney, and Jackie Farry, my best friend and Frances's nanny. Axl Rose was walking through the tent, and Courtney yelled out to him as a total joke, "Hey, Axl, do you want to be the godfather of our child?" Everyone cracked up.

JANET BILLIG Axl Rose was with Stephanie Seymour. He turned to Kurt and said, "You tell your bitch to shut up!" And Kurt looked at Courtney and said, completely deadpan, "Shut up, bitch." Hilarious. Then Stephanie said to Courtney, "Are you a model?" I think she was trying to be mean. Courtney was like, "Are you a brain surgeon?" We laughed and laughed and laughed for days.

AMY FINNERTY Kurt looked at me, and he was like, "I feel scared, like seventh-grade-getting-beat-up-on-the-playground scared."

BRYN BRIDENTHAL Courtney and Axl spent so much time thinking about each other. Years later, when Axl was starting work on the album that would become *Chinese Democracy*, Jim Barber was A&Ring the project. And Axl at one point told me that Jim came to the studio and Axl felt Courtney Love energy coming off of him and made Jim leave. He couldn't work with that energy in the room.

What I found out later, and Axl didn't know then, either, is that Barber had taken up with Courtney. They kept it a secret from me and the company. So for Axl to feel Courtney Love energy coming off Jim Barber's forehead, not knowing that they had a relationship, was sort of like, *Whooooo!* It was just amazing.

Axl would do those kinds of things all the time. This is going to sound ridiculous, but it's true: He's a very spiritual person. Jim's work on the album ended shortly after the Courtney energy came off his forehead. Because Axl thought that Courtney was evil and that her evilness would impact on his record.

AMY FINNERTY When Eric Clapton was singing "Tears in Heaven" at the VMAs, we were on the side of the stage. It was Courtney, me, Kurt, Eddie. Janet was right there, and Jackie. We were all slow-dancing with each other. I was dancing with Jackie, then I was dancing with Kurt, and then I was dancing with Eddie, and then I was dancing with Courtney, and we were all switching partners. There was a moment where we looked at each other and realized that we were all from the same group, we were all from the same movement. I remember Courtney coming up and saying, "We gotta get them"—Eddie and Kurt—"to dance together."

COURTNEY LOVE My memory can be really addled, but I remember for some reason Eric Clapton is onstage, he is playing "Tears in Heaven" about his little son that has fallen out of a window, and I shoved Kurt into Eddie and I shoved Eddie into Kurt, and then I laughed, just chuckled, because it was genius. I loved it. They slow-danced. It was cute.

EDDIE VEDDER We were slow-dancing on a gym floor as though it was a seventh-grade dance. . . . Who led? That's a good question. That's the thing, no one led.

AMY FINNERTY It was such a sweet, sweet, sweet moment because it signified the end of this feud. I remember Janet and I actually jumping up and down and going, "YAY! They made up!" Everything was fine after that.

DAVE GROHL Yeah, some kind of fucking summit. It was so ridiculous; it had blown so out of proportion. I remember the two of them smiling and hugging each other—*(sarcastically)* and then, all of a sudden, Seattle was okay!

DAVE JERDEN The first Alice in Chains record was like a party, and the second record was just all work. We started the record the day the L.A. riots started. It was crazy; we had to shut down production for a week because they had a curfew on the whole city.

JERRY CANTRELL I was actually in a store buying some beer when some guys came in and started looting the place. I also got stuck in traffic and saw people pulling other people out of their cars and beating the crap out of them. That was some pretty scary shit to have to go through, and it definitely affected the overall feel of the album.

DAVE JERDEN Layne was living down in the marina, and during the curfew he was driving from the marina downtown to score is what I heard.

DAVID DUET Before I left Seattle, Alice in Chains was having their big Bumbershoot show and *Facelift* was out. I would stay with Layne and

Demri sometimes, and I had laid on their floor kicking for a couple of days. They were freaked out by it all and didn't understand it. Then I went back to Houston, where I was working at a nightclub, and the phone rang in the office. This was probably '91. It was Layne and Demri and they had to find me to tell me they started doing dope and how wonderful it was, and right then I knew they were goners. You can just tell when you talk to certain people, especially females. You can tell when they're lifers. Very seldom been wrong.

JOHNNY BACOLAS I found out Layne was on heroin after the Van Halen tour in '91. He told me that he had an issue and he couldn't stop. He told me that the first time he did it, he was exhausted and feeling like shit. Someone—I don't want to say who—brought him some heroin because they couldn't find any coke. And Layne tried it, and he said that was the first time he really thanked God. He literally looked up to the sky and said, "Thank you for this feeling."

DAMON STEWART Right after the release of *Facelift*, Layne and I became roommates in Seattle. I had started working for Sony Records at the time, doing a regional A&R job, and with them being signed to a Sony label, it was a little bit awkward for both us. The Sony people were trying to use me as eyes and ears to report back—is he doin' drugs? It wasn't a blatant thing, but it was definitely implied a couple of times that they wanted to know how he was. I can understand that to a degree, but we were pals, and I wasn't gonna play a tattletale game.

He *was* usin'. There was no question about that. Him and his girl-friend Demri both lived with me at the time. They were very discreet about it. There was one time I found a spoon, and it was obvious what it had been used for. I adored the both of them, but we definitely had plenty of conversations that were like, "Look, it's not fair for me to say what's right or wrong for you guys . . ." But I got to the point where I was like, "I can't have this goin' on here and be wonderin' if you guys are gonna wake up or not."

KELLY CURTIS Susan and I managed Alice in Chains together for a bit, but I quit right when it was all happening for them. We had lost Andy to heroin, and there was a lot of that going on with Alice in Chains. I just had a little girl, and I remember Layne was holding her once and he nodded out. And I thought, I don't want to do this anymore. He was a great guy—all those guys were great—but there was a dark cloud over them, and it really affected me. I hated it.

SUSAN SILVER Not that the others weren't heavily into drugs, too, but Layne was clearly so deep—it was so dangerous—that all of our lives centered around how to aid him. It was never about, "How are we going to prop him up to get him on a tour?" I had this conversation with Layne over and over and over after the success of *Facelift*: "Your health is the most important thing. You need to get well. Stop this. You have enough money, you can go buy a cottage on the beach and be there with Demri"—who was also very artistic—"and you can go and create whatever art you want."

DAVE JERDEN During *Dirt*, recording vocals, Layne and I got into arguments. He'd come in loaded on heroin, and I told him I didn't want him to sing on heroin. He could use heroin afterward, but when he sang he had to be somewhat together because he was singing all out of tune on heroin. I remember making a phone call to Layne and I told him, "Listen, I'm not trying to be mean, all I'm trying to do is get these vocals out of you." We didn't have any problems after that.

Jerry and I got along fine. Jerry's morale was good. Sean's always great. At that point they were having problems with Mike Starr. Mike Starr had a song that he wanted on the album, and they didn't wanna put it on the album. Layne sang on it, and Mike said Layne didn't sing it right and Layne got really mad.

MIKE STARR I wrote a song called "Fear the Voices." We did record it, but they didn't let it on the album because Jerry didn't have nothin' to do with the writing of the music. But they put it on the box set later, and it got some recognition and got played on the radio.

DAVE JERDEN And Mike Starr used heroin within my studio one time. He was in the bathroom with Layne, and Layne said, "Stick out your arm," and Layne hit him with heroin. Mike Starr was crawling through the lobby throwing up on the carpet. It was really sad.

MIKE STARR I shot heroin once with Layne during the making of the song "Junkhead." I stayed up all night—we were hanging out with two girls. It felt great, but I decided never to do it again.

DAVE JERDEN Layne was worse off. He had a drug dealer that was hanging out with him the whole time while I was mixing the record. In fact, Layne came in to listen to it, and he brought his drug dealer with him. His drug dealer made some comment about the mix, what he wanted to have changed on the mix, and I blew up. I said, "Fuck you! Who are you?" And Layne told the guy to settle down and shut up. The *drug dealer* had some input on my mix.

JERRY CANTRELL It's a dark album, but it's not meant to be a bummer. Those five songs on the second side, from "Junkhead" to "Angry Chair," are in sequence because it tells a story. It starts out with a really young, naive attitude in "Junkhead," like drugs are great, sex is great, rock and roll, yeah! Then as it progresses, there's a little bit of realization of what it's about . . . and that ain't what it's about.

DAVE JERDEN I was a little concerned we were making an album glorifying drug use. The take I got from people around me was I wasn't glorifying drugs, I was making a record that was showing the horrors of drugs. The band talked to me about where a lot of the songs came from. "Rooster" was about Jerry Cantrell's dad.

MARK PELLINGTON The "Rooster" video was awesome. I heard the song and thought, Wow, this is really epic in terms of its flow and its arc, very cinematic. Jerry was in the process of really trying to heal with his dad. I spoke to Jerry and was like, "Let's go to Oklahoma. Let's make this as personal as you can. I want your dad to be in it."

JERRY CANTRELL ["Rooster"] was all my perceptions of his experiences [in Vietnam]. The first time I ever heard him talk about it was when we made the video and he did a 45-minute interview with Mark Pellington, and I was amazed he did it. He was totally cool, totally calm, accepted it all, and had a good time doing it. It even brought him to the point of tears. It was beautiful.

MARK PELLINGTON When we shot the performance part, Layne was pretty high. I remember Layne wanted to wear this cowboy hat. I was like, "I don't know about the hat." It felt inappropriate for the song; we were shooting them in front of projections of this Vietnam stuff. His eyes were really fucked up, he was totally pinned. It was like, "Wow, guys, he's really fucked-up looking. What do you want to do about this?" Oh, this sweet guy, I knew it wouldn't have been very flattering for him.

So I just put him in sunglasses: "Instead of the hat, how about you wear these?" I said, "God, you look like a badass in these sunglasses. Let's go with this." And it was like, "All right, let's go. Let's get a couple of takes." So it was not without its challenges.

TOM NIEMEYER We did the entire U.S. and Canada with Alice in Chains. The first time was what they called the "shitty cities" tour, when they were warming up for their *Dirt* album tour. Touring with them was absolutely over-the-top: part Spinal Tap, part Disneyland for adults. Porno party at the fuckin' Playboy Mansion. Jimi Hendrix, as big as Janis Joplin. All colors, all shapes, all sizes, all temperatures, all the time.

If you were with those guys on that tour, it could make the most mundane thing, like us walking from here to there, one of the most memorable experiences of your life. And the whole time there's every chemical possible flying through the air, falling out of pockets, landing in your hand, accidentally going inside you somehow.

TIM PAUL (Gruntruck bassist) There were a lot of pranks. It was the *Dirt* tour, so we found a hardware store that was open late and bought these five-pound bags of potting soil and doused Alice in Chains with them right as they were going on. Looking back, it was maybe ill-advised because the poor guys had to play a show with dirt down their throats.

SCOTT McCULLUM Oh, my God, Gruntruck and Alice in Chains were a perfect fit. We started off doing a "shitty cities" tour, basically all of these shitty little towns in the Northwest, in 1992. One time, we were up in Butte, Montana. Jerry's a big outdoorsman, so we went fishing together and caught a bunch of brown trout. We took 'em back to the next show, probably at Missoula, and went to this frat-boy party afterward.

Jerry and I walk in with this bag of fish, looking at all these frat boys and girls, and we're like, "Where's your kitchen?" We just went into the kitchen and started cooking up these fucking trout without even knowing whose house it was.

TOM NIEMEYER You think you're invincible when you're on a tour like that. And for the most part, you are; if you get caught at something, there seems to be somebody there to help get you out of it. I broke a sink completely apart in a club bathroom for some reason. Well, the reason was Jägermeister and coke. The sink *had* to be broken, and I shattered it into a million pieces.

SCOTT MCCULLUM Sean had a little bit of a destructive streak in him whenever he got to a certain point. I heard some stories about televisions going out of windows—very rock-and-roll stuff that got them kicked out of hotels.

TOM NIEMEYER Somewhere, probably outside Bozeman, Montana, there were about 30 people inside this hotel room having fun, watching TV, drinking beers, and the cops come to the door with the front-desk clerk saying, "It's time to quiet things down." Somebody had the door open *this* much, saying, "No, everything's fine in here. Sorry, we'll quiet it down." And Sean's trying to get the door open to yell at the cops, and three or four people had their hands over Sean's mouth, holding him back from saying what he wanted to say.

Once the cops left, it was time for people to leave. I wanted to stay—it was my room—but Sean didn't want me to, so he literally dragged me by the feet down the hall to his room, into the lair of the minotaur or whatever, and on the way there, I'm looking up. He had a beer in one hand and he's filling up the lights, they're sconces, on the walls. He's filling those up with beer, and they're all popping. I don't remember much after that.

. . .

SCOTT MCCULLUM Alice in Chains asked Gruntruck to join another tour, with the Screaming Trees. So we flew into Fort Lauderdale, and met them there. The Screaming Trees weren't there yet. I remember walkin' into that room and seeing those four Alice in Chains guys in a booth, and it was like we were fuckin' little giddy kids. We ran over, and they were gettin' up, and we were all hugging each other. It was like this great family reunion.

This is when I got into hard alcohol and Jägermeister. That same day, Sean grabs me, like, "Hey, good to see ya. Let's do some Jäger!" Goes over to the bartender, and goes, "I want 12 Jäger shots." We proceeded to down six shots each right there in the first five minutes. We get done drinkin' that, and then Layne bought me a Jack Coke. "I've never had a Jack Coke before." Boy, was that a mistake. Jack Coke was my drink for a while.

MATT VAUGHAN So we set off on tour, starting off just as drinkin' buddies again, and within a week it was very obvious this wasn't gonna be just a drinkin' buddy tour. The party reached a level that was not anything I had seen before and some of the guys in Gruntruck hadn't seen before. There was a lot of speed, you knew there was heroin out there. It was just nasty. And Screaming Trees was on the tour, too, so you have the Lanegan element.

KIM WHITE The Screaming Trees got offered the Alice in Chains tour, and I thought it was a terrible idea. Honestly, I thought, You're going to put an alcoholic on the road with a junkie, and when the tour is over you're going to have two junkies. I said that to the label and they were like, "Nonsense." Alice in Chains were huge, and they're like, "You're going to be playing huge arenas, you're going to sell a lot of records," and I was like, "Yeah, but at what expense?"

BARRETT MARTIN That tour was the biggest mistake that we made as a band. We had an entire world tour being booked where we were headlining, and we would have really put ourselves on the map as this big headlining band. But the people at Sony decided that we should tour together because we were both Sony bands. But we were gonna have to open for Alice in Chains, which was ridiculous because we actually were a larger draw than Alice in Chains. They wanted us to open for Alice in Chains and give them street cred and let everybody know that Alice in Chains was a Seattle band, too.

And on top of that, Mark and Layne really got heavily into heroin on that tour, and that was kind of the beginning of the end.

TOM NIEMEYER Lanegan had a tendency to wander off. One night, they told me to go into the club and get the guy, 'cause nobody else could get him to come out in time for the buses to leave.

He told me, "Tommy, come with me. Into the night."

And I was like, *"Whaaat?"*

And he goes, "Look at that!" And we were looking at the skyline from the club we were at. I was like, "But we gotta go, dude." I got him as far as the bus. But he wouldn't get on. He just said, "I have a ride, and I'll meet you there."

MATT VAUGHAN There was a lot of testosterone, masculinity on that tour. You had Lanegan, you had Ben McMillan, Scott McCullum. There were a lot of fights. I remember Lanegan fighting with Mark Nafacy, the soundman. It was after the show, and Lanegan and him were bitching about something. And before you know it, Lanegan rips his jacket off, he throws it at me, and they just started whalin' on each other. Lanegan won the fight. He wasn't afraid. It was so out of control, you couldn't stop it.

And then Lanegan walked off into the hills, and no one saw him for a week and they were basically off the tour until Seattle dates came around. I remember MTV News: "Mark Lanegan is in the hospital, has a stomach flu." That wasn't the case at all—he was *missing.* No one could find him. From what I heard, he ended up meeting some girl and stayed with her.

KIM WHITE A couple of weeks into the tour, I got a phone call from Lanegan saying that he was in a Canadian hospital, on a cot in a hallway, with the number 134 above his head—meaning he wasn't getting out of there for a while. It was around Mark's birthday, and it was the first time that he had done heroin with Layne, and he got blood poisoning. Layne sang for the Trees that night.

There was a *Spin* journalist on the road with them, and I lied to the reporter. At this point, the band had had such a dark reputation, and I don't think we needed to add to that. I said something like there was horseplay around the bus after the show, and Mark slipped and cut his leg and poured whiskey on it and went to bed, and when he woke up his leg was swollen and he had blood poisoning. I made up some phenomenal story.

VAN CONNER There was a lot of debauchery on that tour. There's an old Steinbeck story called "The Harness" about this guy who wears a back brace and his wife is sickly and once a year he goes to town and does all these crazy things at a brothel. *(Laughs.)* That always reminds me of touring. I'd come home, I had a kid, and things were fairly straight there. Alice in Chains were living the true rock-star cliché, excess life. They definitely had the rocker chicks around. Screaming Trees, at least my brother and I, are definitely not ladies' men. We both have had long-term relationships, and we're very nerdy.

JERRY CANTRELL We were like hog wild, man. Totally. We dove into everything. Knee deep.

DAVID DUET Layne and Demri had kind of an open relationship. In the position he was in, it's probably the only way he could've had a lasting relationship. Layne was very true to Demri in his heart, but he related many, many wild touring adventures to me.

GARY LEE CONNER It was nice to go back to the hotel and get away from all that crap. I always hated having to go to the party after the show. That was the worst. I remember one night in Minneapolis, *everybody* was on the bus, either snorting coke or doing something, and I was just like, My God, this sucks!

SCOTT MCCULLUM I never was a heroin user. The harder stuff was done very on the down low. As far as cocaine and speed and stuff like that, I partook quite a bit. On the Alice in Chains U.S. tour, that would always happen in the back of the bus, or whatever hotel room we were staying at. Do some lines and talk bullshit. You got 16 hours until your next fuckin' town, so you sit back there and drink and get kinda crazy.

MATT VAUGHAN Once *Dirt* started to take off, we started going from club shows to larger venues. It would go from a 400-seat club to a 3,000-seat venue. I recall there being more handlers halfway through the tour, and I remember going to Susan, "Why are there more people here?"

They were bodyguards. And I said, "The band's not *that* popular yet that we need this." And she said, "This bodyguard is to make sure Layne doesn't go out at night and that nobody tries to pass him something."

SCOTT MCCULLUM Layne had broken his leg at some point, and he was in a wheelchair for some of the shows. And then he got a cane. And this was significant, because Ben coveted what Layne had.

Layne sorta had this mystical rock persona, always wearing lots of jewelry and piercings and nail polish. And Ben started mimicking him on tour. Somebody pointed it out to me afterward, and I reflected on it: Yeah, all of the sudden, Ben *did* have a cane. All of the sudden, Ben was trying to be this vagabond, gypsy, mystical rock guy. He would shave his eyebrows. He'd paint his body with all these paints and swirls, and wear these really bizarre leather chaps.

MATT VAUGHAN It seemed very paradoxical because here you have Ben McMillan, who is regarded as one of the pioneers of our scene, *imitating* a newbie.

TOM NIEMEYER The cane? Ben wanted to have an excuse to have a limp, essentially. Actually, we gave him one by accident by the end of the tour. He was so drunk and on so many pills on the tour bus one night, and he wouldn't shut up. He kept talking and talking about this girl that he met. It was gettin' to be too much, and he wouldn't take a bath and he was startin' to smell and it was just terrible. So me and the rest of the band shoved him in the back lounge of the tour bus. He had grown to have the power of 50 men at this point, almost like he was on angel dust, and he didn't wanna be crammed back there. He was tryin' to get out and we accidentally slammed this big door, which slid out from the wall, right on his kneecap. So now he had this huge, swollen, bruised knee which made him limp for, I think, forever after that.

He used the cane on the wrong side, though. He walked with a limp, but he was favoring the wrong knee because that was the side he wanted it on. He was a funny, funny guy.

MATT VAUGHAN I left the tour in the middle of the night, five weeks into it. I was disgusted by what was happening. There was a lot of violence among Gruntruck, and there was a lot of hostility and maybe bitterness in that they wanted more than they were getting as a band. Gruntruck went from being beer-drinking guys to drug addicts; I don't know that for sure, but they came back different.

TIM PAUL I didn't party as much as a lot of other folks on the road. After we got back, Ben was not the same Ben from the early days. He was not that working-out-six-times-a-week guy with all the musical gear, making everything happen. I used to tease Ben that he was slowly turning into Jim Morrison; in fact, I called him the Lizard King in later years.

SCOTT MCCULLUM We were supposed to go on the European tour with Screaming Trees and Alice in Chains, but there's conjecture that Layne got so freaked out by Ben, that's why it didn't happen.

BARRETT MARTIN They had to cancel our Paris show because Layne overdosed. And the people were already inside the theater, we'd already sound-checked, the gear was onstage, and Layne overdosed—I think at his hotel, but I'm not sure. He never came to the venue. We escaped out the back of the venue, and they put us in cabs because they thought the audience was gonna tear the place apart. The stage crew were throwing all this swag—the CDs and T-shirts they were going to sell—into the audience, to quell the crowd.

SCOTT MCCULLUM We toured with Pantera after that. Dimebag bought me my first hooker, in Hamburg. But it wasn't that same bond we had with Alice in Chains. Alice in Chains were always like, "You guys are equal." Pantera, there was always that "They're definitely the headliners" kind of thing.

BARRETT MARTIN I remember that Alice in Chains' road crew and the people that produced their show, they were not cool. I mean sometimes we didn't even have any place to go because Alice in Chains had the whole backstage area. Alice in Chains were friendly to us backstage—they were never rude or anything—but they definitely let it be known that they were the big rock stars, and we were the openers. So I actually lost a great deal of respect for them. I did not think that they really got the Seattle thing, which was all independent, DIY, and take-care-of-your-musical-community. And it's because they were on the periphery at the beginning of it.

MATT VAUGHAN That was a nice jacket Lanegan tossed me during the fight. It was a long tweed with a furry collar; a little long in the sleeves, but I wore it all the time. I didn't know what else to do. I didn't know Lanegan's number; no one ever knew how to get ahold of Mark. Two years go by, and I was at a show with my girlfriend at the time. Lanegan comes right up behind me and says, *"Give me my jacket." (Laughs.)*

I was like, "Here you go."

My girlfriend was like, "What was that all about?"

And I'm like, "Well, this hasn't been my jacket, I gotta tell you."

CHAPTER 34
FUCK HOLLYWOOD!

DANNY BRAMSON When we first screened *Singles* to Warner, during the parts when Alice and Soundgarden came on, these three corporate heads in front of us all turned to each other, registering either distaste, scorn, or disappointment, or we didn't know what the fuck. Afterward, in the lobby, we found out they were thinking, Holy fuck! This is a concert movie. This is *Rattle and Hum*. Which was a huge disappointment for Paramount the year before. And it was right then and there that we were brushed aside as "that music concert movie."

I remember the marketing guru of Warner, Rob Friedman, saying, "Look, we'll release your movie, open it in Seattle, San Francisco, and Los Angeles." During that time, Cameron and I got wind of ridiculous things. With Nirvana becoming the iconic band of the moment, these marketing shills at Warner had come up with the new title *Come as You Are,* and unbeknownst to us, had gone and tried to secure a license, I believe, for both the title and song. We got wind of it when John Silva requested that Nirvana be able to screen the movie in Europe. We chose not to send the movie—which we had done organically and naturally, years before the scene ever made it onto the cover of *Time*—to be screened out of context. Digging in our heels led to a continued delay. Suddenly, Pearl Jam was exploding, and Michele Anthony and Donnie Ienner at Sony said, "Danny, Cameron, we can't wait on releasing this soundtrack." They just knew what they had. So we released the soundtrack in the summer of '92, and the album exploded.

CAMERON CROWE *Singles* was in the can for a year before it came out. But the success of the so-called Seattle sound got it released. Warner Bros. said, "If you can get Alice in Chains, Soundgarden, and Pearl Jam to play the MTV party that we can use to publicize the movie, we'll put it out." So I painfully had to try and talk the bands into doing it. Pearl Jam said that they'd do it as a favor to me. So the taping happened, and it was . . . a disaster. It was populated mostly by studio executives and their children, who wanted to see the Seattle sound.

ALEX COLETTI (*MTV Unplugged* producer) The morning of the *Singles* event, we taped a *Smells Like Grunge* video countdown in the hotel in L.A. where the event was taking place. Already everyone kinda hated the term *grunge,* so of course we couldn't have picked a more alienating title for the artists. Dave Abbruzzese and Mike Starr and a few other people did the video countdown. Dave really took to being on camera to the point where it didn't help his relationship with the band. The other guys in Pearl Jam were very reluctant to do anything.

RICK KRIM The party was the day after the VMAs. It was amazing to see the contrast between the night before, where they had to be prim and proper, and the next night, just letting it fly. Ed had some drinks beforehand, and I remember him backstage, wearing an army helmet and kicking beer bottles like he was a field-goal kicker.

DANNY BRAMSON The show started, and Vedder goes out onstage begrudgingly. He's got a bottle in one hand, and he grabs the mic and his opening words are "FUCK HOLLYWOOD!" That set the tone for the entire evening.

RICK KRIM It got a little sloppy onstage. The fire marshals were being difficult, and Ed was calling them out onstage, causing a little ruckus. Eventually it completely broke down and someone had to carry him off the stage and out of the building. I remember taking him to a car and getting him out of there.

DAVE ABBRUZZESE Eddie was actually drunk. I think it was the first time our illustrious leader failed to show up, and it just felt like a joke.

CAMERON CROWE They were playing covers, and somebody got into a fight, and Chris Cornell got into it, and I think Kim Thayil got into it. I remember Eddie yelling, "Fuuuck! What the fuck is this?" and studio executives grabbing their kids and streaming out. I was seeing this whole thing to get the movie released going down the tubes. But *Singles* came out, and the show aired twice, heavily edited. To anybody who taped it off the air, it's a real collectible. Later, we made up T-shirts to commemorate the party and they said on the front SINGLES PREMIERE PARTY and on the back it said NOBODY DIED.

DANNY BRAMSON The soundtrack went from the Top 30 to the Top 20 to the Top 10. It was heartening to read both *The New York Times* and MTV saying that *Singles* was the soundtrack of the '90s and was a really inspiring force for all quote-unquote alternative programming and playlists.

BARRETT MARTIN "Nearly Lost You" ended up being the hit single. I think it probably sold more copies of the *Singles* soundtrack than it sold of our album, *Sweet Oblivion*. Because *Singles* came out first and that soundtrack sold at least a million—I think it was one of those soundtracks that did better than the movie did. *Sweet Oblivion* came out later that year and pretty quickly sold about 300,000 copies.

KIM WHITE When I became the Trees' manager, Susan Silver was pissed, and that was right when the *Singles* soundtrack was being made. Susan was kind of in charge of the soundtrack, and the Screaming Trees were not on the soundtrack. She'll deny that she ever tried to prevent them from being on it. But we suspect it very strongly.

SUSAN SILVER Absolute bullshit. I don't operate that way. Never did, never will. I didn't have an issue with the Trees. Parting ways was sad for me, but it didn't mean that I was out to change the trajectory of their career. Cameron Crowe and his music supervisors had their own vision that didn't have anything to do with my choices. I made no comments about any of that.

KIM WHITE The Trees had gone into the studio with Don Fleming, and one of the first songs that they recorded was "Nearly Lost You." We actually had to waive our sync fee—synchronization fee, what you get paid to be put on the soundtrack—for them to reedit the movie and put that song on the soundtrack. It involved lawyers. "Nearly Lost You" is playing quietly in the background as Kyra Sedgwick's character reveals the results of her pregnancy test.

GARY LEE CONNER We got an offer to do a Budweiser ad. They wanted us to change "Nearly Lost You" to "Nearly Lost a Bud" or something like that. We turned it down, but it was hard, because we were like, "Well, we could use the money." I think it was for $10,000, which actually isn't very much to rewrite our damn song. Nowadays, nobody will even bat an eyelash at doing an ad. But back then, it had a stigma.

ROBERT ROTH Sub Pop was gonna give Truly an unprecedented amount of money to do a one-off record because we were on the *Singles* soundtrack. I heard that Cameron Crowe personally picked the song, "Heart and Lungs." Then a few days before the masters were sent off to press for the *Singles* soundtrack album, a lot of political shenanigans went on with Epic Records, and even though "Nearly Lost You" wasn't actually in the movie, that got put on the soundtrack, and we were bumped. Though our song is still in the actual movie. Basically, we were expendable—we were the only indie band on the album—and even though we were one of the director's favorite songs on the album, it was off.

Oh, it was devastating. We were in the studio at the time that we got the news. That was a big deal. That would've affected our career tremendously. From what I heard, Mark Arm put the down payment on his house because of being on that album.

MARK ARM We had heard about this thing happening and realized there was no kind of Sub Pop representation at the time. Cameron Crowe was married to Nancy Wilson, who'd worked with Kelly Curtis, so that was probably Cameron Crowe's connection to what was happening locally.

Bruce and Steve and I marched over to Cameron Crowe's office one time, and I was psyched to see there was a John Coltrane poster above his desk. You get these ideas that people are mono-dimensional or whatever. I was thinking, Maybe this guy doesn't really know what's happening. But it seemed like he was so psyched that we were there.

There wasn't like an antagonistic fight, like the bands that were managed by Susan Silver and Kelly Curtis versus the Sub Pop bands. The line is blurry anyway, because Soundgarden was on Sub Pop, and members of Pearl Jam were in Green River. There is no actual line. There's no distinct border. Though it was perceived at the time.

So Cameron Crowe put Mudhoney on the *Singles* soundtrack, and in typical wiseass fashion, we wrote "Overblown," taking the piss out of the glorification and aggrandizement of the scene.

EDDIE VEDDER Mudhoney has an amazing song on the soundtrack that is a disclaimer for the whole thing. It's called "Overblown." God, the last verse is just so perfect: "Everybody loves us/we're getting pretty old/can't hold a regular job/long live rock and roll!" Classic! *(Laughs.)*

STEVE TURNER "Overblown" is about rock-star bullshit. There's a lyric about standing onstage with your shirt off, which is a pretty apparent Cornell reference. But it all was in good fun.

CHRIS CORNELL I remember hearing about that song and listening to it, but it didn't make any difference to me. We toured together after they wrote that song. It was nothing I really paid much attention to.

MARK ARM We recorded it for like $164, and we got paid $20,000, so we kept the rest of it.

BOB WHITTAKER We got a pretty good chunk of change up front for that song, and the attorney said, "Don't let anyone know how much you recorded this song for." I think the attorney thought it would upset the producers.

ROBERT ROTH So in the next meeting with Sub Pop, after we find out that we're no longer on the soundtrack, Jonathan and Bruce are like, "Okay, now you have to give us more than one record, or there's no way we're giving you this amount of money." Mark and Hiro weren't anxious to be involved in a long contract again, so that fell out.

Singles was a good film. It was kinda more about people like my brother, who works at Microsoft, than it was about musicians. There were a few of those characters in that movie, like Matt Dillon, but it was kind of a sideline to the love story.

JASON FINN *Singles* was seen as funny by everyone I know. The whole intrusion theory—where it's this special thing we don't want anyone to know about—that doesn't even make any sense. Everybody wants recognition for what they're doing. They came in, they made a silly movie, and worked in some shameless plugs for their friends the bands. Big deal. I enjoyed the Pearl Jam scenes when I finally saw it. I was like, "Yeah, there's Eddie Vedder the drummer. Awesome."

DANIEL HOUSE People here thought *Singles* was a good movie, kinda cheesy. It definitely was an idealized version of the scene. But at least it was fictional. *Hype!* was intended to be an accurate account, and in fact, it ended up being an incredibly accurate account.

DOUG PRAY *Singles* came out when we were building momentum to try to film my movie. Cameron Crowe actually called me and tried to talk me out of making *Hype!* for 45 minutes: "What can you possibly hope to achieve? The scene has already reached its apex. It's everywhere. People are tired of it. Please don't do a movie about this."

For him to make a movie that was basically set in the Seattle music scene and tell me not to make a movie *about* the Seattle music scene, it was like a non sequitur. And I respected him, and it was an honor to be able to talk to him—I'd just graduated from film school and here I am talking to Cameron Crowe! But he was a part of the world of the really big bands who had just made it, who were represented by mega-management. And I was a part of the world that was defined by the small label Popllama, which had nothing to do with them. To me, the smaller bands were as important to the Seattle music scene as Alice in Chains.

CHAPTER 35
A PROBLEM WITH WEIGHTS AND MEASURES

MARK ARM Our recording budgets for the Warners records were about $125,000 to $175,000 each, and we recorded *Piece of Cake* for $30,000 and *My Brother the Cow* for $20,000. That's a fair amount of money left over, and we made a good amount of money touring; we never had to take tour support.

For a while, we were swimming in it. That probably helped me be an ethical junkie. I didn't have to steal anything; in fact, sometimes I would buy drugs for my friends. Of course, there were some times when I didn't have the money, and my second junkie girlfriend was a stripper, so she would go to work. Otherwise, she was living off me. A friend of mine once described her as having "spent a year on the couch." Talk about atrophy, man.

That's the fucking worst of it to me, that I became such a cliché: I was a junkie rock dude with a stripper girlfriend.

COURTNEY LOVE We had this video camera but we could never figure out how to make the battery work, so it's like three years of a marriage over three hours of footage, going over and over and over each other. I've seen four to seven frames of something on there that I'm like, Oh, geez, if that got slowed down and released it would be the biggest—YouTube would break.

But most of it is just Frances on a bed with two extremely stoned parents, and you see Mark Arm walking by for one second. It's at the Four Seasons, and you don't think when you're a parent, particularly a stoned parent—a good parent but a stoned parent—that your daughter is gonna grow up and be a teenage girl and she's not gonna want fucking footage of her two stoned parents while she's naked with no diaper. All we're saying is, "Naked baby, naked baby, naked baby," for like two hours.

That's one thing I have control of is that three to four hours. I've let out some footage, like 30 seconds of Frances and Kurt in the bathroom. There's this really poignant part, when Kurt's in the bathroom with Frances and he's swinging her around and he's being a really good dad, and then you look at where the toothbrushes are, and there's a syringe. But it's the truth, so I'm okay with it.

MARK ARM I was obviously pretty reckless. I was hospitalized a couple of times. I actually saw the keyboard player from Gorilla, this local band—except Curtis the guitar player, they were all like doctors or med students—in the emergency room at Harborview hospital twice. He told me that the second time, a friend of his working with him said, "Man, your friend has a problem with weights and measures."

I OD'd probably five times. If I was alone, I would have been dead for sure. Here's my advice to the kids: Don't do drugs alone. And don't do drugs around people who are afraid to call 911.

On New Year's Eve '92 going into '93, I was at a party. Kurt and Courtney were there and were like, "Hey, we're going to go back to our room, maybe get some dope." This was after I had come back from that tour, and I was just chippin' at that point. My tolerance was pretty low and I had been drinking and went back to their hotel room with Ron Heathman, the Supersuckers guitar player.

RON HEATHMAN We played on New Year's at RKCNDY. Kurt and Courtney showed up. I didn't know them that well. I had seen them a few times because I used to get drugs from Tommy Hansen, too. But after the show, Mark was like, "Do you want to go over to where they're staying?" They were at the Inn at the Market.

We went in, and it was just Kurt and Courtney and me and Mark. I did some and was fully loaded. Kurt was kind of unshaven with the dyed-blond hair and those polka-dot pajamas on. He and I were talking, and I can't remember what we were talking about, but ironically enough the "Come as You Are" video came on MTV while we were sitting there. Kurt, I think he turned the channel or something.

MARK ARM I did some dope, and I decided I wasn't high enough and went to do some more.

RON HEATHMAN We didn't really notice at first, but Mark had gone out. He was turning blue. This wasn't an uncommon occurrence in the Seattle scene, so we're all borderline paramedics at this point. *(Laughs.)* There was the ice-cube-up-the-butt trick, which we didn't have to use that night. Kurt and I traded giving Mark CPR—the pumping and the breathing, the whole nine.

And then Courtney got on the phone and called Jonathan Poneman and was like, "You need to get over here because one of your fucking band members on your fuckin' label"—and at this point, Mudhoney wasn't even on Sub Pop—"is dying and I can't have this fucking coming back on us because they're checkin' our trash!" She's worried about what the media would say. I kind of get that, but let's deal with someone's life first.

I think she called someone else, too. I don't know if it was Danny Goldberg. Kurt's the one that was like, "Will you fuckin' call the paramedics?" Either Kurt or Courtney finally called the paramedics, and we scooped up the paraphernalia and put it in a bag; but it couldn't go in the garbage because they were searching the garbage. The plan was that I'd say it was my room and I was registered under an alias. And I got them into the bathroom or whatever—I don't know exactly where they hid, because I was pretty loaded myself. But I'll never forget Courtney's reaction. It's crystal clear.

MARK ARM I heard that Courtney might have first called Jon Poneman and went, "How do I deal with this?" Eventually they were like, "We got to do something." Thank God. That seems like a weird thing that your first compulsion would be to call someone else. But I'm sure they probably felt pretty hounded by the press. That was around the time of the *Vanity Fair* story. They weren't exactly under the radar.

RON HEATHMAN I pocketed some dope and got Mark out when the paramedics got there.

MARK ARM The next thing I know, I've got the medics working me over, and I went to Harborview.

RON HEATHMAN And it was never to be spoken of again, until almost 20 years later. The saddest part about the whole thing is that the whole time, Frances Bean was asleep on the hotel bed.

COURTNEY LOVE We only stayed at the Market that one time, and they still are weird about me. Mark Arm OD'ing? I don't remember, honestly. Was he still with his Amazon girlfriend? She was cool. She wasn't trying to mack on my husband, she wasn't trying to mack on me, she just wanted all the drugs. Who's this guy? Ron Heathman? No. No . . . Calling Jonathan Poneman? That could be possible. I always trusted Jonathan Poneman for some insane reason.

I remember me not wanting to do any media. That was the media blackout, but I said to Kurt, "You should at least do the gay media," and so he did *The Advocate*. I know that Kurt was taking a lot of dope. He was really frustrated by things. Mark's habit at that point, I don't know.

MARK ARM It was stupid for me to go back for more when I had been drinking and had a low tolerance. It was after that I had decided it was probably better not to hang out with those folks anymore. They moved into that place in Magnolia, where Kurt ended up killing himself, but I never actually went there. I didn't want to get in there. I didn't want to be involved, and I was trying to take care of myself.

But I still fully didn't learn my lesson: I continued to chip throughout the spring until midsummer.

• • •

MIKE INEZ The Ozzy band, we were holed up in Reno, Nevada, mixing the *Live & Loud* album, and I get a call from Sean Kinney out of the blue. We'd done an American tour with Alice, so I got to be really great friends with them. Sean says, "Hey, what's goin' on, Mike?" It was so funny, because Sean's one of those people where you just know when something's fishy. He says, "We need you to come down to Brazil, we're doing Rock in Rio." At this point, I thought Mike Starr was gonna be coming back; there was talk of him going to be with his family, or he was just getting burnt out from being on the road.

I thought it was a temporary thing, so I told Ozzy, "The Alice guys called, and I don't want to leave you hanging without a bass player." And I remember Ozzy's words exactly. He said, "If you don't go, we're gonna have to go to the hospital." I said, "Why?" He said, "It's gonna take them about a week to get my foot out of your ass."

SUSAN SILVER There were continual positions of jeopardy that Mike Starr had put the band in. He had a fantastic mom who did everything to help him, but he got in a lot of trouble. He was constantly putting the band in legal jeopardy, whether it was drugs or selling backstage passes outside the venue, things that he and his dad did together that could have created a lot of ill will for Alice.

There's only so many times you could ask someone, tell someone, threaten someone, and then those guys had to make that decision, which they made on their own. They called me to tell me that they not only had made that decision, they had talked to Mike. This was before Brazil, in Hawaii. The Brazil shows would be his last.

MIKE STARR One time, Layne was so dope sick he goes to me, "Mike, take these two Van Halen tickets and sell 'em and get a hundred bucks for them so I can get well and play the show." Sean saw me do it, and Layne goes, "Don't tell him you sold it for dope for me," so I kept my mouth shut, and they all got mad at me. And Layne said, "Thanks, Mike. Appreciate it."

That's one reason why I got kicked out of the band. Also, Jerry was jealous 'cause I was getting a lot of attention. I was in a magazine, as "sexiest babe of the month." When that came out, I was walking to the bus, and Jerry had the magazine ripped up at his feet. And I was kicked out two months after that.

JERRY CANTRELL We were really sad about it, of course . . . We'd been together for five years, did a couple of records, EPs, been in a movie—we had quite a history together. It was a hard decision to make, but things just weren't working out, so we made the decision to part ways.

MIKE INEZ Sean had said, "You gotta go and get all these shots to go down to Brazil," so I went back to L.A., got the shots, and was gonna fly out to Brazil. Then they said, "Mike wants to do the last two shows here in Brazil, so we'll just meet you in London." I'm like, Oh great, I'm already sick from these vaccination shots!

JENNIFER FINCH When we went to play in South America, we all took the plane—L7 and the Chili Peppers and Nirvana and Courtney—from L.A. We were making these jokes that if that plane goes down, it's gonna be like the Big Bopper and Buddy Holly situation. When the plane landed, everyone said it lost a wheel, but what really happened was they lost the braking system on one of the wheels so it locked and the plane kind of spun sideways. Everyone was just in shock. Anthony from the Chili Peppers kicked the door open and started screaming at the pilot, and then Anthony was pulled off the plane.

Nirvana totally wouldn't talk to each other. Everyone was at the end of their rope with the drug and sickness situation with Kurt. Dave had just started his relationship with a gal he later married who's also named Jennifer. She's really lovely and had long red hair. Courtney was so pissed at me that I didn't marry him. Her quote was, "That could be your house on the hill."

The first weekend was in São Paulo and then the next weekend was in Rio, so there was an entire week off where the promoters just put together all this different really super-fun stuff to do, like scuba diving or going to the beach or going shopping. We all had bodyguards because we had to. L7 were popular down there. Our faces were so public that there were kidnapping threats.

CRAIG MONTGOMERY Rio and São Paulo, that was quite a trip. First we get down there and we play this giant soccer stadium in São Paulo for 80,000 people—it was this festival with Alice in Chains and L7 and some other bands. We were all staying at the same hotel. Lots of drinking. Going to the beach.

Kurt and Courtney were just holed up in their hotel room. The Courtney Love hotel room was a particular kind of disaster; I learned this later on, after tour managing Hole. She brings like two or three giant suitcases full of clothes, and somehow all those suitcases would get opened and everything would get spread out all over the hotel room. And then it's all coated in cosmetics and baby powder, it's just a tornado of clothes and makeup. They just sit in there and order room service, but they don't let the maids in to clean up or take out the dishes. It looks like an episode of *Hoarders.*

COURTNEY LOVE The one time I saw Kurt happy with his job was when we went to Rio. We had a bodyguard, we stayed at a four-star hotel. He hung out with Pearl Jam, Alice in Chains. He blew a line, which is like really tacky, but when in fuckin' Buenos Aires, blow a line. I was like, "Let's have a threesome with a model!" And he was like, "Really?" I'm like, "Yeah!" Did we? I'm not gonna tell you. No, I do not do sex stuff; that's not my jam, and it never has been. But my point was that he had fun mingling with his people.

MIKE STARR After *Dirt,* I never did heroin again, until the day I was leaving the band.

We were touring with Nirvana and the Chili Peppers, and we were playing a big show, a big festival, down in South America. And Kurt had taken me to the bathroom, him and Courtney, and we shot up all night, and Layne didn't know that. And I went to Layne's room and we shot up, and I OD'd.

I wake up, and I'm all wet, and I'm laying over the toilet. I'm in a different room and I'm all wet. And he had had me in the shower and everything—I was obviously blacked out during that whole time. I was flatlined. And he's crying and punching me in the face. I'm like, "What's wrong? What did I do?" And he's like, "You were dead for 11 minutes, Mike."

I got home to California, and after that's when it really began. Because I couldn't forget about losing my band. It was everything to me, and it broke my heart, so I started shootin' again.

CRAIG MONTGOMERY Nirvana decided to use the time in between shows to go into a studio and just get some ideas down for their next album. So we went to this pretty nice studio in Rio, and the band played all the songs they had written for *In Utero,* which was not that many, and nothing was very complete, but I remember we had "Heart-Shaped Box" and a few other songs.

"Heart-Shaped Box" was pretty good. Frankly a lot of it I thought was crap. It was just this improvisational, atonal stuff, just noisy. I could tell that Kurt wasn't at one of his creative peaks at all. It was obvious—and he had said to me and to others—that he just wasn't really excited about Nirvana anymore and he wanted to do something else. They were struggling to get enough material together for an album. And this is something I haven't really ever said to anyone else before, but my feeling was like, Wow, good luck making an album, guys. You're in trouble.

CHAPTER 36
RADIO FRIENDLY UNIT SHIFTERS

STEVE ALBINI I'd been hearing rumors that I was going to be asked to do the Nirvana record for a long time, and I had gotten a couple of random, drunken phone calls from Kurt—I assume it was Kurt, because I later identified that voice—just slurring that he wanted to make a record with me. I got calls from weirdos all the time, so I didn't think too much about it.

Then I started seeing stuff, particularly in the English music press, saying that I was doing the next Nirvana record. It made me uncomfortable, so I actually wrote, I think it was *Melody Maker,* saying, "I don't know where you're getting your information. Nobody has spoken to me about making a Nirvana record. You've published this, and it's now causing me some consternation because people are calling me up and hassling me about it."

Eventually, Kurt called me and said, "If you're up for it, we'd like you to do this record." I said, "Sure." I wasn't a particular Nirvana fan prior to working on that record, but I grew to respect them a great deal, seeing them work and seeing their work ethic, seeing how they gave each other space to do stuff.

DANNY GOLDBERG Kurt was nervous about looking too mainstream after the huge commercial success of *Nevermind,* and I think he thought that Albini would add some punk credibility.

STEVE MANNING I remember seeing Kurt at an all-ages Fluid show at RKCNDY and feeling like he was being more reclusive than in the past. Must've been right after *Nevermind*. He was pressed up against the wall in the back corner. I remember walking outside and two young kids with Mohawks were screaming at him, "You killed punk rock! You killed punk rock!" Kurt was with a girl at the time, and I just remember looking at him and seeing the most dejected look on his face. I didn't feel close enough to him where I could go up and say, "Ah, fuck them, don't worry about it." I've always wished I would've said something.

GILLIAN G. GAAR I didn't even realize that they had disavowed *Nevermind* until reading the book *Come as You Are*. It was mainly Kurt, and to some extent the others. He said he was embarrassed by *Nevermind* and that it wasn't the kind of record he would listen to. He said it sounded closer to a Mötley Crüe album.

BUTCH VIG To me, that record doesn't sound slick at all. It sounds like a band playing their asses off in a room. To me what sounded slick were the metal records that were coming out, like Whitesnake. Nirvana was super-happy with *Nevermind*. Initially I may have been a little hurt by what Kurt said, but I knew that Kurt had to say that because, what can you say, "We sold 10 million records. I loved the way the record sounds"? That's not very punk.

CHRIS CORNELL When all the bands in the Seattle music scene went on to major labels and bigger success, there was this kind of "Let's pretend that we don't wanna be doing this and someone's sort of forcing us to do it" attitude. I think everybody had it, including members of my own band. The only band I didn't see acting like that was Alice in Chains, because they didn't come from that indie-rock world. Everybody else sort of followed the punk-rock bible, and it wasn't part of punk rock to be on a major label, to make money, to make videos, to spend more than $2,000 on making a record, to be on a tour bus instead of driving a van. And yet, that's what everyone was doing.

BUTCH VIG Here's one reason why I knew that Kurt was happy with that record: because he called me up and started bugging me to produce Courtney. He wanted me to do *Live Through This*. Kurt had so much respect for me, and I think that he knew that I could bring out in Courtney what I had brought out in Nirvana with *Nevermind*.

He started calling every night at the studio. I'd be at Triclops working with the Smashing Pumpkins and they'd go, "Butch, Kurt's on the phone." I'd talk to him and he'd go, "Butch, you gotta do Courtney's record, man, you just gotta do it." I was pretty fried from doing the Smashing Pumpkins' *Siamese Dream*—it was super-draining; six months of pretty much working every single day—and there was just no way I could go right into another crazy record. Billy, who had dated Courtney and knew her really well, said, "You don't want to go in a studio with Courtney." That's all he would say.

PATTY SCHEMEL We lived together for a bit, me and Kurt and Courtney, when I first moved to Los Angeles. They had this really great place, but Kurt would just sit in the closet with his guitar and amp in the dark and play. He liked it in there. And the closet backed up against the room that I stayed in, so I could hear it all. That's where I heard all the *In Utero* stuff. The beginnings of "Rape Me" I heard in there.

STEVE ALBINI We did the record at Pachyderm, and I thought it was a plus that it was way out in the boonies of Minnesota. Given everyone's concerns about Kurt falling off the wagon, being in a studio that was 50 miles out of town made that less likely.

I remember we got an awful lot done in the first week. I was very happy with the progress. Everything sounded really good, the band was in really good spirits, Kurt was sober, there were no flare-ups, no incidents, everything seemed kind of normal. There was one pretty funny episode one night where Dave Grohl and Bob Weston—who was there working on the session, as well—got bored, so they took off into this small town, Cannon Falls, Minnesota, and hit a QuikTrip or the 7-Eleven and bought all of the Reddi-wip in the dairy case. And then stayed up all night doing whippets.

When Courtney showed up at the studio later on? It sucked. She's like a fucking lead weight on everything. You know, I don't get any satisfaction talking about that person.

LORI BARBERO When they were at Pachyderm, I took Krist and Kurt to the Mall of America, and Albini kept saying, "You can't go to the Mall of America—you'll get swamped." I'm like, "Nobody is gonna swamp you." Albini's like, "You're gonna be sorry." He was thinking that they were just gonna get attacked.

I took them to this store called Bare Bones in the Mall of America, because I knew Kurt would love it. It was all about anatomy: babies in jars and skeletons and brains and all that. That's where he bought the woman figure on the cover of the album.

Back then, I really stood out with my blond dreadlocks, and I lived in the Twin Cities, so that was my stomping grounds. The only people that approached us were a bunch of kids, and they're like, "You're in Babes in Toyland!" Not one person recognized Krist and Kurt.

STEVE ALBINI We did a lot of prank calls. We called Eddie Vedder, and they had me pretend to be some famous record producer who had worked with Bowie. I told him that I wanted to get him in the studio with a *real* band that could really play. I don't know if he could tell that there was something up or not, but he handled it with a lot of class.

Three days into the session, Dave called John Silva and said that he'd just been hitting the snare drums for three days and that I'd just been moving the microphone around that whole time. At one point, John Silva said, "Well, you know, it's like we said . . ."—and then Dave totally cut him off. It's like he was about to spill the beans on whatever Plan B was.

DAVE GROHL Our A&R man at the time, Gary Gersh, was freaking out. I said, "Gary, man, don't be so afraid, the record will turn out great!" He said, "Oh, I'm not afraid, go ahead, bring me back the best you can do." It was like, Go and have your fun, then we'll get another producer and make the *real* album.

DANNY GOLDBERG So the record came back, and I listened to it and Geffen listened to it and Courtney listened to it and other people listened to it, and my feeling was that the voice was buried. Kurt, he's got a very good, extremely recognizable voice, and he put a lot of care into the words.

STEVE ALBINI When the record was delivered, the record label freaked out. Because it wasn't something that they had been involved in, they were suspicious of it, and they instilled a lot of doubt in the band. The label started this whispering campaign about me and how I'd ruined the record. I was getting calls from journalists saying things like, "I just got off the phone with Gary Gersh. He said you've ruined the Nirvana album." And that was all done as a means of trying to coerce the band to redo the record in a more expensive, more conventional, big-record-label manner.

I got a call from Kurt, and he sort of explained to me what was going down with the record label. I'm not 100 percent certain of this, but the way he was speaking, the way his voice was affected, I had the impression that he was back on drugs, so I wasn't that confident in his decision making. He said, "The record label hates the record, they want us to redo it all. I've been listening to it and maybe there's stuff we could do better. So we'd like to try and remix some stuff." I listened to a dub of the record and was content with it and told him, "If you want to mess around with stuff on your own, it's your record. Whatever makes you comfortable. I don't think I can help any."

DANNY GOLDBERG Kurt lived with it for a few days, and I think a lot of other people told him the same thing, and so he says, "Well, who can we get?" We talked different names and one of them was Scott Litt, who had done R.E.M. Kurt met Scott, and he loved him. Scott ended up remixing "Heart-Shaped Box" and "All Apologies."

STEVE ALBINI They sent me a copy of the record after it was done. I thought it sounded okay. There was very aggressive mastering done. The band had been made so paranoid by the people that worked for them; those people had somehow convinced them that this awesome record they made was terrible.

The hostile publicity campaign that the record label, in particular Gary Gersh, had waged against me actually did have an effect on my business. They made me seem like I was poisonous, so none of the bigger mainstream bands, certainly no one on Geffen, considered using me for their records. On the other end of the spectrum, all the smaller bands that had been my bread and butter started to associate me with this mainstream culture that had been creeping into the underground; Nirvana were viewed with some suspicion by those bands. And there was a certain category of people that didn't know anything about me, that just assumed I'd be out of their price range because I'd worked on this big hit record. There was an extended period there where I had no work. It almost bankrupted me.

*　　*　　*

ELIZABETH DAVIS-SIMPSON I told my dad about playing music, but I didn't really want to tell him the name of the band. He would just say, "It's a dead end. Being in a band is a dead end." And then when 7 Year Bitch got signed to Atlantic, I thought, Here's something I can tell my dad that's going to mean something to him. Because my dad was born in 1912; he's not going to find it significant that we are on tour or we have a show at a club. I was really excited. Finally I can talk to my dad. And I said, "We're signed to Atlantic Records," and my dad said—I'll never forget this—he just said, "You'll find nothing but Jews in the music industry."

I'm not proud of that—my dad was super-racist and sexist and anti-Semitic—but I told that to Danny Goldberg, the president who signed us to Atlantic Records, and he thought that was the funniest fuckin' thing.

VALERIE AGNEW We chose who we wanted for a producer and all that kind of stuff, whereas the label was trying to steer us toward something that would be more commercial. We didn't realize at the time you basically have to get some kind of radio play or else you're not gonna be able to go very far in their system. It means they don't spend a lot of time working on your record, because there's not much they can do with it.

SELENE VIGIL-WILK Tim Sommer was our A&R guy. He was nice, but he was doing Hootie & the Blowfish, too, which kind of threw us for a loop. We just didn't know how to deal with the label because we were still trying to be really DIY, which was sometimes a mistake on our part, because at times we really didn't know what the hell we were doing.

VALERIE AGNEW We got really good advice from Buzz from the Melvins, because they were on Atlantic at the same time as us. He warned us not to expect that all the things they were saying were gonna happen—the whole "yes-man" type of deal—and that we have to really pay attention to the amount of money that was being spent. Don't go accepting a bunch of crazy tour support or big-budget stuff because that's often taken out of your back end, and just don't have any illusions about this.

I can remember seeing the Melvins later when they were playing Lollapalooza and they were touring in a van and the other bands were on a tour bus. We were like, "Why are you guys in a van?" And they were like, " 'Cause we're not gonna spend the money that way. Hell, no. We don't wanna be indebted to the label."

BUZZ OSBORNE It was going really good for us recording for Boner Records. We were doing fine, we were making more money than we ever had. We certainly didn't have anybody knocking on our doors to do records. When we did get interest from a major was when I was recording my solo album—we did these Kiss [themed] solo records. I was actually with Dave Grohl in Seattle, recording with him in this basement that one of his friends had, and Crover called me and said all these majors were interested in signing us. We didn't have a manager, nothing.

DALE CROVER I was out eating breakfast with Kurt—Nirvana might have been in town or something—and he was like, "Do you guys want to be on a major label?"

And I'm like, "Sure, yeah. Why not?" And somehow from that conversation I got hooked up with these lawyer guys who were working for Mudhoney. They pretty much said, "Because of Nirvana and all these other bands, there's definitely interest in other bands from Seattle." Grunge bands, whatever. We were a little leery about it, but these guys were actually pretty straight up.

DANNY GOLDBERG I asked Kurt, "Is there anybody you want me to sign to Atlantic?" He says, "Oh man, sign the Melvins. They're the best band in the world. They changed my life." I would never say no to him about something like that. First of all, I figured his taste was a lot better than mine, but secondly, he had done so much for me just by letting me be his manager.

DALE CROVER Danny Goldberg was at Atlantic, but he still owned Nirvana's management company. He pretty much talked us into signing with his label. He's like, "You guys are already an established band, I know you guys do weird stuff, and that's fine." He was completely realistic about the whole thing. He wasn't some schmoozy A&R guy. We had other meetings with people that were more like, "Yeah, you're a grunge band, you're going to sell a million records!"

BUZZ OSBORNE We got about 25 to 30 offers in total, from a variety of labels. Everything was going crazy. What really pissed me off was all these offers from these indies. Where were you guys when we needed you? So what we're going to do is sign with the biggest label we can. We got a lawyer and signed a deal with Atlantic without even having a manager. I just told them, "Here's what I want." We got 100 percent artistic control, they didn't have to put the records out but they couldn't make us do another one, they couldn't sit on us, they didn't even know where we were recording. It was perfect.

DALE CROVER I think Danny Goldberg might've mentioned something about Kurt producing the *Houdini* record: "I think if you had him do it, you could guarantee that you could sell a bunch more records." At first I was like, "I don't want to do that. It just seems kind of cheesy." But then Buzz was like, "You know, we've never done anything like that before. Kurt might help us in songwriting and doing something completely different."

BUZZ OSBORNE I hadn't been around Kurt for a long time—not really since we had toured with him, when I got the John Silva speech. Kurt played on "Sky Pup" and the last song on the album. He was just completely strung out, and I realized pretty quickly that it wasn't going to work. I went to Danny Goldberg's office in L.A. and said, "Look, Kurt Cobain's strung out." Kurt was really bad, as bad as he's ever been.

DALE CROVER Well, Kurt did nod out a few times. But he definitely tried. But then, we kind of didn't have any songs at the time. We would write a few songs and have him come down. We tried to convince him that "You're really good at melody, and if you got any ideas, you should help us out. You should be involved in the songwriting process."

Nirvana had just done that record with Steve Albini, so Kurt wanted to try some different drum things. But then, after a couple of sessions, he just kind of stopped showing up.

DANNY GOLDBERG Kurt was pretty drugged out. He was also upset that they didn't have songs. Kurt was tremendously committed to the punk culture, but he was a traditionalist when it came to songwriting. He listened to the Beatles a lot. He didn't only listen to Black Flag and the Dead Kennedys and the Melvins.

He was very disappointed that, in his mind, they hadn't prepared for the record the way he prepared for his records. They didn't have material. They were, he felt, more like jamming. I suggested that he cowrite with them, but he wasn't that excited about doing that. Buzz asked him to also. Kurt was kind of possessive about his material. He didn't write for Courtney, either. He liked his good songs to be for him.

Buzz said something about Courtney later on that got Courtney upset. I don't remember what it was. Courtney was all pissed and said, "I want Kurt to take his name off the album." I said, "Kurt, I'd really rather you not take your name off the album." He said, "I'd never take my name off the album, don't worry about it."

BUZZ OSBORNE I said something in the media like, "She's just a fucking gold digger." And they all flipped out about it. So I called up Cobain and said, "Look, I'm sorry."

DAN RAYMOND I know Kurt wanted to divorce Courtney. I heard that come out of his mouth, when he was supposedly producing the Melvins' *Houdini* sessions. He said, "She's running up my credit cards" and something or other and, "I want a D-I-V-O-R-C-E," like out of that country-western song.

COURTNEY LOVE Kurt was Buzz's Stepin Fetchit boy, and Buzz saw himself as some sort of big-deal motherfucker. And you know, Kurt's the best friend I've ever had, and I'm not gonna put up with somebody putting down my best friend and being mean to him.

I don't know anything about Buzz other than one Christmas Eve, which was about 1992. Goldberg signs the Melvins, and we go to San Francisco, and Kurt's got a dependency issue and it has to be monitored. I fuckin' leave to go Christmas shopping, and I leave him in the hands of this girl Debbie, who's someone's girlfriend.

I come to Shirley Temple Black's daughter's house to get my husband, who was intensively doing production notes with Buzz. And Buzz is shooting Kurt up with a big old needle—and all I see is this black, black . . . I know that the heroin in San Francisco is Persian and it's better and it will kill people. Buzz is about to fucking kill Kurt, and I almost broke the needle in his arm. I took that needle out of his arm, squirted the rest in the fuckin' sink, looked at Buzz.

He looked away, and it was one of those very rare looks that you get when you catch somebody doing something very bad. *Very, very bad.* And I don't know what his intention was, but my God, whatever it was, it wasn't right, and I knew it and he knew it and it was really bad. *Very, very bad.* Have you ever been caught in a lie? I certainly have. Someone looks at you and they bust you and it's like, *Ohhh,* and you feel so bad.

And all of a sudden, I've got a blue fuckin' husband and had an overdose on my goddamn hands. It's just like, "You motherfucker."

BUZZ OSBORNE Courtney actually went public saying that I tried to murder Kurt Cobain. That I actually took a syringe of heroin and tried to shoot him up and kill him. Somebody pointed out to me that it was online. That's an absolute fabrication from someone who is insane. It's complete and utter garbage.

The people from Babes in Toyland are friends with her and they said that she would tell them these rambling stories about how I wanted rid of Kurt because I was jealous of his fame, and at that point I was like, "That makes no sense at all. This is the biggest PR guy we've ever had and you think I want to kill him? Why the fuck would I do that?"

She first said these things publicly two or three years ago: "Oh, yeah, Buzz tried to OD my husband." So she waited until *now* to say this? I don't know about you, but if somebody was trying to kill my wife, I probably would have gone crazy over it. I wouldn't wait 15 years to mention it. It doesn't really do much for her case, does it? She's fabricated this bullshit story to drag me through the mud once again.

COURTNEY LOVE I read recently, Kim Gordon—and she was just trying to fucking get to me, so I ignored it—Kim Gordon going in the *NME*, "Yeah, Buzz has some theories on Kurt's death dah dah dah that I agree with." It's like, Kim, I can't wait to see you at the Marc Jacobs store. I'm gonna stick my boot so far up your withered ass! *Jesus Christ.*

BUZZ OSBORNE I think that that's where that came from, because I was having a conversation with Kim Gordon around that amount of time ago, and Courtney probably got word of that. That's why she lashes out with something about me trying to murder Kurt. It's absolute cockamamie bullshit. Anybody that believes any of that stuff needs to have their fucking head examined.

Remember this: How do you know when Courtney Love is lying? Her lips are moving.

COURTNEY LOVE I don't like talking about Buzz. That one story, though, that I wanted to get on the record for a while because it really, really bugs me that he did that and then he goes around and talks about that "Kurt was murdered" nonsense. It's like, you know what, say that to my kid, you asshole.

BUZZ OSBORNE As far as Courtney wanting to take his name off the album, that's news to me. That wouldn't have made any difference anyway.

I fired Kurt from the record. I didn't talk to him about it. I think he was happy to have it go. I don't know how it was worded to him. I think they just let him walk away from it.

DANNY GOLDBERG Was Kurt fired? Not to my knowledge. I wouldn't have tolerated such a thing. He finished his work on it, and he did an okay job. I think it wasn't the romantic thing that he had hoped it would be of working with his idols.

DALE CROVER We did some sessions on our own, and then Atlantic got this guy, Garth Richardson, to come in and help us finish up the record. And it was awesome. It was the most comfortable recording ever.

BUZZ OSBORNE We'd kicked out Lori before because she had a whole bunch of troubles. Joe Preston was in the band for about a year, and then

Lori came back in for a few months maybe, but she never was on the Atlantic contract. Lori's on *Houdini* a little bit, but it's mostly me and Dale; the credits on that record are all wrong, it's nonsense.

I broke up with Lori in '92, I think, for good. Because it wasn't really working, and I was just over it. What was interesting was, when I was done with the relationship with Lori, her dad called me. After having absolutely no interest in what I was doing for years, us being signed to Atlantic somehow legitimized the whole thing in his mind. He said that he didn't see any reason why his daughter couldn't still be in the band. He became really nasty.

And I was like, "Forget it, Charlie! Forget it. It's not gonna happen. You had your chance, fucker, and good-bye!"

Was I afraid of him? Of course, I was. I was thinking, This may be the biggest mistake I've made in my life. I mean, her dad told me stories about strangling Japanese soldiers on the beaches in World War Two. With his *bare hands*.

But I've never been a pussy. I'd made up my mind, and I wasn't about to let that kind of thing stand in my way.

CHAPTER 37
NOTHING WAS THE SAME

STEVE MORIARTY Mia just had a way of connecting with the audience. I always knew when we got up there to play, no matter how dead the audience was or where anyone was in the bar or how big the place was, by about the third or fourth song, everybody in the place would be really close to the stage. She had a way of engaging everybody, bringing them forward to the stage to be part of what's going on. It was *wild*. She would get on her knees and sing to people individually, practically. And it wasn't showy, it wasn't any kind of performance at all, it was just her being her amplified self. People would just be watching her, everybody staring at her and listening for every word that would come out of her mouth.

VALERIE AGNEW We had all been together in L.A. The Gits were down there to talk to Tim Sommer from Atlantic, who was our A&R guy. We had already signed with Atlantic; I'm not sure if the paperwork was finalized, but we'd made the decision. Mia had just done a couple of solo shows down there, which she was really psyched about.

When we were down in L.A., it was the anniversary of Stefanie's death. I remember me, Selene, Liz, and Mia hanging out in the bathroom at the Hyatt on Sunset smoking pot and drinking a toast to Stef. Mia had a lot of encouraging words. And when we came back to Seattle, we were in the Comet and that came up again, so we had a round and did another toast to Stef. And then Mia left the bar, and that was the last time we saw her.

ELIZABETH DAVIS-SIMPSON 7 Year Bitch was about to go on tour with the Gits, and I remember Mia and the rest of the band were there. We're excited about the tour. We're drinking, having a good time . . .

STEVE MORIARTY We had six months of touring planned, in Europe and the U.S. and Canada. We were supposed to tour with L7 and 7 Year Bitch, all together. The pope was visiting the U.S., and we were going to play all the cities the same day that he was visiting them and have a pro-choice, anti-pope tour.

I went home at about 9 or 10 from the Comet, and Mia was just getting there. I was tired. Had to be in the studio the next day. I said, "Don't stay out too late. I gotta go. Okay, bye." And, yeah, that was it. And then the next day, when she was supposed to show up in the studio, she wasn't there.

VALERIE AGNEW I remember Steve calling me and one of Mia's best friends called, looking for her, and they were like, "Piecora's called"—Mia also worked there—"she didn't show up at Piecora's." I was like, What the hell? No way, this can't be happening again! Mia's not using drugs. Immediately the thought went to that, of course. And then Mia's roommate called me and told me that they had found her and that she had been strangled, and that's when the walls came tumbling down.

STEVE MORIARTY So we were looking, looking, looking, and then later that night, someone got up the courage to call the morgue, and they found that she was there. She was wearing her Gits hoodie when they found her.

MATT DRESDNER Obviously my viewpoint is a bit myopic, but it all ended on that day. Innocence was lost. With Stefanie's death and Kurt's death and Andrew's death, they had done it to themselves. Mia was taken from us. But like Stefanie, she was a real magnet for people to come together around. I don't know if the scene ever recovered from losing Mia. There was so much attention given to "Who the fuck did this?" and it took us 11 years to figure it out—and no one was beyond suspicion.

BEN LONDON The nature of the crime—the fact that she was brutally raped and murdered—and the fact that historically with these kinds of crimes it's usually somebody that the victim knows that does them, put everybody, not really in our core group but in the larger group—the second, third circles of our group—under suspicion. Her boyfriend at the time was considered a suspect by the police.

DANIEL HOUSE A lot of people were looking at each other and wondering if that was the person who killed Mia. Suddenly, everything was tainted.

STEVE MORIARTY There was a huge amount of rage at the police for not disclosing that she had been raped. If they released all the information about what happened and it was public knowledge, then it would ruin their line of questioning for suspects. Because the cops hadn't said that this person had raped her, people in the community thought that made them more vulnerable to it. That and the fact that the cops seemed really bumbling, and dismissive and judgmental at first because Mia was a rocker, she had dreads, she was wearing cut-off jeans, and she had been drinking.

DANIEL HOUSE The Gits kept a lot of the details from us. In the same way that they were always mistrustful and paranoid, they knew more details about the case than they were sharing with the label. It took a long time before I found out that Mia had also been raped.

SELENE VIGIL-WILK There were so many different reactions to it. From being totally fed up with the police not being able to find the murderer to friends saying, "Oh, my God, I got hauled into the police. I got taken down and questioned." It was just crazy. Nothing was the same anymore. Not that things were ever particularly safe, but it wasn't dangerous. And now you're gonna walk out of the Comet and get frickin' strangled and left for dead in a frickin' field?

ELIZABETH DAVIS-SIMPSON We developed way more of a hardcore attitude, about not just being feminist through the words we were saying and the way we were acting, but really adapting this fierceness in our own personal lives. Mia was a fierce, street-smart person, so if someone tough like Mia can have that happen to her, it really made all of us feel vulnerable.

I actually got a gun. I had a Lorcin .22, though you probably would have to have someone stand in place and not move for you to do any damage with this little, tiny gun.

STEVE MORIARTY People were buying guns and weapons and carrying them around. They wanted to find the guy and *kill him*. People were raging.

VALERIE AGNEW One of the things that came out of that tragedy was Home Alive, this collective that I cofounded with eight other women. It was a nonprofit to raise awareness about violence against women, but primarily to offer training for people so there was a tangible thing you could do: street-fighting skills, how to deescalate conflicts, weapons training.

Home Alive got its most significant support from Eddie Vedder. He basically set us up with Epic Records. They agreed to release a benefit compilation that raised over $200,000 for the organization and gave us *a lot* of press. He was always very humble about it, and at some point we stopped thanking him all the time, but he really did make an enormous impact. We were able to teach a lot of ass-kicking with that money!

ELIZABETH DAVIS-SIMPSON I was blown away by the support. All these different bands, from garage bands to Soundgarden, contributing to the Home Alive comp.

STEVEN MORIARTY One of the last shows Nirvana played in Seattle was a benefit that I organized to hire a private investigator to find Mia's murderer. TAD was scheduled to headline it, and they told Kurt they were playing it. So Kurt called me and said, "I heard you're doing this benefit. Is there any way we can get on and play?" I was like, "Fuck, yeah!"

KURT DANIELSON The show was at the King Cat Theater, which is a fairly small venue in downtown Seattle. There weren't the greatest backstage facilities, which meant that all the bands and family and friends were cramming into this very tiny room. There was a lot of sitting very close together and there was a lot of tension. And, basically, Courtney and Tad's then-girlfriend Barbara had a little tussle.

You should've seen: There's Tad sitting slumped in his chair, there's Kurt sitting next to him slumped in a chair, those two girls going at it, pulling each other's hair—total catfight—scratching each other's faces. They knocked over a lamp, the carpet catches on fire, nobody gets up to put the fire out, so I put the fire out.

STEVE MORIARTY I remember Courtney Love was high out of her mind. Courtney was walking around and saying there wasn't enough light backstage and she wanted more light. Probably because her eyes were pinned, and she couldn't see in the dark. Tad's girlfriend told her to shut up. Then: "Don't tell me to shut up!" It was just one of those really stupid schoolyard things. It was about, We're trying to be the center of attention, when we're clearly not supposed to be the center of attention.

BENJAMIN REW These are two chicks that fight like dudes, okay? It's no fuckin' hair-pulling and scratching, this is straight-up fuckin' fisticuffs.

JEFF GILBERT I heard screaming. I heard some crashing going on. Kurt comes out, and he's just exasperated. He goes, "Everybody out! This is not cool. Everybody out!" I saw a little bit of it. There were some really funny insults being hurled back and forth, alluding to one or the other's drug habit.

That's when you knew the scene was starting to fall apart. When you'd start having drama queen fights like this. *Really?* The girlfriends are fighting now? It was retarded.

KURT DANIELSON Some months later, we were on tour in Europe. We had a show the night before, and we hadn't slept much and we did interviews all day. Tad hadn't had a chance to eat—he had very low blood sugar—and the English journalist took advantage of the situation by asking Tad some very leading and pointed questions about this incident that occurred at this benefit. And so Tad responded with some rather harsh remarks about Courtney, something to the effect of "That bitch slapped my girlfriend."

And they took this remark and put it in bold-print headlines in the *NME* and I think *Melody Maker,* and Courtney saw these things. We were slated to open for Nirvana in America, along with the Butthole Surfers. But because Courtney saw this, she said to Kurt, "You've gotta kick those guys off your tour." And so Kurt turned around and told Krist to tell me that we were off the tour. Which he did.

COURTNEY LOVE Great, is this Blame Courtney Week? I had a role in removing TAD from the *In Utero* tour? Is this some Yoko shit? I didn't have anything to do with who Kurt took on tour. I remember my physical altercations. I certainly didn't get into a fight with Tad's girlfriend. I didn't know he had a girlfriend. People like to make things up about me: "Oh, she set a fire, and then we did dope . . . and she stole my grandmother's ring." I get that kind of thing a lot.

KURT DANIELSON I was furious. It's like, Jesus Christ! I didn't blame Tad for it, because the reporter pushed his buttons. No matter what we did, it turned out wrong or fucked up or turned into a nightmare where we got sued or we got dropped. It seemed almost pathological, almost like we were doing it on purpose. "How could they have such bad luck?" I heard this many times: "You must have bad karma." Great, I feel better now. I got bad karma. That explains everything.

JOSH SINDER If saying the truth gets you kicked off the tour—oh well, I guess that's how it goes.

*   *   *

STEVE MORIARTY The Gits actually played one of our first shows in Seattle with TAD and Nirvana, at the HUB Ballroom at the University of Washington. There were like 2,000 people there, and we played brilliantly. So they kind of welcomed us to town and showed us out of town. The benefit was great. We made like five grand.

I always knew that we would find the guy who killed Mia eventually. That's how I maintained my wits, really. So when we did, I was obviously really psyched, but it also brought back a lot of repressed and horrible memories. And having to go through the trial was like reopening all those wounds, and I knew that I had to be there and to testify as a witness.

At the time they gathered the DNA from the crime scene, the technology was not created to test it. It wasn't until 10 years later, but the medical examiner who did the autopsy had the foresight to save particular samples, thinking that maybe the technology would catch up one day, and lo and behold, it did. It was the first case in the state that a conviction was made using DNA from saliva from teeth marks.

The guy had gotten a felony assault on his girlfriend who was pregnant. He kicked her in the stomach and gave her a bloody nose. That's when they entered his DNA sample into the database. I think the only reason the cold-case detectives picked up the case—there were only two detectives for the entire region—is because of all that media attention and all those bands and all the organizations, the self-defense group. Joan Jett really went out of her way to help us out. It was a movement.

The guy was as far away from Seattle as you could get—he was in the Florida Keys. He disappeared just as quickly as he appeared in Seattle. He wasn't anyone that anyone knew. He had stalked other women, who came forward during the trial. He was a sociopath and felt no remorse.

ELIZABETH DAVIS-SIMPSON I remember going online to look at a picture of him and thinking for a long time, Do I click the site? Do I do this? Do I look at this fucker's face, the last face that Mia saw? And I did. I looked at his face, and I looked at his eyes. That was pretty intense. He's a monster, huge.

VALERIE AGNEW I wasn't there for the trial because I was out of the country, but Selene ended up testifying. I was there for the sentencing. I accidentally walked into the courtroom behind him at one point. They had him shackled out in the hallway. We were on his heels right behind him. It was totally an intense experience. Man, he's enormous. It was very emotional. I think he got like 36 years. It was so frustrating to know that the amount of time is never enough to compensate for what your friend or her family goes through. But it was at least no longer a question mark.

STEVE MORIARTY The trial was the first time I'd seen the pictures of the crime scene, and it was blown up to the size of a door: where she was laid out and the blood dripping from her mouth. Like horrible, horrible shit in the courtroom, and it sure didn't seem like it was 10 years earlier. It seemed like yesterday.

CHAPTER 38
ALL THE RAGE?

MIKE INEZ I flew over to London with my girlfriend at the time, and Alice in Chains are coming from Brazil, and we scheduled three rehearsals in London. The first day we didn't do anything but smoke hash together. And here is my jumping in the pool for Alice in Chains—I think it was 27 gigs in 32 days and 16 countries. It's so funny, like Layne would say, "All right, here's a song called 'Rain When I Die,'" and then I'd run up to Layne and whisper in his ear, "Which one's that?" He'd sing me a little of the song. "Okay, I got it. Go."

We finished that cycle and I was still thinking it was temporary, and then we got an offer to do this Arnold Schwarzenegger movie soundtrack, which was the first time I ever wrote with Jerry, Sean, and Layne. And then the guys asked me, "Hey, do you want to stick around and be our guy?" Those times things were still going good, and it was just such a pleasure. We used to laugh our way around the world.

SEAN KINNEY I thought a lot of people were gonna be freaked out by the change. But then a lot of people really didn't notice, because they're both Mikes and about the same height. People just thought Mike Starr got tanner and grew his hair more. They didn't even notice. It's like, Goddamn, I don't even have to be here! I was sort of looking around for guys that look like me. *(Laughs.)*

MIKE INEZ We did Lollapalooza '93, with Tool, Rage Against the Machine, Primus, Dinosaur Jr. Babes in Toyland were great. It was just so nice hearing the Fishbone guys reciting poetry on the tour bus or Jerry jamming with Fishbone or those guys jumping up onstage with us. Arrested Development would come up and jam, and Layne loved this German industrial band called Front 242; you'd be backstage getting some catering and kinda waking up and then you'd hear Layne singing with Front 242. That's another one of those tours where life-long friendships were made.

MAUREEN HERMAN Lollapalooza was very tough, because my picture was on the cover of *Entertainment Weekly* for the Lollapalooza issue, along with pictures of Layne and the guy from Arrested Development. People said, "Oh! You must be doing so well." But I had to borrow money from my mom for the rent that month. Our record company was *really* pushing us to take a tour bus, but we preferred to drive ourselves. We were told that no other band on the tour would be traveling in a van and we had to "grow up."

Finally we relented, and because all tour costs are paid by the band or charged against future record sales, and our primary source of tour income, merch, was jacked by Lollapalooza, we walked off with only a couple hundred bucks each.

LORI BARBERO Lollapalooza was really, really fun. All my friends, all together, day after day. I already knew the Fishbone guys, and that was really fun to hang out with them again. Alice in Chains were so great. Layne really liked us, and so he was always hanging out in our backstage room.

MAUREEN HERMAN Layne was so meek and mild-mannered and quiet in person that it was really hard to believe that he was a rock singer. He seemed like a child, and everybody else in the band kind of seemed like a man. He seemed like he didn't fit in. He really didn't hang with his band socially.

NICK POLLOCK Layne got me passes to a Lollapalooza show. I hung out with him all day. There was a guy on the bus who made sure he didn't get any drugs. There was a marked change in Layne's personality then. He was kinda melancholy and really disappearing. We still had a lot of the same conversations and reflections and things like that, but he wasn't there. He was lost.

DAVID DUET When I was living in Texas, Layne called and said he's comin' to play Lollapalooza. He says, "Here's what I need: a bottle of Jägermeister, a bag of pot, mushrooms, bottle of Jack Daniel's . . ." Gives me this long list. When I get on his bus, I'm excited to see him and not really paying attention, so I bring him the bag of stuff and I say, "Okay, here's everything." He's trying to give me the eye the whole time. And then I learn I'm on Layne's personal "clean and sober" bus. *(Laughs.)* His stepdad, his manager, everybody's standing there.

I packed the bag up and left the bus before it was confiscated, and Layne met me like 15 minutes later.

LORI BARBERO Eventually Kat and Layne got in trouble, of course.

MAUREEN HERMAN Layne and Kat started seeing each other on tour, and then when we were in San Francisco, either his girlfriend was in town or he had changed his mind about the situation. Something happened, and he couldn't be hanging with her. I don't know what it was. But they had a falling-out that day, so Kat decides to react to the situation with Layne by doing excessive heroin.

KAT BJELLAND Layne and I hung around the whole time. We weren't going out, just to make that clear. He was like a kindred spirit. We probably had crushes on each other, because I punched him in the stomach once, which is like a third-grader's crush reaction, right? And then he had his minions throw me in a bucket of water before we were supposed to play. I was immature. I kinda liked him, but you just get confused when you're out around the same people all the time.

Let me make this very clear: I never really did heroin on tour. When I came home and I was bored and depressed with money, yeah, that's when I would do it. In my whole career on tour, I'm thinkin', I did it three times. Otherwise, I'd do that thing people do—they kick by drinking themselves to death for at least four days, get through the withdrawal symptoms, and be on their way. At that show in San Francisco, some person from Minneapolis brought it to me. I didn't ask for it. Never really did that onstage before. Really slows things down to a sub-dirge.

MAUREEN HERMAN The San Francisco stop was the day of the *Entertainment Weekly* photo shoot. My mom and my sister came to the show. Kat has to be revived, and then she starts asking for my mom! I'm glad they have a great relationship, but I was just like, "Oh, Christ, Kat! Don't ask for my fucking mom when you OD."

Kat was indisposed, so *Entertainment Weekly* ended up taking pictures of me and Lori, and that's probably how my image ended up on the cover as opposed to Kat's.

. . .

DAVE ABBRUZZESE When Pearl Jam started talking about laying off on doing interviews and stuff, I had a *Modern Drummer* cover already in place to be done. One of those nights on tour in Italy was when I was doin' the last interview with *Modern Drummer.* Kelly said something to the effect of, "You might just wanna lay off of that." And my response was that I'd already committed to it. And Kelly said, "Hopefully you're prepared to deal with the consequences."

If I had to guess at what moment I crossed the Eddie threshold into him makin' a power move to get rid of me, it was probably that one.

ADAM KASPER (producer/engineer) *Vs.* was the first Pearl Jam album I worked on, as an assistant. I've become really good friends with Eddie since, and at that time he was definitely a different guy. I don't know if it was an affectation or what, but he was very moody and serious, and most of the guys in Seattle were pretty lighthearted. Maybe it was because of his fame; it was probably a shock to his system. Basically, you gain a lot of power when you're in that position and everyone is kissing your butt, nobody wants to upset you, and "Can I get you something?" Matt Lukin used to call him the Pope because Eddie would say something and people would cater to him.

EDDIE VEDDER The second record, that was the one I enjoyed making the least. We didn't record it in Seattle, and it was just like being on tour.

I just didn't feel comfortable in the place we were at because it was very comfortable. I didn't like that at all.

JEFF AMENT Recording *Vs.*, there was a lot more pressure on Ed. The whole follow-up. I thought we were playing so well as a band that it would take care of itself. Toward the end it got fairly intense. He was having a hard time finishing up the songs; the pressure, and not being comfortable being in such a nice place. We tried to make it as uncomfortable for him as we could. He slept in the freaking sauna.

BRENDAN O'BRIEN (producer/mixer/engineer) There's a great song we recorded for *Vs.*, "Better Man," which ended up on *Vitalogy*. One of the first rehearsals we did they played it and I said, "Man, that song's a hit." Eddie just went, "Uhhh." I immediately knew I'd just said the wrong thing. We cut it once for *Vs.* He wanted to give it away to this Greenpeace benefit record; the idea was that the band was going to play and some other singer was going to sing it. I remember saying to the engineer, Nick, "This is one of their best songs and they're going to give it away! Can't happen!" And we went to record it, and I'm not going to say we didn't try very hard, but it didn't end up sounding very good. I may have even sabotaged that version, but I won't admit to that. It took us to the next record, recording it two more times, before he became comfortable with it because it was such a blatantly great pop song.

CATHY FAULKNER (KISW assistant program director/music director) Eddie and Jeff appeared on *Rockline*, a national radio show, to coincide with the release of *Vs.* It was being recorded in Seattle, and I was there as an assistant to help make it comfortable for them. After *Rockline*, they came to KISW, and we gave them the airwaves to play whatever songs they wanted and talk about whatever they wanted. I remember how troubled Eddie was about being on the cover of *Time* magazine. He had the issue with him, and a bottle of wine, and he drank the bottle of wine and talked about how stupid it was that for all the things going on in the world they put a musician on the cover of *Time*.

EDDIE VEDDER Maybe I wasn't ready for attention to be placed on me, you know? Also I think it was the practical things that I wasn't ready for, or the legal things that I wasn't ready for. I never knew that someone could put you on the cover of a magazine without asking you, that they could sell magazines and make money and you didn't have a copyright on your face or something.

COURTNEY LOVE Eddie did something insanely manipulative. Well, I don't know if he did it on purpose or not, but I suspect he did. It was gonna be Kurt on the cover of *Time,* only Kurt wasn't going to talk to them. So Eddie said he would talk to them, and then he put it off, put it off, put it off, and at the last minute, when it was going to print, he didn't show up. Eddie pulled the same thing as Kurt, except he was smarter about it. I was so pissed. Kurt was so pissed. It should have been Kurt's *Time* cover.

CHRISTOPHER JOHN FARLEY (*Time* magazine staff writer) I just knew that the next album coming out by Pearl Jam was gonna sell trillions of copies, but at first it was like, "We should probably put Nirvana on the cover," because Kurt Cobain is more of an artiste, the stuff was more thoughtful. So I had many conversations with Walter Isaacson, *Time*'s managing editor at the time, about who would be better, Pearl Jam or Nirvana? The thing is, Nirvana wouldn't talk to me. They kept putting it off, putting it off, and I realized that we were gonna miss the boat. So I said, "Screw it, we'll do Pearl Jam." It wasn't a second-choice kind of thing, because all the time we're thinking, Should we put them both on the cover? Should we put Vedder? Can we get them to pose together? *That* wasn't gonna happen.

I kept hearing things about how Eddie felt *Time* magazine would be overexposure. Maybe it was too mainstream for him. Wasn't the album a Sony release? They promised Eddie would give me a call to talk about things. So I was up all night waiting by the phone, waiting for this guy to call, waiting for Godot. And he never did call. So we did the classic "write-around."

JOHN LEIGHTON BEEZER That cover of *Time* had Eddie Vedder's face screaming into the microphone, and down below it says ALL THE RAGE. Well, okay, that's kind of a pun—yes, it's a fad, so it's "all the rage," but also, he's full of rage. It's like, No, he's not. Well, maybe he is, but that's the guy from San Diego. You can listen to the music all by itself and get the impression that it was angst-ridden, but part of the humor was that we were a bunch of dorks and we would make noises like that. The humor was easy to miss.

NILS BERNSTEIN *Hype!* was cool because you get a sense of everyone's humor, which you don't necessarily get in the music or the media portrayals of it. Like Van Conner is the funniest fucking guy. It still surprises me that people have a sense of grunge being really dark or the result of living in the rain, because to me it seemed to be the most lively, funny, upbeat group of people.

RIKI RACHTMAN When Pearl Jam were on *Headbangers Ball,* they really weren't into the whole thing. *Complete opposite* was Alice in Chains. They always wanted it to be a theme. They went to a mansion in Beverly Hills, where they all had robes on, smoking cigars, with facial masks—I think Jerry Cantrell had cucumbers on his eyelids. Then we went to the water park in New Jersey, and they all came out with Speedos and flippers and snorkels. That's everybody, from Layne to Jerry. They had a blast.

CATHY FAULKNER The famous quote that came out of that radio show was that Eddie wanted to wipe his butt with *Time* magazine.

CHRISTOPHER JOHN FARLEY You gotta take the staples out first if you do that.

Putting Pearl Jam on the cover was a great call because the issue sold really well. Also, the week it came out, that album sold a million copies, the first album to sell in that range.

BILLBOARD ("Sales Suggest Pearl Jam, Nirvana Are Here to Stay," by Craig Rosen, November 6, 1993) The record-breaking debut week of Pearl Jam's "Vs." and the staying power of Nirvana's "In Utero" strongly suggest that the two bands linked to the "Seattle sound" have transcended any such scene and are well on their way to careers that will continue long after "grunge" is a memory . . .

"Vs.," released Oct. 19, racked up first-week sales of more than 950,000, the largest first-week sales figure since The Billboard 200 began using SoundScan data May 15, 1991.

Although Nirvana's Oct. 1 debut at No. 1 with sales of more than 180,000 pales by comparison, "In Utero" has shown staying power that has surprised some observers. This week the album drops to No. 4, but retains its bullet as it experiences a sales gain for the second consecutive week.

COLLEEN COMBS (Kelly Curtis's assistant) Pearl Jam was just getting bigger and bigger. *Ten* was a hit quickly, and then *Vs.* set the all-time-highest first-week sales record. It looked like things were never, ever going to calm down. Eddie didn't go through that building process, the years it takes you to get climatized to what's happening. It was all at once for him. Otherwise, he would know that he couldn't just go out barhopping with somebody on tour.

THE TIMES-PICAYUNE ("Slam Jam: Rocker, Cy Young Winner Team Up in Decatur Street Brawl," by Michael Perlstein, November 19, 1993) A $4 million-a-year major league baseball pitcher, a platinum selling rock singer and a Terrytown waiter converged in a drunken brawl on a French Quarter street just before dawn Thursday and guess who was left standing?

Hint: The rock singer, grunge super-phenom Eddie Vedder of Pearl Jam, was sent to Orleans Parish Prison and booked with public drunkenness and disturbing the peace.

Hint: The pitcher, 1993 American League Cy Young winner Jack McDowell of the Chicago White Sox, was rushed to Charity Hospital and treated for a cut on his head after barroom bouncer Anthony Martinez decided that the social fabric had been stretched far enough.

When the melee ended, local waiter and music aficionado James Gorman, 24, had one-upped two of the hottest celebrities of the year.

"He spit on me for no reason," Gorman said of Vedder, explaining how the scuffle began. "He grabbed me by the throat and started pushing me and that's when things went wild."

EDDIE VEDDER I was with Blackie and Ed from Urge. I talked to this guy for a while, and we tried to walk on. But this guy, he wouldn't let it go. He still had to have more. He still had to cover some more points. And Blackie says, "Look, man, just mellow out, we're going, you know . . ." And this guy's going, "No, no. I got to say one more thing, we gotta talk . . ." and finally I kinda held him against the wall and I . . . spit . . . in . . . his . . . face. Big fuckin' deal. Anyway, then all hell broke loose.

EDDIE ROESER The evening started out innocently enough. We were at Daniel Lanois's studio, and I think we might have met him. We had quite a few drinks and ended up at an extremely crowded bar. Jack McDowell was there as a guest of Eddie Vedder. Eddie's just trying to have a good time, and some drunk guy wants to talk with him and ends up saying something like, "You're not so fuckin' great," and Vedder just fuckin' spit in his face. I think the bouncers took this moment to beat on the out-of-towners.

Before we knew it, the police were there and they had Eddie Vedder in handcuffs. I don't know if they knew who he was, though it was pretty obvious, but I remember they said to Vedder, who was extremely drunk by that time, "Shut the fuck up. Shut your mouth for a minute, and if you're able to be quiet, we will let you go," and he would not do so.

ERIC JOHNSON I got to go bail Eddie out of jail at 5 in the morning. By the time I got there, he'd already made friends with everybody. He was laughing and talking to the other guys in the holding cell. I remember the smell of alcohol when I got there. It almost fuckin' burned my eyes. It was Eddie. He had been having a serious party.

EDDIE VEDDER But I never threw a punch. Thank goodness. Because— who knows?—I could really have hurt him. . . . So there's this guy, a talented and well-respected friend of mine who's lying on the ground unconscious because of this little dick who's saying to me, "You're not my Messiah, you're not my Messiah . . ."

And I'm going, "That's what I was trying to tell you, man. That's what I was trying to *tell* you. I'm not your fuckin' Messiah."

CHAPTER 39
IN THE ROCKET

BEN SHEPHERD I had just put my bags down in our hotel room in London and turned on MTV. I saw the video for "Heart-Shaped Box." That was the first time I'd heard the song, too. I freaked out and was like, "I need to get ahold of Kurt *right now.*"

Yeah, I can feel Kurt. A million miles away, and in one song. One note, one little drain of his voice, that's when I could feel it. It was a bad feeling. Like, It's either him or me. *Kurt, don't.* That's what I felt like. So I tried to get ahold of Kurt for our entire European tour. But no one helped me get ahold of him from our camp. No one paid attention.

ANTON BROOKES I saw Kurt OD a couple of times. The worst one was in New York, when they played Roseland, in '93. And Cali DeWitt, who used to look after Frances Bean, ran into the toilet and Courtney was screaming, and we went rushing into the room and Kurt was just laying in a heap on the floor, next to the toilet, with a syringe in his arm, blue, fuckin' blue. Cali just smacked him in the solar plexus. He didn't even think about it, he just did it. He just ran in and was in motion, and by the time he got to Kurt his fist was in his chest, and Kurt just came to. And then you're trying to get him up and deal with the situation: get him walking, wash his face, get him conscious.

After that, me and Kurt almost came to blows. I had said to Courtney something along the lines of, "He's fucking turning into Axl Rose. Who does he think he is?" And Courtney told Kurt that to get me into trouble. What would *you* say to someone who has just OD'd on a substance called Body Bag? That's what the little sachets of heroin he was using at the time had stenciled on them. After he OD'd, he was getting a massage and the masseur was finding these sachets everywhere. I was going discreetly next door and flushing them down the toilet. There must have been about 10 bags of it. Body Bag, how sick is that?

I think I was within my right to accuse him of selling out a little bit, if you think about what Nirvana was supposed to be about and what they stood for; they did antirape benefits for Bosnia and stuff like that. Nirvana were supposedly right-on, weren't they? They were the voice of a generation, the conscience of a generation. And for all intents and purposes, Kurt mutated into everything he was against. He became your attitudinal rock star, with the tantrums and the plush hotels and everything. And then, for all intents and purposes, Kurt was sucking corporation cock.

Kurt took what I told Courtney really personally, and me and him got into an argument in Central Park, with a photographer about 50 yards away who was just about to do a photo session with the band. I could see the photographer out of the corner of my eye, and he's checking his light meter and taking Polaroids of locations to show the band. And meanwhile, me and Kurt are having an argument, literally nose to nose; I'm a good foot taller than him, so I think he stood on a rock or something. Just screaming at each other. Calling each other every name under the sun.

I told him, "You've become Axl Rose! You've become everything you set out to be against!" He was arguing he wasn't like that. The look in Kurt's eyes said he was probably gonna punch me. I'm thinking, Shit, that guy's got his camera. And the photographer kept looking over at me. He was far enough away not to know we were arguing. There was a journalist nearby, too. We're in the middle of Central Park, and I'm thinking, God, can you imagine if this ends up being in the press: ROCK STAR AND PUBLICIST IN PUNCH-UP? Oh, God, this is gonna be really embarrassing. So I just walked away.

And then that evening backstage, I walked into a dressing room, and we sat down and talked and Kurt gave me a hug and kiss and apologized, and I apologized for saying what I said. Nirvana went from one extreme to the other within a few hours. That evening they played one of the greatest shows I've ever seen.

COURTNEY LOVE I put Pat Smear into Nirvana because Kurt needed someone to make him happy, and no one in that band did. We thought of putting Dylan [Carlson] in, but it was just like, "You'll be dead in a month," which Kurt heartily agreed with. I'm like, "I know someone. He's really fucking funny. I'm not gonna say he's the greatest guitar player in the world, but my God, he will make you laugh."

DAVE MARKEY Kurt was looking for a second guitarist. Pat was working at the SST Superstore on Sunset. The reason why there was an SST Superstore on Sunset in '93 was because suddenly the label was selling millions of records. Directly related to Nirvana's success. Pat, ironically enough, was working for minimum wage at the counter there. He'd recently turned down a position in the Red Hot Chili Peppers. He had a chance at being in a huge band, but because he wasn't a fan, said no. I think that really impressed Kurt, and Kurt invited him to be in Nirvana.

CRAIG MONTGOMERY I didn't do the last *In Utero* tour. I got fired after the second *SNL*. I think that *SNL* taping was the first time I saw Pat play with them. Pat had a lot of credibility because he had been in the Germs, and I think Kurt really just liked having a new personality around.

Technically, I thought the *SNL* show went fine, but then we get back to Seattle and there's a meeting at the rehearsal space and Kurt asks me, "What happened at *Saturday Night Live*?" And I'm like, "What do you mean?" And he says, "People said it sounded bad on TV." And I'm like, "It sounded fine in the control room." Then after I saw a recording of the broadcast, I figured out what he was talking about. What sounded like crap was the way the band played. They had Pat Smear playing second guitar, and like what I was saying about Jason Everman before, what's coming out of his amp is just noise. I don't know what the guy was playing. And if you listen to that, Kurt's guitar is on one side and that sounds like Nirvana, and Pat Smear is on the other side, and it sounds like a random jet taking off. *(Laughs.)* So maybe that's what somebody thought sounded bad, I don't know.

Then I get called into an office by Alex MacLeod, the tour manager, saying I'm not gonna mix the tour.

MARK ARM We did this leg on the first part of the *In Utero* tour. This is our first foray into the arena world, and we're like, Okay, it's our old buddies Nirvana, this will be great.

They're having a dry tour because they're trying to keep Kurt from drinking. But that's not even his problem. He's still doing pills, like massive amounts of pills, and he's just out of his fuckin' head. So they're not letting Dave and Krist drink beer. We got beer in our room on our rider, so those guys would come into our room and drink beer. And in Chicago, we had a bunch of friends backstage, and the beer ran out really quickly. One of our friends goes into catering and grabs a case of beer and brings it back. Catering complains that a case of beer got stolen which sets off this fucking incredible kerfuffle, with their tour manager, Alex MacLeod, calling back to John Silva in L.A., back and forth about the beer, and they're fuckin' pissed off at us. They have to pay for this extra case of beer, which could be how much, 20 bucks or something?

MATT LUKIN Touring with Nirvana was a downer. They were really bummed that they were even there, it seemed like. Kurt was busy, I was busy. Sometimes we'd be in the same room, but we didn't actually hang out very often. Same with Krist. We would hang out a bit, but it wasn't, Hey, old brothers from Aberdeen hanging out! It was more like, they had their shit, we had our shit.

MARK ARM Kurt and I were on the bus between Davenport, Iowa, and Chicago, and Kurt said something like, "I don't know how you do it." At this point, I wasn't doing drugs at all. The one thing I think that really helped me out in terms of stopping was that we went on tour an awful lot, so I was used to quitting, I was used to getting dope sick. I chipped until the summer of '93, at which point I started going out with Emily—who has put up with me ever since—and she asked me if I was ever going to do heroin again. I was all wishy-washy: "*Well . . .* you never know what the future holds." She said, "If you ever do it again, I'm outta here." I was like, "Oh, okay." That was enough of a push for me to finally walk away from that shit.

Kurt was just fuckin' loaded on pills, and I said something like, "You just gotta want to do it bad enough." What I regret not saying is, "You need to dump your junkie wife, because you're not going to be able to do this while you're in a partnership with someone who's also an enthusiast."

ALEX COLETTI Nirvana had agreed to do *Unplugged,* and the first meeting where I give the spiel about what I allow, what I don't allow, was after their show somewhere outside of Boston. When the show was over, we went back into the band room. I was sat next to Kurt. I said, "I just wanted to talk about the show real quick." I had just brought some set drawings and I showed it to him. He had asked for stargazer lilies. He said, "I want more, I want more."

I said, "What's the vibe you're goin' for?"

He said, "You know, like a funeral." But it wasn't like, *bummm,* heavy music plays and foreshadowing.

AMY FINNERTY The day of the *Unplugged* show, they were all nervous. I went to Kurt's hotel before the show and he told me that he felt nervous and uncomfortable with the idea that people had to sit down the whole time and I said, "What would make you feel more comfortable?" He said, "I'd really like to meet some of the kids first." So I bring him to the venue and he came into the studio where we were shooting and went around and he met the kids and hugged them before the performance, which was really sweet.

ALEX COLETTI Word had trickled down beforehand that they're gonna bring guests, and I think that, in our naiveté and my missing the point, it was like, "Oh, he's gonna bring Eddie Vedder out 'cause they're all grunge buddies and they hang out at that one bar in Seattle and it's gonna be great!" It's like, "No. We're bringin' the Meat Puppets." Oh great, I smell ratings! But that was never the point of it, so you trust the artist.

AARON STAUFFER I was in New York, and I got on the list for the *Unplugged* taping. Before the show, I ran into Dave and I told him, "I came to see you guys play." And he kind of gave this face and groaned: "It's not going to be good." It hadn't been good in rehearsal. I was like, "I saw Bob Dylan this week unplugged, so hopefully you guys can live up to that." And he totally gave this look of horror, just like, That is *never* going to happen. But it turned out to be an amazing performance. It brought tears to my eyes.

AMY FINNERTY Everybody there was completely aware that we were witnessing history. I mean there was something about the coolness in the air of the studio, and the set was beautiful, and you could feel the anticipation and excitement not only from the crowd but from the band, as well. Every time they finished a song, you could kind of see this sense of relief on their faces.

ALEX COLETTI They closed with Leadbelly's "Where Did You Sleep Last Night?," and the ending is possibly the most memorable moment in *Unplugged* history. Kurt screams out the final "shiver" with that battery-acid voice, then makes a rubbery, hillbilly-ish face for "the whole." Pauses, takes a breath, stares right into the camera, and hits that final "night through."

AARON STAUFFER And here's the tragedy of that show: The minute the last note finished ringing out, all the record company suits jump on Kurt like fuckin' flies on shit. I couldn't hear them, but I knew what they were saying: "Is this okay? Are we going to do another song?" And my heart just sank for the guy. He's just put on one of the best performances I've ever seen—and I've been to thousands of rock shows—and now he has to deal with these fuckin' leeches making sure that they don't need to shoot some more, because their mouths are so wrapped around MTV's cock.

ALEX COLETTI At the end, I asked them, "Is there anything else you wanna try? We don't have to use it." I didn't even dare suggest "Teen Spirit." And Krist and Dave were kinda brainstorming, and Kurt just looked at me and said, "How do I top that last song?" I remember reaching to my headset and going, "That's a wrap. We're done."

AMY FINNERTY At the end of it, we went back to the hotel, and Kurt said to me, "I didn't do very good." I said, "What are you talking about? That was a historical moment, that was a really incredible performance. Why do you feel like you didn't do very good?"

He said, "Because everybody was so quiet, nobody really clapped that loud and they just kind of sat there." I said something to the effect of, "People felt like they were seeing Jesus Christ for the first time. It was intense for people. They were trying to be respectful by being quiet and just letting you do your thing." And then he kind of got a little smirk on his face and said, "Thank you."

ALICE WHEELER I was with Kurt one time at this show, *MTV's Live & Loud,* and all these record people were around. Their eyes looked different—they had this coldness, like they're out to take advantage of you.

TOM HANSEN Right before the *Live & Loud* show in Seattle, I sold to Kurt and Dylan. We were in my Camaro, under the Alaskan Way Viaduct. We had a conversation in the car where Kurt said he was disgusted with the rock-star treatment he had gotten when he came to New York for the *Saturday Night Live* thing. He just went on a bit of a rant, if I remember correctly. The only verbatim thing that I remember was, "Those fuckers in New York, man."

COURTNEY LOVE Dylan and Lanegan were pretty much the only friends Kurt had. He really didn't have any friends. He liked the dealers, which was gross. He liked being isolated.

I have this thing, me and my manager call it the Rocket. It's what happened to Kurt, it's what happened to me. It's what happened to Eminem. It's what happened to Britney Spears. Instead of just going up in steps—you're an apprentice with a mentor, you learn your craft, you go up to the next level and the next level—you disappear into the Rocket. You have to fight centrifugal force. *Who's our friend? Who's not our friend? Who do we fire? What do we do? What's gross? What's not?*

CHARLES PETERSON Courtney and I had exchanged phone numbers at one point. She actually wanted me to go hang out with Kurt, because he didn't have any friends. It's like, Well, of course, because he's a junkie. It's really hard to hang out with a junkie.

No, unfortunately, it never happened. I went to Frances's one-year birthday party, things like that. But you go over to a junkie's house, and the TV is always on, and every hour or two they're taking extra-long bathroom breaks, there's always people coming and going. Junkies build little junkie worlds.

I'd already been through that with a relationship. Seeing my friends always near death . . . It's tough. Tough. In retrospect, I think, Man, I should've just done it.

SLIM MOON Courtney hated me, she hated Tobi Vail, hated Riot Grrrl, hated Olympia, hated Mary Lou Lord. And I put out Tobi's and Mary Lou Lord's records. One time, Courtney called me at 1 in the morning, and told me, "You're all right, you're all right. You're a Libra. You're just misguided because you've been taken down a bad road by all your awful friends." So she went back and forth; sometimes she claimed not to hate me, but mostly she just hated me by association.

She said, "You should come up and hang out with Kurt and be a good influence." And I said, "Sure," but I think it was just a wasted person saying shit in the middle of the night. I never got any concrete invites to come hang out.

MARK DEUTROM I was playing with the Melvins on the *In Utero* tour. There was a cocooned environment going on with Nirvana. For people who had come from the same small town and apparently had known each other super-well—with Kurt having this whole "I love you guys" thing—there was surprisingly little love expressed. Really, Rush were more friendly when we played a few dates with them. Trent Reznor was more friendly. Gene Simmons was the weird uncle, there every day in our dressing room going, "What can I do for you guys?"

I'm sure stories abound about the legendary last show. At the sound check, Kurt was throwing his guitar and saying, "This is our last fuckin' show." There was a catering area in this venue, and a bunch of phones. Everybody got to sit in the catering area and listen to Kurt on the phone, screaming every expletive in the book at Courtney.

BUZZ OSBORNE The last conversation I had with Kurt was in Munich, after he had the screaming match with his wife. I had told him this before and I basically reiterated, "I think that what you should do is give her everything, and run as if your very life depends on it. Sign everything over to her from this moment on and just be gone. And if you need money, just go out and do a fucking solo tour, play acoustic guitar, you'll be fine." He felt like he was trapped. He was embarrassed by her. He wanted to divorce her. He wanted to get out of it. But he was too much of a mess to get out of it.

Right when they were walking onstage, he said, "I should just be doing this solo." And that was it. I never talked to him again. They canceled the rest of the tour.

DALE CROVER Kurt said he was canceling the rest of the shows because he had laryngitis. While we're still in Europe, they're reporting that Kurt Cobain ODs. Accidental overdose. Took a bunch of pills.

COURTNEY LOVE Kurt had gone all out out for me when I got [to Rome]. He'd gotten me roses. He'd gotten a piece of the Colosseum . . . I had some champagne, took a Valium, we made out, I fell asleep. The rejection he must have felt after all that anticipation . . .

I turned over about 3 or 4 in the morning to make love, and he was gone. He was at the end of the bed with a thousand dollars in his pocket and a note saying, "You don't love me anymore. I'd rather die than go through a divorce." It was all in his head. I'd been away from him during our relationship maybe 60 days. Ever. I needed to be on tour. I had to do my thing.

I can see how it happened. He took 50 fucking pills. He probably forgot how many he took. But there was a definite suicidal urge, to be gobbling and gobbling and gobbling. Goddamn, man. Even if I wasn't in the mood, I should have just laid there for him. All he needed was to get laid. He would have been fine.

DAVE GROHL [Someone] called and said he'd passed in Rome, and I fucking freaked out. I just lost my mind and started wailing. As disconnected as our relationship had become, you just can't imagine real tragedy in your life. Twenty minutes later someone called me and said, "Actually, no, he's not dead, he's awake." How weird. That could have been the happiest moment of my life. When he came home, I talked to him on the phone. We tried to avoid the subject—we were talking about buying minibikes or something, and I told him, "Look, man, I was really scared." He said, "I know. I'm really sorry. It was just an accident." I was trying to reach out to him and tell him that I really cared about him, but it wasn't enough.

DALE CROVER But the shows were getting rebooked. They were advertising it on TV over there! On MTV! We even saw posters about them being rebooked. And we're just thinking, That's really weird. Those shows are already getting rebooked after this guy basically tried to kill himself. What the fuck's going on?

ANTON BROOKES Taking an overdose is a pretty big cry for help, so everyone did what they could to help. Everybody. There's no one in the Nirvana camp with blood on their hands. No one whatsoever.

COURTNEY LOVE It's only known to the inner circle that Kurt's first suicide attempt with a note was in December of '93. It was at home, around Christmas. I did all that shit you do, like CPR, like punching, poking, cold water. He wrote a big note, it was like a few diary pages, a list of reasons why he shouldn't be alive and blah blah blah and how he could never stop doing heroin. It's like, It's the fuckin' '90s. The '90s are going to be gone. Keith Richards does dope or did it for as long as . . . Whatever, it's your lifestyle.

The inner circle? Janet knew about it, Rosemary knew about it, Danny knew about it, David Geffen knew about it.

SUSAN SILVER Courtney and I had touched base several weeks before Kurt died, after there was an incident. She had reached out and said, "You have to help, you have to help, he's gonna kill himself." So I hooked them up with a person that we'd been dealing with, with Layne for intervention. They ended up not using him. They did do an intervention, but it didn't go particularly well.

COURTNEY LOVE Before that last intervention, Kurt dropped the kid. He dropped Frances. Not on her head. He didn't drop her from a great height; he stumbled, he fell, he was too high to be holding the kid, and you don't do that. And I was like, "That's fuckin' it! You can't drop the kid, you don't drop my baby!" I was just fucking outraged.

The great thing about our relationship is that we wouldn't fight at all. We would have eruptions. We had three physical altercations. Around that time, he dragged me by my hair, dragged my cheek on the gravel. He's stronger than me, and I'm strong. He was a tough fucker.

DANNY GOLDBERG Courtney had called and asked for some of us to do another intervention, saying that she felt Kurt was out of control. I was at Atlantic Records and living in New York at the time, so I flew to Seattle with Janet. She found some guy, a big Paul Bunyan kind of guy with a beard, and I think Silva came up and I forget who else was there. Kurt's thing was "Courtney is more fucked up than I am. She should go into rehab, too." "That's not a great excuse for you being fucked up. You can't solve these problems with the way you're fucked up." You know, a regular intervention-type thing.

I wanted to get back to L.A. because I have two kids there and had been away from them. Maybe I should have taken a later plane—I could have had a personal conversation with Kurt. When I did get home, I talked to him on the phone and he was kind of depressed. I put my daughter on the phone—Kurt liked kids a lot—and they talked for a minute. And that was the last I ever spoke to him. I don't know what we could have done, if anything, that would have changed his decision to kill himself, but I'll never stop wondering.

JANET BILLIG The last intervention was bad. It just went on for hours and hours and hours. It was inside, and then it was outside, at the Lake Washington Boulevard house. Everyone said their piece. I can't remember everyone who was there—Silva and Danny and Rosemary, and I think Dylan, Cali DeWitt. We were trying to get them both into rehab. Courtney went to rehab, and Kurt went, too.

JENNIFER FINCH I saw Kurt at Exodus. Just getting him in there and visiting him. He was very disturbed. Very upset. By the way, he never jumped over a fence. Exodus has a no-locked-door policy. You can leave. He chose to leave, and Courtney did her best to try to get someone to find him, cut off all his credit cards.

MARCO COLLINS In '98, I ended up going to rehab at Exodus, the same place in Los Angeles that Kurt went to. There was a little courtyard there where people go out to smoke, where he jumped over the wall to escape. It was a horrible situation, but it's somewhat humorous that Kurt jumped the fuckin' wall instead of just walking around to the exit. The counselors there laughed about it well after the fact. They were like, "All he had to do is walk around to the side door to leave. We're not jail." It was very punk rock of him to escape rehab.

MARK ARM It seemed like something intense was happening in the couple weeks before Kurt's death. Bob Whittaker was hanging out with Krist Novoselic an awful lot, and they would go on these hikes up at Tiger Mountain and they would have these conversations, and then Bob would relay the gist of things to me. He was like, "Maybe you should go talk to Kurt."

And then we went on tour with Pearl Jam. Went from that Nirvana tour, where it didn't seem like people trusted each other and no one was having a good time, to this Pearl Jam tour where the band had circled their wagons and was trying to take care of each other and trying to keep levelheaded about things. The atmosphere was completely different than the Nirvana tour. They went out of their way to hire good people.

CHRIS CORNELL I think Pearl Jam was the band that set the perfect example. Their big video, "Jeremy," propelled them into becoming TV stars and one of the biggest rock bands on the planet, so they stopped making videos, which was proof positive that that wasn't where they wanted to be. And that made a lot of sense to me.

Nirvana doing an *Unplugged* at the time that they did it and making a video for "Heart-Shaped Box," that didn't make a lot of sense to me, because it seemed clear to me that Kurt was pretty disillusioned by the situation that he was being put in. It felt like, If he's so unhappy, he shouldn't be doing this kind of stuff.

MARK ARM I was thinking, I'm going to come back and try to talk to Kurt if I can. I don't think I could have done anything, though. I didn't realize things were at such a severe point for him.

DUFF MCKAGAN I was flying from L.A. up to Seattle, to home. And I get on the plane and Kurt gets on the plane and sits next to me, and we took off and he and I started talking. He told me, "I just took off from Exodus." We talked, y'know, we were drinking. . . . We got to Seattle, we went to baggage claim, and he was pretty down. And a friend of mine, this guy Eddie, met me at baggage claim in Seattle. Kurt and Eddie went out to have a smoke, and my friend Eddie came back in. I said, "Hey, man, maybe we should take him over to the house to-night." . . . So Eddie went back out to get Kurt, and right at that mo-ment his car had picked him up. And he was gone.

LARRY REID I didn't know Kurt real well. The last conversation of any substance I had with him was backstage at this show they played at the Seattle Center Coliseum, in September 1992. His baby was like two months old. Someone brought up Jesse Bernstein. I was really closely associated with Bernstein, who was sort of the poet laureate of the grunge scene. He was this second-generation Beat poet who was really engaging and just crazy as the day is long. He'd killed himself the year before by slitting his own throat.

Kurt said something like, "That's the way I wanna go: Live fast, die young," or words to that effect. I'm paraphrasing. And I just started yelling at him. I think he must've used the word *romantic,* because I remember saying, "There's nothing romantic about it at all!" Then I said, "Yeah, you die and it's fine, but you leave nothing but hard feelings. You've got this beautiful young baby, and you've got a lunatic wife . . ."

He just sort of sheepishly wandered off.

CHAPTER 40
SITTING IN THE RUBBLE

STEPHANIE DORGAN I was so pregnant, I was just taking naps all the time, and I just feel like I heard that gunshot. I don't want to be dramatic—I'm not sure—but it's a really pretty quiet neighborhood and you hear something but you just never put it into context. It would have been in the afternoon a couple of days before they found him. His house was not very far; we were up back behind them. It was totally possible. Again, I don't know. Memory and imagination are next to each other in our brains. That's a fact.

VAN CONNER I was good friends with Dylan Carlson. Him and Mark had been lookin' for Kurt for days. Some P.I. guy had started callin'. Courtney had taken off because of that intervention shit. I ended up driving Mark and Dylan around on-and-off for a couple of days. We went to all these different locations, mostly around the U District. We went everywhere but Kurt's house, which was where he was, it turned out.

AMY FINNERTY I was at work at MTV. The girl who worked there who was responsible for answering the fan phone line said somebody just called and said, "A body has been found at Kurt Cobain's house." I was hoping and praying that it wasn't him, but when someone says, "There's a body there," what do you think, right?

ALICE WHEELER At first, nobody knew it was Kurt. We all thought it was Dylan. I don't know why, because now it seems like there were more warning signs for Kurt. A friend of a friend was on police ride-along in the neighborhood where Kurt lived—I think it was a couple of days before he went to rehab—and they went to his house because Courtney had called. Kurt had locked himself in the bedroom with a shotgun or something. And Dylan was the one who had bought him the shotgun.

DYLAN CARLSON (Earth singer/guitarist) We used to go shooting together. He said he wanted the gun for protection. He had the cash. . . . He insisted on me buying him the gun.

BOB WHITTAKER I was in Seattle, and my friend David called me in the morning, saying, "Is it true?" I said, "What?" He goes, "They're saying on the radio that Kurt's dead." I said, "Oh, my God, I don't doubt it."

I hung up the phone and the next call was from Nik Hartshorne, who was the King County coroner. Nik had been doing all the wrongful deaths in Seattle. We had a lot of mutual friends, and he used to go to shows all the time. We'd had drinks recently, and he asked, "How's Kurt doing?" I said, "Not very good. I wouldn't be surprised if he paid you a visit soon." This was three days before they found him.

When I talked with Nik on the phone I said, "Jesus, I just heard. Are you getting stuck with the autopsy?" And he said, "I just got done." And then he said, "I wish we wouldn't have had that conversation the other day."

KURT LODER (MTV News live broadcast, April 8, 1994) Hi, I'm Kurt Loder with an MTV News special report on a very sad day. Kurt Cobain, the leader of one of rock's most gifted and promising bands, Nirvana, is dead. . . . Cobain's body was found in a house in Seattle on Friday morning. He was dead of an apparently self-inflicted shotgun blast to the head. Police found what is said to be a suicide note at the scene, but have not yet divulged its contents. Cobain, who was 27, had reportedly been missing for about six days, according to his mother.

NILS BERNSTEIN The day Kurt's body was found was horrible. It was total media insanity right off. But in a way, having to deal with the logistics of this media onslaught made it so no one had to just stand around and bum out. There were news crews who somehow got up to the roof deck around the penthouse and then tried to get up to the next level, literally scaling the walls of this building, so they could film inside the Sub Pop office. They were trying to shoot us, as if . . . what would we have been doing? The next day there was a TV reporter and camera person hiding in the bushes at my home.

When you live it and then you see how it's covered, you're like, Wow, that's not accurate, or Oh, the feeling of this was different from how they portrayed it. It makes you wonder, was the Civil War really like people say it was, or is the way we think about it the way that five people who were never part of it to begin with said it was? Was it told by guys who just wanted to be cool 'cause they felt like pussies for not going? It makes you question history.

KERRI HARROP That morning, we had to make the decision: Should we open the Sub Pop Mega Mart? "Okay, yeah, I'll go over and I'll open the store." So around 11, I went over across the street to the store, and already there were people waiting outside, which was something that never, ever happened. Ten people followed me into the store, which automatically packed the place.

And the first guy in, some twentysomething, asks, "Do you have any Nirvana vinyl?" I was so sickened at the thought, and I looked at him and said, "No, we don't." Which we did. You know what, if you didn't have *Bleach* on vinyl by now, why the fuck do you need it now? It was so gross to me.

Within like 10 minutes, the store is a madhouse, and by now there's two or three local news teams there, they want to do interviews. If you're looking for some dramatic reaction for your 5 o'clock news bite, I'm not gonna give it to you. So I called Jonathan: "Jon, it's crazy over here, what should I do?" And he's like, "Close the store."

JANET BILLIG I'd had a skiing accident and I'd just had a second surgery on my knee in New York. My friend Theo showed up. It was ironic that I was so doped up on drugs, I don't remember finding out that Kurt had died. Theo is screaming at the doctor, "You gotta sign her out!" and he's like, "I can't." Theo, who's a big tattoo guy, is like, "I'm taking her!"

AMY FINNERTY So I went to the hospital to get Janet. I was supposed to go pick her up and take her home, and I'm racing all over the place searching for her. I finally find some nurse and I say, "I'm searching for Janet Billig, where is she?" She said, "She just walked out the front door and got into a cab."

I took a cab to her apartment and I walked in and there's poor Janet, straight out of surgery, half out of it, and she said, "Come and sit down." I sat down and I said, "I have to tell you something," because I wasn't sure she'd heard anything. And she said, "Kurt's dead." I said, "Are you sure? Are you sure?" That sort of denial. She said, "I'm sure. Kurt's dead. We have to go to Seattle." We got on the next plane.

KURT LODER We must have gone on the air very quickly. Amy Finnerty was there. She was in tears, and Dave Grohl called; I talked to him briefly off-air. Going live is very expensive, but you had to for this band. I've heard over the years, "That was the first time I heard about it." It's remarkable that television would be the first place you would hear about something, because it took television so much longer to get up and running than it did for radio to do the same. When people say it was the first place they heard the news, I don't know how to feel about that. I don't have any feelings about that.

CHARLES R. CROSS It was a complete onslaught. There were TV reporters stopping by *The Rocket* office. It was like the Lindsay Lohan paparazzi situation that you might see now, but multiplied by having Tabitha Soren outside the building.

There was one point where the receptionist said, "Larry King's producer is on line three," and I'm just so exhausted, I don't want to deal with it, and I go to pick the phone up to tell them I can't talk to them, and instead I'm on the radio live with Larry King. There's Larry King's booming voice: "TELL ME, WHAT IS GRUNGE MUSIC?"

BRYN BRIDENTHAL I just jumped in, with Jim Merlis and Dennis Dennehy, and we handled it. We were the center that the media came to. I don't think that I even looked up or peed or had a drink or anything until about 11 that night.

The first thing I did when I got back to my hotel room was call Axl, because I was afraid of how the news might impact him. He was such an emotional roller coaster, I was afraid that Axl would hurt himself. He felt things really deeply, and he felt a real connection there, even though there was no connection from the other side. I think he had a lot of empathy for Kurt.

I was on the phone with Axl until about 3 in the morning. Ultimately, it was okay, but I don't remember what was said because I'd had so many hours and hours of those kinds of conversations with him. One time, I got off the phone with him and my teeth were chattering and I felt like I was energy inside his head. We were just talking on a level that wasn't in the here and now, that was just pure energy—an out-of-body experience, except that my body acts like it's freezing or something. It was just so intense.

KURT DANIELSON We were opening for Soundgarden in Paris. And then I heard this rumor—word was going around that Kurt had tried to kill himself or had killed himself. Nobody knew if it was a repeat of what had happened in Rome or if this was the real thing. So I called my sister, who's married to Van Conner. Van wasn't able to confirm right away, but he called back and did confirm the news.

KIM THAYIL We were onstage. I go to the side of the stage, grab a beer or whatever, change my guitar, sit down for a bit, towel off—maybe it's a drum solo—and Gary from TAD goes, "Hey, they found a body at Kurt's house. It hasn't been identified yet, but the rumor is that they think it could be Kurt." I thought, It's okay, it's not Kurt. It sounds terrible, but it must have been some weird drug incident, somebody else maybe OD'd at Kurt's house. I told myself that.

So I'm playing the next song, and all of sudden I just felt that chill, I just felt the blood and warmth go out of me. It's an empty feeling that I'm talking about. It was entirely a visceral experience. For some reason, at that point I knew, in spite of my hopefulness, that he was dead.

BEN SHEPHERD And we were all playing the encore, we're all rocking out—me and Chris were particularly having fun together that show. Looked around at the crew, everyone around's kind of dour and worried-looking. And they make this corridor for us to walk through to go to the dressing room, and it's like, instantaneously, they shut the door behind us and everyone was there. The guys from TAD and the rest of the crew and stuff. Kurt Danielson told us. Chris turned to me and said, "I'm sorry," and then he started crying and held me. I was just in shock.

JOSH SINDER We'd just got done doing an interview for a TV show. We were laughing and having a really good time, and then we went back to the club. Tad had his own camera rolling when we found out backstage. The camera is on Kurt Danielson's face and he says, "They just found Kurt's body . . ." On the tape, the camera just points to the ground. And everyone's real silent for a second.

KIM THAYIL I've never seen so many big, hairy, usually rowdy guys in tears and crumbling.

BEN SHEPHERD The thing for Soundgarden was every time there was some personal gain, it was always balanced out by something really dark. We were in Europe when we found out that *Superunknown* was number one in America. Then Kurt dies.

SUSAN SILVER I wasn't with Soundgarden. The guys found out after they got offstage. And the tour manager said they were beside themselves: "They're freaking out, they're destroying the dressing room!" And I said, "Just let 'em go, man."

KURT DANIELSON No, no. I told everybody *before* the show, because we all knew about it when we were onstage. I felt it was necessary that these guys find out from the right person at the right time. And actually, it made for a better show, because we were able to dedicate it to Kurt, and I thought that was important.

I've got severe back problems—I've crushed two vertebrae just thrashing around so much onstage—and my back had gone out on me that day. I remember being onstage in Paris, in all this pain, and I knew that Kurt had killed himself, and I felt like somehow that all this pain I was experiencing was putting me in a place where I could understand him somehow. Of course, I was drinking a lot, just to try to kill the pain, which didn't work at all.

I remember being in a trance and feeling like I was totally detached, like having an astral-projection experience. I suddenly found myself above the stage, watching myself onstage, being above the crowd and kind of floating around up there. And somehow I felt a unity with Kurt. It's really hard to describe—I've never really tried to describe it before. I felt like Kurt was there somehow.

JASON EVERMAN I was in basic training, and one of my drill sergeants came into the barracks at 6 in the morning, standard basic-training bullshit: get down, do push-ups. So everyone in the bay is doing push-ups, the drill sergeant is walking around yelling at everybody. Then he goes, "Yesterday, the singer for Nirvana blew his head off." As he said that, he looked right at me. And he didn't know who I was—I tried to keep that under wraps, because all of the sudden it's not Jason, it's, "Oh, that guy, he used to play with Nirvana."

I don't know why the drill sergeant looked at me. It was kind of interesting. The news didn't surprise me, though. I think anyone with intelligence has grappled with suicide. I was dealing with other stuff at the time—basic training, being a jackass—but I was a little sad. But it's not like I had a lot of time to dwell on it.

DALE CROVER We got off the plane from London in New York, and the first thing our road manager tells us when he met us was, "Kurt Cobain just killed himself." It wasn't a surprise, because he had already OD'd recently.

In London, we'd done some demos for *Stoner Witch*, and we were doing a record—a bunch of weird stuff—at the same time. We were going to call the record *Kurt Cobain*. Yeah, in big letters: *KURT COBAIN*. And in small letters, underneath: Melvins. A big joke. If he hadn't died, we probably would've named it that, and Kurt probably would've been okay with it, too. But after he died, we were just like, "People will think it's some tribute thing." That one ended up being called *Prick*, but not because of him, just because we liked the title.

MARK DEUTROM Our tour manager goes, "Do you want me to send some flowers? What do you want me to do?" Buzz just barked at her:

"I'm not going to send any fuckin' flowers! We're going to play a show." She asked if we wanted to cancel the show, and he just kind of laughed at her like, Man, you don't get it. We're going to play a show. That's how we do it. I think it was Buzz channeling his rage. What better way to salute somebody than doing the most life-affirming thing possible, which is playing?

BUZZ OSBORNE I could believe it, but I couldn't believe it. Whenever you're dealing with people in your life that are junkies, their death never surprises you—you're always pretty much preparing for it. It fucking blows, you know? We had a show that night, and we played it anyway. I wasn't about to stop my life as a result of that stuff. The best thing I can do is be a living example of how that stuff doesn't work.

GRANT ALDEN My girlfriend at the time and I had a vacation planned on the Olympic Peninsula the next day. When we drove through Aberdeen, there was no sign that Kurt Cobain had lived or died. I still think that those church billboards should have said something. There should have been a kind word for that family, and there was nothing. Why not? Well, what they say out here is, "He got above his raising." He was white trash, he got to be a star; he moved away and then he did drugs and he died. They didn't approve of him alive, they didn't approve of him dead.

KRIST NOVOSELIC We were these young people from southwest Washington, ill-equipped. We didn't have the emotional support and the experience at all to deal with this. And we were just whisked away— whisked, whisked up into it, and it went up and up and up and up, like the spaceship *Challenger*. And then it exploded. It's like, Dave and I landed, right? But Kurt didn't.

DAVE GROHL There are some people that you meet in life that you just kinda know they're not gonna live to be a hundred years old. In some ways, I think you kind of prepare yourself emotionally for that to be a reality. It was a terrible surprise. Everybody was totally surprised. And even as much as you prepare yourself for something like that to happen, it doesn't make it easier. It was probably the worst thing that's ever happened to me in my life. I remember the day after that I woke up and I was heartbroken that he was gone. And I just felt like, Okay, so I get to wake up today and have another day, and he doesn't.

* * *

KURT COBAIN (from his suicide note) Thank you all from the pit of my burning, nauseous stomach for your letters and concern during the past years. I'm too much of an erratic, moody baby! I don't have the passion anymore, and so remember, it's better to burn out than to fade away.

KELLY CURTIS I was in D.C. when I heard the news. Neil Young called me, looking for Eddie. He was very upset that someone killed themselves and left a suicide note using the lyrics he had written. He said he didn't mean them in the way Kurt interpreted them. I don't know who he found out from, but he knew about it. It could have come from Courtney. I called Stone and told him to go tell Eddie before he heard it on the news.

EDDIE VEDDER When I first found out, I was in a hotel room in Washington, D.C., and I just tore the place to shreds. Then I just kind of sat in the rubble, which somehow felt right . . . like my world at the moment.

MARK ARM I don't think we said anything at the show that night. We're not very good at grand gestures. It was hard enough just trying to keep our shit together and do the show. The funny thing I remember was reading a review of that show the next day where it talked about how Pearl Jam had lit all these candles onstage in memory of Kurt Cobain. But the previous night they'd had the same candles onstage.

KELLY CURTIS The next day, we went to the White House. The band, minus Dave Abbruzzese, and me and a guy named John Hoyt, who got us into the White House. That was weird.

JOHN HOYT (political and community advisor for Pearl Jam; Pyramid Communications partner) We'd been trying to figure out alternative tour locations. The Clinton administration was looking at a series of base closures, and we thought that if we could do concerts at some of those venues and give some money back to the community that was struggling because of a base closure, that might be of interest. So we ended up setting up a meeting with George Stephanopoulos and some people at the White House.

MARK ARM As a courtesy, Pearl Jam were like, "Yeah, these guys can go along." Me, Matt, and Dan smoked some pot before going. Matt still had a roach with him and the guy who was driving the shuttle bus to the White House started telling some story about how the Secret Service will go through all your shit and how some woman got arrested for having nail clippers or something like that. And I watched Matt's face as the thought process was going on . . .

MATT LUKIN I had another joint that I was going to smoke on the way, but all of the sudden, I realize, We're on our way straight to the fuckin' White House. I got no time to light this thing up. So I ate it. I'm chewing on this fucking joint, and it's all dry. After I'm already really stoned anyway.

MARK ARM [Director of the White House Office of Personnel Security] Craig Livingstone—he popped up in the news later when he got canned for something—was the one who welcomed both bands. And then Pearl Jam went on to meet Clinton. We were hoping to meet him, but I think we knew ahead of time that we weren't going to get the full deal.

MATT LUKIN We got a behind-the-velvet-rope tour. Then some kid recognized us as Mudhoney and asked us for an autograph. So, sure, we gave him an autograph, and as soon as that went down, people just started pouring in, thinking we were Pearl Jam. We're like, "No, no, no, you don't know who we are. You don't want our autograph." And they're like, "No, no, you're Pearl Jam."

DAN PETERS I'm sure once they get home and realize that some guy named Dan Peters signed their piece of paper, they were like, "Who the fuck was that?"

MARK ARM Craig Livingstone told us, "Yeah, we all know how you feel. We lost a good friend here, too"—referring to Vince Foster. It seemed like a really weird thing to say, and kind of insincere.

JOHN HOYT Meeting the president was an add-on. We sat talking to Stephanopoulos, and then Clinton's secretary came in and said, "Would you guys all take a moment to see the president?" There was some concern about a possible copycat effect with Cobain.

NILS BERNSTEIN After Kurt died, a Clinton advisor or someone, I don't remember who the person was, called me, saying, "Clinton's gonna have to address this. Can you give us advice on what might resonate with people that this is meaningful for—what he might talk about or not talk about?"

JOHN HOYT We went into his outer room and hung out for a little bit, and then Clinton came out in his Arkansas sweats. We all went into the Oval Office and did a group photo, and he said that Chelsea really wanted to go to the Pearl Jam concert, but Hillary thought better of it—Chelsea was still pretty young. At the end of it, they asked us to get people out of the room and everyone left so Ed and the president could talk. When Ed left, he turned, and I remember him saying, "See ya, Bill."

KELLY CURTIS We got summoned into the Oval Office, and Clinton asked Eddie if he should address the nation. Eddie said, "I don't think you should address the nation." They didn't know if there were gonna be a bunch of copycat suicides. Eddie thought it was a mistake, and it would draw attention to it.

*   *   *

KERRI HARROP That morning I'd gotten to the Sub Pop office early to finish up this fanzine I was making as our sixth-anniversary party favor. It was six or eight pages, photocopied, and supposed to be this fun little activity book. And the center spread was this cartoon caricature of Kurt, with these starry, dreamy eyes. I purchased these ratty old blond wigs from some thrift store, and was taping locks into the pages of this thing: "Your very own lucky lock of Kurt Cobain's hair!"

We were going to give out fortune cookies, and Nils and I had come up with all these smart-ass fortunes. Twenty different fortunes, and they all related to bands on the label. But there were two that pertained to Kurt. One specifically was P.U. SMELLS LIKE KURT FARTED. Obviously we have no way of knowing which cookies contained the fortune, so we couldn't use them, either. We had like 10 pounds of fortune cookies, which is a hell of a lot! So we had fortune cookies for weeks after. To this day, I can't eat a fortune cookie and not think of that time.

NILS BERNSTEIN Then we had our Sub Pop sixth anniversary at the Crocodile. It basically turned into a wake and was just really horrible. Velocity Girl played, and they just felt like assholes playing cheery music, and the singer got really drunk and ran offstage and disappeared outside somewhere.

SARAH SHANNON (singer for Washington, D.C., area's Velocity Girl) It was just a really bad night for me. I didn't know Kurt Cobain, but I felt pretty sad about it and got a little too drunk and kind of couldn't perform.

MEGAN JASPER I remember walking in and there were cameras everywhere outside. The people inside were just in shock. Everyone was fucked up, fucked up beyond—like really fucked up. People were numbing themselves.

JEFF GILBERT There was kind of an unspoken thing around town that when national media came through here, nobody says *anything*.

Geraldo Rivera and his camera crew of douche bags showed up at RKCNDY one night after Kurt killed himself. The clubs were still full 'cause everybody was hurting; people just needed to be around each other. So here comes Geraldo and his camera crew. Guy at the door tried to charge him cover, he said, "No, we're with the media," and he just busted through. Geraldo was trying to get some interviews from people, and he comes up to Marty Chandler from Panic, a thrash-metal band, and Marty goes, "Hey, Geraldo, pull my finger!" Everybody basically turned around and walked away from Geraldo. He got out of there really quick.

NILS BERNSTEIN Obviously Kurt's death was a big deal to every young person in Seattle. Which really bothered me. I only wanted to see people that knew him. I didn't want to know what the newscaster had to say, what a kid down the street had to say, what display some record store was putting up about him. And within a couple days, I did a total turnaround. The feelings of everyone who knew Kurt are tied up with their experiences with him or their feelings about Courtney, whatever. It felt like people that didn't know him had a purer appreciation for his life and his music.

SUSAN SILVER I was driving when I got the news about Kurt, and I remember the first feeling that I had was the same feeling that I had when Lennon was shot, where it was this huge physical shock and then this overwhelming sense of compassion and protection towards Yoko, and in this case, towards Courtney, regardless of the antics that I'd observed over the years and the mysterious disdain that she had for me.

A few of us started to talk, and there certainly was a need for a public gathering and a private gathering. It occurred to me that it would be a good idea to have the private service at the same time as the public gathering so that the public didn't try to find the private service. There was a church near downtown Seattle that I'd gone to a few times and I called and said this is what had happened in this community—the reverberations are international, there's a real need for a safe place for a smallish group of people to come together and have a service—and they were really open.

MARCO COLLINS I spoke at the memorial at the Seattle Center. We played a tape from Courtney, and it was intense. At the end, when Kurt's music was coming out of this fountain—the speakers were built in—there was this total chilling fuckin' moment of anarchy, where all these kids, fully clothed, just start diving into this fountain. It was just super-fuckin' beautiful.

ALICE WHEELER I met Danny Goldberg and all those people at the funeral. It was really odd, because there were all these guys in suits at the door and they knew who everyone was. They did not look on a piece of paper to see your name or anything, and I'd never met these people before. And then I realized when I got in that there were so few of the rock crowd there that that's how they knew us. Half of the church was his extended family, and then there was a whole group of all the people from L.A., and then maybe 25 rock people. I was surprised 'cause I thought he was a lot more popular than that. I never really thought I was like his super-great friend or anything, but then after the fact it's like, I guess so few people really connected with him.

LORI BARBERO We were pretty close. When Kurt was in Minneapolis, we hung out a lot. His coat got stolen one night, and I gave him that one sweater that he wore all the time, a greenish, brownish V-neck. When I gave it to him, it had thumb holes 'cause I'd been doing that since I was a little kid. When he put it on and put his thumbs through the holes, I go, "I do that to my sweaters," and he goes, "So do I!" He goes, "I've done it since I was a little kid." I go, "Me, too!" I also gave him the jeans with all the patches on them. It still really upsets me when I see pictures of him wearing the sweater and the jeans.

Courtney's not the most complimentary person, but when I went to Seattle for the memorial, she told me, "Lori, Kurt really loved you. He talked about you all the time." Courtney's usually not like that. Thank you for saying that, you know?

ELIZABETH DAVIS-SIMPSON The thing that I remember most about the funeral was Courtney spoke and she quoted from the Bible from Job, and I was really blown away by her ability to speak so eloquently under duress.

JENNIFER FINCH There was a moment when Courtney was giving her eulogy and Frances was just like, "Mommy, where are you?" It was so sad.

SLIM MOON Danny Goldberg gave the most ill-conceived, offensive speech. I like Danny Goldberg. I don't think he's an evil man. Danny's thing was really offensive because he wanted to talk about what a great guy, what a kindhearted, decent person Kurt was, and so he gave examples of something that Kurt hadn't really wanted to do—that Kurt had really objected to on personal-belief-system grounds—that he had begged and cajoled and gotten Kurt to do. Then he gave another example of something that Kurt hadn't wanted to do, that Kurt felt would violate his personal values, that Danny's wife, Rosemary Carroll, had begged and cajoled until Kurt gave in. And then he gave a third story of Kurt really not wanting to do something. I can't remember what they were, but they were all business decisions that some would call "selling out."

It just cemented a lot of people's belief that if you go into the major-label system and you get a big-time manager and you get a big-time lawyer, they just manipulate the crap out of you and convince you to do all types of things that you don't believe in.

DANNY GOLDBERG Courtney asked me to speak. I was thinking about Courtney and about Kurt's mom and about John Silva; those were the people that were on my mind. Just trying to give some spiritual view of things about what he did while he was here and the immortality of the soul, which I believe in. There's no way you can make people feel good about such a horrible, horrible thing, and there's people that felt that Kurt's success was a betrayal of his punk-rock roots, and that I was one of the collaborators in having him go from being a punk-rock artist to an international celebrity who killed himself. The truth is, if it hadn't been me, he would have picked someone else. Kurt wanted to do that.

I'm glad I was the one to have been able to do it, because I loved him and I loved working with him. I don't believe for a minute that Kurt's ambitions were caused by me. I had a lot of visibility, and when you have that kind of visibility—which can be good for you, and it helped my career in many ways—the flip side is people want to be mad at somebody. I'm one of the visible people they can be mad at.

SUSAN SILVER At the end of the service, I went up to offer my condolences to Courtney, and she saw me coming and just turned her back to me and closed this circle of people she was talking with, so obviously she wasn't interested in any sort of contact. Which is fine—it certainly wasn't a day about our potential friendship.

NILS BERNSTEIN Take what you will from the fact that after Kurt's funeral, two of the people closest to him had separate events for people to gather at. Courtney had a party and Krist had a party—they were wakes, I guess—at the exact same time. Krist and Shelli never got along well with Courtney. You chose which one you were gonna go to. Which did I go to? Both. *(Laughs.)* Courtney's was more family, and more of the label and industry people from out of town. It had a much different vibe from Krist's, which was more friends and musicians.

BOB WHITTAKER I didn't go to the service because of the media and all that stuff. But I went to Novoselic's house after, and Novoselic took me out on the porch and read me the eulogy that he had read. I burst into tears and left.

MARCO COLLINS That night, after the memorial, Courtney was with Kat from Babes in Toyland, and she was loaded as fuck, and I remember my radio station called me and said, "Courtney is downstairs in a limo. She wants to come up and all she's saying on the phone is, 'I want to come up there and make you guys stop playing fucking Pumpkins and play Kurt.'" We had been doing 24-hour Nirvana, and at that point we'd started playing other bands again.

The ratings on something like that would be monster—she wanted to use our station as a place to mourn on the air. She does everything in public, that's for sure. I remember going, "Fuck, no, man. She's gonna say a bunch of shit she'll regret later." I was like, "Just tell her to call me," and she called me, but she was loaded, slurring. There's no fuckin' way I was going to let her go on the air at that point. It would have been a fuckin' crime.

KAT BJELLAND I'd gotten a flight out there to go to the funeral and to hang out with Courtney and support her. In the funeral home, I saw him dead, which was more than disturbing. She made me hold his hand. Isn't that gross? I just sat there, frozen. Paralyzed. It was icky, awful. I never told anybody that before, except my friends. I just feel like gettin' it out of my system because I'm sick of holding secrets.

I had a nervous breakdown right after that, when I got home to Minneapolis.

MATT LUKIN Years later, Courtney started talking a lot of shit about Mudhoney not being at Kurt's funeral. I'm like, Fuck that! We were busy! We were on the other coast! My then-wife was there—I guess I was somewhat represented by her. At one point, Courtney invited each of us to pick a guitar of Kurt's: "Go pick up a piece of Kurt's stuff to remember Kurt by." The only one who took her up on it was Steve Turner.

To me, it was like, I knew Kurt, I got my memories. I don't need her to fucking help me out with that.

MARK ARM Getting a guitar of Kurt's? It would make me feel like a vulture, I guess. I spent about a year putting distance between myself and them, so it seemed like a ruse on Courtney's part somehow. Like she's buying us off or something.

STEVE TURNER I ran into Courtney somewhere and she called me a few times and said she really wanted to give me one of Kurt's guitars, how much Kurt looked up to us and all that kind of stuff. So I went over there and basically took some old, ridiculous guitar that wasn't any guitar he played. Courtney seemed just kind of lost and crazy to me.

I kind of regretted it upon walking into the house. It seemed like total zoo chaos. Kurt's mom was there, they had the baby, obviously, there's nannies that were high on drugs. It was like a drug house, a giant mansion with fuckups wandering about. And the guards and the hangers-on and the people that were still trying to get something out of them—the sharks that were living there. I took some stupid guitar at her insistence, and I've never seen her since.

JOHN LEIGHTON BEEZER I'd heard on the news that Kurt and Courtney's house was next to a place called Viretta Park, which is in a neighborhood that I used to live near. So it struck me as odd that I had never heard of Viretta Park before. A couple of days after the suicide, I was driving past the area and I was curious: What's Viretta Park? I was always a fan of out-of-the-way parks to smoke pot in.

I went to the park to smoke some pot, and there were these kids who were definitely sightseeing. They're like, "Do you know where he lives?" Well, he doesn't *live* there anymore. I knew the area pretty well, so I said, "Yeah, you know, I'll show you."

You could see their house on the other side of this hedge, and their windows were open, and the kids are talking really loud, just like tourists, and I said, "Have some respect, there's a widow and child in there." After a few moments, a security guy came through the hedge and said, "Hey, you guys need to keep it down. We're not asking you to leave or anything, but out of respect for the family, you really should keep it quiet."

A few minutes later, Courtney and Kurt's mom come out. And this was weird—they both struck me as if they were on drugs. Kurt's mom in particular looked really—the word I would use is *beatific*. She seemed very peaceful and okay with everything. She rarely talked.

I came to realize Courtney was just a media whore. Even though she'd just lost her husband to a violent suicide, she liked the fact that there were people coming to see her. She had some stuff, a sweater and a pair of rolled-up socks. Unlike the mother, she looked like she had been crying, she looked distraught. Courtney basically said, "Hey, I've got some stuff of Kurt's, and I guess I won't need it anymore, so if you guys want it you can have it." In retrospect, I should've grabbed the sweater. The guy next to me did, and at that point, I'm thinking, Well, I really don't want the socks. It just seemed disrespectful that she was giving away his clothes. You know, if you had a guitar pick of his, that would be nice—that would seem more appropriate. But, no, I don't want a pair of rolled-up socks that was in his sock drawer when he blew his head off.

Then Courtney sat down next to a tree with the mother, and the kids sat in a ring. Courtney was saying things like, "You know, you guys really need to love each other and just appreciate the people in your lives." What I eventually concluded was that she wanted a huge outpouring of kids in that park, that she wanted some kind of "don't forget Kurt" movement to spring up around their house, and she was chumming the waters, basically: "Oh, yeah, if you go there at night, Courtney comes out and gives you some of his stuff." "Really? Wow! Let's get 100 of our friends and go there and chant Kurt's name and hold candles and talk about how great and beautiful Courtney is."

I mean, it was twisted. I felt like an alien visitor. It was all horribly wrong.

PATTY SCHEMEL Courtney has a reputation of not being a nice person. It depends on the situation, though. She's completely self-absorbed. And all that anger that she has is just one big cover-up, because, really, she's just kind of a scared person. I was not threatening to her. I'm not interested in her husband—I'm gay. I'm a drummer. I'm not going to wear the same dress she's wearing. We came from the same place musically. That's why we got along.

ERIC ERLANDSON In our Western society, Courtney's known and she's an archetype—it's like she's this destroyer woman, kind of like a Medusa type. People tend to not like that type of woman, not realizing that we all have that inside us, and the more you hate it on the outside, the more you activate it inside. Deep down inside, she's just a person with a soul, with her own karma, with her own life and her own experiences, and we don't understand what that is and where she came from. You watch *Behind the Music* and think, Oh, now I know her. But you don't know shit.

GRANT ALDEN One of the things I said when I had been asked about the manner of Kurt's death is that I knew the coroner, Nik Hartshorne, and Nik knew me, and Nik knew I had a kind of bully pulpit at my disposal. We never talked about it, and Nik's been dead a long time now, but I absolutely believe that if there had been something wrong with the way Kurt died, Nik would have come to me. By "something wrong" I mean: Did Courtney kill him? Did he really commit suicide? All that bullshit. No. If there had been any irregularities, I am morally convinced that Nik would have raised total hell.

ERIC ERLANDSON A lot of people I know, who I wouldn't expect to say this, ask me, "Did Courtney kill Kurt?" They actually ask me that, because they've watched the movie *Kurt & Courtney*. I'm like, "Wow, I thought I knew you, but since you just asked me that question, I don't really know you anymore." I presume that people would see beyond this problematic documentary. I was in the proximity of Courtney in L.A. at the time, so I don't think she killed him or had him killed. It's pretty clear what really happened.

Also, everybody thinks that Kurt wrote our album *Live Through This*. I treat that like a conspiracy theory, too. I was there for most of the writing of that album, and so I just laugh when people say that. Though Courtney didn't help matters by dragging him in the studio and making him mumble over a couple songs.

PATTY SCHEMEL Right after Kurt died, I went into rehab for the first time and tried to sort everything out. When I got out, Hole's bassist, Kristen Pfaff, calls me up and says, "I'm going back to Minneapolis." We would trade records all the time and she was like, "I have your Live

Skull record, do you want to come over?" I remember saying, "I can't make it." I didn't want to go over there because I was too worried that I might end up getting high. Kristen was using when I was using, but we would try to keep it secret from each other. So I sent my friend to go over and grab my stuff and give Kristen her stuff.

Then I got a phone call that Kristen had OD'd and died, and that was crazy. Crazy. I ended up staying clean for a while, but it didn't last very long.

ERIC ERLANDSON Our album had come out the week after Kurt's death. But Courtney was not in any shape to do anything, so everything was kind of crazy for a couple months. Just as things were starting to mellow out a little bit, Kristen died and there was that tailspin again. With Kurt it was like, Fuck the album, fuck the band, it's over, it doesn't matter. But when Kristen died, it spurred a feeling of, We have to get out of here and go on the road and support this album. The album was so connected to the whole situation, with the lyrics and when it came out and the fact it was called *Live Through This.*

PATTY SCHEMEL Through Billy Corgan we found Melissa Auf der Maur to play bass, and she stepped into this really crazy, toxic, dysfunctional band. On that tour, Courtney would unravel here and there. There was one moment where somebody threw some shotgun shells onstage in Philadelphia or somewhere. We just stopped playing the show. It hurt me bad, but I couldn't even fathom the beginnings of how it felt for Courtney.

COURTNEY LOVE I'll tell you this, if you go and you watch a Hole show—and this happens to this day—after we get offstage, there's this little contingent of boys. They're wearing fuzzy little sweaters and somebody at their school has told them that they look like Kurt, and they stand there and they stare at me. I don't know what they want. They don't want to fuck me. But it is one of the strangest phenomena you'll ever see. They're like wounded children and they just want a hug or something. I don't understand the cult of that, and I've asked my guitarist Micko, because he's English and he grew up with the *NME,* "What is it about Kurt that you fucking think is so great?"

"'Cause he's just fuckin' really cool, man."

I'm like, "What, because he killed himself? *That's* cool? I have a daughter who's fucking never known her father and you think that's cool?"

But there's a part of rock journalism, like possibly yourself, that thinks that's really cool. In fact, the *NME* had Kurt on the cover very recently, with fucking free color-poster pullouts of dead rock stars.

Well, it's not fuckin' cool. It is a cult of death.

CHAPTER 41
FUCKING GREAT PRODUCTS

KEVIN MARTIN Our album came out in July '93, and it exploded that summer. We first met Madonna at a dinner in New York in March of '94. We went to Sfuzzi, an Italian place by her apartment on Central Park West. She was 30 minutes late. All she talked about was sex.

The rest of the band was there, but she just talked to me the whole time. She goes, "Are you a good dancer?" She was sitting right next to me. "You can tell a lot about how somebody fucks by the way they dance."

I'll never forget her saying that. She was very much a provocateur.

SCOTT MERCADO It was weird because she was actually kinda quiet. But then Kevin was talking, and he tends to dominate the conversation. And one point, he poked fun at her for a brief second—I wish I could remember what it was about—and I remember her smiling and saying, "Don't quit your day job," in reference, of course, to the fact that she owned the record label.

KEVIN MARTIN Afterwards, she invited us back to her apartment. We all went. Her place was fucking incredible: Degas, Chagalls, Monets,

Picassos—you name it, it was all there, hanging on the wall. She had a Steinway in the main living room. It was immaculate.

SCOTT MERCADO I was so naive and I'd never seen a bidet before, so I said, "What's this for?" And at the top of her lungs, Madonna goes, "IT'S A PUSSY WASH!"

BARDI MARTIN The thing that struck me the most was she had a really tiny painting on one of her walls by Dalí, maybe six by eight inches. I just remember spending quite a bit of time just looking at it, and it was beautiful.

KEVIN MARTIN At the end, she said, "Okay, I'll see you guys tomorrow. And you, stay"—or "Why don't you stick around for a little bit?" It could have been for a cup of coffee, but you know exactly what she was talking about.

BARDI MARTIN I didn't witness any of that. I was staring at that painting.

SCOTT MERCADO There was a little bit of flirtation there, yeah. I mean, it was all in good fun; it wasn't serious. She's very personable that way.

KEVIN MARTIN I said, "Look, you know I can't stay. I've got a show at Madison Square Garden tomorrow"—we were opening for Rush—"that I'm nervous as hell about. I'm going to bed." If I'd have been single I would've been like, "Sure," but the girl I was dating at the time I was crazy about—and she happened to be Madonna and Freddy's assistant at the label. She ended up becoming my wife. Did Madonna know about me and Renee then? Oh, yeah. Did Renee ever get wind of this? Yep.

At the time, the other assistant who was there was looking at me like, What are you doing? It was very strange. It's very Italian, like a "You don't tell Tony Soprano no sort of thing." *What?* I do.

We saw Madonna again that July, after we had sold a million records, and they gave us our plaques. She was like, "Hi, how are you? What's going on? Congratulations," and then left. It seemed as though that person we had met was turned off and gone. It was like nothing had ever happened.

. . .

KEVIN MARTIN The grunge label was a fuckin' major hindrance to us. We were labeled "grunge lite." They would say, "Grunge-lite band Candlebox." We were lumped in with Bush, Live, Collective Soul. People confused us with Collective Soul all the time. I got divorced in '02 and was dating Zoe, Jason Bonham's sister, briefly. I went over to see her in London and hang out with her, and her brother is like, "I love your band."

I'm like, "Wow, cool. I can't believe you know us."

"Yeah, man: *Duh nuh nuh Nah nuh nuh Nah nuh Nah nuh NAH.* 'Yeah!'"

I'm like, "That's Collective Soul."

RUSTY WILLOUGHBY Flop played a show with Candlebox in Boise. We showed up at the club, and we're in our little crap-ass van, and they had a bus. They were trying to be real nice to us, but we just thought they were jerks because they were in a bus. Who knows, they could've been nice people. But you'd see the lead singer of that band driving around town in his new red Porsche.

KEVIN MARTIN I was so embarrassed to drive my fiancée's Mercedes 190E in Seattle. That's like a toy car. Anybody could afford it, but I was embarrassed to drive it. I thought that I wasn't supposed to have a nice car in Seattle. Your mentality turns into that because you're dealing with what people are writing about you in the press.

Rolling Stone did an article on us, but they didn't want to, so they fuckin' bashed us. It was '94, when we were touring with the Flaming Lips. The guy came out with us for two weeks. Then he just talked shit. During a show, Pete went to kick over his amps, and his guitar tech was tired of fuckin' rebuilding them, so he put some pillows down behind them. The writer is like, "They're so concerned about their gear they put pillows behind it." That's not us.

BARDI MARTIN The drum tech had a cushion that he used to sit on waiting for Scotty; rather than sitting on the hard ground, he sat on a fuckin' pillow or something. The writer had to have known it. He couldn't have been that blind. Can't you find enough shit to throw at this band without actually lying about it?

He basically painted a picture of four undeserving dipshits on the road.

GUY OSEARY Did I ever have discussions with the band about their reputation? Absolutely never. It didn't matter. We were doing great! We did great, we made good fans, we had a good album, we had a good ride. First album sold three and a half million, which is great! That was done week by week by week by week, man.

WAYNE COYNE (singer for Oklahoma City's the Flaming Lips) Candlebox wasn't just the nail in the coffin of grunge. To me, they arrived as *the coffin* of grunge music.

We toured with them for three months at the end of 1994. At the beginning of that phase, they were playing to 4,000 or 5,000 people a night, and by the end, they were playing these giant arenas—hockey rinks, for the most part, that hold 10,000 people—and they're selling them out a couple of nights in a row.

I think we were invited because they thought we made the tour seem more authentic or more cool. And I'm not saying we were cool, or authentic. I think there's an element of, Look, we're Candlebox. You may think we're shit, but we like the Flaming Lips, and doesn't that make us seem cooler?

We all were against it on sort of a practical principle level. We don't like the group, so why would you want to spend three months playing with them? And then you think, Well, we could make some money, and we would be able to play to an audience that would never come to see us otherwise. And I think it worked out great for us. By the end of that tour, our song "She Don't Use Jelly" was being played on the radio everywhere we went. Part of it probably was because we were playing with Candlebox. We would play "She Don't Use Jelly," and the audience that literally hated everything else that we did liked that one song.

KEVIN MARTIN Touring with the Flaming Lips was inspirational. This is a band that blew us off the stage every fucking night. And look at 'em now. If you look at the story of the Flaming Lips, these were four buddies that just started writing really fucking eclectic, weird music with no real agenda. There's no argument, there's no fight, they just keep producing these brilliant fucking records. Candlebox, unfortunately, as good as the songs that we've written are, we're just this fucking disjointed band.

Pete and I argue so much, it's ridiculous. And that's because we weren't friends when we started the band, so we didn't have an understanding of each other's characteristics. We've learned them over the years, but neither of us is really happy with the other person's idiosyncracies. We're like coworkers, exactly. That's a great way to define what Candlebox is. Fortunately, we're coworkers that can produce some really fucking great products.

WAYNE COYNE We saw the clumsiness of their shows and their songs and their identity, and everything about it just seemed like, damn, this is too much, too soon. Candlebox really had nothing. They're just like, We like grunge! We're a big grunge band! I'm not putting it down simply because it's popular; it just wasn't our trip.

The band would offer you cocaine virtually every time you would run into them backstage, like, We're big rock stars, and we're going to do some cocaine backstage. We were by no means straight edge, but we're making $500 a night, they're making $5 million. We're not really rubbing noses with the same people here. And their road crew were guys who six months ago were touring with Mötley Crüe, and it was a very arena-rock mentality.

KEVIN MARTIN When we asked Flaming Lips to open for us, people maybe started to pay attention to what we were doing. That we weren't having bands tour with us to sell tickets. We wanted bands to play with us that we appreciated.

We were always very into being from Seattle, and because we were fortunate enough to have some success, we always wanted to take bands from Seattle on the road with us. We took Sweet Water; we took Green Apple for a few weeks; we took Seaweed for fuckin' six weeks.

SCOTT MERCADO The big three or four bands in Seattle were like, This is our club, you're not invited. Like Alice in Chains, Soundgarden, Pearl Jam. I was still friends with some of them, but they would never take us on tour or anything like that. But at that point, it didn't matter. We were getting offers from Metallica, Living Colour, Rush, so we didn't need to go on tour with them or feel a need to share a stage with them.

I was friends with Sean Kinney, and he told me, "I like your style, you're a great drummer. I just don't like your singer" or "I don't like your music." I admired Sean for saying that, as opposed to talking about us behind our backs. This was actually after we got the gig with Metallica, because Alice in Chains dropped out.

SEAN KINNEY We were rehearsing at the Moore Theatre to get ready for Metallica. Layne was in a treatment place, and we'd been rehearsing ourselves. Nobody had talked to him—he'd been gone all that time. He just showed up, and there were bad circumstances. It just wasn't happening. Lost a lot of trust in him. Lost some trust in each other for a while.

MIKE INEZ I personally have never tried heroin. Everybody points at Layne, but I gotta tell ya, it was all of us. We were doing all kinds of different shit. Just the fuckin' drugs, man. All of us were out of control. It was a really hard time, and that's how we dealt with the pressure and the touring schedule. I wouldn't trade a minute of it for the world, but certainly now, 20 years later, I'm looking back at it going, Okay, maybe my behavior was a little over the top at that time. But, hey, we were four young single guys, just banging chicks on first-class flights. At least we could say we did it.

We had a meeting, and it was really, really, really apparent that we shouldn't go on that Metallica tour. It was one of those times where we needed to go, "Hold on a second. Let's not sacrifice our health—let's not go and literally kill ourselves." For us to say no to Metallica, who were basically our older brothers, is a testament of the love we have for each other.

A poignant moment for me was after that meeting: It was raining outside, and I was walking down the alley one way and Layne was walking the other way. I turned around and looked at Layne, and that's when I had a really big flash, like, Wow, we are not healthy here.

KEVIN MARTIN We opened for Metallica in '94. The end-of-tour party was the most decadent thing I had ever experienced in my life. It was like, mounds of cocaine, strippers, high-class hookers—you got a golden ticket so you can go fuck them if you want. That was not my thing. I've never been with a prostitute. And I quit doing drugs when I was 18, so for me I was a wasted ticket—I ended up giving it to one of our guitar techs or something. I remember going into this back room and seeing this mound of cocaine, a basketball rim around and six to eight inches high.

PETER KLETT Layne wouldn't answer the phone. The story I heard is that they'd call him to leave a message on his answering machine, then they'd call back and it's a different outgoing message, so obviously he was fucking with them. Because of that, we also got their slot on Woodstock.

KEVIN MARTIN We play Woodstock '94, and we're the only band all weekend that's got a record in the *Billboard* Top 10 or Top 20. We go to do a press conference and they introduce us: "This is Candlebox from Seattle. They've got a number-seven record on *Billboard,* they're moving 125,000 units a week, they're really pleased to be here. We'd just like to open the floor to any kind of questions."

Not one person asked a question. We stood there for like two minutes. I finally joked, "Mr. Brokaw?" Everybody turned like Tom Brokaw was there. I was like, Why am I standing here? Nobody gives a shit. The only people that ever cared about Candlebox were the people that bought our records. It hurt, man. It was like, We're never gonna fuckin' win. We're never going to be a reputable band regardless of what we do.

JOHNNY BACOLAS The weekend Alice in Chains was supposed to be playing Woodstock, I went on a camping trip with Layne and a friend of his, and a friend of mine named Alex Hart.

Alice in Chains were having some internal issues. I remember that the guys in the band were calling him and leaving voice messages for him, and he would just disregard them. Layne had other things going on. He was trying to kick heroin that weekend, as well. That was really the reason he went on that camping trip, to try and clean up. We went to Eastern Washington. And that's where we ended up setting up camp, in a town called Twisp. It wasn't much fun for Layne at all. He slept a lot on that trip. We were tending to him to an extent.

Later, we ended up in Lake Chelan, which was a big touristy spot. One night, Layne drank quite a bit, and him and I are on this beach. We ended up sitting at this little bridge over the lake. He was very, very depressed—it was basically the withdrawals—and he was really freaking out. He just grabbed me and started crying. And he told me that he wanted to kill himself. He, in my mind, was considering doing it right there and then at that bridge. We were just sitting there on the concrete, and I'm holding him for dear life.

Alex drives up, and the next thing I remember, all of us are going to the Safeway in Lake Chelan to get beer. Now it's probably 2 o'clock in the morning, and some guy started giving Layne shit. Of all nights to start fucking with him. I can't remember what they were saying, but they were badgering him. Layne clocked one guy in the jaw, just laid him out right in the Safeway aisle where the beer is. We bailed, got in the car, and left.

We ended up going to this parking lot, hiding, and there's probably 30 cars there, all blaring music. People smoking weed and drinking beer. All teenagers. We had the windows down, we were just parked, smoking cigarettes. Some kids recognized Layne, and they were like, "Dude, there's Layne Staley!" And the other guys were like, "No, it's not. He wouldn't be in Lake Chelan."

And they all came up to the car, probably 15 kids, and they're like, "If you're Layne Staley, prove it." And Layne was just looking straight ahead. Sunglasses on, 2 o'clock in the morning, wouldn't even acknowledge them. Finally, one of the guys pulls up in a truck, cranks "No Excuses," and he goes, "If you're Layne Staley, sing along!"

And Layne started singing. Sang the verse, sang the chorus. Nailed it, exactly like it sounded on the record. All the kids were like, "Holy shit, it's fuckin' him!" He sang that, just to be, Get the fuck out of my face! Kind of proved who he was, and then he's like, "Get out of here!" And then we drove off.

SCOTT MERCADO Sean and I talked for a long time and he's like, "You guys probably get bummed by critics not liking you or people in the industry not liking you or people in the grunge scene not liking you. Now you know how I feel whenever somebody comes up to me and says, 'Too bad your band is so fucked up they can't go on tour.'"

JOHNNY BACOLAS The night that he was holding on to me and we were on that bridge there in Lake Chelan, Layne asked me to move in with him. He said, "I don't trust many people. I trust you. Please, would you come live with me?"

CHAPTER 42
SOME IMPLODING GOING ON

JEFF AMENT The first record or two, Ed and I could talk. We roomed together, the whole first year and half that we toured, so we got to know each other fairly well. We were jamming on "Release," and he started to sing this thing, and after we were done he said I need to talk to you and he laid the whole thing on me, acknowledged what had gone on with him and his dad. It was a heavy moment. But now communication was at an all-time low. I responded like I've always responded: just put my head down and played. . . .

STONE GOSSARD *Vitalogy* was the first record where Ed was the guy making the final decisions. It was a real difficult record for me to make, because I was having to give up a lot of control.

BRENDAN O'BRIEN *Vitalogy* was a little strained. I'm being polite—there was some imploding going on.

ADAM KASPER *Vitalogy* was when I started noticing that Eddie was not all too pleased with Dave musically. Dave was an extremely busy player, and Eddie likes a more raw sound. We even recorded a couple songs starting out with drum machines, and that's sort of a slap in the face to a drummer.

And then there was Dave's personality. I'm not really sure during which album this happened, but the classic story is when Dave Abbruzzese accidently knocked over Eddie's guitar, which was a gift from Pete Townsend or something. He breaks it and just leaves a little picture of a boo-boo face on it, like, Sorry, and fuckin' left the studio to go do a drum clinic or some self-promoting bullshit like that. He just had a bit of a rock-star attitude, and that didn't go well with Eddie.

DAVE ABBRUZZESE Breaking one of Eddie's guitars? That never happened. Nope. I never broke nothin'.

COLLEEN COMBS Pearl Jam really were a democracy as a band, but the way the democracy worked was that they were kind of all on the same page about what they wanted. Dave always wanted something different, and he was the only one who wanted something different. He was the person who would want to order a limo and not a town car. And there's nothing wrong with that. But it was kind of a hard place for him to be.

DAVE ABBRUZZESE I really thought we should be playing music instead of participating in that Ticketmaster fiasco. I thought it was a waste of time.

JOHN HOYT What happened with Ticketmaster was that all those extra add-on fees were exorbitant. Pearl Jam has never been concerned just about making money, so they took on the cause. With all the extra charges, it meant that if they wanted to have a $20 ticket, it would cost $26. We were trying to cut deals with Ticketmaster to decrease those charges, but never were able to do it, and finally just said, "Screw it."

COLLEEN COMBS As soon as we started asking questions, we started having problems with booking our tours. Promoters or people we considered friends in business suddenly couldn't help us or wouldn't take a phone call. There were definitely strange things happening in the office. Honestly—and this is going to sound like a bad conspiracy movie—but

I swear there was clicking on the phone line. It seemed like the phones were tapped.

KEN DEANS I can tell you what I told Kelly. I go, "You know, you're fighting the wrong battle." The battle was not with Ticketmaster. Ticketmaster wasn't setting those fees. The promoters are. So the reason why the convenience charge went from a dollar to $3 was because a dollar and a half was going to the promoters. That whole thing was a valiant but misguided effort.

JOHN HOYT Jeff Ament and Stone Gossard testified in front of a House subcommittee about unfair ticket practices, and that became the big national story in all the papers. That elevated it to a completely different level. It was a bit of a circus. There was a fair amount of media, and an awful lot of congressional interns and people wanting to be present for this. There were softball questions and only a couple harder questions, because Ticketmaster had a lot of money and a pretty strong lobby and they put some pressure on members of Congress.

REP. LYNN C. WOOLSEY (Democratic congresswoman from California; during questioning at Pearl Jam's antitrust complaint hearing before the House Subcommittee on Information, Justice, Transportation and Agriculture, June 30, 1994) I have to ask another question that has nothing to do with monopolies. What does Pearl Jam mean or does it have a meaning?

STONE GOSSARD (June 30, 1994, testimony) I am not going to answer that question.

JEFF AMENT That whole thing was a joke. The Department of Justice used us to look hip. Stone and I spent a week with this guy John Hoyt; he was drilling us with serious questions that we were [supposedly] going to get asked, and then it didn't feel like we got to utilize any of it. It made me a lot more cynical about what goes on with the government.

DAVE ABBRUZZESE When those guys were testifying in front of Congress, I was in Indonesia just enjoying being alive. The more I read about the Ticketmaster situation, it's like, It all sounds good and nice, but there are way more important, flagrant injustices we could have latched onto.

JEFF AMENT Dave was a different egg for sure. There were a lot of things, personality-wise, where I didn't see eye to eye with him. He was more comfortable being a rock star than the rest of us. Partying, girls, cars. I don't know if anyone was in the same space. Also, with Dave, musically, when you'd say, "I want this to sound more like the Buzzcocks," I don't think he related to that at all. He was a technical guy, and we all played by feeling, or by seeing bands.

DAVE ABBRUZZESE That statement from him is incredibly disrespectful, and untrue, as well. It's such a crock of shit. I was the only one in the band who had the same girlfriend for eight years. I had bought a car that was used, and I kept it. But he makes it sound like I was the odd man out; it paints a picture of me as being pretentious. Shit, we worked our asses off to be successful. We *were* rock stars. Who cares? Jesus Christ. *(Laughs.)* Doing articles where you're on the cover, and the article is how you don't wanna be on the cover. That's pretentious hypocrisy.

   Forgive me for not giving a fuck about the Buzzcocks. *(Laughs.)* If anyone would've mentioned something like that to me, I certainly would've went and listened to what the fuck they were talking about. There was never an "It should have this or that kind of feel."

STONE GOSSARD It was the nature of how the politics worked in our band: It was up to me to say, "Hey, we tried, it's not working; time to move on." On a superficial level, it was a political struggle: For whatever reason his ability to communicate with Ed and Jeff was very stifled. I certainly don't think it was all Dave Abbruzzese's fault that it was stifled.

DAVE ABBRUZZESE I called Kelly just to check in, and he said he was on the way to the airport with Eddie. They were goin' to New Orleans 'cause Eddie had that court case where he had gotten in a scuffle outside of a bar. I told Kelly, "Hope everything goes well. Tell Ed hello." And he said, "Everything's great. Good-bye. Wait, I think Stone wants to talk to you." So I called Stone up, and he asked if I wanted to meet for breakfast the next day.

When I sat down for breakfast, Stone just looked at me for 30 seconds and then said, "Dave Abbruzzese." Then he had the balls to say it the way he did: "We're looking for another drummer." My reaction was complete and utter disbelief. I was devastated. But I thought that Stone was such a good person. Stand-up, strong. If he wasn't there, it probably would've been a lawyer calling me.

I got home and Mike called and Jeff called. I think it was difficult for everybody in the band, except for the one person I never spoke with after that, which was Eddie. The only time I ever had two words with Eddie since I got fired was two or three years later. I was sitting with Alain Johannes from Eleven on the curb after a Chris Cornell show in Seattle, and Eddie came up to us. He said, "Dave Abbruzzese," and kinda put his arms out in greeting, because he couldn't hide from me. And I stood up and realized how much shorter he was than I remembered. I think it was a one-armed hug. He started rambling and tried to join in our conversation, and he ended up toddling off. There was a little part of me that would've loved to clobber him and another part of me that felt like I already had, just by the fact that I could still sleep at night and I was still proud of everything that we accomplished.

A lot of people have asked me about the stick-man tattoo: "Do you regret it?" When I got it, it was a profound time and I felt free. No matter what would have happened with that band, that tattoo still signifies the same thing to me. I have no regrets at all.

JACK IRONS Eddie wanted me to be in the band earlier, and so did the other guys. I would get a phone call every now and then from Eddie: "We're looking for somebody. Are you interested?" And I would ask him, "How long you gonna be on the road?" And he goes, "Well, we're kind of booked for the next year and a half, off and on." I was committed to Eleven, and my wife and I had just had our baby. The idea of being on the road for that long was hard to swallow, and I still had some traumatic stress from the Chili Pepper days and I was trying to keep my life balanced.

And then in June '94, my wife and I left L.A. We bought a little cabin in Northern California. I didn't know what my future would be with

Eleven at the time. And then in August, someone hipped me to the fact that Pearl Jam were looking for another drummer. So I thought about it, and I realized that it was now or never for me, to at least put myself out there. As I got older and had a family, I knew I had to produce and make money for the future. And it wasn't just about that. This was as *Vitalogy* was coming out and I knew that they didn't want to do it like they did it on *Ten* and on *Vs.* Eddie said the band wasn't going to tour at the same insane pace. And them being successful allows a certain amount of comfort and ease on the road.

I wasn't a shoo-in at that point anymore because everybody had a couple guys they had wanted to try out. I went up to Seattle, and there was an audition process, so to speak, but it did very much help that I was Eddie's guy. We played Neil Young's Bridge School Benefit, and I think at that point I was committed to do the tour in Australia in the beginning of '95. If I went to Australia and I did these gigs and it went well, then we'll just keep going. Eventually, I was in the band.

COLLEEN COMBS If there was ever something that might've caused that band to break up, it might've been the pressure of putting together and pulling off that 1995 U.S. tour. Ticketmaster had contracts with all the major venues, so a band the size of Pearl Jam had to build from the ground up. We hired a company to print our own tickets.

JEFF AMENT We'd be playing parks and racetracks. And somebody would be yelling, "The fence is down a mile in the east corner!" and we'd have one guy trying to fix it. It was absolutely stupid.

ERIC JOHNSON In San Francisco, Eddie got food poisoning. I remember he called me at like 6 in the morning and said he had been sick all night and he needed to go to the hospital right away, so I went up to his room to get him and the telling sign was there was half a tuna sandwich still sitting on the tray. I thought, Eww, that's bad. We were at the hospital for a couple of hours—they put several pints of fluid into him because he was really dehydrated—and then we went pretty much right from the hospital to the show.

We were in a town car, and he was in so much pain that he was on his knees on the little floor well in the back. He was grabbing the seats, and you know how taut the leather seats are—you can't pinch them or grab the leather? He was grabbing wads of leather in his hand and squeezing, he was in so much pain. When he got to Golden Gate Park, one of the guys from Rock Med that's always at the shows gave him a shot that kind of eased him back for a little while.

EDDIE VEDDER I thought I was going to die. We've been in some pretty tense situations as far as crowd control, and usually I pull it off. I think they just thought I was going to pull it off.

I'm not being a martyr or anything, but it was hard. And then I was looking through the set list. Well, maybe I can pull this off or that off. And then it was like, "I can't. I just can't do this. It's crazy." That was one of those low moments. That was a really tough thing. But there was nothing, just nothing, I could do. I'm human.

ERIC JOHNSON Eddie did a couple songs, and then couldn't do any more. Neil had showed up on his Harley and was just gonna play a song with everybody, and he ended up doing like eight or nine songs with the rest of the band.

KELLY CURTIS We were afraid there'd be a riot. Neil just went down and wore 'em out. After that show, Neil said you know what, if it doesn't feel right, go home. And the band looked at each other and said you know what, we feel like going home. So we called it quits and went home.

COLLEEN COMBS We got so much hate mail from fans after that show. It was so discouraging. Can you imagine having a sick day that causes those kind of repercussions? That is a lot of pressure for a person to handle. We worked really hard to make that tour happen.

EDDIE VEDDER Eventually they came out with a press release that basically said, "The Department of Justice has ceased its investigation of Ticketmaster. No further investigation will take place." That was it, after a year of struggle. It was really amazing to be right up close and get absolutely stomped on by a huge corporate entity.

BRETT ELIASON Pearl Jam really believed in what they were doing, and from my point of view, what good does it do to have a big fight like that and just give up? They do walk their talk. They always have, they always will.

KIM WARNICK The Fastbacks touring with Pearl Jam in 1996 was the best thing ever. I lived out the ultimate rock dream. We played huge, huge, huge places. But they don't live the major-rock-star lifestyle. They are as Fugazi as Fugazi. Their whole organization, everything about that band is so right-on, I can't say enough about them. I'm not just talking about the band and Kelly Curtis, I'm talking about everybody who works for them. Everybody.

We had two weeks in the U.S. and then five weeks in Europe. They didn't use Ticketmaster. So we didn't play Madison Square Garden, we played Randall's Island. So it's like, "I know you guys are doing the right thing, but this is the only time I might've been able to play Madison Square Garden. Dammit! Dammit!" But it's hard to be mad at them for that.

BRETT ELIASON In '97, Pearl Jam really didn't tour much. They had time to think about things, which, I'm sure, led them to change their mind and approach about Ticketmaster. In the end, fans really didn't want to go that far out of their way, and it made people grumpy. They were willing to pay the ticket prices. Some fans got it, and some just felt, Why aren't they just playing at the usual place? I think that was part of the reason it ended up being kind of a futile endeavor.

CHAPTER 43
THE MAD SEASON

MIKE MCCREADY We had a lot of meetings [in Pearl Jam] where they would say, "Hey Mike, you're getting way too fucked up." But we're all really good friends and we love each other and I think they actually thought I was going to die, but they never took steps to kick me out of the band, which I can't believe because I fucked up so many times.

ERIC JOHNSON I used to worry about Mike on tour because he'd not be back by 4 a.m. sometimes. I'm not a big sleeper, so I'd be up worrying. A lot of times I'd know Mike was back because I'd see a hotel ashtray kicked over outside an elevator. "Fuck, thank God he's home."

I remember having Abbruzzese run into my room in Ireland, telling me, "You should probably go downstairs in front of the Burger King." "Why?" "Because Mike's out there naked." Mike was always so cute when I would show up, like, "Uh-oh, Dad's here!" But he's totally cleaned his life up; he does really wonderful things for people now.

JOHNNY BACOLAS The point of me moving in with Layne was to be a support for him, to help him to—you know, I don't know what he exactly wanted. He just wanted me around him, and I suppose I probably wanted the same. When I moved in, he laid out the law. He said, "If there's any interventions, I'll never speak to you again." Being 25, 26 years old and not knowing better, I listened. It was pretty dark. It's difficult living with someone that you absolutely love, and you're essentially watching them kill themselves.

But there were also a lot of good times living with Layne. Like when his family or my family would come over and all of us would be hanging out. He and I had a lot of great times just watching movies or jamming on guitars. We'd go grocery shopping together at 4 or 5 o'clock in the morning so people didn't bug him. Layne took me to Eddie Vedder's house in 1995 when Eddie broadcasted a radio show called *Self-Pollution Radio* from his basement. I met Eddie that night, and Layne introduced me to Chris Cornell. And I watched Layne perform with Mad Season.

MIKE MCCREADY A lot of hallucinogenic mushrooms grow in the area around Surrey, England, where we mixed the first Pearl Jam album, and the people there call the time when they come up the "Mad Season" because people are wandering around mad, picking mushrooms, half out of their minds. That term has always stuck in my mind, and I relate that to my past years, the seasons of drinking and drug abuse.

BARRETT MARTIN Mike McCready, who I'd known off and on and had jammed with at house parties, said he wanted to form a band with this bass player, John Baker Saunders, who he'd met at the Hazelden rehab clinic. Mike asked me to come jam with him and Baker, and I said sure, since the Trees weren't doing anything. I immediately liked Baker because he had this blues background—he was from Chicago—and the three of us had this good chemistry. It was just real blues-based rock; it didn't sound grunge and it didn't sound like any of our bands. Mike said that he wanted to find a singer, and he mentioned Layne.

JOHNNY BACOLAS Layne never answered the phone, and we'd never answer the door if someone just knocked. You'd have to let us know you're coming. Mike called and spoke to me, and he's like, "Dude, wanted to come and hang out and say hi to you guys. I just got out of rehab, and I had this idea for this band." I'm the one who let him in the house, and he played Layne these songs. Before they were Mad Season, they were going to call the band the Gacy Bunch. Like John Wayne Gacy, the killer. *(Laughs.)* I remember thinking, That's a pretty cool name, but damn, that's a pretty negative connotation!

Mark Lanegan sang on a couple of songs on the album. He was a good friend of Layne's. I saw Mark Lanegan at the house more than any other of Layne's friends, to be honest with you. At the time, he had his issues. I'd talk to him for five or 10 minutes in the living room, just small talk. He's one of the sweetest guys I've ever met. Zero intimidation factor. Like meeting Bill Cosby or something.

BARRETT MARTIN Even though I'd lost respect for Alice in Chains on tour because of the resonant attitude of "We're the big rock stars," I wasn't opposed to Layne being in the band, because he had an incredible voice and he was always cool. We did a couple of rehearsals with Layne and he was actually clean at that time; he had stopped using heroin. The beauty of that Mad Season record is that we were all sober. We wrote the songs in a couple weeks, played a couple unannounced shows, and recorded the album in about two weeks. It was fast.

BRETT ELIASON I produced, recorded, and mixed the Mad Season album. Layne was not healthy. Heavy, heavy drug use. Such a sweet guy, such an amazing talent. One of the best singers I've ever recorded. He could just stand out there and light it up. The problem was getting him there. We were in cahoots with his roommate, who'd help get Layne off the couch and point him in our direction.

Layne would show up and he'd go back to the bathroom and be doing dope back there and you'd wait for hours before he was ready to come back out. He was pretty open about it. I asked him, "Why? Why are you doing this to yourself?" He said, "I'm either going to drink or I'm going to do dope, and drinking is harder on me."

JOHNNY BACOLAS Either during the making of the record or after, McCready started getting really concerned about Layne. He really wanted Layne to go back to Hazelden, where Layne had been in the past. He knew that Layne really liked this one counselor, whose name was Lowell, kind of a Harley-Davidson biker-type dude. McCready flew Lowell out one day and surprised Layne. Layne agreed to go back to Hazelden, but he only ended up staying for two or three days before flying back to Seattle. That was it for drug rehab.

MIKE MCCREADY I was under the mistaken theory I could help him out. I wanted to lead by example.

JOHNNY BACOLAS Ultimately what happened is Layne's mom and his stepfather, Jim, convinced me that I was essentially enabling Layne, that I was making life a lot easier for him to continue doing what he's doing. Now there was someone that bought him the groceries, took care of the day-to-day affairs of living. Stuff that pretty much anybody that's into heroin that deep seems to neglect. So I moved out after about six or seven months.

TOBY WRIGHT (producer/engineer) I had engineered Alice in Chains' *Jar of Flies* acoustic EP—the first EP ever to debut at number one—which they recorded after they finished that Lollapalooza tour. The third Alice in Chains album, the one with the three-legged dog on the cover, started with me coming up to Seattle and working with Jerry at his house. The strategy between Susan, Jerry, and myself was to get me up there, and as soon as the other members heard I was in town, hopefully their ears would perk up and they'd go, "What's goin' on? What are we doin'?" And that's exactly what happened. It got Sean interested, brought Mike in. All of a sudden, *boom*, we were jamming, and I'd go over to Layne's place and get him.

NICK TERZO The third album was when Alice in Chains accomplished their goal of boxing me out. I heard very few demos. They picked Toby Wright, who I brought in once to engineer something for them. I would not have picked Toby Wright. I think he was more of an engineer, and they could have used a full-on producer again. At the time, I didn't think he had the experience to deal with the challenges he was going to face.

TOBY WRIGHT I had a special relationship with Layne. I had already gone through a phase of smokin' weed and doin' coke and heroin and all that kinda shit, so we could identify with each other and I kinda knew how to talk to him. Which I guess was one reason why I was hired to continue with them. I was able to really get down to some personal is-sues: "Here's a piece of paper and a pencil. Write it all down. Make a song out of your pain, because pain makes for great music."

SEAN KINNEY A lot of the songs that Jerry and Layne wrote, you can hear what they have to say to each other right there. It's spelled out, in a roundabout way. It's a way more malicious and brutal album than *Dirt* was.

TOBY WRIGHT There were so many rumors going on about Layne and his lifestyle at the time: "Layne has gangrene and lost both of his arms." "Oh, my God, he's lost all of his teeth!" But the band never answered any rumor calls, because they didn't think it was anybody's business. There was a lot of speculation that the album would never happen. I heard rumors about some of the record executives betting against the record being made. I was like, Oh, really? Watch this.

NICK TERZO I felt Toby was more of an enabler in a way, too. Because he enabled the label to be shut out. As someone who's being hired by a record label, I think you have to have better diplomatic skills than that. You're serving two masters in a way.

MIKE INEZ Toby was very, very patient. He was such a soldier and just trying to keep the energy upbeat. He's a brother for life. The cover of that album is very gray, and I think that was the general feeling of the band. And Seattle, when we were doing the record, I remember that feeling real gray.

TOBY WRIGHT One of the things that happened when we were recording was the Mad Season record went gold. So at 6 in the morning we were still in the studio with Layne, and the heads of Sony, Donnie Ienner and Michele Anthony, called and were congratulating him. And at the end of the conversation, they said, "Oh, yeah, by the way, you have nine days to get your record done."

So they call him up to congratulate him and then threaten him. *(Laughs.)* So he wrote that into the lyrics. It's the second verse: "Call me up congratulations ain't the real why/There's no pressure besides brilliance let's say by day nine/Endless corporate ignorance lets me control time/By the way, by the way . . ." I think the recording process went another month or two after that.

The band didn't do very much touring on the dog record, but they got offered to do this *Unplugged* show by MTV, in 1996.

ALEX COLETTI Before the show, I went to Alice in Chains' rehearsal space in Seattle. When I walked in, I was happy to see Layne eating a bucket of chicken. He had on fingerless gloves and they were all greasy, so he wouldn't shake my hand, but I got the elbow shake. He was really friendly. Seeing him eating that chicken just blew away my concerns of what condition Layne's gonna be in. He was really in a great place. When he got to New York, I think he was still in good health.

MIKE INEZ Scotty Olson, who played with Heart, was playing with us that night; it was really special to have another energy up onstage with us. We discovered at that show that songs like "Sludge Factory" were even heavier acoustic. Layne that night was so haunting. His voice, especially his performance on "Down in a Hole," it still brings a tear to my eye. There was a couple times I had to pull my eyes off of Layne and remind myself, Hey, I'm at work. Instead of being a fan here, I better concentrate on my bass chords. He was just so mesmerizing.

TOBY WRIGHT I recorded it and mixed the show. It was an amazing performance to watch. With *Unplugged,* you can do a song as many times as you wanna until you capture the performance that you wanna release, but you can't do any overdubs. And Layne kept forgetting the words to "Sludge Factory." It got pretty funny. I think he was nervous because Donnie and Michele happened to be sitting right in front of him.

SUSAN SILVER Alice did a four-show run opening for Kiss. Kansas City was the last show. I remember standing there at the soundboard with the tour manager. As soon as they went on I looked over at him and said, "This is the last time we're gonna see these guys together onstage, Kevan, I just feel it."

MIKE INEZ That was our last show with Layne. That was really just a heartbreaking thing. Dragster races only last a couple of seconds because you can only burn that hot and go that fast for a short amount of time without having to rebuild your motor. And once again, we were there for each other, and it was like, Okay, let's step back and reevaluate.

SUSAN SILVER Layne's situation was heartbreaking over and over, and I didn't realize how it affected me until the daily crisis management was over. I didn't realize how psychically drained I was until after the last record and after those Kiss shows, when they finally stopped touring and stopped being active altogether.

BARRETT MARTIN We had started making a second record for Mad Season; we had 16 or 17 tunes that we were working on. We were gonna do the same thing—have Layne be the main singer and lyric writer, and have Lanegan be involved. But I could never get either of them to come down to the studio. And then McCready had this idea of doing a new band called Disinformation. I guess Lanegan was gonna be the singer, but again, he never showed up, not once. We talked, Mike and Baker and I did, about getting another singer. And then Baker died.

JOHNNY BACOLAS I was at Baker's house probably a week and a half before he died, which was in 1999. He lived in a tiny house over by Green Lake, another suburb of Seattle, and was playing in a band called the Walkabouts. He was really sad that they weren't finishing Mad Season record number two. And I remember that he was kind of stressing financially. He was just really somber. When he first came out of rehab and I met him, he was extremely excited because it was a fresh start. I remember leaving his house that last time feeling, This is not the normal Baker I'm used to. There's just something not right.

BRETT ELIASON Baker had a girlfriend from Belgium who'd gone back to school in Europe, and I think he felt really lonely. He ended up turning back to dope. I've heard this kind of story a few times, where if you do what you used to be able to do, your body can't take it anymore. Baker hit the floor, and the gentleman that was with him was brave enough not to run, and he called 911. But he was dead by the time they got there. He was a sweet man, a smart man. It's crushing. So sad.

BARRETT MARTIN I was the last guy to talk to Baker. I spoke to him on the phone the night he died; we were supposed to meet for lunch the next day, since I hadn't hung out with him in a little bit. I guess that night this dealer came over, and Baker overdosed and died right there on the kitchen floor. And this shows the sleaziness of the drug dealer—the guy didn't even call an ambulance right away. He left Baker in an overdosed state, and then later, I guess, called the cops to say, "You better go check on this guy."

And when Baker died, that was it. The band was done.

CHAPTER 44
THE BOYS WITH THE MOST CAKE

KEVIN MARTIN The making of Candlebox's second album, *Lucy,* was a disaster. Scott wanted to quit the band, but he wasn't telling anybody, so he was playing drums like a robot. Everybody was really unhappy and tired and overworked. When we said no the first time about getting into the studio to make a record, we should've stuck to it. Were we being pressured? Yeah. The label and management were like, "We need to make this record. We need to make this record." To capitalize on the success of the first album, they want you to follow up with it and be able to get it out as soon as you can.

KELLY GRAY Everybody had just gotten done with a tour. They just got beat to death on the road. They weren't ready to make the second record yet. Hindsight being 20/20, if they'd waited six months it probably would've been a lot better.

KEVIN MARTIN Also, nobody would show up to the studio. Why? Because they had a lot of money. People were buying houses, and it's like, "We got a job to do."

SCOTT MERCADO I don't think I was one of those people that would've just flat-out not shown up. Pete back then was obsessed with golf, so if it was sunny out we knew he was gonna be golfing and we weren't gonna be doing music. *(Laughs.)* Also, Pete at that point, that was before he was clean and sober, and he was having a hard time.

PETER KLETT By *Lucy,* I'd be high on coke and all jittery and just wanting to get my tracks done so I could go. I was definitely guilty of calling in sick because I'm fucking hungover and not showing up to the studio, things like that. But sometimes we didn't deserve to be ridiculed and yelled at. Kevin tends to think he was Mr. Perfect all the time.

SCOTT MERCADO The thing is that Kevin won't sing until he feels that everything is right, and if your singer won't sing until everything is right, what are you gonna do? He's very, very, very anal about the drums. I think that's why Candlebox goes through so many drummers. I just felt like, Okay, I'll do it this way, just for the sake of getting it done.

KEVIN MARTIN I think they'd be foolish not to complain about me. The problem was, they don't see me as the bandleader. In the studio, I would be like, "We have a record we're trying to make here. Where the fuck are you guys?" They probably would call me a control freak, but the bottom line is if we decide to get started on something as a band, then that means if you're not showing up you're gonna get your fucking ass handed to you.

BARDI MARTIN I remember being there every day. In my mind, it wasn't about people showing up or not showing up, it wasn't about drugs, it was about not taking the time and the space to write the album that we probably could have written.

KEVIN MARTIN Courtney used to talk shit about us all the time. We saw her on MTV, talking about "stupid bands like Candlebox who ride the coattails of my husband." That started in '93, and after Kurt committed suicide, it was even worse.

COURTNEY LOVE *Nobody* cared for Candlebox. It seemed fake.

Guy Oseary signed two bands that made money out of the 48 bands that he signed to Maverick. The other was Alanis Morissette, and

Alanis was the thing that really, really, really infuriated me. I was still filming *Larry Flynt* at the time that Alanis was selling fucking truckloads, and I forbade Woody Harrelson from mentioning Alanis to me. Candlebox was just sort of gay, but Alanis was a safe version of what I had been doing, and it really, really, really infuriated me.

Maverick tried to sign me. I walked into Maverick, and I felt like, Why are these people looking at me like I'm the Vegas dead Marilyn version of Madonna? I play rock music. This is a ghettoized bunch of shit. It was a joke meeting. I took it because it seemed funny and because Guy Oseary seemed very passionate.

I don't want Madonna being my patron. It's retarded. Do you know anything about the relationship between me and Madonna? *No.* What do you know about my relationship with Madonna beyond me throwing a MAC [compact] at Kurt Loder's head?

PETER KLETT She just hated us for the same reason all the other assholes did. They could not handle the fact that we were successful. Fucking Courtney Love didn't deserve squat, man! The reason she ever became anything was because of her husband. Period. End of story.

COURTNEY LOVE It's not like the film industry, where everyone has to say they love each other when they hate each other. So I might say, "Oh, God, George was wonderful to work with, and Renée is the best actress in the history of the world, and Richard is a fantastic director." But music is an industry where slagging each other becomes sort of a sport, particularly in the British press.

KEVIN MARTIN We did a magazine cover for *The Rocket* in '95 and all dressed up like Courtney—in slips and blond wigs and tiaras and makeup—and the headline was CANDLEBOX: THE BOYS WITH THE MOST CAKE. It was a stab at her. But I had a lot of respect for her and I loved her records, and I still do. Charles Cross wrote the article, which helped to explain a lot of our history and where we came from, but it was a little bit too late for people in the Seattle scene to respect or understand it.

CHARLES R. CROSS We do this funny story with Candlebox, and I didn't know that Courtney Love was going to be pissed off enough about it that she was going to threaten to come blow my toilet up. I was in Portland at a hotel; no one knew where I was, and then the phone rang and it's fucking Courtney Love, and I'm like, "How did you find me?" I still never figured that out. She said, "I'm gonna come blow up your toilet!"

KEVIN MARTIN About two months later, we were on tour in Chicago and Courtney called a friend of mine that she knew from Chicago. He handed me his phone, and she just went off on me for two hours. She was losing her fuckin' mind. I think she was pretty well loaded. "How dare you? You guys are posers and fucking bullshit!"

Everything that came out of her mouth went back to Kurt and how we were riding his coattails. I even made a point to her about that: "You know, you keep using your husband's name. This isn't about your husband. We don't sound anything like Nirvana. You need to understand that article is, more than anything, an homage to you and your credibility as an artist in the scene. And you just need to quit being such a pain in the ass and talking shit about us." In a way we were making fun of her, but she should've found it somewhat flattering that somebody would go that far to parody her.

I don't really remember ending the conversation, just looking at the phone and going, "She's not there." I think she passed out.

JONATHAN PLUM On that second record, the record stores had already ordered a million copies. So it was certified platinum before we even made the record. When it got released, it did ship a million. But what none of us knew at the time was that record stores can actually ship back records. So it shipped a million and went certified platinum, but then they just started getting shipped back.

KELLY GRAY When that record came out, the whole music scene had changed again. It definitely had cycled on to its new thing. It was Green Day then.

JEFF GILBERT Among the metal guys, there was a term that we all used to bandy around. If your band was on the way out, we'd say, "Oh, man, you're Candleboxin'." That meant you were circling the drain, so to speak. This was when their second album came out. The second album kind of sounded like the first one, and the first one was pretty cool, but . . . they never really connected with everybody.

PETER KLETT *Lucy* flopped. Plain and simple.

CHAPTER 45 THE COUP

BRUCE PAVITT Post-Nirvana, everyone thought the indie underground was blowing up. It was on the cover of *Time* magazine; Courtney Love is being taken out by major labels and discovering crème brûlées; everybody thought they could sell a million records. There was a total feeding frenzy. Major labels were approaching all the bands we were working with.

I remember specifically there was a situation—this might be a year after *Nevermind* came out—when our A&R head Joyce Linehan said, "There's this group the Grifters who have typically sold 5,000 records and would like a $5,000 advance," and I'm thinking, That sounds about right. By the time we were done negotiating, we had given them a $150,000 advance. And they wound up selling 5,000 records.

MEGAN JASPER The only time I remember Bruce and Jon really becoming furious with each other was in 1990, when Dinosaur Jr. were shopping around for a label. Both Bruce and Jon were huge fans, and Jonathan said, "Let's offer them a big deal. Not more than the majors, but more than we typically do." But there was no money. That's what flipped Bruce out. He saw that as a step towards that becoming normal, and he said, "No, we can't do that—we don't have that money! Is this what the company wants to be?!"

And Jonathan was saying, "Yes, this is what the company should be like! We have to work with the times. This is a relevant band making great art—let's fucking be a part of it!" Bruce walked away, doing his famous mannerism we'd always imitate, where he'd put his hand on his forehead and put his head back and his eyes would get huge.

They were yelling at each other. And that was that moment that it was clear to me that these guys had different visions and different paths they were on.

BRUCE PAVITT After the suicide, we sold half a million copies of *Bleach*. It was a weird feeling that because of the suicide you're able to pay your bills. As the money was coming in, the label was growing. And as the label grew, it became more departmentalized. I felt that Sub Pop was becoming more corporate. We had brought in a marketing person from a major label. I remember she came in one day and said, "There will be no more brainstorming," and I felt less empowered to be creative.

I personally felt if we continued to spend at the rate we were that we would once again be in a situation where we would be desperately low on funds, and I initiated the idea of working with Warner Bros. I thought, Why not just go for it, as opposed to creating a corporate culture, spending all your money, and going out of business? Jonathan was kind of apprehensive about it, but we got on the same page. Dana Giacchetto was our money manager; Sub Pop was his first really big account. He was a very persuasive and charming guy.

Around November '94, we actually talked to Microsoft about doing a joint venture. That was an unusual approach. Dana's idea was Microsoft is in Seattle, they have tons of money, they are in media, and if we went to other labels and said, "We're negotiating with Microsoft," that would move things along. It was a very smart move. Microsoft said, "Sub Pop, you're cool, but we're not interested in working with record labels," and that was it. However, to the people at Warner, we were talking to Bill Gates, the richest guy in the world, and maybe they should offer more money—which they did.

RICH JENSEN I know there was a period in 1990 where Sub Pop was taking meetings with various executives at major labels to talk about partnership deals and asset sales, but that quieted down during the collapsed period and it didn't really get going again until about '93, and eventually the deal was consummated with Warner Music in '95. It was a pretty remarkable, historic deal that basically provided a lot of money without too many strings attached. It was $20 million for a minority stake, noncontrolling interest of 49 percent. I think the deal ended up being four times what we expected—we had been thinking $5 million.

BRUCE PAVITT After Dana engineered this deal, everyone wanted to work with him. He went on to manage Leonardo DiCaprio's money. Later, it became known that he never did go to business school and didn't have a business degree, and he wound up going to jail for a couple of years for embezzlement.

MEGAN JASPER Post-grunge, Sub Pop's roster was all over the map: there was Plexi, who were glam; Mike Ireland; the Blue Rags, who were blues; Damien Jurado; the Supersuckers; Combustible Edison; Velocity Girl. I heard a lot of people asking, "What's going on?" There was confusion about what kind of label it was; it was in the process of evolving into something else.

LOU BARLOW (singer/guitarist for Westfield, Massachusetts's Sebadoh; bassist for Amherst, Massachusetts's Dinosaur Jr.) With Sebadoh's third Sub Pop record, *Harmacy,* things just went wrong. They'd hired people from big labels to do radio promotion and get placement for us on shows like *Friends.* They were trying to get our wannabe–hit single "Willing to Wait" to play when Ross and Rachel were splitting up or something.

The only reason I wasn't comfortable with it was because I knew that we as a band were flawed in a way that would prevent us from reaching that kind of level. The drummer that we had was just a friend of ours who could barely play, and drums are the texture that really determine whether it's gonna reach the next level. We'd even hired a producer who, during the course of *Harmacy,* was begging me, "Fire your drummer! You've got to do this!" And I was like, "We're sticking with Bob. He's a friend."

Sub Pop was becoming corporate, and trying to play the game on that level. There just weren't any returns on it. They lost a lot of money on us, and I think they lost even more on the Supersuckers.

NILS BERNSTEIN There was the major-label idea that we need a few huge bands to float all the small bands. So they have this huge radio department, with locations all over the country, which kept growing, as if, if we just make ourselves big enough, we will somehow compel a hit to occur. And that's where I think it got a little irresponsible. A lot of money was spent to no avail. Bruce's leaving was a really gradual process over many years. He was more and more gone from the office, and then he was entirely gone, and then he became officially gone.

ART CHANTRY There's only about 10 people who got rich in the Seattle scene, like millionaire-level. And this includes people who ran record labels. Bruce Pavitt, bless his heart. I've said a lot of harsh things about Bruce, but I think of them as funny things, in a very black sort of way. But when it came to helping the community, he is one of the only guys who didn't take the money and run. He actually helped his friends. Say, if somebody wanted to start a restaurant, he would finance it. He would loan people money to go back to school. There's a lot of guys that would not have survived if he hadn't come back and helped them. And I gotta say, there's a spot in heaven waiting for him for that.

BRUCE PAVITT My relationship with Jon was becoming more distant. I had married, I had a kid, so I was less available for travel and for inter-action; we used to do a lot of brainstorming and theorizing about stuff when we traveled. Jon and I are different people, but we had a good chemistry with regards to envisioning and creating things together. I couldn't relate to the corporate culture, so I officially resigned in April 1996. In December, some employees came to me and said, "Bruce, we really miss you, and the company is becoming unbearable." This was the beginning of "the coup."

JONATHAN PONEMAN What I had heard was that Bruce was meeting with some employees at Linda's Tavern, which Bruce and I co-own. The fact of the matter was Sub Pop was not a very nice place to work at that point. Bruce had the good sense of having checked out years ago. I had the impulse to move the label forward. In retrospect, I was very depressed, very tired. I had gotten involved in certain spiritual pursuits; I was trying to distract myself from the growing mess that was Sub Pop.

This was all going down in a period of my life that was very difficult, because my father was dying, and the very week of the coup, my father died. Also, we had ongoing tenuous relationships with Warner and we were borrowing money and we had all these satellite offices that just weren't managed in a very practical manner. So the company was exceedingly bloated. It was all the bad things about a major label, with the inefficiency of an indie.

LOU BARLOW During that period, I got into Seattle to play a show, and I was in this coffee shop on First Avenue, and they were laying out the new stack of either *The Stranger* or the *Seattle Weekly*, and there's a big picture of Bruce and Jon on the cover, with the headline WHAT HAPPENED? or THE BIG SPLIT. The story detailed the collapse of their relationship, and one of the first things it blames is how poorly the Sebadoh record sold after how much money they spent on it. We only sold 90,000 copies of *Harmacy*, which would have been great had we not spent $120,000 on a video for "Willing to Wait" and had the song remixed by some big-league cheeseball mixer.

BRUCE PAVITT Jon had set up a meeting with Warner to get a bunch of money. My point was, "Before we borrow more, let's think about restructuring and reconsidering how money is spent." I still owned 25 percent of the company and told him I was going to go to Warner and tell them to stop funding the label. Jon was extremely pissed off. He then fired the four people I wanted put in positions of more responsibility. I felt that Nils Bernstein, who's now the publicist at Matador, was the one person who could get along with everybody, the one person who had a very sane perspective on what an indie label should do and how money should be spent. I felt very strongly if Nils was in there as a president or general manager, the label would be in a much stronger position. I didn't think Rich Jensen was doing that. He was a friend of mine, but I think he was losing perspective.

RICH JENSEN Bruce was at home and launched a surprise attack. I was totally sympathetic to the idea of hacking back at that bloat. They put three quarters of a million dollars behind the Supersuckers, and I thought that was absurd. Similar number for this glam band from L.A., Plexi, that was gone after a year. That was nuts. At the time I was very disappointed in Bruce. I wish that we could've had a friendly conversation before he put people in the position of being fired.

NILS BERNSTEIN I was one of the four fired. Around that time, we had written, but not yet sent, a letter to Warner about changes we wanted. I understand why Jonathan did it—we were undermining him.

JONATHAN PONEMAN I may have overreacted, but these people were meddling in my affairs. If this letter would have been sent off, I would have been profoundly humiliated at best.

BRUCE PAVITT When the people were fired, they had to sign gag orders in order to get compensation. So they couldn't even talk to the press. That was not very punk rock, in my opinion. After that, I didn't really communicate with Jon, except through attorneys, for seven years.

ANNA WOOLVERTON (Sub Pop Records receptionist) It really felt like a divorce. Everybody was so suspicious of everybody else. There was a lot of crying. I remember during the coup, I just sat at my desk and cried, because I was so bummed out that it had to be like that.

JONATHAN PONEMAN The coup was a wake-up call. I owe everyone in that situation a debt of gratitude, because it set us on a course of restructuring that a lot of record companies are doing now—shrinking and becoming more efficient. I think we're so successful right now by staying within our budgets, minding our overhead, signing bands that mean something to people, not being overly ambitious, being respectful of the artist.

DANIEL HOUSE C/Z was courted for a really long time by Relativity Entertainment Distribution, RED, part of Sony. We had a really good distribution setup through a number of nonexclusive arrangements.

And we sold directly to retail, as well, and we were a profitable company. We weren't making money hand-over-fist, but we were not laden with debt. RED, in some sort of desperate need for indie cred, kept chasing us and chasing us and said, "We can get your records in places that you're not being represented," meaning the chains, big-box stores. Our concern was that our foundation, the mom-and-pop indie stores, didn't get compromised. And they assured us, "No, no, no, that won't happen." So we finally did a deal with them in 1993, and they fucked us sideways and frontways and backwards.

They wanted to use us to go, "See? We have C/Z," to get other labels to come on board. All of a sudden our records weren't getting into any of those mom-and-pop stores anymore. So our entire base of where we sold our records was not being served, and we were not allowed to sell directly to them anymore. And RED was loading 300 copies of a CD into one Sam Goody, the kind of store that people who were trying to get our kind of music never went to. In nine months, I went from being debt-free and in the black to laying everybody off, myself included.

About a year later, I got this deal with Zoo Entertainment through BMG, where they gave us money that ultimately allowed me to pay down the rest of the debt that was outstanding. It was a pretty good deal, but unfortunately, it only lasted a year because Volcano did a hostile takeover of Zoo and basically shut Zoo down, and we stopped getting money.

At this point, it just seemed like, This isn't fun anymore, this is fucked, it's too much of a fight. What's the point? I said if I'm gonna do anything else, I'm gonna have it be a hobby, like how I started. And the last record I put out on C/Z was in 2001; it was the Skin Yard odds-and-sods record called *Start at the Top*. I figured Skin Yard was what got me into the whole thing, so that would be a good way to step away. I haven't put out a record since.

CHAPTER 46
70 PERCENT OFF ALL FLANNEL

JACK ENDINO Mark Arm had gotten clean at some point before I started recording *My Brother the Cow*. He said, "This is the first record I'm going to do clean and sober, so I'm a little worried." That record probably restored his confidence, because he was fine.

Mark was never any problem to deal with in the studio at any point. I never had any idea that he was doing drugs, because Mark was a very functional person. There wasn't any of this being late, not showing up, any of that bullshit you get with junkies. He wasn't the typical junkie, as far as that goes.

DAVID KATZNELSON *My Brother the Cow* is all about the movement itself. You could look at that album as marking the death of grunge. It talks a lot about not only Kurt's death, but what happens to a scene when it is majorly marketed, when big business buys in, when a lot of the members of the scene buy into the idea of big business, when the music gets corrupted, when friends get famous and forget where they came from. It's a very, very dark look at one band's attempt to remain consistent with their beliefs while the world around them has changed.

The song "Into Yer Shtik" caused a lot of problems. The CEO of Warner Bros. at the time was Danny Goldberg, who was the former manager at Gold Mountain, and Courtney Love called him one day and said, "I am so destroyed at the fact that there's that one line in the song," which was, "Why don't you go blow your brains out, too?" That song wasn't about Courtney. That song was actually more about the business side, the exploiters, and it was kind of ironic that Courtney assumed it was about her.

COURTNEY LOVE I don't think I ever listened to that song, but it just hurt my feelings. That's really mean. Why would you do that? What are you doing? Unconsciously playing into some Byzantine notion of pre-Rome, where if someone committed suicide the widow has to get buried alive next to the fuckin' husband? Thanks, assholes. It shocked me that someone of Mark's intellect would do that, and even Matt Lukin and even Steve. When I toured with them, we had such a good time. I *loved* Dan Peters. Dan Peters and me fuckin' broke fuckin' Budweiser bottles over our heads together.

DAN PETERS There's a lot of references in that song. We played in Chicago one time, and Steve Albini was at the show, probably not there to see us. I'm like, "Hey, Steve, my name is Dan, I play for Mudhoney. I hear you just recorded my buddies in TAD. Just wanted to say hi." He gave me some offhanded dismissal. I was pissed, and I told Mark about it. And Mark, sometime later, walked up to Steve and was like, "Hi, my name is Mark. I really dig your shtick."

STEVE ALBINI I don't remember that incident, but I could totally imagine myself being dismissive to somebody else. I was kind of a prick back then.

MARK ARM That's what got the ball rolling in the back of my mind— the idea of people trying to live up to something that they think they are supposed to be, instead of trying to be a natural human being. Steve Albini's not in that song necessarily. But it applies. It applies to all kinds of people, not just musicians.

JACK ENDINO Everybody thought it was about Courtney. I remember asking, "Mark, is this what I think it is?" He said, "No, it's not who you think it is, and I'm not going to tell you who it's about." And that was it. I never got anywhere asking Mark what his lyrics were about.

MARK ARM The song has three little stories, and one is about Layne. I think Emily witnessed this—supposedly Layne was at the Mecca Café and his hands were all bandaged. He'd just come out of the hospital because he punched through a window or something. If you listen to the second Alice in Chains record, it's all songs about being a junkie. He went from dabbling with this thing to having it become a major part of his persona. That's the one who "Made his myth/Now he's trapped."

DAVID KATZNELSON The hubbub started before the album came out. In fact, the way I found out about it was pretty surreal: Mudhoney was in the building at the time, and it was Mark Arm's birthday. We were bringing the cake to him with the candles, and I got a call from Danny, and he was very upset because he had gotten this call from Courtney. He had no idea Mudhoney was even in the building.

MARK ARM Another is about this woman Janet Billig. When we first met her, she was totally antidrugs, wouldn't work with anyone who was a junkie. And when she started working for Gold Mountain, with Kurt and Courtney, all of a sudden she just let her ethics totally slip. Either she was starstruck or the job meant so much to her that she wanted to please her bosses.

DAVID KATZNELSON Danny and I had a conversation that evening, which culminated in a conversation over lunch the next day. The end result was that he was fine with the release of the record. He understood that there were a lot of emotions going on in the community and also understood the song wasn't about Courtney.

MARK ARM The other one was Eric Erlandson, who was going out with the 19-year-old actress, which would be Drew Barrymore. I think it's more about this 19-year-old girl, who thought this guy in Hole was all that. Because if he wasn't in Hole, he wouldn't have stood a chance with her.

ERIC ERLANDSON Really? I'll have to go look at the lyrics. I met Drew in L.A., we hooked up together in Seattle, and within six months or so we moved in together in L.A. Two people had just died—Kurt and Kristen—and I wanted to get the hell out of Seattle. She was bringing a little sunshine. I don't care if people in Seattle didn't think it was a "cool" move. When you love somebody, you love somebody.

MATT LUKIN Danny Goldberg told our A&R guy, "I don't want to meet those guys. I don't ever want to shake their hands. I don't want to have my picture taken with them." And I'm like, "Oh, really? That's all I've been dreaming about my whole life, is to have my picture taken with Danny Goldberg!"

STEVE TURNER Obviously there's some Courtney stuff in there, but there's also the Stone Temple Pilots in there. 'Cause I think we were reading some fashion magazine article focusing on their stylist and the band's singer demanding some outfit he wanted to wear or some such bullshit. I put out the "Into Yer Shtik" seven-inch on my label, Super Electro Sound Recordings, and remember cutting up parts of that magazine article to use on the back of the sleeve. Here it is: "Then her pager beeps. It is Polyester Pilot"—I changed the dude's name—"the band's moody singer, and he wants 'something pink.' And not just pink, he says. Pink, fuzzy, and still sort of masculine. 'I'll find it,' she says."

I'm sure they're lovely people, but at the time it was like, "Man, they can't be serious."

JEFF SMITH I remember Mark saying he figured they hadn't really made it because there was no fake Mudhoney song on the first Stone Temple Pilots album. Beavis and Butt-Head were like, "Hey, Eddie Vedder got a new haircut!" "What, this *isn't* Pearl Jam?" It had a fake Alice in Chains song, a fake Nirvana song. That record is almost like a best-of-Seattle.

DAVID KATZNELSON *My Brother the Cow* sold crappily. There was a backlash against grunge. The backlash didn't touch Soundgarden, it didn't touch Pearl Jam, because they were no longer grunge bands, they were pop bands. They had been accepted by a whole other audience.

MATT CAMERON With "Black Hole Sun," we brought out the psychedelic elements of Soundgarden and that kind of ferocious element, as well. We had a huge hit with it. *Superunknown* was a huge, huge record for us, and getting on the radio for the first time with a pop hit just cemented the success. I felt like we had infiltrated the system with our sound. We didn't compromise at all.

STEVE TURNER The reviews for *My Brother the Cow* were just *horrible*. We made a big, grungy record, and I think we even used the word *grunge* in the press packet. We were just being funny because we knew it was probably gonna be savaged. Grunge had been in everybody's face and there was a horrible tragedy that came out of it and there was also the new punk explosion—Epitaph bands, Offspring, Green Day—that was getting the younger kids.

Because we were a grunge band and Kurt was dead and we hadn't hit that kind of success anyway, not only was it an old thing, but we were failures, also-rans. It made total sense to me, but it was all bullshit game stuff. Some of the English press people that we thought were kind of friends with us, they wouldn't even talk to us anymore—they did the cold-shoulder thing. It was like, They take that shit *serious*?

Dave Grohl made his first Foo Fighters album and people were *ecstatic* about that. Because they were looking for something to rise from such a tragedy. It got *crazy* hype in Seattle at first.

DAVE GROHL After Kurt's death, I was about as confused as I've ever been. To continue almost seemed in vain. I was always going to be "that guy from Kurt Cobain's band" and I knew that. I wasn't even sure if I had the desire to make music anymore. I received a postcard from fellow Seattle band 7 Year Bitch, who had also lost a member.

ELIZABETH DAVIS-SIMPSON When Kurt died, we wanted to reach out to Krist and Dave to share some things that we wished someone had told us, or things that we learned from our experience when Stefanie died. I remember everyone contributing a few paragraphs. The basic sentiment was, "We know that you might feel like, Fuck all of this, and just stop playing music, but you should not feel that way and you should keep on playing."

DAVE GROHL That fucking letter saved my life, because as much as I missed Kurt, and as much as I felt so lost, I knew that there was only one thing that I was truly cut out to do and that was music. I know that sounds so incredibly corny, but I honestly felt that.

STEVE TURNER After that, more of the fun music from the area was getting attention: the Presidents of the United States of America, "Flagpole Sitta" by Harvey Danger. We've been around for a while—it's okay for people not to be ecstatic for us anymore.

JACK ENDINO The circus left town, and the town had a grunge hangover. Basically, the music scene kind of woke up groggy and went, "God, where's the truck that hit us? What happened? Oh, guitars, I don't even want to look at a guitar now."

The first sign of that? Probably Britpop. I don't even remember the bands that were involved. One of them got popped for ripping off Wire. Elastica? Yes. They're completely forgotten now. But, yeah, that became the next big thing, and in Seattle, the biggest band were the Presidents, who had nothing to do with grunge, even though they have an ex–Skin Yard drummer in the band. But they were huge!

DAVE DEDERER The people at *The Rocket* and the scenesters hated us, but normal people just started to find out about us; it was truly word of mouth in the beginning. When Jason joined the band, Love Battery had just signed a major-label deal with A&M after three records for Sub Pop. The Presidents was just a joke side band for him. Everybody he knew was basically telling him that the Presidents was stupid and a waste of his time.

KEVIN WHITWORTH It was obvious there was a strain between the two bands, and that Jason was gonna have to go with one or the other. And he really has always wanted to be famous, and good for him. He's a character. He should be famous. When Love Battery worked on songs, he used to say, "We're never gonna go anywhere!" "We're not trying to go anywhere, we're just trying to make this a decent song right now." He was very impatient.

DAVE DEDERER We were nominated for a Grammy two years in a row, and we lost to Nirvana and the Beatles. At the '96 Grammys, I thought it was so funny that Pearl Jam won and they got up onstage and Vedder said it didn't mean anything.

EDDIE VEDDER (accepting the Grammy for Best Hard Rock Performance for Pearl Jam's "Spin the Black Circle," February 28, 1996) I'm gonna say something typically "me" on behalf of all of us. I don't know what this means. I don't think it means anything. That's just how I feel.

DAVE DEDERER I'm in the audience and Chris, Jason, and I just looked at each other and laughed. Because it was so absurd and self-conscious and silly. Nobody goes out and starts a band and goes through the nightmare of making records and promoting them and going on tour, which is hard fucking work, unless they want to sell records. That said, Pearl Jam managed to survive and thrive and work together, and that's no mean feat—I have a lot of respect for what they've done.

At the Grammys, Tupac and Snoop Dogg were sitting in front of me and my wife and they got up literally every 10 minutes to go blow dope in the lobby. Every 10 minutes, they'd look at each other and smile, leave, and come back five minutes later just reeking. I saw Ed Vedder up there sayin' that shit and tryin' to be cool. I'm like, Okay, that's silly. And then you look at someone like Snoop Dogg and you think, Okay, that guy is actually a badass. That guy actually is cool.

JACK ENDINO There was a period there in '95, '96 where I thought, Maybe I'm going to have to find another career here. There's no more bands to record! The scene died! It's gone, it's over. Maybe that was just a flash in the pan back then, and I'm going to have to either start recording really bad bands or I'm going to have to find some other line of work. So I started recording people in other countries, because people wanted me as a producer there.

TIM HAYES I moved away from Seattle in '90 and came back in '96. When I got back, the life had been sucked out of a lot of people I knew. They weren't out looking for new bands. They were just relying on their old bands, like Mudhoney, to keep them going. I love Mudhoney, but they're what people already knew. My friends were holding on to the past a little bit. With some people I would say it was a function of their age, but I think it was more because the industry had permeated the scene with so many shitty bands, like Candlebox and Alice in Chains.

LANCE MERCER When the scene died down, the musicians and other people in the business who didn't make it had to back up and reevaluate. I always say they had to either put on the orange apron, the green apron, or the blue apron: Home Depot, Starbucks, or Kinko's.

CHARLES PETERSON In some ways, with a lot of photo editors, my career died when Kurt did. So I needed to go and reinvent myself and validate myself as a photographer. I went and did some traveling to Southeast Asia. I just needed to put it away for a while.

Then around 2001, when it was the 10th anniversary of the release of *Nevermind*, I started getting more requests, and I started pulling out the files and going through stuff, and just going, My God, there's some good work in here that nobody's ever seen. Or old work that nobody's ever seen properly. That's when I sat down with my friend Hank Trotter, and we designed my book *Touch Me I'm Sick*. And it keeps going. I keep selling Nirvana photos on a weekly basis. It's a little bit weird, living with this dead guy.

. . .

KURT DANIELSON We were dropped from Giant when we were in Europe with Soundgarden. What screwed things up with Giant wasn't really the way it's been told—as being because of the poster with Clinton on it. Have you seen that poster? I don't know who did it; it was somebody in connection with the European tour. It was a black-and-white photograph of Bill Clinton making a speech. And his hand gestures and facial gestures were perfect for the insertion of a fake joint, and there was a quote on the bottom saying "THIS IS HEAVY SHIT," referring to TAD's music, of course. It was hilarious.

Unfortunately, somebody at Giant didn't have a sense of humor and thought it was a politically damaging thing, even though not that many people saw it. Giant used that poster as their excuse to drop us. But more important than that was that we had a manager at the time who was less than trustworthy, let's just put it that way. All we can surmise is that he must have caused more problems than solutions when he dealt with Giant. And we weren't selling a lot of records.

We got a new manager, Jonny Z, who originally was Metallica's manager, and he got us onto Elektra/East West. Gary had left the band, and we were back on the road again, promoting *Infrared Riding Hood*, the last record, when they cleaned house at East West.

JOSH SINDER Then TAD got dropped a final time. I left because I didn't like other people's attitudes. Everybody was getting fucked up too much. At the end, there was a lot of drugs, and things weren't going good. I started playing with Gruntruck.

MIKE MONGRAIN (TAD drummer) My first show with TAD was August of '96. At that point, it was a band in decline. I liken it to stepping on the *Titanic* about five minutes post-iceberg. And I rode that bitch to the bottom, yeah.

It was tough on Tad and Kurt because so many of their peers—and I'm speaking here as an outsider seeing it from the inside—had done so well. All the bands that they started with were living in big houses and making their mortgages. TAD and Soundgarden and Nirvana and Alice in Chains all came up together, and TAD was always passed over for that one big promotion. I don't think anybody was ever explicit about it, but every now and then you would see flashes of anger and resentment. It was the only thing I could attribute it to.

And there were so many crappy bands getting on the grunge band-wagon that were kind of a joke. I always had a serious distaste for bands like Stone Temple Pilots and Bush. They were capturing the essence of what was going on, at least the sound, but they were missing some-thing. Something that was tongue-in-cheek and humorous and ironic, like TAD or Mudhoney. I never caught a shred of humor in anything the Stone Temple Pilots or Bush were doing. They were being serious rockers, copping a sound and missing the irony.

RON RUDZITIS After Kurt died, the big media thing was, "Grunge is dead, along with Kurt Cobain." Yet the biggest bands on MTV were people like Bush, who were blatant Nirvana rip-offs. I felt a lot of re-sentment, going, "Well, what the fuck?" How can some bands like Bush, which is just a fuckin' Nirvana wannabe, get all this exposure, when the bands that actually started that sound are getting left in the dust?

Our major label very unceremoniously dropped us. Maybe there's a reason why Love Battery never made it big—because I'd be dead by now. I have to try and look at the bright side. *(Laughs.)* If I had all that disposable money, I really doubt I would've quit drugs.

KURT DANIELSON Tad and I had difficulty in communicating because we were both doing a lot of drugs. It seemed easier just to continue doing a lot of drugs than to deal with the problem of the band. My first marriage was falling apart, the band was falling apart, I had chronic pain issues, and instead of facing those problems, I just escaped. The pain that resulted from my back injuries, plus migraines, led me to experiment with all kinds of painkillers and eventually with heroin, so I became a long-term opiate addict. The heroin started about '95 or so.

TAD DOYLE I liked coke a lot, and I found that I couldn't afford it that much, so I went for the cheaper version of that, which was crystal meth and glass. I was taking cash advances on my credit card to go buy more. And I'd only leave at night. I was becoming essentially an addicted vampire. I had a police scanner that I bought that I'd listen to 'cause I was sure they were coming after me someday—that's how far it went.

MIKE MONGRAIN I wanted to try to nudge us in a direction that was post-grunge. TAD had already been going in a more melodic direction, but it just didn't have the cohesion yet. I thought, Let's continue in that direction, with some more refinement. I remember when we were on tour in the Netherlands in '97, we walked past a department store and there was a display in the window. It had a whole bunch of flannel shirts hangin' in the window with a humongous sign that said 70 PERCENT OFF. I was like, "Guys! Look at that. Let that burn into your brain. That's the reality."

KURT DANIELSON The question of "Should we continue or should we break up?" was on the table for a month or two, and finally Tad and I had a conversation in 1999 and we decided, "Let's just break it up."

DAN PETERS I was actually shocked that we lasted as long as we did on Warner Bros. We knew when we were making *Tomorrow Hit Today* it was going to be our last record for the label. God love Dave Katznelson; he fought tooth and nail to get that record made. Warner Bros. had gone through a lot of changes, and he was pretty much told by the people that had taken over the label, "Why do you want this record to be made?" So that record was released into obscurity. They released it—I think. I do have a copy of it.

MATT LUKIN The rest of the band claims *Tomorrow Hit Today* was my best bass performance. And I go, "That's kind of funny, because that's when I cared the least about it." But I guess a lightbulb shines brightest right before it burns out.

A month or two after we got back from Japan, Mark came over to the house for something, so I broke it to him. I go, "Look, Turner took the wind out of my sails a few years ago with the going-back-to-school thing. And I really haven't been able to get motivated since. I've tried." He goes, "Yeah, we kinda noticed."

I started working carpentry. I remember coming home from the first job I had by myself. I thought, This is fucking great. I'm going home, it's 5 o'clock, I get to spend the rest of the night at home doing nothing. No one's deciding if I'm going to work tomorrow or not. Of course, that turned into just being like everything else, a big headache. I can decide what I want to do when the bills are paid. Until they're paid, I can't decide anything.

RICK GERSHON (Warner Bros. Records/A&M Records publicity executive) Mudhoney's last record for Reprise, *Tomorrow Hit Today,* I remember nobody stood up to be counted when that record came down the pike. I put my hand very high in the air and said I would be honored to work with Mudhoney. And the two years or so that I worked with them, it was one of the most satisfying experiences of my life, musically, personally, professionally. They are such an amazing band and such bright musicologists.

I always found it very ironic and sad that Mark Arm had a day job at the Fantagraphics comic-book warehouse in Seattle. To me, it just wasn't fair. They were the band that should've become rich and famous. And then written some really funny songs about becoming rich and famous.

DALE CROVER Pretty much from when we signed on to do our last record for Atlantic, everybody was gone. Danny Goldberg wasn't there anymore. Our A&R guy, Al Smith, was gone. We made *Stag,* and I thought, This is the best record we've ever done. I don't know why they wouldn't be able to sell a shitload of these records! But the people at the label at that point just had no idea what to do with our band.

VALERIE AGNEW I remember us feeling like we had more problems on an independent label than we did when we were on a major label. Once we were doing a record with Atlantic, it felt easier in some ways. We learned later it was because they didn't give a shit about us!

SELENE VIGIL-WILK Contrary to popular belief, we didn't get dropped by Atlantic. We broke up because we were having our own internal stuff going on. Things were just really intense. There was a lot of death—other very close friends of ours who weren't popular musicians—and a lot of freaking emotion.

VALERIE AGNEW We probably *would* have been dropped had we continued. But I think Atlantic would have been willing to work with us still if we had been a little more agreeable the next time around with business-type suggestions. But we really got to a point where we couldn't agree on some business stuff and we were arguing about our creative direction, which was new for us. And we were being very ambitious, trying to work together and not be living in the same city. Selene was in L.A., and Elizabeth and I were in San Francisco. And Roisin had quit the band, so we also had a new guitar player come into the mix. I think the combination of all those things made it really hard to be on the same page.

BUZZ OSBORNE When Atlantic picked up the option for the third album, I just about couldn't fucking believe it. The big money would've come on the sixth and seventh records, I believe. Not that this wasn't good money. It was like 150 grand, you know?

I saw the writing on the wall with *Stag*, and we went ahead and recorded another record without them knowing. So that the second that they dumped us, that we were legally done, we could have an album come out. No waiting time, no down period where people think that you broke up, no sitting around wondering what to do. And then, if they wanted us to do another record, we'd go, "Okay," collect the advance, sit around and pretend that we're recording, and then give them that record. It was flawless.

Finally, I got to the point where I called up our A&R guy, Mike Gitter, who'd essentially told us, "I'm in charge of all the older bands that nobody else wants to work with." I couldn't get him on the phone, so I told his assistant, "Tell Mike Gitter that we want him to drop us off the fucking label immediately." Get a call back from him in five minutes. I told him, "Just drop us. We know it's going to happen. Just drop us now. It's fine." A couple weeks later, we find out that we're done. So we got dropped from Atlantic, put out the *Honky* record about a month later, hit the road, and toured for the next year.

And that just pushed us into the next era of our band. Today, I think we're better than we've ever been. We work all the time, and we never stop.

MARK DEUTROM On *Honky*, which we recorded for Amphetamine Reptile after Atlantic didn't pick up our option, there is a tune called "Laughing with Lucifer at Satan's Sideshow," which seemed to epitomize the major-label experience for us, and probably a few other bands, I would imagine. The voices on this are actually the band's manager, David Lefkowitz, and a woman, I can't remember who, quoting real statements made to us by individuals in some of the higher positions at Atlantic, after Danny Goldberg had left. Such chestnuts as "You should consider yourself lucky—any other major label would have dropped you by now" and "The people here in Radio just don't like your band."

I think "Laughing with Lucifer" is truly the epitaph on the tombstone of grunge. Major labels brought it to the planet, exploited it, and then killed it when it was used up, like any self-respecting corporation would do.

NICK TERZO I got to Maverick in the summer of '96. Guy wanted me to meet with Candlebox and get the material right for the third record. Peter and Kevin definitely butted heads, and there was a lot of disinterest from the public, too. I just felt like we could never get the material quite where it should be for that third record. The album came out, and nothing really happened. I was finished by the time it came out; because of the tension between the partners at Maverick, I was out of there by the spring of '98.

The label knew what Candlebox had done for them in a nascent part of their lives, so I think there *was* a loyalty there. I bet the band didn't feel that—they would have felt neglected—but I really think any other band would have been dropped after the second record. Maverick did the right thing. I think they felt Candlebox were part of the family there. It's a different vibe there.

GUY OSEARY When they signed, immediately I went, "Thank you, thank you, thank you. Thank you for believing in me and giving me a chance to show you what I do and helping me build this future." So I'm very grateful to Candlebox. A year later we're gold, the year after that we're triple-platinum-plus, and after that it's lots of stuff internally with the band. I'm not really privy to all the details.

SCOTT MERCADO I got tired of all the arguing. After the *Lucy* tour, I walked into a rehearsal situation, and Kevin was playing drums with Pete and Bardi. And again, because Kevin's controlling . . . I saw him there, and I was in a very bad mood that day. I'm like, "I just can't do this anymore, guys. I'm sick of this. I'm sorry." They understood. I mean, they weren't really happy in the band, either.

DAVE KRUSEN In '95, I took over for Eddie Vedder on drums in his then-wife Beth's band Hovercraft. I really loved it, but I didn't make any money and I had a daughter with my now-ex-wife to support. Then Kevin Martin called me saying that Candlebox were having some problems and Scott was leaving the band, so I left Hovercraft and joined Candlebox in '97.

We went to L.A. and recorded *Happy Pills,* and once we were on the road nonstop for months, it got to where everybody was in a screaming match every day and somebody was gonna quit the band every day. It just felt like the whole thing's gonna friggin' implode anyway, so why am I gonna wait till the last second? So I jumped ship, and then Bardi left right after I did.

KEVIN MARTIN After the first tour on *Happy Pills,* which would've been the fall of '98, I went to Maverick and talked to Freddy and Guy. I said, "You know, you guys got to fucking show us some sort of commitment here, because we are losing faith in you as a label." They said, "Everything's fine. We're working the record." I'm like, "You're not."

Maverick dropped the ball. They fired the whole promotion staff right before we released the record. I have no idea why. We never got a straight answer from them about it. I think it was egos—Guy and Madonna were trying to buy Freddy out of the company. I told them, "You're gonna cause this band to break up." And by '99, the band was so imploded because of all of the shit we'd dealt with that we were like, "Look, we gotta fuckin' walk away before we kill one another."

Until March 2011, I didn't get royalties from the first three Candlebox records. Before then, I was still paying for a fourth Candlebox record that was never delivered to Maverick. The label didn't exist anymore, but they were still collecting the money. In order to get out of the contract, I had to agree to pay back my quarter of the fourth-record advance. Unfortunately, it's usually the singer who gets stuck signing that agreement. I'm sure that Scott, Pete, and Bardi are fine with it, because they've been getting royalties all along.

My now-ex-wife Renee told me I should've slept with Madonna. It was one of the fights that we had: "If you had slept with her, your career wouldn't be this way! You wouldn't have to sign this agreement!" At the time, she was incredibly frustrated with the position that we were in. Yeah, that tension helped me out the door.

JACK ENDINO Gruntruck continued to play throughout the '90s. Got a song on MTV and everything. They'd got it into their heads that if they could just get off Roadrunner somehow, they could get a major-label deal. What commenced was years of legal nonsense, of them trying to get out of their seven-album deal with Roadrunner. But by the time they did, nobody cared about them anymore. They continued playing, halfheartedly recording, but it fell apart. By the time the thing happened with Ben, which was the early 2000s, Gruntruck was not really active.

Ben had a history of increasingly heavy hard-drug use and seriously hard drinking. But, oddly enough, that was a red herring. What took him out was a blood-clotting disease that ran in his family. He had an internal blood clot that actually took out a good chunk of his internal organs—his liver, part of his spleen, a huge chunk of his intestines. Basically, blood flow cut off, and he had to have this incredibly invasive surgery. He was literally in a coma for weeks. Full, complete life support. This guy's going to die. He is done. I remember going to see him at one point, and his body was so swelled up with fluids, he looked like a whale. You couldn't even recognize his face.

CAM GARRETT He died there, really. They brought him back. The blood clot had killed most of his colon, and they took most of his colon and part of his pancreas out. They gave him less than a five percent chance to live, but he lived another seven years. He was always in pretty fragile health after that. A lot of people thought it was his lifestyle. He had been to rehab a couple times.

JACK ENDINO Ben was never the same. He lost a good third of his body weight, it aged him tremendously, and he literally was missing part of his diaphragm as part of the end result. He never had the full vocal power after that. Although Gruntruck tried to get back together, did a little recording with me, did a few shows, ultimately nothing seemed okay.

SCOTT MCCULLUM He'd fight alcoholism and drug abuse, deteriorate, get back on his feet. Finally, he had kidney failure in 2008. I knew that his life expectancy was greatly diminished and he could go at any time, but I was still shocked when that happened. Especially since we were going to get back together and put together arrangements for some music he'd been working out.

DANIEL HOUSE Ben died of complications of diabetes. I visited him several times at the hospital and spoke to the doctor several times. At the risk of saying things that will piss people off, the doctor told me that Ben had what was called alcohol-induced diabetes. As much as his death was officially due to complications with diabetes, I think the unofficial reason is years and years of heavy drinking and doing a lot of drugs.

CAM GARRETT He was just in his forties. About a year before he died, I was doing a light show for Love Battery, and this guy came up and set his drink by my projectors, and I kind of shooed him away. What I didn't realize at the time was that it was him. I didn't even recognize him. He was so gaunt. He should have told me, "Hey, it's me, Ben." But he didn't. He just kind of slunk away. I think he felt so terrible, and he was really miserable there at the end.

CHAPTER 47
FELL ON BLACK DAYS

BEN SHEPHERD Was making *Down on the Upside* a difficult experience? Yeah. For me, the love of my life was leaving. I think we were working on tracking the day that she left me. I can't remember what the song we were tracking is called now—it's one of my tunes, too. The rest of the band seemed to be chugging along. But we were writing different; we didn't jam as much as we used to. It turns out, thinking about it and hearing all the stories later on, there was a massive lack of communication going on.

SUSAN SILVER Chris and I weren't talking to each other. Chris had definitely become a bad emotional wreck during those times. There was some sort of transition going on that unconsciously or not—I don't know, because he didn't say—maybe he wanted to do something different and hadn't identified it yet. He was unhappy with how things were going on the record, and then he'd just come home and curl up on the floor in a ball and sob.

FRANK KOZIK Soundgarden, they were super-nice guys. I did a music video for them, for "Pretty Noose," which was from their last album.

You could tell that those guys were getting really burned out by the mechanism at that point. They definitely didn't want to do the dog and pony show one more time for this fucking video.

So I was like, "Okay, if you were not a rock star and it was a Saturday afternoon, what would you be doing?" And the big guy with the beard was like, "I'd be shooting pool," so he was shooting pool. And the other guy was like, "I'd be riding my motorcycle," so he'd be riding a motorcycle.

I asked Cornell, "What would you be doing?" and he was like, "I'd be sitting here getting shitfaced."

CHRIS CORNELL During the *Down on the Upside* period, I was drinking all the time. I was playing shows drunk. I would have a keg cup full of vodka with ice before I walked out onstage. And I wasn't aware enough to understand that that wasn't good. I wasn't singing as well or playing as well. I had a couple bad episodes. It wasn't anything new or unusual for someone in a rock band, but for me it was—the band was so important to me and on all the early tours with Soundgarden I never drank on the road.

STUART HALLERMAN By the time there's whiskey on the band's rider, during the last few years of the band, the whole scene turned into a different thing. Instead of having a few beers, they were kind of soused sometimes. Ben, his mean streak would show up. Chris actually got into some moodiness that I had never seen before. It just wasn't as golden and pure as it used to be.

FRANK KOZIK The way it worked with the video was this weird dude, who was the label-slash-MTV guy, came in and was like the producer or something. The guy was a retard. He was asking Cornell, "Can you take your shirt off?" Cornell was like, "I don't want to be the pretty guy with the shirt off. I want to be the asshole." He just really wanted to go have a cheeseburger and not take his shirt off.

So the compromise was, okay, he'll take his shirt off, but only in the context that he's just brutally raped and murdered his girlfriend in the video. It got filmed, and then they cut that part. They refused to show the video in the U.S., except when MTV had the show where they'd air the *weird* videos once a month or whatever.

MATT CAMERON I think we were yearning to be a smaller band or just a band that was completely about the music. I know that's completely cliché and hokey, but success can really tear the good times apart. I think it manifested itself in the touring that we did for *Down on the Upside*. Sometimes there was a disconnect between us and the audience. I got the impression that sometimes it felt like a chore for Ben or Kim to be up there. There was some infighting, and it wasn't a good feeling overall.

SUSAN SILVER The bigger the band got, the bigger everybody's tendencies got. Matt took on more and more of a leadership role; Chris became more and more withdrawn. Kim's a peacemaker—he wanted everything to be good with everybody—but all the responsibilities of the business and touring seemed to overshadow his availability towards playing, so it seemed like he was having less fun.

Ben always had his wild-card moments, but at that point they tended to be more explosive, more dangerous sometimes. He was hostile towards the audience. "How dare you like me?" was the energy that he put back towards people. If they were being too overly appreciative, he'd find a way to spit on 'em.

SOOZY BRIDGES In February of '97, Susan gifted us all—family and people close to her—tickets to come to Hawaii and see Soundgarden play the last show of their tour. At the show, Chris was amazing; his voice was really on top.

CHRIS CORNELL The bass rig wasn't working in sound check, and I remember thinking, Oh, that's not a good sign. It was a mystery why it stopped, but it was one of those things where they got it working now so it will be okay. What inevitably happens is when you start playing, whatever the mystery was will show up again.

BEN SHEPHERD My fuckin' gear was dead. I'm not going to stand up there like some dumbass monkey and pantomime the songs. Let them finish the fuckin' set. I remember smashing my bass on the stage and seeing everyone else there gasp, and my daughter, who was nine years old then, was standing there laughing. She was having the time of her life.

I go backstage and Kim goes back there with me. I'm like, "Kim, you've worked really hard. You got to go back out there and finish this show, man." Susan tried to interrupt us at one point, and I slammed the door and said, "Get the fuck out of here! This is between us. This is *band* talk."

SUSAN SILVER Everybody walked offstage and into the dressing room, and I'm following them in there. And as Ben got in the dressing room, he spun around and we were staring in each other's face, in a dead eye lock, and he had his fist up in a punching position. We stared at each other for a good 30 seconds and I turned around and walked out.

BEN SHEPHERD I finally told Kim, "I'll go with you back out there." He walks back up to the stage, and I didn't. I totally tricked him. Because he was so loyal to me—I'm his brother—unless I tricked him, he wouldn't have gone back out there and finished.

SUSAN SILVER Kim was extremely upset and thrown off by the whole thing, and I went to Matt and Chris and said, "Two choices: Stop it now or you guys can go back up there and perform." By that time, Ben was gone. Matt and Chris went back up there and performed a few acoustic songs; I don't think Kim went back out.

KIM THAYIL It was nothing that unusual. We had live performances that would sometimes end in tantrums or breakdowns. Sometimes it was Ben and at times it had been Chris, at times it had been me. But the band did not break up then, though people characterized it as that. It just happened to be the last scheduled show of the tour. The band broke up a couple months later.

MATT CAMERON I came back to my house from a long walk with my dog and I saw Chris's truck in my driveway, and I was like, Awesome, Chris came over, man. He hasn't come over to my house in a long time. Maybe we're gonna start working on some new music.

I get into the house and my wife informs me that Chris is waiting for me in the basement. I'm like, "That's strange. Why isn't he in the living room?" I remember he smelled like he had been up for days drinking and smoking cigarettes—it was just a total waft of alcohol. I was really happy to see him. I played him some music I'd been writing for Soundgarden. So he listened politely, and he just said point-blank, "I'm leaving the band." I was kind of relieved, in a way. I just didn't know how we were going to rebuild after that last show in Hawaii.

BEN SHEPHERD Chris Cornell shows up in my driveway. I had just played a gig with Devilhead, Brian and Kevin Wood's band, and I got a bunch of the rocker guys to come over to my house. Chris had come to visit me before, but I thought, Oh, that's strange. He has a bottle of MacNaughton's with him, and he comes into the house, like, "Hey man, what's going on?"

A friend of mine who was there said, "Today's the day the Beatles broke up." It was the anniversary. And we all drank to that. And then Chris goes, "Can I talk to you?" And I go down to the car with him, and that's when he said, "I'm leaving." I spat on the ground—just like when I got asked to join the band—and said, "All right." But to me, it seemed like, What's the point? We shouldn't break up. We should all just take time and live for a while.

KIM THAYIL Chris decided that he wanted to move on with his career. I was relieved. Most of our breaks we did songwriting or preproduction. There was a lot of tension trying to maintain the schedule, the expectations, the success. We were in our mid-thirties. People are married, have girlfriends, other friends and family, just a lot of things to pay attention to. We needed to attend to those things.

SUSAN SILVER I knew Chris was extremely unhappy. That night after the Hawaii show, he was so flipped out he wouldn't even talk about it. The basic sentiment was, "I never want to tour with those guys again." There was no conversation about it after that. As he told me later, it was to protect me and my position with the band and not put me in a potentially uncomfortable or maybe even legally difficult situation. He got a totally separate lawyer and went about all of it with great focus. After he went to each of their houses, he came home and told me what he had done. And then got really drunk.

ERIC GARCIA (assistant for Chris Cornell/Susan Silver) With Chris, it got pretty dark. I think it started during Soundgarden, towards the end. He went into severe depression, drugs and alcohol. It was odd. I remember a conversation I had with Sean Kinney about it, and Sean was like, "What the fuck is Chris doing?" We were talking about the fact that Chris was going off the deep end at the wrong time. This is shit that you're supposed to be doing when you're like 25, you know? It was like if you knew somebody and then they ended up being exactly what they said that they never wanted to be.

CHRIS CORNELL It was mentally, physically, and spiritually a fucked-up point in my life. I was waking up and drinking a glass of vodka just to get a dial tone. My marriage wasn't working at all, and rather than face that, I turned to constant inebriation and then drugs.

BEN SHEPHERD It's hard to become a civilian again. I feel like I just disappeared. My honey had just left me, my band had just broken up, and then my band Hater broke up, so I had nothing but three separated ribs from a stunt that I'd pulled—diving into a moving van my friends were driving and landing on the stick shift. Then I got addicted to pain pills like an idiot.

Three separated ribs and no band, no honey, no point of living in Seattle at all. I don't know why I ever stuck around this shithole city. I should've gone adventuring around. But I didn't. I did nothing, besides squander my life and my money.

Pretty quickly after that it got to be the lowest point in my life. I ended up OD'ing on liquid morphine by accident, because I didn't know what it was. A guy I knew gave it to me. I go, "Oh, well," and I slammed it. That night I think I was on 30 Valium, 14 scotches, 6 whiskeys, and 8 beers. Used to do that every night. Sometimes I was up to 50 Valium.

I got dropped off in the cab at home. My friends were in the cab and I could hear them laughing, driving away. I realized as I took the next step up my driveway, Oh, fuck, I've gone way too far. I was like, What is that? It was the ground and the trees and the hill. I realized I was laying on the ground. And the next thing I know, I woke up five days later. In my bed. Somehow I must've made it there.

That was two weeks after Soundgarden broke up. I think. Because ever since we broke up, I haven't cared about dates. Ever since Chris broke the band up, I don't even know what year it was, I don't even know how many months it's been, because I had no honey anymore, had no band anymore. I didn't care.

So I've lost track of everything, I'm absolutely disorganized all the time. Time is irrelevant.

. . .

BARRETT MARTIN The Trees tried to record with Don Fleming again right after we got back from that Alice in Chains tour in '93. This time, we were recording in Seattle because we all wanted to be there with our wives, girlfriends. Van had a couple kids. We were kinda burnt, and I don't think the songs were as good as they could've been. And Lanegan just couldn't sing. He tried, but it just wasn't working, because he had other priorities.

DON FLEMING (producer; singer/guitarist for New York's Gumball/Velvet Monkeys) They had really been on the road a lot; I think that that was the initial problem. We probably should've done what we did with *Sweet Oblivion* and just demo first, and then go back and say, "All right, let's work on these, or write six more." And instead, we went in and just tracked what was available. In my mind, drug use wasn't the problem; if that was going on, I didn't see it. The problem was not having a great set of songs.

MARK LANEGAN Everyone wanted to put out the record to capitalize on *Sweet Oblivion*. The timing was certainly right, but the music wasn't, and I just thought, You know what? This is not good. And it wasn't good because of me. I didn't come to the party, I didn't involve myself— I went through the motions, but I didn't invest any of myself into it. I just didn't have the strength. After all the touring, and because of some other personal problems, I didn't have anything to give to it. I was empty. I tried, but the end result was: It sucked.

BARRETT MARTIN We had started working with Peter Mensch and Cliff Burnstein from Q Prime; they manage Metallica and all those bands. They were like, "You know, you guys need a little more time to rest and write more songs, and then let's revisit this." So we scrapped the Seattle sessions.

I think that if we had gotten *Dust* out within a year or two of *Sweet Oblivion,* it would've done better, but four years went by during which Lanegan was battling heroin problems. I went back to work, back to doing construction.

GARY LEE CONNER That was the worst time of my entire life, around '94, '95. We had to do something. We weren't about to break up, because the band was our whole life financially. I rented the bottom part of a house in Ballard, and sat there for two damn years writing songs. And first it was like, Okay, Mark's going to come over, and Van's going to come over, and we're going to work together. And unfortunately, the first few times we tried that, Mark was asleep on the bed in the other room, and every once in a while we're like, "Hey, how does this sound?" "Okay."

I wrote literally 200 songs over that period of time, and most of them were utter crap. Sometimes Van would come over, and Van was working on some stuff himself, but he was home with his family, so it was hard for him to work full-time on it.

Every night, I'd get a call at some point from Mark, and it'd be, "What are you doing?" He'd always say, "Bring me a tape." So then I had to drive across town in the middle of the night. Usually when I'd get to his apartment, a hand would come out, he'd grunt, maybe say hello, and take the tape. I maybe went in his apartment one time that entire two years.

VAN CONNER I don't want to blame anybody. I was probably carin' more about drinkin' then. Lee would have blowups if we'd be fucking around—maybe I'd be drunk or maybe Mark would disappear for a few days—but through it all, Lee just kept plugging away.

GARY LEE CONNER By the time we got to mixing *Dust,* it was '96. Things had changed, musically. Nirvana was gone; Pearl Jam was big, but they weren't like what they were. It was kind of flavor of the week then. What's going to be next? At the time, it was bands like Prodigy—it was going to be electro, or whatever the hell they were.

Dust ended up selling 100,000 or 150,000 records. Which was good, but we'd always been used to the next record doing better than the last one. We got Lollapalooza, and we were like, Whoa! At that time, that was a big deal. But things had changed, plus Mark was not doing very well. It's not real fun being on tour with him, because he's looking for drugs all the time. This is an example of what it was doing to the band: Right before Lollapalooza, we were playing some shows by ourself . . .

BARRETT MARTIN We were in Cleveland, and the irony was, we played one of the best shows of our careers. We played for like two hours at least, way beyond what was expected, and we were taking requests. Lanegan was in a really good mood. We never took requests, you know? And at one point he was doing question and answer; he was on a bar stool just talking to a thousand people.

Backstage, Van and Lee started arguing about something ridiculous, and I basically said, "Oh, come on, you guys, knock it off. That was a great show." And I said something like, "Lee, stop whining."

And every now and then Lee would spaz out and do something. And he threw a beer bottle—a full beer bottle—really flung it at me, and it almost hit me in the head. Except I saw it out of the corner of my eye, and I ducked. It grazed the back of my head and stuck in the Sheetrock. That's how hard he threw it. If it would've hit me in the head, it would've done some damage.

GARY LEE CONNER Mark kept wanting to borrow money from me. So I would give him a couple hundred bucks or something, and Van and Barrett were like, "Maybe you shouldn't give him money for drugs." At that point, it wasn't just heroin, it was crack and shit like that. And he's going to ghettos and telling us about almost getting killed in a knife fight.

I couldn't tell Mark no, really. He was just going to get mad and stomp off, and it's not real fun to have him mad at you. I got really upset, and I threw a bottle at the wall. Man, I almost hit Barrett in the head. I just cringe when I think what could've happened.

VAN CONNER We said something to Lee that made him mad—I don't know what it was. He threw the bottle at Barrett's head, and then he picked up another bottle to throw it, so we had to jump on him to stop him, and he fought his way over to the kitchen area of the dressing room.

BARRETT MARTIN Van leaped out of his chair and tackled Lee. And I jumped up, too, but Van and Lee were already on the floor, or starting to fall down. I was somehow in the middle of it, or like right next to them, and the melee knocked this refrigerator over. And the refrigerator fell on me. I probably should've just let them go at it and stayed out of the way! The refrigerator did not hurt me—I didn't break any bones. I just kinda pushed it off me. And then it turns into this urban myth that Barrett was almost crushed under a refrigerator.

VAN CONNER Everybody was tired of dealin' with drug issues and personality problems. We fought like we always did, but we would fight about things that weren't real. I remember hearing the answering machine message say something and going psycho-ballistic, and the next day listening to the same message and it said something different. Because I was fucked up, I heard it how my mind interpreted it. Just shit like that, where you get crazy paranoid. A lot of ego, too. And low self-esteem. Ego and low self-esteem at the same time.

BARRETT MARTIN Van and I and Lee agreed that we couldn't keep touring like this. We're doing the shortest set we can legally get away with. So I went and saw Peter Mensch in New York and said, "Look, man, if we keep playing shows like this, sooner or later something very bad is gonna happen. Mark's gonna overdose or worse, and that is the end of the Screaming Trees. We really should not even be on the road at this point." And he agreed. So we stopped.

GARY LEE CONNER We knew that we needed to get off Epic, because it wasn't really helping us much. They had advanced us $1 million. We negotiate with them, and they sent us a letter saying, "You are off Epic. You owe us a million dollars for those records, but forget about it. If you sell records, it'll go against it, otherwise . . ." So basically, we got away with a million dollars from Epic, even though I never saw a damn thing for it, except for several kinda bad videos and two pretty good records.

We mostly stopped doing stuff in '96, though we played a few other shows after that. Mark would nosedive, then get up, then nosedive again.

BARRETT MARTIN It took a while for Mark to get sober, and he finally did. He went to rehab, actually at Courtney's urging, so I have to give her some credit for that.

COURTNEY LOVE I love Lanegan. To this day, I love Lanegan. *Love* Lanegan. LOVE him! I've never met a creature more noble and quiet and seriously cool than Mark Lanegan. I sent Dylan and Mark to rehab, but I separated them. I had to make a calculation, which is a little vicious of me, about which one I thought had the best chances of succeeding, so I sent Dylan to the really hardcore one, Cri-Help, and I sent Mark to Los Encinos. Mark got better.

MARK LANEGAN I mean, there was a time when I thought I didn't have any choice in the matter, when I spent almost a year in various "situations": jail, rehab, halfway house. And just through the sheer fact that I wasn't able to get outside, so to speak—and also because I really just did not want to live that way any longer—for me it wasn't hard. It was the end of a nightmare that had lasted for years and years. I had always hoped that I would be able to stop, but I never was able to. Eventually, I was. A lot of that had to do with changing my way of thinking on a great many things; again, some battles you just have to give up. I was pretty stubborn, I thought I could do a lot of things myself. Nobody likes to believe that they need anybody's help in anything, and the smarter you are—and I'm not smart—or the tougher you are—and at times I thought I was pretty tough—the more trouble you have. The smartest guys I ever met are not around anymore, because they thought they could think their way out of an unthinkable situation, and the tough guys have to just be beaten up repeatedly, and some guys just never do make it out.

GARY LEE CONNER By the time we played our last-ever show, which was the opening of that Experience Music Project in Seattle in 2000, Mark was cleaned up and doing pretty good. The main thing I remember about the EMP show: $65,000. That's how much we got paid. That was the most we ever made. It was a good show. We got Josh Homme from Kyuss to play with us again; he'd played keyboard and guitar with us when we toured for *Dust*, and that was a nice addition.

Mark didn't even tell us this was going to be our last show. I remember sitting in the dressing room and he was telling someone else it was going to be our last show. Nobody was that surprised, because we'd spent the last two years trying to get on another label. We'd done two demos on our own and another one with some big-time producer. Nobody seemed interested.

CHAPTER 48
LOST NINE FRIENDS WE'LL NEVER KNOW

JACK IRONS I got worn out touring. I have the whole sensitivity, bipolar thing that I live with. My wife and I, we had another child. I just couldn't keep up with everything. That was a slippery slope for me at the time. I fell down.

It's an anxiety disorder. You're having irrational anxieties—like your life's being threatened. You can't get onstage in front of 30,000 people and play your best for two or three hours that way. When I was in the midst of it, I was always looking to figure out what the cause was, but the reality is that it was my own body chemistry. That's the imbalance part. I stopped sleeping during the Australia tour of '98. We had a big American tour coming up in the summer and I just realized I wasn't going to make it. I had to make a choice for my health and my longevity and my family versus my career and, honestly, there was no way around it.

That was a very traumatic time and I think it was hard for all of us. It wasn't anything personal. There's no doubt that Matt Cameron proved to be a very worthy addition to the band and deservedly is there. How do I say it? It all happened exactly as it should have. Years later, my life's a lot easier. I definitely might find myself in a situation that has me doing some touring someday. There's absolutely no comparison between the place I was at when I had to leave and where I'm at now. It's like being on fire versus being a little bit warm.

BRETT ELIASON Jack was struggling personally, and he wasn't on his game at all. He is a great musician, but he just didn't have the energy to bring that night after night, and he'd get lost in the arrangements, and tempos were going up and down, and he just wasn't capable of being the drummer that he is. Having Matt join reignited the band.

MATT CAMERON After Soundgarden, I was just questioning things, like, Did I do or say something wrong? Did I play something weird? I was working with John McBain on Wellwater Conspiracy and doing other sessions, but I always kind of thought that Chris was gonna go do a solo record and then we were gonna get back together. Then I was asked to tour with Pearl Jam in the summer of '98.

KELLY CURTIS Matt said, "Sure, I'll do it," and the changeover was really nice. The hysteria started to go away. That was the first non-drama tour in our life.

MATT CAMERON I was a little noncommittal at first, but after that first tour, I realized Soundgarden wasn't going to get back together— Chris seemed pretty happy doing what he was doing and I heard reports that he was into drugs. Pearl Jam was a lot less volatile than Soundgarden was. I felt like there was a more workmanlike professionalism with Pearl Jam, which I found refreshing. The fact that I knew all the Pearl Jam guys really well made the transition a lot easier. Things were going great.

I'd played Roskilde once before with Soundgarden, and it was a really cool festival. It was always one of the best-organized festivals, too. It's in Denmark, where everyone is beautiful-looking and has good healthcare and nice teeth, and it's just like, what a weird place for this freak accident to happen.

EDDIE VEDDER . . . Right before we went on that night, we got a phone call. Chris Cornell and his wife, Susan, had a daughter that day. And also a sound guy left a day early, 'cause he was going to have a child. It brought me to tears, I was so happy. We were walking out onstage that night with two new names in our heads. And in 45 minutes everything changed.

BRETT ELIASON I was mixing that Roskilde show. It was a stormy, really windy, rainy night. A lot of people, great big crowd. Outdoor shows with wind, they don't ever go very well. It sounds like the P.A.'s being put through a flanger, wind is blowing everything all over the place. The crowd was crunching up, as they always did for the band. Apparently, the ground was uneven, it was very muddy, and people started to go down because of the side-to-side movement of the audience. The front crunch will crush you, but it doesn't drop you. Going side to side you lose your footing and can get pulled under, and apparently that had happened to a bunch of kids.

STONE GOSSARD Well, this particular show, the barrier was 30 meters away; it was dark and raining. They'd been serving beer all day long. People fell down; the band had no idea.

BRETT ELIASON A security guard had seen a hole where a kid had been and was smart enough to react. He said something to our stage manager, who ran to our production manager, Dick Adams, and said, "I think we have a problem out there." Dick ran straight onto the stage and told Ed in the middle of "Daughter." Ed stopped the band and he asked this huge crowd to take a step back, and they did. He asked them to take another step back, and they did. And that's when they saw a bunch of bodies on the ground.

I remember watching Ed drop to his knees. At that point, Dick corralled the band and got them offstage.

BILLBOARD ("Loss of Life Fails to Halt Festival; Nine Killed as Crowd Rushes Stage During Pearl Jam Set," by Kai R. Lofthus, July 15, 2000) OSLO—Danish police have confirmed that the organizers of Denmark's Roskilde Festival will not face prosecution following the death of nine concertgoers at the event June 30. A spokesman for the authorities tells Billboard that they regard the tragedy as an accident and not a criminal case.

The fans, aged between 17 and 26, died as a result of a crowd crush during Pearl Jam's headline set. Another 30 people were hospitalized.

STONE GOSSARD We were part of an event that was disorganized on every level. Mostly I feel like we witnessed a car wreck. But on another level, we were involved. We played this show, and it happened. You can't be there and not have some sense of being responsible. It's just impossible. All of us spent two days in the hotel in Denmark crying and trying to understand what was going on.

NANCY WILSON I got a call in the afternoon from Kelly, who was freaking out, and he told me everything that happened firsthand—how they saw people being hauled off the stage right in front of them that were already dead. We were crying on the phone together because rock and roll is not supposed to be a war zone.

KELLY CURTIS The reason those people died was that no one could get word out what was happening. It was just chaos. There was a lot of Danish press that said we were inciting moshing. It wasn't during a crazy part of the set; it was during "Daughter."

EDDIE VEDDER The intensity of the whole event starts to seem surreal, and you want it to be real. So you sit there with it, and you cough it up and redigest it. You still want to pay respect to the people who were there or the people who died and their families. Respect for the people who cared about you. A friend of an Australian guy named Anthony Hurley asked if I would write something for the funeral. That was just hands-down the hardest thing I've ever had to do—not really knowing what was appropriate, not knowing how the family or friends felt; maybe I'm the last person they'd like to hear from. But it meant a lot to them, and it really helped me. I think it also helped the rest of the guys. Hurley had three younger siblings, and they said he really cared about our band, and that's why he was in the front. And that he was actually doing something he loved during his last minutes. His sister and a friend of his—who was with Anthony that night—came to Seattle and saw our last two shows. And that was nice, spending time with them. . . .

JEFF AMENT Some of us thought maybe we should cancel the [North American] tour. I felt if we cancel, what are we running from? It made us deal with it every day on some level, and that was the most positive thing we could do. The shows were all reserved-seating, which made it a lot easier. At first, it was hard to look at the crowd. A couple of kids I saw at Roskilde, they're burned in my memory forever. Sometimes, when you're looking at a crowd, you can't help but see those faces.

The Vegas show on the U.S. tour was pretty heavy. That afternoon was the first time we'd played the Mother Love Bone song "Crown of Thorns." Kelly and Susan Silver and my parents are there, my whole family, and all of a sudden, playing that song, it was the first time I properly reflected on what we'd gone through and what a journey it's been. And that moment was reflected in a purely positive way, feeling blessed, happy to still be playing music.

NANCY WILSON I saw them in Seattle, the last show of their whole tour. It was incredible. All these incredible versions, different versions of songs, different grooves on songs, big long jams. Pretty much every person during the whole show sang every lyric to every song. And every time Eddie would glance over or look over to our section, every arm went up. Afterwards, I went backstage and Eddie came up to me and was having a million feelings, you could tell, 'cause it was the end of the whole tour, the "life and death tour." I said, "I just got so emotional during your show. That was maybe the best show I've ever seen." I saw tears come into his eyes and he was like, "Yeah, I know," and gave me this big hug. It meant so much to him that the night was so good.

CHAPTER 49
MY FRIEND, BUT NOT
MY FRIEND

KURT DANIELSON TAD did a Midwestern leg of the Alice in Chains tour in '93; they were dates making up shows that had been canceled in the past due to Layne's drug problems. Layne was on his best behavior because he had been in rehab recently and he was clean and he wanted to stay that way. They had a bodyguard with him at all times who was supposed to help him. But I saw Layne on other occasions, around '96, '97, when he was definitely way back into being a junkie. Not only that, but smoking a lot of crack. I can remember one time in particular, at another musician's apartment—and by this time I was also doing heroin, and that's why I was there.

The coffee table was covered with a mound of used needles that were glazed with blood. It was sad, really sad, because next to that there was a mound of charred Chore Boys—that's the steel wool that you get if you want to smoke crack, you put that in a glass pipe. And on the couch were rosettes of crumpled tissue paper stained with blood. The couch cushion was uncomfortable, and when you lifted it up to look what was there, you found a gun. A pistol. And there was a street guy sitting in a corner, he was from somewhere else. He was completely destitute, a

full-on junkie, just hanging out with his idols. And then in the bathroom, you would find the walls splattered with blood. Suddenly you
find yourself in a Burroughs novel that Bukowski had a hand in.

I was hanging out there for a few hours and talking to Layne. We
shared some reminiscences about the tour. And the rest of it was drug
talk, anecdotes, and puns. He was good at making puns and he was
punning on the name Yasmine Bleeth at the time. I forget exactly what
it was. But his mind wasn't working quite right, and what seemed like
an ingenious pun to him was not quite so funny. What it indicated to
me was sort of the mental depletion caused not so much by heroin but
by the crack. The crack is what fucks with your head and really causes
lasting damage. That was an insight that showed me what could happen
if you follow that path long enough, but I was just starting, so it didn't
deter me whatsoever.

PATTY SCHEMEL I always hoped to see Layne at a meeting. I really liked
him a lot. The last time I saw him was probably in '95. It's funny because we were both at the dealer's house, and we were talking and he
said, "Do you want to go get some coffee?" I thought it was the *weirdest*
thing because the *last* thing I wanted to do was something normal like
get coffee. I was like, "No, doing this is just fine with me," sitting here in
this dope dealer's house. But I liked that: Let's be normal for a second.

JAMES BURDYSHAW Demri had started lookin' kinda ragged for a
young person. I knew she was really into dope deep at that point, and
one time I saw her on the bus and she pulled up her shirt and showed
me her scar from when she was on the hospital table and they had to
massage her heart back to life. She almost died from doing a speedball.
A month after I saw her on the bus, she was dead.

TOM HANSEN Demri ended up getting endocarditis, which is an infec-
tion of the lining around your heart. It happens a lot to drug addicts.
When Demri passed, Layne really took that hard. She was really sweet
and really cool.

JOHNNY BACOLAS I recall many nights when I was living with Layne,
Demri would come to the house and after I'd go to bed, she would
just open my door, sit at the edge of my bed with a bag full of potato

chips, chew really loud, and just talk. It didn't matter if I was exhausted. She didn't ask me, she didn't care. "So anyways, yesterday I ran into so-and-so and blah blah blah. Did you hear this new record by this band?" And I loved it—I thought it was so cute. If a kitten's in your bed clawing you, it's a kitten, you know?

After I moved out from Layne's, I didn't have much contact with Demri. After she died, in '96, it seemed like Layne went into a darker place. He moved to the U District, to a condo right above this tavern called the Blue Moon. The Blue Moon was kind of notorious, at least when I was a teenager, as the place to go buy drugs. That kind of clientele. And part of me wondered if he moved there because he didn't have to drive anywhere and it was easy access. Then again, all the dealers would come to his house anyway, because, hey, he was Layne Staley. Once he moved to that place, I didn't talk to him. I don't think many people did, to be honest with you.

DAVE JERDEN I was making an Offspring record years later, in 1998, and they were planning a box-set record of Alice in Chains with some new songs. I stopped production on Offspring and got Alice in Chains into my studio. Layne didn't show up until midnight or later, and the band had already been there cutting stuff. My engineer Bryan Carlstrom was so burned out, he said, "I can't work anymore tonight." So there was a big fight.

At that point, Jerry was in complete control of the band, and he yelled at Layne and said something to him like, "Shut up!" And the reaction from Layne was pretty bizarre. He turned into this little kid—he wasn't like the Layne of old. Like he was being reprimanded by his mother or father.

MIKE INEZ At that point, we weren't keeping a whole lot of contact with each other. We were all pretty scattered. That was a tough session. We were in Los Angeles, and I just remember wishing I was in Seattle. Why? Because the vibe is completely different in L.A. Especially during those times, with the people we were hanging out with, it was dark for us.

DAVE JERDEN That was a Friday night, and I had an understanding I had Layne till Sunday, and Layne all of a sudden says to me, "I have to be back in Seattle for a wedding." They left and Susan called and *completely* dumped on me. She started yelling at me: *"Your whole career was based on Alice in Chains!"*

Rolling Stone called me up and wanted to know what the story was, and I gave them my side. The big thing that I said was during the making of *Dirt* I wasn't there to be Layne's friend, I was there to be his producer. And what I meant by that was I wasn't there to enable him to use drugs—I was there to get him to sing, to make that record. And that got blown all out of proportion.

MIKE INEZ It wasn't working, and the vibe that Dave created for us in the studio was not the vibe we needed at that time. We ended up going back to Toby.

TOBY WRIGHT When I came back to work with the band on the box set, it was all about getting some music done, so I was focused on that instead of anything that might be bad happening around them, to keep a positive influence and to keep creativity flowing.

The only time I actually used Pro Tools with the band was during the two new songs, because Jerry and Layne had gotten to a point where they wouldn't go into a room together. There was something going on between them, I'm not sure exactly what it was. It was really none of my business. Layne would come in and sing, and then Jerry'd come in and listen to that and say, "Oh, that's horrible." Thank God for Pro Tools, because for me it was an editing nightmare.

SUSAN SILVER The last time I saw Layne? It was at a soundtrack recording session, which took him 10 hours to get to. People were waiting and wondering and worrying, and Todd Shuss, who used to work for me and who Layne would answer the phone for, picked him up and brought him to the studio. And when he finally got there around midnight, Layne was as sweet and funny and unaffected and mischievous as always.

ERIC GARCIA The thing about Layne is, especially toward the end, that I'd just hear all these horror stories about how he was and where he was at. The last time I saw him, I had to drop some stuff off at his condo. At the time, he was doing some soundtrack work. And he came down to meet me, and he was kind of frail-looking and he was wearing gloves, which I thought was odd because it was kind of summertime.

But his brain was firing on all cylinders. We were just shooting the shit really, but he was funny and articulate, and his eyes were alive. He's obviously having a good day at that point, I guess. It was weird, because I expected to basically see a hollow shell of a guy with sunken eyes, talking really slow, on the nod or something like that. But he wasn't. There was still a light on; he was still there.

SUSAN SILVER In the last couple years, Layne was *extremely* isolated. I don't know who he saw, but of the people that I know, it was really only Todd who saw him. I was dealing with my family problems at that point. By late '99 I was in my own private hell. The new primary drug addict in my life was my husband, and I was also going through fertility treatments and eventually got pregnant in late '99. Meanwhile, Alice was not active; Jerry had another manager, and he was struggling with his own addiction.

RODERICK ROMERO I was Krist Novoselic's best friend for five years, after Kurt's death. Krist really tried to help Layne, 'cause obviously he'd already lost Kurt, so it was like . . . Krist is one of the most caring and kind and sincere people on the planet. He would show up at Layne's apartment, and bring food to him. Layne wouldn't let anybody in; he had surveillance cameras. Krist would come back and say, "I dropped more food off for him. *Fuck.*" I'd say, "Well, anytime you want me to go with you . . ." He said, "It's just kind of freaky. You don't want to." He really cared. It was like, maybe he could help save somebody.

NICK POLLOCK The last time I ever saw Layne was probably a year and a half before he died. I was living up on Capitol Hill with my first wife after finishing college, getting my design degree, and I was walking into QFC on Broadway, and I see this guy shuffling around. He looks like an 80-year-old man with this obviously fake curly wig on and weird-ass mismatched clothes. Looking like a homeless person. Looking like he was just nuts. I think it was a disguise. But I caught his profile, and I'm going, "Oh, my fucking God." I knew who it was, and I came around the corner and his back was to me, and I go, "Excuse me." And he turns around and he looks and he goes, "Nick!" and he gives me this big hug.

I was in such shock because he was like a skeleton. His skin was gray. I don't remember him having any teeth. We had a nice conversation—"Let's get together," the usual things that people say—but this is surreal. This is a nightmare. I don't even know who I'm talking to. My friend, but not my friend. I was in such shock. I went home, and I just bawled my head off.

JEFF GILBERT Layne sequestered himself and did nothing but play video games and do drugs. I bumped into him probably about six months before he died, in the U District. He looked like an 80-year-old version of himself. He looked very jaundiced. He wore a leather jacket down to his fingertips to cover up all the needle marks. He had a knit hat on, pulled down, and his eyes were so sunken in, just dark. Smelled pretty ripe. I gave him a hug, and we talked for a while. I said, "Damn, man, you need to get out in the sun." That was my attempt at humor. But I felt this horrendous amount of sadness for him. He was a dead man walkin'.

MIKE INEZ Me and Mark Lanegan would go by Layne's apartment and knock on his door. We didn't get an answer, and we'd call him, just trying to put as many lines in the water as we could.

SUSAN SILVER Sean would call Layne all the time. But it didn't matter—he could call Layne every day for six months and Layne still wouldn't respond. Not because there was any animosity; it was just like Layne was in that cloud.

TOBY WRIGHT I had spoken with Layne by phone three or four times like three weeks before they found his body, which turned out to be a week before he died. I had sent him a track—I was working with a band called Taproot, and they really, really wanted Layne to sing on this one song, and he had agreed to do it. He sounded excited on the phone because this band was a big fan of his, and he was like, "Wow, I get to perform again." Some of the members of Taproot wanted to be there when he recorded, but he wanted complete privacy.

MIKE STARR He died the day after my birthday. And I was with him all that day, on my birthday, trying to keep him alive. I even asked him if

I could call 911, and he said if I did he would never talk to me again. And of course, I didn't know he was gonna die, or I would've called 911 anyways.

I wish I wouldn't have been high on benzodiazepine. . . . [Layne] just said, "I'm sick" . . . He was agitated because I was too high. He used to get mad at me when I took 'em. He'd be like, "You're an idiot on these pills." And then I got mad at him, and I said, "Fine, I'll just leave." And his last words to me were, "Not like this, don't leave like this." I just left him sitting there. His last words were, "Not like this." I can't believe that. I'm so ashamed of that.

KURT DANIELSON Layne had access to resources that allowed him to get in much deeper than most people ever could, unless they're an ingenious thief. When you heard about his death, it wasn't such a surprise. What was sad about it was that his body wasn't found immediately, but only after many days, which indicated the level to which he'd been cut off from everybody else.

MIKE STARR I went home and I blacked out on benzodiazepine. I just blacked out for the whole two weeks.

SUSAN SILVER I got a call that there was some concern because Layne hadn't been heard from for a while. Maybe his bank statement came in, and there hadn't been the usual pattern of activity. Both Laurie Davis, who was the bookkeeper for the business-management firm Alice was with, and I had an innate sense that something was wrong. And Laurie mentioned it to Sean, who also runs heavily on intuition, and he was gonna go over there and try to get into Layne's building and break down the door. I immediately felt the gravity of it and told him he needed to sit tight and we needed to get the family involved.

IANN ROBINSON (MTV News reporter; MTV News report, weekend of April 20, 2002) The rock world lost one of its more honest voices this weekend when Alice in Chains front man Layne Staley was found dead in his Seattle home on Friday. He was 34. Seattle police say they responded to a call from one of Staley's relatives, asking them to check on his well-being since he hadn't been seen in two weeks. Police then discovered a body, later identified as Staley, that had been deceased for at least a few days, surrounded by intravenous-drug paraphernalia.

SEAN KINNEY It's like one of the world's longest suicides. I'd been expecting the call for a long time, for seven years, in fact, but it was still shocking . . .

MIKE INEZ I had just come home to Big Bear Lake, California, and I was really in a bad spot because my best friend in the world, Randy Castillo, the drummer of the Ozzy band and basically my mentor, died. He got smoking cancer in his jaw, and it spread throughout his body. Either the day I got back from his funeral in Albuquerque or the next day, I get a call from Sean. He said, "Are you sitting down? Layne's gone." "Oh, my God, you're kidding." That was one of the lowest points I think I've ever been in my whole time of existence.

TOBY WRIGHT My wife at the time and I were from Los Angeles and we were on our way to the Burbank airport to go to Seattle—to get the studio together and capture Layne's performance—and my phone rang and it was Susan saying that they had just found Layne dead. We all cried, and I said, "Well, I'm actually on my way to Seattle right now." And she said, "Well, keep on comin'," for the memorial.

JEFF GILBERT There was a public gathering at the Seattle Center around the fountain. Whenever anybody dies, that's where everybody goes. The local radio station came down and blasted music out. I ran into Chris Cornell and Eddie Vedder, and they were walking around on the outside of the crowd. And I was glad that people were stayin' the fuck away from them, givin' them some room. Eddie was tremendously distraught. I gave Chris a hug and said, "You doin' okay?" He said, "I'm never okay with this."

MIKE INEZ The private service was on this island, so you had to take a ferry there. I remember sitting with Chris Cornell, smoking cigarettes at the front of the ferry, just totally silent, listening to the waves hit the boat.

NANCY WILSON Layne's memorial was another amazing communal thing. We went out to kind of a resort somewhere in the San Juans, and me and Ann and Chris Cornell sang together. It was hard to get through it; it was an emotional moment, but a really great moment. We did a Bob Dylan song called "Ring Them Bells," which Layne had sung with us for one of Heart's albums.

I remember when Layne had finally agreed to sing with us on "Ring Them Bells," we were like, "This will be great! Let's have a moment!" He was like, "Oh no, you can't be in the control room when I'm singing. You have to go away." He was too shy to be singing where Ann Wilson might be listening. We went out to dinner or something and came back, and he didn't want to be there when we heard it, so he left. He was just like that.

JERRY CANTRELL Was there more I could have done to help Layne? I don't think so. I think we all cared about each other a lot and dealt with each other pretty realistically, but we were grown men at that time and you live your life the way you're going to live it. So I don't think there was anything anybody could have done. He made a choice and stuck with it, and it didn't turn out very well, obviously. It's not like nobody did anything or nobody cared, that would be a ridiculous statement.

SEAN KINNEY It felt like when Layne passed away, he largely got swept under the carpet. They just kinda discounted everything he was. . . . It made me really sick when he'd just passed away, and we'd been up for another Grammy, and they convinced us to go. . . . And during those shows, they play a collage of all the people who passed away, and they didn't even put him up there. I remember us lookin' at each other and just gettin' up and leaving.

JERRY CANTRELL "Died of a heroin overdose. Junkie." That's the only thing anybody ever fuckin' wrote, and to see that start to fade and people realize what the guy contributed and the amazing talent that he was—and nobody's ever gonna know personally what kinda fuckin' guy he was. We do, and he was so fuckin' cool and badass. It's cool he's taken on an Obi-Wan kinda of thing: He's more powerful in death, and he's gained a lot more reverence.

MIKE STARR (died March 8, 2011, of a suspected drug overdose) When the band formed, we all became brothers, especially me and Layne. Me and Layne definitely bonded. Over what? We wanted to be rock stars. Every time I'd walk into the jam room I'd look at Layne and he'd look at me and we'd get these big smiles. Everyone was funny as hell. We all laughed a lot. As a band, we were always really good. Layne was, Jerry was, Sean was. They were great. I was a lucky guy to play with them.

One time, Jeff Ament came up to me and said, "Every time you guys walk in, it's all four of you, you're always together." I was like, "That's right, man. We're the Four Musketeers, man."

We lived our band. That was our only focus in life.

EPILOGUE
THE COSMIC BROTHERHOOD OF ROCK

JOHN BIGLEY I got a phone call from Bruce Pavitt. I haven't talked to him in a year or two, and this must have been 1989, 1990. I'd bought a house near where I went to high school and went and hid for a while. He's goin', "I don't know if you were paying attention to this, but the shit is *goin' on, man*. I would strongly recommend you take a long hot bath and think about what you're doing, because shit is happening and you should be part of it." He gave me this wicked pep talk.

"Yeah, I know what's goin' on."

"Like national press."

"What?!"

He said, "Let's talk about signing you"—he wanted us to reform the U-Men or something similar—"and hop on this fuckin' thing. Call Tom. Fuck it!" He was very excited.

And? I don't know . . . I don't feel like it's a lost opportunity. I don't regret not hopping on the train. I do wonder what would have happened to my life differently had we continued on under those circumstances. Morbid curiosity more than anything. We were a little off-center as far as the music goes. I don't know if there's that much to ponder, really.

CHARLIE RYAN We were thrilled for everybody's success. My father called me one day and he's reading a review of Nirvana in the paper, and he's like, "You know these guys, right?" I'm like, "Yeah, you know, we were playing the same places."

"I don't understand this. How come all these guys are making all this money and you're not gettin' nothin' out of it?"

I said, "Well, you know, Dad, we have our artistic integrity."

He slammed the phone down. He hung up on me.

He always busted my balls about the money: "So, you know these Soundgarden guys, and you know the Pearl Jams?" "Yeah, Dad." "And these guys all make millions of bucks?" "Yes, Dad." "But let me guess, you got your artistic integrity?" "That's right, Dad."

When I was playing with Cat Butt, we were on some Sub Pop record, so we got these crummy little checks sent to us for years. One year, I framed this and gave it to my dad for Christmas. The letter says, "I'm pleased to enclose mechanical royalties for blah blah blah." And look at how much the check was for: one dollar and 48 cents. My dad actually hung it up behind his couch. He thought it was hysterical.

JOHN BIGLEY Nirvana did two nights with the Butthole Surfers at the Seattle Center Arena. Peter Davis, this tour manager guy, called me and said, "Man, I got a band playin' with the Buttholes and Nirvana, and I'm gonna be in town, and if you don't show up you're fuckin' dead. I'm gonna come and burn your house down." He was adamant about me goin' to it. I had gone fully screaming in the opposite direction. Just wasn't going to shows in general, after going to shows five, six nights a week for seven years. The scene had started getting a little intense, I thought. Just the gravity of it all. I haven't seen Peter in some years and went, and it was a very heavy night, catchin' up with the Butthole Surfers and doin' the whole backstage thing.

Backstage, bodyguards and A&R guys in the mix. Fully like, fuck me, laminates and like, "Could I get you something?" "Sure." That whole trip. I met Courtney through Peter. It was a cordial, somewhat brief encounter. I watched Nirvana's set; I went out on the side of the stage, and there were thousands of people. They were just *on it*, man. *In Utero* had been out not that long, and I was just knocked out by how tight they were. I haven't seen them in five, six years. The last concert I'd seen at that place was Van Halen open for Black Sabbath. Kurt is standing where Ozzy Osborne stood, Tony Iommi and Geezer Butler. This is fucking *wild.*

I go backstage at the end of the set. Talkin' to Greg, one of my friends that was in the Crows. And this memory is very vivid: these two metal doors, tile floor, cinderblock painted-white walls—the backstage bunker trip. And the door—*crashhh,* and this army of people come in. Krist's head is stickin' up in the middle of it all. There are a couple bruiser-type guys, and guys in suits—the full-on Geffen fuckin' army, 25 to 30 people around, ear pieces and all this shit. Like, Whoa. They come through the door, and Kurt's in the middle of the whole crowd, wearing one of those striped shirts. He walks by and noticed me and goes, "John? Bigley? Did you come to our show?"

"Yeah."

"What'd ya think?"

"Fuckin' rockin', man."

He goes, "Cool. Thanks, man." He shakes my hand and he goes, "Hey, what I do, you do," and he said some sort of cosmic brotherhood of rock thing. I didn't fully understand it myself at the time. It was kind of a musician buddy pat on the head. He was always wearing Melvins and Scratch Acid shirts—seemed to be highly aware of that which came before him. I'd never heard that kinda shit from him to me. I'd only met him very briefly before. It was flattering. And he goes, "Thank you, and please come back and have a drink and meet my wife." I said, "I just met her a little while ago. She seems really nice."

Half this group of people with him are standing there, tapping their toes, like, Let's keep it movin' here. It was only two or three minutes. He goes, "Cool, see you back there." And then they're all *whoosh,* goin' down the hallway. Greg's like, "What the fuck was that?" We go walkin' back later, and Kurt and Courtney had split, so I didn't get a chance to talk to them more.

A few months later, I bumped into Charles Peterson, a friend of Kurt's. He gave me Kurt's phone number and said, "Hey, Kurt said he saw you. He said it was really cool. He said you should call him sometime, go up to his house and chill out." Kurt had bought a house in Duvall, up north. "It's really beautiful and laid-back, and it would be cool if you guys could chill."

"Yeah, neat."

Two weeks later, three weeks later, I was laying in bed with a broken jaw and arm. Bicycle accident. Lost a bunch of teeth, had some pretty serious surgeries. Heavily medicated. Val, my girlfriend at the time, called me from work and said, "Turn on the radio! Turn on the radio! They found Kurt dead."

"Kurt Cobain?"

"Turn on the radio!"

And that's that.

ACKNOWLEDGMENTs

An oral history is nothing without its voices. So first and foremost, a heartfelt thanks to all the people who were generous enough to share their grunge era memories with me. Obviously, it would have been impossible to put together a book of this nature without you. I'd like to give special thanks to a few interviewees who provided invaluable assistance over the course of the three years I spent working on this project: Mark Arm, Robert Scott Crane, Jeff Gilbert, Buzz Osborne, Susan Silver, and Kim Thayil.

I am deeply indebted to my agent, PJ Mark, who pitched me the idea of doing this book after reading my oral history of Sub Pop Records that ran in *Blender* magazine back in summer 2008. He's been a tireless advocate for this project and patiently talked me down after many a book-related crisis. Also, huge thanks to my editor, Sean Desmond—who brought tremendous enthusiasm and a seemingly unflappable nature to this project and edited my manuscript with a light, deft touch—and everyone at Crown who rallied behind this book.

Much gratitude to my photo editor, Christine Reilly, for assembling the many rare and wonderful images in these pages. Thanks to all the photographers who provided images for the book, in particular Valerie Broatch, Paul Hernandez, and Alice Wheeler. High praise to my crack team of audio transcribers—Cynthia Colonna, Larry Fitzmaurice, Marissa Graziadio, Diana Salier, Megan Stride, Kate Thuma, and Jessica Vaysman—without whom I could not have done this.

All my love (and many apologies) to my incredible wife, Bonnie, who tolerated my taking Grunge as a mistress and supported me throughout the entire process. Thanks to my family—my father Jay and step-mother Marilyn, my brother Fred and his wife Andrea—for their love and support.

Many thanks to my former *Blender* editors in chief Craig Marks (for hiring me) and Joe Levy (for his guidance and support), plus my former colleagues David Carthas, Victoria De Silverio, Josh Eells, Chris "Goldteeth" Ehrmann, Lizzy Goodman, Tyler Gray, Rob Tannenbaum, and Rory Walsh for providing me with contacts and/or book-writing tips.

Thanks to fellow authors John Cook, David Peisner, Marc Spitz, Katherine Turman, Eric J. Weiner, and Jon Wiederhorn for their advice and generosity, and much gratitude to my friends who offered manuscript critiques and moral support: Elizabeth Champ, Miles Hutton, Jeff Jackson, and Gregg Lauer. I'd also like to give shout-outs to the proprietors and fellow denizens of Room 58, my writing sanctuary, and Sonja and Andy Hoven, who provided me with a Seattle sanctuary. And many thanks to Jeffrey Kleinberg, for keeping me sane.

Thanks to the following people for all their efforts in connecting me with interviewees: Andrea Ball, Nils Bernstein, Jenny Dalton, Marie Walsh Dixon, Kent Eby, Bobby Gale, Rick Gershon, Jessica Gronvold, Kate Jackson, Bennett Kaufman, Carol Kaye, Jeannie Kedas, Miranda Lange, Steve Manning, Steve Martin, Brian McDonald, Michael Moses, Pam Nashel Leto, Elaine Schock, Gina Schulman, Monica Seide, Steve Sherr, Staci Slater, Gillian Smith, Andrew Steinthal, Aimee Tyo, Nicole Vandenberg, Amanda Van Goethen, Terry Wang, Beth Winer, Emily White, and Bob Whittaker.

I'd like to acknowledge Jacob McMurray of the Experience Music Project for all his help with, and enthusiasm for, this project. Also, thanks to the following for their assistance with research and source materials: Charles Batho (Archived Music Press), John Bigley, Carrie Borzillo, Stevie Chick, Jennifer Clay, Charles R. Cross, Chris Gill,

Regan Hagar, Brian Hiatt, Kristin Jones, Paul Jones (FooArchive .com), Martin Kuiper (FaceCulture.com), Jennifer Kutsher, Al Larsen, Clemens Marschall (*Rokko's Adventures*), Maire Masco, Andy Savage, Herman Stadshaug, Dave Wulzen, and the New York and Seattle public library systems.

For reasons of structure, the following people I interviewed are not quoted in the book, though I sincerely appreciate the time they took to speak with me: Michael Alex, Danny Baird, Valerie Broatch, David Dorrell, Jan T. Gregor, John Hawkley, Jane Higgins, Jeff Kleinsmith, Dave Lipe, Chris Monlux, Nigel Pulsford, Reyza Sageb, Dave Sirulnick, Greg Stumph, Whiting Tennis, and Elizabeth Wurtzel.

Also, my humble apologies to anyone I may have failed to recognize here for his or her contributions to this project.

Finally, my sympathy goes out to the friends and family of the two interviewees who passed away as I was nearing completion of this book: Ricky Kulwicki and Mike Starr.

CAST OF CHARACTERS

DAVE ABBRUZZESE Pearl Jam drummer

VALERIE AGNEW 7 Year Bitch drummer

MICHELLE AHERN concertgoer; Robert Scott Crane's ex-wife

STEVE ALBINI recording engineer; singer/guitarist for Big Black (Chicago)

SAM ALBRIGHT Velvetone studio/label owner

GRANT ALDEN *The Rocket* newspaper managing editor

JEFF AMENT Pearl Jam/Temple of the Dog/Mother Love Bone/Green River/
    Deranged Diction bassist

JOHN MICHAEL AMERIKA (né Mike Hutchins; deceased) Cat Butt
    guitarist

JULIANNE ANDERSEN Supersuckers/Gas Huffer booking agent

DAWN ANDERSON journalist; *Backlash* zine publisher; Jack Endino's ex-wife

MICHELE ANTHONY Sony Music president

MARK ARM (né Mark McLaughlin) Mudhoney singer/guitarist; Green River singer;
    Mr. Epp and the Calculations guitarist/singer; the Thrown Ups drummer

KRISHA AUGEROT Kelly Curtis's assistant; Green Apple Quick Step comanager

JOHNNY BACOLAS Alice N' Chains/Second Coming bassist

PETER BAGGE *Hate* cartoonist

LORI BARBERO drummer for Babes in Toyland (Minneapolis)

LOU BARLOW singer/guitarist for Sebadoh (Westfield, Mass.); bassist for
    Dinosaur Jr. (Amherst, Mass.)

SAMUEL BAYER "Smells Like Teen Spirit" video director

JOHN LEIGHTON BEEZER the Thrown Ups bassist; the Blunt Objects guitarist

NILS BERNSTEIN Sub Pop Records publicist

JOHN BIGLEY U-Men/the Crows singer

JANET BILLIG Hole manager via Gold Mountain Entertainment

KAT BJELLAND singer/guitarist for Babes in Toyland (Minneapolis)

CHARLES ALDEN BLACK (d. 2005) father of Lori Black; husband of Shirley Temple Black; businessman

LORI BLACK (a.k.a. Lorax) Melvins bassist; daughter of Charles Alden Black and Shirley Temple Black

DON BLACKSTONE Gas Huffer bassist

DANNY BLAND Cat Butt guitarist; Best Kissers in the World/Dwarves bassist; Sub Pop Records booking agent

CHAD BLAKE (a.k.a. Slam Hate) concertgoer; posterer

KURT BLOCH Fastbacks/Young Fresh Fellows guitarist

DAN BLOSSOM Feast guitarist

JENNIE BODDY Sub Pop Records publicist

TIM BRANOM Gypsy Rose singer

DANNY BRAMSON *Singles* music supervisor

BRYN BRIDENTHAL Geffen Records publicity head

SOOZY BRIDGES intern for Kelly Curtis/Ken Deans; club booker

ANTON BROOKES U.K. music publicist

ROBIN BUCHAN U-Men bassist

PETER BUCK guitarist for R.E.M. (Athens, Ga.); Stephanie Dorgan's ex-husband

JAMES BURDYSHAW Cat Butt guitarist; 64 Spiders guitarist/singer

MATT CAMERON Pearl Jam/Soundgarden/Hater/Temple of the Dog/Skin Yard drummer

KELLY CANARY Dickless singer

JERRY CANTRELL Alice in Chains guitarist/singer; solo artist

DYLAN CARLSON Earth singer/guitarist; Kurt Cobain's close friend

ROSEMARY CARROLL Nirvana/Hole attorney; Danny Goldberg's wife

TINA CASALE C/Z Records label/Reciprocal Recording studio cofounder

MATT CHAMBERLAIN Pearl Jam drummer

CHAD CHANNING Nirvana drummer

ART CHANTRY *The Rocket* newspaper art director; Sub Pop Records freelancer; album/poster designer

FRANCES BEAN COBAIN daughter of Kurt Cobain and Courtney Love

KURT COBAIN (d. 1994) Nirvana singer/guitarist; Courtney Love's husband; Frances Bean Cobain's father

ALEX COLETTI *MTV Unplugged* producer

MARCO COLLINS KNDD DJ

COLLEEN COMBS Kelly Curtis's assistant

GARY LEE CONNER Screaming Trees guitarist

VAN CONNER Screaming Trees bassist

JOHN CONTE the Living/the Blunt Objects singer

BLAINE COOK the Fartz/10 Minute Warning/the Accüsed singer

BILLY CORGAN singer/guitarist for the Smashing Pumpkins (Chicago)

CHRIS CORNELL Soundgarden singer/guitarist; Temple of the Dog singer; solo artist; Susan Silver's ex-husband

GERARD COSLOY Homestead Records label head

WAYNE COYNE singer for the Flaming Lips (Oklahoma City)

ROBERT SCOTT CRANE Soundhouse Recording Studio owner; Michelle Ahern's ex-husband

CHARLES R. CROSS *The Rocket* newspaper owner/editor in chief; Kurt Cobain biographer

DALE CROVER Melvins/Nirvana drummer

CAMERON CROWE *Singles* director; Nancy Wilson's ex-husband

KELLY CURTIS Pearl Jam/Mother Love Bone manager; Heart tour manager; Ken Deans's business partner

BLAG DAHLIA singer for Dwarves (San Francisco)

KURT DANIELSON TAD/Bundle of Hiss bassist

PETER DAVIS tour booker; *Your Flesh* zine editor in chief/publisher

ELIZABETH DAVIS-SIMPSON 7 Year Bitch bassist

KEN DEANS production manager; Kelly Curtis's business partner

DAVE DEDERER the Presidents of the United States of America "guitbassist"/ singer

FREDDY DEMANN Maverick Records cofounder

MATT DENTINO the Shemps guitarist

LINDA DERSCHANG Linda's Tavern/Basic clothing store owner

MARK DEUTROM Melvins bassist/soundman; Alchemy Records cofounder; producer

MICHAEL DEWITT (a.k.a. Cali DeWitt) Frances Bean Cobain's nanny

MIKE DILLARD Melvins drummer

MATT DILLON *Singles* lead actor

STEPHANIE DORGAN the Crocodile club owner; Peter Buck's ex-wife

GORDON DOUCETTE Metropolis club cofounder; Red Masque singer/ guitarist

TAD DOYLE TAD singer/guitarist; Bundle of Hiss guitarist/drummer; H-Hour drummer

DONNA DRESCH Screaming Trees bassist; Team Dresch guitarist/bassist; Chainsaw Records founder

MATT DRESDNER the Gits bassist

DAVID DUET Cat Butt/Girl Trouble singer; U-Men roadie

GREG DULLI singer/guitarist for the Afghan Whigs (Cincinnati)

ROISIN DUNNE (now Roisin Ross) 7 Year Bitch guitarist

BRETT ELIASON Pearl Jam soundman; producer/mixer

JACK ENDINO producer; Skin Yard guitarist; Dawn Anderson's ex-husband

ERIC ERLANDSON guitarist for Hole (Los Angeles)

JASON EVERMAN Nirvana guitarist; Soundgarden bassist

JONATHAN EVISON (a.k.a. Munkeyseeker) March of Crimes singer

BRUCE FAIRWEATHER Mother Love Bone/Green River/Deranged Diction guitarist; Love Battery bassist

CHRISTOPHER JOHN FARLEY *Time* magazine staff writer

PERRY FARRELL singer for Jane's Addiction (Los Angeles); Lollapalooza festival cofounder

RAY FARRELL SST Records promotion department head; Geffen Records/DGC A&R and marketing executive

CATHY FAULKNER KISW assistant program director/music director

JENNIFER FINCH bassist for L7 (Los Angeles)

JASON FINN the Presidents of the United States of America/Love Battery/Skin Yard/Fastbacks/Feast drummer

AMY FINNERTY MTV director of music programming and talent relations

STEVE FISK producer; keyboardist for Pell Mell (Berkeley, Calif.); solo artist

DON FLEMING producer; singer/guitarist for Gumball/Velvet Monkeys (New York)

ED FOTHERINGHAM the Thrown Ups singer; illustrator

CHRIS FRIEL Shadow/Goodness drummer

RICK FRIEL Shadow singer/bassist

GILLIAN G. GAAR journalist/author

ERIC GARCIA assistant for Chris Cornell/Susan Silver

SUZI GARDNER guitarist/singer for L7 (Los Angeles)

CAM GARRETT photographer; SCUD cofounder; Ben McMillan's first cousin

DAVID GEFFEN Geffen Records/DGC head

CLAUDIA GEHRKE the Vogue club booker

MARC GEIGER Lollapalooza festival cofounder; talent agent

GARY GERSH Geffen Records/DGC A&R executive

RICK GERSHON A&M Records/Warner Bros. Records publicity executive

JEFF GILBERT journalist; KZOK DJ; concert organizer

GREG GILMORE Mother Love Bone/10 Minute Warning/the Living drummer

DANNY GOLDBERG Gold Mountain Entertainment founder/president; Nirvana/Hole manager; Atlantic Records president; Warner Bros. Records chairman/CEO; Rosemary Carroll's husband

MICHAEL GOLDSTONE PolyGram Records/Epic Records A&R executive

KIM GORDON bassist/singer for Sonic Youth (New York); Thurston Moore's wife

STONE GOSSARD Pearl Jam/Temple of the Dog/Mother Love Bone/Green River/Brad/Satchel/March of Crimes guitarist

KELLY GRAY producer; Queensrÿche/Myth guitarist

KERRY GREEN Dickless guitarist

DAVE GROHL Nirvana drummer; Foo Fighters singer/guitarist; drummer for Scream (Washington, D.C., area)

DEAN GUNDERSON Cat Butt bassist

REGAN HAGAR Malfunkshun/Brad/Satchel drummer

ROSS HALFIN photographer

STUART HALLERMAN Soundgarden soundman; Avast! Recording studio owner/
operator

KATHLEEN HANNA Bikini Kill singer

TOM HANSEN the Refuzors/the Fartz guitarist; heroin dealer

CHRIS HANZSEK C/Z Records label/Reciprocal Recording studio cofounder;
producer

KERRI HARROP Sub Pop Records sales and retail employee

TIM HAYES Fallout Records store owner

GIBBY HAYNES singer for Butthole Surfers (Austin, Texas)

TOM HAZELMYER Amphetamine Reptile Records founder; U-Men bassist

RON HEATHMAN Supersuckers guitarist

FAITH HENSCHEL-VENTRELLO KCMU music director

MAUREEN HERMAN bassist for Babes in Toyland (Minneapolis)

DAVE HILLIS producer/engineer/mixer; Mace guitarist

DANIEL HOUSE Skin Yard/10 Minute Warning bassist; C/Z Records owner

JOHN HOYT political and community advisor for Pearl Jam; Pyramid
Communications partner

DAVE HUNT (d. 2009) Malfunkshun drummer

REED HUTCHINSON Feast guitarist

DON IENNER Sony Music chairman

MIKE INEZ Alice in Chains bassist; Ozzy Osbourne band bassist

JACK IRONS Pearl Jam/Red Hot Chili Peppers/Eleven drummer

STEVE ISAACS MTV VJ

MARC JACOBS fashion designer

AARON JACOVES A&M Records West Coast director of A&R

MEGAN JASPER Sub Pop Records receptionist-turned–executive vice president;
Dickless singer

RICH JENSEN Sub Pop Records general manager; musician

DAVE JERDEN producer

CALVIN JOHNSON K Records cofounder; Beat Happening singer/guitarist

ERIC JOHNSON Soundgarden/Pearl Jam tour manager

JAIME ROBERT JOHNSON (a.k.a. Crunchbird) singer/guitarist

BARRETT JONES Nirvana drum tech; Laundry Room Studio owner/operator

AL JOURGENSEN front man for Ministry (Chicago)

NEAL KARLEN journalist; Babes in Toyland biographer

ADAM KASPER producer/engineer

MARK KATES Geffen Records/DGC head of alternative promotion

DAVID KATZNELSON Warner Bros. Records A&R vice president
ANDY KESSLER (a.k.a. Joe Spleen) the Gits guitarist
SEAN KINNEY Alice in Chains drummer
PETER KLETT Candlebox guitarist
FRANK KOZIK poster artist; video director
RICK KRIM MTV director of musical talent
DAVE KRUSEN Pearl Jam/Hovercraft/Candlebox drummer
RICKY KULWICKI (d. 2011) guitarist for the Fluid (Denver)

XANA LA FUENTE Andrew Wood's fiancée
MARK LANEGAN Screaming Trees singer; solo artist
AL LARSEN Some Velvet Sidewalk singer/guitarist
MIKE LARSON Green River manager
MICHELLE LEON bassist for Babes in Toyland (Minneapolis)
PETER LITWIN Coffin Break guitarist/singer
KURT LODER MTV News anchor
BEN LONDON Alcohol Funnycar singer/guitarist
COURTNEY LOVE singer/guitarist for Hole (Los Angeles); Kurt Cobain's widow;
    Frances Bean Cobain's mother; actress
MATT LUKIN Melvins/Mudhoney bassist
JOHN LYDON (a.k.a. Johnny Rotten) singer for Public Image Ltd./Sex Pistols
    (U.K.)

STEVE MACK singer for That Petrol Emotion (U.K.)
ALEX MACLEOD Nirvana tour manager
MADONNA pop singer; Maverick Records cofounder
STEVE MANNING Sub Pop Records publicist
TRACY MARANDER photographer; Kurt Cobain's ex-girlfriend
DAVE MARKEY *1991: The Year Punk Broke* documentary director
BARDI MARTIN Candlebox bassist
BARRETT MARTIN Screaming Trees/Mad Season/Skin Yard drummer
KEVIN MARTIN Candlebox singer
MAIRE MASCO Pravda Productions partner; *Desperate Times* zine cofounder
PONY MAURICE Feast singer
SCOTT MCCAUGHEY Young Fresh Fellows singer/bassist/guitarist; Popllama
    Records/Egg Studios employee
MIKE MCCREADY Pearl Jam/Temple of the Dog/Mad Season/Shadow
    guitarist
SCOTT MCCULLUM (a.k.a. Norman Scott): Skin Yard/Gruntruck/64 Spiders
    drummer
DUFF MCKAGAN bassist for Guns N' Roses (Los Angeles); played various
    instruments in Fastbacks, the Fartz, the Living, 10 Minute Warning, the
    Vains, many more

BEN MCMILLAN (d. 2008) Skin Yard singer; Gruntruck singer/guitarist; Cam Garrett's first cousin

SCOTT MERCADO Candlebox/Sky Cries Mary drummer

LANCE MERCER photographer

BRET MICHAELS singer for Poison (Los Angeles)

LILLY MILIC Top Hat Records store owner; Garrett Shavlik's wife

COURTNEY MILLER *The Rocket* newspaper advertising manager

MIKE MONGRAIN TAD drummer

CRAIG MONTGOMERY Nirvana/TAD soundman

SLIM MOON Earth guitarist; solo artist; Kill Rock Stars label founder

THURSTON MOORE singer/guitarist for Sonic Youth (New York); Kim Gordon's husband

STEVE MORIARTY the Gits drummer; OK Hotel club booker

JOE NEWTON Gas Huffer drummer

TOM NIEMEYER the Accüsed/Gruntruck guitarist

KRIST NOVOSELIC Nirvana bassist; Shelli Novoselic's ex-husband

SHELLI NOVOSELIC (now Shelli Hyrkas) Krist Novoselic's ex-wife

BRENDAN O'BRIEN producer/mixer/engineer

TOMIE O'NEIL soundman; RKCNDY club co-owner/comanager

BUZZ OSBORNE (a.k.a. King Buzzo) Melvins singer/guitarist

OZZY OSBOURNE singer for Black Sabbath (U.K.); solo artist

GUY OSEARY Maverick Records A&R scout–turned-partner

RICK PARASHAR producer; London Bridge Studio cofounder

DEMRI PARROTT (d. 1996) Layne Staley's girlfriend

TIM PAUL Gruntruck bassist

BRUCE PAVITT Sub Pop Records cofounder

JOHN PEEL (d. 2004) BBC Radio 1 DJ

MARK PELLINGTON video director

DAN PETERS Mudhoney/Nirvana/Screaming Trees/Feast/Bundle of Hiss drummer

CHARLES PETERSON photographer

ERIK PETERSON (a.k.a. Erok) Cat Butt drummer

KRISTEN PFAFF (d. 1994) bassist for Hole (Los Angeles)

BOB PFEIFER Epic Records senior vice president A&R; Hollywood Records president

MARK PICKEREL Screaming Trees/Truly drummer

HUGO PIOTTIN (now known as Poki Piottin) Metropolis club owner

DEE PLAKAS drummer for L7 (Los Angeles)

JONATHAN PLUM producer/engineer; London Bridge Studio co-owner

NICK POLLOCK Alice N' Chains guitarist; My Sister's Machine singer/guitarist

JONATHAN PONEMAN Sub Pop Records cofounder

DOUG PRAY *Hype!* documentary director

TOM PRICE U-Men/Cat Butt/Gas Huffer guitarist

BARBARA DOLLARHIDE PRITCHARD C/Z Records public relations and marketing director

CHRIS PUGH Swallow guitarist/singer

RIKI RACHTMAN host of MTV's *Headbangers Ball*

TONY RANSOM (a.k.a. Tone Deaf) U-Men bassist

DAN RAYMOND Melvins "hanger-on"

DAVE REES Malfunkshun bassist

LARRY REID U-Men manager; co-owner of Roscoe Louie/Graven Image galleries; Tracey Rowland's husband

BENJAMIN REW musician; TAD roadie

TRENT REZNOR front man for Nine Inch Nails (Cleveland)

IANN ROBINSON MTV News reporter

JOHN ROBINSON singer for the Fluid (Denver)

EDDIE ROESER (a.k.a. King Roeser) singer/bassist/guitarist for Urge Overkill (Chicago)

RODERICK ROMERO Sky Cries Mary singer

AXL ROSE singer for Guns N' Roses (Los Angeles)

JIM ROSE Jim Rose Circus Sideshow founder

ROBERT ROTH Truly singer/guitarist

TRACEY ROWLAND co-owner of Roscoe Louie/Graven Image galleries; Larry Reid's wife

RON RUDZITIS (a.k.a. Ron Nine) Love Battery/Room Nine singer/guitarist

CHARLIE RYAN U-Men/Cat Butt/the Crows drummer

SALTPETER bassist for Dwarves (San Francisco)

STEFANIE SARGENT (d. 1992) 7 Year Bitch guitarist

JOHN BAKER SAUNDERS (d. 1999) Mad Season/the Walkabouts bassist

PATTY SCHEMEL drummer for Hole (Los Angeles)

SARAH SHANNON singer for Velocity Girl (Washington, D.C., area)

GARRETT SHAVLIK drummer for the Fluid (Denver); Lilly Milic's husband

BEN SHEPHERD Soundgarden bassist; Hater singer/guitarist; March of Crimes guitarist

ALEX SHUMWAY (a.k.a. Alex Vincent) Green River/Spluii Numa drummer

JOHN SILVA Nirvana/Sonic Youth manager; Gold Mountain Entertainment partner

SUSAN SILVER Soundgarden/Alice in Chains/Screaming Trees/U-Men manager; Chris Cornell's ex-wife

TRACY SIMMONS (a.k.a. T-Man) Blood Circus bassist

JOSH SINDER TAD/Gruntruck/the Accüsed drummer

ROB SKINNER Coffin Break bassist/singer

SLASH guitarist for Guns N' Roses (Los Angeles)

PAT SMEAR Nirvana/Foo Fighters/Germs guitarist

JEFF SMITH (a.k.a. Jo Smitty) Mr. Epp and the Calculations singer/guitarist

TABITHA SOREN MTV News reporter

EDDIE SPAGHETTI Supersuckers singer/bassist

DONITA SPARKS singer/guitarist for L7 (Los Angeles)

LAYNE STALEY (d. 2002) Alice in Chains/Mad Season/Alice N' Chains singer; Demri Parrott's boyfriend

MIKE STARR (d. 2011) Alice in Chains bassist

ANNA STATMAN Geffen Records/Slash Records A&R representative

AARON STAUFFER Seaweed singer

DAMON STEWART KISW DJ; Sony Music regional A&R scout

KEN STRINGFELLOW the Posies singer/guitarist

SCOTT SUNDQUIST Soundgarden drummer

JOSH TAFT video director

SUSIE TENNANT DGC Records Northwest promotion representative

NICK TERZO Columbia Records/Maverick Records A&R executive

KIM THAYIL Soundgarden guitarist

GARY THORSTENSEN TAD guitarist

JIM TILLMAN U-Men/Love Battery bassist

EVERETT TRUE *Melody Maker* newspaper writer; Nirvana biographer

MIKE TUCKER U-Men roadie

STEVE TURNER Mudhoney/Green River/Mr. Epp and the Calculations/the Thrown Ups guitarist

CONRAD UNO Popllama Records founder; Egg Studios owner; producer/engineer

CHRIS UTTING (a.k.a. Criss Crass) the Vains singer/guitarist; the Living drummer/guitarist

TOBI VAIL Bikini Kill drummer; Kurt Cobain's ex-girlfriend

SCOTT VANDERPOOL KXRX/KCMU DJ; Room Nine drummer

MATT VAUGHAN Gruntruck manager; Easy Street Records stores owner

EDDIE VEDDER Pearl Jam/Temple of the Dog singer; Hovercraft drummer

BUTCH VIG producer; drummer for Garbage (Madison, Wis.)

SELENE VIGIL-WILK 7 Year Bitch singer

KIM WARNICK Fastbacks singer/bassist; Sub Pop Records receptionist

ALICE WHEELER photographer

DENNIS R. WHITE Pravda Productions partner; *Desperate Times* zine cofounder

KIM WHITE Screaming Trees manager

BOB WHITTAKER Mudhoney manager

KEVIN WHITWORTH Love Battery guitarist

STEVE WIEDERHOLD (a.k.a. Steve Wied) TAD drummer

RUSTY WILLOUGHBY Pure Joy/Flop singer/guitarist

ANN WILSON Heart/the Lovemongers singer; Nancy Wilson's sister

NANCY WILSON Heart/the Lovemongers singer/guitarist; Ann Wilson's sister;
Cameron Crowe's ex-wife

ANDREW WOOD (d. 1990) Mother Love Bone singer; Malfunkshun singer/bassist;
brother of Brian and Kevin Wood; Xana La Fuente's fiancé

BRIAN WOOD musician; brother of Andrew and Kevin Wood

KEVIN WOOD Malfunkshun guitarist; brother of Andrew and Brian Wood

REP. LYNN C. WOOLSEY Democratic congresswoman from California

ANNA WOOLVERTON Sub Pop Records receptionist

MATT WRIGHT Gas Huffer singer

TOBY WRIGHT producer/engineer

HIRO YAMAMOTO Soundgarden/Truly bassist

NEIL YOUNG Canadian singer-songwriter

MIA ZAPATA (d. 1993) the Gits singer

NOTES

All interviews conducted by the author between 2008 and 2011, unless noted otherwise below.

CHAPTER 1: Something Crazy's Gonna Happen
11   *What were all the police cars doing at the recreation center* "Vandalism at the Recreation Center," Laurelhurst Community Club newsletter, January 1982.

CHAPTER 2: The Gospel According to Buzz
23   *I remember hanging out at Montesano, Washington's Thriftway* Kurt Cobain, *Journals*, Riverhead Trade, 2003, pp. 56–57.
25   *It was like a revelation* Jim Berkenstadt and Charles R. Cross, *Nevermind: Nirvana*, Schirmer Trade Books, 1998, p. 17.

CHAPTER 5: Screaming Life
55   *At the time I was growing up* Alec Foege, "The End of the Innocence: Chris Cornell of Soundgarden," *Rolling Stone*, January 12, 1995.
56   *I went from being a daily drug user at 13* Ibid.
61   *The beginning of me thinking maybe I should get out there* David Peisner interview with Chris Cornell, 2010; © David Peisner.

CHAPTER 7: A Third Sound

81 *The fact that none of these bands could open* Dawn Anderson, *Deep Six* record
    review, *The Rocket*, June 1986; © Murder Incorporated.

85 *And her boyfriend, from behind, grabbed me* Andy Savage, Jodi Brothers, and
    Steve Migliore, KNDD interview with Jeff Ament and Matt Cameron, aired
    November 6, 2000.

86 *Went up to get paid afterwards* Ibid.

CHAPTER 8: The Four Weirdest Guys in Ellensburg

90 *When I was a kid, I got caught shoplifting* Charles R. Cross, "Screaming Trees,"
    The Rocket, July 24, 1996.

CHAPTER 10: Sounds Like Throw Up Looks

115 *Stone and I were on the side of the stage* Brendan Mullen, *Whores: An Oral
    Biography of Perry Farrell and Jane's Addiction*, Da Capo Press, 1995,
    pp. 151–52.

CHAPTER 12: Touch Me I'm Sick

143 *I remember my mom, when I showed her the record* *TAD: Busted Circuits and
    Ringing Ears* documentary, directed by Ryan Short and Adam Pease, King of
    Hearts Productions, 2008.

CHAPTER 13: He Who Rides the Pony

145 *He was going to live on the island with his parents* Lonn M. Friend,
    "Heroes . . . and Heroin," *RIP*, July 1992.

147 *Stone and I had known Andy a long time* Brian Hiatt interview with Jeff
    Ament, RollingStone.com podcast, 2006.

CHAPTER 14: Bands That Will Make Money

158 *It put the other three guys in the position* David Peisner interview with Chris
    Cornell, 2010; © David Peisner.

162 *[The tractor] was coming right for my balls* Keith Cameron, "Death Valley
    Blues," *MOJO*, October 2004.

163 *We didn't have a damn thing in common* Ibid.

CHAPTER 15: The Music Bank

170 *I wasn't really close to my dad* Jon Wiederhorn interview with Jerry Cantrell,
    1995; © Jon Wiederhorn.

170 *I never had a whole lot of money* Chuck Dean, "Chain Letter," *Ray Gun*,
    December 1992–January 1993.

170 *I met Layne again at a house party* Martin Kuiper video interview with
    Jerry Cantrell and Sean Kinney, FaceCulture.com, January 11, 2010;
    © FaceCulture 2010.

171 *I first met Layne around 1985* Chris Gill, "Dirt," *Guitar World*, November 1999.

172 *Layne was playin' with another band* Martin Kuiper video interview with Jerry Cantrell and Sean Kinney, FaceCulture.com.

CHAPTER 16: Where's the Grog?

183 *Mark used to try to mythologize Sonic Youth's profile* David Bevan, Jonathan Cohen, Corey duBrowa, Andrew Earles, Jason Ferguson, Matthew Fritch, Tim Hinely, Pat Hipp, Bruce Miller, and Noah Bonaparte Pais, "Superfuzzy Memories," *Magnet*, Summer 2008.

CHAPTER 17: Create Your Own Myth

195 *I hate Mr. Epp & the Calculations!* Mark Arm, *Desperate Times*, letters section, July 22, 1981.

199 *The one show of this tour that really sticks in my mind* Carrie Borzillo, *Eyewitness Nirvana: The Day-by-Day Chronicle*, Carlton Books, 2000, p. 36; used with author's permission.

CHAPTER 18: Incompatible Individuals

202 *We just decided to drive straight home* Carrie Borzillo, *Eyewitness Nirvana: The Day-by-Day Chronicle*, Carlton Books, 2000, p. 39; used with author's permission.

CHAPTER 19: All About Kicks

211 *We played another show in the West* Krist Novoselic, "Twenty Years After the Wall," SeattleWeekly.com, November 3, 2009.

CHAPTER 21: Raise Your Candle High

234 *I loved Mother Love Bone* Eric Weisbard with Jessica Letkemann, Ann Powers, Chris Norris, William Van Meter, and Will Hermes, "Ten Past Ten," Spin.com, August 2001. Reprinted with permission from *Spin* magazine. All rights reserved.

234 *We were crammed in a smallish living room* Chris Cornell, "Essence of Dreams," ChrisCornell.com blog, October 13, 2008.

CHAPTER 22: A Bright, Clear Sound

243 *I was looking forward to being able to write* BJ Shea, KISW interview with Chad Channing, November 3, 2009.

244 *When we were auditioning [Jason]* Mike Gitter, "Soundgarden: Behold, the Grunge Messiahs," *RIP*, January 1992.

CHAPTER 23: Good Luck in Your Future Endeavors

252 *The first phone call that I had with Kurt* Foo Fighters, *Skin and Bones* DVD, RCA, 2006.

252 *This girl sits down and she plays* Ibid.

CHAPTER 24: Sick of Crying

264 *I was sitting around at a party with Pete Droge* Jeff Gilbert, "Alive: Pearl Jam's Mike McCready Says Goodbye to Drugs and Alcohol and Is a Better Man for It," *Guitar World*, April 1995; © Jeff Gilbert.

265 *I was going through a major identity crisis* Eric Weisbard with Jessica Letkemann, Ann Powers, Chris Norris, William Van Meter, and Will Hermes, "Ten Past *Ten*," Spin.com, August 2001. Reprinted with permission from *Spin*. All rights reserved.

267 *Jack sent me three of their songs* Jennifer Clay, "Pearl Jam: Life After Love Bone," *RIP*, December 1991; used with author's permission.

268 *I'd never been in a situation where it clicks* Weisbard et al., "Ten Past *Ten*."

268 *The minute we started rehearsing* Ibid.

268 *I never knew my real dad* Cameron Crowe, "Five Against the World," *Rolling Stone*, October 28, 1993.

270 *I had written "Say Hello to Heaven"* Weisbard et al., "Ten Past *Ten*."

272 *Within our own community, there was* Charles R. Cross, "Chain Reaction," *Classic Rock*, July 2006.

275 *I was trying out the camp counselor thing* Jonathan Bernstein, "Crowe's Feat," *Spin*, September 1992.

277 *Acting was really uncomfortable* Phil West, "Insiders Wonder Whether Movie Will Change Seattle's Music Scene," *The Seattle Times*, September 17, 1992.

280 *Recording* Ten, *we probably did "Even Flow" 30 times* Weisbard et al., "Ten Past *Ten*."

280 *The first time I mentioned Pearl Jam [as a band name]* Ibid.

CHAPTER 25: The Final Countdown

285 *In August of 1990, I found myself laying on my stomach* Comments during performance at Joe's Pub, New York, December 15, 2010.

288 *You open the cell door and boom* Michael Azerrad, *Come as You Are: The Story of Nirvana*, Main Street Books/Doubleday, 1993, p. 178.

289 *"More low end!"* Nathaniel Penn, "The Moment We Found Nirvana," *GQ*, June 2011.

292 *Originally we wanted L7 to be the cheerleaders* Videos That Rocked the World, episode one, aired on Fuse, November 26, 2007.

292 *I go, "Well, why don't we have the cheerleaders"* Ibid.

CHAPTER 26: Punk Breaks

303 *In 1990,* RIP *magazine comes out* David Peisner interview with Chris Cornell, 2010; © David Peisner.

305 *[Axl] was always hidden somewhere having a personal crisis* Austin Scaggs, "Q&A: Chris Cornell," *Rolling Stone*, July 28, 2005.

305 *February 1, 1992, was our last show with Soundgarden* Slash with Anthony Bozza, *Slash*, It Books/HarperCollins, 2007, p. 347.

CHAPTER 27: On the Corner of Dopey and Goofy

308 *Nirvana pulls off an astonishing palace coup* Paul Grein, "Nirvana Achieves Chart Perfection," *Billboard*, January 11, 1992.

309 *I remember walking into their hotel room* Michael Azerrad, "Territorial Pissings: The Battles Behind Nirvana's New Album," *Musician*, October 1993.

311 *I remember after the New Year's Eve 1991 show* Eric Weisbard with Jessica Letkemann, Ann Powers, Chris Norris, William Van Meter, and Will Hermes, "Ten Past Ten," Spin.com, August 2001. Reprinted with permission from *Spin*. All rights reserved.

311 *In San Diego we were playing with Nirvana and the Chili Peppers* Ibid.

CHAPTER 29: Bile Hog!

336 *It made us feel like playing those huge shows* Cameron Crowe, "Five Against the World," *Rolling Stone*, October 28, 1993.

338 *We had to hide him in the dressing room* Stevie Chick, "Where to Start with . . . Screaming Trees," *Kerrang!*, December 10, 2005.

343 *Just looking for attention, I guess* Eric Weisbard with Jessica Letkemann, Ann Powers, Chris Norris, William Van Meter, and Will Hermes, "Ten Past Ten," Spin.com, August 2001. Reprinted with permission from *Spin*. All rights reserved.

CHAPTER 30: The Emperor's New Flannel

347 *All subcultures speak in code* Rick Marin, "Lexicon of Grunge: Breaking the Code," *The New York Times*, November 15, 1992.

349 *I wore shorts year round* Eric Weisbard with Jessica Letkemann, Ann Powers, Chris Norris, William Van Meter, and Will Hermes, "Ten Past *Ten*," Spin.com, August 2001. Reprinted with permission from *Spin*. All rights reserved.

352 *We were fired from Perry Ellis* Marc Jacobs talk, moderated by Patricia Mears, deputy director, The Museum at FIT, March 22, 2010; part of the Fashion Talks series presented by the French Institute Alliance Française.

352 *Marc sent me and Kurt his Perry Ellis grunge collection* Rachel Strugatz, "Courtney Love on Birkins and Sex," *WWD*, July 21, 2010.

CHAPTER 32: Strange Love

364 *The 20 words that shook the record business are found* Steve Hochman, "POP MUSIC: The Ruckus over the Vanity Fair Profile," *Los Angeles Times*, August 16, 1992; copyright © 1992, *Los Angeles Times*. Reprinted with permission.

365 *In a statement by Love and Cobain* Ibid.

369 *What I wanted to do was drop my pants and pull it out* Renée Crist, "The Magnificent 7," *Spin*, July 1993.

371 *[Reading] was a pretty strange experience* Alan Light, "Foo Fighters' Pilot Roosts with Vultures," *The New York Times*, November 13, 2009.

373 *Nirvana gets introduced, and we start playing our prank* Krist Novoselic, "What Really Happened at the 1992 MTV Music Video Awards," SeattleWeekly.com, November 18, 2008.

373 *It was at that time that Eddie took it over* Eric Weisbard with Jessica
     Letkemann, Ann Powers, Chris Norris, William Van Meter, and Will
     Hermes, "Ten Past *Ten*," Spin.com, August 2001. Reprinted with permission
     from *Spin*. All rights reserved.
374 *I felt that with any more popularity we were going to be crushed* Brian Hiatt,
     "Eddie Vedder's Embarrassing Tale: Naked in Public," RollingStone.com,
     June 20, 2006.
376 *We were slow-dancing on a gym floor* Brian Hiatt, "The Second Coming of
     Pearl Jam," *Rolling Stone*, June 29, 2006.
376 *Yeah, some kind of fucking summit* Eric Weisbard et al., "Ten Past *Ten*."

CHAPTER 33: Into the Night
377 *I was actually in a store buying some beer* Nick Bowcott, "Seattle Do Nicely:
     Jerry Cantrell," *Guitarist*, April 1993.
380 *It's a dark album* Katherine Turman, "Digging Out of the Dirt," *Los Angeles
     Times*, August 1, 1993.
380 *["Rooster"] was all my perceptions of his experiences* Jerry Cantrell, liner notes
     for Alice in Chains' *Music Bank* box set, Columbia Records, 1999.
385 *We were like hog wild, man* Jon Wiederhorn interview with Jerry Cantrell,
     1995; © Jon Wiederhorn.

CHAPTER 34: Fuck Hollywood!
390 Singles *was in the can for a year before it came out* Eric Weisbard with Jessica
     Letkemann, Ann Powers, Chris Norris, William Van Meter, and Will
     Hermes, "Ten Past *Ten*," Spin.com, August 2001. Reprinted with permission
     from *Spin*. All rights reserved.
391 *They were playing covers, and somebody got into a fight* Ibid.
393 *Mudhoney has an amazing song on the soundtrack* Jeff Gilbert, "The Mouths
     That Scored: Pearl Jam's Eddie Vedder and Soundgarden's Chris Cornell
     Reflect on Their Success," *Guitar World Presents Nirvana and the Seattle
     Sound*, 1993.

CHAPTER 35: A Problem with Weights and Measures
400 *We were really sad about it, of course* Jason Roberts, "A Sound Called Alice,"
     Guitar, December 1993.
401 *We were touring with Nirvana* to *"You were dead for 11 minutes, Mike."*
     Loveline with Mike & Dr. Drew, radio interview with Mike Starr,
     February 16, 2010.

CHAPTER 36: Radio Friendly Unit Shifters
406 *Our A&R man at the time, Gary Gersh, was freaking out* Phil Sutcliffe, "King
     of Pain," *Q*, October 1993.

CHAPTER 38: All the Rage?
422 *I thought a lot of people were gonna be freaked out* Jon Wiederhorn interview
     with Sean Kinney, 1995; © Jon Wiederhorn.

425 *The second record, that was the one I enjoyed making the least* Eric Weisbard with Jessica Letkemann, Ann Powers, Chris Norris, William Van Meter, and Will Hermes, "Ten Past *Ten*," Spin.com, August 2001. Reprinted with permission from *Spin*. All rights reserved.

426 *Recording* Vs., *there was a lot more pressure on Ed* Ibid.

426 *There's a great song we recorded for* Vs. Ibid.

426 *Maybe I wasn't ready for attention to be placed on me* Ibid.

428 *The record-breaking debut week of Pearl Jam's "Vs."* Craig Rosen, "Sales Suggest Pearl Jam, Nirvana Are Here to Stay," *Billboard*, November 6, 1993.

429 *A $4 million-a-year major league baseball pitcher* Michael Perlstein, "Slam Jam: Rocker, Cy Young Winner Team Up in Decatur Street Brawl," *The Times-Picayune*, November 19, 1993; © 2010 *The Times-Picayune*. All rights reserved. Reprinted with permission.

429 *I was with Blackie and Ed from Urge* Allan Jones, "I'm Not Your Fuckin' Messiah," *Melody Maker*, May 21, 1994.

430 *But I never threw a punch* Ibid.

CHAPTER 39: In the Rocket

439 *Kurt had gone all out for me* David Fricke, "Life After Death," *Rolling Stone*, December 15, 1994.

439 *[Someone] called and said he'd passed in Rome* Austin Scaggs, "On an Honor Roll," *Rolling Stone*, July 28, 2005.

443 *I was flying from L.A. up to Seattle* The Last 48 Hours of Kurt Cobain, TV documentary, directed by John Dower, World of Wonder, 2007.

CHAPTER 40: Sitting in the Rubble

445 *We used to go shooting together* Steven Goldsmith and Dan Raley, "Friend Innocently Bought Shotgun for Cobain," *Seattle Post-Intelligencer*, April 15, 1994.

445 *Hi, I'm Kurt Loder with an MTV News special report* MTV News live broadcast, April 8, 1994.

451 *We were these young people from southwest Washington* Video interview with Krist Novoselic, November 18, 1999, courtesy of Experience Music Project Oral History Program.

451 *There are some people that you meet in life* Jo Whiley, BBC Radio 1 interview with Dave Grohl, November 8, 2009.

452 *When I first found out, I was in a hotel room* Robert Hilburn, "He Didn't Ask for All This," *Los Angeles Times*, May 1, 1994.

CHAPTER 41: Fucking Great Products

470 *We were rehearsing at the Moore Theatre* Jon Wiederhorn interview with Sean Kinney, 1995; © Jon Wiederhorn.

CHAPTER 42: Some Imploding Going On

473 *The first record or two, Ed and I could talk* Eric Weisbard with Jessica Letkemann, Ann Powers, Chris Norris, William Van Meter, and Will

Hermes, "Ten Past *Ten*," Spin.com, August 2001. Reprinted with permission from *Spin*. All rights reserved.

473 *Vitalogy was the first record where Ed was the guy* Ibid.

473 *Vitalogy was a little strained* Ibid.

475 *I have to ask another question* "Pearl Jam's Antitrust Complaint: Questions About Concert, Sports, and Theater Ticket Handling Charges and Other Practices," from the hearing before the Information, Justice, Transportation and Agriculture Subcommittee of the Committee on Government Operations, House of Representatives, June 30, 1994.

475 *I am not going to answer that question* Ibid.

475 *That whole thing was a joke* Weisbard et al., "Ten Past *Ten*."

476 *Dave was a different egg for sure* Ibid.

476 *It was the nature of how the politics worked in our band* Ibid.

478 *We'd be playing parks and racetracks* Dave Simpson, "Pearl Jam: 'People Get That This Means Something,'" *The Guardian*, August 13, 2009.

479 *I thought I was going to die* Brad Kava, "Vedder Days," *San Jose Mercury News*, November 3, 1995.

479 *We were afraid there'd be a riot* Weisbard et al., "Ten Past *Ten*."

479 *Eventually they came out with a press release* Ibid.

CHAPTER 43: The Mad Season

481 *We had a lot of meetings* Jeff Gilbert, "Alive: Pearl Jam's Mike McCready Says Goodbye to Drugs and Alcohol and Is a Better Man for It," *Guitar World*, April 1995; © Jeff Gilbert.

482 *A lot of hallucinogenic mushrooms grow in the area* Ibid.

484 *I was under the mistaken theory I could help him out* Charles R. Cross, "The Last Days of Layne Staley," *Rolling Stone*, June 6, 2002.

485 *A lot of the songs that Jerry and Layne wrote* Jon Wiederhorn interview with Sean Kinney, 1995; © Jon Wiederhorn.

CHAPTER 46: 70 Percent Off All Flannel

503 *After Kurt's death, I was about as confused as I've ever been* Capitol Records press release, Foo Fighters biography, 1995.

503 *That fucking letter saved my life* Ibid.

508 *I liked coke a lot* TAD: Busted Circuits and Ringing Ears, documentary, directed by Ryan Short and Adam Pease, King of Hearts Productions, 2008.

CHAPTER 47: Fell on Black Days

516 *During the* Down on the Upside *period* David Peisner interview with Chris Cornell, 2010; © David Peisner.

517 *The bass rig wasn't working in sound check* Ibid.

520 *It was mentally, physically, and spiritually a fucked-up point* David Peisner, "Alive in the Superunknown," *Spin*, September 2010.

521 *Everyone wanted to put out the record to capitalize* Jason Fine, "Hot Band: Screaming Trees," *Rolling Stone*, August 22, 1996.

525 *I mean, there was a time when I thought I didn't have any choice* Stevie Chick, "Mark Lanegan," *Loose Lips Sink Ships*, February 2004; © Stevie Chick.

CHAPTER 48: Lost Nine Friends We'll Never Know

527 *Matt said, "Sure, I'll do it"* Eric Weisbard with Jessica Letkemann, Ann Powers, Chris Norris, William Van Meter, and Will Hermes, "Ten Past Ten," Spin.com, August 2001. Reprinted with permission from *Spin*. All rights reserved.

527 *Right before we went on that night* Ibid.

528 *Well, this particular show, the barrier was 30 meters away* Ibid.

528 OSLO—*Danish police have confirmed that the organizers* Kai R. Lofthus, "Loss of Life Fails to Halt Festival; Nine Killed as Crowd Rushes Stage During Pearl Jam Set," *Billboard*, July 15, 2000.

529 *We were part of an event that was disorganized* Weisbard et al., "Ten Past *Ten*."

529 *The reason those people died* Ibid.

529 *The intensity of the whole event starts to seem surreal* Ibid.

530 *Some of us thought maybe we should cancel* Ibid.

530 *I saw them in Seattle, the last show* Ibid.

CHAPTER 49: My Friend, but Not My Friend

536 *He died the day after my birthday* *Loveline with Mike & Dr. Drew*, radio interview with Mike Starr, February 16, 2010.

537 *I wish I wouldn't have been high* *Celebrity Rehab 3*, "Family Weekend" episode, aired on VH1 February 18, 2010.

537 *I went home and I blacked out* Ibid.

537 *The rock world lost one of its more honest voices this weekend* MTV News report, weekend of April 20, 2002.

538 *It's like one of the world's longest suicides* Charles R. Cross, "The Last Days of Layne Staley," *Rolling Stone*, June 6, 2002.

539 *Was there more I could have done to help Layne?* Mark Eglinton, "Alice in Chains Interview: Jerry Cantrell on Fighting Back to the Top," thequietus .com, November 16, 2009.

539 *It felt like when Layne passed away* Martin Kuiper video interview with Jerry Cantrell and Sean Kinney, FaceCulture.com, January 11, 2010; © FaceCulture 2010.

539 *"Died of a heroin overdose"* Ibid.

ABOUT THE AUTHOR

Mark Yarm is a former senior editor at *Blender* magazine. He has written for *Wired, Men's Health, Esquire,* Salon.com, and many other publications. He lives in Brooklyn with his wife, Bonnie. For more information, visit MarkYarm.com.